PENGUI

GEORGE ORWELL: A LIFE

ofessor of Politics at Colchester, the Univer-
for mature part-time students. He
educated at School, Univer
en, the London S Economics, as ar-
vard. ved for four years in North America before teaching
at the London School of Economics and then Sheffield University. He has also lectured in Germany, Holland, Israel, New
Zealand and Eastern Europe.

His other books include *The American Science of Politics*; *In
Defence of Politics* (Pelican edition, 1964), which has sold over
250,000 copies and has been translated into German, Spanish,
Italian and Japanese; *Crime, Rape and Gin*, reflections on contemporary attitudes to violence, pornography and addiction; and
Political Theory and Practice. He was chairman of the working
party which produced the Hansard Society's influential report,
Political Education and Political Literacy. He is currently working
on the political relations of the British Isles.

Joint editor of the *Political Quarterly* from 1965 until 1980, he
has written for the *Observer*, *New Statesman* and other papers,
and reviews regularly for the *Guardian*. He has reviewed plays
for *The Times Higher Educational Supplement* and the *New
Review*, and is a frequent broadcaster. This book was the *Yorkshire Post* Book of the Year for 1980.

BERNARD CRICK

GEORGE ORWELL:
A LIFE

PENGUIN BOOKS

Penguin Books Ltd, Harmondsworth, Middlesex, England
Viking Penguin Inc., 40 West 23rd Street, New York, New York 10010, U.S.A.
Penguin Books Australia Ltd, Ringwood, Victoria, Australia
Penguin Books Canada Ltd, 2801 John Street, Markham, Ontario, Canada L3R 1B4
Penguin Books (N.Z.) Ltd, 182–190 Wairau Road, Auckland 10, New Zealand

—

First published in Great Britain by Secker & Warburg Ltd 1980
First published in the United States of America by Little, Brown and Company, Inc.,
in association with the Atlantic Monthly Press 1981
Published in Penguin Books in the United States of America by arrangement
with Little, Brown and Company, Inc., in association with the Atlantic Monthly Press
Published in Penguin Books 1982
Reprinted 1984, 1987

—

—

Excerpts from the following works by George Orwell are reprinted by permission of Harcourt
Brace Jovanovich, Inc.: *Animal Farm; Burmese Days; A Clergyman's Daughter; The Collected
Essays, Journalism and Letters of George Orwell,* Volumes 1–4; *Coming Up For Air; Dickens,
Dali and Others; Down and Out in Paris and London; Homage to Catalonia; Keep the Aspidistra
Flying; Nineteen Eighty-Four; The Road to Wigan Pier; Shooting an Elephant; Such, Such Were the
Joys;* copyright 1933, 1934, 1936 by George Orwell; copyright 1945, 1946, 1949, 1950, 1952,
1953 by Sonia Brownell Orwell; copyright 1946, 1949 by Harcourt Brace Jovanovich, Inc.;
copyright © Sonia Pitt-Rivers, 1961, 1962; copyright © Sonia Brownell Orwell, 1968, 1977;
copyright © Sonia Orwell, 1974

Made and printed in Great Britain by
Richard Clay Ltd, Bungay, Suffolk
Filmset in Monophoto Ehrhardt

CONTENTS

LIST OF ILLUSTRATIONS

ACKNOWLEDGEMENTS

FIRSTLY I must thank the late Mrs Sonia Orwell who in 1972 granted me unrestricted access to all of George Orwell's papers. I must also say clearly that the opinions expressed in this book are mine alone and that in no sense is this an official biography, nor is it likely to be the last life of George Orwell that is written (all perspectives change over time), even if the first to have unlimited rights of quotation from all of his published and unpublished work.

Because there were still some restrictions on access to parts of the Orwell Archive at University College, London, I have sometimes quoted at greater length from material not included in *The Collected Essays, Journalism and Letters of George Orwell* edited by Sonia Orwell and Ian Angus (four volumes, Secker & Warburg, London, 1968) than economy of style might otherwise dictate.

I wish to thank Mr Ian Angus, the Librarian of King's College, London, who, while Deputy Librarian of University College, London, was in charge of the Orwell Archive. While collecting material for the archive, with admirable energy and skill, he interviewed and corresponded with many people who had known Orwell, some of whom were dead by the time I began work. Ian Angus generously made his own interview notes as well as the Archive's correspondence available to me, let me use a day-to-day chronology of Orwell's life that he had compiled, and helped me in numerous other ways. He is working, with Mr Ian Willison of the British Library, on a definitive bibliography of George Orwell. It is necessary to say clearly that he is in no way responsible for the use I have made of his help, and again that the opinions expressed in this book are mine alone.

With similar qualifications, I thank Professor Bernard Bergonzi and Mr Julian Symons, who read the manuscript for the publishers, for giving me their detailed criticisms as well as making very helpful general points, as did Mrs Celia Goodman and Professor Barbara Hardy, both of whom read through it all at my earnest request, patiently and helpfully. My good friends, Irene and Roland Brown, also read the manuscript closely and sceptically.

Audrey Coppard has been my Department's research assistant at Birkbeck College during almost the whole of this work, giving me, by the sufferance of my colleagues, a lion's share of her time. She helped with the research and typed the manuscript in its different stages, but only after reading critically and helping to tighten every chapter. Without her literary experience, common sense and mixture of faith and irony I would have lost my way many times, or could have produced several volumes of unreadable length. My former Department Secretary, Mrs Pat Culshaw, held the fort while I was otherwise engaged, and in temporary retirement helped with some final typing.

Anne Daltrop came to work with us as the first draft was completed and checked all quotations and footnotes with great skill. And she and Audrey Coppard have read the proofs with me efficiently and impersonally. Two former part-time research assistants in my Department at Birkbeck also helped: Deirdre McKellar transcribed notebooks, etc.; Jasmina Ljuhar listed Orwell's writings which are not included in *The Collected Essays, Journalism and Letters*, and she searched for and transcribed marginalia in his books (disappointingly few, incidentally). The comments of two members of my seminar proved especially helpful, those of Dr Robert Klitzke on Orwell's political writings in the period 1936 to 1939 (not fully represented in *The Collected Essays, Journalism and Letters*), and of Miguel Berga on Catalonia and Spain, and I want to add that I have found the editorial and production staff at Secker & Warburg most helpful and perceptive.

Mrs Janet Percival, who is in charge of the Orwell Archive at University College, has an extraordinary knowledge of it and an untiring practical helpfulness. Without her help and that of her cheerful colleagues in the Manuscripts and Rare Books Department, progress would have been much more difficult and even slower. Some libraries are a pleasure to work in.

Also I must thank Birkbeck College for a term's leave of absence; and the Nuffield Foundation for giving me a small grant towards travel and research assistance.

Now must follow a long and necessarily undifferentiated list of those who granted me interviews, wrote me helpful letters, put me on a trail, or allowed me to quote from unpublished letters or documents in their ownership or possession. Their precise help appears in the footnotes.

Eileen Aird, the late Evelyn Anderson, Lord Ardwick, David Astor, His Excellency Maung Htin Aung, Sir Alfred Ayer, Noreen Bagnall, the late Roger Beadon, Anne Olivier Bell, Miguel Berga, Lucy Bestley, Richard Blair, Francis Boyle, Melvyn Bragg, Lord Brockway, James Brodie, Jonathan Brown, Jacintha Buddicom, Amy and Jerry Byrne, Professor John Cohen, F. J. R. Coleridge, Dennis Collings, the late Cyril Connolly, Lettice Cooper, Stafford Cottman, Constance Cruikshank, Henry Dakin, Donald Darroch, Kate Darroch, Mary Deiner, Kay Dick, Rodney Dobson, Patricia Donoghue, the late Avril Dunn, William Dunn, Christopher Eastwood, Bob Edwards, MP, Kay Ekevall, Valerie Eliot, Sir William Empson, David Farrer, Tony Farringdon, Mabel Fierz, Michael Foot, MP., Frank Frankford, Tosco Fyvel, Frank M. Gardner, Percy Girling, Livia Gollancz, Jose Gomés, Celia Goodman, Geoffrey Gorer, the late Andrew Gow, Ruth E. Graves, Sir John Grotrian, Jim Hammond, Rosalind Henschel, the late Rayner Heppenstall, David Holbrook, the late Inez Holden, Lydia Jackson, M. D. Jacobs, Tom Jones, G. D. Kennan, Jon Kimche, Denys King-Farlow, who also kindly gave permission for two of his photographs of Orwell to be used, Colin Kirkpatrick, Helmut Klause, Arthur Koestler, Joan Lancaster, Baroness Lee of Asheridge, David McAvoy, James MacGibbon, Sally Magill, the late Philip Mairet, L. W. Marrison, Carlton Melling, Edward Mendelson, the late Henry Miller, Jane Morgan, Frank Morley, Malcolm Muggeridge, Joan Mullock, Michael Meyer, Sir Roger Mynors, Margaret Nelson, Rosalind Obermeyer, David Owen, MP, Harry Pearce, Henry Pelling, Captain Maurice Peters, Professor Richard Peters, Ruth Pitter, Paul Potts, Anthony Powell, the late Sir Herbert Read, Vernon Richards, Alan Rimmer, Tony and Betty Rozga, Sir Steven Runciman, Brenda Salkeld, Professor John Saville, George Scharrat, L. J. Bahadur Singh, Stephen Spender, Victor Stacey, Corin Hughes Stanton, H. S. K. Stapley, Geoffrey Stevens, George Strauss, Professor

Gleb Struve, Henry Swanzy, Julian Symons, Dr Lola S. Szladits, Fred Urquhart, Sir Anthony Wagner, Nicolas Walter, George Wansbrough, the late Fredric Warburg, Susan Watson, Dame Veronica Wedgwood, Dame Rebecca West, the late Myfanwy Westrope, Baroness White of Rhymney, B. T. White, Ian Willison, and George Woodcock.

Also I thank the following for giving permission to quote from published materials in copyright:

George Allen & Unwin (Publishers) Ltd, extract from *Truth About a Publisher* by Sir Stanley Unwin; Campbell, Thomson & McLaughlin Ltd, extract from *The House of Elrig* by Gavin Maxwell; Jonathan Cape Ltd, extracts from *Jonathan Cape, Publisher* by Michael S. Howard; Cassell Ltd, extracts from *My Life and Soft Times* by Henry Longhurst; Collins Publishers, extracts from *Part of My Life* by A. J. Ayer and *Chronicles of Wasted Time* by Malcolm Muggeridge; *Commentary;* Constable Publishers, extract from *The Unknown Orwell* by Peter Stansky and William Abrahams; Lettice Cooper, extract from *Black Bethlehem;* Curtis Brown Ltd, extract from 'Some Are More Equal than Others' (*New Writing*), by John Morris; Peter Davies Ltd, extracts from *Almost a Gentleman* by Mark Benney; William Dunn, extracts from an essay and broadcast of the late Avril Dunn; Valerie Eliot, extract from letter by T. S. Eliot to George Orwell; *Encounter;* Faber & Faber, extract from 'Spain' by W. H. Auden; Freedom Press, extract from *Freedom*; John Freeman, extract from *Editor* by Kingsley Martin; Tosco Fyvel, extracts from essays; Victor Gollancz Ltd, extracts from *The Left News*, readers' reports and Victor Gollancz's writings; David Higham Associates Ltd, extracts from *More Memoirs of an Aesthete* by Sir Harold Acton, *I Am My Brother* by John Lehmann, *The Whispering Gallery* by John Lehmann, and *Infants of the Spring* by Anthony Powell; James MacGibbon, extracts from *The Holiday* and letters by Stevie Smith; Macmillan London and Basingstoke, extracts from *The Republic and the Civil War in Spain* by B. Bolloten, and poems by Rudyard Kipling, 'The Road to Mandalay', 'MacDonaugh's Song' and 'Take Up the White Man's Burden'; Sally Magill, extracts from a manuscript 'Orwell at Wallington' by the late Jack Common; *Morning Star*, extract from *Daily Worker*; *New Statesman*; A. D. Peters & Co Ltd, extracts from *Fugitive from the Camp of Victory* and *A Theory of My Time* by Richard Rees; Deborah Rogers Ltd, extracts from *Enemies of Promise*, © 1938 and 1948 by Cyril

Connolly, and *The Evening Colonnade*, © 1973 by Cyril Connolly, and *Previous Convictions*, © 1963 by Cyril Connolly; Anthony Sheil Associates Ltd, extracts from *The Crystal Spirit* by George Woodcock, and *Dante Called You Beatrice* by Paul Potts; Neville Spearman Ltd, extract from *My Friend Henry Miller* by Alfred Perles; Julian Symons, extract from 'An Appreciation'; Weidenfeld (Publishers) Ltd, extracts from *Grace and Favour* by Loelia, Duchess of Westminster, and *The World of George Orwell*, edited by Miriam Gross; George Woodcock, extract from *The Writer and Politics*.

If I have accidentally omitted to acknowledge any copyright material, I apologize profusely.

Numerous BBC programmes, based on interviews with old friends, have been made about Orwell since his death, notably those produced by Rayner Heppenstall, Malcolm Muggeridge, and Melvyn Bragg. This material has been extremely valuable, but questions of copyright of great complexity arise. I thank the BBC for their permission to consult transcripts of the broadcasts, and apologize if in using some extracts I have accidentally infringed any copyright of some of those recorded or of their heirs whom I have been unable to trace.

Bernard Crick
Birkbeck College
University of London

Publication of a life of such a famous near contemporary has inevitably stimulated the offering of new evidence which I can now add in this revised edition. André Deutsch and George Mikes have given me important material on the publication of *Animal Farm*, Reg Groves on Orwell's relations with British Trotskyism, Nicolas Walter on his relations with British anarchists and Dr Howard Nicholson on his last illness. And many helpful reviews and letters have led me to correct or clarify points of fact and to remedy infelicities of style. So additional thanks are particularly due to, among many who wrote to me: Sydney D. Bailey, Dr Ernest Colin-Ross, Dr John Field, Alaric Jacob, Betty O'Halloran, Andrew Roberts, Dr R. E. F. Smith, Robert D. Thornton and Iris Walkland.

In tribute to Orwell I decided seven years ago to deed the British volume rights of this book to establish a 'George Orwell Memorial Trust'. The objects of the trust are to help either young writers on projects that Orwell would be likely to have approved of had he lived or else research students of Birkbeck College and of University College London to study topics connected with him.

BRC
April 1981

INTRODUCTION

Orwell's Achievement

What kind of biography have I tried to write, and about what kind of man? The questions are not wholly separable. It makes a difference, obviously, if one is writing about a statesman, a theologian, a scientist, an actor or a writer of a certain kind; one's initial assumptions about one's subject must affect the way one goes to work and the kind of evidence one looks for, even though working through the evidence inevitably modifies those assumptions. The reader is entitled to frankness about the author's preconceptions (although frankness too can be a self-deception – straightaway, a typical Orwellian dilemma).

Eric Blair, with his odd combination of writing from experience, his autobiographical asides, his imagination as a writer (easy to underestimate), his common sense and common man honesty, the man's love of privacy and yet the writer's cultivation of a public image as George Orwell, raises unusual problems that seem to demand – or at least to excuse – some otherwise pretentious preliminaries before one presents what one has tried to do: simply to write as straightforward and informative a life as possible.

I saw and still see Orwell as someone who fully succeeded, despite his tragically early death, in the task he set himself in mid-career. He succeeded in such a way that he moved, even in his lifetime, from being a minor English writer to being a world figure, a name to set argument going wherever books are read. In 1946 he wrote in 'Why I Write': 'What I have most wanted to do throughout the past ten years is to make political writing into an art,' adding that 'looking back through my work, I see that it is invariably where I lacked a *political* purpose that I wrote lifeless books and was betrayed into purple passages, sentences without meaning, decorative adjectives and humbug generally.'

Orwell came to see himself as a 'political writer', and both words were of equal weight. He did not claim to be a political philosopher, nor simply a political polemicist: he was a writer, a general writer, author of novels, descriptive works that I will call 'documentaries', essays, poems and innumerable book reviews and newspaper columns. But if his best work was not always directly political in the subject matter, it always exhibited political consciousness. In that sense, he is the finest political writer in English since Swift, satirist, stylist, moralist and stirrer, who influenced him so much. The mature Orwell called Swift 'a Tory anarchist', forgetting that he had once used the phrase of himself when asked, as a young man, where he stood.

Orwell's reputation and influence have increased since his death and show no sign of diminishing. The actual life of such a writer is, alas, only half the story. His greatest influence has been posthumous and has been for liberty and tolerance, but not as passive things to be enjoyed, rather as republican virtues to be exercised: the duty of speaking out boldly ('the secret of liberty,' said Pericles, 'is courage') and of tolerating rival opinions not out of indifference, but out of principle and because of their seriousness. And plain speaking always meant to him clear writing: communality, common sense, courage and a common style. He saw his literary and his political values as perfectly complementary to each other, he could not conceive of them being in contradiction – even if plain style sometimes limited the kind of literature he could enjoy as well as the development of his own more theoretical ideas. His own style became a cutting edge which, with much trial and error, by fits and starts, he slowly forged into a weapon of legendary strength. He made common words sharp, made them come to life again until under his spell one thinks twice before one uses any polysyllables, still less neologisms.

So in the term 'political writer' the second word is as important as the first. Obscure, pretentious or trendy language was to Orwell always a sign of indecision or of deceit, as much when used by private men as by party hacks. For though Orwell and Johnson have many characteristics in common, such as tenacity and pugnacity, an original affection for English letters and an abiding concern for the dignity and well-being of unfortunate writers in poverty, yet Orwell's views on language would imply that Johnsonian ponderosities of style often masked a Tory mixture of deference and evasion.

He became a Socialist (somewhat later than people think) and denied fiercely, whether in reviewing a book by Professor Hayek or in the story of *Animal Farm*, that equality necessarily negates liberty. On the contrary, he stood in that lineage of English socialists who, through Morris, Blatchford, Tawney, Cole, Laski and Bevan, have argued that only in a more egalitarian and fraternal society can liberties flourish and abound for the common people.* It was a tradition that stressed the importance of freely held values, to which the structural arguments of Marxism were, at best, only marginal. Yet his influence has been to reprove backsliding socialists, to sustain democratic Socialists (he always capitalized it thus) and to win back Communist fellow-travellers rather than to convert non-socialists. Many liberals seem unimpressed by Orwell's socialist values, taking what they want from him, admiring him rather abstractly as a *political* writer, but not wanting to come to terms with the content of his politics, with his actual views about the needs of humanity (always humanity, and not just Europeans) and the constraints of a capitalist, acquisitive society. Some either ignore his socialism or espouse a legend that by 1948 and in *Nineteen Eighty-Four* he had abandoned it – what one may call the *Time-Life* and *Encounter* view of Orwell. Part of his anger against the Communists was not only that they had become despots who squandered human life and despised liberty, but that they were also discrediting democratic Socialism. There is really no mystery about the general character of his politics. From 1936 onwards he was first a follower of the independent Labour Party and then a *Tribune* socialist; that is, he took his stand among those who were to the Left or on the left of the Labour Party: fiercely egalitarian, libertarian and democratic, but by Continental comparisons, surprisingly untheoretical, a congregation of secular evangelicals.

What was remarkable in Orwell was not his political position, which was common enough, but that he demanded publicly that his own side should live up to their principles, both in their lives and in their

---

* A. W. Wright names Orwell in this company in his recent *G. D. H. Cole and Socialist Democracy* (Clarendon Press, Oxford, 1979), p. 263.

policies, should respect the liberty of others and tell the truth. Socialism could not come by seizure of power or by Act of Parliament, but only by convincing people in fair and open debate and by example. He would take no excuses and he mocked pretentious talk of 'ideological necessity'. Truth to tell, he made rather a name as a journalist by his skill in rubbing the fur of his own cat backwards. At times he was like those loyal and vociferous football supporters who are at their best when hurling complaint, sarcasm and abuse at their own long-suffering side. Sometimes, of course, it is deserved; and it may always be said to keep them on their toes. Small wonder that some of Orwell's fellow socialists have at times been tempted, like Raymond Williams in his Fontana Modern Masters study, *Orwell*, or like Isaac Deutscher in his polemic against *Nineteen Eighty-Four*, to doubt whether he should be on their terraces at all. But he chose to and he was, whether they like it or not or would prefer quieter spectators. At most times there was a touch of the true Jacobin about him rather than the John Stuart Millite.

Certainly to call Orwell a supreme political writer, both for what he said and how he said it, is to point only to his major talent and influence. There were other good things as well. He began as a novelist and was planning a new novel when he died. Later he repudiated his early novels, except *Burmese Days* and *Coming Up For Air*. *A Clergyman's Daughter* has some good parts but, overall, is embarrassingly bad. *Keep the Aspidistra Flying* won some good critical notices and is still very readable, but it seemed an interesting and promising book, rather than integrated and fully successful. Both these books were self-consciously 'literary': he was, indeed, 'betrayed into purple passages' when he 'lacked a political purpose'. *Burmese Days* was written far more directly from experience and had a clear political purpose, anti-imperialist (though not necessarily socialist, as is commonly supposed – he was a late developer, both politically and artistically). *Coming Up For Air* was received by most reviewers much as *Keep the Aspidistra Flying* had been, but second opinions are now beginning to see greater depths in it, a true novelist's craft, a greater detachment from his own person than appeared at first sight; and certainly it is a comic and satiric *tour de force* not merely in the tradition of Dickens and Wells but as good as any but their very best.

He developed as an essayist. Much critical opinion now locates his genius in his essays. There is much to be said for this view, especially if *Down and Out in Paris and London*, *The Road to Wigan Pier*, and *Homage to Catalonia* can be treated as long essays, since they are all as unusual a mixture of description and speculation as one of them is of fact and fiction. His best essays are by no means all political, though those on politics and literature, language and censorship have become classics of English prose, anthologized and translated throughout the world, even where they are not supposed to be read. A small history could be written of *samizdat* and illegal translations of such essays and of *Animal Farm* and *Nineteen Eighty-Four* (read behind the Iron Curtain as angry satire rather than a pessimistic prophecy). 'Shooting an Elephant' and 'A Hanging' are similarly famous and must each year arouse political reflection for the first time in many new readers, who are often reading them in innocence simply for their good English in respectable language schools or cautious English classes throughout the world.

In his essays on 'Boys' Weeklies', on violence ('Raffles and Miss Blandish') and on pornography ('The Secret Life of Salvador Dali'), he was a moralist who made pioneering studies of unsophisticated, as well as of intellectual, literature to expose anti-humanitarian values. But in the same essays he also pointed to traditional decencies which he believed are more secure among the common people than among the power- and prestige-hungry intellectuals. And there are many short essays that appear simply to entertain, but also lead us by humour and irony to reflect upon, or simply to gain compassion and understanding for, tolerable human failings, oddities and imperfections. While angry at injustice and intolerance, he never seemed to ask too much of ordinary people: his anger centred on the intellectuals, precisely because they hold or influence power and should know better. His politics were Left-wing, but many of his prejudices were conservative. And he wrote about many positive values that have nothing directly to do with politics, love of nature above all: he did not wish to live in a world in which everything could be manipulated, even for the public good. He was capable of literary criticism of the highest order. No one who cares for Dickens and Swift can ignore these two essays; and 'Lear, Tolstoy and the Fool' is a brilliant reproof of one moralist by another for being monumentally silly, and defends the play of art such as Shakespeare's from the Tolstoyan grumbles (so close to the

Leninist) that Shakespeare 'is boring and frivolous' and 'where does he really stand?'. Orwell championed and understood James Joyce's *Ulysses* at a time when some traditional intellectuals denounced it as meaningless filth and honest customs officers seized it to the applause of the *Daily Mail* and the *Express*, though his voice reached few people then. Far more effectively, he praised the art of Henry Miller whose cynicism and deliberate apoliticism he cordially detested. He made simple but bold distinctions between the artistic excellence of figures as diverse as T. S. Eliot and Rudyard Kipling and the inhumanity and bleak pessimism of their politics. It took rare courage and discernment to defend giving a prize to Ezra Pound while condemning him utterly as a person: a Fascist, a war-criminal and a most foul anti-Semite and racialist. Most critics still skirt around the double issue; Orwell waded in with both feet flying, and he was right, horrible old Ezra could sing. He defended with an essay, money and personal activity the gentle British anarchists when in 1944 the police picked on them and the National Council for Civil Liberties ignored them. (The NCCL was then Communist-dominated, no Orwellian paranoia that.)

Not merely was he, in his long and formal set-pieces, a great essayist; he was also a brilliant journalist. He was not outstanding as a reporter when the *Observer* sent him to report events and conditions in France and Germany at the end of the war, and to cover London in the General Election of 1945: he could not reproduce, as it were, the descriptive part of *The Road to Wigan Pier* in miniature – that needed more time and space. But he excelled in the short, characterful and speculative essay. He was a master of column journalism, knocking off quickly straight onto the typewriter three or four topics to a printed page, some serious and provocative, some quirky, comic or perverse. His seventy-six 'As I Please' contributions to *Tribune* – where he was a tribune indeed, protesting, denouncing, needling, nagging, mocking, teasing, and celebrating – became a model for young journalists for their mixture of profundity and humour, their range and variety, and for their plain, easy colloquial style. The model has not always been a fortunate one; it takes an Orwell to do it successfully, someone with a great store of reading and experience, amused and relaxed, working smoothly and fluently but at considerably less than full power, showing no signs of strain to achieve the effect or to fill the space. He made his column a continuing education for his readers, and I have met some old political activists who remember him for that alone and who never read his books.

Specific themes recurred throughout his journalism and essays: love of nature, love of books and literature, dislike of mass production, distrust of intellectuals, suspicion of government, contempt for and warnings against totalitarianism, advice on making, mending or growing things for yourself, anti-imperialism and anti-racialism, detestation of censorship, and praise of plain language, plain speaking, the good in the past, decency, fraternity, individuality, liberty, egalitarianism and patriotism. I list them in no particular order because, although a 'characteristic' and finite list (for instance he rarely discussed music, theatre, opera, art, schools, sport, travel, Whitehall, Westminster, political gossip, scandal, 'Society', or sex – some columnists today would wonder what was left), he never reduced them to any system and it is not always easy to see what they have in common; nor did he always seem aware of obvious contradictions that could arise.

His patriotism is important. He was almost alone among Left-wing intellectuals in stressing the naturalness and positive virtues of loving, not exclusively but none the less intensely and unashamedly, one's native land. He held this view because of his rather old-fashioned radicalism that links his 'Tory anarchist' or individualist phase to his final socialist period. The whiff of Cromwellian powder or dust from Cobbett's *Rural Rides* seems never far from his nostrils, like that horse of whom God boasted to Job: 'He saith among the trumpets, Ha Ha; and he smelleth the battle afar off, the thunder of the captains and the shouting.' He was indeed, a 'revolutionary patriot'. For he saw our heritage and the land itself as belonging to the common people, not to the gentry and the upper middle classes. It was their land because, as in the rhetoric of Wilkes, in the beliefs of the Chartists and in the philosophy of John Locke, they had mixed their labour with the land. He held this view before the War, even in his anti-militarist, quasi-pacifist mood: it was neither an overreaction to accepting the necessity of war in September 1939 nor a lapse back to Edwardian jingoism. Like Cobbett he fought against 'the great Thing', what Cobbett also called 'the Establishment', and part of his anger was that 'they' had tried to monopolize patriotism, so that, for instance, the greatest revolutionary hymn in the language, Blake's 'Jerusalem', could come to be sung at Tory conferences without perceived incongruity. But part of his anger was reserved for those intellectuals who had yielded the native field without a fight, departing for a shallow cosmopolitanism or, worse, staying at home to mock. He was intellectually but never socially intolerant of pacifists on this score. He rejected their policies but defended their principles and liked their company. He confessed to a liking for the 'rather jingoistic' ballad of 'Admiral Benbow' because there was, he said, a tradition that old Benbow had risen from the ranks and remained a friend of the common seaman.

Orwell was careful, amid all his diatribes, to distinguish between *patriotism*, as love of one's own native land (so that anyone who grows into that love can be a patriot), and *nationalism*, as a claim to natural superiority over others (so that States must naturally consist of one nation and seek to exclude others). It is typical that he makes this distinction, which is of extraordinary importance, briefly and almost in passing, neither elaborating it theoretically nor exploring its implications. But it is clear, deliberate, and it is there in his essay 'Notes on Nationalism' of 1945.

Certainly there was a gentler patriotism in Orwell which preceded his socialism and stemmed from his love of English literature, customs and countryside. In many ways he remained socially conservative, or as his friend Cyril Connolly put it in a famous aphorism, 'a revolutionary who was in love with the 1900s'. Orwell said of himself in 'Why I Write' of 1946, the same essay that declared himself to be a political writer: 'I am not able, and do not want, completely to abandon the world-view that I acquired in childhood. So long as I remain alive and well I shall continue to feel strongly about prose style, to love the surface of the earth and to take pleasure in solid objects and scraps of useless information.' He would tease the fierce readers of *Tribune* by writing a column on the beauty and longevity of a Woolworth sixpenny rosebush or an essay on the mating habits of the common toad. His socialism embraces both memory and nature.

He is a specifically English writer and a specifically English character, both in his seeming amateurism – sometimes truly amateurish – and in his eccentricities. He lived and dressed as simply as he came to write, and in some ways as oddly. But he was never insular. He was steeped in French and also in Russian literature through translation, though hardly at all in German. He knew more about European and colonial politics in the 1930s and 1940s than most of his literary contemporaries, or politicians for that matter. He followed contemporary American writing closely but knew little about American history and politics – had he known more he might have avoided misunderstandings when *Animal Farm* and *Nineteen Eighty-Four* were published in America. His other best works came to be reprinted and translated well and widely. He had things to say which are still of universal significance, more so than those of some far more systematic philosophical and academic thinkers. And something of his characteristic style, discursiveness and colloquial ease, the buttonholing directness, the zeal to write for a broad, rather than a purely intellectual public, must come across even in translation, for his style has influenced a generation of young writers in Germany, Japan and Italy, for instance, who do not all read him in the original. Throughout the world 'Orwellian' means this English essayist's manner as well as the quite different connotation that 'Orwellian' has gained from *Nineteen Eighty-Four*.

He is also, perhaps in the very security of his Englishness (it is Englishness, not Britishness, incidentally), a writer of historical stature on English national character. His *Lion and the Unicorn* and his later reworking of some of the same themes in *The English People* are among the few serious studies of the English national character, quite different from the celebratory banalities of Sir Arthur Bryant, Sir Winston Churchill, or even Dr A. L. Rowse. He did not merely write about the manners of the English, but attempted to assess the matter of Britain in the light of our history; who we were and what we *should* do as a people. He offered a moral and sociological stocktaking, both patriotic and radical, worrying about what was happening to England, the degradation and selfishness of its inhabitants and the despoliation of its landscape; but always having hope in the common sense of the common people and pleasure in their pastimes. American intellectuals have often, almost obsessively, at times masochistically, addressed themselves to the question of 'what is an American?'. English intellectuals have kept well away from such speculation, offering little more than smug asides and rude jibes. Now, amid new uncertainties, not just psychological but directly political, such as doubts about the laws of citizenship and the unity of the United Kingdom, we are finding the need for such assessments. Those writing such books will have to start where Orwell left off.

Some literary friends in Orwell's last years of fame never understood his politics nor accepted the importance he attached to politics in general. Cyril Connolly, for instance, often urged Orwell to get away from his political journalism and back to the writing of real novels. Such English intellectuals themselves represented that divorce of political and literary sensibility which Orwell's life contradicted and which so many of his essays railed against. In France, Germany and in the United States it had long been more customary for intellectuals to be viewed as public figures and to make their views known on public questions, sometimes pompously and pretentiously, on occasion ignorantly, but it was both accepted and expected that they should do so. When English intellectuals did commit themselves, as did some but by no means all in the 1930s (legends grow and are fostered), they tended, Orwell considered, to go to extremes, to go overboard, to act with an irresponsible enthusiasm and ignorance like boy scouts on an afternoon's outing, not as mature men journeying through life. In 'Inside the Whale' he struck savagely at W. H. Auden in those terms. The polemicist exaggerated and, as regards people, sometimes hit out crushingly at the wrong enemy. But he was basically right. Many English intellectuals who considered themselves political had, in fact, a divided sensibility and double standards. They tolerated, expected and practised a reckless and passionate sincerity and a crudeness of judgement in politics, even called for it, of a kind that they would not tolerate for one moment in literary writing or in literary criticism. Sense and sensibility were for art, and anger and authenticity were for politics. But Orwell developed a political sensibility of an ancient kind, if rare in the industrial modern world, that without being precisely philosophical and analytical was reflective and conceptually imaginative as well as polemical and activist.* Whether he knew it or not he lay close to the Graeco-Roman republican roots of European civilization which assumed the indivisibility of citizenship and culture, whereas so many of his friends believed in separation and wasted

* Two of Orwell's friends have understood and written well about the precise quality of his political writing as political sensibility: George Woodcock in *The Crystal Spirit: A Study of George Orwell* (London, 1967) reprinted by Minerva Press, New York; and Julian Symons, 'Orwell, a Reminiscence', *London Magazine*, September 1963, pp. 35–49, and 'An Appreciation', being a postscript to the Heron Books (London, 1970) edition of *Nineteen Eighty-Four*, pp. 317–45.

many words rationalizing their own alienation from the public realm.

So as well as a political writer, Orwell was a political thinker of genuine stature. *Nineteen Eighty-Four* can be seen as a 'development model', of a kind familiar to economic historians and social scientists, challenging comparison, in its ironic logic and internal consistency, with Thomas Hobbes' *Leviathan*, the masterpiece of English political philosophy. The governing régime is a wickedly clever and plausible synthesis of Stalinism and Nazism. *Nineteen Eighty-Four* is to the disorders of the twentieth century what *Leviathan* was to those of the seventeenth. Orwell chose to write in the form of a novel, not in the form of a philosophical tractatus. He would, indeed, have been incapable of writing a contemporary philosophical monograph, scarcely of understanding one. He was what Oxford dons sometimes call 'an untrained mind' (that is, untamed). He sailed boldly and skilfully, reached and explored some important destinations, but he had not the least idea of the theories of navigation or of naval architecture. To theorize about political developments in the form of a novel rather than as a treatise has advantages in reaching a wider public and for intuitive understanding, but disadvantages in credibility and explanatory precision.

Hobbes believed that a breakdown in good government would cause a return to a hypothetical state of nature, a condition of violent anarchy where the life of man is 'solitary, poore, nasty, brutish and short'. Orwell believed that a breakdown in good government (by which he meant a breakdown in liberty, tolerance and welfare) could cause a leap forward into a hypothetical world order of one-party total power, a kind of State that the world had never seen before. He thought it would be unique in that the vestiges of genuine ideology, whether Communist or Fascist, would have withered away and yet merged in a single hierarchy of oppression and propaganda motivated by a desire for pure power: 'If you want a picture of the future of humanity imagine a boot stamping on a human face – for ever.' Memory would be abolished, history rewritten and language controlled.

Orwell had first formulated the concept of totalitarianism shortly after his escape from Spain. He argued that common factors were emerging in Stalinism and in Nazism concerned with the retention and extension of power by the inner party élite. These lead the state to mobilize all society as if for perpetual and total war, a common process more important than the vestigial and nominally antagonistic ideologies. Koestler, Borkenau, Silone, Malraux and Orwell all established this usage and began to develop the theory at about the same time, 1936 to 1940 (as far as I can discover, quite independently of each other). They were all political and literary intellectuals in 'the continental manner', as the Englishman Orwell was to say of the others. They set out this theory and acted upon it. It was to be a decade and a half before the scholars and the academics 'invented' or 'discovered' the totalitarian thesis and elaborated it at length, notably Hannah Arendt in her *Origins of Totalitarianism* (1951) and Carl Friederich and Zbigniew Brzezinski in their *Totalitarian Dictatorship and Autocracy* (1956). Arendt nowhere refers to *Nineteen Eighty-Four* although it anticipates many of her conclusions.

If one takes the term 'political writer' in its broadest sense to include philosophers, statesmen, publicists and pamphleteers who might claim to be secure in the canon of English literature, three names seem indisputably pre-eminent: Thomas Hobbes, Jonathan Swift, and George Orwell. The intellectual historian might make some claims for Edmund Burke, J. S. Mill or William Morris, but Burke and Mill, while fine writers indeed, seem too narrow in their range, sonorous but pedestrian compared to the nominated three; and to read Morris after Swift and Orwell is to condemn him as being too consciously literary by far, however original and influential were many of his ideas. Hobbes was a philosopher, grinding and grounding every point, but also indulging in a vast polemical irony that makes *Leviathan* a masterpiece of baroque prose. Swift was a pamphleteer and the supreme satirist, able to satirize knowledgeably philosophy and theology as well as party politics, but not himself philosophical; and his style was a forceful blend of classical form and colloquial diction, so that *Gulliver* is a masterpiece of Augustan prose. Orwell in one work approached the importance and the scale of Hobbes, but he had none of his philosophical knowledge or disposition; and in many others of his works he learned consciously from Swift how colloquiality and formality can be mingled both for comic and polemic effect, and in so doing evolved his own flexible plain style which, while not the most beautiful modern English prose, is certainly the best model of English writing for a hundred and one different purposes. Orwell's common style rested on the questionable assumption that all knowledge can be reduced to common sense. But if he did not have the philosophical sophistication of Hobbes, yet his common sense saved him from Swift's bitter pessimism, at times hatred of humanity. For the thing about common sense is that one believes that other people, quite ordinary people, have it too.

The achievement is more important than the man. The main theme of a biography might therefore simply be how he came to hold the original and heterodox views of *Homage to Catalonia, Animal Farm* and *Nineteen Eighty-Four*. But that would be too narrow, excluding not only a picture of the life he led but also the achievement of the writer. Many of the best essays would get lost. And the essays raise at once the peculiarly Orwellian problem of the image of the writer and the character of the man. The very image he came to exhibit or established is complex, for such a simple man (so it is said). To hold Orwellian views and to write in an Orwellian manner mean different things. How could the essayist Orwell, revelling in natural variety, produce the Orwellian vision of a totally machined society? The common-sense answer is that being a writer of great ability, he adopted another style and mode of writing when he wanted to warn against the *possibility* of something happening. But if one reads *Nineteen Eighty-Four* before any other book of Orwell's or is told that it was his last testament, then one may well believe that it is a prophecy or forecast of the future, not simply an awful warning. Then there is, indeed, a contradiction between the two images of Orwell, and so people have presumed a change of character and of values in his last years. I examined this view very carefully, since it was commonly held and important, but I am bound to say that I found no evidence for it.

Some people still underestimate him as a writer. Why identify the final and utter pessimism and defeat of Winston Smith with the milder pessimism of the author? Why identify the shallow and imperceptive nostalgia of George Bowling in *Coming Up For Air* with George Orwell's loving, but knowing and measured, even half-ironic nostalgia? Mere names mislead. With what other novelist would so many readers and critics so confidently identify characters with author? Is the man so simple or does his art lull or gull some of his readers into simplicity? Perhaps the trouble arises from the nature of the essayist who appears to talk about himself so much, about *his* experiences and *his* prejudices. How closely related is that 'George Orwell' to Eric Blair who became known as George Orwell? The art of the colloquial essayist, himself constantly and amusingly breaking the normal divide between fact and fiction, between the real person and the persona, this is well enough understood; but it can make things difficult when the same man is also a novelist; it can actually encourage critics and readers to think of Winston Smith as what Orwell thought he himself might become. Suppose there was, however, an Orwell mask that got stuck upon the private and modest person, Eric Blair? Does that diminish the performance?

'Orwell' sets many traps both for himself and for his readers. The question is only important, of course, if one is primarily concerned with the man. Some have said that the man is more important than his writings, meaning the example of the life he led. I do not share this view. A biographer should not, in any case, accept such absolute disjunctions between 'character', 'circumstances' and 'works'. Also the view diminishes his works. I suspect that when his old friend, Sir Richard Rees (in his *George Orwell: Fugitive from the Camp of Victory*, Secker & Warburg, London, 1961), called him 'almost saintly', it was because he was never as happy with the content of Orwell's writing as he hoped to be.

Some have found an easier solution to this problem of the literary Orwell and a real Orwell. But I have found no evidence that a man called Eric Blair changed character when he came to call himself for the publication of the first book, 'George Orwell'. I have observed, however, a more subtle and gradual process, that Julian Symons first noted, by which Blair came to adopt the Orwell part of himself as an ideal image to be lived up to: an image of integrity, honesty, simplicity, egalitarian conviction, plain living, plain writing and plain speaking, in all a man with an almost reckless commitment to speaking out unwelcome truths: 'liberty is what people do not want to hear.' But a public image of Orwell grew up even in his lifetime which was like a vulgarized version of this somewhat ideal image. It presented Orwell as the corporal of the awkward squad, that perennial difficult fellow who speaks unwanted home truths out of order, asks embarrassing questions, pricks the bubbles of his own side's occasional pomposity, who goes too far in all this, making the whole Labour movement sound like a swarm of pacifist, naturist, fruit-juice-drinking cranks, and loses his own sense of humour when he cannot appreciate that a pack of lies is ideological necessity, or that an election address is necessarily humbug. 'If you look into your own mind, which are you,' Orwell once asked, 'Don Quixote or Sancho Panza?' George Woodcock began his study of Orwell with that quotation.

But I must explain why I do not think that one can look into Orwell's mind, or minds – or anyone else's. The best that a biographer can do is to understand the relationship between the writer and the man, between Don Quixote and Sancho Panza, by examining their journey together in detail, always remembering that what they did together and how they reacted to what happened along the way will tell us more than constantly analysing and re-analysing their 'characters' and the difference between them.

Biography and 'Character'

What kind of biography, then, have I tried to write about a man with this kind of achievement? I began with the naïve idea that the main task would be to know the character of Orwell as well as humanly possible, while all the time working away at the facts, so that by knowing him, understanding his inwardness, entering into his mind, I could supply his motivations, perhaps even correcting his own later accounts of them, and make sensitive suppositions (i.e., guess) at what was happening when documentation was lacking. But simultaneously reading a lot of 'good biography' and beginning to grapple with the evidence for this book, not in any rational order (as I had hoped) but simply as it came, dictated by ease of access to papers and the proximity or age of certain witnesses, I grew to be sceptical of much of the fine writing, balanced appraisal and psychological insight that is the hallmark of the English tradition of biography. It may be pleasant to read, but readers should realize that often they are being led by the nose, or that the biographer is fooling himself by an affable pretence of being able to enter into another person's mind. All too often the literary virtues of the English biographical tradition give rise to characteristic vices: smoothing out or silently resolving contradictions in the evidence and bridging gaps by empathy and intuition (our famous English 'good judgement of character' which, compared to the French stress on formal criteria, lets us down so often); and this all done so elegantly that neither contradictions nor gaps in the evidence are apparent to any but scholarly eyes carefully reading the footnotes or cynically noting their lack. None of us can enter into another person's mind; to believe so is fiction. We can only know actual persons by observing their behaviour in a variety of different situations and through different perspectives. Hence the great emphasis I found myself placing on reporting the views of his contemporaries at unusual length and in their own words, neither synthesizing nor always sensitively resolving them when they conflicted. Wyndham Lewis once remarked that good biographies are like novels. He did not intend to let the cat out of the bag.

Some good bad biographies appear to be, epistemologically speaking, novels indeed. That is the extreme of the empathetic fallacy. A contrary extreme is a purely empiricist presentation of the evidence, such as one can find in biographies written by professional historians. But they too deceive themselves if they think to avoid selectivity simply by offering a commentary on extracts from original archives. Rather than produce a symbolic distillation called 'basic character', they throw a cloud of dust – called facts – in our eyes. Common sense suggests that one can and must characterize Henry VIII, Wallenstein, Shaftesbury, Woodrow Wilson or Lloyd George, indeed offer rival contemporary characterizations too, but without abandoning the evidence and the chronicle of events for the seductive short-cuts and pseudo-certainties even of 'empathy', still less of literary psychoanalysis.

One has only the evidence that one can find. Which papers survive and which do not is largely accidental; there is no neat proportionality between the records and periods of Orwell's life. His letters to his agent, for instance, survive and are a continuous series from 1930 to 1949, but his agent's letters to him, which would add much to the tale, were foolishly destroyed. Orwell was not the kind of man to keep intimate diaries or to write long personal letters. For most of his career he was too strapped for cash, too hard pressed earning a living by book-reviewing and column journalism to have done so, even had he wished; and to say that he was careless about preserving copies of letters he did write would be to imply that he should have seen some point in doing so. Orwell's ambitions as a writer were modest and what he valued was publication. He was not born to the literary purple of the Bloomsbury group, whose every scribbled note to 'come to tea on Tuesday' seem to contain phrases of wit, malice or insight written in the knowledge or hope that one day they would be published or be useful to some relative writing a biography. Which is the more valuable record of a state of mind, or interesting human document: a file of self-conscious literary letters carefully preserved by the sender, or a few hasty but argumentative letters sent without copies to a friend who happens not to destroy them? Gaps in the evidence are inevitable and should not be disguised either by expanding with surmise what we do not have, or by contracting, for the sake of balanced chapter lengths, what we do have.

Thus the texture of this biography is necessarily lumpy and uneven, both because I quote so much, to let Orwell and his contemporaries tell their own tales as far as possible, and because the sources are so uneven and bear no relationship to the relative importance of events in his life. Of course one tries to fill gaps, or to find other sources of evidence. Any scholar will know the ghastly disproportion of time one spends searching for people or papers that one is relatively unlikely to find compared to the speed and economy with which one assimilates an important section of a large and well-ordered correspondence in an archive. But when one does have to speculate, when a gap in the evidence seems crucial to the coherence of other parts of the record, one should simply say so clearly. I use words like 'probably' and 'possibly' and 'might' as little as possible, but do so when coherence dictates. A biographer has a duty to show how he reaches his conclusions, not to pretend to omniscience; and he should share things that are moot, problematic and uncertain with the reader.

The need to present conflicts in evidence rather than to resolve them all neatly is particularly acute because there is so much good writing about Orwell by famous men of letters who either only knew him in the last few years of his fame, or did not in fact pay much attention to him before. They are eye-witnesses of a few years but can only speculate about and offer hearsay evidence for the long formative years when he was struggling to succeed as a writer. As poets and novelists, they do not always make the distinction clear, so I have always sought and, when I could find it, preferred the direct evidence of people who knew him at the relevant times. A good memory has nothing to do with literary abilities. Indeed sometimes when people have published their memories of someone, their writings act as a block to any further memories and, when interviewed, they simply repeat and defend, consciously or unconsciously, their published position.

A reader has observed that my stress on externality, standing outside Orwell, noting his behaviour, noting contemporary characterizations of him but not claiming to be able to get inside him and to *know his character*, creates an alienation effect. Perhaps so, for the trouble with the empathetic approach to acting, Brecht argued, was that in trying to create the illusion of being someone else, the character is then fixed, frozen and unchallengeable. The audience loses any critical distance and must accept or reject totally the character as portrayed. But both human freedom and good art demand not a suspension of disbelief, but a critical awareness that an actor is acting and that the part could be played in other ways; more generally, that the world could be other than it was and is. So also with an actual human life and a biography. I interpret Orwell's character while feeling acutely aware that other sensible people (who actually knew him) see him rather differently. And yet we cannot substitute 'context' for 'character'. We may understand a person better by knowing more about their history and background, but however much we know there is no inevitable inference from these antecedent facts to what someone actually writes. Childhood experiences, for instance, may limit, but they do not determine. Freedom, imagination, will and chance are all at play throughout life, especially in someone as self-conscious as Orwell: we must be as much on our guard in biography against the danger of reducing everything that happened to character or psychology, as we should be that the need to establish a context does not produce a crude reduction of events to economic structures.

Interpretations about character can even be perceptive and correct, and yet misleading about the actual course of someone's life. Sonia Orwell spoke for many of his friends when she said in the Introduction to *The Collected Essays, Journalism and Letters*: 'If political events had made less impact on him, he would have lived in the country, written a book – preferably a novel – a year, pursued his interest in the essay form and, when money was badly lacking, done straightforward book reviews which, he said, he enjoyed writing ... War made him a political activist ...' But so it did and political events did have a great impact on him – or should one say it was not in his character to ignore them? If we are too confident in our judgements of character we end up by writing instead of history a kind of speculative teleology: what he should have done had he lived differently or longer.

Each of us may even speculate that we have a 'true character' which is not fully realized in our actual life. Orwell himself began a poem in 1935 'A happy vicar I might have been/Two hundred years ago', but the poem goes on to point ironically to the impossibility of this when '... born, alas, in an evil time'; and when he quotes this poem himself in his 'Why I Write' of 1946, it is to say that 'the Spanish war and other events in 1936–37 turned the scale and thereafter I knew where I stood', that what 'he most wanted to do' was 'to make political writing into an art'. Alas, indeed, the only life one can write about is the life someone actually led in reaction to actual events in a particular 'evil time', not about 'true character'. Otherwise biography descends into psycho-drama, just as so many people in an ultra-individualistic culture can waste so much of their sensibility and frustrate so much of their life in wondering who they 'really are'. Our human identity consists in relationships, not in inwardness.

I realize that the externality of my method runs the risk that I appear unsympathetic to Orwell, putting him in the box, as it were, under oath and treating his testimony critically. I would rather run this risk, however (liking him very much, but admitting, not surprisingly, that the works are greater than the man), than pontificate about character and states of mind. Sympathy must be present in a biographer – otherwise one would grow sour living for so long with someone one disliked; but sympathy is not, once again, a reliable short cut to establishing, so far as is possible, what actually happened at the time. An honest biographer must be more dull than he could be, must repress proud inclinations to 'recreate a life' or to imagine too often what someone 'really felt' on some crucial occasion.

If not on 'states of mind' and 'character', then on what threads have I come to hang this biography? Basically I found that I was looking more and more at his occupations, what he was doing to stay alive, and at his bibliography. Once he was determined to be a writer, everything seems secondary to the production of his books and essays. With someone else, circles of friends might be the thread, but not with Orwell: he was grudging with his time, had developed solitary habits in school and Burma, kept different circles well apart; they were all secondary to his passion to write. The main tale must be of how his books and essays came to be written and of how they were published.

This again swung me away from internality towards externality, from the British tradition of the inward eye and what Dr Johnson called 'domestic privacies' (when he virtually invented biography as an English literary mode), towards something closer, I discovered, to the French tradition of literary biography: an account of a subject's public life and of the impact of his works. Certainly this shift has some surprising consequences. What of childhood and the time before works are published? I believe that many English biographers have unnecessarily perplexed themselves by trying to demonstrate that the child is always father to the literary man, when on any cool appraisal of first publications we must often be as astonished at the unpredictable discontinuities from childhood as with the few slender analogues. We have not yet emancipated ourselves either from literary Freudianism or from the cultural belief of the English upper middle classes that school-days are necessarily crucial, whether for good or ill (sometimes this belief amounts to a cult of permanent adolescence). However I discover to my surprise that the amount of space I have actually given to his childhood is greater than I had intended. The difficulty is that there have been so many theories about his mature work based upon thinly supported surmises about his childhood and particularly his schooling, that I have had to spend a disproportionate amount of time in order to reach an essentially negative conclusion. Truth often has to deal in dull negations, unlike the glittering results of intuition and characterology.

This volume is not, however, a 'Life and Times' either: such a formula, unless a man has a great effect on events, is mainly padding. I am worried enough that people sometimes treat a full biography as an *introduction* to the subject's writings, but to think that a biography could also provide a political and social history of the twentieth century is absurd. I have written as briefly as possible, thinking of the general reader but assuming that he has read some Orwell already and has at least a background knowledge of the political and literary history of our times. Yet it is not literary criticism either, not 'Life and Works'. This distinction is not crucial, however – only a self-denying ordinance to prevent elephantiasis. How the books came to be written and published is the central theme of the biography of any writer, but not necessarily a full appreciation of the books themselves, seen as texts and symbolic structures. The line is not always easy to draw, it depends on the nature of the writings: none of Orwell's works raise the same problems for a biographer as do the major works of Joyce or Proust. So I have only discussed the texts when strictly relevant to biography – which, in fact, is often. None the less a biography must have limited aims.

Right from the beginning I realized how complex was the relationship between Orwell's life and his writings. All of his books except the last two are obviously based upon his own experiences, and it is clear that he deliberately went out to gain experiences in order to write about them. This is customary and raises no problems in writers of travel books. But Orwell was primarily a traveller through his own land, through his own society and his own memories. As V. S. Pritchett said, he was 'a writer who has "gone native" in his own country'. Even beyond that double relationship, however, I soon saw that if the autobiographical quality of his novels became a common-place of criticism from shortly after his death, it has been less often grasped how extraordinarily creative and imaginative were his 'documentaries'. *Down and Out in Paris and London*, *The Road to Wigan Pier*, and *Homage to Catalonia*, as well as essays like 'A Hanging', 'Shooting an Elephant', and 'Such, Such Were the Joys', his essay on prep school, raise similar problems – indeed the latter is the most puzzling of all his works to locate accurately between fiction and non-fiction. Each of his documentaries is on a different footing and will be looked at separately. Do we think of documentaries as necessarily conveying the literal truth about the 'I' who pretends to be what the author must know he never can be, 'a camera'? Should we rather not try to gain some critical distance from the documentary technique by exploring the author's intentions biographically as well as by examining the literary result. (Otherwise, we may, like that humble sea-captain, write to the author demanding to be shown where Lilliput is upon the map. Did Orwell witness a hanging and shoot an elephant?) Intentions and results are not always the same. I will seek to show, for instance, that there is little reasonable doubt what effects he *intended* to achieve in both *Animal Farm* and *Nineteen Eighty-Four* about which, for works written in such clear and simple English, interpretations have varied so greatly.

'Though he invented nothing, he altered everything,' was George Painter's conclusion about the relationship of *A la Recherche du temps perdu* to Proust's own life. Reading this remark crystallized my feelings that a biography of Orwell was needed, despite the seeming straightforwardness of his own autobiographical passages and the chronological progression of the four volumes of *The Collected Essays, Journalism and Letters*, precisely in order to understand his literary achievement better. For Orwell had said in *The Road to Wigan Pier* of his earlier *Down and Out in Paris and London* that 'Nearly all the incidents described there actually happened, but they have been re-arranged'. I cannot entirely agree with Sonia Orwell when she said in her influential Introduction to *The Collected Essays* that all his novels except *Animal Farm* and *Nineteen Eighty-Four* 'contain *straight* descriptions of himself' or that 'a whole chapter of *The Road to Wigan Pier* suddenly turns into *straight* autobiography' (my italics). Some critics, particularly when commenting on 'Such, Such Were the Joys' have not distinguished between the rare autobiographical 'I' and the more common storyteller's 'I'. ('Were you really present when all those events occurred at Simla, Mr Kipling? "Plain Tales" indeed!') To question the literal truth or straightforwardness of some of his writings is not to question his honesty and his integrity, but is rather to notice how his skill as a writer and his persona as a public figure have made some of us willing to accept his partly imagined worlds as literally true. It is easy to underestimate the literary achievement of his 'documentaries'* and to confuse his straightforwardness as a person (the first and last impression he made on so many people) with the seeming-simplicity of his major writings.

One of his oldest friends fell into this trap. The late Sir Richard Rees, his first literary executor, wrote to Sonia Orwell (28 January 1950) advising against publication of 'Such, Such Were the Joys':

... it is such a bad piece of writing, far below G's standard. If one knows, as I do, that he was already past his best when he wrote it, one does not allow it to shake one's confidence in his ability as a reporter of his own experiences. But if one did not know that, one might well wonder after reading it whether what he reports in *Down and Out in Paris and London* and *Wigan Pier*, and *Catalonia*, should be taken seriously.

If he had not dismissed it as a bad piece of writing and made a questionable assumption about when it was written, he might have been led

* No one has written a scholarly study of the documentary as a fashionable genre between the two wars, its conventions about fact and fiction and its links both with social research and the realistic novel.

to wonder whether he was right simply to praise his friend for 'ability as a reporter of his own experiences'. Not all reporters write so well and raise moral issues. On Rees' line of reasoning, *Down and Out* would have been a greater work of art but Orwell a worse man if it could be proved that he had never been to Paris. Orwell's documentaries were all far more subtle and difficult to allocate between the Fiction and the Non-Fiction shelves than Rees appreciated. Rees had his friend somewhat patronizingly typecast, a kind of Douanier Rousseau of English Letters.

The problem of genre and truth is important in reading 'Such, Such Were the Joys' as evidence of what happened at his prep school and of how he reacted to it at the time. The problem is even more acute because some have read into the essay a direct relationship with *Nineteen Eighty-Four*, have reduced the novel to a self-dramatization of trauma at his prep school, strengthening this case by assuming, from the chronological position in which it is printed in *The Collected Essays*, that he wrote the essay immediately before the fatal writing of his last great book. If this were so, the end is indeed in the beginning and an orderly chronological narrative becomes impossible. *Nineteen Eighty-Four* is then evidence on the character of his formative years and St Cyprian's is the key to understanding the government and psychology of Airstrip One in *Nineteen Eighty-Four*. This thesis lies like a booby-trapped road-block across any progress towards a sensible understanding of Orwell's life and achievement, so I have to devote virtually the whole of a chapter to clearing up these confusions. A short preliminary chapter draws attention to the ambivalence of his memories of childhood. I have learned in these researches to have a great scepticism about the accuracy of memory, about both states of mind and facts, unless supported by some external evidence.

To move from the achievements to the man is also to remember that the man expressed a wish in his will that a biography should not be written. Such a wish is bound to be forlorn, as the executors of Hardy and Kipling found. Attempts to enforce such wishes only lead to biographies being written without proper access to sources. Why did he make such a wish, however? Perhaps he simply disliked those sensation-mongering kinds of biography of which he had read and reviewed so many. But he once wrote to John Atkins, his predecessor as Literary Editor of *Tribune*, that he thought that a truthful biography was impossible 'because every life viewed from the inside would be a series of defeats too humiliating and disgraceful to contemplate'. This suggests that he thought of biography as trying to view 'from the inside', as primarily concerned with Samuel Johnson's 'domestic privacies'. These 'privacies' were once noble and pathetic, advantages or obstacles to be overcome on the road to authorship and fame; since Lytton Strachey they have become the exposure of personal inadequacies, warping or shaping future writing. But whichever mode of privacies was to be pursued, the ancient or the modern, or to put it crudely (and precisely) in Orwell-like terms, whether an official life or a hatchet job, his objection would be the same: its irrelevance to what he valued, his writings, not himself. He had no great secrets to hide, he simply valued his privacy and despised irrelevant effort. At times he almost literally cared for his writing more than his life, certainly more than his comfort and physical well-being. He was both a brave man and one who drove himself hard, for the sake, first, of 'writing' and then more and more for an integrated sense of *what* he had to write.

He might, of course, have withdrawn his objection had he known that with the passage of time some of his writings could be badly misunderstood because of mistaken beliefs about the nature of his life. And he might have objected less to a way of writing biography that looks at the writer's position as a public figure: 'in France a far more classical, mandarin, Eliotesque idea has prevailed, emphasizing . . . the *clericature* of the writer', as Ian Willison has put it: 'This implies an indifference to domestic privacies in themselves on the part not only of the author but of the serious reader as well.'* Orwell with his vivid attacks on 'intellectuals', but with his high-minded view of the political and moral responsibilities of men of letters, deserves to be treated in this manner rather than in the Johnsonian. But the disjunction between English and French biography is one of emphasis, tempered by fact, not a total separation. If the domestic privacies are relevant to understanding the writings or the public role of an author, then they must be fully treated and not ignored; but if they are not relevant, they need not be examined and therefore, for the sake of clarity and economy,

---

*I am grateful to Ian Willison for showing me his 'Authors and their Publishing Histories: the Case of George Orwell', to appear in a forthcoming number of *Publishing History*. I take from him the point about Johnson and the contrasting French tradition.

should not be examined. In fact I explore domestic privacies a great deal, but only because of the kind of writer that Orwell was: not simply a novelist, but an essayist and a journalist who dealt with private morals in an autobiographical vein quite as much as he dealt with public issues. Mild disparities between personal conduct and public preachment are sometimes revealed, but not of a kind that should discredit a man – unless foolish claims are made to saintliness or to total honesty and openness on all occasions. It is always easy simply to drop the preachments and to lead a life of full and empty acquisitive zeal and material comfort. Prying into his 'domestic privacies', discovering the full measure of the pain and difficulties that he underwent, have heightened my initial respect for the man as well as for, above all else, the writer.

Orwell was unusually reticent to his friends about his background and his life, his openness was all in print for literary or moral effect; he tried to keep his small circles of good friends well apart – people are still surprised to learn who else at the time he knew; he did not confide in people easily, nor talk about his emotions – even to women with whom he was close; he was not fully integrated as a person, not quite comfortable within his own skin, until late in his life – and he was many-faceted, not a simple man at all. So for all these reasons the famous honest and straightforward man, George Woodcock's 'crystal spirit', appears as enigmatic, and has positively challenged and provoked his contemporaries to attempt, both in his own brief years of fame and in some remarkable obituaries and posthumous essays, to characterize him. There has been astonishing agreement either that the man was more interesting than much of his work or else that the work could only be understood by accurately characterizing the man. There are many such characterizations, nearly all beautifully written, but they differ significantly.

What I have come to believe through this work is simply this: that one can say less that is meaningful about the real character of the man than is usually assumed in the English biographical tradition and yet more that is true about the kind of life he led than is often supposed. The labour of writing a biography, like the education of a child, involves a prolonged and strange mixture of love and critical distance, of commitment and restraint.

CHAPTER ONE

'AND I WAS A CHUBBY BOY'

WHAT kind of childhood did he think he had? In the brief days of his fame and towards what proved to be the end of his life, George Orwell grew a little less cagey and more mellow about the past than hitherto. The last book review that he wrote in 1948 for the *Adelphi*, which had published his first book review of 1930, was of the third volume of Sir Osbert Sitwell's autobiography. As unpredictable as a good essayist should be, he praised this account of aristocratic life. Sitwell 'has never pretended to be other than he is,' unlike, as Orwell's regular readers would now almost expect him to say, 'a whole literary generation ... pretending to be proletarians'.

There is now a widespread idea that nostalgic feelings about the past are inherently vicious. One ought apparently to live in a continuous present, a minute-to-minute cancellation of memory, and if one thinks of the past at all it should merely be in order to thank God that we are so much better than we used to be. This seems to me a sort of intellectual face-lifting, the motive behind which is a snobbish terror of growing old. One ought to realize that a human being cannot continue developing indefinitely, and that a writer in particular is throwing away his heritage if he repudiates the experience of his early life. In many ways it is a grave handicap to remember that lost paradise 'before the War' – that is, before the other war. In other ways it is an advantage ... One is likelier to make a good book by sticking to one's early-acquired vision than by a futile effort to 'keep up'. The great thing is to be your age, which includes being honest about your social origins.[1]

In the same year Orwell, writing from his bed in Hairmyres Hospital, East Kilbride, to his friend Julian Symons, reflected on children and childhood with a kind of cheerful gloominess, very much the mark of the man:

They're awful fun in spite of the nuisance, and as they develop one has one's own childhood over again. I suppose one thing one has to guard against is imposing one's own childhood on the child, but I do think it relatively easy to give a child a decent time nowadays and allow it to escape the quite unnecessary torments that I for instance went through. I'm not sure either that one ought to trouble too much about bringing a child into a world of atomic bombs, because those born now will never have known anything except wars, rationing, etc. and can probably be quite happy against that background if they've had a good psychological start.[2]

Many times George Orwell referred to the torments of his childhood. Most people writing about him have accepted that he had a uniformly unhappy childhood, and some have built upon it. The posthumously published account of his prep school days, 'Such, Such Were the Joys', is so unhappy and so horrific a picture of institutional despotism that some have seen it, rather than the political events in Europe of the 1930s and 1940s, as the origins of *Nineteen Eighty-Four*.[3] Notice, however, that Orwell in the letter to Julian Symons uses the plural, 'quite unnecessary torments', as if to stress different events and incidents, whereas use of the singular would have implied a general process or a permanent condition, whether physical or psychological.

One close childhood friend actually called him 'a specially happy child', and chides the mature artist for retouching, indeed distorting, his own childhood to give depth to his later, as she sees them, morbid political preoccupations.[4] 'Specially happy' is a large and dubious claim, except perhaps for the vacations from prep school. Yet experience is not always all of one piece, particularly for children who have little control over their immediate environment; and nor is behaviour. In some situations a child is happy, in others regularly unhappy; and it is a commonplace that he or she 'behaves quite differently here than at home'. Other things that Orwell wrote about his childhood carry connotations explicitly more mixed, torment and happiness, shame and nostalgia.

Odd things triggered his memory. 'The other night a barmaid informed me that to dip your moustache into your beer ... turns it flat,' which led the Literary Editor of *Tribune* in 1944 to tell his readers that he had a notebook with a long list of fallacies that were taught to him in childhood as if they were scientific fact. He gave them a few examples. Here is the full list, for he did have such a notebook.[5]

That you will be struck dead if you go into church with your hat on.

That you can be had up for putting a stamp on a letter upside down.

That if you make a face and the wind changes, you will be stuck like that.

That if you wash your hands in the water that eggs have been boiled in, you will get warts.

That there is a reward of £50 for spending a night in the Chamber of Horrors at Madame Tussaud's.

That bats get into women's hair, after which the women's heads have to be shaved.

That if you cut yourself between the thumb and forefinger, you get lockjaw.

That powdered glass is poisonous.

That bulls are enraged at the sight of red.

That swans can break your leg with a blow of a wing.

That if you tell a lie, you get a spot on your tongue.

That people who have a touch of the tarbrush can be detected by their fingernails.

That orientals are not subject to sunstroke.

That dogs are good judges of character.

That all toadstools are poisonous.

That pigs cannot swim because if they do they cut their throats with their trotters.

Thus in a traditional country like England even the middle classes have their folklore: most of these will be familiar to English readers. But even if all such recall is induced memory tainted by later events, the picture of childhood he evoked by his list has humour and pleasure in it as well as pain; or at least – another Orwellian trademark – the bizarre and the ordinary intermingle as he looked at his own country as if he were a traveller from afar. Also he had an acute sense both of how fragmentary is an adult's recall of childhood and of how fragmented are the perceptions of a child.

In the same notebook of 1943 or 1944 (which also contained an early outline of *Nineteen Eighty-Four*) he began some notes about the fragmented nature of children's sexual beliefs. It is unclear whether they are notes towards a story or whether they are simply autobiographical, but the theme, while mainly condemnatory, also carries notes of sad comedy and willing nostalgia.

Very early in life they believed that the doctor brought the baby with him in his black bag, but at 8 or 9 (or perhaps somewhat later) they had learned that it had something to do with the man's and the woman's sexual organs. They nevertheless had to rediscover this knowledge after having more or less possessed it and then passed through a period of ignorance. Thus at the age of six, B. had played with the plumber's children up the road, until his mother found out and stopped him, and their play was largely sexual. They played at 'doctors', and also at 'mothers and fathers' (coming from a more crowded home the plumber's children were more precocious in this) and both boys and girls inspected each other's sexual organs with great interest. Yet at about 9 years of age B. seemed to have forgotten all about this and had to have it explained to him by a schoolfellow of the same age. The schoolfellow's explanation was: 'You know those two balls you have – well, you know. Well, somehow one of them gets up into the woman's body, and then it grows into a baby.' This remained the sum of B.'s knowledge for several years. The whole subject made him feel so sick that he disliked thinking about it. In order to be a daredevil and impress younger boys, he used the two words 'bugger' and 'fuck', but attached no concrete meaning to them. But at about 13 he thought more frequently about sexual intercourse, chiefly because of the constant references to it in classical literature and the Bible, but it still disgusted him. As his practical knowledge of the subject was derived from rabbits, he believed up to the age of 15, or nearly 16, that human beings do it in the same attitude as animals. At 15 he suddenly discovered that sex was attractive after all, and began masturbating; but he had no lifelike image of sexual intercourse for a year or more after this. Till the age of 16 he continued to believe that babies were born through the navel, and he only learned of menstruation at the age of 18. For several years after beginning to masturbate, he believed that this would lead to insanity, but this did nothing towards curing him of the habit.

Such ignorance and repression were, indeed, typical of an Edwardian child. Yet the interpretation, the boy feeling so sick that he disliked thinking about it, is the reflection not merely of a grown man but of a writer possibly beginning in his notebooks to shape a character, largely or partly autobiographical. To argue from this kind of evidence that there was a 'hidden wound'[6] which later damaged him is both to assume that there was damage – the reader will have to judge – that calls for such an explanation, and to underestimate how much a writer can re-imagine and re-interpret his past in order to establish the right mood for his next major piece of writing. How terrible was the mental damage caused to many by Victorian and Edwardian sexual repression and hypocrisy, but also how heartening that so many grew out of it relatively unscathed. (We must neither judge by ideal standards nor make psychological bricks from wisps of biographical straw.)

A few years later he again remembered 'the plumber's daughter' in some fragments of an unfinished poem in the same 'hospital notebook' that he used in 1948 to make some final notes towards the revision of *Nineteen Eighty-Four*:

> 'Twas on a Tuesday morning
>   When the pants hung on the line,
> The month was April or it might be May
>   And the year was nineteen-nine.
>
> We played the games that all have played,
>   Though most remember not,
> And the plumber's daughter, who might be seven,
>   She showed me all she'd got ...
>
> Round as a pudding was my face
>   That now is lean/worn and sad
>
> How long did that idyll last?
>   Not even as long as spring
> I think the May was still in bloom
>   When I did the deathly thing.
>
> I met those children on the road
>
> But I said it, yes, I said it,
>   Roman
> 'I mustn't play with you any more,
>   My mother says you're common.'
>
>   still as uncommon
>   As any in the land;
> As solid as Gibraltar Rock
>   My aitches still do stand
>
> But since that day I have never loved
>   Save those who loved me not
>
> Now what is the moral of this tale?

I would swing the great wheel back
   On my finger has not   The enemy in the
Nor faltered on the trigger   looking glass
   But let it be written
The world's decline
   The skies were bluer and seas were greener
The stickleback had a rosier breast
   A bluer egg than now a sharper joy
When good King Edward ruled the land
   And I was a chubby boy.

A sick and solitary man amuses himself by recalling his childhood and, despite the obvious irony of sky, stickleback and egg all being brighter, this is far from gloomy memory. There is no hint of sexual shame even, for it is quite clear that the 'deathly thing' is not his sexual encounter with, but his social rejection of the plumber's daughter: 'My mother says you're common.' Otherwise they simply 'played the games that all have played/Though most remember not.' He was, indeed, a revolutionary in love with the Edwardian era. Certainly the verses refer to a time before he went to prep school as recounted in 'Such, Such Were the Joys'; but both accounts come from a mature man and are different perspectives on his own childhood. Who can say which was his dominant view, still less which was true? But it is likely that both happiness and misery were present.

This prelude on memory is only a warning that we all resurrect and reinterpret our past according to our present perspectives; Orwell is no exception. Memory unsupported by documentation is not to be trusted, though it has to be used when other evidence is lacking, but carefully and critically.

Eric Arthur Blair[7] was born at Motihari in Bengal on 25 June 1903, five years after his sister Marjorie, who was born at Tehta in Bihar. His father, Richard Walmesley Blair, was in the Opium Department of the Government of India. The opium trade with China had been legalized as a government monopoly from 1860. Richard had joined it at the age of 18 and *The History of Services of Gazetted and other Officers Serving under the Government of Bengal* showed in the bare lists of its subservient second volume, 'Medical, Police, Educational and Miscellaneous Departments' (The 'also rans'), that the poor gentleman had been on the move nearly every year from post to post from when he joined the Service in 1875, first as Assistant Sub-Deputy Opium Agent, then as Sub-Deputy Opium Agent, until he retired at the age of 55. For nearly twenty years he moved posts annually, and they were not good postings. Once he did six years at Tehta in the 1890s, but the only other long spell in one place was at Monghyr, a posting that lasted from a year after his son's birth until his retirement.

Life had not dealt Richard Blair, as he might have put it, particularly good cards. His great-grandfather Charles Blair (1743–1820) had been a rich man, an owner of plantations and slaves in Jamaica, who had married into the aristocracy; but his fortune had dwindled away by the time his tenth and last son was born. So Eric's grandfather, though a godson and cousin of the Earl of Westmorland, was under the disagreeable obligation of having, as that last child, to earn his living. After one year only at Pembroke College, Cambridge, Eric Blair's grandfather left for the Empire, being ordained a deacon in the Church of England in Calcutta in 1839 and a priest in Tasmania in 1843 – very much the period of Cobbett's gibe that the Empire was a system of out-door relief for the indigent sons of the British aristocracy. There is a family tradition that he stopped off at the Cape on his way home to England on leave, got to know a family called Hare and actually became engaged to one of the older sisters. Returning from leave, he stopped off intending to marry the girl but found that she had already married someone else. 'So he said,' related Eric's sister Avril, '"Oh well, if Emily's married it doesn't matter – I'll have Fanny", and Fanny at that time was 15. I believe they played with dolls after her marriage.'

In 1854 Eric's grandfather returned to England to become Vicar of Milborne St Andrew in Dorset, probably the last aristocratic patronage that his branch of the family was to enjoy. Thus his son Richard had to fend for himself from the age of 18. He chose 'the Service' – as the alien administration of the huge Indian sub-continent called itself – and not the Church, but without public school or university advantages (one of twelve children, he had been educated at home for economy), he could not get into a favoured or fashionable branch of the Service, nor did he rise particularly fast in the humble Opium Department, to judge by those postings and gradings. He retired on his pension with no family inheritance beyond some monogrammed silver and a few pieces of furniture.

Perhaps the best bit of luck that Richard Blair had was his marriage. He married in 1896, at the age of 39, Ida Mabel Limouzin who was 21. She had been born in Penge near London, then a semi-rural, new residential suburb (as painted by Camille Pissarro). Her mother was English and her father French, and she had lived most of her life until marriage in Moulmein, Burma, where her father kept up a business, founded by his father, as teak merchant and boat-builder, but later lost much of his money speculating in rice. Her mother, a woman of strong character and considerable intelligence, was still very much alive when her grandson, Eric Blair, went to Burma in 1922. Ida Blair, eighteen years younger than her husband, was a more lively, unconventional, widely read and in every way a more interesting person (all her grandchildren agree). Why did they marry? The evidence is lacking; no papers or letters of either of them survive relating to that period. The opportunities for marriage were very limited in the small British communities in the minor postings, or were somewhat now-or-never, frantic and hasty affairs (by home standards) in the summer hill stations. The situation and views of 'Mrs Lakersteen' and her daughter in Orwell's *Burmese Days* may reflect something of his mother's situation, perhaps even of two contrary poles in her character: the vaguely artistic, as in Mrs Lakersteen, trying to lead a Bohemian life in Paris; and the resignedly conventional, as in Elizabeth herself, hating poverty, her mother's fads, set on marriage, respectability and security.

Ida Limouzin was a realist who could make light of, even be merry in, difficult circumstances. Incompatibilities of age and temperament were taken for granted in those days as part of the institution of holy matrimony. Eric's parents can hardly have been actively happy together but if it had been asked of either of them in the language of the day, 'Were they happily married?', the genuine answer would have been 'Yes'. He was plainly a tolerant and easy-going man, no martinet or domestic tyrant to crush a young girl's spirit. A woman could have done far worse. Perhaps he did not approve of all her opinions, but then in the tradition of the Opium Department itself he would have extended to her the kind of official tolerance for indigenous deviations which he exercised in his administrative capacity – within, of course, the well-known institutional limits of matrimonial propriety and power.

Ida Blair took their two young children back to England, as was then quite common, some time in 1904.* They settled temporarily in a house called Ermadale in Vicarage Road, Henley-on-Thames, in Oxfordshire, leaving it in April 1905 for another, slightly larger, rented home, The Nutshell, Western Road. Richard Blair did not see them again until 1907, when he was given three months' leave on his final promotion from Sub-Deputy Opium Agent, second grade, to Sub-Deputy Opium Agent, first grade. Avril was conceived at this time. He returned to Monghyr before she was born and did not rejoin his family until his retirement, four years later. This arrangement would not have been thought of as anything extraordinary. Nearly all the 'Anglo-Indians' (the British in India) saw the advantages of bringing up even younger children in England despite, it was a commonplace to note, the inevitable fall in the standard of living and of services, the perennial servant problem. From now on Ida Blair kept house with a non-resident daily, neither a cook nor a parlour-maid even, thus doing much of the work herself, an arrangement that she perhaps thought a fair price to pay for the greater liberty of being 'home' (if nowhere in particular) at last. Such years of separation enabled Ida to prepare a good home for her husband's eventual retirement. Perhaps there were also specific worries about Eric's health that kept Mrs Blair in England.

No letters or papers of his mother's survive from Eric's early childhood, except her diary for 1905 when he was 2 years old.[8] The entries consist of five- or six-word notes, ten or a dozen at most, on what she did each day; though often there are none. It throws some light, none the less, on her character and on Eric's health. She seems to have had a lot of visitors, both French and English relatives including her sister Nellie and her brother Charles, and new friends; and she went off on

---

* Not in 1907, as both Peter Stansky and William Abrahams say in their *The Unknown Orwell* (Constable, 1972), p. 12, and Ian Angus in the Chronology to *The Collected Essays, Journalism and Letters of George Orwell*, edited by Sonia Orwell and Ian Angus (Secker & Warburg, 1968), Vol. I, p. 543. Jeffrey Meyers in *The Reader's Guide to George Orwell* (Thames & Hudson, 1975) goes on about the effect on Eric Blair of his non-existent first four years in India, following T. R. Fyvel in his seminal essay, 'A Writer's World', *World Review*, June 1950. The evidence to the contrary is a diary of Ida Blair's for 1905 in the possession of a niece and the photograph of Eric at about three in an English suburban garden. They were all misled by Avril Blair, reminiscing confidently of a time before she was born.

small visits frequently. She walked, played bridge and tennis, and took up photography and developed her own plates.

Monday, 6 February: Baby not at all well, so I sent for the doctor who said that he had bronchitis ...
Thursday, 9 February: Baby improving every day now.
Saturday, 11 February: Baby much better. Calling things 'beastly'.

Who, one may well ask, had been calling things 'beastly' so that a not-quite 2-year-old repeats it? Admittedly the weather was bad.

Sunday, 26 February: Horrid day, didn't go out at all.

And only on 6 March, 'Baby went out for the first time today for more than a month.' In June Baby Eric was flexing his muscles, for his latest 'feat' was to climb into the garden from the drawing-room window. And his mother went off visiting friends, to play a round of bridge and tennis in Tunbridge Wells, but also 'went to tea with Mrs Cruikshank at the prison' at Winchester. Was she just playing the tourist, or possibly visiting a Suffragette friend of her sister Nellie, who was active in the movement? Ida was no more than a sympathizer. In London she watched Wimbledon tennis, also heard a lecture by the Lord Chief Justice at the Mansion House, saw Sarah Bernhardt ('"Angels", simply splendid'), and went to 'Paddington Baths' (Porchester Hall, presumably) with her sister Nellie. But on 29 July 'got a wire from Kate saying Baby was ill, got the wire at 8.30, while bathing and I was in the train at 9.10.' All was well, but there was an undercurrent of nervousness about Baby's health throughout. In August, at Frinton-on-Sea, he paddled for the first time and enjoyed it, but became ill and was taken to the doctor immediately on returning home. And again in November.

So worries about Eric Blair's chest condition, which was to harry him all his days, began early. His mother appears to have been, in the very nicest sense, a bit of a gadabout. The diary gives the impression of a woman who could be very protective towards her children, but not ever present, perhaps over-compensating when at home. Certainly at that time, when Richard Blair must have been sending back much of his pay, they were not hard up, even if they were not well off. Orwell's own monody in *The Road to Wigan Pier* on the horrors of genteel poverty will need to be taken with a pinch of salt. It cannot be accepted as primary evidence about his childhood feelings, only as evidence of how the writer could skilfully shape his memories for literary and polemical effect.

He claimed no memories whatever, of course, of life in India. The earliest memory he recalled or admitted to is in his essay 'Why I Write' of 1946:

I wrote my first poem at the age of four or five, my mother taking it down to dictation. I cannot remember anything about it except that it was about a tiger and the tiger had 'chair-like teeth' – a good enough phrase, but I fancy the poem was a plagiarism of Blake's 'Tiger, Tiger'.[9]

A good mother for a writer, indeed, to take dictation and to read William Blake to a child so early; but, of course, that is the kind of first memory one would have in writing such an essay. The essay went on, however, to take a more general view of his formative influences:

I was the middle child of three, but there was a gap of five years on either side, and I barely saw my father before I was eight. For this and other reasons I was somewhat lonely, and I soon developed disagreeable mannerisms which made me unpopular throughout my schooldays. I had the lonely child's habit of making up stories and holding conversations with imaginary persons, and I think from the very start my literary ambitions were mixed up with the feelings of being isolated and undervalued.

(The name of his 'familiar', his sister Avril remembered, was 'Fronky', and she was often told what he had said to Eric.) His next sentence, however, is much more obviously coloured by his experiences in the late 1920s and early 1930s: 'I knew that I had a facility with words and a power of facing unpleasant facts, and I felt that this created a sort of private world in which I could get my own back for my failure in everyday life.' Whatever sense of failure, rather than simply of inadequacy, that he may have had as a small boy, was a very different thing from the acute sense of failure of the unsuccessful writer of the 1930s.

At the age of 5 he was sent, like his sister Marjorie before and sister Avril after him, to a small Anglican convent school in Henley. He never referred to it, but he must have done very well for them to recommend him for a scholarship to a crack prep school. Avril was taught to read and write by a Marjorie Dakin whose brother Humphrey was later to marry Marjorie Blair. The Dakins and the Blairs remained close to each other.

A few odd memories of early childhood appear incidentally in George Orwell's essays. 'The earliest song I can remember, which must have been in 1907 or 1908, was "Rhoda Had a Pagoda". It was an inconceivably silly song, but it was certainly popular.'[10] Also he remembered searching in a cupboard at about that time and finding a bustle; they had to tell him what it was, since it was already antique.[11] And at 6, there was 'the plumber's daughter', already lightly touched upon, recalled so fully in her erotic glory in his unpublished notebooks, but also more guardedly in 'Such, Such Were the Joys' and in the autobiographical chapter of *The Road to Wigan Pier* where he relates that he was separated from her by his mother because she was 'common'. Again this is a selective use of memory. In his notebooks he admits both charges, the sexual and the social – for the context seems to be that of making notes towards future novels; but in *The Road to Wigan Pier* the context is severely political, so only the social charge is mentioned. The account in 'Such, Such Were the Joys' is subtly different yet again.

At this time I was in an almost sexless state, which is normal, or at any rate common, in boys of that age; I was therefore in the position of simultaneously knowing and not knowing what used to be called the Facts of Life. At five or six, like many children I had passed through a phase of sexuality. My friends were the plumber's children up the road, and we used sometimes to play games of a vaguely erotic kind. One was called 'playing at doctors', and I remember getting a faint but definitely pleasant thrill from holding a toy trumpet, which was supposed to be a stethoscope, against a little girl's belly. About the same time I fell deeply in love, a far more worshipping kind of love than I have ever felt for anyone since, with a girl named Elsie at the convent school which I attended. She seemed to me grown up, so I suppose she must have been fifteen. After that, as so often happens, all sexual feelings seemed to go out of me for many years.[12]

But if the advertisement for 'Sunnylands' in the local newspaper is to be relied upon, the Anglican nuns only took children from 'five to eleven years old'. Children are not very good at estimating ages. She may have been more of the age of the village girl paid a few pence to take Eric for walks on holidays or weekend afternoons. On the other hand, the novelist George Orwell became adept, he thought, at disguising his use of real people by slight shifts of age, name or locale (as the minimum necessary for decency's sake).

Another little-known autobiographical fragment also refers to himself at 6 years old and again shows the pointed use he made of memory. In a review of Arturo Barea's *The Forge*, he wrote:

When I read that last phrase, 'the civil guards never attack the gentry', there came back to me a memory which is perhaps out of place in a review, but which illustrates the difference of social atmosphere in a country like England and a country like Spain. I am 6 years old, and I am walking along a street in our little town with my mother and a wealthy local brewer, who is also a magistrate. The tarred fence is covered with chalk drawings, some of which I have made myself. The magistrate stops, points disapprovingly with his stick and says, 'We are going to catch the boys who draw on these walls, and we are going to order them Six Strokes of the Birch Rod.' (It was all in capitals in my mind.) My knees knock together, my tongue cleaves to the roof of my mouth, and at the earliest possible moment I sneak away to spread the dreadful intelligence. In a little while, all the way down the fence, there is a long line of terror-stricken children, all spitting on their handkerchiefs and trying to rub out the drawings. But the interesting thing is that not till many years later, perhaps 20 years, did it occur to me that my fears had been groundless. No magistrate would have condemned me to Six Strokes of the Birch Rod, even if I had been caught drawing on the wall. Such punishment was reserved for the Lower Orders. The Civil Guards charge, but they never attack the gentry.[13]

The 'long line of terror-stricken children' sounds like stretching a good tale too far. But there was indeed a brewer, called Simmons, who was a magistrate and also a friend of his mother's; Ida Blair's diary has his girls coming to tea and Avril remembered them too. Such a tale was not likely to be pure invention and had probably been told or re-told to him by his mother, before his subsequent national and class-comparative literary embellishments.

In *The Road to Wigan Pier* (which was *his* road) he gave an account of the class prejudices instilled into a middle-class child: that the working classes were stupid, coarse, crude, violent and '... it is summed up in four frightful words which people nowadays are chary of uttering, but which were bandied about quite freely in my childhood. The words were: *The lower classes smell*.' His account of the special peculiarity of the 'lower-upper-middle' class rings true:

People in this class owned no land, but they felt that they were landowners in the sight of God and kept up a semi-aristocratic outlook by going into the professions and the fighting services rather than into trade ... Theoretically you knew all about servants and how to tip them, although in practice you had one, or at most two, resident servants. Theoretically, you knew how to wear your clothes and how to order a dinner, although in practice you could never afford to go to a decent tailor or a decent restaurant. Theoretically, you knew how to shoot and ride, although in practice you had no horses to ride and not an inch of ground to shoot over.[14]

However, while it may have been sociologically true for him to say 'In the kind of shabby-genteel family that I am talking about there is far more consciousness of poverty than in any working-class family above the level of the dole', yet 'shabby-genteel' was not an accurate description of his own home in the 1910s and 1920s with his father on a pension of £438 10s per annum. And the famous 'a shabby-genteel family is in much the same position as a family of "poor whites" living in a street where everyone else is a negro'[15] would be ludicrous if he were talking about the Blairs. His identification with the shabby-genteel was an imaginative device by the writer of a documentary, those years later, intended to convince working-class readers that he too could feel, equally authentically, class-consciousness, indeed could perceive through it the grim comedy of false-consciousness. Not to be rich enough to be a landowner or to adopt an aristocratic way of life was not to imply a necessary shabby-gentility (unless everything else was shabby by way of contrast and relative deprivation): the Blairs were comfortably in the middle. Mrs Blair did not seem to mind, but perhaps Mr Blair had lingering aristocratic pretensions noticeable by his son.

Eric's basic memories were real and intense but the use he made of them should not deter us from taking a commonsensical view of what his early childhood, while still going to the local school, was probably like. Generally it was more ordinary and pleasant than he would later allow. In 1940 he reported that the earliest political slogan he could remember was 'We want eight and we won't wait' (eight Dreadnoughts) and that at 'seven years old I was a member of the Navy League and wore a sailor suit with "H M S. Invincible" on my cap.'[16] Being a 'member' may have meant no more than putting pennies in a collection-tin and wearing a flag; and middle-class children wore sailor suits simply as a convenient and hard-wearing fashion. Some connections with a pride about sea power, certainly; but to associate every child who ever wore a sailor suit with the Navy League may only be what was called in those times 'artistic licence'.

We know also that he was greatly fond of animals and that dogs, cats, rabbits and guinea pigs abounded. Wherever he settled in later life small menageries appeared, though rationalized, as it were, by utilitarian function. The 1905 diary makes clear, by the social comings and goings for teas, walks and parties of his then 7-year-old sister Marjorie, that he would not have lacked for human company either when he reached her age, even if he was, as some evidence suggests, of a shy and solitary disposition long before going to prep school. The Blairs were a family for outings. If his mother dashed off for short visits, the daily help, his mother's relatives or friends, his older sister, or a local girl, would take him out for walks, rough walks, veritable expeditions of exploration through woods or down the riverbank. When his mother returned, she would arrange more ambitious outings: everything by the season, blackberrying, hazelnut-gathering, picking wild fruits and flowers for wine-making and preserves; or boating on the River Thames. And at some epochal moment, the Dakin boys (whose father was the family doctor) began to take him fishing with them. They were older than him, but they did it for Marjorie's sake: no Eric, no Marjorie. All his life he retained the boyish pleasure and skill of coarse fishing, and the symbolisms of fish and fishing were to surface in his novel *Coming Up For Air*. The nostalgia of George Bowling for a happy Edwardian childhood in the opening pages of Part II of *Coming Up For Air* can be seen as very much George Orwell's own. 'Lower Binfield' is recognizably Henley. 'If I shut my eyes and think of Lower Binfield any time before I was, say, eight, it's always in summer weather that I remember it ... Most sweets were four ounces a penny, and there was even some stuff called Paradise Mixture, mostly broken sweets from other bottles, which was six. There were Farthing Everlastings, which were a yard long and couldn't be finished inside half an hour. Sugar mice and sugar pigs were eight a penny ... A whole lot of the kinds of sweets we had in those days have gone out.'[17] And, thinking of sugar and spice and all things nice, could 'Katie' in the same book, whom 'when we were very small mother used to pay ... eighteen pence a week to take us out for walks in the afternoon' have been 'Elsie' of the convent school with whom 'I fell deeply in love'? He calls her 'Katie Simmons' in the book, saying indeed that her father worked at a brewery. The name of the real owner of the brewery in Henley in the 1900s had been Simmons – whose close friendship with their mother, Avril hinted much later, neither she nor Eric liked. Some infant intuition or jealousy? Orwell's memory of Lower Binfield/Henley before the age of 8 'always in summer weather' was almost as much a symbol of the good society or 'the golden country' as was that one day that Rousseau tells us of in his *Confessions* (the only perfect day) when he picked apples in complete contentment and innocence with two young girls.

Orwell attributed his feelings of being lonely and out of it, despite all the other children and the outings, because of the five-year gaps between himself and the other two children, to being 'the middle child'. Five years is a big gap, indeed, between children, especially an older boy and a younger sister; even though an older sister tends to cross the gap by playing Mother vigorously, sometimes whether the young boy wants it or not. Marjorie seems to have done no more but no less than was usual. Note that he spoke of 'two children' rather than (more precisely and concretely as became his style) 'two girls'. He did grow up until 8 entirely among women, having seen his father only for three months when he was 4. He remained deeply fond, if very undemonstratively, of his mother and his two sisters all his life; but there may have been some ambivalence in his attitude. In appearance and manners he might seem a military or colonial gentleman-bachelor, but all his life he made friends more readily with women than with men; and the friendships were usually returned, although there is some lack of perceptiveness in his treatment of women, both as novelist and person. There may have been a feeling of some smothering of the very boyish boy at home; and then a sense of betrayal when pitched out so young to the brutal male world of boarding school.

In the last year of his life he was to write an isolated passage in a notebook, which could be simple reminiscence or it could be drawing from memory towards some story shaping in his mind:

The conversations he overheard as a small boy, between his Mother, his aunt, his elder sister and their feminist friends. The way in which, without ever hearing any direct statement to that effect, and without having more than a very dim idea of the relationship between the sexes, he derived a firm impression that women *did not like* men, that they looked upon them as a sort of large, ugly, smelly and ridiculous animal, who maltreated women in every way, above all by forcing their attentions upon them. It was pressed deep into his consciousness, to remain there until he was about 20, that sexual intercourse gives pleasure only to the man, not to the woman. He knew that sexual intercourse has something to do with the man getting on top of the woman, and the picture of it in his mind was of a man pursuing a woman, forcing her down and jumping on top of her, as he had often seen a cock do to a hen. All this was derived, not from any remark having direct sexual reference – or what he recognized as a sexual reference – but from such overheard remarks as 'It just shows what beasts men are.' 'My dear, I think she's behaving like a perfect fool, the way she gives in to him.' 'Of course, she's far too good for him.' And the like. Somehow, by the mere tone of these conversations – the hatefulness – above all the physical unattractiveness – of men in women's eyes seemed to be established. It was not till he was about 30 that it struck him that he had in fact been his mother's favourite child. It had seemed natural to him that, as he was a boy, the two girls should be preferred.

The least this passage suggests is that some of his guilt feelings and complex about being an ugly and smelly child pre-date his experiences at prep school; and that there may have been some basic ambivalence towards his mother, feeling over-protected and smothered but also, as man child, unwanted.

Certainly one of his nieces saw something that may have been a little worrying, at least to a boy, in her grandmother Ida Blair, as well as something good. She talks of Ida in Southwold in the late 1920s but it is recognizably the same woman, half emancipated, half artistic, and the same kind of household as in Henley in the 1910s:

We [Blairs and Dakins] always feel rather up in arms about this image of Eric living his early life under 'shabby genteel' conditions. Shabby, perhaps, genteel, never.

My impressions of my Grandmother Blair's house in Southwold are of an extremely comfortable, well-run establishment. Quite small but rather exotic. The furniture was mostly mahogany, perhaps second hand but everything blended. Rainbow silky curtains, masses of embroidered stools, bags, cushions, pin cushions done by my grandmother, interesting mahogany or ivory boxes full of sequins, beads, miniature tracts, wooden needle-cases, amber beads, cornelian and ivory, small boxes from India and Burma. Fascinating for children.

Most of the work of the house was done by my grandmother with the able assistance of Mrs May, a tiny Suffolk woman ... Mrs May arrived after breakfast which my grandmother and Aunt Avril took in bed, one at the head, one at the foot. Earl Grey tea, toast and Patum Peperium. The dachshunds usually sat on the bed, which delighted and scandalized us ... Mrs Blair was so very much younger than her husband, and was so very much more intelligent and on the spot, that she more or less discounted him, at any rate when he was at Southwold. They had separate rooms and separate interests but got along quite amiably. He was always considered at meals and his favourite foods, especially puddings, were provided. Otherwise he was rather out of things. He was a very sweet-tempered man but not a patch on Mrs B.

She usually referred to men as 'those brutes'. 'Do you know what those brutes have done?' re dustmen, butchers, etc.

So that the children were rather self-reliant and undemonstrative emotionally, with a boarding-school term and a fairly reserved holiday. Of course I only knew Mrs B. as a grandmother and she may have been different as a young woman.[18]

There is little doubt from whom Baby Eric learned his first recorded word, 'beastly'. 'Those brutes' is mainly a contemporary *façon de parler*, yet there is some ground for thinking that in his early childhood he might have suffered some tension from being pulled two ways between the over-protectiveness of a conventional mother and the up-and-away over-practicality of the woman on her own who might have quite liked to have been almost a *femme libre*. Some balance seems wanting which may perhaps account both for his ambivalence towards his childhood and for his odd mixture of aloofness and gregariousness. Always we have to allow that, for the purposes of mature writing in adult life, he skilfully stressed and polarized idyllic or oppressive images as the subject matter demanded. His niece made another remark that fortifies the belief that social, not sexual, guilt, the desertion of 'Elsie', dominates the childhood reminiscences of his notebooks.

Class was a greater problem ... I think a lot of Eric's hang-ups came from the fact that he thought he ought to love all his fellow-men; and he couldn't even talk to them easily. My father was the same sort of age and background and he could never speak of anyone without first placing them classwise ...[19]

CHAPTER TWO

THE JOYS OF PREP SCHOOL
AND THE ECHOING GREEN

AT no more than 8 years old the time came when every upper-upper-middle-class boy was sent away to school, even the sons of what Orwell called his own class, the 'lower-upper-middle class'. He defined the 'lower-upper' as being the upper-middle class short of money, not really hard up, no discomfort, but not able from their own resources to play the full role expected of them by themselves and others, both from the education they received and the status they still enjoyed. Thus education was an investment as well as a mark of status. For colonial civil servants without either property or – in Richard Walmesley Blair's case – family patronage, education was especially important, it was not just the 'ladder of advancement', it had to be climbed even to stay still in the same place. Entry to all the careers, the Church, the Army, and the Civil Service, and of course the professions, depended on having had 'a good education', to the end of school at 18, though at that time not necessarily university. It was 'school' that counted, and school was the private secondary institution from the ages of 13 or 14 to 18. To get boys into the 'right school' was the business of preparatory schools. Under the competitive pressure of the children of the growing professional classes, the so-called public schools had in the last decades of the nineteenth century raised their entrance standards appreciably, as if to bring status and achievement somewhat more into alignment. Even the sons of the landed aristocracy now commonly had to go through a prep school. So these preparatory schools were recent foundations; and even though they aped the ways of the more ancient foundations which they sought to supply, they were frankly utilitarian in character. They tried to be useful and their recruitment of fee-paying boys depended on their success ('reputation' was the customary word) in getting their little charges into 'good schools'.

This led to them being eager to get some bright children as a leaven to the merely wealthy or the well-connected. Best that a child had all these attributes, of course, but the world was imperfect. A balance had to be struck. All their products would get somewhere if they could pay, for the supply of ancient and ancient-looking public school foundations was also increasing to meet the demand. The prep schools would attract 'the better sort of pupil' if they could get a few children a year into the 'great schools', among which Eton College and Harrow School stood at the top of the educational and social hierarchy. These figured prominently in the head master's report in the school magazine, a document much scrutinized by parents and potential customers. Indeed, half-holidays would be given to the boys to celebrate scholarships to the great schools, so hundreds of letters home would spread the glad news widely and quickly.

Eric, strongly recommended by his local convent school, was taken on at half-fees by St Cyprian's, one of the newest but most successful preparatory schools. He was to stay until he was 13. Mrs Blair must have made the application in the spring of 1911, interviewing and being interviewed by the head master and owner of the school, Mr Vaughan Wilkes, and the real power behind the throne, Mrs Wilkes. Could the Blairs have afforded it without the scholarship? Mr Blair was soon to retire and return home on a pension of £438 10s per year. Eric's full fees would have been £180. (By way of comparison, consider that in 1913–14 the average annual wage of a skilled manual worker was about £100, of a clerk about the same, of a manager about £200, and of the higher professions about £330.)[1] Marjorie and Avril were both sent away at a later stage, at the age of 11, to a girls' boarding school at Oxford, a decent enough place but by no means famous or front rank. So Eric's scholarship of £90 per year must have turned 'extraordinarily difficult' into 'just possible' and may have made the difference between his younger sister being sent away at all rather than educated locally. The scholarship was confidential and was kept secret even from Eric. His contemporaries did not know. But as he got near his public-school exams, Mr Wilkes told him, perhaps to shame him into working even harder.

The school was only twelve years old in 1911 and already had a reputation for getting scholarships and places at Harrow or other leading public schools. The fees of £180 a year were high, yet with only about a hundred boys in the school, spread over four or five years, with ten teaching staff as well as a matron, a drill sergeant and the Wilkes themselves, both of whom taught, value for money was plainly given in terms of very small classes and intensive teaching. However mechanical the teaching, and it was very mechanical, small numbers made up for a lot. St Cyprian's was just outside Eastbourne in Sussex, a fashionable and very respectable south-coast summer resort, and even then a town favoured for retirement among the prosperous middle class. The school occupied two large, late-Victorian William Morris-style houses, in extensive grounds very near to Beachy Head, the beautifully smooth chalk down and the steep cliff overlooking the English Channel.

St Cyprian's had a good sprinkling of aristocracy as well as of upper middle and professional middle classes. Some 'old boys' strongly deny that there was any snobbery either in the school or in the attitudes of the Wilkes. Henry Longhurst (the famous amateur golfer and commentator) claimed in his memoirs 'to have grown up absolutely "classless"', citing as proof that the Wilkes 'cheerfully accepted the rather uncouth offspring of a modest, though worthy, retail house furnisher'. Longhurst recalls with pleasure that among his particular school chums were Lord Mildmay, 'among the last of the Corinthians of steeplechasing', and 'Reggie', Viscount Malden, heir to the 8th Earl of Essex.[2] Also a contemporary at St Cyprian's, Cyril Connolly recalls 'an awful lot of nobility' as well as a Siamese prince and some sons of South American millionaires.[3] The school was hardly 'classless' so much as a good mixer of the complicated top section of the English, Scottish and Anglo-Irish class system and their wealthy foreign clients. The facts of social composition are not in question; only subsequent opinions are in fierce and irritable contradiction about what opinions and attitudes the boys had back then. On one thing, however, all accounts agree: the food was awful and inadequate, as was the heating and the sanitation. The code, of course, was an austere one and, to make matters worse, it was soon to be wartime. Hard conditions were accepted as part of 'the building of character', the official ideology through which even the oppressors themselves came to believe in the self-sacrificing altruism of this most unlikely form of commercial enterprise – as did their pupils when they went out to govern the Empire or to 'help the family' by taking a job in the City. Henry Longhurst actually meant to defend the old school against 'abuse' like Orwell's and Connolly's when he ended his chapter on St Cyprian's 'on a lighter note'. He relates with pride as well as superficial irony that a contemporary had just written to him: 'It may amuse you to know that my brother attributes the fact that he emerged absolutely sane and fit from five years as a prisoner of war solely to having been at St Cyprian's.'[4]

Orwell's own testimony survives in two forms: the famous and virulent 'Such, Such Were the Joys' (of uncertain date*) and some twenty-two simple boyish letters to his mother, all but one written in his first fifteen months at St Cyprian's, all that remain of the required weekly letter home during his four years there. Both sets of evidence need careful handling: the essay is a polemical essay intended, like 'A Hanging' or 'How the Poor Die', to have a direct effect on the reader – one cannot assume that it is all literally true; and the letters were censored or 'gone through' by an adult hand, nominally to correct errors of fact and spelling, and were written in that knowledge. Here are his letters from the first term.

September 14 [1911]

Dear Mother, I hope you are quite well, thanks for that letter you sent me I havent read it yet. I supose you want to know what schools like, its alright we have fun in the morning. When we are in bed. from E. Blair.

'Supose' is corrected in the adult hand – they did not always bother, but it showed both parent and child that (as Orwell taught us to say) big brother was watching.

October 8 1911 Sunday

My dear Mother,

I hope you are quite well. I am top in arithmetic, and I have been moved up in Latin. I cannot quite read your letters yet, but I can read Margies. How is Togo, [a terrier], we had a magick lantern the other day. It is Kirk-

---

* Commonly thought to have been written in 1947 just before he began to write *Nineteen Eighty-Four*, but all that is certain is that he sent it to his publishers then. Several factors point strongly to an earlier composition. See Appendix B.

patricks birthday today he is eight years old, Last time we played football I shot seven goals.

from E. Blair

P.S. I forgot to tell you I had a letter from Margie and I will write to her soon.

Togo was the family dog and Colin Kirkpatrick became a banker and businessman, who finally settled in Rhodesia.

Nov. 5

My dear Mother

Thank you very much for that shilling you sent me and my album. We had the thee Matches yesterday we won two and lost one, while the Matches went on we went for a lovely walk on the Downs, and called Smallman picked up ten shillings on the road.

On Sunday it is halfterm. Will you please send me Margerys adress. Next time you write to Auntie Hay and ask her to send me stamps.

lots of love from E. Blair

Thank you for the 1/- you sent me

Nov. 12

My dear Mother

What kind of weather are you having? We are having lots of rain, but it is not raining this morning. but it is very dull. Will yoou please send me one of one or two of the new penny stamps for I have not got one yet.

The swimg races were on Monday, and a boy called Murray started last in a race and won by a good deal. I was third in the race, I had a rathe tight bathing dress on and could not swim a bit fast.

I am second, in Arithmetic, and this week I am first in Latin. And I am 8th in French.

We are breaking up on the 20 Dec: that is on a Vensday. Give my love to Avril, and to Father.

Much love from

E. Blair

'First' is corrected by the adult hand to read 'second in Latin'. They were evidently given weekly placings. Notice how scores and placings in lessons and games are all mixed in together, seemingly of equal importance. This weird synthesis of team spirit and of individual competitiveness could truly be said to epitomize the blending of a capitalist and an aristocratic ethic, so typical of these schools.

[no date. November 19?]

My dear Mother
I hope you are quite well!, please send my stamp album as soon as you can.
We played 3 Malches yesterday, and lost all.
It is a lovely day quite warm.
Give my love to Avril
Much love from you son.
Eric Blair xxxxx

[no date. Nov. 26?]

My dear Mother,
I hope you are quite well. I am second in Latin and first in arithmatick and third in history.
Iits raining like mad this morning and at about five aclock this morning and the house rattled like paper with the wind.
There is an aufly naughty boy hear called Lesly Cohen he has only just had his seventh birthday. We have had severl nice games of football this week.
x.x.x.x.x.x.x.x.xxxxxxxxx
from your loving son
E. Blair

He was more sportive than he later made out, though he did have recurrent bronchitis even then and 'a stomach cough', but they told him that it was 'nothing' and that he could 'run it off', like getting a second wind after a stitch. He said later that he had loathed football, but had quite liked cricket and swimming, adding typically that 'these had no prestige value'.[5]

Dec. 2

My dear Mother, I hope you are alright.
It was Mrs: Wilkes birthday yesterday, we had aufel fun after tea and played games all over the house. We all went for a walk to Beachy-Head.
I am third in Arithmatick.
'Its' very dull today, and dosent look as if its going to be very warm. Thank you for your letter.
It is getting very near the end of the term, there are only eighteen days more. On Saturday evening we have dncing, and I am going to say a piece of poetry, some of the boys sing.
Give my love to Father and Avril. Is Togo alright. We had the Oxford and Cambridge Matches yesterday. Cambridge won in the first and third, and the second did not have a Match. I am very glad Colonel Hall has given me some

stamps, he said he wold last year but I thought had had forgotten. Its a beastly wet day today all rain and cold.

I am very sorry to hear we had those beastly freaks of smelly white mice back. I hope these arnt smelly one. If they arnt I shall like them.

From your loveing son, E.A. Blair.

This letter was heavily corrected. One of the trade-marks of George Orwell was to be, according to one's judgement, either an obsessive or a salutary frankness about the most neglected of our five senses, smell. From his earliest days he grew to associate smell with oppression.

These letters have no literary merit. So there would have been little point in printing them in *The Collected Essays, Journalism and Letters*. But if they had been, then there might have been some second thoughts about accepting as literal rather than as figurative truth Orwell's later account of the great terror of first term at prep school. There is no evidence of disturbance in these letters. Granted that one would not expect anything critical of the school, even of the food, in letters that the child knew were read by the Wilkes; but a child in terror would write more briefly and in safe and easy stock phrases, not so chattily and spontaneously.

The only real evidence of any trauma at being torn out of the comfort of the womanish home into the barbaric and totally un-private boys' world of corridors, cubicles, caning and cramming is provided by what Orwell himself was to say in 'Such, Such Were the Joys': 'Your home might be far from perfect, but at least it was a place ruled by love rather than by fear ... At eight years old you were suddenly taken out of this warm nest and flung into a world of force and fraud and secrecy, like a gold-fish into a tank full of pike.'[6] Confident assertions that there was a trauma that marked and warped him for life, somehow *explaining* (often explaining away) the most uncomfortable parts of his future writing, have become a commonplace of critical writing on Orwell; but they are highly speculative, often attempts to use psychological explanations to short-cut a slow and detailed examination of his adult experiences, some of which may have affected his adult beliefs. Those who are confident that they can find a psychological 'hidden wound' in the young Eric and then locate *Nineteen Eighty-Four* on the map as a version of St Cyprian's, as if the vision of totalitarianism arose from prep-school terror and sufferings, may be disguising their own lack of perception of the political horrors that Orwell said were under their own noses, far more dangerous, dramatic and objective, in their shared contemporary world of the 1930s and 1940s.[7]

Boys of his class expected to go away to school and can have been under no illusions, unless there was no talk with other children, that it was anything other than a pretty rough, uncomfortable and often painful experience; but on the other hand, lots of fun and games were to be expected, lots of other boys, sport, heroes, and lots of books to be read. He appears to have been a great reader before ever he went to St Cyprian's. This by itself may have alienated him more from many of his contemporaries, as it did Cyril Connolly, than hypothetical traumas (which then, *ex hypothesi*, every boy would have suffered). The school authorities needed scholarship fodder but the mass of brute boys would mock and harry 'the swots' and 'the bookish'.

His mother had given Eric on his eighth birthday Swift's *Gulliver's Travels*. This was one of the most important introductions he ever had. He remembered finding the parcel the night before his birthday and being so eager to read it for himself that he began secretly then and there. It must have been an expurgated child's edition, for precocious though he was, his parents would not have given him the original, even if he could have understood it. In the days of his fame, when he was being freely compared to Swift, he was to claim that 'From a very early age, perhaps the age of five or six, I knew that when I grew up I should be a writer.'[8] George Orwell was to say to Dean Swift in an 'Imaginary Interview' (a wartime broadcast) that Gulliver has 'lived with me ever since so that I suppose a year has never passed without my re-reading at least part of it. And yet I can't help feeling that you have laid it on a bit too thick. You were too hard on humanity, and on your own country.'[9]

The same problem of laying it on too thick arises with Orwell's own essay, 'Such, Such Were the Joys', which he described to his publisher as being 'autobiographical' (certainly so libellous that it could not be published in Great Britain until after Mrs Wilkes' death in 1967 aged 92).[10] Swift could well have replied, '*Tu quoque*, Sir'. Was he too hard on his teachers and on himself? Did St Cyprian's really lead him to believe that by their 'law I was damned. I had no money, I was weak, I was ugly, I was unpopular, I had a chronic cough, I was cowardly,

I smelt'?[11] How much was the essay pure autobiography and how much a polemical short story written in the first person and drawn from experience? None of Orwell's novels and documentaries is entirely clear as to its genre. The reader must either lower his guard completely or constantly be on guard against assuming too readily that he is faced with either undiluted 'fact' or undiluted 'fiction'. The problem arises, in part at least, because Orwell's talent as a writer grew slowly and relatively late. He fed on his own early experiences but in so doing he changed them creatively. 'I base these generalizations on what I can recall of my own childhood outlook. Treacherous though memory is,' he himself warned at the end of the essay, 'it seems to me the chief means we have of discovering how a child's mind works. Only by resurrecting our own memories can we realize how incredibly distorted is the child's vision of the world.' The animus of 'Such, Such Were the Joys' cannot be rejected as evidence of what actually happened and of what his feelings were back then at prep school as distinct from the time of writing; but the piece cannot be accepted fully either. It must be handled both emphatically and critically.

The title came from a line in 'The Echoing Green', one of Blake's *Songs of Innocence*, some of which his mother had read to him when a young child.

> Such, such were the joys
>   When we all, girls and boys,
> In our youth time were seen,
>   On the Echoing Green.

As the mature Orwell fully realized, an echoing green is a more complex metaphor for the relationship between artistic and literal truth than, say, 'holding a mirror up to nature', or any delusion of 'I am a camera'. If he mocked myths of childhood joy unbounded, he was surely well aware that by using such a quotation as the title of his essay he was drawing attention to the fact that the author was creator, not remembrancer. Echoes both repeat and distort.

Certainly he came to blame the place (and such places) greatly. In 1938, he wrote to Cyril Connolly: 'I'm always meaning one of these days to write a book about St Cyprian's. I've always held that the public schools aren't so bad, but people are wrecked by those filthy private schools long before they get to public school age.'[12] And he told readers of *Tribune* two years later, in reviewing a novel of Stephen Spender's, *The Backward Son*:

It is about a 'prep school', one of those (on the whole) nasty little schools at which small boys are prepared for the public school entrance examination. Incidentally these schools with their money-grubbing proprietors and their staffs of underpaid hacks, are responsible for a lot of the harm that it is usual to blame on the public schools. A majority of middle-class boys have their minds permanently lamed by them before they are thirteen years old.[13]

Did he include himself for once among the hypothetical 'majority of middle-class boys' whose minds were 'wrecked' or 'permanently lamed'? Certainly in the period between Burma and Spain he suffered from feelings of failure and of guilt, but it is not clear that he himself attributed this to prep school more than to imperial service and, even if he did, it is doubtful if this was the full story. Other things were to happen, and not to happen, later. Only a narrower point is crystal clear: that he loathed the anti-intellectualism of learning by rote. He saw the bad methods of St Cyprian's as intellectually stultifying and oppressive.

Certainly Cyril Connolly regarded 'Such, Such Were the Joys' as the 'key to his [Orwell's] formation'.[14] Biographical evidence from Orwell's novels can also support Connolly's judgement. Some of Eric Blair's experiences must have gone into the character of Gordon Comstock, the poor and bitter anti-hero of Orwell's *Keep the Aspidistra Flying* written in 1935:

Even at the third-rate schools to which Gordon was sent nearly all the boys were richer than himself. They soon found out his poverty, of course, and gave him hell because of it. Probably the greatest cruelty one can inflict on a child is to send it to school among children richer than itself. A child conscious of poverty will suffer snobbish agonies such as a grown-up person can scarcely even imagine.[15]

'Money' was to worry him, like Gordon Comstock, all the days of his life, until the success of *Animal Farm*. He too despised a world 'infected with the mania of owning things' and gone 'money mad': but also he realized that independence for a writer depended on earning some. Fear of exposure of his dependence on the secret scholarship, with which Mr Wilkes threatened him, would indeed, at every stage of his schoolboy and most of his adult life, have been agony. And it was an agony that he never forgot, but he put it to good use to understand the psychology of the poor and the oppressed in his early writings and, later on, to champion their causes.

The very first sentence of 'Such, Such Were the Joys' began the symbolic anecdote from which all the other themes of the essay (cruelty, favouritism, snobbery and wealth, bad teaching, filth and bullying) radiated. It is about bed-wetting. 'Soon after I arrived at St Cyprian's (not immediately, but after a week or two, just when I began to be settling into the routine of school life) I began wetting my bed.' And after two or three such hideous offences, he tells us, he was warned that he would be caned. The warning took place in a curiously round-about way. Mrs Wilkes called him back from leaving tea to where she was sitting with a lady visitor, 'an intimidating, masculine-looking person wearing a riding habit', as if to introduce him.

'Here is a little boy,' said Flip, indicating me to the strange lady, 'who wets his bed every night. Do you know what I am going to do if you wet your bed again?' she added, turning to me. 'I am going to get the Sixth Form to beat you.'

The strange lady put on an air of being inexpressibly shocked, and exclaimed, 'I-should-*think*-so!' And here there occurred one of those wild, almost lunatic misunderstandings which are part of the daily experience of childhood. The Sixth Form was a group of older boys who were selected as having 'character' and were empowered to beat smaller boys. I had not yet learned of their existence, and I mis-heard the phrase 'the Sixth Form' as 'Mrs Form'. I took it as referring to the strange lady – I thought, that is, that her name was Mrs Form. It was an improbable name, but a child has no judgement in such matters. I imagined, therefore, that it was she who was to be deputed to beat me. It did not strike me as strange that this job should be turned over to a casual visitor in no way connected with the school. I merely assumed that 'Mrs Form' was a stern disciplinarian who enjoyed beating people (somehow her appearance seemed to bear this out) and I had an immediate terrifying vision of her arriving for the occasion in full riding kit and armed with a hunting-whip. To this day I can feel myself almost swooning with shame as I stood, a very small, round-faced boy in short corduroy knickers, before the two women. I could not speak. I felt that I should die if Mrs Form were to beat me. But my dominant feeling was not fear or even resentment: it was simply shame because one more person, and that a woman, had been told of my disgusting offence.[16]

He then wet his bed again, was denounced by the matron and beaten by Mr Wilkes. Does this sound plausible? Surely the general points do, to which he reverts several times: both the cruelty and the 'almost lunatic misunderstandings which are part of the daily experience of childhood'. It is a telling, sad and comic instance of 'how incredibly distorted is the child's version of the world'. But, as he said to Swift, 'I can't help feeling that you laid it on a bit thick.' Something like that must have happened; but misheard as 'Mrs Form' and with a fantasy riding-whip? 'Mrs Form' sounds like a stock figure in Victorian and Edwardian pornographic novelettes. But no such lady can be found in such literature.[17] There is no reason to doubt that he was beaten for bed-wetting, which is barbarous enough, but the trimmings may belong more to a story in the first person, a polemic against the folly of inducing a sense of guilt about nameless (natural) things, and against the general harshness that could lead to disturbances far worse than bed-wetting: these are the point of the essay, not the most un-Orwellian (as we will see) gratuitous self-revelation. There is, however, one other piece of evidence on the bed-wetting and the beating. A very eminent Old St Cyprianite whose memory seems excellent has annotated the margins of an earlier published account of Eric Blair's life at St Cyprian's. His notes are full of fierce denials and disagreements, particularly where the account follows Orwell closely, for he defends the old school passionately and uncritically. Even so, twice he admits that there was a bed-wetter who was publicly beaten; but it was not Blair, he asserts, it was another little boy who later became a colonel in the British Army and a holder of the Victoria Cross.[18] Several boys, of course, could have been beaten for this same offence of nature. But whatever the literal truth, why should not a polemical essayist transpose events for dramatic effect?

Cruelty was certainly a characteristic of the school, particularly in relation to the arbitrariness and uncertainty of punishment, as illustrated by the beating for bed-wetting, to whomever it occurred. The head master, nicknamed 'Sambo', 'a round-shouldered, curiously oafish-looking man, not large but shambling in gait, with a chubby face which was like that of an overgrown baby, and which was capable of good humour', beat him, said Orwell, with 'a riding-crop', intoning as he did so, 'you dir-ty lit-tle boy', keeping time with the blows. But it was a mild, first beating, so he cockily told the others in the corridor as he came out. But 'Flip', as Mrs Wilkes was nicknamed, heard him and ordered him back. 'This time Sambo laid on in real earnest. He continued for a length of time that frightened and astonished me – about five minutes it seemed, ending up by breaking the riding-crop. The bone handle went flying across the room. "Look what you've made me do!" he said furiously, holding up the broken crop.'[19]

Again this somewhat suspicious riding-crop. In those days an ordinary bamboo cane was, as children's comics still testify, almost always held in the teacher's hand or left lying prominently on his desk, even when not much used, a symbol of power and authority, much like an army officer's dress-sword. When the earlier account paraphrases this, my marginal commentator comments, 'NOT TRUE! You sod!!! LIBEL!' And he means not merely that it was not Blair who was beaten, but that riding-crops were never the chosen medium of chastisement. Also, to push common sense to a point of absurdity, consider the 'about five minutes'. Intoning Mr Wilkes' phrase for rhythm, going as slowly and heavily as one can with a stick, it is hard to achieve a slower rate of fire than twelve strokes to the minute. 'Six of the best', as Orwell would have known, was traditionally reckoned the maximum punishment, enough to raise weals, often to break the skin bloodily. Five minutes would have been as bad as a naval flogging at the Nore or Spithead, and would have put the victim in the infirmary for days. Orwell's actual words, however, were 'about five minutes – it *seemed*'. Perhaps a beating could seem that long, but the innocent reader need not accept as gospel what is more likely to be either semi-fictional polemic against such real abuses of authority, or else in part a fantasy.

The school was harsh and Blair was caned from time to time, as caning was then common; he hated the place deeply for those cruelties, particularly for the arbitrariness and injustice of them. The terse 'Not True' of the marginal annotator against any passage that speaks of general unhappiness of small boys at prep school, particularly one of this kind, is unconvincing; although, of course, small boys can be 'up' one minute and 'down' the next. Indeed, the whole rhythm of boarding-school life was somewhat manic-depressive, collective exultation alternated with collective gloom. Head masters at morning assembly would one day extol some scholastic, athletic or even national victory, and the next day condemn sin and corruption enough to depress anyone. Small boys would think, after masturbation or nocturnal emission, of suicide one day and of winning a race and becoming a hero on the next. Some writers truly have a point when they claim that boarding schools commonly institutionalized, as it were, both manic-depressive and sado-masochistic impulses. Yet individuals react differently: such broad terms never explain an individual's 'character'.

Consider the passage in Orwell's essay that follows the episode of the second beating. He says that for the first and only time this beating reduced him to tears. Not because of the pain but:

... because of a deeper grief which is peculiar to childhood and not easy to convey: a sense of desolate loneliness and helplessness, of being locked up not only in a hostile world but in a world of good and evil where the rules were such that it was actually not possible for me to keep them.

He knew that bed-wetting was 'wicked' but also that it was 'outside my control'.

Sin was not necessarily something that you did: it might be something that happened to you. I do not want to claim that this idea flashed into my mind as a complete novelty at this very moment, under the blows of Sambo's cane: I must have had glimpses of it even before I left home, for my early childhood had been not altogether happy. But at any rate this was the great abiding lesson of my boyhood: that I was in a world where it was *not possible* for me to be good.[20]

This is, indeed, the world of a totalitarian state, truly of *Nineteen Eighty-Four*. But it is also the reflection of a mature writer. Was it possible for any boy of eight to have thought that? Could Orwell really have thought that he thought it then? Which is more plausible: that he is here untypically exposing the roots of his own psychology, or that he is transfiguring imaginatively aspects of his early experiences into what was soon to become the helplessness of Winston Smith?

Favouritism was rampant. The boys spoke of being 'in or out of favour' with 'Mum' Wilkes. Orwell disliked her so much that he asserts that the habit of addressing her as 'Mum' was 'Probably a corruption of the "Ma'am" used by public schoolboys to their housemasters' wives',[21] as if not wanting to recognize the far more obvious derivation, or to sully the sacred name of 'Mother'. To be officially 'Mum' was plainly part of her bag of tricks: to be matriarch with all the boys 'under her thumb' and also have them as 'one of the family'. She liked to be both stern schoolmistress cramming them for her beloved Harrow

History Essay Prize – an infectiously enthusiastic teacher, one Old Boy has said – and, on occasion, *woman*: comforting, indulgent, and understanding. In other words, she was capricious, vain, volatile and inconsistent as well as genuinely caring for her charges. As Cyril Connolly put it: 'On all the boys who went through this Elizabeth and Essex relationship she had a remarkable effect, hotting them up like little Alfa-Romeos for the Brooklands of life.'[22] Later Connolly polished yet more wicked epigrams about her.

Both Orwell and I were dominated by the head mistress of our private school; it was this remarkable woman who dished out rewards and punishments, who quoted Kipling and inculcated patriotism, who exalted character and moral courage and Scottish chieftains in kilts. We learnt the father values from a mother, we bit the hand that fed us, that tweaked the short hairs above the ear. But it was a woman's hand whose husband's cane was merely the secular arm. Agonizing ambivalence![23]

Above all, her capriciousness: 'even the nickname "Flip" suggested some primitive goddess of fortune.'[24] But it also suggests 'flip-flop'; and though Connolly ignores or does not notice the vulgarism, Gavin Maxwell has roundly stated that: 'She was a stout woman in middle age, with a well-developed bust from which her nickname was derived ... "Here comes Flip", someone would say, "... flapping nicely, eighty to the minute, everything in clockwork order."'[25]

'I conclude that St Cyprian's was a very good school indeed,' wrote Henry Longhurst despite the fact, he added, that three celebrated contemporaries (Connolly, Orwell and Maxwell) 'have written so vitriolically about it as to make one wonder whether we are writing of the same institution'.

It is true that Mum Wilkes' dominant and sometimes emotional character caused one's whole existence to depend on whether one was 'in favour' or otherwise, and indeed the expression became a normal part of one's daily life without, so to speak, the inverted commas. If you were in favour, life could be bliss: if you weren't it was hell, and no doubt this should be chalked up on the debit side. On the other hand it taught you the hard way one of *the* lessons of life – if you don't 'look after Number One', no one else will.[26]

With friends like that, what need had Mrs Wilkes of such a trio of detractors?

Gavin Maxwell, in fact, only spent a year at the school and that ten years later; but it was much the same. He read and relished Connolly's Elizabeth and Essex metaphor: 'Flip would have liked to have kept me in favour but I was just too much of an oddity for a busy woman to cope with.'[27] He might have all the blood of the border barons in him, Percys and Maxwells, but he was a very nervous and distraught little boy. He took it hard when on one occasion, being out of favour, Flip bellowed publicly, 'Matron, I think Maxwell is working that cold of his to death, he can start football again today and cold baths again tomorrow.'

Because I was as over-sensitive as a hermit crab without a shell, these thrusts hurt far more than I believe Flip ever intended them to; she was, I think, basically a kindly person and certainly an extremely efficient one. But she was using her standard technique on very unstandard material and instead of my being hotted up by [St Cyprian's] I was slowly reduced to a jelly.[28]

He summed it all up by saying that he had been 'through a prison sentence that ended in escape, however ignominious'.[29] Certainly it is not unreasonable to suppose that some never escaped from such an experience. Both Cyril Connolly and Colin Kirkpatrick remember Eric Blair as being generally out of favour, confirming his own account.

The experience of snobbery and wealth furnished another battle-ground between old boys of St Cyprian's. 'St Cyprian's was an expensive and snobbish school which was in the process of becoming more snobbish,' wrote Orwell, 'and, I imagine, more expensive.'[30] 'Snobbery,' writes a contemporary, 'we didn't know what the word meant.' 'One of the charges levelled against the Wilkes family by the critics I have mentioned was that of "snobbery",' writes Henry Longhurst, 'in that they liked to have in the school the offspring of the aristocracy, and indeed I think they did, but for the life of me I cannot see why they shouldn't.' Of course, one may reply to the anonymous contemporary, that it is not a question of acting in a way you then called 'snobbish', but of acting in a way that others could reasonably call snobbish. Yet one must concede, as Orwell did by lack of complaint against Eton, that sometimes right at the top, in high status schools, clubs, regiments and colleges, there is an almost republican equality among the élite: high status in English society can bridge wide variations of income. At its best, St Cyprian's was probably like that, but surely too new, uncertain, *arriviste* and pushy a place to be secure? Orwell asserted that 'the rich boys had milk and biscuits in the middle of the morning', and that there were differentials in the very small amounts of pocket money doled out by the Wilkes and charged on the bill. No one else can remember this, even those who broadly agree with Orwell. But his account of the boys quizzing each other and boasting about their parents' incomes rings true; at least none of the surviving contemporaries denies that it 'sometimes' went on. But Orwell's 'I doubt whether Sambo ever caned any boy whose father's income was much above £2,000 a year' is less likely to be descriptive sociology than the arresting pseudo-precision of the skilled essayist.

The Wilkes themselves played the money card in two obnoxious ways. First, Mr Wilkes revealed to Eric that he was on reduced fees ('You are living on my bounty') to spur him to work harder for a good scholarship; and second, he told him that if he didn't win this scholarship, he must leave the school at 14 'and become, in Sambo's favourite phrase, "a little office boy at forty pounds a year"' – the ultimate horror of falling among the poverty-stricken genteel, the world of Gordon Comstock and his sister indeed. But this fear probably arose only in his last year in the school. There is little doubt, however, that even if the boys were reasonably egalitarian among themselves at most times, the Wilkes, for the survival and expansion of the school, had to work pretty hard at pleasing the kind of well-off and well-connected parent whose example would be followed in where to get the male offspring crammed and prepared for public school. Their task was made easier because most of the parents would have regarded spartan conditions, strict discipline and stoic behaviour as essential parts of the building of character; indeed, of Empire too. Eric Blair certainly suffered inwardly, even if not from outward abuse, at knowing how marginal he was in this strange world that tried to blend competitive careerism with the ethic of an unambitious English gentleman batting at number eight in a village cricket match.

Filth as a characteristic of the school impressed itself on his adult mind.

Whoever writes about his childhood must beware of exaggeration and self-pity. I do not want to claim that I was a martyr or that St Cyprian's was a sort of Dotheboys Hall. But I should be falsifying my own memories if I did not record that they are largely memories of disgust. The overcrowded, underfed,

74

underwashed life that we led *was* disgusting, as I recall it. If I shut my eyes and say 'school', it is of course the physical surroundings that first come back to me: the flat playing field with its cricket pavilion and the little shed by the rifle range, the draughty dormitories, the dusty splintery passages, the square of asphalt in front of the gymnasium, the raw-looking pinewood chapel at the back. And at almost every point some filthy detail obtrudes itself. For example, there were the pewter bowls out of which we had our porridge. They had overhanging rims, and under the rims there were accumulations of sour porridge, which could be flaked off in long strips. The porridge itself, too, contained more lumps, hairs and unexplained black things than one would have thought possible, unless someone were putting them there on purpose. It was never safe to start on that porridge without investigating it first. And there was the slimy water of the plunge bath – it was twelve or fifteen feet long, the whole school was supposed to go into it every morning, and I doubt whether the water was changed all that frequently – and the always-damp towels with their cheesy smell; and on occasional visits in the winter, the murky sea-water of the local Baths, which came straight in from the beach and on which I once saw floating a human turd. And the sweaty smell of the changing-room with its greasy basins and, giving on this, the row of filthy, dilapidated lavatories which had no fastenings of any kind on the doors, so that whenever you were sitting there someone was sure to come crashing in. It is not easy for me to think of my school-days without seeming to breathe in a whiff of something cold and evil-smelling – a sort of compound of sweaty stockings, dirty towels, faecal smells blowing along corridors, forks with old food between the prongs, neck of mutton stew, and the banging of doors of the lavatories and the echoing chamber-pots in the dormitories.[31]

That Orwell warns us, so honestly, against 'exaggeration and self-pity', is not to conjure that possibility away. Again the evidence conflicts. Connolly concurs: 'blue with cold, haunting the radiators and the lavatories, and waking up every morning with the accumulated misery of the mornings before.'[32] The contemporary disagrees, saying that the baths in question were both clean and modern. 'Murky sea-water' coming 'straight in from the beach' – but could anything have been fresher in those days before widespread pollution? To picture the sea itself being filthy or corrupted by one random turd is laying it on a bit thick. It is reminiscent of the polluted ponds and rivers of his novel, *Coming Up For Air* (1939), which symbolizes a whole civilization gone sour and decadent. As to the foul food, again the most fervid defender of the school against Orwell, Connolly and Maxwell has this to say:

At that age you don't ask many questions. You take life for what it is, and on the whole, by today's standards, it was pretty spartan, not only from the point of view of washing in very cold water and having to do a length of the swimming-pool every morning, followed by P.T., which put me off every form of artificial physical exercise for life, but also because the food rationing was far less expertly managed in the First War than in the Second ... It is one of the more merciful dispensations of providence that one tends to forget the hard times and remember the good ... Some of the scars remain, but not many. Among them I should put the cold pewter bowls of porridge with the thick slimy lumps, *into which I was actually sick one day and made to stand at a side-table and eat it up*; the liquified orange-coloured maize pudding with the coarse husks floating on the top ...[33]

Henry Longhurst surely kicks a decisive own-goal: nothing in Orwell's account is as horrible as that. Orwell may have laid it on thick, but there is little doubt that his identification of filth with oppression and squalor with tyranny began so early, and so plausibly.

Bullying was rife. Orwell tells of being constantly bullied by a boy in the top form and of resolving to sneak up on him and hit him hard by surprise. He did, bloodying his mouth. The boy then challenged him to fight and Eric kept on refusing, out of fear he said, and feeling doubly guilty that he was breaking 'rules' both against surprise attack and against refusing legitimate challenges. To his surprise, the boy did not attack him out of hand, indeed thereafter left him alone. He said it then took him twenty years to realize that 'the weak in a world governed by the strong' *must* 'break the rules, or perish ... have the right to make a different set of rules for themselves.' Although the story sounds almost too good to be true – old George making out that young Eric was an effective anti-hero – his admission that he drew the moral much later is impressive: he does not pretend that this is a first step on the road to his believing in a socialist revolution. Something like it must have happened. Sardonic about it all though he became, he was not a purely passive resister. This incident would have been in his penultimate year in school. But before that too he had been a target for bullying. Sir John Grotrian, a year behind him at school, has written:

My memories of Blair are of a time when he was an unhappy little boy at prep school. Both my brother and he, as intellectuals, were not infrequently 'mobbed' by the school's gang of philistines and, in great fear, were reduced to tears and then laughed at; and I as an onlooker, to my everlasting shame, had not the guts to attempt to defend them. What would have been the use I argued. Outnumbered by twenty or thirty to one, how could I have quelled the mob?

And poor Blair didn't only suffer physically from his contemporaries. Mrs Wilkes herself, frequently in a rage of impatience while teaching the children, was not above resorting to violence. She used to reach out and pull the boys' hair, as though that would be any kind of an aid to learning or remembering. For that reason, Blair told us, he kept his hair very well greased so that the teacher's fingers would slip off! His hair was quite straight and butter coloured, his complexion cream. His face was moon shaped and all too often streaked with tears.[34]

This is poignant and impressive evidence, especially as Grotrian had not read anything of Orwell's and had never heard of 'Such, Such Were the Joys', nor yet Connolly's *Enemies of Promise*. It is confirmed in some notes that the contemporary (a year senior to Blair) prepared:

To be absolutely frank, he was NOT popular among the majority of our 'little hooligans'!!! Nevertheless I always liked Eric and I believe he liked me ... He was *very* UNordinary. He seemed to think about things in a much more sophisticated and mature manner than we did. I think he appreciated that I thought of him like this. He had a temper which could be very easily aroused by 'little hooligans' – but I remember that on several occasions I – as head boy – stood and drove the hooligans off. NO, he was not popular, but neither was he *generally* disliked. I think it was just a matter of him seeming to be years ahead of the rest of all of us – mentally. I think he was 'bullied' by the younger ones and this probably infuriated and affected him. I don't know about his private family life – but may be because his mother remained at home while his father returned to India, had something to do with it.[35]

The 'it' is his general view that 'Such, Such Were the Joys' was a monstrously unfair and unbalanced attack on the school. And he plainly thinks that Eric should have put up with the bullying and not taken such a belated revenge, even on the assumption that it was Eric himself who was flogged for bed-wetting. Nevertheless, if the attitudes are different in these two accounts, the facts are much the same and are equally damning. But again the essential 'offence' of Eric seems to have been, not as George makes out, lack of money and social insecurity, but of being intellectual, bookish, a swot, mentally superior. It is a wonder these Philistines did not kill Cyril Connolly.

What Orwell most disliked was simply the bad teaching. All the barbarity and psychological stress could have been forgiven if not forgotten if the Wilkes had valued learning for its own sake and not, as he constantly stresses, for its cash value. 'Over a period of two or three years the scholarship boys were crammed with learning as cynically as a goose is crammed for Christmas.' But 'with what learning!' he says. The whole 'evil' process was 'frankly a preparation for a sort of confidence trick. Your job was to learn exactly those things that would give an examiner the impression that you knew more than you did know, and ... to avoid burdening your brain with anything else.' They were prepared in the classics in a 'flashy, unsound way', never reading a book through, only the kind of passages that might come up in the exam as an 'unseen translation'. He then used, and kept, Entick's *English–Latin Dictionary* – in which he wrote his name in Greek – published in 1820 and unrevised.

History was taught 'as a series of unrelated, unintelligible but – in some way that was never explained to us – important facts with resounding phrases attached to them'. He recalled 'positive orgies of dates, with the keener boys leaping up and down in their places in their eagerness to shout out the right answers, and at the same time not feeling the faintest interest in the meaning of the mysterious events they were naming'.[36] He felt strongly enough to tell the – possibly indifferent – Indian listeners to the BBC's wartime Eastern Service all about this: 'I used to think of history as a sort of long scroll with thick black lines ruled across it at intervals. Each of these lines marked the end of what was called "a period", and you were given to understand that what came afterwards was completely different from what had gone before.'[37] He also regaled the readers of *Tribune* in 1947 with an account of how bad history teaching is in private schools.[38]

Gavin Maxwell's account confirms the factualist frenzy: 'a young master ... loped up to the blackboard and wrote his first question, "Who beat De Gras?" This struck me as a funny and naïve simplification of the issue ... it was one of my first recognitions of weakness, woolliness.' Maxwell suffered particularly because they expected him to have instant recall of every date in Scottish and border history, his ancestors having been in on so much of it.[39]

All in all, the school seems to have been a pretty despicable place. Orwell's description of it seems truthful, but it is not literally accurate, and his account of his own relationship with it, of its effect on him, is either semi-fictional or heavily overdrawn. He was able to keep a greater distance than the essay suggests, as if even in those days he had developed both a tendency to be against authority and an ability to preserve himself from its influence. Some of Orwell's later rage at the school may have been due to a puritanical feeling of time so badly wasted – brutality and strain without intellectual compensation; and, at that period, the sheer disappointment of a small boy who naïvely and genuinely liked books. Much of his rage was highly rational. 'Such, Such Were the Joys' was no *Émile*, but it was a considerable tract on what education should not be. Fifty years later it so stung a distinguished Fellow of Trinity College, Cambridge, old Andrew Gow, who had been Blair's tutor at Eton, that he wrote to Sonia Orwell:

I did not know that you were collecting his works, but I hope, if so, that you do not intend to reprint that essay about his private [prep] school ... It shocked me profoundly. I knew the Wilkes's and the school quite well ... and the essay is monstrously unfair. It was quite a good school: Mr W., though a rather stupid and probably idle man, was genuinely keen on it and his boys; Mrs W., capable, energetic, and motherly, probably really ran it ... No doubt G. (and Cyril Connolly) being rebels, resented being mothered, and G. seems from the essay to have acquired an inferiority complex because he was taken at a reduced fee. I could understand his having written thus venomously just after leaving but if the date on the essay is correct it was written long afterwards and I was horrified at his having nursed his rancour so long. I cannot believe that he would ever have published it himself and think it would be a disservice both to him and to the W.'s to resurrect it.[40]

And when, a few years before, David Farrer, the partner of Fredric Warburg, Orwell's final and most faithful publisher, had actually visited Mrs Wilkes to explore the possibility of publishing the obviously libellous piece, he reported: 'I am bound to say that she produced ample evidence in the form of letters, testimonials, etc., to substantiate her denunciation of the story, which I suspect is a gross distortion of what actually took place.'[41] Gross distortion?

What finally emerges from 'the Echoing Green', that is, the highly complex relationship between moral truths of his adult 'Such, Such Were the Joys' and the facts of his actual career at St Cyprian's (does not the full quotation warn of such complexity?), is the common ground of the two experiences of brutality, injustice and oppression. But the oppression of St Cyprian's was not in a *totalitarian* mode – completely unenvisaged by anyone in the 1910s and Orwell recognized it, though among the very first, only after 1936 – but rather in an old-fashioned *autocratic* mode. Autocracy was shock enough in what was supposed to be a cultivated school in a civilized parliamentary democracy. Under autocracy inner dissent can be maintained beneath the cover of politic conformity; but his picture of totalitarianism was of a world in which all privacy was denied and which had to be resisted if individualism was to survive. Such a distinction was important to Orwell in his last years. His experiences at prep school prepared him to reject imperialism when he went to Burma and to side with the underdog, for ever afterwards, with empathy and understanding. But they did not directly form the imaginative roots of *Nineteen Eighty-Four*, even though *some time* just before writing that book, his least autobiographical novel, he wrote or revised an apparently autobiographical essay, as if to get the feeling for Winston Smith in his world of no escape from doing evil. The essay exploited and reinterpreted his own past for both literary and polemical effort, in the light of later knowledge.

Jacintha Buddicom, the author of *Cat Poems*, knew him well in his teens and wrote a book about their childhood friendship in which she actually claimed that 'he was a specially happy child'. She cast shrewd doubts on the literal accuracy of the great polemic against prep schools.[42] A reviewer in the *New Statesman* had represented her as saying that the essay was 'a pack of lies'. In her reply, which was not published, she wrote,

Orwell's 'Such, Such Were the Joys' is not a pack of lies! It is a story in the form of an autobiographical sketch written in the first person: a story so brilliantly told that it is popularly believed to have happened word for word – as some incidents undoubtedly did.[43]

She is probably right; but it is simply impossible to be sure. All that is clear is that if he intended it to be literally truthful, then memory played him some curious tricks, but that none the less it was a brilliant polemic – not entirely about the past.

CHAPTER THREE

LEARNING AND HOLIDAYS

HIS real prep-school days, though he disliked the experience and detested such a broiler-house of a school, may thus have been less terrible and have had less lasting effect on his character than long afterwards he made out. The English upper classes tend to exaggerate the effect of their school-days, whether for better or for worse. And they did not fill his whole life. The experience was of an autocratic, not of a total, institution. This distinction became very important to the mature man. Letters home, for instance, were important, and if necessary the censorship could be avoided simply by posting a letter in town. Gavin Maxwell sent a desperate letter to his mother to take him away; she did. Long afterwards Lord Clark's son wrote home similarly, and was moved on. Holidays, after all, were long and were almost wholly enjoyable. There were glad moments of peace and solitude remembered, at school as well as at home, when he was alone with his books: 'the joy of waking early on summer mornings and getting in an hour's undisturbed reading (Ian Hay, Thackeray, Kipling and H. G. Wells were the favourite authors of my boyhood).'[1]

His weekly letters home only survive to just beyond his ninth birthday. There are the same remorseless weekly listings of position in class, always near the top, of football scores and anxious inquiries about the dog, cats, guinea pigs and the humble white mice at home. Spelling slowly improves. 4 February 1912: 'I have been in the sickroom again because I got an aufel cold. Yesday of course everything iced and boys went and skated, but I was stuffed up in the sickroom and I couldent get a bit of peace to read for Leslie Cohen kept on worrying and in the end I had to go and read to *him*.' On 11 February he asks for draughts to be sent and 'some of those peas that were left over frome the bags because theres a boy here who's got a kind of cannon that has to have those peas to shoot ... I am second in everything in my lessons.' And on 18 February, anxiously, 'If there are any tadpoles in the rain tub please dont let any leeches in, because I certainly dont want to come home and find that all the tadpoles are eaten up by the beasts of leeches.'

3 March brings the usual placings and animal inquiries but also a dramatic account of being in goal with a first accidental touch of Orwellian style: 'I had to be jolly quick to pick them up and kick them, because most of the chaps the other side were in aufel rats and they were runing at me like angry dogs. From you loving son, E. A. Blair.' And on 17 March 'The was a fairly big ship wrecked some way out, and you can see the masts sticking up.' May brings long walks over the Downs which he says, even in 'Such, Such Were the Joys', brought back 'good memories of St Cyprian's amid a horde of bad ones'. 2 June brings a request: 'a gunmetal watch for my birthday' and 'shall soon be wanting my bathing dress soon if you send me one of my old pairs dont send those beastsley things that come all over my body'. Further cricket scores follow in the middle of the month and then his last two letters of the school year.

30th of June 1912

My darling Mother,
I hope you are alright.
Thank you very much for the ripping little watch you sent and the Little Paper, thank Father for the book for me and some one sent me a knife and some-one else a box of toffy and someone else a cake that looks as if it is a seed one.
I am 2nd in Latin and 4th in English and 6th in History and Geography and 5th in French and 11th in Arith.
With lots of love from Eric Blair.

21st July

My darling Mother,
I hope you are alright. Will you please ask to the tobaconest to sell you some cigarette cards he will give you a good many for about four-pence.
We had two matches yesterday in the 1st we lost, in the II we won they made 52 and we mad 246, one of our boys mad 90.
With lots of love from
 Eric Blair. P.S. I send my love to everybody at home and give Guissy [Avril's piebald guinea pig] my love.

'There were wonderful midsummer evenings,' he recalls even in the essay, 'when, as a special treat, we were not driven off to bed as usual but allowed to wander about the grounds in the long twilight, ending up with a plunge into the swimming bath at about nine o'clock' (it cannot always have been icy and filthy).

Then the contented school holidays, family holidays, back to school, but only three of the next term's letters survive (and then, indeed, only one more at all from St Cyprian's). Two are routine but the third is full of high matters:

My darling Mother,
I hope you are quite well. We have had a Magic Lantern Lecture on Thursday and a Fancy Dress Dance on Friday, I went to the dance as a footman with a red velvet coat, and a white silk flowered waist-coat, and red silk trousers, and black stockings and a lace frill, and a wig.
One of the boys went as a priate, three as revelutionests, one went as a sun flower, and one as Puss in Boots, another as a frog, and one as the White Rabbit in Alice in Wonderland, and a lot of other things. I am 2nd in Latin this week, and 2nd in one of my English forms, and 3rd in Arithmetic, 7th in French and my other English form. We played four matches yesterday and won in them all. I hope Marjorie is quite well now, and that everybody likes the house in Shiplake. please give Avril my love and Guissy as well, and pleas write to me when you are not too busy and tell me all about the new house.
With lots of love from
Eric Blair

'Three revelutionests' indeed, and the costumes would have come from the school: one imagines black cloaks, black beards, round black bombs with fuses, a red scarf or handkerchief, a box of matches and Russian accents? And after the summer holidays, his family, his father now home, had moved into a larger house at Shiplake, 'Roselawn' in Station Road, but only two miles from the former house at Henley.

Before 1914 and the Great War, the summer holidays were spent in Cornwall, either at Looe or at Polperro. An old Mrs Perrycoste of Polperro had been brought up by Richard Blair's mother, Eric's grand-mother, who survived her husband by many years. He had died in 1867, over thirty years before Richard Blair had had his first child at 41; and Eric's grandfather had been born in 1802, a hundred and one years before Eric (how extraordinary the life-spans and successions of children with old fathers). Mrs Perrycoste's children, Honor and Bernard, played with Marjorie, Avril and Eric. 'We used to have a lovely time down there, bathing,' Avril reminisced in a BBC programme in 1960, 'we had some friends down there with children who were almost cousins really, and we used to go rock-climbing and all the sort of usual pursuits and he always seemed perfectly happy.' She remembered Eric, the Perrycoste children and herself going down a lane at Polperro where a headless ghost was said to lurk; and as a precaution they carried sprigs of rowan and a leaf from the Prayer Book. Eric was always interested in ghost stories. Jacintha Buddicom has said that she is surprised that he never edited an anthology of them. Apart from these Cornish visits, said Avril:

We never really played much together as children because five years' difference in age does make a great difference at that time of life, but I do remember interminable games of French cricket when he always seemed to be in and we were always vainly trying to get him out. But it has been said that he had an unhappy childhood and I don't really think this was in the least true, although I must admit that he did give out that impression himself.[2]

Avril Dunn's testimony carries conviction when she herself reminds us of the age gap. He would not have talked to her about the dark side of St Cyprian's, but plainly no disturbances carried over into his behaviour to mar the holiday pleasures, no aggressive tantrums such as one would expect if St Cyprian's had been a total hell, quite as black as he later painted it, or, even if so, if he had not been able to cope with it.

The school year of 1913–14 brought that new boy to St Cyprian's who was to be such a welcome ally or solace against 'the philistines' and 'the hooligans', who was to follow him to Eton, and then to resume a friendly and helpful acquaintance in the mid-Thirties which would last until Orwell's death: Cyril Connolly. If there are some tensions between 'Eric Blair' and 'George Orwell', Cyril Connolly was, right from his first appearance on the prep-school scene, all surviving contemporaries agree, Cyril Connolly. Connolly saw himself as standing for aestheticism and romanticism and Orwell for independence and 'an alternative to character, Intelligence': Cecil Beaton 'showed me another, Sensibility ... from Orwell I learnt about literature, from Cecil I learnt about art,' he wrote in *Enemies of Promise* – the school being one such enemy. How much, indeed, children learn for themselves and get from their friends, not the learning facts by rote but the love of ideas, problems and curious things. Cyril and Eric both wrote poetry and exchanged their poems: 'I would compare [my poems] with Orwell's and be critical about his, while he was polite about mine.'[3]

Miss Buddicom thinks that Orwell in his essay was simply trying 'to go one better' than Connolly's disparagement of the school in his chapter. Connolly's chapter is indeed almost as cruel a tract as Orwell's essay. The time-scale of it is, however, unreliable, for he attributes views to 9- and 10-year-old boys only plausible in precocious 12- and 13-year-olds. He reads back into early days what they were like when they were at Eton.

The remarkable thing about Orwell was that he alone among the boys was an intellectual, and not a parrot, for he thought for himself, read Shaw and Samuel Butler, and rejected not only [St Cyprian's] but the war, the Empire, Kipling, Success and Character.[4]

Certainly he did not reject the War, Empire and Kipling in 1914. On the contrary, the War led to his first attempt at publication, in the *Henley and South Oxfordshire Standard* in that September when aged 11. They published his submission promptly – he was not always to be so lucky with manuscripts – on 2 October 1914.

AWAKE YOUNG MEN OF ENGLAND

Oh! give me the strength of the Lion
  The wisdom of Reynard the Fox
And then I'll hurl troops at the Germans
  And give them the hardest of knocks.

Oh! think of the War lord's mailed fist,
  That is striking at England today:
And think of the lives that our soldiers
  Are fearlessly throwing away.

Awake! Oh you young men of England,
  For if when your country's in need,
You do not enlist by the thousand,
  You truly are cowards indeed.

The metre owes a debt to Robert Service even if the language is sub-Kipling at his wartime worst. The last letter of his from St Cyprian's which survives asks for copies of this poem.

[n.d.]

Darling Mums,

Thanks for your letter. Today there was a whole holiday, and we took our dinner out to East Dean, and went to have tea at Jevington. The tea was unspeakably horrible, though it did cost 1/6. Thanks most frightfully for the two bob you sent me: it will be especially useful in one way; because you see, when I'm given my money at the end of term, I shall probably be given a crisp, crackling, and dirty ten-shilling note, so that I can put it and your postal order into a letter and send them straight off to Gamages. Then I'll get the things in about a week, I hope. If I do go and get mumps, which is quite probable, it will muck up things considerably. However, let's hope I won't. Do you think they'll have these things in stock at Gamages? Because I found them in the Christmas catalogue. I do hope poor little Roy [a pet dog] will live through all right: I've a sort of presentiment that he will. By the way, do you think you could send 2 copies of the paper they've offered to take my poem in? It doesn't matter much if you don't, but still I should like it. It was ripping on the picnic we went today, – I've never drunk water from a bucket drawn straight up from a well before. We did this at a farm where six of us went with a master to buy milk. By the way, I have 3 catterpillars now, as my partner made over his stock to me. They're called Savonarola, Paul, and Barnabas. Please give my love to Father and Avril and everyone.

Your loving son

Eric

When copies of the newspaper arrived, Mrs Wilkes read the poem aloud to the whole school: he was suddenly in favour. If the 'little hooligans' and the Philistines had gone for him that night, who would have blamed them? They were a patriotic mob, however. But either he was not a good courtier, or luck deserted him. For despite the poem and his winning the prize 'for the best list of books taken out of the library', when he and Connolly were caught reading either something of Somerset Maugham's or Compton Mackenzie's *Sinister Street* (two separate incidents seem to have got conflated in memory), they fell from favour just as suddenly – Blair never to recover it, said Connolly.

Could Shaw and Butler have been read before Eton? Connolly's memory tended to push things back. ' "Of course you realize, Connolly," said Orwell, "that, whoever wins this war, we shall emerge a second-rate nation" ' [5] was more probably said, Connolly later considered, at Eton rather than St Cyprian's. Yet they were both reading books beyond their years. It is at least possible that he tackled them then. Orwell recalled in a letter to Julian Symons in 1948 his great admiration for H. G. Wells as a writer:

... he was a very early influence on me. I think I was ten or eleven when Cyril Connolly and I got hold of a copy of Wells's *The Country of the Blind* (short stories) and were so fascinated by it that we kept stealing it from one another. I can still remember at 4 o'clock on a midsummer morning, with the school fast asleep and the sun slanting through the window, creeping down a passage to Connolly's dormitory where I knew the book would be beside his bed. We also got into severe trouble (and I think a caning – I forget) for having a copy of Compton Mackenzie's *Sinister Street*.[6]

But despite this stronger diet, his patriotism broke into print once more in the *Henley and South Oxfordshire Standard* on 21 July 1916. Mrs Wilkes had set the theme of 'Kitchener' for a poetry exercise or competition to mark the death of the War Lord when the *Hampshire* sank on his secret journey to Russia. (Connolly's offering was also modelled on Gray's 'Elegy'.)

KITCHENER

No stone is set to mark his nation's loss
　　No stately tomb enshrines his noble breast;
Not e'en the tribute of a wooden cross
　　Can mark his hero's rest.

He needs them not, his name untarnished stands,
　　Remindful of the mighty deeds he worked,
Footprints of one, upon time's changeful sands,
　　Who ne'er his duty shirked.

Who follows in his steps no danger shuns,
　　Nor stoops to conquer by shameful deed,
An honest and and unselfish race he runs,
　　From fear and malice freed.

This was to be his last publication for twelve years. And could this possibly have been youthful cynicism, simply to get back into favour or into print again? Unlikely, but possible. His sardonic, odd-man-out attitudes were certainly established and apparent by his last two years in prep school. And yet patriotism does strange things to a fellow, particularly the higher patriotism aware of death and sacrifice, when contrasted with the more vulgar jingoism moved only by revenge and paltry pride.

Certainly his 1914 poem rings completely true. His sister's first memory of him

. . . was at the beginning of the First World War, in fact I think it was actually the day war broke out and he would have been about eleven then and I suppose I was six and he was sitting cross-legged on the floor of my mother's bedroom talking about it in a grown-up manner and I was knitting him a school scarf . . .[7]

Later he professed to have been unmoved by 1914. 'Such, Such Were the Joys' hardly mentions the War. And in 'My Country, Right or Left' (1940) he claimed that 'nothing in the whole war moved me so deeply as the loss of the *Titanic* had done a few years earlier'.

Of the outbreak of war I have three vivid memories which, being petty and irrelevant, are uninfluenced by anything that has come later. One is of the cartoon of the 'German Emperor' (I believe the hated name 'Kaiser' was not popularized till a little later) that appeared in the last days of July . . . Another is of the time when the Army commandeered all the horses in our little country town, and a cabman burst into tears in the market-place when his horse, which had worked for him for years, was taken away from him. And another is of a mob of young men at the railway station, scrambling for the evening papers that had just arrived on the London train. And I remember the pile of pea-green papers . . . the high collars, the tightish trousers and the bowler hats, far better than I can remember the names of the terrific battles that were already raging on the French frontier.[8]

He would be oddly forgetful if his first publication was not among his vivid memories. More likely that by 1940 he was being deliberately and skilfully selective, to deflate vulgar patriotism before stating a case for a kind of common-sense, populist patriotism. Back then, however, it was the voice of Kipling, not yet rejected, that spoke through the child.

Towards the end of the summer holidays in 1914, just after the outbreak of War in August and when Eric was 11, a fortunate event occurred for Orwell biography. Jacintha Buddicom (aged 13), her sister Guiny (7), and brother Prosper (10), were playing French cricket at the bottom of their garden when they saw, close to the fence in a neighbouring field, a boy standing on his head. As this was a feat they had not seen before, one of them, polite but curious, asked, 'Why are you standing on your head?' The boy replied, 'You are noticed more if you stand on your head than if you are right way up.'⁹ They all became friends on the spot, though the right way up: not a holiday passed, until Eric left Eton in 1921, without their seeing each other almost daily and they frequently went away on holiday together. Mrs Buddicom got to know Mr and Mrs Blair quite well, particularly Mrs Blair. Mr Buddicom, an Oxford science graduate who had lectured at the London Hospital and Birkbeck College and who dabbled in a wide range of pursuits from Egyptology to market gardening, deserted his family in 1915 to start a new life in Australia. Jacintha Buddicom's account of her friendship with the Blairs creates the impression that she came to rely on Eric for a lot of talk about books and learning that she would have liked to have got from her father. Her book, *Eric and Us*, may be florid and sentimental to some literary tastes, but it is a convincingly detailed account of their childhood. If its perspective is rose-tinted and its vision somewhat myopic (for it was always holiday), yet it is no more so than 'Such, Such Were the Joys' is deliberately depressive. Even if her personal comments on his subsequent career and books (they never met again after 1921) are *obiter dicta*, irrelevant to her genuine biographical evidence, yet they too have in them a bustling common sense and a good feel for the customs of the period. Only early in 1949 did she realize that the George Orwell of *Animal Farm* which she had read and enjoyed was Eric Blair, her vanished childhood friend; and when she wrote to him, he replied at length from his sickbed, warmly and nostalgically – clearly the relationship had been close and real.

Her account, moreover, is well-documented from family letters, photographs and diaries, and the manuscript of her book was read by Avril who thought it 'a very fair assessment of Eric's childhood'. Yet Avril, of course, also only saw the holiday Eric, and neither she nor Jacintha were inclined to take 'Such, Such Were the Joys' too seriously, perhaps not seriously enough. If he was not as desperately unhappy at St Cyprian's as he made out, it was more horrible than either his sister or Jacintha ever supposed. Either he kept a stiff upper lip – as school indeed taught him to, or he was simply unable or unwilling even as a boy to communicate his private griefs easily.

The Buddicom children found Mr Blair a tired, reserved and rather forbidding man, though they liked his wife. They always addressed them formally as Mr or Mrs Blair, never as 'Uncle Richard' or 'Auntie Ida' as was the custom for young children with parents of close friends. They seldom played in the Blairs' garden, but nearly every day with Eric and Avril in their own. Theirs was a much larger garden with a wild end and a croquet lawn, on which bicycle polo took place as well as more orthodox ways of using the croquet balls and mallets. 'The Blairs' was a much more conventional laid-out garden, with a potent if unwritten notice: *Keep off the flowerbeds.*'[10] Mr Blair became the secretary of the local golf club, a post that carried a small stipend, and spent a lot of time playing, possibly the one thing that he had in common with his wife's brother, Charles.

'The Blairs, though certainly not demonstrative, were nevertheless a united family, and their home seemed to us to be a happy one. I do not think Eric was *fond* of his father,' writes Miss Buddicom, 'although he respected and obeyed him, but without any doubt he was genuinely fond of his Mother and sisters, especially Avril.' In the years to come he never lost touch with his mother and Avril, even though he never confided in them. Miss Buddicom notes perceptively that when in 1944 Eric was to name his adopted son Richard – after Richard Rees, in fact, not his father – 'he did not avoid the name'. 'He did not like his own name Eric,' she wrote, for it reminded him of the prig in *Eric, or Little by Little*, the Victorian boys' story, 'a book he deplored'.

Miss Buddicom remembered him as 'a naturally reserved and rather self-contained boy' and Avril remembered him as 'an aloof, undemonstrative person' – and added quickly 'which doesn't necessarily mean to say that he had a blighted childhood and developed a "death wish" as so many big biographers seem to think'.[11] Yet not so aloof or reserved that he couldn't stand on his head when he wanted to attract attention and make friends.

What Eric and Jacintha had in common were bookish, literary tastes. While the others looked after young livestock – both households seemed to have been teeming with fecund pets – they played a game together which they called 'Set Piece Poetry'. A subject was chosen by them in turn, sometimes specific words, chosen at random, were to be included, and sometimes a specified form or metre and a maximum length was set. In each contest, 'undictionary' words could be obligatory, optional or forbidden. Eric was particularly good at coining undictionary words and was more prolific and prolix than she.[12] Poetry was, indeed, to be important in the aspirations of both the boy and the man.[13]

All the children together played many different pencil-and-paper word-games, like 'Ladders' and 'Hangman', and lots of card-games, particularly Rummy and Cheat, as well as the tireless, timeless Ludo, Snakes and Ladders and Halma. Chess was thought too serious. Of all indoor pastimes and educative games typical of that time, nothing musical is mentioned. Eric seems to have been as good as tone-deaf and like the rest of the family to have had neither ability nor interest in music. All the children were collectors, in their season and fashion, of stamps, coins, cigarette cards, birds' eggs (the code was never to take more than one and then only if there were several), and pond life. Eric also collected in an album seaside picture-postcards purchased at East-bourne, largely of ladies with big bottoms; but he also had a manilla envelope with cards judged too vulgar for the eyes of the Buddicom girls. (He may have still had this collection in 1941 when he wrote 'The Art of Donald McGill', the classic critique and appreciation of vulgar postcards as folk art.)

The only time Jacintha and Eric quarrelled was when he and Prosper killed 'a beautiful hedgehog' and attempted to bake it in clay as they had heard the gipsies did. The Buddicom cook was not happy when she found the corpse in the oven, and she actually gave notice when they set up on top of the kitchen stove an amateur 'whisky-still' which blew up while she was having her afternoon rest.[14] Eric and Prosper were fond of 'chemical experiments'. They made gunpowder. They put some in a bonfire in the garden which didn't ignite. So Eric went up and gave it a questing poke and it did. They escaped with singed eyebrows, blackened hands, faces and clothes, and parental wrath. Car-pentry was then a common pursuit but Eric and Prosper did *not* indulge in it: Eric's later do-it-yourself enthusiasms and practicality plainly had no early, formal basis. They all went fishing, although only the boys were serious about it, essaying flies on occasion rather than worms or bread. 'Where are the English coarse fish now?' complained George Bowling in *Coming Up For Air*. 'When I was a kid every pond and stream had fish in it. Now all the ponds are drained, and when the streams aren't poisoned with chemicals from factories they're full of rusty tins and motor-bike tyres.[15] They went shooting for rabbits over common land or fields belonging to neighbouring farms. Eric loved the countryside and the simple country pursuits.

Orwell was to write in 1945 in the *Evening Standard* a light, nostalgic essay on toys with the somewhat gloomy title, 'Bare Christmas for the Children'. It was a wise and gentle polemic against manufactured toys in favour of playing with real things and making one's own toys. But somewhat inconsistently, two manufactured items – anything but do-it-yourself – were also commended:

One of the greatest joys of my own childhood were those little brass cannons on wooden gun-carriages ... The smallest had barrels the size of your little finger, the largest were six or eight inches long, cost ten shillings and went off with a noise like the Day of Judgement. To fire them, you needed gun-powder, which the shops sometimes refused to sell you, but a resourceful boy could make gunpowder for himself if he took the precaution of buying the ingredients from three different chemists.

And an even more surprising sentiment for a war-weary Christmas followed from reckless Uncle George:

One of the advantages of being a child thirty years ago was the light-hearted attitude that then prevailed towards firearms. Up till not long before the other war you could walk into any bicycle shop and buy a revolver, and even when the authorities began to take an interest in revolvers, you could still buy for 7s. 6d. a fairly lethal weapon known as a Saloon rifle. I bought my first Saloon rifle at the age of ten, with no questions asked.[16]

The rifle was a .22 calibre. He would have already used such a gun in the St Cyprian's cadet corps under the instruction of the school ser-geant (old army men sometimes found cosier niches, then and now, in prep or public schools than as theatre commissionaires). Boys would have gone into the all but compulsory Officers Training Corps (the OTC) in their public school already able to shoot at both fixed and moving targets.

Jacintha remembers no great financial stress around the Blairs, and chides Eric for harping on this theme:

His parents' finances were doubtless straitened when Mr Blair retired and Marjorie's school fees had to be found as well as Eric's; but when we knew the family they did not seem drastically impoverished. The children had the usual little treats that we had, and Eric had enough pocket-money to buy quantities of books for me as well as for himself. He had a gun, a fishing rod and a bicycle, like Prosper and his contemporaries, and the Blairs went for seaside holidays . . .

There was no harping on inferiority and poverty by Eric *then* . . . The picture painted of a wretched little neurotic, snivelling miserably before a swarm of swanking bullies, suspecting that he 'smelt', just was not Eric at all.[17]

She has remarked that she finds the 'I' of his essay much closer to the anti-hero of *Keep the Aspidistra Flying* than to the Eric Blair she knew. He would imitate and mimic the masters at school, but she caught no note of bitterness, only of facetious rudeness, perhaps of a slightly cocky superiority. 'He used to tell hilarious anecdotes in the holidays,' she remarked, 'and laughed at the school heads for being prune-and-prism snobs.' He seemed to have no other friends around Shiplake and Henley, nor did school friends come to stay with him in the holidays nor he with them, as was often the custom. But in talking about books, he occasionally and appreciatively quoted the dicta of a friend whom he never named but referred to as 'C.C.'. Even in the relative garrulity of youth, the habit was growing in Eric of keeping his different worlds and different friends apart.

Above all they talked about books, read books, bought, borrowed and swapped books incessantly. 'He said that reading was good preparation for writing: *any* book could teach you something, if only how to write one. Of course, Eric was always going to write: not merely as an author, always a FAMOUS AUTHOR, in capitals.'[18] Wells was one of his favourite authors. In the Buddicom house there was a copy of *A Modern Utopia* which had been owned by Jacintha's run-away father, who had met H. G. Wells. Eric borrowed it so often and admired it so much that eventually it was given to him. He liked ghost stories and detective stories, admired Hornung, Conan Doyle's brother-in-law, and thought it 'a good thing' that Holmes and Raffles should be in the same family. Swift, Thackeray, Dickens, Charles Reade, Ian Hay and Kipling were much read, as was Shakes-peare. Later, but more probably during Eton days, he read Butler, Sterne, the whole of Wells, and Shaw – professing disappointment at the latter; but he may have begun these secularist readings even at prep school in his last year. Jacintha remembers that among short stories he took particular pleasure in Edgar Allan Poe's 'Premature Burial', James' 'The Turn of the Screw', Kipling's 'Baa Baa Black Sheep' and

Wells' 'Slip under the Microscope' and 'The Country of the Blind'. And 'though Eric and I were far too old for it,' they liked Beatrix Potter's *Pigling Bland*, her sister's book: he read it to her twice over to cheer her up when she had a cold.[19]

Not merely was Eric devoted to reading Shakespeare:

Eric used to write him, constantly concocting long historical dramas in blank verse, which he was to read aloud to me with different voices for the different parts. Gruff and manly for the heroes: alternatively ultra-plebeian or mincing la-di-dah for the villains ... And a squealing falsetto for the female characters ... which often dissolved us both into such helpless giggles that Eric was unable to continue his recital. I once suggested that I should 'do the ladies' but Eric declined this well-meant offer: he would not allow his sacred screeds out of his own hands. I never *saw* these Masterpieces – he only read them to me.[20]

This all confirms his account in 'Why I Write' (1946) of his early facility.

Apart from school work, I wrote *vers d'occasion*, semi-comic poems which I could turn out at what now seems to me astonishing speed – at fourteen I wrote a whole rhyming play, in imitation of Aristophanes, in about a week ... But side by side with all this, for fifteen years or more, I was carrying out a literary exercise of a quite different kind: this was the making up of a continuous 'story' about myself, a sort of diary existing only in the mind. I believe this is a common habit of children and adolescents. As a very small child I used to imagine that I was, say, Robin Hood, and picture myself as the hero of thrilling adventures, but quite soon my 'story' ceased to be narcissistic in a crude way and became more and more a mere description of what I was doing and the things I saw. For minutes at a time this kind of thing would be running through my head: 'He pushed the door open and entered the room. A yellow beam of sunlight, filtering through the muslin curtains, slanted on to the table, where a matchbox, half open, lay beside the inkpot. With his right hand in his pocket he moved across to the window...' This habit continued till I was about twenty-five, right through my non-literary years. Although I had to search, and did search, for the right words, I seemed to be making this descriptive effort almost against my will, under a kind of compulsion from outside. The 'story' must, I suppose, have reflected the styles of the various writers I admired at different ages, but so far as I remember it always had the same meticulous descriptive quality.[21]

In 1915 the Blairs moved back into Henley, to 36 St Mark's Road, a smaller, semi-detached house, easier to run in wartime conditions, with Marjorie itching to get away to war work, old Blair trying to get into the

Army, and domestic help hard to find. (But two miles' distance made little difference to the children's meetings, thanks to bicycles. Indeed, after he left prep school, wartime conditions threw them together even more in the vacations.) Just before the move, the Buddicom girls remember Mr Blair often interrupting their play to call Eric to finish his special holiday task in time to catch the last post. For his last two years in school he was receiving special tuition, even by post in the holidays, to try for a scholarship. He did the work without grumbling, conscientiously, and came when he was called. He never told them, however, that Mr Wilkes had goaded him with reminders that he was at St Cyprian's on reduced rates. He loyally supported the hopes of his parents, so far at least.

The last two years at St Cyprian's he worked, and was worked, harder than ever. With so much that he himself wanted to read, quite apart from the scholarship fodder, his lifelong habit of hard and constant work was being established. He must have felt that he would betray his parents and possibly the Wilkes if he slacked off on the scholarship grind, but would betray himself if it stopped his general reading. So he probably worked and read twice as hard as a normal child. These two years were, also, the first two years of the Great War. The lack of any real reference to the War in his essay on St Cyprian's is surely conclusive that its 'meticulous descriptive quality' was a literary realism, not unvarnished autobiography. For school-life changed in many ways: drilling took up a lot of games-time; the boys visited army hospitals competing with old ladies to give Woodbine cigarettes and small comforts to wounded Tommies; and the lower forms were taught *en masse* to knit balaclava helmets, trench-comforters and (like Sister Susie of the song) socks for seamen. Shortage of food and coal must have made the winters specially hellish. Neither Connolly's nor Orwell's accounts allow for this. They can hardly not have noticed the reality of the War, for the slow litany of the names of dead former pupils began to be read in the chapel on Sunday nights; but they were probably repelled by the way all such occasions and incidents would have been, if things ran true to form, seized on almost with relish as yet more, indeed supreme and god-given, 'tests of character'. But within all this, it was 'business as usual' – the great Asquithian war slogan – as regards preparation for public-school scholarship examinations.

The Wilkes thought that Blair was possible material for the highest mutual prize of all, a scholarship to Eton. But knowing the competition was both plentiful and fierce, they hedged their bets by entering him for Wellington College, which was possibly marginally easier than their usual main target, Harrow. In February 1916 he sat the Wellington scholarship exam successfully. None the less, he went to Eton in the spring, accompanied by Mr Wilkes himself (so important these matters were – like a young athlete with his coach), to sit their two-and-a-half-day examination. A contemporary remembers that the death of Kitchener was actually announced during the middle of one of the examinations! The results were published in June.

Now Eton was a curious place. The scholarship boys, the King's Scholars, no more than seventy in number, constituted 'College', an intellectual élite living in some of the oldest buildings of the school. Each annual entry was 'an election' to College, usually ten to thirteen boys, depending on how many of the seventy left that year. Blair came 14th in the competitive examination, not high enough to ensure a place that autumn for the Election of 1916. But it was reasonable to think that there would be room after Christmas if he held on, particularly since boys were leaving early for the army as the blood-letting reached its intensity and the supply of 'suitable officer material' diminished rapidly. Wilkes was confident enough to proclaim a full day's holiday in his honour to celebrate the success (and thus to advertise it to other parents). Blair stayed on at St Cyprian's until December 1916, waiting for Eton. He must have been somewhat in favour at that time, for his poem on the death of Kitchener was published in July and found its way to Mrs Wilkes' scrap-book.

One wonders what he did that last term, whether they let him read much on his own, or if they carried on the hated cramming exercises out of habit or lack of alternative – like the offensives of Haig and Foch. This could have marked the beginning of that slackening-off in schoolwork, the resting on his oars, which was to become so apparent at Eton. For it was to Eton he eventually went; although as nothing came up at Christmas, he took up the Wellington offer which was still open, and spent nine weeks of the first term of 1917 there.

He did not like Wellington at all. He found the militaristic spirit of this famous army school abhorrent. He had looked forward to more privacy, but had to live in the Blücher dormitory whose cubicles had low sides and thin walls, noisy and insecure. He was placed only 13th out of 31 boys in his class after these weeks. All he later remembered with any pleasure was skating on the lake. So when a letter came from Eton, telling his father that there was now room for him to join the Election of 1916, he immediately accepted. And almost certainly the Eton scholarship was, from his father's point of view, a better one financially. So just before his fourteenth birthday in May 1917, Eric Blair joined Eton College.

Farewell to St Cyprian's, but not for ever, since he was to write about it. But let Cyril Connolly now have his last afterthought, writing in 1972 in a review of *The Unknown Orwell*, by Peter Stansky and William Abrahams:

When I read this account of Orwell's school days, drawn so largely from his and mine, I was at first enchanted as by anything which recalls one's youth but when I went to verify some references from my old reports and letters I was nearly sick ... In the case of St Cyprian's and the Wilkes whom I had so blithely mocked I feel an emotional disturbance. I received a letter of bitter reproach from Mrs Wilkes after *Enemies of Promise* which I have never dared to re-read and when, after the death of my own parents, their papers descended to me I found evidence of the immense trouble she had taken to help me win my scholarship to Eton despite the misgivings of my father which had to be overcome. The Wilkes were true friends and I had caricatured their mannerisms ... and read mercenary motives into much that was just enthusiasm.[22]

So affected was he, that he had actually attended her funeral in 1967, which was conducted by her son: 'Nobody spoke to me.' Indeed in 1968 he had written (reviewing *The Collected Essays, Journalism and Letters*):

I have reported ... a certain softening in my own attitude to St Cyprian's. This was due to getting possession of my school reports and Headmaster's letters to my father, and some of my own letters home. They revealed a considerable distortion between my picture of the proprietors and their own unremitting care to bring me on. At this point I hear Orwell's wheezy chuckle, 'Of course, they knew they were on to a good thing. What do you think our propaganda value to them was as winners of Eton scholarships – almost as good as being an "Hon"' ... and perhaps ... Mrs Wilkes ... used too much physical violence and emotional blackmail, and ... vented some personal bitterness on the boys. Yet she was warm-hearted and an inspired teacher. The worldliness

97

and snobbery of the Wilkes which Orwell so much condemns was characteristic of the competitive middle class of the period, not a singular aberration.

None the less, he concluded the review:

It has been suggested by Mr Gow [who taught them at Eton] that Orwell and I were rebels who would be bound to criticize any educational institutions; but this is to underrate the voodoo-like quality of St Cyprian's. Gavin Maxwell found it unchanged ten years later and I have heard of old boys who taught their children to shake their fists at the now deserted playing fields, as they drove past.[23]

What effect did all this have on Orwell's character which, Connolly had said, 'was already formed by the time he had arrived at Eton'?[24] He summed up Eric Blair's young life:

Something that does come out throughout ... that he enjoyed every moment of it, he liked fives and football at school, he liked walking and 'natural history', he liked reading, arguing and debunking, his eyes were made to glitter with amusement, his mouth for teasing, his schoolboy chubbiness persisted until his face grew cavernous from two pneumonias. And he was emotionally independent with the egotism of all natural writers; his friendships were constant but seldom close.[25]

Indeed by the time Eric Blair left St Cyprian's, 'George Orwell' is only discernible in him (with much hindsight) as someone already solitary and reserved. Possibly he was 'emotionally independent' even before he reached the school. Except in the essay, only very rarely would he admit that it had influenced and affected him (as some sad people talk about almost nothing else) in some small ways. Most of his childhood memories in talks to his friends were about books, ideas and interesting and odd external things. If at prep school he was not perhaps altogether without religion or religious feeling, yet he was already an instinctive rationalist and anti-romantic. He had become very tight and secretive too. These latter traits, which stayed with him all his life, may well have been an instant reaction to the hostile world of prep school compared to the easy informality and comfort of his mother's home. Yet as a small boy, virtually without a father, among women – and those women somewhat hostile about men – he may have already found the world regarding him as an odd man out and have learned to keep himself within himself even before going away to school.

The main point, however, is that taking holidays as well as school, freedom as well as constraint, no terrible harm seems to have been done, as he himself claimed; or if some harm there was, it was not as black as he painted it, and the world and he might have been the poorer without it.

CHAPTER FOUR

ETON: RESTING ON THE OARS

(1917-21)

IT is a truth universally acknowledged that going to Eton 'marks a man for life'. Etonians and non-Etonians at least agree on this. One suspects deliberate perversity in Orwell's own terse entry of 1942 for *Twentieth Century Authors*: 'I had been lucky enough to win a scholarship, but I did no work there and learned very little, and I don't feel that Eton has been much of a formative influence in my life.'[1] Much of the evidence, however, points Orwell's way. There are contrary opinions to relate and the evidence can be interpreted differently; even if Eton did not have a 'formative influence' there is more evidence about what he was like while at Eton than there is either for St Cyprian's or Burma. But to say a great deal about Eton is not necessarily to say much about Orwell.[2]

When Sonia Orwell once remarked to Anthony Powell that George was not a typical Etonian, Powell replied that, on the contrary, he was; that what she found missing in Orwell was Oxford and this was what made all the Etonians who went up to Oxford so different from Orwell. But what did Powell mean by 'a typical Etonian'? True answers may lie in negatives: a typical Etonian was not the accepted picture of the typical public-school man, ostentatiously conceited and conformist. Secure and unrivalled at the very top of the English social hierarchy, Eton permitted tolerance and eccentricity to thrive more than in other public schools. Orwell wrote no essay on Eton, only a few glancing references; but they are relatively favourable, even though they stress its snobbery and money-consciousness. In 1948 he reviewed a book on Eton for the *Observer*, typically not mentioning that it had been his own school:

Whatever may happen to the great public schools when our educational system is reorganized, it is almost impossible that Eton should survive in anything like its present form, because the training it offers was originally intended for a landowning aristocracy and had become an anachronism long before 1939 . . .

It also has one great virtue . . . and that is a tolerant and civilized atmosphere which gives each boy a fair chance of developing his own individuality. The reason is perhaps that, being a very rich school, it can afford a large staff, which means that the masters are not overworked . . .[3]

Several times he was to condemn the prep schools as being worse than the public schools.[4] That 'one great virtue' of tolerance was, however, more plausible in relation to College than to the School as a whole. An entry had been made in the 'College Annals' in 1902 by Ronald Knox (later the famous wit and Catholic priest) which was often quoted by Blair's contemporaries: 'College shows a healthy spirit of anti-nomianism – the surest proof of internal soundness.'

College was, indeed, a very different place from the rest of the School. Seventy scholars enjoyed endowments founded by Henry VI: the new State had needed new servants outside the old aristocracy. The rest of the School numbered some nine hundred boys called the Oppidans. The Collegers were all King's Scholars receiving tuition, board and lodging and recreational facilities for £25 a year each ('exorbitant', Blair told his friend, Denys King-Farlow) compared to the £100 paid by the Oppidans.[5] College was thus an intellectual élite thrust into the heart of a social élite. Institutional prestige attached to College; they lived in the oldest Tudor buildings of the Foundation under the Master in College, while the rest of the School lived in Houses of less antiquity, scattered around the town of Eton. Furthermore, the Captain of the School was always a Colleger. The Collegers tended to look down on the Oppidans as aristocratic Philistines and athletic hearties, and the Oppidans looked down on the 'Tugs' as being middle-class 'Saps' (Etonian for swots) living in villas in Tooting. In fact, within the Oppidans there was plutocracy as well as aristocracy and brains as well as brawn; and within College there would have been no one whose parents could not have afforded to have sent him to the kind of prep schools which prepared him in Latin and Greek for the scholarship examinations; and there would have been quite a few from the upper classes who had won scholarships. Not all the blood had run thin. The boys knew that they were stereotyping each other; but the stereotypes none the less were pursued with tribal relish. Oppidans and Collegers, however, were united by what even Christopher Hollis, MP, was to call 'a childish arrogance' towards the outside world – even if they made it less evident to others than did more insecure public schools.[6] The exclusions bred a feeling of equality and fraternity among themselves.

The basic social unit was the Election, not graded classes but all those who entered in the same year – it was somewhat the same form of social organization as a Zulu impi. They lived together, ate together, were mildly oppressed or positively persecuted by the Election above, did the same in turn to those below them, and, being few in numbers, knew each other well. Denys King-Farlow was in Blair's Election:

Blair ... had a large, rather fat face, with big jowls, a bit like a hamster. Best feature, I suppose, about him was he had slightly protruding, light china-blue eyes. I asked him how he'd liked Wellington, what he'd thought of switching over to Eton. He immediately said, 'Well, it can't be worse than Wellington. That really was perfectly bloody.' That struck me as not quite the right way to talk. His mother used to come down from time to time to school and afterwards he would run her down very much and also run down his rather sticky old father. He thought his mother was a frivolous person who wasn't interested in any of the sort of things that he thought people should be interested in and his father wasn't apparently interested in anything. He'd been the first person I personally had ever heard running down his own father and mother. Even more outrageous had been the jeering comments that he would cheerfully offer in public on the appearance and get-up of the parents of other boys when they visited the school.[7]

The antinomian spirit needed little encouragement in Eric Blair. Perhaps he was making it his character 'not to be easily impressed', as each strove to establish a character, as growing boys will, to show their mettle in a world of elders. He made plain that he was not impressed by Eton and most of his contemporaries were not much impressed by anything else about him. His criticism of his parents was real enough and unusual enough to excite comment; but if he implied that he was breaking from family loyalties, that was only his boyish pose. This facetious aggression did reflect some feelings of being socially marginal, something carried over from prep school, even if there were other boys in the College whose parents' sense of social status also ran a bit ahead of the cash flow available.

Something of his scepticism towards authority was shared by most of his Election. College always 'rather prided itself on a good crop of loners and odd ones', but right from its beginning the Election of 1916 had a revulsion against corporal punishment. 'No practical action could be taken but the strength of viewpoint was clear,' said another member of the same Election. 'A good deal of the punishments handed out by Sixth Form depended on people expecting them and accepting them, but we made clear from the beginning that we didn't like it and thought times were changing.'[8] Such liberal ideas were in the air even before the 1914 War, were crystallized by the hard conditions of war-time, and were precipitated into action immediately after the War.

As a latecomer, it must have taken more time for Blair to establish his 'character' in a characterful Election; but on the other hand, he could benefit by their collective experience, already veterans of two halves (at Eton, three halves make a year) of defensive warfare against their seniors; and he could count himself lucky to have missed two-thirds of the year when fagging, the doing of errands and other small tasks, was required for 'Sixth Form' (the top ten boys in College, in scholastic order, and effectively the house prefects). Each boy in his first year had a partitioned cubicle off a common hall, 'Chamber' (thereafter a room of his own), so some privacy was possible. There were initiation rites but these were mild: Blair had to do no more than stand on a table and sing – he sang 'Coming Down from Bangor', an old American student comic song; and he sang it not well but tolerably, enough to avoid being pelted with books, apples or whatever was to hand.[9] There was some bullying, but far less than at St Cyprian's and less in College than in some of the Oppidan houses. He was not an obvious target: his half-withdrawn, sardonic character or pose was recognized early and respected.

Sir Roger Mynors (later Professor of Latin at Cambridge and then Oxford) remembers him conveying from the start that he knew a lot already, did not care much to be taught, vaguely 'thought it all a racket' and was 'against authority the whole time', but without in any way being either especially or pathologically solitary or a leader of dissent. Such attitudes 'were not uncommon'. 'What was odd and interesting about Blair was his slightly aggressive attitude ... and the entertaining way he argued.' Mynors remembers that when they were first introduced to Plato's *Dialogues* – talk quite unlike anything else they had ever encountered, all the endless distinguishing, describing and arguing – he found that just like Blair: 'he would argue about anything all night.'[10] Another contemporary made the same Socratic comparison: 'He was a strong arguer, he put different sides of the case; there was his habit of worrying whether he had seen all sides of a case that distinguished him from many others then.'[11] Mynors suggests that Blair 'was prominent in bringing into College the solvent represented by Wells, Shaw and Samuel Butler, and before that, Gibbon and Sterne'. Sir Steven Runciman (later the historian of the Byzantine Empire) confirms that Blair right from his first year was the spokesman of this sceptical, rationalist tradition; and although most of them were to read Shaw, Wells and Butler for themselves, none that he knew appeared to have known about them before coming up to Eton. Bright boys educate themselves. The system was still religious, the new Head Master of Eton in 1916 (C. A. Alington) was in Orders, and social conventions as well as the rigid curriculum made it difficult for masters to introduce 'new' and critical ideas. Cyril Connolly was once rebuked by a master for reading *Tristram Shandy* because 'Sterne talks smut against his own mother'.

Memories recall much talk and its style and intensity, but who can remember precisely *what* was said sixty years ago or more, in Chamber at night, or while waiting to bat, or while lying in the hay by the then unpolluted Thames at 'Athens', a favoured spot, after swimming? Swimming was Blair's favourite 'activity', though never a competitive 'sport'. Yet two firm if random memories are interesting. King-Farlow remembers that 'he was an awful bore about money', or perhaps an embarrassing realist already; and Runciman remembers that right from the beginning (and he was probably closer to Blair than anyone during their first two years at Eton) he talked about wanting to go East one day. Perhaps his mother had fired his imagination about her youth in Mandalay. And two tales are revealing. Christopher Hollis has related one of them at length, but others think he gilded the lily (he was two Elections ahead of Blair, so really not close at all). In essence it is that Blair made an image in soap, not in wax as Hollis says, of an older boy to whom he took an irrational dislike; and that as the soap washed away, disasters struck the unfortunate elder.[12] A pretty odd thing to happen and a pretty odd thing to do, was the general feeling. The trap that Blair laid for Sixth Form was ingenious if obvious: should they punish him for insolence, they would be mocked for superstition. The other tale of his first year is that he killed a jackdaw, with a catapult. Jackdaws are not common birds, no humble sparrow they. Mynors was with him at the time and says, 'He was the only person I knew who might have done such a shocking thing.' They dissected it together and split the gall-bladder which splashed all over them: Mynors was never to forget the smell. So, unlike the case of the soap effigy, the hidden powers were to revenge themselves on the sceptic Blair, already especially sensitive to smells.

After that one term or 'half' at Eton, he gave the Buddicom children 'very favourable accounts', certainly compared with 'beastly Wellington', when he came home for the summer holidays in 1917.[13] Jacintha thought that he seemed interested and happy. 'Interested', certainly, but in the school as an activity, in the people he was meeting and the books, once again, that he could read for himself; not so much, if at all, in the official offerings of the Classics curriculum. His learned and distinguished contemporaries would agree with her girlhood memory: 'Once he was safely installed at Eton he had rather given up working: he said he deserved a rest after the intensive effort at St Cyprian's.'[14] That was his tutor's judgement and memory. A. S. F. Gow (1886–1978), later a Fellow of Trinity College, Cambridge, when an old man would strongly deny that he ever saw anything special in Orwell, indeed remembered him as 'always a bit of a slacker and a dodger'.

If school was now 'O.K.', 'tolerable', 'all right', holidays became golden. Removed from the necessity of cramming half the day, he filled them with reading and country activities. There is no longer any need to doubt Jacintha Buddicom's shocking dictum that 'Eric was a specially happy child' – at least in the holidays. The friendship with the Buddicom children continued to be close. Eric and Avril spent part of the Easter holidays and much of the summer with them at their aunt's house, Ticklerton Court, a small estate with half a dozen farms near Church Stretton in Shropshire, that most beautiful and varied of the shires. Close to the Welsh border, the Long Mynd (Welsh for mountain) above Church Stretton, is high, bare, ridge-broken moorland, with many sudden and steep descents into wooded valleys. Looking east, the whole of the Midlands, industrial Wolverhampton and Birmingham, are visible on clear days, and often by the red glow of furnaces at night. Shropshire has green valley after valley, farm after farm, villages, ancient churches, fortified houses and castles; and only fifteen miles from Church Stretton lie Ironbridge and Coalbrookdale, the ruined cradle of iron manufacture and the Industrial Revolution. This is speculation, of course, but it is possible that this peculiar physical mixture of moorland, pasture and industry, and this social mixture of 'county' England (almost nowhere is more famed for huntin', fishin' and shootin' than Shropshire) and industrial England, had some effect on Eric Blair's imagination and George Orwell's later concerns with the antithesis between industry as progress and welfare and the countryside as tranquillity and felicity. Shropshire was Housman country. By the time he was seventeen, Blair knew by heart most of the poems in *A Shropshire Lad*. His own literary name was to carry both a geographical association with unspoiled rural beauty and a verbal association with the very basis of industry.

The children remember Aunt Lilian Buddicom as 'very knowledgeable in both natural and ordinary history, archæology and botany, and the byways and bygones of Shropshire in general'. And if she did not know the answer to a question, she asked her friend, Miss Henrietta Auden (the poet's aunt, though no childhood meeting between Eric and Wystan is recorded). A letter from Aunt Lilian to Jacintha's mother in August 1917 tells of 'Ted', the house's or estate's general handyman, taking out Prosper and Eric for their first rabbit shoot: 'A single-barrelled gun, so there is not the risk of a boy firing off a *second* barrel while the other is running forward to pick up the game, and Ted keeps the cartridges in his pocket, only handing out one at a time.' A reassuring letter for a mother about part of a gentleman's education. She liked having all the children there, 'they seem such great friends', but also 'Eric has a bit of a cough. He says it is chronic. *Is this really the case?* I don't remember it before.'[15] And Eric and Prosper fished for perch.

They liked the journeys to and from Shropshire. The train stopped at Banbury where an attendant sold Banbury cakes on the platform. Eric could show a high-spirited facetiousness. Jacintha remembers him once asking Prosper very loudly 'whether his *spots* had come out?'

When this tactic had failed to get them a compartment to themselves, he swung from the luggage rack, scratching himself and declaring that he was an orang-outang; but the supernumerary lady passenger kept her nerve and threatened to 'call the guard if you don't get down at once, you naughty boy!'[16] Stock tales or gospel truth? The spots routine is in Jerome K. Jerome's *Three Men in a Boat* that many of us read in childhood, so perhaps reading the story gave Eric the idea. But whether Eric actually swung from the rack or not, the tale is in character. But there may have been another side to railway journeys for 'the upper middle classes without money':

Once when I was thirteen, I was in a train coming from a market town, and the third-class carriage was packed full of shepherds and pig-men who had been selling their beasts. Somebody produced a quart bottle of beer and passed it round; it travelled from mouth to mouth to mouth, everyone taking a swig. I cannot describe the horror I felt as that bottle worked its way towards me. If I drank from it after all those lower-class male mouths I felt certain I should vomit; on the other hand, if they offered it to me I dared not refuse for fear of offending them – you see here how the middle-class squeamishness works both ways.[17]

Shortly after Eric returned to Eton in September 1917, now with a room of his own, there were big changes on the Blairs' home front. They were on the move again, for Mr Blair had joined the Army and Mrs Blair took a clerical job in the Ministry of Pensions in London. She let the house at Henley and found rooms for herself and Marjorie in London at 23 Cromwell Crescent, Earls Court. At 60 years old, Richard Blair was thought by his family to be the oldest second lieutenant in the British Army. He was put in charge of the mules in a camp and depot near Marseilles. The Opium Service can have had little to do with mules: if his posting had any relevance to his experience, it would be that Marseilles was a staging-post for troop movements inward from India and outward to the Balkans, Mesopotamia and Palestine. None of Eric's contemporaries at Eton can remember him mentioning that he had a father in the Army. By now habitually reticent about his family, he may have found his father's posting ludicrous and his age embarrassing. When George Bowling in Orwell's novel *Coming Up For Air* (1939) became a second lieutenant, he was given eleven tins of bully beef to guard in a forgotten military dump on the north coast of remote Cornwall. Parents can embarrass their children while doing the very things they sometimes hope will most impress them.

Being at school in that 'Great War' must have been a peculiar experience. Orwell later made only the most glancing references to it, even amid the very few references he makes to his period at Eton. Boys of course do take things in their stride and have no experience with which to compare the normal and the abnormal. Runciman remembers learning that boys whom he had known by sight, who had left school promptly at 18, had been killed. 'There was an unreality which made us all, I think, unwilling to look ahead.' There was the growing roll call in Chapel of the dead: of the 5,687 Etonians who served in the War, 1,160 were killed and 1,467 wounded, an extraordinarily high proportion of dead both in relation to the wounded and to the total number who served: such officers went in at the head of their men. On the other hand, school life continued much as before. Food was awful and monotonous, but never totally inadequate; old masters stayed or came back as young ones left for Flanders; but cricket and football, Classics and Confirmation instruction, rivalry and friendship, went on much as before, dominated far more by school tradition and the nature of boys than by 'the great events outside'.

At the beginning of the Second World War, Orwell reminisced:

... If you were alive during that war, and if you disentangle your real memories from their later accretions, you find that it was not usually the big events that stirred you at the time. I don't believe that the Battle of the Marne, for instance, had for the general public the melodramatic quality that it was afterwards given ...

Of the middle years of the war, I remember chiefly the square shoulders, bulging calves and jingling spurs of the artillerymen, whose uniform I much preferred to that of the infantry. As for the final period, if you ask me to say truthfully what is my chief memory, I must answer simply – margarine. It is an instance of the horrible selfishness of children that by 1917 the war had almost ceased to affect us, except through our stomachs.[18]

He said that they simply did not realize at the time that the little red flags that they moved backwards and forwards on the large map in a school-room represented great pyramids of corpses.

The War did demand, however, that more school time be given to the Officers' Training Corps. While OTC was in practice compulsory, Orwell remembered it thus: 'Among the very young the pacifist reaction had set in long before the war ended. To be as slack as you dared on OTC parades, and to take no interest in the war, was considered a mark of enlightenment.'[19] But this essay of 1939 was a polemic against pacifism, reflecting his own recent change of mind. And he may be confusing the wartime period with post-war reaction. At the time he would hardly have seen the 'reaction' as pacifist, but simply as teasing those in authority, nor seen lack of interest in the war as 'a mark of enlightenment'; rather that it did not impinge that much on the immediate and egocentric world of boyhood in boarding-school. His contemporaries do not remember any pacifism. Christopher Eastwood mainly recalled 'Eric as a most unwilling member of the OTC', as he was himself. So 'I followed his example in getting in the Signal Section, which was the refuge of the lazy and the inefficient. It had the particular advantage that as there was a certain amount of equipment one didn't have to march on field days.' Later he said that Blair 'didn't stand out as a strong dissenter, except in not doing things: there were a lot of strong dissenters, but Blair's way was to put the puttees on crooked, not to polish the brass, to look sardonic rather than to act.'[20] Others, however, give Blair a more positive although certainly sardonic liking for the OTC. One says, 'nature made him poor material for the OTC and he was delighted to exploit it – the anarchist in him came out.' Another remembers him liking the OTC for the camping, excursions, field-craft, map-reading and rifle-firing, and thought that Blair shared the same view as himself: a dislike of the attitudes implicit in OTC, but a liking for the activities. King-Farlow recalls that while Blair enjoyed 'playing the lone wolf', he discovered with surprise that he was 'an admirable stablemate under dripping canvas' and commended 'the excellence of his military mucking-in'. The anarchic discipline of the Corps appealed to him. As he rose in the school he entered and then took charge of the Signals Section, which allowed for initiative and thus constant uncertainty about where they were, or ought to be. Once, when Blair decided it was too hot to be in uniform, he led his section behind a distant hay-stack and in shirtsleeves read them *Eric, or Little by Little*, whose ethic he detested so cordially, read it with mock seriousness for the whole of a long and undisturbed summer afternoon.[21]

He also preferred the disciplined anarchy of the river to the competitiveness of the cricket field, so he became, in Eton parlance, a 'wet-bob' rather than a 'dry-bob'. He was strong but not skilled, both in rowing and swimming. As he began to grow tall (at 16 he was five feet eight, and by 18 was six feet one), some of his fellows thought that he had to resort to deliberate incompetence to avoid the risk of being drafted into any of the school crews. His idea of being a wet-bob was to lie in the sweet hay at Athens, watch the river flow on, 'reading, conversing about Life, trying to memorize Theocritus or Gibbon'. Five or six of his Election shared these tastes: '... also our self-appointed jester, Cyril Connolly, whom we had, disregarding a strict College custom, taken up from our junior election year. Blair, knowing Connolly from preparatory school ... warned we could expect to hear plenty about a "Connolly's (probably no family connection) marrying in 1758 the second Duke of Richmond's third daughter". We did.'[22]

He was actually photographed at Athens in school clothes aggressively smoking a cigarette: that was offering a reckless hazard to fortune. And he caught pike from the Jordan (a small tributary) and cooked them himself – 'quite legal but somehow challenging and far from the done thing'.

Odd scraps of conversation have lingered in a contemporary's memory. 'You know, Wansbrough, my uncle says that a good way to score off someone is to nail a dead fish underneath a table; very difficult to find.' 'You know, Wansbrough, my uncle says that there's need to develop a circular piece of paper for lavatory seats in order to avoid the risk of the accidental contraction of VD.' If Uncle Charles' proposal was at least a generation ahead of its American conception, the unreal problem it was trying to solve was already part of the lore of adolescent boys. Perhaps this myth was necessary as an alternative explanation to the family if VD was caught – at a time when desire for a first experience was unhealthily balanced by belief in almost certain infection: another piece of false physiology frequently inserted into depressive sermons at boarding-schools.

The shadowy Uncle Charles Limouzin seems to have played the part of 'man of the world' for his nephew. By then, separated from his wife, he was secretary of a golf club near Bournemouth, and Eric and Avril would sometimes spend a few days of their holidays with him. The Christmas holidays of 1917 found them with nowhere to go. Sub-tenants at the Henley house had not vacated in time for the holidays, as they had promised, and the flat at Earls Court was too small. Mrs

Blair wrote to Mrs Buddicom asking her to have Eric and Avril with her for Christmas, 'most dreadfully cool of me asking you this, but these are such extraordinary times that one is forced to do out-of-the-way things'. A pound a week each was settled upon, and the same thing happened the following Christmas.

The school year continued. Days were full and hard. There was 'Early School' at half-past seven, a class before breakfast, then three hours of lessons and an hour with, or doing work set by, their tutor. Three afternoons a week began with organized games followed by two more hours of classes or preparations; and three afternoons were called half-holidays, in fact devoted to sport but this was not compulsory if the boy was not in a team or if he adopted some approved alternative activity. As regards lessons, the official offerings interested Eric far less than his outside readings. In his first year he was a Classical Specialist, as were most of College; this meant, typically, seven lessons a week of Latin, six of Greek, three of French, three of Mathematics, three of Science, two of English and one of Divinity. He came low in all the class lists. In the Summer Half of 1918, he moved up a form, but changed from Classical Specialist, the class of the potential Oxford and Cambridge scholarship winners, to the less demanding Classical General. Collegers moved up a form each year, never, like some Oppidans, repeating a year, but they were taught in divisions graded by ability subject by subject, together with the rest of the school. So he soon found himself mainly among Oppidans during the teaching hours, being outpaced by the rest of his Election, save one. The classes were small, so even the laziest boys were worked hard and there were preparations to do every evening; but, to judge by results, Eric must have practised a sullen or sardonic passive resistance to enforced learning – albeit with tantalizing and short-lived fits and starts of interest and performance. None of his termly reports survive. One imagines that there must have been a lot of heartfelt, not banal or stock, 'Could do better if he tried' comments. His cynicism towards the official offerings must have been obvious, for when Connolly got bad reports speaking of his laziness and cynicism, his parents were inclined to blame it on Blair's influence. This must have been a hangover from prep school, for 'now I hardly saw him' and 'Orwell was rather aloof', and they soon moved in quite different circles in Eton as Connolly skilfully climbed the social heights.[23]

Somehow time was found for literary activity. Jacintha Buddicom insists that at this time he always had a 'quiet but absolute determination on his own ultimate career. It was always "When I am a *Famous Author*"' and they discussed the best bindings for a collected edition.[24] There is no reason to doubt that such holiday-fantasizing took place, but who can be sure whose fantasies they were and whether or not some irony in him, even then, escaped her? But he would not have talked like that to friends at Eton, and certainly the *Election Times* (Mynors as editor, King-Farlow as art editor, and Blair as business manager) gave no evidence of genius. It was a handwritten set of pages to be lent for reading at a cost of one penny; or copies could be furnished for sixpence (there were no takers, mercifully, for that part of the service).[25] Only one issue of this erratic occasional publication survives, that of Monday 3 June 1918, with three contributions almost certainly by Eric Blair: a comic poem, 'The Wounded Cricketer', which tells of a wet-bob forced to play cricket, struck on the head by the ball, then resting contentedly in the grass; a comic, sentimental, indeed slightly sententious story, 'The Slack-Bob', about a boy who pretends to be in the Rowing Eight to impress some sisters and, when they invite themselves down on Open Day, has to pretend to be injured – it ends, 'Moral: honesty is the best policy'; and a laboured parody of Sherlock Holmes, with Lestrade as the villain, 'The Adventure of the Lost Meat Card'. These stories are no worse, but certainly no better, than one might expect from any educated boy of not quite 16 – clever, quite well-written, but no touch of character or distinctive style, indeed slightly out of character, nothing in the least agin-authority, sardonic or Swiftian, rather as if the ugly fairy 'Literature' had grasped the adolescent rebel's hand when he reached for a pen. And perhaps not yet so much of a rebel, anyway: all that is clear from these literary remains is that their author indulged in a mild mockery – almost 'affectionate mockery' – of the system, and, from what his contemporaries remember, that he was a willing and paid-up member of the Awkward Squad rather than an apprentice to the Revolution.

Just before Blair went back to school in September 1918, Jacintha Buddicom remembers a long conversation they had while picking mushrooms in the woods near Henley. She had recently been sent as a boarder to Oxford High School, but entered very late and imperfectly prepared. None the less, she was full of enthusiasm for Oxford University and claims, 'I had fired him with my own enthusiasm.' He admitted that he had 'rather given up working' and felt he 'deserved a rest' after the intensive effort at St Cyprian's, 'but that he was more than willing to reapply himself to his studies given an incentive, and intended to start a campaign for parental permission'.[26] How marvellous it would be to be at the University at the same time, for she would need at least an extra year at school to catch up on Latin and Greek of which, alas, she had nothing. Again, there is no reason to doubt the accuracy of this account. A florid style does not infallibly mean a pretending heart, nor does a plain style always certificate the literal accuracy of an honest soul. But a different construction could be put on her account: that she had fallen in love with Oxford as a place, was very serious and yet totally unrealistic about university entrance, while he was affably joining in her game. He might occasionally have shown a little resolve to do something about it himself, but not much – which would account for the observed disparity between his potential and his performance. Yet it seems unlikely that he 'intended to start a campaign for parental permission'. That sounds like the author Miss Buddicom preparing the ground for her passionately held view that in 1920–21 only old Mr Blair prevented Eric from going to university. In fact, he prevented it himself, if he ever really intended to try to get there rather than just talking of Oxford as part of an adolescent game of make-believe.

Not that Jacintha was 'all dreams'. In some ways she must have been a tough-minded girl. For instance, she took over her father's religion, or rather turned his agnosticism into pantheism, telling a shocked and incredulous house mistress that she was willing to worship the Christian god for a week or two, so long as they could also pay honour to some others. This explains the title of a poem that Eric sent her at Oxford from Eton that autumn.

THE PAGAN

So here are you, and here am I,
Where we may think our gods to be;
Above the earth, beneath the sky,
Naked souls alive and free.
The autumn wind goes rustling by

And stirs the stubble at our feet;
Out of the west it whispering blows,
Stops to caress and onward goes,
Bringing its earthy odours sweet.
See with what pride the setting sun
Kinglike in gold and purple dies,
And like a robe of rainbow spun
Tinges the earth with shades divine.
That mystic light is in your eyes
And ever in your heart will shine.

She replied to this literary tribute with a calm and prudently technical discussion of the rhyming scheme, together with a few suggested amendments.

When I wrote back I suggested it should have been *unarmoured souls*, not *naked* souls – it was our minds, our hopes, our dreams, that were confided so freely and so guilelessly: we were not cavorting around in the altogether. And I would have preferred *veil* to *robe* which is too man-made for a natural phenomenon. He agreed with those amendments, and later wrote them into my copy – with the original two words crossed out. He said that would make it 'more authentic' than re-writing the whole poem; more like 'more trouble-saving'.[27]

Remember that she was two years older than he, and that there were four children in the relationship. However important literature was to her, and as a bond between them, who is to weigh and on what scales its relative importance compared to the rabbit-shooting, fishing and pyrotechnics with her brother Prosper? In 1918 both a romantic and a common-sense boy alternately appeared: it would be many years before these aspects of him fused creatively.

Yet on return to school in his third year at Eton, he did try to change direction, even if the results were no better. For a year he tried Science, mainly Biology. The grounds can only have been negative, since he was in the lowest possible set for Mathematics, but perhaps he felt it was a chance to make a fresh start. This meant a change of tutor, from Andrew Gow to John Christie (then school-mastering to prove that he could work before entering into his inheritance, Glynde-bourne, which he transformed into the opera house). As he did no better, Blair changed back the following year.

By this third year his character in his Election was fully established.

He appears as 'Cynicus' in a contemporary's literary diary in 1918-19, though only as one of the 'Stoa', the lookers-on: he does not figure in the pretentious dialogues at all.[28] It would be during this time that he interviewed each member of the new Election (earlier he would not have been senior enough, later he would have compromised his dignity). As Christopher Hollis related:

Mr Noel Blakiston, who was a few years Orwell's junior in College, has told me of his first meeting with him ... in a cricket match. Orwell came up to him with a paper and pencil in his hand. 'I'm collecting the religions of the new boys' said Orwell. 'Are you Cyrenaic, Sceptic, Epicurean, Cynic, Neoplatonist, Confucian or Zoroastrian?'
'I'm a Christian,' said Blakiston.
'Oh,' said Orwell, 'we haven't had that before.'[29]

This was the year in which he was prepared for confirmation in 'the Church by law established'. He was confirmed. It was almost as conventionally compulsory as OTC (only a clear *religious* antipathy from a parent could get them out of it), though it is fair to say that religious belief with most adolescents then was as deep as patriotism; and they were as capable of distinguishing between religion and the ludicrous aspects of the Church, especially compulsory chapel, as they were between patriotism and military stupidity. Despite his youthful cynicism and lifelong anti-Catholicism, throughout his life he was to like traditional hymns and the language of the Anglican rituals: certainly he set his last friends a problem they had not anticipated by asking in his Will to be *buried* according to the rites of the Church of England and not to be cremated.

His mother went up to see him confirmed, one Saturday at the end of November 1918, by the Rt Revd Charles Gore, then Bishop of Oxford.[30] Normally boys were prepared by their tutors, but as neither Gow nor Christie was in holy orders (nor especially holy), Eric was prepared by John Crace, the Master in College.

The 'Master in College' at that time had neither the status nor the authority of the house masters. To have a master living in College at all was a comparatively recent innovation (Collegers had traditionally been very much a law to themselves) and Crace was a somewhat ineffectual representative. The tutors often ignored Crace, and Sixth Form thought they needed no help from him to look after discipline.

Certainly Blair's respect for Crace and even for Gow could have been greater. King-Farlow remembers Blair disparaging 'Granny Gow's' love of Homer as sentimentality and his erudition in Italian painting (he later became a trustee of the National Gallery) as 'escapist posing'; he also remembers Blair making up a ribald song which referred to some of 'm'tutor's' physical characteristics, noticeably tufts on his cheek in the naval manner and a 'characteristically cautious' way of sitting down.

> Then up waddled Wog and he squeaked in Greek:
> 'I've grown another hair on my cheek.'
> Crace replied in Latin with his toadlike smile:
> 'And I hope you've grown a lovely new pile.
> With a loud deep fart from the bottom of my heart!
> How d'you like Venetian art?'[31]

Which at least is better as verse than 'The Pagan' is as poetry.

He had it in for Crace. Andrew Gow said that Blair 'made himself as big a nuisance as he could' and 'was a very unattractive boy':

There is one thing I remember vividly. Blair left about in his burry [desk] an empty cigarette carton. Crace, the Master in College, saw it. Crace was a man of high principles. He refused to pick it up himself. He sent for Blair to pick it up, and found it was a dummy. Angry, Crace complained and sent him to me. I said there was no rule against having empty cigarette cartons; but sent for Blair none the less and ticked him off as being a bloody nuisance.[32]

Nearly sixty years later, Gow still showed some pleasure at Crace having met his match in officiousness. Hollis tells the tale of Crace saying to Blair, 'Things can't go on like this. Either you or I will have to go.' 'I'm afraid it will have to be you, Sir,' answered the boy. King-Farlow doubts very much if this is true. Others had heard the tale, but it is, again, a stock tale both in schools and in the armed forces. Such things got attributed to Blair. But King-Farlow attests to the truth of a far more dangerous and slightly unsavoury attack on Crace somewhat later. John (or 'Jan') Crace had a tendency to be overfond of some boys. So King-Farlow and Blair smuggled into the Personal Column of another school magazine, *College Days*, on 1 April 1920, the advertisement 'A.R.D. – After rooms – Janney'. 'A.R.D.' was plainly recognizable as the boy in favour at that moment.[33] Again, though Crace was furious, it was a baited hook, for to punish the slanderer would be to broadcast the accusation.

One oddity of the schoolroom, Runciman remembers, was that he and Blair were taught French by Aldous Huxley. He filled in for a year (as the first chapter of *Antic Hay* witnesses) for one of the twenty masters away on active service. 'He taught us rare and strange words in a rather reflective way. Orwell and I enjoyed him, although he was an incompetent, a hopeless teacher. He couldn't keep discipline and was so blind that he couldn't see what was happening, so was hopelessly ragged. Blair didn't like that, he found it cruel. Perhaps that's going a bit far. Blair, though he always had wit and irony, was lacking in lightness of humour, anything that savoured of frivolity.' Yet they learned something from Huxley:

At first we thought his voice affected, but soon some of us were trying to copy it. Above all it was his use of words that entranced us. Eric Blair ... would in particular make us note Aldous's phraseology. 'That is a word we must remember,' we used to say to each other ... The taste for words and their accurate and significant use remained. We owe him a great debt for it.[34]

In the autumn of 1918, as Blair shot up in height, he was pressed into the extraordinarily complex Eton games of Foot-Ball, weird enough when played 'in the Field', incredible as well as violent 'at the Wall' – a brick wall 120 yards long with a playing-area alongside it only 7 yards wide, which made goal-scoring difficult ('shies' could and would be scored commonly). The manuscript book 'The Annals of Lower College Foot-Ball', Volume 13, first mentions him on 28 September 1918: 'Soon after, owing to a gross mistake by our goal [Blair], the ball was kicked just behind our calx line ... Blair was conspicuously bad.' 2 October, 'Blair did not kick it out with any success.' 5 October, 'Blair was very slack.' 15 October, 'Blair was not at all energetic.' 26 October, 'Blair was good in the first half, bad, very bad in the second' ... 'Blair did poorly behind' ... 'Blair must play harder' ... 'Johnstone* and Blair were very bad.' Then he vanishes from the records for a month, a bare note that he played on 6 December; and the rest is silence. He had made his point, it seems, for that year at least.

---

* That Johnstone, Kenneth Johnstone, who remarked in 1976, 'Who on earth would have thought that Blair would have turned into Orwell? Wouldn't have picked him out as someone likely to set the world on fire.'

Christmas was again spent with the Buddicoms at Quarry House, Henley. Ida Blair in the spring of 1918 had moved into a small flat at 23 Mall Chambers, Notting Hill Gate, in London, visiting Avril on Saturdays at her boarding-school in Ealing and occasionally having Marjorie for weekend leaves. Marjorie had become a dispatch rider (motorbikes) for the Women's Legion, stationed at Warminster at an Australian Army headquarters. Mrs Blair wrote to Mrs Buddicom affectionately of 'her chicks' but seems to have done little to find them a nest all together for Christmas and, still more surprisingly, neglected even to visit them. She declined Mrs Buddicom's invitation to visit on Boxing Day, 'we are to go to my sister's for that day', and on 21 December she sent Christmas presents by post and hoped to see Eric one Saturday before the end of the holidays. Yet on 10 January she wrote: 'I won't be able to see the children this week after all . . . my husband is coming home today, and as the flat is so tiny we could not possibly all squeeze in, so will you keep the children to the end of the holidays?'[35] There is something very odd here. Since Henley was only an hour by train from London, why did she not even visit them one weekend afternoon, or would it not have been possible in the circumstances for the Buddicoms or neighbours to have put her up too? She had got back from London quickly enough years before when Baby Eric was ill.

Eric and Avril must have felt neglected. It is almost as if she did not wish to see them. Eric had told King-Farlow that his mother was a 'frivolous person', meaning 'not serious'. But was that all he meant? One can only speculate. Could she have had a secret friend in Notting Hill? Or was she just being convivially selfish and enjoying the company of her lively sister's circle more than her own children in the few precious days' leave at Christmas from the Ministry of Pensions? Certainly she seemed to age rapidly after her husband's return at the end of the War and their move to a coastal retirement town, as if she too was retiring. Avril would never admit that there was any oddity about this Christmas spent apart. But she was only twelve then and was loyal to her mother later, remaining at home all the long, and for her rather empty, 1920s and 1930s. In those years she blamed her brother for wasting his chances and not repairing the family fortune; and she never blamed her mother for anything, even when after his death she read his books, grew to understand them, grew far more appreciative of him, and could talk about the family with a degree of dispassion. Marjorie appears to have married her childhood friend, Humphrey Dakin, as quickly as she could and left home with no ambitions to do other than that, though the break from home was a natural one and visits took place. Humphrey Dakin's father was attracted to Mrs Blair, but she seems to have kept him at a distance, or so his grandchildren believe.

That Christmas, Eric was stirred to romantic passions once again. He gave Jacintha a special poem with some pomp and circumstance at the first opportunity of 'adequate privacy'.

> Our minds are married, but we are too young
> For wedlock by the customs of this age
> When parent homes pen each in separate cage
> And only supper-earning songs are sung.
>
> Times past, when medieval woods were green,
> Babes were betrothed, and that betrothal brief
> Remember Romeo in love and grief –
> Those star-crossed lovers – Juliet was fourteen.
>
> Times past, the caveman by his new-found fire
> Rested beside his mate in woodsmoke's scent,
> By our own fireside we shall rest content
> Fifty years hence keep troth with heart's desire.
>
> We shall remember, when our hair is white,
> These clouded days revealed in radiant light.

That seems to have been going too far, or were they still only playing their old game of poems for all occasions? She tells her readers firmly:

But that was Eric's idea, which was unfortunately and regrettably never mine. He was a perfect companion and I was very fond of him – as literary guide-philosopher-and-friend. But I had no romantic emotion for him. The two years between a girl of seventeen and a boy of fifteen, as a beginning, are just the wrong two years. At fifteen, he was certainly too young to be married: but at seventeen I *might* have been marriageable to someone older.[36]

'Eric's idea' seems, reading the poem closely, real enough, especially since far from 'parent homes' penning 'each in separate cage', his mother's scatty or flighty arrangements for the holidays penned them in the same gilded cage. And did he see himself as having, even there, just as at St Cyprian's and Eton, 'to sing for his supper' – or is that fourth line only a desperate search for a *suitable* rhyme for 'young'?

Either at Easter or Christmas 1918, Eric saw Shaw's *Arms and the Man:*

... the theatre was full of soldiers fresh from the front in France. They saw the point of it, because their experiences had taught them the same thing. There is a passage early in the play where Bluntschli is telling Raina what a cavalry charge is really like. 'It is,' he says, 'like slinging a handful of peas against a window pane: first one comes; then two or three close behind him; and then all the rest in a lump.' Raina, thinking of Sergius, her lover, charging at the head of his regiment, clasps her hands ecstatically and says: 'Yes, first comes One! The bravest of the brave!'

'Ah,' says Bluntschli, 'but you should see the poor devil pulling at his horse!' At this line the audience of simple soldiers burst into a laugh which almost lifted the roof off.[37]

And he added (broadcasting in 1943) that he saw it acted a second time in 1935, at an experimental theatre before a highbrow audience who did not laugh at all at Bluntschli's line: 'War was far away and very few people in the audience knew what it was like to have to face bullets' (as he himself was soon to learn in Spain). Shaw was one of his mentors, but Blair's scepticism came to see a shallowness in Shaw and allowed no demi-gods in a humanist cosmology.

His copy of *Plays, Pleasant and Unpleasant* (1906) survives and the margin is peppered with sarcasms, not from any clear political position, but cynically to prick bubbles in the great man's rhetoric.[38] Said Shaw, '... modern Italy had, as far as I could see, no more connection with Giotto than Port Said had with Ptolemy.' '*True*' said Eric. 'I am no believer in the worth of any "taste" for art that cannot produce what it professes to appreciate' – '*nonsense*' said Eric. When Pshaw sees Ibsen leading 'the unsatisfied younger generations' towards 'unspeakably giddy' heights, Cynicus primly demands, '*Higher than Shakespeare, Homer, Dante, Plato?*' And when the old performer says: 'Bad theatres are as mischievous as bad schools or bad churches: for modern civilization is rapidly multiplying the class to which the theatre is both school and church,' Blair coldly inquires '*Do you approve of this?*' When the revolutionary argues for theatre subsidy, that 'commercial limits should be over-stepped' to keep 'the public in constant touch with the highest achievements of dramatic art,' Eric, with a whiff of Tory scepticism, adds, '*and the drains and the universities and the hospitals and the golf links.*' 'I see plenty of good in the world working itself out as fast as the idealists will allow it' elicits a scathing *'Indeed?';* '... we should all get along much better and faster' attracts *'Where to?';* and the peroration that we should move from imagination and passion to 'a genuinely scientific natural history' is sunk by that short *'Ah!'* which plainly connotes the sarcastic discovery of folly revealed. Nothing shows more clearly how much Blair was agin authority than this mocking of the mocker, irreverence to the great Irreverent Shaw, but from a standpoint not as close to socialism as he later suggested, however familiar he was with socialist ideas, however many of their arrows he borrowed to fire off against 'authority'. Yet he was no mere sceptic: a sense of justice and of individual rights – perhaps of 'individualistic' rights would be better – comes across from memoria of him at school. He was 'more of a republican than a liberal,' Sir Steven Runciman recalled. At least the Classics teachers had had that effect: they went into the Augustan era for its literature but their moral values were all those of the Republic.

Orwell vividly remembered the 'so-called peace celebration in 1919':

Our elders had decided for us that we should celebrate peace in the traditional manner by whooping over the fallen foe. We were to march into the school-yard, carrying torches, and singing jingo songs of the type of 'Rule, Britannia'. The boys – to their honour, I think – guyed the whole proceeding and sang blasphemous and seditious words to the tunes provided.

Others confirm this account, indeed go further and speak of it as a riot to demand the resignation of the officer in charge of the OTC that spread into the streets of the town. Some bitterness against 'the authorities' was involved, but mainly it was a facetious rag, hardly an example of 'the queer revolutionary feeling of that time', as Orwell makes it, looking back from 1937.[39]

That Easter, 1919, Aunt Lilian Buddicom wrote to her sister: 'I had better not ask Eric ...' Servant problems. 'I am afraid even if we have a house parlour-maid *three* young people would be too much for Mrs Butler', the good cook they were desperately trying to keep.[40] And that summer the Blairs went down to Polperro again and only Prosper Buddicom came with them. Perhaps there was a deliberate cooling-off period between the amorous Eric and the apprehensive Jacintha. Richard Blair was demobilized, they got the tenants out and opened up the house at Henley again, although for a while they kept on the flat in Notting Hill for Aunt Nellie Limouzin and Marjorie to use.

September 1919 saw the beginning of his fourth year at Eton. Science had proved no more interesting to him than Classics, so he retreated back into the so-called General Division, taking Ancient History, French (his best subject), Geography, Latin, Divinity and Shakespeare – a general education for the non-university streams. At the end of the school year he lay 117th down on the form list of 140 boys. Only one of his Election in College did worse.

Gow became his tutor again. There comes a small but curious conflict of testimony. King-Farlow in his written reminiscence says: 'Gow recognized in the stubborn, wilfully unattractive embryo-Orwell qualities for which most other masters had no time, finding him indolent and often "dumb insolent". He set out to encourage and make Blair compose, not the weekly essays exacted by most tutors, but fables, short stories, accounts of things liked and detested.'[41] Stansky and Abrahams, following King-Farlow, have Gow perceiving 'under the shyness and surliness ... an authentic intelligence' ('*I didn't*', says Gow); Blair as being 'privately ... fond of Gow' ('*I doubt very much*'); and moreover keeping in touch with him 'over the years' ('*Not true*'). Also they have it that 'It was the custom for four or five boys in the Election to gather in Gow's room on Sunday evenings, bringing with them to read aloud essays, poems or stories of their own' ('*Untrue. Rubbish. I cannot imagine how they got this*'). 'In fact I saw them for Sunday private [group tutorials],' said Gow, 'and in the mornings too – didn't read essays but a book together. I remember doing the whole of *Paradise Lost* with 'em and even miraculously getting into *Paradise Regained*.' In 1976 he still seemed angry with Orwell for 'wasting time' and 'slacking', but above all for having written and sought publication for 'Such, Such Were the Joys'. All the same, two years after Gow went to Trinity, Orwell visited him in 1927 on his return from Burma; but only that once. And Gow was to visit Orwell once also, on his deathbed at University College Hospital in 1950 – though Gow claims that this was accidental: 'I was visiting a pupil of mine and heard that Orwell was there, and I occasionally believe in being charitable.'[42] Perhaps more than occasionally, for when he became a Fellow of

Trinity he soon established an undergraduate literary circle, somewhat in the manner of Lowes Dickinson.[43] Perhaps he did once have some hopes for Blair, but if so he kept them very well concealed: the old sceptic, crippled in everything but mind and memory, still felt and showed bitterness that Eric Blair had wasted his own chances and Gow's time and had 'written thus venomously' about St Cyprian's.

Yet whether Andrew Gow had once basked in a literary circle of admiring youths (as he was to do when he went to Cambridge) or simply gave a stern tutorial, the reading of *Paradise Lost* had impressed and influenced his rotten apple. In 'Why I Write', Orwell recounted:

When I was about sixteen I suddenly discovered the joy of mere words, i.e. the sounds and associations of words. The lines from *Paradise Lost*,

So hee with difficulty and labour hard
Moved on: with difficulty and labour hee.

which do not now seem to me so very wonderful, sent shivers down my backbone; and the spelling 'hee' was an added pleasure.[44]

When Eve considers whether or not to tell Adam of her new knowledge, she thinks that withholding it will 'render me more equal, and perhaps/ A thing not undesirable, sometime Superior' (IX 823–5). Orwell was to put this thought more pithily in *Animal Farm*, 'All animals are equal but some are more equal than others', so something must have stuck in his mind from the Sunday morning periods with Gow.[45]

Another favourite book of this time, to judge by his marginal annotations, is also somewhat Miltonic, Shelley's *Prometheus Unbound*.

On a battle-trumpet's blast
I fled hither, fast, fast, fast,
'Mid the darkness upward cast.
From the dust of creeds outworn,
From the tyrant's banner torn,
Gathering 'round me, onward borne ...

has in the margin '*Courage, even in defeat*'.

... I alit
On a great ship lightning-split,
And speeded hither on the sigh
Of one who gave an enemy
His plank, then plunged aside to die.

'*Self-sacrifice only possible through suffering*' annotates Eric, relishing the lost fight and integrity amid the losing side. His marginalia on Shelley are in the same hand and of the same period as his comments on Shaw, but rather different attitudes are shown, assumed or tried: romantic not cynical.

Suffering was resumed both in the Field and at the Wall, but not excessive self-sacrifice. 'The Annals of Foot-Ball' for that Michaelmas Half had 'Blair did nothing much but cool, which is rather a general fault ... Blair only sneaked and cornered ... Blair was better at long than he has hitherto been elsewhere ... Blair did not help his other walls enough ...' ('To sneak' was merely to be offside.)

In the Christmas holidays the Blairs were all together again back in St Mark's Road, Henley-on-Thames, his father resuming his part-time job as secretary of the local golf club. Several times Eric bicycled over to tea at the Buddicoms at Shiplake and Jacintha visited the Blairs more frequently, she remembers, than the year before. Two teenagers talking about literature together, even if they looked a bit sweet on each other, were less nuisance to Mr Blair than when five younger children had played noisy games. Eric gave her *Dracula* as a Christmas present, together with a crucifix ('he knew I would not be likely to have one') and a clove of garlic, both of which vampires dislike. And in the Easter vacation both families were again near each other. A diary of Prosper's (then at Harrow) for 1920 shows that out of twenty-six days of the holiday, Eric was with them for twenty-one. But the actual entries are all about shooting expeditions, which were not Jacintha's cup of tea, except for some games of roulette, two visits to the cinema in Reading, and a successful bomb-making. One would hardly expect his diary to record his sister's talks with Eric on literature, but it at least shows that he and Eric had an independent time-consuming friendship based on quite other grounds.[46]

Years later, Orwell in *Tribune* recalled having seen (it must have been one of those Christmas vacations) both Marie Lloyd and Little Titch, legendary figures of the music-hall. He tried to outboast Mr Harold Nicolson who had recalled in the *Spectator* having seen the Czar.

One day I was walking past Windsor Castle [near Eton] when a sort of electric shock seemed to go through the street. People were taking their hats off, soldiers springing to attention. And then, clattering over the cobbles, there

came a huge, plum-coloured open carriage drawn by four horses with pos-
tilions. I believe it was the first and last time in my life that I have seen a
postilion. On the rear seat, with his back to the carriage, another groom sat
stiffly upright, with his arms folded. The groom who sat at the back used to
be called the tiger. I hardly noticed the Queen [Queen Mary], my eyes were
fixed on that strange, archaic figure at the back, immobile as a waxwork, with
his white breeches that looked as though he had been poured into them, and
the cockade on his top-hat. Even at that date (1920 or thereabouts) it gave
me a wonderful feeling of looking backwards through a window into the nineteenth century.[47]

(And so might the postilion have thought if he had looked at the Eton
boy.)

He must have gone up to London, togged up in the traditional tails
and waistcoat, to attend the Eton–Harrow cricket match at Lord's
Cricket Ground in July that year. King-Farlow claims that he and Blair
netted £86 at the match by publishing a special issue of *College Days*,
in content much like the *Election Times* (even re-using some old
material), but printed and therefore able to solicit snob-appeal advertisements from big firms.[48] Jacintha came to the match too, chap-
eroned by an uncle who was a member of the MCC. Aunt Lilian wrote
to her complaining that she had neglected her patient and paying uncle
in favour of flirting with Eric. And he had watched the Henley
Regatta in June from the Buddicoms' punt, enjoying a general Regatta
exeat, on the passing excuse of watching the Eton Eight all swing, swing
together.[49] Dissenter though he was and self-conscious about lack
of money among Oppidans, this did not stop Blair from observing
the great social occasions as he got nearer the top of the school.

A more Orwell-like occasion occurred after the annual OTC camp
at the end of July on Salisbury Plain. He headed straight for Polperro
in Cornwall to join his family on holiday. The letter describing his
adventure has been reprinted in *The Collected Essays, Journalism and
Letters*, but it became so characteristic that it is worth recalling here.

My dear Runciman
I have a little spare time, & I feel I *must* tell you about my first adventure
as an amateur tramp. Like most tramps, I was driven to it. When I got to
a wretched little place in Devonshire, – Seaton Junction, – Mynors, who had
to change there, came to my carriage & said that a beastly Oppidan who had
been perpetually plaguing me to travel in the same compartment as him was

asking for me. As I was among strangers, I got out to go to him whereupon the train started off. You need two hands to enter a moving train, & I, what with kit-bag, belt etc. had only one. To be brief, I was left behind. I despatched a telegram to say I would be late (it arrived next day) & about $2\frac{1}{2}$ hours later I got a train: at Plymouth, North Rd, I found there were no more trains to Looe that night. It was too late to telephone, as the post offices were shut. I then made a consultation of my financial position. I had enough for my remaining fare & $7\frac{1}{2}$d over. I could therefore either sleep at the YMCA place, price 6d, & starve, or have something to eat but nowhere to sleep. I chose the latter. I put my kit-bag in the cloak-room & got 12 buns for 6d: half-past-nine found me sneaking into some farmer's field, – there were a few fields wedged in among rows of slummy houses. In that light I of course looked like a soldier strolling round, – on my way I had been asked whether I was demobilized yet, & I finally came to anchor in the corner of a field near some allotments. I then began to remember that people frequently got fourteen days for sleeping in somebody else's field & 'having no visible means of support', particularly as every dog in the neighbourhood barked if I even so much as moved. The corner had a large tree for a shelter, & bushes for concealment, but it was unendurably cold; I had no covering, my cap was my pillow, I lay 'with my martial cloak (rolled cape) around me'. I only dozed & shivered till about 10c, when I readjusted my puttees, & managed to sleep long enough to miss the first train, at 4.20 by about an hour, & to have to wait till 7.45 for another. My teeth were still chattering when I awoke. When I got to Looe I was forced to walk 4 miles in the hot sun; I am very proud of this adventure, but I would not repeat it.[50]

He was to repeat it, however, and to write about it in a style recognizably based on the same technique of detailed description, granted that it was more mature and flowing. Note that he could have stopped at the YMCA. Not quite as in Jack London's *The People of the Abyss* which he knew well, but it was a good enough first shot at 'tramping'.

He spent with his family the first part of the holiday but saw a good deal of Prosper in mid-August when they returned to the Thames Valley, although Jacintha was away visiting an uncle. There may have been mild parental concern. She says she saw little of him that holiday. Prosper's diary records the usual successful shooting and merciful failures when 'the nitro-Glycerin would not precipitate'. Jacintha returned and Eric went with the Buddicoms to Ticklerton in Shropshire for ten days over the end of August and the beginning of September. Again, Prosper's diary fills the days with shooting and fishing. 'While they shot,' wrote Jacintha, 'I usually led a Social Life with Auntie Lilian, visiting various neighbours.'[51] She and Eric probably blew a little hot and cold. She certainly disapproved strongly of shooting wild animals. She may have been somewhat jealous of Eric spending so much time with her brother and the gun rather than talking literature with her; but then, on the other hand, he may have been apt to grow too warm in his advances. Like most ages, theirs was seen as a specially dangerous age.

In the Michaelmas Half of 1920, he still followed his General Course, concentrating on History and Classics. His work was no better. What interested him most was still not found in the curriculum. English literature, for instance, was not a major subject; he only took a few periods of English lower down the school and much of that was grammar, although there had been one course of Shakespeare. This does not mean that the school thought that there were no other great writers of English: it was assumed partly that a cultivated English gentleman would and should read such things in his leisure time, and partly that English would be introduced by Classics teachers for frequent translation of difficult passages into Greek and Latin. (Boys learned to write good English through the easier task of translating from the Classics.) Some familiarity with English literature was thus induced as well as assumed, and even the assumption was not unrealistic. College *was* a cultivated place and there were intellectuals even among the Oppidans. There were two or three spare hours each evening and two or three half-days each week, if boys were not fanatical about sport. Before the blessings of radio and television there were fewer distractions from a sheer bulk of constant reading.

The rapes and adulteries of the Greek gods and the violence and madness of Roman Emperors were part of 'Classics', not of life, and there might have been nervousness about officially teaching much of English literature, certainly favourites of Blair's like Swift and Sterne, in case literature got confused with life. The morals of the pagan world were studied coldly by Christian masters – was this cultural schizophrenia or true scholarship? Habits of precise and dispassionate observation resulted; and perhaps it was more rewarding to discover much of one's native literature, both ancient and modern, by and for oneself.

'At the age of seventeen or eighteen, I was both a snob and a revolutionary. I was against all authority,' wrote Orwell in *The Road to Wigan Pier*, 'I had read and re-read the entire published works of Shaw, Wells and Galsworthy (at that time still regarded as "dangerously advanced" writers) and I loosely described myself as a Socialist.' He said that he 'had not much grasp of what Socialism meant' and 'no notion that the working class were human beings'. He could 'agonize over their sufferings' through the medium of books: 'Jack London's *The People of the Abyss*, for instance' – but 'I still hated them and despised them when I came anywhere near them. I was still revolted by their accents and infuriated by their habitual rudeness.' Orwell also said, looking back at this period: 'I seem to have spent half the time in denouncing the capitalist system and the other half in raging over the insolence of bus-conductors.'[52] But these references to socialism are a deliberate and considerable exaggeration, designed to fit the events of 1937 rather than to be an accurate memory of 1918. And the anti-hero's moan in *Keep the Aspidistra Flying* that 'Every intelligent boy of sixteen is a Socialist. At that age one does not see the hook sticking out of the rather stodgy bait ...'[53] might also be drawn from experience, but experience reinterpreted for a purpose, not simply recalled.

He remembers that year being set a general knowledge paper in school of which one question was, 'Whom do you consider the ten greatest men now living?' And as an example of that same alleged 'queer revolutionary feeling of that time' as the Peace Celebration or OTC riot, he recalls that fifteen out of sixteen in the class included Lenin in their list.[54] But with ten votes each in 1920, even Etonians could not ignore Lenin. From their Classics they would not read 'great man' as necessarily meaning 'good man'. The memories of five contemporaries are that Blair was 'against authority' but did not then claim to be a socialist. He used socialist ideas, on occasion, but as a way of annoying authority, not standing behind them solidly for the Cause. When he finally found where he stood politically in 1936 he tended to re-read or rather re-write parts of his own past.

Some of the books he was reading around 1918 must have been still in his mind thirty years later in 1948/1984. In H. G. Wells' *The Island of Dr Moreau* the animal slaves chant of their surgeon-maker-torturer:

> His is the House of Pain.
> His is the Hand that makes,
> His is the Hand that wounds,
> His is the Hand that heals.

And in Jack London's *The Iron Heel*, the captured revolutionary is told by 'the Boss' the same bleak secret that O'Brien was to reveal to Winston Smith:

We will not reply ... in words. Our reply shall be couched in terms of lead. We are in power. Nobody will deny it. By virtue of that power we shall remain in power ... This, then, is our answer. We have no words to waste on you. When you reach out your vaunted strong hands for our palaces and purpled ease, we will show you what strength is. In roar of shell and shrapnel and in whine of machine-guns will our answer be couched. We will grind you revolutionists down under our heel, and we shall walk upon your faces ... As for the host of labour ... in the dirt it shall remain so long as I and mine and those that come after us have the power. There is the word. It is the king of words – Power. Not God, not Mammon, but Power. Pour it over your tongue till it tingles with it. Power.[55]

Wells and London stayed with him all his life, both for what they wrote and for whom they wrote: socialists trying to reach the middle class, not intellectuals or literary men writing for their fellows.

Blair, back in 1920, was tall and weighty and even though now he was eighteen and near the top of the school, he had not the power to avoid going to the Wall again. And to the Field Game: 'The Annals of Foot-Ball' of Eton College begin familiarly enough on 22 September, 'Blair did not overwork himself', and 27 September: 'The behinds, especially Blair, kicked out too much'; but on 6 October 'The feature of the first half was a superb goal neatly shot by Blair from the halfway line ...' And from then on he did not look back, having probably decided that it was more trouble to play badly than to play well. 'For them, Blair, Turner ... were best', '... Then the keeper scored off a good penalty kick by Blair ... Meynell, at short, aptly backed up by Blair ...' 'Blair was competent' ... 'Blair kicked very well' ... and 'Blair kicked and kept competently under considerable pressure'. Also, to round off his sporting career, he enjoyed playing Fives – and he must have learned to play squash (on the two College courts), for we hear of him playing squash in Mandalay, as well as football in Moulmein.

In the first part of the Christmas holidays, Eric joined his family, at first at Henley but then also at Notting Hill. Prosper's diary for 20 December notes that 'we went up to town to Natural History Museum and Olympia Fair with Eric'. On 24 December 1920, Mrs Buddicom remarried at the Henley Register Office, so presumably it was not the best time for one of Eric's usual visits. Yet on 28 December, Eric wrote to Prosper accepting an invitation to come to Quarry House from 17 January to the end of the school holidays; but Prosper fell ill and the visit had to be cancelled. In his letter, Eric noted chattily that 'we are going to the *Blue Lagoon* this afternoon and the *Beggar's Opera*'[56] – everyone at Eton seemed to have been talking about Nigel Playfair's famous revival of John Gay at the Lyric, Hammersmith. This production's mixture of harsh satire and nostalgia suited the post-war mood; and it was apt to the budding Orwell, both romantic and cynical. He went to stay with cousins of his father in Suffolk. One of them remembers finding him 'a very quiet boy, difficult to entertain, who didn't seem interested in anything'.[57] Curious and unexplained, his being parked out, when normally the parents of boarding-school children 'make up for it' in the vacations. But he did find something to interest him, as an undated letter sent to Prosper towards the end of that holiday tells:

Thanks for your letter. It was most awfully good your shooting the two snipe & the woodcock. You ought to get at least one of them stuffed, I think. I have bought one of those big cage-rat traps. This place is overrun with rats. It is rather good sport to catch a rat & then let it out & shoot it as it runs. If it gets away I think one ought to let it go & not chase it. If they are threshing the corn while you are there, I should advise you to go – it is well worth it. The rats come out in dozens. It is also rather sport to go at night to a cornstack with an acetylene bicycle lamp & you can dazzle the rats that are running along the side & whack at them – or shoot them with a rifle. I rather wish I had my rifle here, as there are no rabbits ...[58]

Thus Blair bought the cage that eventually was thrust at the face of Winston Smith in *Nineteen Eighty-Four*. And the rat seems to be the devil to be striven against in a child's own created world of domestic animals.

Prosper's illness turned out to be serious, a bad attack of chicken-pox that affected his heart. Eric visited his friend at Shiplake during the Easter holidays when Prosper was convalescing. Jacintha neither recorded nor remembered events or incidents concerning Eric, literary or ballistic. Perhaps she felt that her brother had taken him over.

They were together again at the Eton–Harrow match in the Summer Half, when Eric and King-Farlow made such a huge second killing with commercial advertisements for their magazine *College Days* (King-Farlow claims that they netted £128) that the authorities declared against the profit motive. There was to be no more exploitation of the sacred event. The standard of the publication (apart from the offending advertisements) was not high, no sign of literary genius in Blair's several contributions, only of cheerful endeavour. The year before he had contributed, *inter alia*, 'The Photographer' which began:

> Not a breath is heard, not a moving of lip,
> As his hand stays posed on the shutter.
> And only the gnat on the neck gives a nip,
> As we think of the words we mayn't utter.

And in 1921 came an 'Ode to Field Days', which began:

> Hills we have climbed and bogs that we have sat in,
> Pools where we drenched our feet in mid-December,
> Trains we have packed, woods we have lost our hat in,
> When you are past and gone, we will remember.

And which continued for several more verses.

That summer trouble came to a head between the senior Election and the rest of College led by Blair's Election, who were now themselves about to enter Sixth Form. Cyril Connolly claims that Blair was beaten by Sixth Form when he was 18, nominally for being late for prayers, but in fact for being 'uppish'. He and King-Farlow were beaten 'on the most flimsy pretexts'. King-Farlow has denied this strongly. He said that he even threatened Connolly with a libel action in the 1930s for repeating the tale.[59] He was working in America at the time and thought it would be damaging for anyone to think that virtually a grown man would allow himself to be treated in such a degrading manner. No one else can remember it, though Blair had been beaten lower down the School, as had most of his Election, both individually and as part of collective punishment. Connolly's memory must be at fault for, by his eighteenth birthday, Blair was in Sixth Form and capable of administering canings himself; or perhaps he transposed an incident.* There is no doubt, however, that the Election of 1915 had been remarkably traditional, reactionary even, about matters of discipline and Sixth Form privilege, while Blair's Election of 1916 was far more liberal and relaxed, used the cane very little, and almost dismantled the privileges of Sixth Form and College Pop (not to be confused with the prestigious and powerful institution of the Eton Society, 'Pop'). The Election below them went so far in liberalism as to create, as people saw it at the time, 'an inevitable reaction' later. That particular reaction was led, equally inevitably, by Quintin Hogg, later Lord Hailsham.

Connolly relates a shocking tale. When the customary votes of thanks were moved at the end of term to those members of College Pop who were leaving, including the President, Treasurer and Secretary, the Keepers of College Wall and Field, the Cadet Officer of the O T C, and the Captain of the School himself, 'name after name was read out, proposed and seconded, the ballot box passed . . . blackballs extracted, and the transaction noted down in "Annals" – not one of the previous years' officers received a vote of thanks' (a solitary black ball was enough to negate such a vote).[60] Connolly makes it sound a great event in the records of College. Mynors says that he does not remember it, that if it did take place (and the notes in the Minute Book are *said to be* clear, and Eton is careful about access to its records) 'it must have been a storm in a tea-cup'. Others remember 'something of the kind', less precisely than Connolly.

A feature of 'College Annals' is a 'Retrospect' written by the Captain of the School. Perhaps the blackballing explains why no Retrospect was written for 1920–21, but the Captain's entry for 1921–2, when Orwell entered Sixth Form for his last term, throws some light on the troubles of the times:

* I have deliberately made as little use as possible for Eton of *Enemies of Promise*, Connolly's small masterpiece explaining why he never produced a great one. It raises the same problems as Orwell's 'Such, Such Were the Joys' in respect of literal, historical accuracy. His scholarly contemporaries view the accuracy of his memories with sceptical eyes.

The past year has been conspicuous more for alterations in the general tone of College than for any remarkable achievements. It has always been the hope of my own Election to destroy the inter-election enmity, as it existed a few years ago, to abolish the scandals of College Rag, to reduce the numbers of beatings to a minimum, and generally to substitute a more harmonious system of government for the old methods of repression and spite. All but one of the *ancien régime* Election left last summer, and we were given an almost free hand ... It is too early to judge the success of these experiments, and the inward predictions of the 'old man' may be verified, but I can at least honestly record that the College has been in every way *happier* this year than at any time in the last six years. The Master in College, though disapproving in many ways of our 'lack of discipline' has been very helpful and tactful ...

Two years later, his successor wrote:

The whole reaction from the over-severe discipline of six years ago has gone too far, as reactions do ... We should have been more careful that in casting out this one devil we did not make way for seven worse devils – for in-discipline and anarchy ...[61]

And this young 'old man' went on to deplore that there had been 'two parties' in Sixth Form leading to 'the destruction of discipline in the College'. 'Politics' then became a regular feature of the 'Annals', and the issues were those of discipline and corporal punishment.

'The Glorious Fourth' is for Eton the Fourth of June, King George III's birthday, not the Fourth of July. It is a kind of Open Day. Sixth Form (ten Collegers and ten Oppidans *in toto*), stuffed into court dress with knee-breeches, silver buckles and silk stockings, gave the 'Speeches', readings in fact. Blair read a morbid passage from 'The Suicide Club' stories in Robert Louis Stevenson's *New Arabian Nights*. Stansky and Abrahams see this, together with his colours for the Wall Game and election to College Pop, as 'not contemptible items in an Eton dossier'.[62] But contemporaries, reading what they say, despite their careful use of a negative, think they exaggerate. Sixth Form was small, so everyone had to orate. It was not a chosen honour. College Pop was still a debating society with a reasonably open membership. And historically the Wall Game was very much a College-dominated affair in which height and weight would help determine the composition of the team – Blair did develop skill, but that was a bonus; the 'Colour' was for being, not becoming. Academically, he was near the bottom of the lists, placed 138th out of 167 in the Eton July examinations.

There was no denying that it had been an undistinguished career, but also, despite what he said later about Eton being such a snobbish place, one that he had rather enjoyed. As Osbert Sitwell once claimed in *Who's Who* that he was educated at home from Eton during the holidays, so Orwell – who only made *Who's Who* in the year of his death – could well have claimed that he had educated himself outside the school rooms while at Eton.

The time for boyhood pastimes and lack of care about earning a living was rapidly drawing to a close: one last vacation before one last term.

In the summer of 1921, the Blair family gave up the house at Henley. Richard Blair stayed with relatives in Suffolk while house-hunting for a final retirement place that he could afford – assuming that no more wars called for his services. The Buddicoms, too, had given up their house to live in Harrow, so that Prosper, with his weakened heart, could enjoy the milder régime of a dayboy. The two families combined to rent a house for the summer, Glencroft in Rickmansworth outside London. It was a hot summer. A tennis court went with the house, and there were bicycles and a gramophone. A nearby reservoir gave good fishing, and there was a billiards hall in the village ('Men Only') into which Eric and Prosper often retreated. There was a last exchange of tender poetry between Jacintha and Eric. He wrote:

> Friendship and love are closely intertwined,
> My heart belongs to your befriending mind:
> But chilling sunlit fields, cloud-shadows fall –
> My love can't reach your heedless heart at all.

And she replied:

> By light
> Too bright
> Are dazzled eyes betrayed:
> It's best
> To rest
> Content in tranquil shade.[63]

There was a last burst of Buddicom pressure that 'Eric should go to Oxford' which both his father, whose heart was not set on such things, and Eric, whose heart was not set on them enough to want to swot, knew was impossible without his winning a scholarship. Jacintha relates:

So when Mrs Blair sided with Eric in a desperate last-minute stand for a final last-minute chance of Oxford, our mother backed them up in some vigorous correspondence with old Mr Blair, strongly advocating that Oxford was 'the proper thing' for a boy. She told them that 'at whatever sacrifice' she was determined that Prosper should be given the opportunity. But Mr Blair was adamant: nothing could alter his own equal determination that Eric should *not*. Eric frequently sat in on these discussions, especially whenever an epistle from Mr Blair was read out, when he was not engaged in outdoor pursuits with the others.[64]

But Eric almost certainly did not, in later years certainly did not, share Jacintha's enthusiasm. Some time during this period the idea of simply following in his father's footsteps must have occurred, which was then, after all, a most ordinary thing to happen, in any class or condition whether the boy welcomed it or not.

In the new Michaelmas Half, Richard Blair went to Eton to talk to Gow about possible careers for his son. Andrew Gow remembered Mr Blair telling him that Eric could not go to Oxford without a scholarship; and that he told Mr Blair that Eric 'did not stand the slightest chance of getting a scholarship' – which settled the matter. And sixty years later Gow fumed that Eric would have brought 'disgrace on College' had they even put him forward for a scholarship examination, since he had done 'absolutely no work for five years'.[65] He volunteered further that he thought Miss Buddicom's account 'of his wanting to go and being able to go but his father stopping him' was 'rubbish'.[66]

Eric must have known the score, even if his friend was still hoping, and Jacintha still thinks that he missed something. If he felt any sense of loss, he never said so to anyone who can remember it, nor wrote about it; and, after all, only a minority from Eton as a whole in those days went on to university, though a majority of boys from College did. To have been to Eton at all was a good enough beginning for most careers. The idea of serving in India or Burma would have come up quite naturally and from the family, especially with his maternal grandmother still in Mandalay. Gow was sure that the school did not recommend the police; certainly he did not. The Indian Police was a poor service, already tainted in the liberal press with hangings and floggings; but for the Imperial Civil Service itself one needed university-level qualifications, and of the lesser services the Police would seem more interesting than, say, Forestry, Public Health, Roads or the wretched Opium Department. Such a choice does not demand psychological speculation. Runciman remembered him saying even before he entered Sixth Form that he did not want to go to university, he wanted 'to go back' to the East. Uncertain where he belonged, it was as if he wanted to go back to where he was born, even before his memory.

There is a lot of Orwell himself in his character of the failed and bitter writer, Gordon Comstock, in *Keep the Aspidistra Flying*. Comstock curses a rejection slip: 'Why be so bloody mealy-mouthed about it? Why not say outright, "We don't want your bloody poems. We only take poems from chaps we were at Cambridge with ..." The bloody hypocritical sods!'[67] This has been read by some literary critics as a proof of jealousy and of regret that he did not go to Oxford. But critics forget that such accusations are often true, that Orwell is right to attack nepotism; and also there is a lot that is not autobiographical in Gordon Comstock. Orwell may never have felt *that* bitter, but he was Comstock enough in condition and thought to know how a Comstock would feel. 'Probably the greatest cruelty one can inflict on a child,' muses Comstock, 'is to send it to a school among children richer than itself. A child conscious of poverty will suffer snobbish agonies such as a grown-up person can scarcely even imagine.'[68] If this cap, indeed, fitted Orwell tightly, it did so at St Cyprian's more than at Eton. There is no sign or complaint of his being similarly unhappy and constrained at Eton. College was an intellectual aristocracy, not a plutocracy. He did go on a bit about money, as King-Farlow remembers, but it was largely a good middle-class rant about 'not getting value for money'. Yet compared to most of his fellows, he was abnormally aware for his age of the difference that money makes to a person's life. All in all, however, if his career at Eton had been unsuccessful by College standards, he had got a lot out of it, in terms of reading and self-confidence. And he had not been unhappy; he had simply stood aside from official enthusiasm and had, indeed, flexed his muscles in practical scepticism of authority. He emerged with all the 'wrong attitudes', precisely those that were so good for a social critic to have; and his peculiar genius as a writer might well have been damaged by going on to university – certainly to Oxford or Cambridge.

He was one of the awkward squad, but a proud member. There was no sign then, however, that when the last great game is played at the Wall or in the Field with the courtiers, the careerists, the imperialists, the parlour creeps, the backstair crawlers, the arse-lickers, the toadies, the money-grubbers, the City men, the complacent and sleekly successful (all words to be used by Orwell), against God's great awkward squad of unorthodox, dissident Englishmen, that Eric Blair as George Orwell would have had a place in that team, not at the top of the list, but turning out none the less with Skelton, Lilburne, Swift, Defoe, Sam Johnson, Hazlitt, Cobbett, Dickens, William Morris and Bertrand Russell.

The last term in school must have been somewhat unreal once a decision had been made about his future career. He was in Sixth Form but it was not an Election for throwing its weight about. He seems never to have used the cane. He *did* have a fag, but made little use of him, let him off lightly. Sir Anthony Wagner (later Garter King of Arms) remembered him as 'kind and nice, very withdrawn, a very pleasant, kind and decent fagmaster'.[69] He saw him only as a rather dim figure, at the bottom of the academic list of seniority in a brilliant Election, 'else someone more interesting might have picked me up; I didn't think of him as particularly interesting'. 'I must be careful not to remember more than I can remember,' added Sir Anthony with professional rectitude. All he can clearly remember Blair saying to him was, rather shyly, 'Come and work in my room if ever you like, if you find things too noisy in Chamber.' He too confirms that Blair's Election had a very relaxed attitude to discipline, they inaugurated a libertarian phase: 'This was all very well in most ways, but in other ways it led to bullying they didn't know about by relaxing their grip on the College.' The paradox of imperial power was present even then. And when Blair left, he gave Wagner as a farewell present Robert Service's *Rhymes for a Rolling Stone*.

Before Blair left, he did one memorable thing. In a match at the Wall he passed the ball long and accurately for Bobbie Longden to score a goal. John Lehmann arrived at Eton only just in time to witness – in what he thought was (and set down in his memoirs as) the great St Andrew's Day game against the Oppidans: 'that extremely rare event, a goal scored in the Wall Game, and to make it more exciting for me it had been scored by my fag-master, Bobbie Longden, with the aid of George Orwell. "Wasn't it wonderful?" I wrote in the same letter, and added, as if to make sure my parents assented in the same view of the matter, "It was perfectly splendid ..."' But, alas for the fallibility of human memory, Lehmann was wrong: the records show that it was only a practice match.[70]

Eric Blair must have been mildly pleased to show that he could if he would but mostly he had shown that he would be damned if he would if told he had to.

CHAPTER FIVE

AN ENGLISHMAN IN BURMA

(1922–7)

NOT even an old Etonian could simply waltz in and join the Imperial Indian Police. The public examination marked the bureaucratic phase of imperialism. 'Off to the crammers with him' was a general parental cry among the competitive middle classes. In December 1921, the same month that Eric left Eton, his parents moved yet again, Mrs Blair's sixth move since leaving India in 1904. This time it was to Southwold, in Suffolk, on the east coast. The family stayed there until the Second World War, though with several changes of house. So it was to a crammer in Southwold that Eric went in January 1922, six months' hard labour to prepare for several papers of the India Office's examinations at the establishment of Mr P. Hope, MA ('late scholar of King's College Cambridge and for many years Sixth Form Master at Dulwich College').

Southwold is a small, modest resort town. It had little then of the wealth of Eastbourne, Bournemouth and other favoured south-coast resort-cum-retirement towns, but it was becoming popular with Anglo-Indian families, wanting somewhere cheap but decent and comely – perhaps genteel is the right word – to retire to. So it already boasted a crammer that could specialize in the India Office exams. From old Blair's point of view, this must have been yet another damned expense, albeit a necessary investment in a secure and respectable future. To him, it would seem natural, a proper end to the preparation that had begun at St Cyprian's and to which Eton was probably an irrelevance – any public school would have done; but it might have been a disappointment nonetheless that Eric had not done well enough at Eton for a university scholarship.

Southwold had been recommended to the Blairs by the parents of Kathleen O'Hara who was a friend of Ruth Pitter (the future poet), whom Ida Blair and Marjorie had got to know while living at Mall Chambers, Notting Hill. Ruth Pitter remembers Eric when he was still a schoolboy of 17 at Eton. 'I knew at once he was an interesting person. He looked at me with his very keen look, his eyes were an exact pair. He told me afterwards with all the impudence of Eton – Eton for ever when it comes to impudence, he was only 17 and I was 22 – "I wonder if that girl would be hard to get." No, he told me afterwards. He would not have dared to say that at the age of 17.'[1] Eric, in fact, grew to dislike Southwold because of its many elderly and Anglo-Indian inhabitants, but he kept on returning to it – so strong was the family link. He met many young people of his own age, notably Eleanor Jaques (1906–62), the daughter of the family next door who had come from Canada (with whom he was to have, some years later, a brief affair), and Dennis Collings, who was to marry Eleanor. (Collings, born in 1905, was a friend of Eric's from 1921 when his father became the Blairs' family doctor. He was later an anthropologist and went East in the Colonial Service.)

A fellow student at the crammer, who used to play tennis with Avril, remembers that 'A very beautiful young lady ... became very attracted to Blair and they saw a lot of each other, but he was very shy and I think she became a bit too much for him.' Also 'Blair and a rather wild young man who had, I think been expelled from Malvern somehow fell foul of the Borough Surveyor'; they found out the date of his birthday and 'by way of a present they sent him a dead rat with birthday greetings and signing their names'.[2] Mr Hope promptly expelled them from his academy, but it was near the end of term and Blair had already sat his examination.

The India Office's examinations consisted of compulsory two-hour papers in English, English History, Mathematics, French and three options. Eric chose Latin, Greek and Drawing. And if these hurdles were crossed, there was a medical and a practical test in horse-riding. No letters, reports, or administrative papers from his Burmese days survive, all that is left for history is bare files of entry forms and examination results.[3] Crace sent a formal reference from Eton, with a tinge of donnish sarcasm in it: 'I do not know at all what is required by the authorities for candidates in the Indian police. I send a formal certificate which is probably all that is necessary.' Evidently few if any Etonians, certainly none from College, had trod the road to Mandalay before. His father gave his formal permission and signed the usual undertaking to meet the cost of Eric's uniform.

The exams took about a week in all and were highly competitive. From the questions asked it appears that their standard, however, was closer to an 'Ordinary Level' in England today rather than the 'A' or Advanced Level: certainly not an equivalent to university-entrance standard. In the English paper, for instance, he was asked to 'Write a character sketch of an old gamekeeper, or a retired colonel, or an old farmer'; a letter to a relative about a trip to the theatre; a 250-word précis of a passage on the battle of Sedgemoor; to name and describe three members of the Cabinet, and several similar snippets. The History paper included questions on 'Who was the greatest Prime Minister since Pitt?' and (more imaginatively) 'If Nelson had lost Trafalgar?' And in Drawing the candidates were asked to copy a picture so that it would be 'useful to an officer', and to draw from memory 'a chair at an angle, a hut or a bucket'. Twenty-six candidates went forward to the medical and riding test, Blair being placed seventh on the examination list; but after the riding test, he was ranked twenty-first from a successful twenty-three. Practical necessities of getting round their districts were, after all, weighed more heavily than knowledge.

He had listed his choices in order of preference as Burma, United Provinces, Bombay, Madras and the Punjab. He gave as reasons that he had relatives in Burma and that his father had served in United Provinces. He was one of three assigned to Burma: it did not rank high in the pecking order of the India hands. They regarded its problems as peripheral to those of the great sub-continent, even though they re-sisted claims to give it administrative autonomy.

On 27 October 1922, Blair sailed for the East on SS *Herefordshire*, from Birkenhead to Rangoon. New arrivals and departures are the set pieces of biographies, but so often it all has to be made up: there is no way of knowing what frame of mind he was in or quite what burden, if any, he thought he was carrying, this difficult, interesting, independent-minded, self-contained 19-year-old, committed only to scepticism towards authority and a love of literature but hardly of learning. Was he leaning over the rail, watching old England recede behind him, et cetera, in a Kiplingesque spirit of adventure, excitement and dedication?

> Take up the White Man's burden –
> Send forth the best ye breed –
> Go bind your sons to exile
> To serve your captives' need;
> To wait in heavy harness,
> On fluttered folk and wild –
> Your new-caught, sullen peoples,
> Half-devil and half-child.

Or was he doggedly doing the only thing that then seemed possible, dutifully following his father, but brooding morbidly that he probably wouldn't like it? Quite possibly both sets of ideas were competing in his mind. His feelings may well have swung between such poles. What is implausible is that he went out placidly as if it were the natural thing to do and a normal culmination of his education. Some sense of 'service' was probably in his mind, but more likely as a role to be played, whether sadly, gladly or sourly – something not quite in character. Hindsight must be avoided. It is sheer speculation to picture him as masochistically sacrificing his promise to a poor Service to atone for guilt about privilege, or to punish his father for pushing him through such ambitious, competitive and socially condescending schools. For one thing, there was no sign of particular promise, despite an exceptionally well-developed ironic eye. None the less, he probably had a greater sense than his father of entering into a career that would be an incongruous end to his education. Most of the education of George Orwell, in fact, still lay ahead of him.

Long years afterwards he remembered two incidents from the voyage out which, he claimed, influenced him. Notice that they are both memories of observing and watching, not of discussion or direct involvement. He was to tell hungry readers of *Tribune* in 1947 about meals of 'the stupendous kind' they had 'nearly a quarter of a century ago' when 'I was travelling on a liner to Burma ... ships of this line were mostly manned by Indians, but apart from the officers and the stewards they carried four European quartermasters whose job was to take the wheel'. As a young man, he looked up to them 'as godlike beings on a par with the officers'. One day he came up from lunch early and saw a quartermaster 'scurrying like a rat along the side of the deck-houses' with a half-eaten custard pudding from the passengers' table 'partially concealed between his monstrous hands'.

Across more than twenty years I can still faintly feel the shock of astonishment ... this sudden revelation of the gap between function and re-ward – the revelation that a highly-skilled craftsman, who might literally hold all our lives in his hands, was glad to steal scraps of food from our table – taught me more than I could have learned from half a dozen Socialist pamphlets.[4]

The memory and the shock sound genuine, but it took him another ten years at least to see it in such a specifically socialist perspective. He also added to the other memory a good anti-racialist moral.

When the other day I read Dr Ley's statement that 'inferior races, such as Poles and Jews' do not need so much to eat as Germans, I was suddenly re-minded of the first sight I saw when I set foot on the soil of Asia – or rather, just before setting foot there. The liner I was travelling in was docking at Colombo, and the usual swarm of coolies had come aboard to deal with the luggage. Some policemen, including a white sergeant, were superintending them. One of the coolies had got hold of a long tin uniform-case and was carry-ing it so clumsily as to endanger people's heads. Someone cursed at him for his carelessness. The police sergeant looked round, saw what the man was doing, and caught him a terrific kick on the bottom that sent him staggering across the deck. Several passengers, including women, murmured their approval.[5]

He reached Rangoon in November, the steamer coming right up the wide, mud-coloured but deep Irrawaddy river, past the oddly con-trasting black smokestacks of the Burmah Oil Company's refinery and the tall gold spire of the Shwe Dagon pagoda, one of the oldest and most holy of Buddhist shrines. He and another trainee who had travelled out with him spent a few days in Rangoon on the customary round of courtesy calls to high officials; and they then took the train to Mandalay, a sixteen-hour journey, north-bound for the Burma Provincial Police Training School. Since 'the pacification' of Burma in the 1880s, the railway had replaced the old river route of Kipling's lines:

> On the road to Mandalay,
> Where the old flotilla lay,
> With our sick beneath the awnings when we
> went to Mandalay!

They were met at the station by Roger Beadon, the third successful
Burma Police candidate that year, who had come out ahead of the
others to meet his father. (Beadon was the same age as Blair and lived
to tell his tales until 1975.) He took them to the Police Mess which was
adjacent to the Training School. The Police Mess was reckoned to be
the best of the regimental and administrative clubs in Mandalay. The
ground floor was a large club-house, and above were six bedrooms,
three reserved for the probationary ASPs (Assistant Superintendents
of Police). The Police School was primarily for the training of Cadet
Sub-Inspectors, mostly native Burmese school graduates (but including some Shans, Karens and Arkanese, as well as a few Indians
and Chinese).

The English probationary ASPs led a life apart, with only a small
amount of instruction in common. They polished up their own drill
privately – they had already done it to a high standard in their school
OTCs; but then practised taking command and drilling on the native
cadets. 'We had one pip and thought ourselves very important,'
Beadon remembered – though he defended fiercely the whole system
against 'the slurs' and 'malice' of Orwell in his novel, *Burmese Days*
(Beadon had read this when still in Burma).

[Blair] didn't speak very much about his past, I mean, he was very quiet ...
He always looked as if his clothes would never hang on him properly, he was
long and thin and I always felt rather lugubrious, very tall for his age; and
as I say, his clothes just sort of fell on him, you couldn't make him tidy however hard you tried. And he was a very pleasant fellow to know, but he kept
very much to himself. I was very fond of going down to the club and
playing snooker and dancing and what have you, but this didn't seem to appeal
to him at all, he wasn't what I would call a socialite in any way, in fact I
don't think he went to the club very much ... I think he mostly read ... or
stayed up in his room.[6]

Others confirm that he was not disliked, did nothing provocative at
the Training School, but was an unclubbable man, a solitary and therefore 'an eccentric'. This was plainly so, but again there were material
as well as psychological factors: the Mess was terribly expensive. 'We
all left the school heavily in debt,' said one senior officer. And the time
was to come when probationers without private means could not
afford to join the club.[7] Whatever the causes, a vicious circle could
set in: unclubbable men got poor and lonely postings, which could

increase their eccentricity, unsociability or 'melancholy' – think of the strange quotation from *As You Like It* that Orwell used as a legend to *Burmese Days*: '... this desert inaccessible/Under the shade of melancholy boughs.'

One of his mildest later remarks on Burma was 'five boring years within the sound of bugles' – a sound which must have saddened him like Housman rather than filled him with elation like Philip Sidney. The bugles, in fact, would only have been in the first year, while he was living in the cantonment in Mandalay. The days consisted of cramming in the morning, drilling in the afternoon, and drinking at night. Blair substituted reading for drinking.

He had come to Burma at an interesting time. Until the Great War, relations between educated Burmese and the British authorities had generally been quiet. Nationalist sentiments began to spread during the War mainly through Buddhist monks and a body called the Young Men's Buddhist Association, which was moving away from its early, westernizing intent to copy the YMCA movement. Discontent and national sentiments flared up, though still far short of claiming independence. In 1919, Burma, although administratively a province of India, had been specifically excluded from the reforms of the Government of India Act. This measure was to introduce to India, following the Montagu-Chelmsford proposals, a system of dual government or 'Dyarchy' by which Indians were given representation in elected assemblies as well as having higher posts in the civil service open to them. Important areas of government and financial control were still reserved to the occupying power, yet it was considered a great step forward in India, the beginning of a process of deliberate education towards eventual self-rule – perhaps by the end of the century; and its absence in Burma was bitterly resented. A former Lieutenant-Governor of Burma, Sir Herbert White, had in 1913 condemned as 'pernicious cant' the view that 'our mission in Burma is the political education of the masses'; we are there, he said, to bring 'law and order to parts of barbary and to maintain them there'. At best the political ideas of English imperialists were as Professor Stokes was to characterize them: 'the belief that political power tended constantly to deposit itself in the hands of a natural aristocracy, that power so deposited was morally valid, and that it was not to be tamely surrendered before the claims of abstract democratic ideals, but was to be asserted and exercised with justice and mercy.'[8] (Blair would at first have shared this theory in principle, while in practice coming to think as an ex-Etonian that the type of Englishman and Scot who came to Burma did *not* constitute a 'natural aristocracy' who would govern with 'justice and mercy'.)

Burmese resentment took the form of a boycott of British goods. Young Buddhist monks plunged into politics, going round with small canes with which they beat anyone breaking the boycott. In 1920, Rangoon College was raised to the status of a full university; but an effective student strike took place, spreading to the schools, when it became clear it was intended to teach, above all else, obedience and loyalty. The new university was to be tightly controlled to prevent it becoming anything like the University of Calcutta, thought to be the cradle and hotbed of Indian nationalism. By 1923, however, the British Government had given way, with its usual shrewd conservative practicality, and the Indian reforms were extended to Burma; but the damage had been done. Rebellion and civil disobedience were avoided until the 1930s, but the old mutual trust had broken down. Unrest was endemic; as so often licensed freedom made things worse.

There was no real fear of violence, however, and British police and civilian administrators still rode or trudged around the country with only a few native escorts, sometimes almost alone. The military presence was small (two battalions of British and ten of Indian infantry). All the same, there was a general atmosphere of hostility. Orwell gave a careful and far from exaggerated picture of it in his essay of 1936, 'Shooting an Elephant'. There is no record of Blair making friends among any of the young nationalists. Many of the British old hands were, of course, upset and intolerant of the Burmese because of their seeming ingratitude at 'all that was done for them' and the granting of Dyarchy. And many of the old and new hands had been coarsened and rendered impatient – as with the Black and Tans in Ireland – by their experiences in the Great War. Flory, the 'hero' of *Burmese Days*, rants on to himself:

In the end the secrecy of your revolt poisons you like a secret disease. Your whole life is a life of lies. Year after year you sit in Kipling-haunted little Clubs, whisky to right of you, *Pink'un* to left of you, listening and eagerly agreeing while Colonel Bodger develops his theory that these bloody Nationalists should be boiled in oil. You hear your Oriental friends called 'greasy little babus', and you admit, dutifully, that they *are* greasy little babus. You see louts fresh from school kicking greyhaired servants. The time comes when you burn with hatred of your own countrymen, when you long for a native rising to drown their Empire in blood. And in this there is nothing honourable, hardly even any sincerity ... You are a creature of the despotism, a pukka sahib, tied tighter than a monk or a savage by an unbreakable system of tabus.[9]

Did Blair initially have such intense feelings of hidden revolt against being 'a cog in the wheels of despotism', as he later wrote?

At least one different thought may have run through his mind in the early days at the Police School. A group photograph has survived with thirteen men and one dog in it, including one Burmese: all with topees, Sam Browne belts and swagger sticks. Their names and ages survive. All, except Beadon and Blair, were of an age to have served in the Great War. Blair had at first 'written off' 1914–18 as 'a meaningless slaughter':

But the dead men had their revenge after all. As the war fell back into the past, my particular generation, those who had been 'just too young', became conscious of the vastness of the experience they had missed. You felt yourself a little less than a man, because you had missed it. I spent the years 1922–27 mostly among men a little older than myself who had been through the war. They talked about it unceasingly, with horror, of course, but also with a steadily-growing nostalgia.[10]

He came to reject imperialism while in Burma, but probably not at once, only gradually; meanwhile he did his duty with distaste. For his anti-imperialism would never imply anti-patriotism. At first he must have half-admired these men with their campaign ribbons and decorations, however little he shared their values and their tastes. And the British Army, and colonial services, were used to and reasonably tolerant of solitary eccentrics who read books. Sometimes in lonely posts it was the only thing to do if you were not to ruin yourself with drink, women or – the deepest fear of all out East – opium. Many a military man or civilian even has wished that he was a bit more bookish.

An Assistant Superintendent of Police would spend 'nine months at the ... Police Training School during which time he will be instructed in law, languages and police accounts and procedure'.[11] They then plunged straight into field postings, although on probation for a further fifteen months.

We saw each other every day [said Roger Beadon], we attended instructions in law, Burmese and Hindustani, and we used to have to do an hour's Burmese and then switch right over to Hindustani ... but what shattered me more than anything else was that whereas I found it very difficult, it didn't seem to worry him [Blair] at all, I mean when I, we, should be attending class, he was probably up in bed reading, so whether he had a flair ... for Eastern languages I don't know, but he certainly could speak it extremely well for I'm told that before he left Burma, he was able to go into a Hpongyi Kyaung, which is one of these Burmese temples, and converse in a very high-flown Burmese with the Hpongyis, or priests, and you've got to be able to speak Burmese very well to be able to do that.[12]

Two odd tales also stuck in Beadon's mind. He had taught Blair to ride a motorbike and Blair purchased a huge American machine, very close to the ground, so that when he, six foot three, sat on it, his knees came up to his chin. Once they headed for one of the gates of Fort Dufferin, each on their own machine, but Beadon suddenly realized that it was not open. He shouted a warning 'but it didn't react on him and he didn't quite know what to do, he wasn't very mechanically minded I think, so he just stood up and the bike went straight on between his legs and hit the thing and came down ...' Also Beadon once suggested 'a tiger-shoot'. He had a Luger Parabellum automatic pistol and Blair borrowed the Principal's shotgun. They went out fifteen miles on their motorbikes, then roused a villager to drive them about all night in a bullock cart (presumably the bullock doubled up as bait). They sat in the back with cocked guns. 'We didn't see a tiger and somehow I don't think the gentleman in charge of the bullock cart ever intended that we should. I think if we had that possibly Mr Blair or Mr Orwell would not have existed ...' No wonder the old India hands doubted that their compatriots in Burma were pukka sahibs. 'Tiger shooting on a motorbike with a pistol!' It was only a grander version of killing a jackdaw with a catapult at Eton.

They completed their exams successfully enough in January 1924 and got their first postings. Only one piece of 'practical' training had interrupted this course of law and languages. They were posted for a month to a British regiment up-country at Maymyo. The second autobiographical chapter of *The Road to Wigan Pier* (1937) was to recall in a curious context one incident from this month: that of class prejudice and smell. He said that he had been brought up to believe that 'the lower classes smell',[13] but that he felt towards the Burmese none of the prejudice that he did towards 'the lower classes at home'. 'When you have a lot of servants you soon get into lazy habits, and I habitually allowed myself, for instance, to be dressed and undressed by my Burmese boy. This was because he was a Burman and undisgusting: I could not have endured to let an English man-servant handle me in that intimate manner. I felt towards a Burman almost as I felt towards a woman.' (In *Burmese Days*, of course, the body-servant was a woman, as was very common in the outposts.) This led him to remember that:

When I was not much past twenty I was attached for a short time to a British regiment. Of course I admired and liked the private soldiers as any youth of twenty would admire and like hefty, cheery youths five years older than himself with the medals of the Great War on their chests. And yet, after all, they faintly repelled me; they were 'common people' and I did not care to be too close to them. In the hot mornings when the company marched down the road, myself in the rear with one of the junior subalterns, the steam of those hundred sweating bodies in front made my stomach turn. And this, you observe, was pure prejudice. For a soldier is probably as inoffensive, physically, as it is possible for a male white person to be. He is generally young, he is nearly always healthy from fresh air and exercise, and a rigorous discipline compels him to be clean. But I could not see it like that. All I knew was that it was *lower-class* sweat that I was smelling, and the thought of it made me sick.[14]

He certainly had no illusions about the British soldier in Burma: 'They develop an attitude towards "the niggers" which is far more brutal than that of the officials or business men. In Burma I was constantly struck by the fact that the common soldiers were the best-hated section of the white community, and judged simply by their behaviour, they certainly deserved to be.'[15] Perhaps this was just counter-propaganda to the assumed popularity of Tommy Atkins in those four lines of verse that everyone knew (if they knew little else) about Burma:

> By the old Moulmein Pagoda, lookin' eastward to the sea,
>> There's a Burma girl a-settin', and I know she thinks o' me;
> For the wind is in the palm-trees, and the temple-bells they say:
>> 'Come you back you British soldier; come you back to Mandalay.'

*

His first posting took him far from Mandalay, to Myaungmya, a small and primitive town in the alluvial Irrawaddy Delta, a grim contrast to Mandalay and with a notoriously difficult Superintendent of Police. There is general agreement among his surviving contemporaries that it was a rotten first posting, and indeed that none of his subsequent five postings, except one close to Rangoon, was brilliant. The duties were demanding for a still fairly green 20-year-old. He was expected to run the office at the district headquarters; to supervise all stores and records; to organize the training school of locally-recruited constables; to oversee the headquarters staff (between thirty and fifty men); to arrange escorts for hearings and trials, night patrols, and generally to take charge when his superior was touring the sub-divisional headquarters, away for days on end. Blair cannot have made a great success of it – or more likely he got on badly with his superior officer – for although it was regarded as a temporary training post, he was transferred in less than three months, which was exceptional.

Since there was an American Baptist Missionary College nearby, it was probably there that the small incident occurred which he describes in *The Road to Wigan Pier* as leading to a large doubt. An American missionary was watching one of Blair's native sub-inspectors bullying a suspect. 'Like most Nonconformist missionaries he was a complete ass but quite a good fellow ...' He turned to Blair and said, 'I wouldn't care to have your job.' 'It made me horribly ashamed. So that was the kind of job I had! Even an ass of an American missionary, a tee-total cock-virgin from the middle West, had the right to look down on me and pity me.' He recalled the misery of the prisoners, the scarred buttocks of the men who had been flogged with bamboo sticks and the howling of women and children as their menfolk were led away under arrest: 'Things like these are beyond bearing when you are in any way directly responsible for them. I watched a man hanged once; it seemed to me worse than a thousand murders. I never went into a jail without feeling ... that my place was on the other side of the bars.'[16]

Again, there could be some hindsight here. It took him some time to realize on which side of the bars both head and heart lay. The mature Orwell would have known Voltaire's dictum that 'when one man is imprisoned unjustly, the only place for a just man is in prison'. But his own remark went far beyond that: he was not talking about the personal guilt or innocence of the imprisoned and down-trodden Burmese, but of their needless suffering under a system of despotism and alien rule. Plainly, however, even at the time many things were shaking and worrying the conventional side of the convictions of Eric Blair.

The first piece of writing that shows the distinctive style and powers of Orwell, the essay, 'A Hanging', describes one of these. It was written before he took a pseudonym, was published in the *Adelphi* in August 1931, and was signed Eric A. Blair. It has the terror of a Goya coupled with the precise, mundane observation of a Sickert, showing how men can turn even violent death into routine and habit. Even the victim turns aside to avoid splashing his feet in a puddle a few yards from the rope.

It is curious, but till that moment I had never realized what it means to destroy a healthy, conscious man. When I saw the prisoner step aside to avoid the puddle, I saw the mystery, the unspeakable wrongness of cutting a life short when it is in full tide. This man was not dying, he was alive just as we were alive.[17]

When did he witness it? None of the few surviving contemporaries can remember such an incident, but then the very point of his narrative was the ordinariness of the unnatural act. It could have been any one of the 116 hangings in 1923, the 145 in 1924, the 162 in 1925, or the 191 in 1927. No administrative records survive, only aggregate statistics.[18] Did he witness a hanging at all? The old hands feel fairly certain it would not have been part of a young ASP's duties; but he could have watched a hanging if he had asked. The tale does not make clear what the narrator is doing. Orwell told a friend, Mabel Fierz, sometime in the early 1930s, and also told his housekeeper, Susan Watson, in 1946, that 'it was only a story' – this after they had praised it and tried to get him to talk about it. And a year later he said the same to his sister. Yet not only did he write in *The Road to Wigan Pier* that 'I watched a man hanged once; it seemed to me worse than a thousand murders', but he repeated this to readers of *Tribune* in 1944: 'I watched a man hanged once. There was no question that everybody concerned knew this to be a dreadful, unnatural action.'[19] There could have been another hanging which he witnessed *and* 'A Hanging' could be, indeed, a brilliantly artful short story.* His denials could have been simply to stop unwelcome and morbid conversations, for he disliked talking about his work, even his past work.

None of his letters home from Burma survive. He wrote three letters to Jacintha Buddicom but she lost them. All she can remember was that 'The first was a long one, in the strain "you could never understand how awful it is if you hadn't been here" – very disconsolate but unspecific.' He did not explain how and why, and she wrote back suggesting he should leave if it was that awful. He replied that he couldn't leave, then wrote a final letter at greater length 'but it seemed guardedly. I got the impression that perhaps correspondence might be censored.'[20]

His next posting, for the second half of 1924, was to Twante, further east in the Delta. There might have been two or at the most three other Europeans there. He spent most of the time on tour in the villages, inspecting sub-stations, checking with and on village headmen who exercised minor police powers, constantly on the move with a small retinue of housemen, cook, orderly and two or more constables.[21] Even ASPs had powers of summary jurisdiction, so he settled minor problems on the spot, while larger matters called for his decision whether to send them in front of a magistrate. Blair spent long hours listening to bizarre and wholly partisan evidence, sometimes translated, sometimes in the vernacular; always trying to keep things to the point, trying to simplify wildly complex divergent and digressive issues and evidence – in other words, he was sent out to exercise rough and patient justice.

> Take up the White Man's burden –
>   In patience to abide,
> To veil the threat of terror
>   And check the show of pride;
> By open speech and simple,
>   An hundred times made plain,

* 'I watched a man hanged once.' Is this repetition simply coincidental with the metre of Eliot's Sweeney declaiming, 'I left her there in a bath' – a poem he was to praise several times for its attempt to find a popular style, for example, *The Collected Essays, Journalism and Letters*, Vol. II, pp. 198 and 334? There is also an echo of Swift in *A Tale of a Tub*: 'Last week I saw a Woman *flay'd*, and you will hardly believe, how much it altered her Person for the worse.'

> To seek another's profit,
> And work another's gain.

'By open speech and simple': could Kipling's words, or rather the situation they describe – speaking with patient clarity in another language or slowly for translation – have begun to create his characteristic style?

Blair attended the village churches of the Karens. A contemporary thought this odd, for although converts to Christianity by the American Baptist Mission, the Karens conducted their services in their own language. He may have learned Karen, some of his contemporaries think he did. He had a greater interest in and facility with languages compared to his contemporaries in the Police. ('In my life, I have learned seven foreign languages, including two dead ones.'[22])

Twante, like both Myaungmya and his next posting, Syriam, was on the alluvial plain: flat, featureless, with mangrove swamps, paddy fields, mosquito-infested and stinking of oil. It was nothing like the lush jungle vegetation of mid and upper Burma which he described so warmly and excitedly in *Burmese Days*, as if to comprehend that exotic landscape was to understand the Burmese character. It must have been these depressing delta landscapes which he had in mind in *The Road to Wigan Pier*:

I find that anything outrageously strange generally ends by fascinating me even when I abominate it. The landscapes of Burma, which, when I was among them, so appalled me as to assume the qualities of a nightmare, afterwards stayed so hauntingly in my mind that I was obliged to write a novel about them to get rid of them. (In all novels about the East the scenery is the real subject-matter.)[23]

This is an interesting instance of how the writer picks one typical landscape, from a variety of landscapes, to suit the purpose and the mood of what he is writing at the time.

A more senior officer who visited him while in Twante found him 'tall, good-looking, pleasant to talk to, easy of manner'; but 'he did not give the impression of being in any way remarkable'. Another found him 'a shy, diffident young man ... obviously odd man out with other police officers, but longing, I think, to be able to fit in.' He would visit a colleague in a neighbouring post on his motorbike, along roads 'only fit for bullock carts' but his only interest appeared to be in shooting imperial pigeons.[24] The main problem for anyone in these posts arose from isolation and loneliness. While in Mandalay in 1923 Blair be-friended a sad and interesting character, Captain H. R. Robinson, who had been seconded from the Indian Army to the Burma Police, where 'he was axed in 1925,' wrote Orwell much later, 'and settled down ... in Mandalay, where he devoted himself almost exclusively to smoking opium, though he did have a brief interlude as a Buddhist monk and made unsuccessful efforts to float a gold mine and run a car-hiring business.'[25] After blinding himself in an unsuccessful attempt to blow his brains out (in March 1925) this pioneer hippie drop-out lived to write a book about it. Orwell could find no certain explanation in Robinson's account of why 'a young, healthy and apparently happy man' should give himself up to such a debilitating habit, but 'the clue is possibly to be found in the earlier part of the book which describes [his] adventures as a frontier magistrate among little-known tribes in the north-east corner of Burma'. What one finds is an account of total isolation amid constant – not threat precisely, but uncertainty and pres-sure. 'Rather lonely,' said Captain Robinson.[26] Every policeman had this experience to some degree. Alcohol was the socially acceptable anodyne, even if as harmful as opium. Blair, incidentally, could have earned no bonus marks for knowing such a man as Robinson.

Twante was not, in fact, all that far from Rangoon, twelve or so miles, a slow journey down a canal. Plainly Blair had very little time off, but on at least one afternoon he did get into Rangoon, for a curious incident occurred. Maung Htin Aung, who was until recently Vice-Chancellor of the University of Rangoon, recalls:

It was November 1924. I was a freshman at University College, Rangoon, and Blair was serving at a small town across the river from Rangoon. One after-noon, at about 4 p.m., the suburban railway station of Pagoda Road was crowded with schoolboys and undergraduates, and Blair came down the stairs to take the train to the Mission Road station, where the exclusive Gymkhana Club was situated. One of the boys, fooling about with his friends, accidentally bumped against the tall and gaunt Englishman, who fell heavily down the stairs. Blair was furious and raised the heavy cane which he was carrying, to hit the boy on the head, but checked himself, and struck him on the back instead. The boys protested, and some undergraduates, including myself, sur-rounded the angry Englishman. Although undergraduates, we were not much older than the schoolboys, for the age of admission to the university was sixteen. The train drew in and Blair boarded a first-class carriage. But in Burma, unlike India, first-class carriages were never taboo to natives, and some of us had first-class season tickets. The argument between Blair and the undergraduates continued. Fortunately, the train reached Mission Road station without further incident, and Blair left the train. He must often have pondered on the tragic consequences that could have followed had he not controlled himself. Blair was, of course, merely reflecting the general attitude of his English contemporaries towards Burmese students, especially those from the National Schools.[27]

The Vice-Chancellor speculates that Orwell must have based on this the incident in *Burmese Days* when the choleric Ellis lashes out with a stick at jeering boys, blinding one of them and provoking a dangerous riot.

Need one draw quite the same moral from this little incident, however, as Maung Htin Aung, who sees it as proving the propensity of Europeans to lash out with sticks at natives? 'Fooling about', 'accidentally' bumping into the Englishman 'who fell heavily down the stairs'. Which of us, having a stick, would not then – ? And if there was a sadistic streak in Blair, he 'checked himself'. Would a railway station in Rangoon not have had a police constable, or officials who could have been summoned? Para. 357 of *The Burma Police Manual* for 1899 states that 'One policeman is usually posted at smaller railway stations.' It seems very Orwell-like for Blair not to have summoned help and, instead, to have carried on arguing with the students in a railway compartment. Not quite the typical behaviour of the pukka sahib. Certainly he himself later recalled his 'bad conscience' at the remembered faces of 'servants and coolies I had hit with my fist in moments of rage (nearly everyone does these things in the East, at any rate occasionally)'.[28] The parenthetical generalization is more likely to be literally true than the 'I' of George Orwell's narrator. Perhaps he did not hit natives with his fist but certainly he saw a lot of it done and felt it painfully, as if every time he had done it himself.

His third and longest posting, which was to last for nine months, until October 1925, was at Syriam. This was even more awful, for although it had a good number of European residents, it was the site of the Burmah Oil Company's refinery: the fumes and the smell were everywhere and vegetation was poisoned for miles around. His job was dull and routine, that of being responsible for the security of the refinery. Again he had a difficult and probably bullying superior, one who sneered at him for having been to Eton. Old Etonians were rare birds in that corner of Empire. Orwell later commented that in Burma 'the all-important thing was not whether you had been to one of the right schools but whether your skin was technically white. As a matter of fact most of the white men in Burma were not the type who in England would be called "gentlemen"', although they lived like gentlemen, 'had servants, that is, and called their evening meal "dinner"'.[29]

A civilian chemist at the refinery, L. W. Marrison, put up Blair and his superior, De Vine, for a few nights while their *dak* (bungalow) was being repaired. He remembers De Vine introducing Blair as 'a highly educated sort of chap, ha, yes; Blair was eaten and bought up, ha, ha, sorry, brought up at Eton.' Blair took this with the sort of blank expression which indicated that he had heard it all before. Marrison imagined that Blair and De Vine, although obviously incompatible, got on reasonably well, for 'De Vine seemed to me no worse than rather insensitive'. It seems more likely that they did not get on very well. Marrison remembers that five of them sat on the veranda after dinner in their pyjamas, drinking and singing and that he *thinks* the singing was started by Blair (perhaps in self-defence against conversation or by way of satire), who sang 'Zipping Zyder through a straw-haw-haw'. 'One remark of Blair's I do remember distinctly: he deplored the fact that "there weren't any good bawdy songs about nowadays". He did give me the impression that he was a very typical public school boy (I am Grammar School and London University), devoid of snobbery but with a slight pose of nonchalance under all circumstances, deprecating enthusiasm.' 'Pose' or not, Orwell's nonchalance is noted again and again: under fire, in air-raids, in a whirlpool, and expressionless but patiently interested in the wildest of unlikely company. Marrison and Blair had some revolver practice together – 'he wasn't a very good shot' – and Marrison told him that he had been reading Aldous Huxley's *Crome Yellow* and *Leda*, and had been much impressed. 'We discovered,' he wrote home to his parents, 'that we were the only people in Burma who ever read books.' But Blair made no literary judgements that he remembered, nor 'betrayed any desire or determination to write himself', only 'he told me two facts I didn't know – that Huxley had been a master at Eton and that he had been nearly blind'.[30] Even on meeting in such a wilderness a man of literary tastes, Blair was not the kind of person to unburden himself or even to talk intellectually; but courteous enough, mark, to offer two odd and evidently interesting facts.

Much of the company was, indeed, very coarse. An old Burma hand of the Irrawaddy Navigation Company, who knew Mrs Limouzin (Eric's grandmother in Moulmein), recalls that at about that time the Governor's wife had decreed throughout Burma (unofficially but authoritatively) that white officials and residents were to marry their Burman 'keeps' or concubines or cast them out. The habit was widespread, as with Flory and his Ma Hla May in *Burmese Days*. 'But the American oil men at Syriam, a tough and gambling lot,' said my ageing informant (as soon as his sister had left the room), 'when they had heard the news simply sent a telegram unsigned and *en clair* to Government House, saying, "No cunt, no oil".' He remembers Blair only vaguely as standing quietly in the background in bars and messes, 'a tall, thin and rather nervous-looking young man'.[31]

Syriam had two great advantages, however: the work was far less demanding than in Twante and it was located only ten miles by river from Rangoon. Blair could get there easily for an evening, an occasional weekend, even for the afternoon, to visit restaurants, acquaintances and, above all, Smart and Mookerdum's Bookshop, to which each P. & O. liner brought the latest books and even literary periodicals from England. He later told his friend, Richard Rees, the proprietor of the *Adelphi*, that he knew the journal then, but thought it a 'damned rag' and used it for revolver practice in his bungalow garden. Orwell may have been teasing him or claiming the credit of a converted Philistine as well as of an ex-imperialist: for he certainly bought and read it then. He mentioned nothing in his writings of what else he was reading, and Smart and Mookerdum's ledgers of customers' accounts vanished during the Japanese occupation. There is only a later reference to the state of his lifelong love-hate relationship with Kipling. 'I worshipped Kipling at thirteen, loathed him at seventeen, enjoyed him at twenty, despised him at twenty-five, and now again rather admire him.'[32] So he enjoyed him when he was in Burma and despised him when he left; but it seems that he kept on reading him. His friend, Captain Robinson, the opium addict and failed suicide, wrote: 'I found myself repeating [as he squeezed the trigger] some lines of Kipling – "Just roll on yer rifle and blow out yer brains/And go to yer Gawd like a soldier".[33]

Blair too had read Kipling a lot and Kipling could be all things to all men. Obviously Blair had brooded on the antithesis between Kipling the annalist of and apologist for imperialism and the Kipling with almost a Brechtian feeling for the hard lot of the common soldier and his empathy for those who were officially his inferiors or enemies – Gunga Din, even Fuzzy-Wuzzy: 'You're a pore benighted 'eathen but a first-class fightin' man.'

Consider the *Plain Tales from the Hills* and other imaginative stories in the first person, drawn from the author's own experiences. Consider also the Kipling who wanted to be H. G. Wells, writing about modern inventions; from that technocratic Rudyard, Orwell drew much for the many and complex sources of *Nineteen Eighty-Four*. Kipling's story for instance, 'As Easy as A.B.C.' (1912), has: 'The A.B.C., that semi-elected, semi-nominated body of a few score persons controls the planet. "Transportation is civilization" our motto runs. Theoretically we do what we please, so long as we do not interfere with the traffic and all it implies.' A tale which ends with MacDonough's song:

> Whether the state can loose and bind
>   In heaven as well as on earth;
> If it be wiser to kill mankind
>   before or after the birth –
> These are matters of high concern
>   where state-kept schoolmen are;
> But Holy State (we have lived to learn)
>   endeth in Holy War.

> *Once there was The People, Terror gave it birth;*
> *Once there was The People and it made a Hell of Earth ...*

Orwell was to write a very derivative poem about the end of Empire (see p. 170). Kipling's 'With the Nightmail' ('a story of 2,000 A.D.') is also about 'the A.B.C. and a world technological and bureaucratic despotism'. Even among the oeuvres of the Puckish, rural Kipling an early story of the 1890s, 'A Walking Delegate', concerns 'a yellow horse' from the West trying to stir up rebellion among farm animals in Vermont against 'the Oppressor', man, although his ingrate overtures are turned down. The yellow horse is rejected as a work-shy trouble-maker.[34] *Animal Farm* is that world turned upside down.

The imperial, Kiplingesque side of Blair came out that summer in Rangoon when he met Christopher Hollis, who had been two years ahead of him at Eton.[35] Hollis passed through Rangoon on his way home from an Oxford Union debating tour of Australia and New Zealand and heard that Blair was there from a friend who had played squash with him.

We had a long talk and argument. In the side of him which he revealed to me at that time there was no trace of liberal opinions. He was at pains to be the imperial policeman, explaining that these theories of no punishment and no beating were all very well at public schools but that they did not work with the Burmese – in fact that

> 'Libbaty's a kind o' thing
> Thet don't agree with niggers.'

He had an especial hatred ... for the Buddhist priests, against whom he thought violence especially desirable – and that not for any theological reason but because of their sniggering insolence ... If I had never heard or read of Orwell after that evening, I should certainly have dismissed him as an example of that common type which has a phase of liberal opinion at school, when life is as yet untouched by reality and responsibility, but relapses easily after into conventional reaction.[36]

Hollis comments that afterwards he realized, when he had read 'Shooting an Elephant' and *Burmese Days*, that there had been a struggle of two minds going on of which he only saw one that evening. Perhaps, but Blair may have been partly playing a role and partly pulling Hollis' leg, thinking him a glib and priggish liberal, Oxford Union to boot; so that he probably gave him the 'realist' line, half from the divided heart but half from the satiric tongue in cheek. Even at Eton Blair had shown an almost Dr Johnson-like pleasure in pugnaciously defending an improbable position in argument. The squash-playing mutual friend (E. F. Seeley [1901–75]) 'whom Blair insisted on befriending', turned out to be an old Etonian, although Hollis discreetly concealed this from his readers, for he was 'greatly cold-shouldered by Rangoon society for having married an Indian lady'.[37]

Seeley years later told two American scholars that Blair had fre-quented the waterfront brothels.[38] This could be confirmed by a conversation which Harold Acton had with Orwell in Paris in 1945: 'I prompted him to reminisce about his life in Burma, and his sad, earnest eyes lit up with pleasure when he spoke of the sweetness of Burmese women ... He was more enthusiastic about the beauties of Morocco, and this cadaverous ascetic, whom one scarcely connected with fleshly gratification, admitted that he had seldom tasted such bliss as with certain Moroccan girls ...'[39] This evidence is very hard to handle. Blair's confession to the old Etonian in Rangoon may have been braggadocio, a shy young man keeping his end up; but on the other hand, his friend Captain Robinson wrote about visits to brothels, not naming his companions, particularly to the house of a poor Indian schoolteacher who had set up shop with three of her sixth form. Acton's remarks could well be spiced with malice against a rather normal heterosexual and by then married man whose moral seriousness discomforted him. The Moroccan admission, even if actually said, is unlikely – and Orwell knew whom he was talking to and may have been trying to embarrass him. (Even Dr Johnson once debated whether intercourse with a Duchess would give, in principle, more pleasure than with her serving maid.)

When Roger Beadon visited Blair briefly at his next Burma posting, 'as for female company, I don't honestly think I ever saw him with one, he certainly was not like me – I had an eye for anything that was going'.[40] This is hardly conclusive, and Ma Hla May in *Burmese Days* is a convincing character, if lightly drawn. It really would be surprising if he had not known women – either in the brothels or with a concubine or 'keep' in his bungalows, as was so common.

He wrote two poems, either at the time or shortly after he left Burma (for they are both improperly on Burma Government writing paper), which may throw some light on this matter. The first seeks to be profound and the second to be cynical.

THE LESSER EVIL

Empty as death and slow as pain
The days went by on leaden feet;
And parson's week had come again
As I walked down the little street.

Without, the weary doves were calling,
The sun burned on the banks of mud;

Within, old maids were caterwauling
A dismal tale of thorns and blood.

I thought of all the church bells ringing
In towns that Christian folks were in;
I heard the godly maidens singing;
I turned into the house of sin.

The house of sin was dark and mean,
With dying flowers round the doors;
They spat the betel juice between
The rotten bamboo of the floors.

Why did I come, the woman cried
So seldom to her bed of ease?
When I was not, her spirit died
And would I give her ten rupees.

The weeks went by, and many a day
That black-haired woman did implore
Me as I hurried on my way
To come more often than before.

The days went by like dead leaves falling,
And parson's week came round again.
Once more devout old maids were bawling
Their ugly rhymes of death and pain.

The woman waited for me there
As down the little street I trod;
And musing on her oily hair,
I turned into the house of God.

This raises the same problems as his love poems to Jacintha Buddicom.
How literally are they to be taken? Or how purely conventional are
they? The second, if equally wicked, is less guilt-ridden.

ROMANCE

When I was young and had no sense
    In far-off Mandalay
I lost my heart to a Burmese girl
    As lovely as the day.

> Her skin was gold, her hair was jet,
>   Her teeth were ivory;
> I said 'For twenty silver pieces,
>   Maiden, sleep with me.'
>
> She looked at me, so pure, so sad,
>   The loveliest thing alive,
> And in her lisping, virgin voice,
>   Stood out for twenty-five.

The ambiguity of the young man's humorous cynicism is how we must leave it. In any case, first experiences are not always as important in real life as in the conventions of modern autobiography and biography.

> Ship me somewheres east of Suez, where the best is like the worst,
> Where there aren't no Ten Commandments an' a man can raise a thirst;
> For the temple bells are callin', an' it's there I would be –
> By the old Moulmein Pagoda, looking lazy at the sea.

At the end of September 1925 he was posted on to Insein, still close to Rangoon, but now ten miles north, amid lush vegetation – very different from the bleakness of the Delta. There was a sizeable European community there and a club. Blair was Assistant Superintendent at quite a large police headquarters. After the boredom of guarding the oil refinery, he was back on the real job that he now knew well, mostly in headquarters, but quite often touring the outposts. The district had the second biggest prison in Burma, so this could have been the scene for 'A Hanging'. The snag about Insein, however, Beadon recalls, was that the Superintendent had the reputation of being a bully and probably was. Beadon thinks that it is this that may have 'turned Orwell against Government service' – almost certainly, by now, far too narrow a view of his smouldering discontents. This post (where he served for six months) and his next two merge together in the club and town Orwell imagined and reconstructed in *Burmese Days*.

Even those bloody fools at the Club might be better company if we weren't all of us living a lie the whole time [declaims Flory] ... the lie that we're here to uplift our poor black brothers instead of to rob them ... We Anglo-Indians could be almost bearable if we'd only admit that we're thieves and go on thieving without any humbug.[41]

A fellow had to put in an appearance at the club each evening, whether civilian or official; but Blair remained unclubbable and was firmly labelled 'eccentric'. Roger Beadon visited him there – what proved to be their last meeting: 'he had goats, geese, ducks, and all sorts of things floating about downstairs, whereas I kept rather a nice house – it rather shattered me, but apparently he liked that – and that was his sort of idea of ... it didn't worry him what the house looked like.'[42]

'His idea of what?' I later asked Roger Beadon.

'Oh, of living naturally, as some people call it, I suppose I meant to say. Not going native, mind. I don't mean that; more "bohemian". Didn't seem to give a damn. Thought it "practical", I suppose. Seemed a ruddy mess to me.'[43]

Blair remembered things that Beadon would not:

In Burma I have listened to racial theories which were less brutal than Hitler's theories about the Jews, but certainly not less idiotic ... I have often heard it asserted, for instance, that no white man can sit on his heels in the same attitude as an oriental – the attitude, incidentally, in which coal-miners sit when they eat their dinners in the pit.[44]

He describes the character Ellis in *Burmese Days*: 'Any hint of friendly feeling towards an Oriental seemed to him a terrible perversity. He was an intelligent man and an able servant of his firm, but he was one of those Englishmen – common, unfortunately – who should never be allowed to set foot in the East.' And he has Ellis ranting:

Sitting down at table with him as though he was a white man, and drinking out of glasses his filthy black lips have slobbered over – it makes me spew to think of it ... Here we are, supposed to be governing a set of damn black swine who've been slaves since the beginning of history, and instead of riding them in the only way they understand, we go and treat them as equals. And all you silly b—s take it for granted. There's Flory, makes his best pal of a black babu who calls himself a doctor because he's done two years at an Indian so-called university. And you, Westfield, proud as Punch of your knock-kneed, bribe-taking cowards of policemen ...[45]

The last remark implies that the Burma Police were seen by some of the civilians as not being tough enough. Certainly Blair would have been torn almost daily between his sense of justice and his knowledge of European opinion; and then there was the growing element, very clear in *Burmese Days*, of exasperation at crooked Burmese, particularly when educated officials let their own side down in front of his unpleasant countrymen. When, years later, he reviewed Maurice Collis' almost classic *Trials in Burma*, he said that: 'it brings out with unusual clearness the dilemma that faces every official in an empire like our own ... in theory he is administering an impartial system of justice; in practice he is part of a huge machine that exists to protect British interests, and he has often got to choose between sacrificing his integrity and damaging his career.'[46] We do not know whether there were such specific incidents that occurred during Blair's duties, or whether all his duties began to take on this colour in a systematic way. Whether or not he had close Indian or Burmese friends, like Flory's Dr Veraswami in the novel, who were forbidden the club, we simply do not know.

At that time, the Governor had ordered all the ordinary clubs to open their doors to some, at least, senior native officials, but there must have been foot-dragging in the outposts and even ostracism in the Mandalay, Rangoon and Moulmein clubs. A famous incident arose from all this, which may have suggested the very different one in *Burmese Days*. The Gymkhana Club at Rangoon stood outside such edicts. They fielded a Rugby team. There was only one snag: they had only one opponent, the garrison in Rangoon. And in 1924 even the garrison could not find fifteen good men and true, fit and white. So they fielded U Tin Tut (the brother of Maung Htin Aung who had had the scuffle with Blair at the railway station). He was a civil servant who had been commissioned in the Army during the Great War and was a member of the English Bar. More to the point, he had played Rugby for Dulwich College and Cambridge University. He was the best player present. But after the game, he was refused the use of the showers and told that only Europeans could use the club house. This caused a greater stir among Burmese officials and journalists than many a casual act of discrimination towards their poorer fellow country-men.[47]

In April 1926, Blair moved to Moulmein. This was the third largest town in Burma, an important port and trading centre with a large European and Eurasian community. He was ASP at Police Head-quarters, No. 2 again. There must have been some congenial company, but by that time his dislike of the Service was hardening into hatred.

He felt himself ground between the hatred of his fellow-English and Burmese hatred of him. He begins his famous essay, 'Shooting an Elephant':

In Moulmein in Lower Burma, I was hated by large numbers of people – the only time in my life that I have been important enough for this to happen to me. I was sub-divisional police officer of the town, and in an aimless, petty kind of way anti-European feeling was very bitter. No one had the guts to raise a riot, but if a European woman went through the bazaars alone somebody would probably spit betel juice over her dress. As a police officer I was an obvious target and was baited whenever it seemed safe to do so. When a nimble Burman tripped me up on the football field and the referee (another Burman) looked the other way, the crowd yelled with hideous laughter. This happened more than once. In the end the sneering yellow faces of young men that met me everywhere, the insults hooted after me when I was at a safe distance, got badly on my nerves. The young Buddhist priests were the worst of all. There were several thousands of them in the town and none of them seemed to have anything to do except stand on street corners and jeer at Europeans.[48]

It was indeed a case of:

> Take up the White Man's burden –
> And reap his old reward:
> The blame of those ye better,
> The hate of those ye guard.

The story tells how against his better judgement he shot an elephant that had killed a man but was a perfectly quiet, docile and recoverable investment by the time he came on the scene. He shot it because the huge crowd expected him to and he had 'to impress' the natives: 'seemingly the leading actor of the piece; but in reality I was only an absurd puppet pushed to and fro by the will of those yellow faces behind me. I perceived in this moment that when the white man turns tyrant it is his own freedom that he destroys.' That is a profound moral epigram, and whether 'this moment' was 1925 or 1936 hardly matters. Even if it was 1925, the same story gives a second motive for shooting the poor brute beast: 'to avoid looking a fool'. He had the thought in his mind that if something went wrong and the elephant turned on him, trampled him to death, some of them would laugh and 'that would never do'. Once leaders are laughed at, their authority is gone. He was protecting not just his own skin but the whole mystique of white domination.*

The hatred must have got harder and harder to endure, even if it only took the physical form of tripping and spitting – particularly if he liked playing football and talking to Buddhist priests. 'When I went round Moulmein in 1935 after reading *Burmese Days*,' recalls Maung Htin Aung, 'I found that only a handful of people could recollect anything about him, and they remembered him merely as a sporting and skilful centre-forward who scored many goals for the Moulmein police team.'[49] There is something disparaging in this, something a trifle suspect in his anecdotes, for he was upset that *Burmese Days* appeared to score off his fellow-countrymen. He does not seem to have recognized that in *Burmese Days* Orwell showed the British putting the ball into their own net. Orwell's way of overcoming prejudice and championing the Burmese was not to idealize them but to say, like Mark Twain, 'God damn the Jews, they are as bad as the rest of us!'

His grandmother, Mrs Limouzin, was living in Moulmein as well as an aunt who was married to a high official in the Forestry Service. He must have visited them before, but he never mentioned them in any of his later references to Burma; nor did he admit their existence when he talked to friends about Burma in later years. Indeed none of his later references to Burma are autobiographical: they are all in a polemical context, a context in which personal safe-havens or family obligations are not relevant. But it is odd that none of his subsequent friends, to some of whom he did talk about Burma, remember him mentioning the Limouzins. He only once referred to his grandmother

---

* Whether he actually shot an elephant or not does not seem quite so important as whether he saw a hanging, or was flogged for bed-wetting. One old Burma hand, R. C. Chorley, with whom he went pigeon-shooting in Twante, thinks he remembers reading in the *Rangoon Gazette* that Blair had been called in to shoot a rogue elephant; but he also thinks that he may have read 'Shooting an Elephant'. The files of that paper have been searched but are incomplete, so this cannot be verified. It is worth recalling that the essay or story proudly headed *Penguin New Writing* in 1940, edited by John Lehmann, who had first published it in 1936 when it was written. Twelve of the fourteen 1940 contributors wrote in a similar, ambiguous, first-person descriptive vein, a then fashionable genre which blurred any clear line between fiction and autobiography – truthful to experiences but not necessarily to fact. It even included Isherwood's 'A Berlin Diary', with its famous, influential and absurd 'I am a camera with its shutter open, quite passive, recording, not thinking.'

in correspondence, and then derogatorily. He did make it appear, on several occasions in his life, as if he was more isolated than was in fact the case. Also he had a habit of keeping different groups of friends very much apart. Often in later years people were astonished to discover who else he knew. Perhaps he learned this habit in Burma: the Roger Beadons, the Captain Robinsons, and the old Etonians with Indian wives would hardly mix either with each other or with his grandmother. Also the habit of the observer, apparent even in school-days, was growing stronger: he could observe people better in their own habitat by not mixing them. It might have spoiled the effect of his own literary first-person character if the reader knew that there was, for instance, a grandmother in Moulmein, or a favourite aunt in Paris, or that the employers at the Hampstead bookshop were close friends of that same aunt, Nellie.

In Burma Blair was isolated, lonely and desperate – to a deliberate degree; and this also became his later literary trade-mark and was perhaps also his self-image at the time. If he was still telling stories to himself, but had for the moment given up young dreams of being a writer, he may yet have been thinking what he would have written if he were 'a writer' rather than a duty-ridden policeman.

The Limouzin family had been in Moulmein in the teak and timber business since the earliest days of the colony. Moulmein had been ceded to the British as early as 1826. Eric's grandmother was English, though her husband was French. She had been educated in France, though born in Burma, and had grown up bilingual – even if she spoke, to Eric's disgust, not a word of Burman. The family had once been very wealthy, but had lost money in rice speculation. By Eric's time in Burma they were comfortable, well-off, not rich but affluent enough to entertain a lot: 'At Homes' for tea twice a week, dances and tennis parties. Mrs Limouzin was a leading figure in the British community, an intelligent, talkative, slightly eccentric lady, given to wearing the colourful and loose-fitting Burmese robes. She is well-remembered by those she entertained as having a zest for mixing slightly unlikely types: ranks, orders and ages, officers, officials and civilians – a few Indians and Burmese even. But no one can be found or survives who knew her well. Several people remember being introduced to her grandson, but hard as they try, cannot honestly remember much about him; only a shy, tall young man, very much in the background, not fully at ease.

One officer, seven years older than Blair, remembers meeting him with two ladies at a sports meeting, and the elder (almost certainly Mrs Limouzin) asking his advice about Eric, as if it was common knowledge that he was unhappy in the Service.[50] He remembers simply replying that he should get out while he was still young enough to take up another profession. There may have been more to it than that. A distant cousin of Blair's said that her aunts, whose families had all served in the East, used to keep in touch with family news in the old days. 'Reports came back about Eric's odd behaviour, but I cannot remember any details, but it all upset the various relations.'[51] 'Odd behaviour' implies more than solitariness, but it may have been no more than refusing to take up invitations, snubbing 'useful people' to whom his grandmother would obviously introduce him, in the way most careers were advanced. The urge to fail may have been growing, but there is no reason to see it at that time as any more specific than unhappiness with the Burma policeman's lot. Success or promotion might have made inner withdrawal or actual resignation more difficult.

Knowing how close to life were not only characters but also names in Orwell's first novels – to the terror of his publishers and their lawyers, particularly over *Burmese Days* – 'Mrs Lackersteen' of the novel (the snobbish Elizabeth's mother) and Mrs Limouzin of life are too close to be coincidence. Mrs Lackersteen has tried, pathetically and unsuccessfully, to lead an artistic (or arty) life in Paris. She dies and her daughter is taken in by her brother and her sister-in-law, also called Mrs Lackersteen, who as proper Memsahib devotes herself to marrying off her sister's child. Eric may well have seen an unresolved ambivalence between the bohemian and the conventional in his own mother; and it might have been even more apparent in his grandmother. If there is anything of Mrs Limouzin in the two Mrs Lackersteens, he plainly did not like her, seeing her as domineering and pretentious. ('Superficial' is perhaps another adjective that might be applied, for 'lacquer-sheen' is a Joycean type of pun; and we know that he had read *Ulysses* before writing his first two published novels.) 'My grandmother lived forty years in Burma and at the end could not speak a word of Burmese – typical of the ordinary Englishwoman's attitude,' he told a correspondent twenty years later, and linked this to the 'disgusting social behaviour of the British'.[52]

'How comforting to think Eric is near Mother,' or 'At least that sensible sister of yours can keep an eye on him,' his parents may have said. But young Eric may not have seen it quite that way.

His last post was at Katha which he reached two days before Christmas 1926. It was in Upper Burma, luxuriant jungle, open hills and river meadows, exotic with flowers and vegetation, and a dry, not too hot, atmosphere – very different from the steamy Delta. Katha was undoubtedly the landscape of *Burmese Days*, although the characters had been picked up all along the road from Mandalay and the heat had been intensified. His work was much as before, but by now it seems that he had had enough. Blair had come morally to reject the system of alien rule, not merely to say, as Balfour murmured, 'Better self-government than good government', but to see the corrupting effect on his fellow Englishmen of exercising autocratic government, with racial prejudice redoubling old class prejudice.

There is no knowing when this incident occurred or even if it definitely did occur, as he relates it in *The Road to Wigan Pier*:

I remember a night I spent on the train with a man in the Educational Service, a stranger to myself whose name I never discovered. It was too hot to sleep and we spent the night in talking. Half an hour's cautious questioning decided each of us that the other was 'safe', and then for hours, while the train jolted slowly through the pitch-black night, sitting up in our bunks with bottles of beer handy, we damned the British Empire – damned it from the inside, intelligently and intimately. It did us both good. But we had been speaking forbidden things, and in the haggard morning light when the train crawled into Mandalay, we parted as guiltily as any adulterous couple.[53]

His specific feeling of a breaking point must have come like Flory's in the novel:

Flory pushed back his chair and stood up. It must not, it could not – no, it simply should not go on any longer! He must get out of this room quickly, before something happened inside his head and he began to smash the furniture and throw bottles at the pictures. Dull, boozing witless porkers! Was it possible that they could go on week after week, year after year, repeating word for word the same evil-minded drivel, like a parody of a fifth-rate story in *Blackwood's*? Would none of them *ever* think of anything new to say? Oh, what a place, what people! What a civilization is this of ours – this godless civilization founded on whisky, *Blackwood's* and the 'Bonzo' pictures! God have mercy on us, for all of us are part of it.[54]

Flory, of course, did stand it longer – until his suicide. Blair went home on leave that summer probably still uncertain whether to resign or stick it out, but leaning, amid turbulent wave and counter-wave of feeling, towards resignation. Even to resign could have induced guilt feelings. He had a strong sense of duty. A man with a protestant conscience in that sort of situation fears that his replacement will be worse for the natives than he. Besides, what alternative career did he have?

He rejected the system so much that he imagined with lurid relish its total collapse. This awful poem was composed either just before he left or just after, for it is again, fittingly, written on Burma Government paper.

> When the Franks have lost their sway
> And the soldiers are slain or fled,
> When the ravisher has his way
> And the slayer's sword is red;
> When the last lone Englishman dies
> In the painted Hindu towers,
> Beneath ten thousand burning eyes
> In a rain of bloody flowers, again
> Moving more westward to the lands we know
> When the people have won their dreams,
> And the tyrant's flag is down,
> When the blood is running in streams
> Through the gutters of London town:
> When the air is burst with the thunder
> And crash of the falling thrones,
> And the crack of the empires torn asunder ...
> Is it not dreadful for us to contemplate
> These mighty ills that will beset the world
> When we are dead and won't be bothered with them?
> Do not these future woes transcend our own?
>
> Dear Friend: allow me for a little while
> To speak without those high and starry lies ...
> Not all the screams of twenty thousand victims
> Broken on the wheel or plunged in boiling oil
> Could pain me like one tooth in my own head;
> And secondly, I do not care what comes
> When I am gone, though kings or peoples rot ...
> I care not if ten myriad blazing stars

Rain on the earth and burn it dead as stone;
    I care not if God dies.
And all because
    Frankly, and look at it which way you will,
This life, this earth, this time will see me out,
    And that is about all I care about.

The distance between the apocalyptic first part and the second, young man as cynical writer (Somerset Maugham?) part, is both extraordinary and incongruous. But part of the genius of Orwell was to be this ability to be both a European Jeremiah, a stern and condemnatory prophet, and an English Montaigne, a humorous and humanist annalist of local oddities.

When he recalled in 'Why I Write' that his childhood habit of making up a 'continuous "story" about myself, a sort of diary existing only in the mind' continued 'till I was about twenty-five, right through my non-literary years',[55] he was obviously counting Burma as part of that 'non-literary' period, despite the two highly unpublishable poems.

Having served for five years, he would be due for leave that November. He applied to go earlier on medical grounds, though what they were was not stated. So he was given leave for five months and twenty days out of India from 12 July 1927. 'He resigned ... chiefly because,' said the dust-jacket of the American edition of *Burmese Days*, 'he disliked putting people in prison for doing the same things which he should have done in the circumstances.'[56] This precise sentence must surely have come from Orwell himself. Notice 'should' instead of an expected 'would': thoughts of rebellion, but no acts of rebellion. 'I gave it up,' he was to write in an author's guide, 'partly because the climate had ruined my health, partly because I already had vague ideas of writing books, but mainly because I could not go on any longer serving an imperialism which I had come to regard as very largely a racket.'[57]

Did Burma ruin his health? There is no knowing. On the one hand, there is his football at Moulmein, and centre-forward at that; and on the other, his unspecified sick leave. His one good posting to Katha could have been for its mild, dry climate. When he went into a sanatorium in Kent in 1938 for several months, he wrote to Cyril Connolly, 'There isn't really anything very wrong, evidently an old TB lesion which has partly healed itself and which I must have had ten years or more.'[58] Unless he is referring to 1929, when he was in hospital in Paris, a haemorrhage *could* have occurred while he was in Burma. He was not well on his return, but nobody thought that his health was 'ruined', and a contemporary photograph still shows a somewhat full face, no longer 'chubby', but markedly different from the narrowed, lean face of the mid-1930s onwards. Something may have happened, but 'the climate ruined my health' could be exaggeration, symbolic of what imperialism does to you, or a measure of his hatred of it as 'a racket'. In *The Road to Wigan Pier* he had a bit more to say about this aspect of his resignation – which, even allowing for hindsight, surely gives a fair picture of how he must have felt on the voyage back home:

I had reduced everything to the simple theory that the oppressed are always right and the oppressors are always wrong: a mistaken theory, but the natural result of being one of the oppressors yourself. I felt that I had got to escape not merely from imperialism but from every form of man's dominion over man. I wanted to submerge myself, to get right down among the oppressed, to be one of them and on their side against the tyrants.[59]

During his leave in England, Blair resigned, and there is a flurry of correspondence in an India Office Services & General Department file because he gave no reason, even though his request to resign was supported by 'the local office' of the Government of India. The Department saw no reason to refuse his request, nothing discreditable was known about him, he was not leaving the Service in order to avoid prosecution in Burma. But on 17 March 1928, a Mr P. H. Dumbell signed a Minute on behalf of the Secretary of State saying that, arising from the Blair case, reasons, when known, should be stated in future cases.[60] The file was closed (only to be reopened briefly for a security vetting in 1938).

Let Blair have the last word on why he resigned. In 1929 a small, French radical journal, *Le Progrès civique*, asked 'our contributor, E. A. Blair, whose inquiries into "the miseries of the British worker" our readers have already been able to appreciate' to say something on the causes of the troubles in recent years in the British Indo-Chinese territories. His article, although flat and descriptive, and translated back from a French translation, is none the less worth quoting from at some length – as his contemporary view of his Burmese experience, or as close to it as we have, without the artistic shaping of his later development.

(4 May 1929)

... The government of all the subject Indian provinces is necessarily despotic because only by a certain amount of sabre-rattling can the British Empire hope to hold on to a population of many millions of subjects. But such despotism is hidden. It clothes itself in a mask of democracy. The first motto of the English, when called upon to govern an oriental people, is, 'Never let a European do what an Oriental is able to do' ... In this way peace is maintained with the certain co-operation of the educated, or semi-educated, classes, from whom there might have been the risk of revolutionary leaders emerging. One does not have to live in Burma for long to see that Britain is complete master of the country. The Burmese, like some of the Indian provinces, have a parliament – always the show of democracy – but this parliament in reality does not hold any power ... At the same time, while showing that the British government rules the Burmese in a despotic fashion, it should be borne in mind that it does not mean they are unpopular. The English have constructed roads and canals – in their own interests, sure enough, but the Burmese have profited from them – they have built hospitals, opened schools, and maintained national order and security.

It should be remembered that the Burmese are simple peasants, busy working on their land. They have not yet reached the intellectual level necessary for nationalistic activity. Their village is their world, and inasmuch as they are left to till their fields, they don't care too much whether their rulers are black or white ...

Now, as in the rest of the Orient, contact with Europeans is creating the need, not known before, for manufactured goods. The English have stolen from the Burmese in two ways:

Firstly, they have taken the natural resources. Second, they have taken upon themselves the exclusive right to sell them manufactured goods which they are not able to make themselves. And the Burmese are also, little by little, being taken into an era of industrial capitalism without ever being able to become capitalists themselves ...

To sum up, if the English have rendered any service to Burma, it has had to pay for it very dear. Up until now, they have not too much inflamed the Burmese, because they do not yet feel the need. They are still at the beginning of a period of transition when they are changing from peasants to industrial workers ...

They ... find themselves placed under the protection of a despotism which offers them protection, but which would abandon them instantly should the need arise. Their relation to the British Empire is that of slave to master. Is the master good or bad? That is not the point: enough to state that his authority is despotic and, let us say the word, self-interested.[61]

So at the end of his Burmese days a specific hatred of imperialism is clear which he soon turned into a general critique of autocracy of any kind. His solitary condition in Burma strengthened what was already there from schooldays, solitary but highly individualistic characteristics and strong psychological distrust of authority of any kind. The passages from *Le Progrès civique* show that he was familiar with socialist ideas and used them. This may appear to contradict what he said immediately after 'the simple theory that the oppressed are always right' passage in *The Road to Wigan Pier*: 'On the other hand I had at that time no interest in Socialism or any other economic theory.' He exaggerates. He was familiar with socialist ideas and interested in them, but this does not mean he had as yet espoused them. He used them for political effect but his own standpoint was still individualistic. To read the *Le Progrès civique* article and *Burmese Days* carefully, without hindsight, is to find simply and splendidly an individualist protest against alien rule and autocracy. The protest is compatible with libertarian socialism, with Millite liberalism or even with Tory anti-imperialism (of the 'little Englander' persuasion) – or with no developed political position at all. In those far-off days plenty of Tories still disliked exploitative capitalism.

Rayner Heppenstall remembers that when Eric Blair first presented himself to the *Adelphi* offices in 1930, he 'described himself as a Tory anarchist, but admitted the *Adelphi*'s socialist case on moral grounds'.[62] Orwell was to use the same phrase of Swift ('a Tory anarchist like Swift'), and Richard Rees, who knew Orwell well and helped him much in the 1930s, was to use the phrase directly of Orwell himself. This does not argue that politically he was Tory, only that the Burma experience as such did not turn him socialist; and that there was in Blair a tolerant respect for indigenous cultures, coupled with a cynicism about the (largely liberal) civilizing mission, which was typical of that rare but interesting bird, the Tory anti-imperialist: 'live and let live', or 'if govern we must don't rationalize it by interfering with their culture'.[63]

Of the voyage home nothing is known, except that he got off the P & O liner at Marseilles and returned to London via Paris, as was quite common. Almost certainly he visited Aunt Nellie, the one aunt, intellectual and bohemian, he had always liked. She was living in Paris with a prominent Esperantist. We know Blair was in Marseilles a few days before 23 August 1927 because:

A few days before Sacco and Vanzetti [the Boston anarchists] were executed I was standing on the steps of one of the English banks in Marseilles, talking to the clerks, while an immense procession of working people streamed past, bearing banners inscribed, '*Sauvons Sacco et Vanzetti!*' etc. It was the kind of thing one might have seen in England in the eighteen forties, but surely never in the nineteen twenties. All these people – tens of thousands of them – were genuinely indignant over a piece of injustice, and thought it quite natural to lose a day's wages in order to say so. It was instructive to hear the clerks (English) saying 'Oh, well, you've got to hang these blasted anarchists', and to see their half-shocked surprise when one asked whether Sacco and Vanzetti were guilty of the crime for which they had been condemned.[64]

A symbolic return to Europe indeed. The Sacco and Vanzetti case raised just the same issues as had many a humble trial in Burma.

CHAPTER SIX

GOING NATIVE

IN LONDON AND PARIS

(1928–31)

WRITING for an American reference book during the Second World War, Orwell summed up his life in the next few years thus: 'When I came back to Europe I lived for about a year and a half in Paris, writing novels and short stories which no one would publish. After my money came to an end I had several years of fairly severe poverty during which I was, among other things, a dishwasher, a private tutor and a teacher in cheap private schools.'¹ He told Ukrainians in a Preface to *Animal Farm* slightly more than he saw fit to remind Americans: 'I sometimes lived for months on end amongst the poor and half criminal elements who inhabit the worst parts of the poorer quarters, or take to the streets, begging and stealing. At that time I associated with them through lack of money, but later their way of life interested me very much for its own sake.'²

To begin with, though, he had to tell his father and mother not only that he was resigning from the Service, which to them, if catastrophic, was at least understandable, but also that he was determined to become a writer. Just how one earned a living from that was by no means clear, nor could any evidence be seen of any ability in that direction. They only noticed that he had left for Burma a boy but come back a man: more mature in every way, with a moustache and with darker hair. He talked warmly of the landscape and the jungle, but let it be known that he disliked the people in Burma. He appeared untidy, smoked and dropped cigarette ash all over the place, as if he was still amid servants and bamboo floors. His sister Avril remembers her mother being 'rather horrified in a way', which is Blair understatement. After all, her own family had been in Burma for three generations. Eric was their only son and a lot of hopes had been put into his career. There is little doubt that his father, easygoing as he appeared, must have been as angry as he was astounded. Had he not spent his whole life doing what had to be done, even joining the Army at 60? Now this son of his says he does not *like* it, and wants to *write*. Eric later complained to a friend that his father neither understood nor appreciated him; but his friend thinks that he was none the less anxious, for the rest of his father's life, to impress and please him in every respect except that of giving up his ambition 'to be a writer'.[3]

Eric followed his family down to Polperro in Cornwall only a few days after his return from Burma. Some of the tension may have been eased in a holiday atmosphere, perhaps by the presence of other relatives; and perhaps even by illness. His sister Marjorie's daughter Jane was with them, then aged 6. She has a distinct and vivid memory of her uncle Eric in bed, seeming to be very ill and being nursed by her grandmother. Whatever happened, he soon recovered and there was no lasting dispute between Eric and his parents. In spite of professing dislike for Southwold, his parents' house there became his main base camp for the next few years.

There was little emotional warmth between any of the Blairs, but the loyalties were great. At least, he assured his parents, he would be no charge on them. He would have had five months' salary as well as some savings, having largely steered clear of the clubs in Burma; and he meant to live cheaply until his first writings were published. Before he embarked on his new career, Blair went up to Cambridge to ask advice (somewhat surprisingly, for he had never written to him all the long years in Burma) from his old tutor, Andrew Gow, now a Fellow of Trinity College. Gow remembered little about the visit, except that Blair came to tell him that he had resigned from the Burma Police, was thinking of pursuing a literary career, but wanted to take advice first. 'I seem to remember,' Gow said, 'that as he seemed fairly determined and had nothing else in mind, I said in a rather noncommittal way that he might as well have a try.' He stayed the night in College and Gow remembers that he sat him next to A. E. Housman at High Table, who asked him about Burma.[4] It is hard to interpret this incident, except to say that Blair must have felt respect or affection for Gow. He can hardly have hoped, however, for a deep colloquy about what to do with one's life, that was out of character for both men. He may have sought reassurance to bolster up his father, some slight support, or at least not a complete condemnation of the idea of 'writing'. The meeting does show that he did not reject Eton utterly and in principle. There are also vague memories from two of his Election that he attended a small reunion dinner that autumn, said next to nothing, conveyed that he did not care much for Burma, but gave no hint of resignation from the Service. He never seems to have attended any other Eton function, nor sought Gow's advice again.

There was another backward glance. A fortnight was spent in Shropshire, visiting Ticklerton as a guest of Aunt Lilian at the same time as Prosper Buddicom. 'Completely unavoidable circumstances prevented me from joining the party,' wrote Jacintha.[5] Their break had probably already taken place. 'You were such a tender-hearted girl, always full of pity for the creatures we others shot and killed,' he wrote from hospital in 1949. 'But you were not so tender-hearted to me when you abandoned me to Burma with all hope denied.'[6] The tone is part teasing, as of calf-love recalled; but Jacintha did not join the party in Shropshire, and neither of them made any attempt to look each other up until, in 1949, she belatedly realized who 'George Orwell' was. They never saw each other again after 1922. In any case, Eric's visit to Shropshire suggests that he had been as much of a friend to Prosper as to Jacintha.

The problem arose of where he was to live while he wrote. He sent a letter, quite out of the blue, to Ruth Pitter, a family acquaintance whom he had met only once. She and her friend Kathleen O'Hara had lived in Mall Chambers, Notting Hill after the War and had got to know Ida and Marjorie Blair then; but now they were living in the Portobello Road.

To my surprise, I had a letter from him at this time, asking if I remembered him. He wanted us to find him a cheap lodging. We found a bedroom in a poor street, next door to a house our employers used as an arts and crafts workshop. I have a clear picture in my mind of Orwell lugging some heavy suitcases into our workshop house; no doubt to sort out the contents more easily than he could have done in the cramped bedroom next door. He was now a very tall man; he had the same rather formidable, perhaps defensive, look; and the very wide *terai* hat he was still wearing made him look still more imposing. He was far from well, even then. I don't think the tropics suited him, but I think he was also sick with rage. He was convinced that we had no business to be in Burma, no right to dominate other nations. He would have ended the British Raj then and there.

That winter was very *cold*. Orwell had very little money indeed. I think he must have suffered in that unheated room, after the climate of Burma, though we did, rather belatedly, lend him an oil-stove. He said afterwards that he used to light a candle to try and warm his hands when they were too numbed to write. Oh yes, he was already writing. *Trying* to write, that is – it didn't come easily. At this time I don't think any of his friends believed he would ever write well. Indeed, I think he was unusually inept. We tried not to be discouraging, but we used to laugh till we cried at some of the bits he showed us. You must remember that we were hard-working women, older than he. To us, at that time, he was a wrong-headed young man who had thrown away a good career, and was vain enough to think he could be an author. But the formidable look was not there for nothing. He had the gift, he had the courage, he had the persistence to go on in spite of failure, sickness, poverty, and opposition, until he became an acknowledged master of English prose.[7]

What is remarkable is that having determined to become a writer, Eric Blair did not just begin to lead the life of a 'writer': he actually sat down and started to write. Here was the first sign of great tenacity in his character – unless his sticking it out in Burma so long or refusing to succeed at Eton were earlier instances. But as for the writing itself, Ruth Pitter remembers:

He wrote so badly. He had to teach himself writing. He was like a cow with a musket. A cow with a musket. He became a master of English, but it was sheer hard grind. He used to put in a fair number of rude words in those days and we had to correct the spelling. I would have thought an Old Etonian knew every word there was and a few more. He certainly couldn't spell the London rude words.

We lent him an old oil-stove and he wrote a story about two young girls who lent an old man an oil stove ... I remember one story that never saw the light of day ... it began 'Inside the park, the crocuses were out ...' Oh dear, I'm afraid we did laugh, but we knew he was kind, because he was so good to our old sick cat. We used to ask him for a meal now and then. I've often thought lately, God forgive us, why didn't we ask him oftener.[8]

Only one fragment clearly of this period survives, written on his dwindling stock of Burma Government paper. It is a scenario and a few trial pages of dialogue for a play.

Scene I A mean and poverty-stricken room which is painted on a curtain half-way down the stage. In the middle is a small bed with a pale child lying on it flat on its back and apparently asleep. There is a low table beside the bed on which are half a loaf of bread, a medicine bottle and a ragged picture paper. To the right of the stage is a double bed with ragged sheets ... Facing up to the table is a dilapidated armchair in which FRANCIS STONE sits opening letters. His wife, LUCY STONE, leans over the head of the bed. STONE announces that the letters are all bills, amounting to nearly £40, while all the money he has is 7s.4d ...

STONE is a man of about 33, good looking, but with a weak and rather cynical expression. His voice is dreary. He is obviously much his wife's intellectual superior, and this makes for misunderstandings between them ... The clothes of both are good but battered. Their shoes are very old.

Baby will die if they don't get money for 'a very expensive operation', but Francis will be damned before he'll write advertising copy for 'Pereira's Surefire Lung Balm' (premonitions of *Keep the Aspidistra Flying*) because the firm are swindling crooks, the substance is noxious, and, besides, he's got his artistic integrity to consider. When his wife reminds him of Baby's needs, he suggests that for her to prostitute herself would be no worse than the job she wants him to take. Then the scenario turns abruptly from naturalism to expressionism (premonitions of *A Clergyman's Daughter*). 'Everything goes dark, there is a sound like the roaring of waters. What actually happens is that the furniture is removed'; and we are in a timeless prison cell, in something like the French Revolution, with POET, POET'S WIFE and CHRISTIAN who 'sits ... reading a large book. He has a placard inscribed DEAF round his neck.'[9] It is only a fragment. The laughter of the girls, if they read that, is understandable. (Only one more play was ever attempted, indeed completed and performed, and that was for a very special occasion.) There is, however, only one way to begin to write and that is to begin to write. But to write about what?

He had the 'courage and the persistence', says Ruth Pitter; and she meant both in sticking to his writing and in seeking out and physically involving himself in a new subject-matter. The relationship between his writing and his concern with poverty and degradation is complicated. Let us consider carefully what he himself said about this period in *The Road to Wigan Pier* (with all the warnings, once again, that he was writing in 1936 and for 1936):

I was conscious of an immense weight of guilt that I had got to expiate. I suppose that sounds exaggerated; but if you do for five years a job that you thoroughly disapprove of, you will probably feel the same ... I felt that I had got to escape not merely from imperialism but from every form of man's dominion over man. I wanted to submerge myself, to get right down among the oppressed; to be one of them and on their side against their tyrants. And, chiefly because I had had to think everything out in solitude, I had carried my hatred of oppression to extraordinary lengths. At that time failure seemed to me to be the only virtue. Every suspicion of self-advancement, even to 'succeed' in life to the extent of making a few hundreds a year, seemed to me spiritually ugly, a species of bullying.[10]

The 'guilt' is real enough but there is no reason, no clear evidence from his childhood indeed, to warrant a wholly psychological rather than a political and social interpretation; for it *is* bad to oppress other men and arbitrary power and privileges *do* corrupt; and to write about the condition of the poor and oppressed it *is* sensible to share it, even if only for a time, not simply to observe it. He could reinterpret and reinforce what he had seen and experienced in his early schooldays in the light of what he had seen in Burma, but that was still not enough. He had to share a sense of failure, not just opt out. His suspicion of success and his cult of failure contained, however, some common-sensical reservations. He did want to succeed as a writer, to prove himself a success to his family, to his father particularly (his younger sister was convinced); and money was important, even just to keep alive. He had no other support and was too proud to be dependent on his family (though not too alienated to stay with them quite often); and knowing their sole dependence on his father's pension, he probably wanted to make some contribution to the expenses of the home, which he was never able to do. Success 'as a writer' did not for a long time appear to lie in concentrating on political and social themes. Yet Richard Rees, who knew him well in the 1930s and published most of his early essays, reviews and poems in the *Adelphi*, had 'Fugitive From the Camp of Victory' as the sub-title of his book, *George Orwell*. He obviously saw much of Orwell in Gordon Comstock and 'the cult of failure': that any kind of success in capitalist civilization means selling out *both* on others and on oneself (though Gordon mainly feared selling out on himself and Orwell mainly feared selling out on others). Orwell certainly held these views for a while, but backdates them, only coming to hold them after continued failure to get major works published. His hatred of oppression did not necessarily mean joining the oppressed, only finding out more about them. But in order to find out one has to be with them.

The word 'unemployment' was on everyone's lips. That was more or less new to me, after Burma, but the drivel which the middle classes were still talking ('These unemployed are all unemployables', etc, etc) failed to deceive me. I wonder whether that kind of stuff deceives even the fools who utter it. On the other hand I had at that time no interest in Socialism or any other economic theory. It seemed to me then – it sometimes seems to me now, for that matter – that economic injustice will stop the moment we want it to stop, and no sooner, and if we genuinely want it to stop the method adopted hardly matters.[11]

Again, there is a little bit of retouching here. As the *Progrès civique* article (already quoted on p. 173 above) on Burma shows, he may not have been a socialist, but it was untrue that 'I had at that time no *interest* in Socialism or any other economic theory' (my italics). He was claiming credit in 1936, Salvation Army style, for the dramatic virtues of a recent convert from sin, rather than for a commitment that, in fact, followed a long period both of rational consideration and of inward fear that 'to go political' would destroy, rather than in his odd case enhance, his artistic ambitions.

He himself said in *The Road to Wigan Pier* of his down and out days that to move from a concern with unemployment to living from time to time among tramps was far from wholly sensible (several critics drive this blow home, never noticing that he made the point himself, the mature man of 1936 smiling at the sincere muddles of the youth of 1927).

I knew nothing about working-class conditions. I had read the unemployment figures but I had no notion of what they implied; above all, I did not know the essential fact that 'respectable' poverty is always the worst. The frightful doom of a decent working man suddenly thrown on the streets after a lifetime of steady work, his agonized struggles against economic laws which he does not understand, the disintegration of families, the corroding sense of shame – all this was outside the range of my experience. When I thought of poverty, I thought of it in terms of brute starvation. Therefore my mind turned immediately towards the extreme cases, the social outcasts: tramps, beggars, criminals, prostitutes. These were 'the lowest of the low', and these were the people with whom I wanted to get into contact. What I profoundly wanted, at that time, was to find some way of getting out of the respectable world altogether.[12]

So finally he sallied out one winter evening from Notting Hill to Limehouse Causeway and, having to screw up his courage greatly, entered a 'Good Beds for Single Men' common lodging-house, probably Lew Levy's 'kip'. A drunken young stevedore lurched towards him, Eric thought he was in for trouble, but: '"Ave a cup of tea, chum!, Ave a cup of tea" . . . It was a kind of baptism.'[13]

A few weeks later, having picked up a certain amount of information about the habits of destitute people, he went on the road for the first time. The conscience of the scrupulous and fastidious man forced him to move into a world of dirt and squalor, but he did so with keen and stimulated discernment, even humour, not pain all the way. All this was to emerge in *Down and Out in Paris and London* (1933). He began his tramping experimentally and voluntarily before becoming genuinely 'down and out' eighteen months later in Paris, contrary to what he said in his own short summary. When he submerged, he knew that he could always surface again, and he always did; but while he was submerged he shared the life of tramps and destitutes totally, without compromise. The experience that went into 'The Spike', his first characteristic and important essay to be published, his account of a night in a casual ward or hostel for tramps, occurred during this period at Notting Hill.[14]

In exploring the East End, Blair was following in Jack London's footsteps, quite literally. In 1902 Jack London, already a famous writer, had spent a similar first night when he submerged himself in the slums of East London to write *The People of the Abyss*, a book that Blair had read at school and which obviously influenced his choice of how and where to find his 'lowest of the low' (Jack London's very phrase). Several precedents existed of writers or social investigators submerging themselves for a while in the East End[15] (indeed, Jack London nervously broke his cover on his first night in the underworld, and said, when asked who he was, that he was a social investigator). None, however, had been more likely to go native than Eric Blair, so hard up and unestablished, even though with no clear purpose in mind. Obviously he knew that somehow he would use these experiences for his writing, but one should not assume that the desire to write predominated over his feelings of guilt and his plain desire to be – if not of – at least with and among the oppressed. He may have thought of his Rangoon friend Captain Robinson attempting to lead the life of a mendicant Buddhist monk. As part of his education as a social moralist, now clearly beginning, it was an admirable step to move among tramps, outcasts and the wretched of the earth; but as a sociology of unemployment and poverty it was, as he came to see, misleading, even slightly ridiculous. At first he was to carry over some of the attitudes of patronage as well as of pity with which he had viewed the Burmese poor. For a while he 'went native in his own country' and carried the cross of class as heavily as he had done that of race. Only a sense of common purpose can create true fraternity, neither pity, guilt, conscious humiliation nor a writer's curiosity.

Blair's experiences were real and were more intense, various and sustained than those of Jack London in his English sojourn. But two years later, when he came to write about them, several literary borrowings from London were used to express experiences common to them both. Each man had begun by going into a poor second-hand shop and buying, with some difficulty, a set of ragged old clothes:

No sooner was I out on the streets [wrote London] than I was impressed by the difference in status effected by my clothes. All civility vanished from the demeanour of the common people with whom I came into contact. Presto! in the twinkling of an eye, so to say, I had become one of them. My frayed and out-at-elbow jacket was the badge and advertisement of my class, which was their class. It made me of like kind, and in place of the fawning and too-respectful attention I had hitherto received, I now shared with them a comradeship. The man in corduroy and dirty neckerchief no longer addressed me as 'sir' or 'governor'. It was 'mate', now – and a fine and hearty word, with a tingle to it, and a warmth and gladness which the other term does not possess. Governor! It smacks of mastery and power ...[16]

Dressed as I was [wrote Orwell], I was half afraid that the police might arrest me as a vagabond, and I dared not speak to anyone, imagining that they must notice a disparity between my accent and my clothes. (Later I discovered that this never happened.) My new clothes had put me instantly into a new world. Everyone's demeanour seemed to have changed abruptly. I helped a hawker pick up a barrow that he had upset. 'Thanks, mate,' he said with a grin. No one had called me mate before in my life – it was the clothes that had done it.[17]

The borrowing is obvious, but so is Orwell's improvement of the anecdote: the greater sharpness and precision of his style, his tying of the accolade 'mate' to a precise incident (which shows him, indeed, as 'mate', not just observer). And the style is more honed down to the subject, apart from the old-fashioned, somewhat literary word both men use: 'demeanour'.

If his choice of tramps as guides into the underworld of poverty had a literary induction, yet in following that road so far he showed courage, tenacity and originality.

Ruth Pitter recalls he was in poor health when he came back from Burma, and he had a bad foot, some kind of infection, that his land-lady dressed for him. But this did not stop his East End ventures and tramping; and he dressed like the tramps, no concessions, even in the coldest weeks of winter. She remembers (though this is possibly an occasion after he returned from Paris, because she says that by then he had had several bouts of pneumonia):

... one perfectly horrible winter day with melting snow on the ground and an icy wind. Orwell had no proper overcoat, no hat, gloves, or muffler. I felt quite sure he was in what is called the pre-tubercular condition. And here he was, exposing himself to such weather in totally inadequate clothing ... I made an open attack on him, trying to get him to take proper advice and attend to his health. All in vain. He would never face the facts. On one occasion he *was* tested for TB, but the result proved negative, or so he said. He never had proper treatment until it was too late.[18]

Some time that winter he decided to go to Paris to write and in the Spring of 1928 he did. If he discussed his motives with friends or rela-tives, none remembers it now. The narrative of *Down and Out* plunges straight in, with no explanation of how the author or the 'I' character got there or who he is, and the autobiographical section of *The Road to Wigan Pier* leaves out the Paris period completely. This section of the book was, of course, about the author's attempt to overcome his class prejudice and to assuage the twin guilt of class privilege and imperial domination. It also leaves out his equally determined attempt to be a writer. It is as if having climbed the ladder, he kicked it away.

A young man in Paris at that time could take on, it can be fairly surmised, one of two romantic roles: dissipation and *joie de vivre*, or the life of a poor writer. With Eric Blair, no doubt it was the latter – though perhaps he hoped for a dash of the former. Certainly, ten years later, he was to admire the craft of Henry Miller who combined them both with princely plenitude, and was to enjoy meeting him, even putting up with being teased about taking all the burdens of the world upon his shoulders. Almost certainly Blair went in an earnest frame of mind. But with no literary contacts in Paris and with the economic recession already under way, he could not have chosen a worse time to go than 1928.

In Paris he wrote a lot but earned very little. He only sold a few pot-boiling articles to minor journals in Paris and London: he had no luck with his real writing, short stories and novels. In the autumn of 1929 Blair ran out of money and was reduced to taking a job as a dishwasher for a few weeks in a fashionable hotel on the rue de Rivoli. He was writing a great deal in Paris, work that neither got published nor has survived. Evidence of what else he did is sadly lacking. No one who knew him can now be found and only one reminiscent letter survives from a friend of his Paris days. If occasionally he sat in the literary cafés of St-Germain-des-Prés, there is no sign that he sought the company of other writers, established or apprentice; and he must have lived, even before he became destitute, a very quiet, simple and solitary life.

Apart from *Down and Out* itself, all he published on his Paris days was an introduction in 1935 to the French edition (called *La Vache enragée*) and in 1946 most of one of his finest essays, 'How the Poor Die'. Like 'A Hanging' and 'Shooting an Elephant', this was a documentary short story, the merit of which does not depend on its factual, historical veracity. The essay or story begins: 'In the year 1929 I spent several weeks in *Hôpital* X, in the fifteenth *arrondissement* of Paris' – one of the few facts that can be confirmed, even though the stay was only for two weeks (7-22 March) according to the register of the Hôpital Cochin.[19] Orwell explained to readers of *La Vache enragée* the motives for his retreat from Burma and advance on Paris:

It was a job for which I was totally unsuited: ... I gave in my resignation in the hopes of being able to earn my living by writing. I did just about as well at it as do most young people who take up a literary career – that is to say, none at all. My literary efforts in the first year barely brought me in twenty pounds.

His motivations were made out to be as purely literary as for the different purposes of *The Road to Wigan Pier* they were presented as purely political. He continued:

I set off for Paris so as to live cheaply while writing two novels – which I regret to say were never published – and also to learn French. One of my Parisian friends found me a room in a cheap hotel in a working-class district which I have described briefly in the first chapter of this book ... During the summer of 1929 I had written my two novels, which the publishers left on my hands, to find myself almost penniless and in urgent need of work ... So I stayed on in Paris and the events which I describe in this book took place towards the end of the autumn of 1929.[20]

The actual period covered by *Down and Out* can be no more than ten weeks of his eighteen months in Paris; and of the rest of that time practically nothing is known.

Down and Out raises by now familiar problems. How much can it be read as literal autobiography? '*Nearly all* the incidents described there actually happened, though they have been rearranged,' he was to write in the autobiographical chapters of *The Road to Wigan Pier*.[21] This is close to the mingled claim and disclaimer of Robert Tressell in the Preface to *The Ragged Trousered Philanthropist* ('which has always seemed to me a wonderful book'[22]): 'I have invented nothing. There are no scenes or incidents in the story that I have not either witnessed myself or had conclusive evidence of.' And again, in the introduction to *La Vache enragée* Orwell said: 'As for the truth of my story, I think I can say that I have exaggerated nothing except in so far as all writers exaggerate by selecting. I did not feel that I had to describe events in the exact order in which they happened, but everything I have described did take place at one time or another.'[23] He immediately added that he refrained, as far as possible, from drawing individual portraits of particular people. 'All the characters I have described in both parts of the book are intended more as representative types ... than as individuals.' Since much of the interest of the Parisian section of *Down and Out* is meant to be sustained by his gallery of Dickensian or Gogolesque characters, this disclaimer somewhat contradicts the 'everything ... did take place' of *La Vache enragée* and strengthens the 'nearly all' of *The Road to Wigan Pier*. In 1944 Orwell remarked on how much the American chapters in Dickens' *Martin Chuzzlewit* are a mixture of the travel book and the novel: 'a good example of Dickens' habit of telling small lies in order to emphasize what he regards as a big truth.'[24] *Down and Out* can perhaps best be read in that light. Few other writers would have worried about it so much.

The true critical response is not to use words like 'lies' and 'truth' at all (even if the author does), but simply to appreciate the processes of a growing creative imagination. But Blair's and Orwell's *own* preoccupation with claiming as much for literal truth as he honestly, decently could, shows how much he intended his writings to be social, or 'political' in a broad sense, even before he became clearly a 'political writer'. For the reader of a 'political' work is suspicious that 'the facts' may be made up: and it is then crucial whether they are or not. The confusion arises because it seems (from the evidence of the kind of writing he was attempting) that his motives in coming to Paris were primarily literary, but that his successes, when they came, arose from looking back over this period in a more political manner.

To follow the account in *La Vache enragée:* '... one of my Parisian friends found me a room in a cheap hotel in a working-class district.' This was 6 rue du Pot de Fer, which figures as 'rue du Coq d'Or'. (This closeness and euphony between real and invented names was to worry his future publishers greatly.) It was undoubtedly working-class, but Hemingway had earlier described it as 'the best part of the Latin Quarter', meaning the most typical. 'It was quite a representative slum', said Orwell in *Down and Out* – which was an exaggeration, certainly if it were compared with Belleville, Ivry or La Villette, the classic Paris slums, or with Whitechapel, Limehouse and Vauxhall in London, which he had already begun to explore.[25] 'Quite a representative slum' was consistent with the narrative of *Down and Out*, but not with the predominantly literary motives with which he went to Paris.

Orwell peopled his hotel with 'eccentric characters'. He saw poverty as producing eccentricity: 'there are plenty of other people who lived lives just as eccentric as these' in 'our quarter'. Some of the characters ring true, like Henri who has retreated into the sewers and dumbness after his girl, for whom he went to prison, was unfaithful; but others seem to be stock figures, like Charlie, 'a youth of family and education', who for five whole pages is allowed to recount the hoary old fantasy of raping a procured virgin in a luxurious room, furnished totally in red, hidden among decrepit, rat-infested cellars. The story is incongruous among the simpler tales of poverty that Orwell told so well, almost as if he were trying as a desperate plunge to make that book sexually sensational as well as socially serious. He pictured 'the cheap hotel' simply as a slum boarding-house. Perhaps it was. Certainly it was the very cheapest kind of hotel possible. Eric Blair would have heard, through the 'walls as thin as matchwood', some such things as George Orwell was to relate: the fighting, the weeping, the whoring, the drunken singing, the pissing and soft shuffle of rent defaulters trying to get in and out without being spotted by the concierge. Inhabitants of such places were in constant terror of not being able to pay the rent and in continual debate about which pawnshop gave the least bad rates. Yet most of the characters drawn or mentioned in *Down and Out* have come down in the world from the middle classes: they are not representative, ordinary French working men and women. They · are Russians, Algerians, immigrants, transients and drop-outs of all kinds, even including an Englishman who lives in the hotel on a remittance for half of each year, drinking four litres of wine a day, and the other six months living respectably with his parents in Putney. So to call it a 'representative slum' is either an exaggeration or a relative term. Paris like St Cyprian's is an 'echoing green'. 'Poverty is what I am writing about, and I had my first contact with poverty in this slum.'[26] This is not autobiographically true. This is the fictional voice of George Orwell: it is more dramatic for the hero not to be prepared for what he encounters when his money runs out. Eric Blair however already knew poverty from London and was writing about 'The Spike' in Whitechapel while in the cheap hotel in Paris.

Who was the friend who found him the room? In none of the narratives or conversations remembered by his friends did he mention that Aunt Nellie was in Paris – his favourite relation, the bohemian of the family. What is more likely than that she found it for him (as she was to find him a job four years later in a bookshop in Hampstead)? As a bohemian but sensible lady, sadly expert in making a little money go a long way, she would have found him precisely this type of cheap room in a cheap hotel in a poor and cosmopolitan quarter but not in a slum. (He could, of course, have moved deliberately from a better place that was found for him into a far worse place that he found for himself – as he later did in Wigan.) Nellie Limouzin had moved back to Paris from England to live with and to care for her lover, Eugène Adam, a stalwart of the Esperanto movement. He had founded the *Sennacieca Asocio Tutmonda* (the Workers Esperanto Association of the World) some time in 1928. He was born in Brittany but would neither write nor speak French, only Esperanto. If everyone spoke one tongue,

the curse of Babel would be at an end, there would be no more conflict between nations, no more war, hence inevitable and lasting universal peace. He had been a Communist, but had turned Socialist after a
visit to Moscow.[27] Orwell told a friend in his last years that as a young
man he had gone to Paris partly to improve his French, but had to
leave his first lodgings because the landlord and his wife only spoke
Esperanto – and it was an ideology, not just a language.

Eric must have seen a good deal of his aunt and her lover, even
if he did not stay with them for long and was too proud to sponge
off them when he went broke; or perhaps they were as hard up themselves. Fellow Esperantists described them as living in a small top flat
in a poor building in a middling district. Here is once again Blair's
early trait of tightness or caginess about his friends and his sources.
In part, this was already deep in his character, a consequence perhaps
of being the odd man out at school and of having parents who were
not emotionally demonstrative. However, this secretiveness may well
have been strengthened by the kind of writing which was beginning
to turn Blair into Orwell, the documentary essay (ambiguously fact or
fiction), which could so easily portray (and betray) friends and
acquaintances. This must have worried him because all the time he
seemed to believe that he was short of material, so that he was under
pressure to use almost everything that was at hand. He underestimated
his own artistry and creative powers of imaginative invention. He was
as yet naïve enough as a writer to have felt as guilty about using friends
as he would about 'making up' characters in a 'true narrative'.

Another important and obvious possibility in 'the suppression' of
Aunt Nellie and Eugène Adam from all later accounts of Paris is that
they were, if not full-blown cranks, certainly crankish. And when
George Orwell emerged from Eric Blair, he wore the clothes of common sense. By 1936 he came to believe that the main business of
political writing and practical politics was to catch the ear of the lower
middle classes whom he believed should be the natural leaders of the
people, and who were equally victims of capitalist exploitation and
illusion. So in *The Road to Wigan Pier* there is the magnificently comic
and violent tirade against the pollution of Socialism by 'cranks' (as good
as anything in the early novels of H. G. Wells); but all this earlier time,
indeed all the early years before his great fame, he had mixed a lot
with such people, liking their individuality and tolerant eccentricity.

He was then more than a little bohemian himself, despite his moral earnestness. Later he made no mention of such people, even though he was exposed to their ideas (without fully sharing them) earlier than is usually thought and than he would ever admit; precisely the ideas, in this case, if the speculation is correct of a Left-wing anti-Communism, posing hopefully as the nucleus of a popular mass movement, but in fact small if vastly intellectual, and with a dash of anarchism. The bookshop proprietors in Hampstead that he was later to work for were also Esperantists of the same political persuasion as their friends, Nellie Limouzin and Eugène Adam. And Orwell was to have a passing phase of interest in Basic English, seen as a rival to Esperanto but to serve the same great pacific purpose.[28]

What was he writing? Possibly some character sketches from the world of tramps and beggars, but mainly he pursued conventional literary ambitions of short stories and novels. His first publication, however, since the schoolboy patriotic poems was a journalistic potboiler: an article in *Le Monde* on 'La Censure en Angleterre'. He described in a competent but unoriginal way some of the anomalies of contemporary censorship, particularly of the stage, and the robustness of many of the classics. He ended, however, on what was to prove a more characteristic and strongly libertarian note (though of the style we can say nothing for the original English is lost):

What conclusions can we draw? We can only say that this casual and arbitrary censorship that England suffers today is the result of a prudery which would suppress (except for the snobbish fear of a great reputation) Chaucer, and Shakespeare, as well as James Joyce. The reason for this prudery can be found in the strong English puritanism which does not find filth repugnant but which fears sexuality and detests beauty. Nowadays it is illegal to print a swear word and even to swear, but no race is more wont to swear than the English. At the same time, however, every serious play on prostitution is likely to be banned from the English stage just as every prostitute is likely to be prosecuted. And yet it is a known fact that prostitution is as widespread in England as elsewhere. There are signs that this state of affairs will not last for ever. One can already perceive a little more freedom in writing than there was fifty years ago. If a government dared abolish a literary censorship we would find that we have been misled for several decades by a small minority and a century after its abandonment we can be sure that this strange institution, moral censorship in literature, would seem as remote and as fantastic as the marriage customs of central Africa.[29]

On 29 December 1928 his first English publication appeared: 'A Farthing Newspaper', in *G. K.'s Weekly* (G. K. Chesterton), an ironic account of a French Right-wing attempt to produce a nearly-free newspaper. It was also signed 'E. A. Blair'. It is an ephemeral piece, but crisply and colloquially written:

And supposing that this sort of thing is found to pay in France, why should it not be tried elsewhere? Why should we not have our farthing, or at least half-penny newspaper in London? While the journalist exists merely as the publicity agent of big business, a large circulation, got by fair means or foul, is a newspaper's one and only aim. Till recently various of our newspapers achieved the desired level of 'net sales' by the simple method of giving away a few thousand pounds now and again in football competition prizes. Now the football competitions have been stopped by law, and doubtless some of the circulations have come down with an ugly bump. Here, then, is a worthy example for our English Press magnates. Let them imitate the *Ami du Peuple* and sell their newspapers at a farthing. Even if it does no other good whatever, at any rate the poor devils of the public will at last feel that they are getting the correct value for their money.[30]

The pithy use of ordinary phrases like 'fair means or foul', 'ugly bump' and 'poor devils'; the irony of the last sentence; and even the pseudo-precision of '*doubtless* some of the circulations have come down', these are the devices found frequently in his famous essays. His first journalism was thus closer to his mature style than were his early novels. It seems as if he then regarded his journalistic style as merely workmanlike and still strove to achieve a 'literary style'. It took him some years to discover that he already possessed something much finer than what he thought he was still seeking. The style is distinctively radical, but again not necessarily socialist: the populist stylistic devices and the political contempt for 'big business' were quite at home precisely where he published them, in the militantly individualistic pages of *G. K.'s Weekly*.

Two or three other slight articles appeared in French for the small Radical journal, *Le Progrès civique*, including the political one on Burma. Two letters from a Monsieur Pierre Yrondy of *Le Mont-Parnasse* thanked him for '*votre "ballade"*' ('*c'était extrêmement amusante*') and for '*des articles d'humour* "AYANT TOUJOURS TRAIT AU QUARTIER MONTPARNASSE"' and hoping that he would be a regular contributor 'when the resources of the journal allow'. They may never have allowed, indeed it may never have been launched, for no trace of the article or of the journal can be found.

His income from such journalism was not nearly enough to live on. He did some private English teaching, but clients were hard to find and keep, he said in *Down and Out*.

All we know about his literary aspirations is from three letters from a literary agent, the McClure Newspaper Syndicate of New York and London.

19 February 1929

Dear Mr Blair

I received your letter of the 17th inst., and I would very much like to see the proposed new book when it is typed. It seems to me that a better judgement could be made after perusal of the whole. Have these stories ever been serialized at all? – possibly their length would be against this.

I should not be sanguine about the Tramps and Beggars book, but one never knows. Maybe at some future time you will shoot it across to me, though of course if it is political, that would be rather against it.

Our charge is 10% (Ten Percent) for all of your work placed. I will let you know when I am next in Paris, and then we three can probably meet.

Yours very truly,
L. I. Bailey[31]

The reference to a book on 'Tramps and Beggars' is important, for it shows that he was already either at work on or thinking of such a book based purely on his English experience, even before his real period of destitution in Paris and specifically his experience of the hotel which probably moved him to write a whole book on Paris – certainly it is the most vivid and original part of the eventual manuscript. He did, indeed, write his essay, 'The Spike', or at least a version of it, while in Paris. He sent it to Max Plowman at the *Adelphi* in August 1929 (though it did not appear until April 1931, a few months before the first of his great essays, 'A Hanging').[32] The second letter reads:

23rd April 1929

Dear Mr Blair,

It's too bad that I have not written earlier regarding the stories you sent me. Since my little jaunt I have been inundated with work, and that must serve as the excuse for my apparent neglect. I have just got through the Mss., and in parts am enormously impressed.

Allow me to start at the bad end!

'THE SEA GOD' I found to be immature and unsatisfactory. It was difficult to believe that the end of the story had been reached. I think, too, that you deal with sex too much in your writings. Subjects a little less worldly would have a greater appeal!

'THE PETITION CROWN' You have very good powers of description, but this power becomes tedious when a page of description could be much more effective in a few brief sentences. Stories of action will much more readily find a market than slow-moving, descriptive (no matter how beautiful) ones will. Sex here again *ad lib*!

'THE MAN IN KID GLOVES' impressed me very much, and I consider it an extremely clever story. It holds the attention of the reader and strikes a crisp note.

I think these writings would stand a greater chance if they were published in a book than serialization would afford. However, I want to try one, if not more, on an Editor friend of mine and get his views.

Do not be angry with me for my, perhaps, too frank criticisms, but you wished for this, and there it is!

It was nice to meet you in Paris, and I enjoyed our little chat tremendously. I trust you are keeping fit.

> With kind regards,
>> Yours sincerely,
>> L. I. Bailey
>> for THE MCCLURE NEWSPAPER SYND.[33]

PS Very best regards to Miss Limouzin.

Bailey presumably knew that he had not been 'keeping fit', that earlier that year he had been in Hôpital Cochin in the rue Faubourg Saint-Jacques with pneumonia, a terrible experience of human degradation, even allowing for any possible exaggeration in his essay of 1946, 'How the Poor Die'.

Bailey's last letter was in June, reporting failure to place 'The Man in Kid Gloves'. This still leaves it unclear what the 'two novels' were about to which Orwell refers in the Preface to *La Vache enragée*. From the letter of 19 February, there seems to have been a finished 'new book' about to be typed and a proposal for one on tramps and beggars. The letter of April discussed a number of short stories. Could they have been 'the book'? Could 'tramps and beggars' have been first thought of as a novel − just as *A Clergyman's Daughter* was to re-use some of the tramping material? Perhaps one or other of the novels remained in his head, or Orwell may have been simplifying a more complicated programme. Ruth Pitter remembers that he had written a lot which he destroyed that previous winter in London. It is conceivable, so hard did Blair work, that in eighteen months, even allowing for the two weeks in hospital and the ten weeks as *plongeur* (dishwasher), he had finished two novels as well as all the other work mentioned in the letters. What is clear, however, even from the titles of the short stories, is that he did not then see himself as predominantly a political writer and was thrashing around for themes. He wanted to be a writer but was unsure what to write about. Had these early works been published he might well have remained both in a literal and an intellectual sense merely Eric Blair.

One of the two novels projected could have been something that grew into his first published fiction, *Burmese Days*. Twenty-one pages of manuscript survive which, by handwriting and paper, were either written in the winter of 1927–8 in London or during 1928–9 in Paris, and are either part of a longer, missing manuscript or a trial run for sections of 'The Tale of John Flory'. It is in the first person and 'the author', John Flory, seems to be writing his autobiography in prison, awaiting execution indeed, as a cautionary tale or final confession. It begins, in fine black humour, with 'My Epitaph':

Goodness knows where they will bury me, – in their own graveyard I suppose, two feet deep in a painted coffin. There will be no mourners, and no rejoicers either, which seems sadder still; for the Burmese celebration of a funeral with music and gambling is nicer than our beastly mummeries. But if there were anyone here whose hand could form the letters, I would like him to carve this on the bark of some great peepul tree above my head.

John Flory

Born   1890

Died of Drink 1927

Here lie the bones of poor John Flory
His story is the old, old story.
Money, women, cards and gin
Were the four things that did him in.

He has spent sweat enough to swim in

Making love to ~~married~~ stupid women;
He has known misery past thinking
In the dismal art of drinking.

195

> O stranger, as you voyage here
> And read this welcome, shed no tear;
> But take the single gift I give,
> And learn from me how not to live.

So the prime villain is drink. Had he in mind the old *Hints on the Preservation of Health for Officers in Burma*? It must have been, indeed, as the manuscript conveys, no joke: tongues loosened by alcohol, drinking to reduce tension, spewing out racial prejudice. The effects of alcohol addiction on lonely and frustrated men were quite as bad as those of opium addiction. The first paragraph of the rest of the manuscript gives the flavour of the writing:

For awhile I abandon autobiography & commence fiction writer [sic] That is for the main facts of the story here told are known to me, & I have supplied the rest out of my imagination. I take so much trouble because this chain of events led to my downfall; not however by any real poetic justice, but simply through coincidence. Nevertheless I am, after all, here in Nyauglebiu through my own fault, for if this mischance had not come my way, there was bound to have been some other. My own temperament & way of living had made sure that I would fall into any trap of this kind that fortune laid me.[34]

Flory appears to have been mixing too freely with Burmans, plying them and being plied with drink; and he seduces the wives of his friends, notably the wife of his best friend, Lackersteen. Adultery arises from convention and boredom rather than from affection and passion. Flory also remembers his childhood, a remote father whom he did not see much of until he was about nine, though a solitary man of bookish tastes (as it were old Blair recast). Faced with these twenty pages, a publisher's reader would want to see much more before proceeding to contract: the writing is heavy-handed, though there are some fluent passages and the tone is notably more experimental and ambitious (as a book about a book being written) than was the happily more conventional final version.

He wrote without any success as regards his literary aspirations and with only a very limited success in the journalism that he counted on to keep him going. He must have hoped to get work on a regular basis with *Le Progrès civique* after they had carried two or three of his articles between December and May, but it did not happen. When he collapsed with pneumonia in February 1929, probably brought on by

cold, undernourishment and overwork, he even tried to keep on writing
from hospital (since he gave that address in writing to an editor) despite
the pain, the noise, the filth and the bureaucratic callousness, all so
precisely set down in 'How the Poor Die'. He did a bit of English
tutoring when he came out of hospital, but that was spasmodic and unreliable. Rejection slips must have piled up – much as Gordon
Comstock relates in *Keep the Aspidistra Flying*: every time you eat, terrible decisions have to be made; buying the cheapest things, you always
feel cheated; buying always small quantities, you are cheated; and you
sit waiting for the letters that never come – you begin to get obsessed
about money, both hating your dependence on it and desiring it
desperately. 'A letter, please God, a letter! More footsteps. Ascending
or descending? They were coming nearer, surely! Ah, no, no! The
sound grew fainter.'[35] Even a stamp costs two bread rolls.

6 rue du Pot de Fer
Paris 5
22 September 1929

Dear Sir,
  During August I sent you an article describing a day in a casual ward. As a
month has now gone by, I should be glad to hear from you about it. I have
no other copy of the article, and I want to submit it elsewhere if it is no use
to you.
                                        Yours faithfully
                                        E. A. Blair

There must have been many more such letters. Max Plowman at the
Adelphi eventually took the piece and began to send Blair books to review, but only after he had left Paris.
  In all his letters and essays there are only two most casual references
to incidents in his Paris days. He told readers of *Tribune* in 1947
that he had been at Foch's funeral in 1928 and that the appearance
of Pétain had caused a great stir in the crowd: 'His appearance
impressed me so much that I dimly felt, in spite of his considerable
age, that he might still have some kind of distinguished future ahead of
him.'[36] Most readers would not have given the columnist credit for
such forethought, nor would he expect them to: it was a nice piece of
deliberate hindsight to create a dramatic irony at a moment when
Pétain of Vichy was ending his distinguished life in prison. Somewhat

more revealing of how he spent his time other than attending funerals, he was to tell a friend that he remembered the *Deux Magots*, the famous literary café in St-Germain-des-Prés: 'I think I saw James Joyce there in 1928, but I've never been able to swear to that because J was not of very distinctive appearance.'[37] Here he cannot be accused of stretching a tale and he was far too shy and proper a young man to force himself on anyone famous. And yet he did go to the café.

A glimpse of a reasonably normal young writer's life in Paris can be gained from the only surviving letter from an acquaintance of those days, that reached him during his final illness:

I can hardly expect you to remember me after more than twenty years, but I have always enjoyed recalling those Saturday evenings in Paris, when we took turns about the dinner, and the hours of good talk later in my little cluttered place in Rue de la Chaumière.

You showed me sketches then of your experiences – some of the material I recognized when *Down and Out in Paris and London* came out. Perhaps I was your first critic . . . I believe your Aunt, Mrs Adam, went back to England? I treasure the memories of my years there, including the very good talk of a tall young man in a wide brimmed pair of Breton hats, who was as kind as he was keen of mind.[38]

Leading 'the writers' life' came to an end one day when his money ran out and his last slender store was stolen. There are two versions of this theft. In *Down and Out*, a young Italian compositor, who is made to pay a week's rent in advance because Madame does not like the look of him, manages to prepare some duplicate keys; and on the last night 'he robbed a dozen rooms including mine. Luckily he did not find the money that was in my pockets, so I was not left penniless. I was left with just forty-seven francs – that is seven and tenpence.'

The other version is what he told a friend, Mabel Fierz, as she was to relate it in a broadcast:

In fact, on the question of girls, he once said that of all the girls he'd known before he met his wife, the one he loved best was a little trollop he'd picked up in a café in Paris. She was beautiful, and had a figure like a boy, an Eton crop and in every way desirable. Anyway, he had a relationship with this girl for some time and came a point one day he came back to his room, and this paragon had decamped with everything he possessed. All his luggage and his money and everything.[39]

Whichever version of Blair's misfortunes is the more creditable (and Orwell may have favoured the Italian over the girl not to upset his family too much), the theft does lead him to give us in *Down and Out* an exact accounting.[40]

Before the theft he had 450 francs left and was earning 36 francs a week from English lessons. There were then 6 francs to the shilling or 120 to the pound. He had paid 200 francs in advance, fortunately, for a month's rent and reckoned that with the other 450 francs plus English lessons 'I could live a month' (that is, continue writing for a month), during which time he could find some work, as a guide or an interpreter (that is, he was still reasonably well-dressed and present-able). After the robbery, he had to cut his expenditure down to 6 francs, or a shilling a day, to last out a month, rather than the expected 13 francs a day. He got caught in a vicious circle. Not finding work, he had to pawn his good clothes; and having pawned them, he could only apply for the lowest jobs of all. 'Boris', with his hopes to be head waiter and to take Blair with him if a fellow émigré's awful restaurant ever opened, may or may not have existed. But Blair did end up as *plongeur* – working thirteen hours a day, probably through October, November and the first part of December 1929 in a grand hotel. There is not the slightest doubt about this, and the account rings all too true. He could have pulled out earlier. Aunt Nellie was in Paris and his family were not short of five pounds to get him home. But he stuck it, probably both out of pride and for the experience of poverty and al-most his only experience of work as the working class understand the term. The first version, indeed, of *Down and Out* that he submitted for publication was noted in Faber and Faber's register for 14 December 1931 as 'A Scullion's Diary'.

He was to defend the accuracy of his account of the hotel kitchen in a letter to *The Times* of 11 February 1933 against a Monsieur Possenti, '*restaurateur* and *hôtelier* of 40 years' experience'.[41] And there is a bizarre confirmation of the nature and servility of his job in, of all un-likely places, *Grace and Favour: The Memoirs of Loelia, Duchess of Westminster*.

We often stopped for a day or two in Paris – a town Benny much preferred to London. Looking back I think that Benny must have had a permanent suite in the Hotel Lotti, as we always had the same rooms. The staff bowed before him and hastened to gratify his slightest whim.

Years later, at a party, I met a frail-looking man who said, 'You won't remember me, but I have a very vivid recollection of you and your husband.' He then told me that he had worked at the Hotel Lotti. Late one night Benny had rung the bell for the floor waiter and asked for a peach. It turned out that there was not a peach in the hotel so my friend, who was an apprentice waiter, was sent out into the streets and, under threat of instant dismissal, told not to return without at least one peach. Of course all the shops were shut, so he wandered forlornly about (I tell the story as he told it to me) until he saw a small greengrocer's with a basket of peaches in the window. Desperately he rattled the door, pounded on it, but all in vain. He dared not go back empty handed, so, as the street was quite deserted, he picked up a cobble stone from a heap where the road was being mended, smashed the window, seized a peach and dashed back to the Lotti, happy to think that he had kept his job. However, soon after that he gave up trying to be a waiter and became a writer. His name? George Orwell.[42]

One wonders if she was aware that, like her Benny, Orwell was an old Etonian.

By the end of the year he returned home. In *Down and Out* he says that a friend 'B' had written that he could get a job for him, looking after a 'congenital imbecile' and he then sent him a fiver to get his clothes out of pawn and a ticket home. This sounds contrived. There was to be such a job for a short while near Southwold, though simply with a backward boy, which means that the offer would, more likely, have come from family or their friends in Southwold. Certainly he would have been hard pressed to have saved the fare from his *plongeur*'s salary – 750 francs a month (about £6).

On the face of it, Paris was an abject failure. None of his literary work found publishers and he must have had so little confidence in it, on re-reading it, that he destroyed nearly everything shortly afterwards. When he found a good agent, two years later, none of the titles in the McClure Newspaper Syndicate correspondence recurs. But there were some competent pieces of journalism which, though mere pot-boilers in motive, did begin to show that colloquial, easy, plain style that became his genius; and to show it more obviously than in many rather overwritten passages that occur in his first two published novels. There was at least the first version of 'The Spike' in which the journalism is undoubtedly literature. And, as was to happen again, from his very ill luck or lack of luck, good was to come. Somehow he was to capitalize sensibly on all his misfortunes. The experience in the hotel gave him the germ of the idea that led to *Down and Out* as his first published book. He seems at first to have dropped the idea of an English book on 'Tramps and Tramping', although he revived it, tacking it on rather awkwardly to the French material, when he got the opinion from Cape's that 'A Scullion's Diary' was interesting but a bit thin. Even so, *Down and Out* has a lot of padding, all those long florid anecdotes told by one of the characters, like the scarlet brothel story and the equally stock, rather nasty, indeed positively anti-Semitic anecdotes about the swindling Jew who is himself swindled over the facepowder that looks like cocaine. But there was enough, more than enough, in a different style to show an unusual and unusually honest sensibility. He wrote very directly, not theoretically, about poverty, and with a mixture of compassion and anger – however uncertain it is what derived from experience and what from imagination. The style of *Down and Out* was not, however, what Blair had intended when he determined to be a writer, and he did not give up the more conventional literary ambitions and manner easily and all at once: but that workmanlike style was to become the man.

This is to anticipate, for when he returned to England, in time for Christmas 1929, he at first seemed to resume his former life of spells of writing between spells of tramping, but with a few odd jobs between, as if nothing had happened; and perhaps he thought that nothing had happened except a period of failure.

The Christmas of 1929 can hardly have been a jolly occasion at the Blairs' home in Southwold. Return home was a defeat for Eric, his tall presence, if not quite a disgrace, was more a misfortune to the family than a blessing. Their friends commiserated with them. The prodigal had returned, but empty-handed. Rationally he must have known that success does not come overnight, but he must also have wished to return with something to show for his time in Paris, apart from pneumonia, a pile of rejection slips, a little journalism and lots of experience (the name, as Oscar Wilde remarked, that we give to our mistakes). He had returned home, once again, and home was not a long-loved family house, as the Buddicoms or his friends at Eton had, but a small, rented house in an out-of-the-way seaside town, the retirement home of his 73-year-old father and his 55-year-old mother. A grown man of 26 at home and virtually jobless was hardly comfort or support to such a quiet and by now wholly conventional household. Moreover, it was a town which he specifically disliked, his sister Avril remembered, for the presence of so many Anglo–Indian families with the kind of racial prejudices that had appalled him in Burma. And Avril, though only 21, was already carrying (later conversations with her would suggest) a stern and reproachful air of seeing Eric as loafing around, trying to write while life was passing her by, she thinking of what she could have done with his opportunities instead of having to work in a tea-shop (though a very nice and modestly profitable one, incidentally, quite unlike the wretched situation of the hero's sister in *Keep the Aspidistra Flying*).

Perhaps it is surprising that he returned home at all. Ties of family, however, are not always those of positive pleasure or affection. If they were 'worrying about him', he might have felt guilty at not going home unless he had a positive reason to be elsewhere – even if he felt still more guilty when he was at home. While still consumed by the guilt and curiosity that was to drive him back, time and time again in the next two years to live among the tramps, he nevertheless returned home each time simply because it was difficult, almost impossible, to write while on the road. Being at home at least gave him the time to write up his experiences. Besides, he was not simply loafing about. Someone had indeed found him a job tutoring a backward boy in Walberswick, just across the river by chain ferry from Southwold. He held this job until the spring, then became vacation tutor-companion to the three Peters boys, sons of neighbours, in three successive vacations. Their father was in India; their mother knew what Eric had been doing, but thought him a gentle, harmless, if misguided 'Bolshie' soul.[43]

All in all, he felt uncertain of himself, guilt-ridden and gloomy. He let it be known that he was writing a book about his experiences in Paris. Everyone had to understand that. He finished the first version of *Down and Out* in October 1930 and called it 'A Scullion's Diary' so it must have been solely on Paris.[44] On the strength of the *Adelphi* accepting 'The Spike' (though it was not published until a year later), and two pieces on English tramps for French journals, Blair wanted to be thought of as studying English low life in a serious fashion. This enabled him to slip away without subterfuge; and if his parents did not like the thought of him being on the road, they accepted it. Also his pride, though not his pocket, was sustained by a few book reviews which came his way from Max Plowman who was literary editor of what was now called the *New Adelphi*, after Richard Rees took over the editorship, though not ownership, from Middleton Murry whose platform essentially it was (it soon, however, reverted to its shorter name).

The *New Adelphi* sent him Lewis Mumford's *Herman Melville* to review, and he put a lot into it:

We see him as an overworked man of genius, living among people to whom he was hardly more than a tiresome, incomprehensible failure. We are shown how poverty, which threatened even when he was writing *Moby Dick*, infected him through nearly forty years with such loneliness and bitterness as to cripple his talents almost completely.

He put into it more than he intended. But any biographical biter is soon bit by Blair's next remark: 'The criticism which sets out to interpret – to be at the deepest meaning and cause of every act – is very well when applied to a man, but it is a dangerous method of approaching a work of art. Done with absolute thoroughness, it could cause art itself to vanish.'[45]

His next review offered praise of Edith Sitwell's study, *Alexander Pope*, but with a stern warning that love of musicality in poetry should not excuse lack of sense or positive banality; and even more boldly his next review took on J. B. Priestley's *Angel Pavement* as being heavily written, fatuously optimistic, and pleasant enough overall but nowhere near the standard of Dickens, to whom Priestley was being compared. How much better, says Blair, would Bennett, Conrad, Hardy or Wells have tackled the same theme. 'Mr Priestley's work is written altogether too easily, not laboured upon as good fiction must be – not, in the good sense of the phrase, *worked out*.' Blair did not intend to make the same mistake, but if Priestley had noticed his early novels, he could well have thrown the same review (apart from the optimism) back at Blair. Yet this is the writing of a man who was no flincher, no respecter of persons, who would take on lions and lionesses of any shape or size, although he was as yet showing more ability in critical than in imaginative writing.

Jack Common from Tyneside, one of the few authentic English proletarian writers, was in 1930 27 years old and working as 'circulation pusher' for the *New Adelphi*. He recalls his first meeting with Blair:

One name that interested me much was that of 'E. A. Blair'. He wrote no-nonsense reviews and vivid pieces that looked like sections from a coming book. Already a legend was shaping about him. He was not as other Bloomsbury souls, they said, he was an outsider, a rebel, a tramp, he lived and wrote in the bottom-most underworld of poverty. A man to look out for then, a man to meet.

He was sitting in Katherine Mansfield's armchair one dusky afternoon (late in 1930) talking to Max Plowman and Sir Richard Rees, our editors, and like that, seen at that low level from which one took in first the scrub of hair and curiously ravaged face, he looked the real thing: outcast, gifted pauper, kicker against authority, perhaps near-criminal. But he rose to acknowledge the intro-duction with a hand-shake. Right away, manners – and more than manners, the process euphemistically called 'breeding' – showed through. A sheep in wolf's clothing, I thought, taking in the height and stance, accent and cool built-in superiority of the public school presence. Of course the effects of social drilling that showed on him were to some extent libellous. He was an Eton man, I learned later, one of a kind that often stray into contexts not their own to become the catalysts of change, extra consciences to the 'movement', whatever it is. All the same this man Blair was a letdown to me that day.

Our next encounter was not so negative. It was just before Christmas I re-member. I happened to be alone in the office, which must have been dis-appointing for him, but I offered the traditional Bloomsbury hospitality of the cup of tea and cigarette, the seat before the gas-fire where seventeen asbestos columns glowed like the thrones of wicked emperors flaming eternally in Hell. I think we probably talked about Christmas, the curse of it, that is, to people who are poor enough already without having the extra burden of cele-bration. Anyway it is certain that he was tempted to launch out with one of the statements he loved to use for shock value and which made him appear like an over-long *enfant terrible* in decay. 'I would like to spend Christmas in gaol,' he said.

Later on when he was Orwell, one would have agreed that was the ideal festive season setting for him. But in this far-off, callow 1930 he de-valued the suggestion for me by his follow-up. He had thought of starting a bonfire in Trafalgar Square.

Now this was just the trifling, undergrad sort of stunt which irritated me because it mocked the rebellions of the truly destitute. Was Eric just a phoney then? Or anyway an amateur pauper?[46]

There followed a hostile and suspicious conversation, both men doubtless hoping that someone more interesting and congenial would drop in; but an odd reply to a banal question charmed working-class Gruff into instant appreciation of lower-upper-middle-class Grum:

But how did he come to write for the *Adelphi*? He was in Burma, he said, up against petty minds and starved for intellectual debate. The *Adelphi* was one of the periodicals he subscribed to. Not that he was a loyal supporter of the Murry crusades and outlook. Often the magazine disgusted him. Then he'd prop it up against a tree and fire his rifle at it till the copy was a ruin.[47]

Such direct lit. crit. appealed to Common, and he and Blair remained good friends for many years. Blair provocatively described himself then to the *Adelphi* circle (that is, to those who tried to keep up with, or at least follow, Middleton Murry's syntheses of aestheticism, post-Impressionism, Nietzsche, D. H. Lawrence and socialism) as 'a Tory anarchist'.[48] Blair and Rees became friendly through the *Adelphi* – they had been at Eton at the same time, but Rees was an Oppidan and had not known Blair at all. Rees was already a painter, author and critic of modest reputation, but most of all he was a keen seeker for new ideas and a kindly helper, both by his editing and from his own income, to many young writers of the time.

Edouard Roditi, the novelist and poet, met Orwell at this time through Jack Common and describes contributors to the *Adelphi* as:

... a curiously composed group, closely knit though we had few real ideas or beliefs in common ... all still rather confused, more distrustful of traditional beliefs than yet converted to any new beliefs. Some of us had some knowledge of Marxist literature; others, some acquaintance with Freudian theory, others again, some awareness of DADA and Surrealism. But nothing had jelled yet in our minds, so that we could still discuss new ideas quite freely as none of us had yet adopted a firm stand on anything, though some of us were already moving towards the ideology of the Independent Labour Party.[49]

From April 1930 Blair resumed his tramping. He had various 'drops' in London where he would leave his better clothes and don his rags, sallying out sometimes for a few days, sometimes for a week or two. The only 'drops' known about for sure are Ruth Pitter's studio, later Mabel Fierz's house in Hampstead Garden Suburb, and Sir Richard Rees' elegant flat in Cheyne Walk, Chelsea.

Ruth Pitter remembers laughing at Blair as he changed in and out of character, with him 'looking daggers at us, daring us not to laugh, but we did'. Her sister called him 'your dirty beau'. But most of all she remembers his poverty. They would occasionally go out for a cheap meal together, just good friends – as they were – but the slightest miscalculation could bring great embarrassment. 'You know, he would go out and hadn't enough money, and fit to die with chagrin when I put my hand in my pocket and put money in his hand. He hated it, poor soul.' As he did when her legs gave out and she insisted on paying for a bus, rather than always agreeing that she 'enjoyed walking' and would 'walk everywhere for preference'.

His wanderings took him beyond the slums of London. He got down into Kent and out into Bedfordshire and Essex, even a short venture into Suffolk – dangerously near home ground. He lived rough, exactly as the tramps did, and never carried more than a few shillings on him, indeed did not possess in all more than a few pounds. Only once do we hear of him surfacing while on a 'trip' or tramp. Brenda Salkeld was the same age as Eric and gym mistress at a girls' school near Southwold. They had met in 1928 through Avril Blair, and became close if independent-minded friends. She admired his intelligence and enjoyed talking to him, almost being tutored about modern literature. Yet she was impatient at his tramping. Miss Salkeld says that she always objected that it was not real tramping because he could get out of it at any time. He was trying to be with tramps but was not really a tramp. She told him he was being silly. He dropped in at her family's home in Bedfordshire when he was tramping, and they sent him straight upstairs to have a bath. Her mother said that it was very funny behaviour: if he wished to be a tramp then he could not call on respectable families; and if he called on respectable families, he could not be a tramp.[50] And after his death a legend was to grow among the young that Orwell had joined the tramps 'back then' much as Count Tolstoy had joined the peasants. But all this was a misunderstanding. He never claimed to have become a tramp, only to have been among tramps and in so doing have freed himself from certain prejudices, particularly those class prejudices relating to physical contact and dirt.

Tramps are not really very dirty as English people go, but they have the name for being dirty, and when you have shared a bed with a tramp and drunk tea out of the same snuff-tin, you feel that you have seen the worst and the worst has no terrors for you.[51]

The understatement does not conceal the terror, revulsion and disgust that he steeled himself to contain if not overcome. But to overcome class prejudice is not, he himself argued, to become classless.

Some time that spring or early summer of 1930 he spent a month or two in Leeds with his elder sister Marjorie, and her husband Humphrey Dakin – the same Dakin who long ago had taken young Eric fishing in Henley. His reception of this penniless, jobless and, in his eyes, work-shy failure of a brother-in-law had a similar cold tolerance about it; indeed, there seems to have been some positive dislike. Perhaps it stemmed from his memory that when he was sweet on Marjorie as a boy, she always felt it her duty to bring, he loved to recall, 'stinking little Eric' along with her, who 'was a sneak, full of "nobody loves me" and torrents of tears at the age of five or six'. Dakin enjoyed rattling on in later years about the impracticality of his late brother-in-law and his alleged lack of knowledge and concern for working people in the early 1930s. He would claim that when he took Eric out with him to pubs in Bramley, the working-class suburb of Leeds in which they then lived, he was a 'skeleton at the feast', did not know how to pass the time of day with anyone and that one publican had said: 'Don't bring that bugger in here again.' But he paid a grudging tribute to his brother-in-law's obsessiveness with writing.[52] Eric would finish supper, chat stiffly for a few moments, then go upstairs to a small room and type away, often throughout the night. He was working on the first version of *Down and Out*.

Blair's nephew and two nieces remember 'Uncle Eric' from when he was a frequent visitor in the early 1930s. Their mother's fondness for her brother was evident. He did not talk down to the children, so did not embarrass them like many adults; indeed he treated them very much like adults – in all kindly but rather remote. He did not play with them much since 'he appeared to be always busy', but when he did, he joined in just as if he were another child, neither 'showing them' nor dominating them.[53] They, too, remember the typewriter going on and on, 'tap, tap, tappety tap', said one of the nieces (which is curiously a line of a tramp's song that Orwell mentions in an essay).[54]

His niece, Jane, remembers an almost legendary family journey for a weekend in a cottage on the Yorkshire moors. They had a goat. She thinks it was because her sister had difficulty retaining food as a baby, and somebody thought goat's milk would help. (Before tubercular-tested milk became common, some people took to goat's milk if they feared TB or thought that it was in the family. Orwell kept goats in Wallington in the late 1930s.)

In the front of the car sat my mother with Lucy on her knee, in the back seat sat my brother aged about 4, myself aged about 7-8, our pug dog Taurus, our cat ... two or three guinea pigs and a kid goat called Blanche in a straw fish-basket with her head sticking out. Rugs and food baskets and the usual clamour. And behind the driver, on the back seat, sat Eric, quite unruffled and amiable, although disassociated from any responsibility, with his knees up near his ears, reading French poetry.[55]

How different from the ménage of a Woolf, a Murry, an Orage or a Lawrence.

Her father went further than a humorous 'disassociated from any responsibility'. He saw Eric Blair as almost fecklessly inept in prac-ticalities, either shirking his share of domestic tasks or somehow getting them wrong – as for example actually double-trenching Humphrey Dakin's allotment to get the clay out on top, when he had been asked merely to turn over the top soil lightly. He claimed to have given Eric ten shillings a week on these visits, and to have expected him at least to be useful about the house.

Such bitterness on small things thirty years later suggests some jealousy and that either these visits had been a source of tension between him and his wife, or that a major row between him and Eric occurred some time later. His reactions were not confined to comments within the family. Years later he was prepared to air his views on the BBC:

I often wondered what the clue to Eric's character was. Rather diffidently I put forward the theory that he disliked his fellow men. Intellectually. He forced himself to think of his fellow men with compassion. And put on an excellent act, you know, of being a friend of the poor; but I think he was partly ashamed and partly angry about having to put up with being so hard up. He was the last man in the world who would ever scrounge or do anything dishonour-able ... But I think that he wanted money in order to lead a more pleasant life and get away from poverty.[56]

The producer cut all of these recorded impieties out of the final broad-cast.

One of the three boys whom Blair tutored in Southwold made a far more favourable and favoured offering to the BBC. Professor Richard Peters' (Professor of Philosophy at The Institute of Education, London) reminiscences were broadcast, and they are worth quoting at length. Mature critical judgement obviously filters his memory of childhood, but his elder brother (a senior civil servant) gave much the same account.

We gathered that Eric Blair ... was rather a strange fellow but very nice. He was very kind to his mother and helped her with the washing up; but he had given up a very good job with the Burmese Police and had chosen to do a year's trip as a tramp without any subsidy from home ... and now he was writing a book all about it. You can imagine that we felt a bit apprehensive ... I vividly remember the first impression of him as he came up the garden path ... a tall spindly young man with a great mop of hair on top of a huge head, swinging along with loose, effortless strides and a knobbly stick made of some queer Scandinavian wood. He captivated us completely within five minutes. He had a slow disarming sort of smile which made us feel that he was interested in us yet amused by us in a detached impersonal sort of way. He would discuss anything with interest, yet objectively and without prejudice. We knew nothing of politics and cared less. I have only the vague impression that he thought most politicians wicked people and that making money entered into it rather a lot. But his remarks on these subjects were without rancour. He commented on the actions of politicians in the same sort of way as he commented on the behaviour of stoats, or the habits of the heron.

He was a mine of information on birds, animals, and the heroes of boys' magazines. Yet he never made us *feel* that he knew our world better than we knew it ourselves ... He entered unobtrusively ... into our world and illuminated it in a dry, discursive, sort of way without in any way disturbing it. He never condescended; he never preached; he never intruded. I remember him saying that he would have sided with the Cavaliers rather than with the Roundheads because the Roundheads were such depressing people. And I can now understand what he meant. For temperamentally he was a Cavalier, lacking the fervour and fanaticism of the Puritan ... He was never noisy and lacked the dogmatism of the insecure. I can only remember him getting indignant on one occasion when he told us how he thrashed a boy whom he caught blowing up a frog with a bicycle pump.

His attitude to animals and birds was rather like his attitude to children. He was at home with them. He seemed to know everything about them and found them amusing and interesting. Perhaps he thought of them like children as uncorrupted by the pursuit of power and riches, living for the moment and caring little for organized exploitation of each other. He infused interest and adventure into everything we did with him just because of his own interest in it. Walking can be just a means of getting from A to B; but with him it was like a voyage with Jules Verne beneath the ocean. He had of course, nothing of the hearty technique of the adolescent scoutmaster or the burning mission of the enthusiast. Neither had he the attitude of the guide on a conducted tour. A walk was a mixture of energy, adventure, and matter of fact. The world, we felt, was just like this . . .

These walks had often a definite purpose. Perhaps we would walk along to a nearby broad to attempt to get near a swan's nest or to find plovers' nests on the hillside . . . We went fishing in the mill-pool at Walberswick . . . He also told us how he used to kill eels by firing at them with a 12 bore shot gun . . . We helped him, too, to dig a couple of tumuli in the search of prehistoric remains, though I think that all we found was a soldier's button . . .

But of all the activities which we indulged in with him, the one that stands out in my memory most is the making of bombs. We used to call him by the somewhat irreverent title of 'Blarry Boy' and we coined a kind of war-cry . . . : 'Blarry Boy for Bolshie Bombs' would echo through the house and my poor mother would look anxiously out of the window to see which part of the garden was going to disappear next. My grandmother, I remember, nearly had a stroke when a grassy mound blew up just by the sitting-room window. George Orwell taught us a very special way of making gunpowder . . . the same energy and detached interest went to making and firing a bomb as to looking for a redshank's nest. We had to get every detail just right; we must not hurry; we must get into a really safe place before we pulled on the cotton. Nature was intriguing but predictable; we had to learn the way she worked or we would suffer.

We had another game in which he would also join with quiet nonchalance. We would stalk each other in the sand-dunes armed with small sand-bags. His calm precision was formidable. This was our world and it also seemed to be his. He was merely the boy who played the game with his head.

I suppose the nerve and quiet confidence with which he played this and other games was the quality in him which we admired most . . . The picture I shall always carry of him is of a tall loveable man striding nonchalantly across a girder about 18 inches wide on which the old disused railway bridge at Walberswick was suspended. I must confess that I was pretty frightened just jumping from sleeper to sleeper with the river [Blythe] swirling through the mudbanks about 30 feet below. But there was he walking as calmly as you like up to the apex of this girder miles above our heads. He told us that he had often wheeled a bicycle across . . . [57]

Professor Peters' reminiscences leave no doubt that Blair was a man among boys, but was he – Dakin doubts – a man among men? Dakin's view is suspect as motivated by personal dislike and jealousy. But his children, who liked their uncle Eric very much, also pointed to his ineptness and his withdrawal from domestic obligations and practicalities, a view also in sharp contrast to that of the Peters brothers.

But probably there was truth on both sides. Blair could behave very differently to different people. He had a typical public-school self-sufficiency which could make him appear cold and aloof, could lead to a certain lack of empathy with people, though not with ideas; but on other occasions, he was sweet and gregarious – when the situation was created on his own terms. Emotionally he did find it difficult to relate to strangers, however bravely and hard he forced himself to do so, as with tramps and derelicts, both morally and intellectually. His habit of keeping his different circles of friends apart and telling them little about each other was growing. He could appear almost a different man in different circumstances. From the earliest days, even when his fame was at its most modest, people seemed challenged to describe his character: there are some fine characterizations, and they can differ remarkably.

Richard Peters' comments on Eric Blair's politics, or lack of them, are also interesting, as is his favouring the Cavalier over the Roundhead. It strengthens the view that at this stage, despite the quasi-Marxist article on Burma in *Le Progrès civique*, his anti-authoritarianism and anti-imperialism took a 'Tory anarchist' form, rather than anything specifically or even latently socialist.

In the summer of 1930, while sketching on the beach at South-wold, Blair met Mabel Fierz, who was to do him a considerable service: both saving the manuscript of *Down and Out* and finding it a publisher. Her husband, Francis Fierz, was an engineer, and they had a nice house in Hampstead Garden Suburb, a four-rooms-up and three-down kind of place, as arty and intellectual-looking as they themselves. Mabel was a seeker and an enthusiast, a natural subscriber to A. R. Orage's *New Age*, which had moved from socialism to mysticism through Social Credit, and to Middleton Murry's *Adelphi*, attending the Summer Schools in the 1930s as his circle tried to keep up with his latest complete answers to the greatest Questions – if only the questions had not changed so often too. In the eyes of the world she might appear as a wee bit of a crank, of the genus Orwell railed against in *The Road to Wigan Pier* as discrediting socialism; but her enthusiasm was good for him and she was inclined to help him. When she positively decided to help him, as she had helped other young writers in a modest way, she would not be denied since all her geese were swans: she bullied friends for introductions, she bullied editors of small journals, gave a meal and a bath at almost any time, searched for cheap digs, and offered the spare room for short visits – a Garsington of Golders Green. She was to bring two particularly difficult geese together, George Orwell and Rayner Heppenstall.[58]

The immediate result of this meeting was, however, only that he received and accepted invitations to stay in Golders Green. He made use of this quite a lot in 1931, both as a base camp for his tramping and to spend some time in London, living reasonably conventionally, to extend his acquaintance with Richard Rees, Max Plowman, Edouard Roditi and Jack Common. It was the custom at the *Adelphi* to send books to reviewers, but also for young would-be reviewers like Blair to call, like commercial travellers, to see what the literary editor had on his shelves. 'You ask what kind of thing I like reviewing,' he replied to a note from Max Plowman. 'If you ever get any book (fiction or travel stuff) on India, or on low life in London, or on Villon, Swift, Smollett, Poe, Mark Twain, Zola, Anatole France or Conrad, or anything by M. P. Shiel or W. Somerset Maugham, I should enjoy reviewing it. Please excuse a post office pen.'[59] But this was hardly to push himself. In spite of a stiff and awkward manner with ordinary working people (there is no reason to discard all of Humphrey Dakin's testimony) and having to force himself to muck in with the tramps (who would not? but who would do it at all?), Blair made no attempt to use Old Etonian connections to further his literary career. He did not, as many unknown young men determined to make a career of letters, Orage in the 1900s and Middleton Murry a little later, seek to draw himself to the attention of great names. He knew none of the Bloomsbury group nor the Garsington Manor circle, and did not try to; he came to know Richard Rees simply through submitting his manuscripts to the magazine. When Cyril Connolly resumed their boyhood friendship in the mid-1930s, Orwell was, if still hard up, already a writer with a small reputation of his own. His famous literary friends came in the days of his fame, not in the days of struggle. If anyone can claim, besides Richard Rees (who, gentle man, never claimed any such thing), to have been his patron, it was Mabel Fierz. Above all, she radiated absolute confidence in what he was writing. She was the only Lady Ottoline Morrell he ever had.

The other Southwold friends, Brenda Salkeld, Dennis Collings and Eleanor Jaques were each closer and more natural friends, admiring Eric's intellectuality, talking earnestly but with open minds, yet pursuing their own interests and careers. While liking him very much as a person, they probably did not think Eric had much hope as a writer and in any case, there was nothing they could do to help his new career as a writer.

Edouard Roditi saw a good deal of Blair in 1931. They shared a taste for taking a cheap Chinese meal in Limehouse and then wandering around London together watching people and often talking to them at coffee-stalls. On several occasions they walked all the way back from the East End to Ebury Street in Pimlico where Roditi lived.

Often ... we stopped in Trafalgar Square and listened to people there. I can remember Orwell repeating phrases he had heard there so as to memorize them. I was with him when we first met the original of Mrs Wayne [in *A Clergyman's Daughter*] and he subsequently discussed at great length with me her insistence on having seen better days as a straw of respectability to which she desperately clung. He remarked that such people could never become revolutionaries ... Orwell and I were both equally shocked by the apparent indifference of the middle and upper classes to the dreadful phenomenon of unemployment and sheer destitution. In the busy crowds of daytime London, this phenomenon was less striking.[60]

Orwell, he remembers, admired George Gissing's realistic novels and put him on to that poor man's *The Odd Women* especially. (*A Clergyman's Daughter* was beginning to stir in the writer's mind.)

By October 1930 he had finished 'A Scullion's Diary' and began or resumed work on *Burmese Days*. The original manuscript on Paris, which has not survived, was in the form of a diary and shorter than what we now know, only about 35,000 words. He submitted it to Jonathan Cape (whose chief reader at that time was Edward Garnett) and they told him that it was too short and fragmentary, so Blair set to work expanding it.[61] Perhaps the original was only about his time as *plongeur* and he added material on the inhabitants of the cheap hotel where he lived. In any case, he made the additions, and re-submitted; but it was turned down by Cape again. He must have put a lot of work into the revisions, for it did not go to a second publisher until 14 December 1931, when 'A Scullion's Diary' appeared in Faber and Faber's register. It is entered as rejected by 25 February 1932. Sir

Richard Rees had commended it to T. S. Eliot but Eliot took the same view as Cape's reader – though his letter did not close the door completely:

February 19th 1932

Eric Blair Esq.
    Westminster Chambers
       Westminster Bridge Road
Dear Mr Blair,

I am sorry to have kept your manuscript. We did find it of very great interest, but I regret to say that it does not appear to me possible as a publishing venture. It is decidedly too short, and particularly for a book of such length it seems to me too loosely constructed, as the French and English episodes fall into two parts with very little to connect them.

I should think, however, that you should have enough material from your experience to make a very interesting book on down-and-out life in England alone.

With many thanks for letting me see the manuscript.

    I am,
       Yours faithfully
         T. S. Eliot[62]

None of the readers' reports survive, nor internal memoranda at Cape's, so it is not clear when the book became, in form at least, 'comparative', quite when the English material was added let alone expanded. The two sections do not, indeed, fit together as a narrative and neither is it all of a piece stylistically. The Paris half has passages both of purple literary Blair and of plain-style Orwell. The London passages both hang together better and are plain style throughout, hence probably written later. It obviously underwent great changes in the year or more between its first submission to Cape and its rejection by Eliot. But the version that earned Eliot's pernickety rejection must have been substantially the same as that which Victor Gollancz so shrewdly was to accept.

Getting so near to acceptance, not once but twice, may account for his dejection. Otherwise it seems a bit arrogant or depressive virtually to abandon a manuscript after it had only been turned down twice – and by the two most distinguished literary publishers of the day. (When the same two firms did the same thing in 1944, Orwell just kept on trying with *Animal Farm*.) Did he send it to them out of confidence or naïveté? He abandoned the manuscript, but fortunately at

Mabel Fierz's house, telling her to destroy it, to keep the paper clips, or do what she liked with it. She did. She bore it in person to a good literary agent, Leonard Moore of Christy and Moore, and seems to have fairly stood over him until he promised to read it. Moore cleverly saw that it would appeal to the new, radical and ambitious, somewhat brash and challenging house of Gollancz. This is to anticipate. What is interesting at this stage, however, is that his most sustained period of tramping, to and from the hopfields of Kent in August and September 1931, came *after* the submission of the *Down and Out* or 'The Scullion's Diary' manuscript to Cape.* He did not tramp to Kent for the book.

The hop-picking trip, however, was not a sudden impulse. Some time in the summer, Blair wrote a letter to Brenda Salkeld to arrange a meeting – nominally a teasing, but perhaps a somewhat edgy, sarcastic letter:

I don't know what condition I shall be in. I suppose you won't object to a three day beard? I will promise to have no lice anyway. What fun if we could go hopping together. But I suppose your exaggerated fear of dirt would deter you. It is a great mistake to be too afraid of dirt.
　　Best Love,
　　Eric[63]

He wrote to Dennis Collings from Mabel Fierz's house on 16 August to tell him about a ghost he had seen in Walberswick churchyard (a figure that just disappeared – 'presumably a hallucination'). He went on to say that 'I haven't anything of great interest to report yet about the Lower Classes'; but announced that he had made arrangements to go hop-picking. And a letter of 12 October contained 'Hop-Picking', an essay written in diary form, not published in his lifetime.[64]

He started off at Lew Levy's kip in Westminster Bridge Road again. 'It is exactly as it was three years ago, except that nearly all the beds are now a shilling instead of ninepence. This is due to interference by the LCC [London County Council] who have enacted (in the interests of hygiene, as usual) that beds in lodging houses must be further apart.'

---

* It is extraordinary how many people know of Orwell's hop-picking yet think that *Down and Out* contains an account of it, rather than part of *A Clergyman's Daughter* and the essay or memoir on which part of it was based, but only published after his death (see *The Collected Essays, Journalism and Letters*, Vol. I, pp. 52–71).

The sturdy individualist favours the tramps against the municipal bureaucrats. Blair spent the next night with the 'hundred to two hundred' tramps and destitutes in Trafalgar Square. This becomes, with a simple change of sex, Dorothy's foul ordeal in Chapter 3 of *A Clergyman's Daughter*. He spent one night in another kip, a dirt-cheap sevenpenny one in Southwark, and there he met 'young Ginger', also bound for the hop-fields of Kent, and they worked and returned to London together. Ginger is plainly 'Nobby' of *A Clergyman's Daughter*. The adventure began on 25 August. He and Ginger were several days on the road before beginning picking from 2 to 19 September. Blair noted that the pickers were of three types: East Enders (mostly costermongers) in families, having a working holiday, gipsies, and 'itinerant agricultural workers with a sprinkling of tramps'. But he did not describe them much further, limiting most of his observations to the conditions of work as they affected himself and Ginger/Nobby. He did not mention or was not aware that 1931 was the worst year in memory for low prices, unemployment and bankruptcy in the hop-picking industry, exacerbated by ruinously bad weather.[65] His was a tramp's eye view of ''opping'. But he noted that being tramps they got a fair amount of sympathy, 'especially among the fairly well-to-do people'. He told of a costermonger and his wife being like father and mother to him. 'They were the kind of people who are generally drunk on Saturday nights and who tack a "fucking" on to every noun, yet I have never seen anything that exceeded their kindness and delicacy.' For they offered him food which they pretended, not to make it seem like charity, would otherwise be thrown away.

Thus Blair had had some brief contact with the genuine working class, not just the eccentric sub-culture of the tramps. The image of 'the proles' had been born (also a Jack London word), even with their cheerful songs.

> Our lousy hops!
> Our lousy hops!
> When the measurer he comes round.
> Pick 'em up, pick 'em up off the ground!
> When he comes to measure
> He never knows where to stop;
> Ay, ay, get in the bin
> And take the fucking lot!

On 19 September Blair and Ginger headed back to London, having made twenty-six shillings for eighteen days' work. Until 8 October he stopped in another of Lew Levy's kips, that in Tooley Street. Several mornings he and Ginger earned a few more shillings by helping the porters at Billingsgate fish market; and he spent the rest of his time in Bermondsey Public Library writing up the narrative of his experiences. 'The dormitory was ... disgusting, with the perpetual din of coughing and spitting – everyone in a lodging house has a chronic cough, no doubt from the foul air. I had got to write some articles, which could not be done in such surroundings, so I wrote home for money and took a room in Windsor Street near the Harrow Road.'

From Windsor Street, a poor street in West London, swept away by the bulldozers in the 1960s, he resumed the literary life. Even before sending the manuscript of the book to T. S. Eliot at Faber's, Blair had written two letters to Eliot 'as Richard Rees tells me that he has spoken to you on my behalf', asking if he could translate a French novel for them, Jacques Roberti's *A la belle de nuit*, the story of a prostitute. Not optimistic, Blair asked if they had any other French books to be translated: 'I am anxious to get hold of some work of this kind.'[66] In fact he was becoming anxious to get work of almost any kind – compatible with getting some writing done.

Before poverty drove him to take a job, Blair made one last foray into the underworld. He tried to carry out the festive wish he had expressed to Jack Common on their first meeting: to spend Christmas in prison. A week or two before the Christmas of 1931 he went down the Mile End Road in East London one Saturday afternoon in his tramp's clothing and with four or five shillings in his pocket. As soon as the pubs opened, he spent all but twopence on filling himself up with beer and whisky. The tall man was soon picked up by the police as he reeled along the pavements of Whitechapel, wide though they are – another ruined gentleman drowning his sorrows in drink. Getting arrested on a Saturday ensured spending Sunday in the crowded cell, observing and remembering, before being brought before the Bench on Monday. As 'Edward Burton' he was fined six shillings, which he could not pay (having been careful not to have money on him), so he settled down to enjoy a few sociologically interesting days 'inside'. But to his great annoyance he was thrown out at the end of the afternoon. Whatever the beaks might say, the coppers plainly had a better use for their cell, or perhaps they saw that he was not, after all, their usual type of customer and suspected a spy from some philanthropic body. Not satisfied, Blair spent some money and headed for the Casual Ward or 'Spike' at Edmonton in North London. He reckoned that by turning up there when drunk and thus committing a specific offence under the Vagrancy Act he would get a more stern sentence. 'The porter, however, treated me with great consideration, evidently feeling that a tramp with enough money to buy drink ought to be respected.'

During the next few days Blair made several more attempts to get arrested, this time by begging under the noses of the police; 'but I seemed to bear a charmed life – no one took any notice of me.' Perhaps the spirit of Christmas had entered into the police. So, not wanting to do anything serious enough to lead to an inquiry into his identity, Blair gave up.[67] He never said how successful he was as a beggar. The tension must have been great. It was one thing to move among tramps as a ruined gent, quite another all on one's own to have to wheedle food and small coins out of ordinary people in the street.

He never published his memoir on his brief imprisonment, except to take one image from it for the prison scene in *Keep the Aspidistra Flying*, and then similarly in *Nineteen Eighty-Four*: a man defaecating in a small crowded cell into the WC, the flush of which did not work.[68] The stench symbolizes both despotism and degradation. The memoir reads like a companion piece to 'The Spike', which was then ready for publication. Perhaps some of the language was too strong, or perhaps the attitudes to the police coupled with the language put the fear of prosecution into Richard Rees. For instance, scrawled on the wall of the Black Maria was, Orwell reports, the couplet 'Detective Smith knows how to gee, Tell him he's a cunt from me'. (To gee is to be a stalking horse or *agent provocateur*, often in relation to sexual offences.)

From Windsor Street there was sent a would-be comic, but in result a somewhat morbid and self-pitying, letter to Brenda Salkeld about the epitaphs in the vast Kensal Green Cemetery nearby: 'The thought entered my mind that all those tombstones and epitaphs are, after all, a last attempt on the part of the corpse to get himself noticed.'[69]

Blair, with his money running out again, must have begun to feel that he was turning into a tombstone just sitting there writing and waiting. The last straw may have been when a 'poisonous, but one must live' new magazine, *Modern Youth*, for which he had had two short stories accepted, not merely failed either to appear or to pay up but had all its copy seized by the printers when their bill was not met. So he even lost the stories.[70] Mabel Fierz had already persuaded him to try an agent, and he realized in the new year of 1932 that something had to be done. He had seen enough of utter poverty to realize that to surrender to it would destroy him both as a man and as a writer. He had been close to the edge of the abyss. He had lived hard among the very poor and had morally identified himself with gaining understanding and justice for the underdog; but to surrender to any nascent death-wish or desire for secular martyrdom – there was a morbid streak in his character – would be both self-defeating and contrary to the common-sense streak that was also in his character. Besides, as a shrewd friend of later years judged: 'His crucial experience . . . was his struggle to turn himself into a writer, one which led through long periods of poverty, failure and humiliation, and about which he has written almost nothing directly. The sweat and agony were less in the slum-life than in the effort to turn the experience into literature.'[71]

So he had to find a job. But it had to be a job that left some time for writing. The outcome, as for most other needy young writers, was almost inevitable: the bathos of private school-teaching. Mabel Fierz claims to have found him the job, probably through a scholastic agency. It was to give him a new model for autocracy; and to revive such memories of prep school.

CHAPTER SEVEN

HARD TIMES OR STRUGGLING UP

(1932–4)

THE decision to seek a job did not mean that Eric was throwing in the sponge in the struggle to become a writer. It was a reasonable response to the realization that his book was not going to rescue him from poverty in time. How poor he was is shown by his move some time around Christmas 1931 from Windsor Street, Paddington, a poor but clean and decent lodging, to 'Westminster Chambers, S.E.1', slum properties on the wrong side of the river from Westminster. This was the model for the bug-ridden 'frowsy attic' in the 'filthy kip' by Lambeth Cut to which Gordon Comstock sinks in *Keep the Aspidistra Flying*.

There it was that he received T. S. Eliot's final letter of rejection from Faber's on 19 February 1932. This must have plunged him into depths of Comstock-like dejection. The place, anyway, was too foul to work in. And he, unlike Gordon Comstock, had no 'Rosemary' to come down and drag him back by her pregnancy into a salutary or ironic compromise with 'the money god'. Eleanor, by then torn between Dennis Collings and Blair, did not play that part. Perhaps he sat hoping that she would, but she did not. Eric had to and could save himself.

He made one more slightly ignominious retreat before taking up his teaching job, which was to begin after Easter. He went back up to Leeds to resume tap-tapping away with his welcoming and indulgent older sister, but also to endure his brother-in-law nagging away at him about the need to have some pride in himself and to get a proper job. The local branch librarian in Leeds remembered Blair, because he used the library a lot during this visit. The librarian recalled him as a 'compel-

ling personality', though looking 'thin and ill', with nervous movements: 'not ... very communicative, and it seemed that he was, not
exactly confused, but in the process of rearranging himself.' A librarian
might draw a clear distinction between 'rearranging' and 'restocking'.
Eric used the library mostly to read newspapers and magazines, but
he browsed among the fiction shelves. The librarian introduced him
to Robert Tressell's *Ragged Trousered Philanthropist* and obtained
for him Aldous Huxley's recently published *Brave New World*. Blair
advised the librarian to read *Madame Bovary*. He has not yet done
so.[1]

On 26 April 1932, Blair wrote to Leonard Moore from The Hawthorns, Station Road, Hayes, Middlesex, where he was to teach until
Christmas 1933. (The address changed after 1 July 1932 to Church
Road, Hayes, but it is still the same corner house.) In this letter he gave
an account of the misfortunes that had befallen 'Days in London and
Paris'; he asked Moore if by any chance he were to get it accepted to
'please see that it is published pseudonymously, as I am not proud of
it'; told him of a novel he had begun several months before, and 'shall
go on with next holidays' (plainly *Burmese Days*); asked to exclude from
their agreement any articles or book reviews, though he promised (or
threatened) 'a long poem describing a day in London which I am
doing'; and sadly asked if he could get him any more translation work
from the French – 'I could also translate old French, at least anything
since 1400 A.D.'[2] And he said he was very busy.

He was very busy. For he was 'head master' of the school, The
Hawthorns, which consisted of fourteen or sixteen boys between the
ages of 10 and 16. There was only one other master, also as new and
as unqualified as Blair. Legends grow. A recent biographical study of
Orwell rashly imagined a 'prep school ... like St Cyprian's in its
academic objective – to prepare boys for public schools – though a day
school and less grand in its social pretension'.[3] And a recent play in-
flates it still further into a boarding prep school complete with a Victorian Gothic chapel and masters sitting in book-lined studies.[4] In
truth it was not preparatory but terminal: it took boys who had nowhere
else to go, who could not get into grammar school and whose lower-
middle-class parents could not afford even a minor public school, but
whose concept of being middle class at all depended on keeping their
children out of the local authority schools, however poor the local

private school. The Hawthorns did not prepare the pupils for university matriculation but for the examination of the Senior College of Preceptors (acceptable in commercial offices for salaried and pensionable clerical work). It was originally a pair of Edwardian small houses, The Briars and The Hawthorns. They were turned into one house during the First World War as The Rectory, but then became two again when the new Rectory was built: The Hawthorns became the school, 'Hawthorns High School for Boys', some six or seven rooms standing amid early nineteen-twenties, cruder, pseudo-Tudor ribbon-development houses. Two of the rooms were used for teaching and the rest for the family of the proprietor and Blair as head teacher and lodger. The proprietor, Mr Derek Eunson, was too uneducated to do the teaching himself but ran the school precariously as a small business and also had a job at the HMV gramophone factory. If Uxbridge, like Illyria, had been on the sea-coast, it would have been a cheap hotel, not a school. The previous head teacher had just been removed for some minor financial fraud. As one of the boys remembers, 'the school was a proper hoodwink'. (When Orwell came to write about Dorothy's school-teaching experience in *A Clergyman's Daughter*, this became heightened into 'the dirty swindle ... called practical school-teaching'.)

He was certainly an odd fellow and one who lived almost entirely within himself. It was obvious that his head was full of interesting and amusing thoughts and not infrequently these would get the better of him and his face would be creased with irrepressible smiles. Rarely, however, did he reveal the details to those in his company.

He was a great nature lover and took delight in taking some of us lads (after school hours) to search for Puss Moth caterpillars eggs on the Black Poplar or to collect marsh gas from some stagnant pond. He taught me the rudiments of oil painting and gilding. In fact, he had wide interests which he delighted to share with anyone who cared ... He wrote a school play and produced it in full hand-made costume with modest success in a local Hall at the end of the school year.[5]

He remembered Blair's 'inward laughter'. Blair gave the boys a lot of his spare time. He mixed with them unselfconsciously. Mr Stevens recalls a remarkable man 'who seemed to think of the boys as friends – when he was trying to get an answer out of someone he would poke him gently in the stomach with a ruler'. He kept a large stick by his desk which 'he used fairly often'. Mr Stevens had a taste of it: 'I couldn't

sit down afterwards and had bad bruises for a week. He really hit hard.'
If there was a sadistic streak in Blair, the cane was a very ordinary
part of school life in those happy days. 'Nobody bore any ill will,' the
pupil concluded. Blair once offered sixpence from his own pocket as
a prize for anyone who could spot a ludicrous misspelling in a local
laundry window. 'He was always doing little things like that.'

Apart from Blair using the cane to keep the natives in order, the
picture presented is much the same as that by the Peters brothers in
Southwold: of a kindly man who shared his thoughts with the boys
and, punishments apart, treated them more as equals than any adult
they had known. Mr Stevens is emphatic in his memory that Blair told
the proprietor's son, who also attended the school, that he was working
on a book about tramps and his experiences of being poor in Paris.
This might have gone over well with the boys, but to admit that he
had lived among tramps could have scared the parents greatly – particularly after what had happened to his predecessor (he must have
known). Perhaps he was being naïvely honest, or perhaps it was part
of the 'inward laughter' that he was imagining the parents weighing
'tramp' in the scales against the new head master being an 'Old
Etonian', a Colleger too – if they could have understood such things.
Etonians were rarely tramps.

The reference to working again on *Down and Out* dates and confirms
Mr Stevens' memory. Good news had come from Leonard Moore.
Gollancz would publish it, subject to certain revisions being made.

Victor Gollancz had had an enthusiastic report from his reader,
Gerald Gould:

This is an extraordinarily forceful and socially important document, and I
think it most certainly ought to be published ... I know nothing about the
author but I am absolutely convinced of his genuineness. Nobody could have
made up the experiences which he describes. He may, of course, have embroidered a little here and there, but substantially this is a true picture of conditions which most people ignore and ought not to be allowed to ignore ...
The picture is convincing and personally, although I found it utterly disgusting, as of course it is meant to be, I also found that it held my attention
far more closely than the ordinary novel ...[6]

He warned strongly, however, about obscenity, blasphemy and libel.
But Gould pointed to what would appeal to Gollancz: an important
and genuine document that people should not be allowed to ignore.

Gould's report is dated 16 June 1932. Gollancz wrote to his solicitor, Harold Rubinstein, the very next day. (Rubinstein was of the family firm that were to achieve such prominence in publishing law.)

17/6/1932

My dear Harold,

DAYS IN LONDON AND PARIS by Eric A. Blair

This is an extraordinary and important book. It is also full of possibilities of libel, running to thousands of pounds. Do you see any way in which it can be made watertight from that point of view? The obscenity can, I think, be satisfactorily dealt with.

Yours ever,
Victor[7]

Rubinstein responded quickly, full of sympathy with the book, but insisted that every name be changed and checked with the author, and that all f— blanks became simple blanks; and warned that even references to the filthiness of unnamed coffee-stalls and unspecified Salvation Army hostels could be perilous. Blair went to see Gollancz as soon as he had heard from his agent, Moore, and he 'gave me a full account of the alterations he wants made in the book. Names are to be changed, swearwords etc, cut out.'[8] He got to work in his room at The Hawthorns on yet another, but now the last and minor, revision of the manuscript. He made no protest at the cuts and was thoroughly businesslike and practical in correspondence. Gollancz did not like 'Days in London and Paris' as a title. Blair wrote back to suggest 'Lady Poverty', and he added: 'I think if it is all the same to everybody I would prefer the book to be published pseudonymously. I have no reputation that is lost by doing this and if the book has any kind of success I can always use the same pseudonym again.'[9]

This seemed a sensible decision to make, and there is no great mystery associated with his change of name nor yet any change of style, belief or personality. He did not have much confidence in the book, the parts are, indeed, so much better than the whole; and he took this view of all his writings in the 1930s (except for *Homage to Catalonia*), and only *Animal Farm* ever lived up to his own high standards and intentions. While his parents had known about his tramping and knew vaguely what he was writing about, he could by using a pseudonym shield them somewhat if they found his book upsetting, or if it was denounced by the reviewers as scandalous. Knowing that his next book would be on Burma, the need to spare and protect the family was even greater. If the books failed, he could continue his literary career by still using 'Eric Blair' for the reviews and articles which were now appearing not only in the *Adelphi* but in the *New English Weekly* and the *New Statesman and Nation* too. Also he did not like his own name, particularly 'Eric'. Certainly when the name 'George Orwell' began to be well known, it acted as a kind of ideal image to himself and he grew late in life towards a more balanced, integrated and yet public personality, somewhat different from the more contradictory and prickly young man. But though some critics have made much of his change of name, have implied a contemporary change of personality, and have pointed to 'the deeper and less easily defined forces at work',[10] there is no evidence at all for these psychological speculations and what cannot be 'easily defined' had best be ignored.

He told Moore and was to tell Eleanor Jaques that he 'was not proud' of the book; he probably felt that he had revised it too much so that the freshness and immediacy had been lost. Also he had hoped that his first major publication would be a novel: he was in two minds whether *Down and Out* was journalism or literature. It was long before he realized that his documentaries were better than most of his novels. Also Blair was uncertain where he stood, indeed uncertain whether to make a stand, and if so whether it should be politically, morally or aesthetically (he had still had a hope that he would turn out, after all, to be really a poet). The *Adelphi* was exposing him to new ideas and new uncertainties. Middleton Murry threshed around, looking for answers and redefining '*the* questions' (relieved by now of editorial work by both the spasmodic energy and the steady cash of Sir Richard Rees). The librarian in Leeds had been shrewd to notice that 'he was, not exactly confused, but in the process of rearranging himself'. Acceptance of the manuscript did not lift a general cloud of gloomy conviction, such as diffused all of his novels, that he was bound to fail. He shared at least some of the thoughts of his future character, Gordon Comstock, in *Keep the Aspidistra Flying* who 'liked to think that beneath the world of money there is that great sluttish underworld where failure and success have no meaning; a sort of kingdom of ghosts where all are equal. That was where he wished to be, down in the ghost-kingdom, below ambition.' This was not just simple pessimism; he genuinely valued art more than success.

An odd episode occurred in this time of intellectual uncertainty while Blair was at The Hawthorns: he began to attend church. This may have been a false start at 'rearranging himself' or simply because, as he told Eleanor Jaques:

Hayes ... is one of the most godforsaken places I have ever struck. The population seems to be entirely made up of clerks who frequent tin-roofed chapels on Sundays and for the rest bolt themselves within doors. My sole friend is the curate – High Anglican but not a creeping Jesus and a very good fellow. Of course it means that I have to go to Church, which is an arduous job here, as the service is so popish that I don't know my way about it and feel an awful BF when I see everyone bowing and crossing themselves all around me and can't follow suit.[11]

He makes a joke of it in his letters of June and July to Eleanor, who was firmly Humanist. These letters, though full and friendly, are signed, 'Yours, Eric A. Blair'; and he keeps up the joke even in October, after the summer vacation in Southwold, when their relationship changed.

I take in the *Church Times* regularly now and like it more every week. I do so like to see that there is life in the old dog yet – I mean in the poor old C. of E. I shall have to go to Holy Communion soon, hypocritical tho' it is, because my curate friend is bound to think it funny if I always go to Church but never communicate.[12]

But which friend was he deceiving? Or was he uncertain himself?

The curate's widow, Mrs Madge Parker, remembered Blair well and was shocked at the idea that he was not in Communion. He served for her husband at Mass, as they firmly called it, twice a week. He attended Sunday services and on several occasions had helped her husband administer the last rites to the dying.[13] Blair went fairly far if he was just obliging friends. He washed up after Church Guild meetings and often took tea or supper with them in their kitchen, helping with domestic tasks for the church, chopping wood and filling coal-buckets: 'you know, the kind of person who fits into a kitchen and helps you with everything in your own house, didn't stand on ceremony.' She remembers him as giving a lot of time to the boys out of school hours, and Mr Stevens remembers Eric bringing church ornaments into school for them to paint and gild (which thus confirms Mrs Parker's memory). Eric observed that the crown of the statue of the Blessed

Virgin Mary was tarnished, sought permission and successfully cleaned her in onion water – which alarmed and impressed them. He gave Eleanor a much funnier version of the same story – also gilded: 'promised to paint one of the church idols, a quite skittish-looking BVM ... and I shall try and make her look as much like one of the illustrations in *La vie parisienne* as possible.'[14]

Mrs Parker is indignant at the idea that he was not a genuine believer. She argues that her husband looked him over very carefully indeed (in view of what had happened to the previous head teacher – one of her sons had been a witness) when he tried to get the names of the local clergy back on the school prospectus. On the other hand, they had other concerns that drew them together. The Parkers had started in a working-class parish in Birmingham, and the curate was to spend the rest of his life in industrial chaplaincies. They were deeply concerned with the plight of the unemployed. The Hayes and Uxbridge area had exceptionally high unemployment in that bleakest of years. Blair asked them a lot about industrial conditions and told them a lot about his journeys among tramps and destitutes. Mrs Parker remembers that he made one short tramping trip while at Hayes. The three of them had seen and remembered the United Dairies pouring fresh milk down the drain because nobody could afford to buy it. If they were not fully socialists at that time – her memory is uncertain – she is none the less sure that they were each to become so soon. And she and her husband were, like Eric himself, serious without being solemn: they kept in their garden 'the Holy Goat', which they taught Eric to milk.

All this could have been reason enough for friendship and therefore for his church attendance. Yet he contributed an unsigned review that June to *New English Weekly* on Karl Adam's *The Spirit of Catholicism*, which he praised as being more informative than most English Catholic polemic, 'free from silly-cleverness', while he warns that the Catholic Church must be taken seriously, for its 'dogmatic intolerance' is a more proper target for anti-clerical feeling than 'the poor, unoffending old Church of England'.

The reviewer is thus determined to show that there are good grounds to be anti-Catholic, but also that he is fair to individual thoughtful, non-polemical Catholics. He is not anti-religious. He studiously reserves his own position. This may be a case of the dog that did not

GEORGE ORWELL

bark. In a letter he mocks a 'moribund hag who stinks of mothballs
and gin' who has to be helped to the altar to take communion 'lest
the Devil should happen to slip in at some moment when she is in
mortal sin' (so close to Dorothy's thoughts in *A Clergyman's Daughter*);
but in the same letter to Eleanor, one of the passionate phase, he says
casually that he is 'reading a book called *Belief in God* by Bishop Gore
– late Bishop of Oxford, who confirmed me, and seemingly quite sound
in doctrine tho' an Anglican'.[15] Gore was a Christian Socialist.

A poem published in March 1933 in the *Adelphi*, though obviously
written in 1932, wavers somewhere between the psychologically pessimistic and the existentially religious. The first two verses are conventionally Georgian both in tone and content:

> Sometimes in the middle autumn days,
> The windless days when the swallows have flown,
> And the sere elms brood in the mist,
> Each tree a being, rapt, alone,
>
> I know, not as in barren thought,
> But wordlessly, as the bones know,
> What quenching of my brain, what numbness,
> Wait in the dark grave where I go.

The third and fourth verses take on something of the tone and deeper
sentiments of T. S. Eliot in *The Waste Land*, while the language is
reminiscent of Anglican hymns:

> And I see the people thronging the street,
> The death-marked people, they and I
> Goalless, rootless, like leaves drifting,
> Blind to the earth and to the sky;
>
> Nothing believing, nothing loving,
> Not in joy nor in pain, not heeding the stream
> Of precious life that flows within us,
> But fighting, toiling as in a dream.

And the eighth and last verse:

> So shall we in the rout of life
> Some thought, some faith, some meaning save,
> And speak it once before we go
> In silence to the silent grave ...[16]

228

is indeed, enigmatic and ambivalent, 'some faith' but 'a silent grave'.

Whatever was happening, or did not quite happen, none of these themes occur again explicitly anywhere else in his writings or letters. 'George Orwell' was to be a clear Humanist, even a Rationalist with a pronounced anti-Catholicism, even though one with an ironic attachment to the liturgy, the humane political compromises and the traditions of the Church of England.

Religion was not his main preoccupation that summer in Southwold. Dennis Collings, certainly Eric's 'best friend in Southwold', best male friend that is, was courting Eleanor Jaques at the time, though working in Cambridge. The three of them often went walking together when at home. Brenda Salkeld occasionally joined them, though as Eric's friend – she was not so close to the other two as they were to each other and to Eric. Some time that summer Eleanor and Eric grew very much closer.

36 High Street
Southwold

18 August 1932

Dearest Eleanor,

Do not forget, Tuesday, 2.15 by Smith's bookshop. And, as you love me, do not *change your mind* before then. If you are at church on Sunday, pray for good weather on Tuesday. If it *does* rain, can you meet me same time and place after all, and we will go somewhere or other. Till then, all my love,

Eric

p.s. Please send me a line to reassure me that you have not changed your mind.[17]

Eric was soon to enjoy what may have been his first serious *affaire*. It was not without its difficulties, geographical and economic as well as the need to avoid hurting his friend Dennis Collings.

Much of that summer he and Avril camped out together in Montague House, a property in the High Street that Ida Blair had just bought with a small family legacy on her mother's death. Eric never called it 'Montague House', putting '36 High Street' on his letters, unlike the rest of the family. His parents had let their old house in Queen Street to summer visitors and were staying with Marjorie. 'Eric and I' wrote Avril, 'moved into Montague House . . .'

GEORGE ORWELL

It had very little furniture in it, because most of our furniture was in the other house. Eric was writing away hard all day, and I was out. I was at that time working in a tea-shop in the town and came back pretty late at night. For some unknown reason, we only had two electric-light bulbs. I don't know why we didn't buy any more, but we each had one, and we used to take them round from room to room plugging them in wherever we wanted them.

When he wasn't writing, Eric was trying to distil some black treacle and water and make rum. He'd fermented this black treacle and water and was busily boiling it up in a kettle. Out of the spout of the kettle, or fixed on the spout of the kettle, there was yards and yards of rubber tubing, criss-crossed across the kitchen, slung up on chairs and draped over the sink. Every time you had to move from the gas-stove to a cupboard or to a table, it was a sort of hurdle. Eventually the stuff did come out distilled at the other end as pure alcohol. When we tasted it, it had the most frightful taste of rubber tubing.[18]

Even if his sense of propriety towards his parents' property had allowed, he could hardly have enticed Eleanor into all that mess. And Avril would not have stood for it either, neighbours described her at this time as 'a bitter pill' ('wickedly amusing at the expense of other people'). He had to conceal his brief love affair from his sister.

In September he was back at the school and Eleanor was in South-wold. He wrote to her in October that he was going up to town for a night or two to see how the sleepers on the embankment got on at that time of year. He mentioned the food riots in Lambeth, believing that some of his old friends would have been involved. Dennis Collings had asked him up to Cambridge for half-term, but he could not get away: he did not want to tell Dennis that there were 'two or three people at Cambridge whom I'm not anxious to meet'. (More likely it was Dennis himself.) They exchanged gossip from Southwold: he 'was sorry to hear about poor old Crick', the proprietor of the local cinema at which Mr Richard Blair attended every new film – having run into some trouble over income tax – 'another sign of the bad times of course.' He recalled the summer: 'It was so nice of you to say that you looked back to your days with me with pleasure. I hope you will let me make love to you again sometime, but if you don't it doesn't matter, I shall always be grateful to you for your kindness to me.'[19]

The tone is stilted and restrained, he was plainly not at ease writing about sexual and personal matters. The 'doesn't matter' and 'always be grateful' can be read two ways: as either a kindly, decent fairness, or as conveying self-pity, perhaps even veiled reproach – as if to suggest that she thought he was not good enough for her and was only doing it out of kindness.

Their letters that autumn and into the next year are full of frustrated attempts to meet. They did meet in London for a matinée of *Macbeth* at the Old Vic. He hoped she would be able to get a job in London; she did; but Hayes was still fifteen miles from the centre of the city. 'If we had even passable weather, how would it be to go out some Sunday into the country, where we could go out for a long walk and then have lunch in a pub? London is depressing when one has no money ... When we were together you didn't say whether you were going to let me be your lover again. Of course you can't if Dennis is in Southwold, but otherwise? You mustn't if you don't want to, but I hope you will. Write soon ...'[20] He was plainly humiliated by his penury in trying to conduct a love affair over a long distance. But he pursued her even into December for a walk from Uxbridge and lunch at Denham in Buckinghamshire. 'Letting you pay for my meals,' Gordon Comstock was to exclaim. 'A man pays for a woman, a woman doesn't pay for a man.'[21] The planning and the topography in the letters are very close to that of the sad excursion in *Keep the Aspidistra Flying* when Gordon Comstock does succeed, more or less, in making love in the woods to his reluctant Rosemary, but then is caught out by the price of a set tea in a pretentious hotel and is humiliated by having to borrow the bus fare home. If these incidents in the novel came as close to what he actually did as the topography undoubtedly does to where he actually walked, they would have taken place the following summer. 'I think it would be nicest if we went somewhere where there are *woods*, seeing what the weather is like, e.g. to Burnham Beeches,' he wrote to Eleanor on 6 June 1933.[22]

School kept him busy. Successive letters tell the tale: 'I have managed to put in an hour or two at my own work, also frantically busy with a play the boys are to act at the end of term ... I've done no other writing, except part of a mucky play the boys are to act later ... Besides all the usual school work, I have had to write and produce a play – am now in the throes of rehearsing it – and what is worst of all, have had to make most of the suits of armour etc. for the boys to act in.'[23] He made them in the evenings out of glue and brown paper, just as the heroine of *A Clergyman's Daughter* was to do. One of the young

actors so liked the play that he preserved the script lovingly. It is a
school play.

KING CHARLES II

ACT I

Scene: an inn near Worcester. It is the evening of the battle of Worcester,
1661 [sic]. Present in the Inn are the landlord, Mr Giles, the oldest inhabitant
of the village, his granddaughter, Lucy, and George Burton, a labourer.

MR GILES (setting down his mug): You've been a-watering that beer again,
landlord.
LANDLORD No, not I.
MR GILES It don't taste as it did when I were a boy.
     I mind the time, in good Queen Bess's reign (a booming noise.
     All except Mr G look towards the window).
BURTON Hark! Did you hear that? The guns!

A Mr Burton, it will be remembered, was last heard of being thrown
out of Whitechapel Police Station despite his refusal to pay the six
shilling fine for being drunk and disorderly. The play ends:

MESSENGER Sir! Sir! The king's escaped! His ship has left the harbour. They
    fired that shot as they crossed the bar. The soldiers arrived there
    just a minute too late.
CAPTAIN CHAMBERS Ten thousand curses . . .
SIR JAMES DIGBY Good people all, this is a joyous time
     When our good king, long in most dangerous plight
     Is safe at sea and bound for friendly France.
     We'll honour it with song, and silver too
     Sir Edward here and I will give you all
     To drink good health unto his majesty.
     Long may he flourish, and soon come the day
     When the usurper Cromwell ends his sway;
     Peace, freedom and prosperity shall reign
     When England has her own true king again!
     Come, sir, if you've a song, let's hear it.[24]

Private school teachers had to commit such jolly atrocities to keep their
jobs. A Christmas play in the Church Hall was the school's main public
advertisement. If the school could not attract more boys, it would soon
be done for. What is interesting, however, is that Blair took the Royalist
side against, so the play implies, the miserable, narrow-minded, kill-

joy, life-hating Puritans. That this was not tongue in cheek to please the royalism of the suburbs is suggested by Richard Peters' memory that Blair told them that he would have favoured the Cavaliers against the Roundheads. In *A Clergyman's Daughter* the school play also involves Charles II and Oliver Cromwell, who is made to sound ridiculous in the children's words and accents. (' 'Alt! I 'old a pistol in my 'and.') On the edge of socialism though he was, there was still something to his joke – was it? – to the *Adelphi* staff that he was a 'Tory anarchist'. Richard Rees was to use the phrase of him, and Orwell was to use it of Swift.

Private school teaching must have been a bit like life in the Burma Police: periods of taxing over-activity followed by spells of utter boredom and a constant doubt as to whether one was doing any good at all. In September Blair gave Brenda Salkeld a vivid description of the English Suburban Sunday *entre deux guerres*:

I am writing as I promised, but can't guarantee an even coherent letter, for a female downstairs is making the house uninhabitable by playing hymn tunes on the piano, which, in combination with the rain outside and a dog yapping somewhere down the road, is rapidly qualifying me for the mental home.

I have spent a most dismal day, first in going to Church, then in reading the *Sunday Times*, which grows duller and duller, then in trying to write a poem which won't go beyond the first stanza, then in reading through the rough draft of my novel [*Burmese Days*] which depresses me horribly. I really don't know which is the more stinking, the *Sunday Times* or *The Observer*. I go from one to the other like an invalid turning from side to side in bed and getting no comfort whichever way he turns.[25]

Some things have changed very little.

Though publication of *Down and Out* was planned by Gollancz for the first week in January and proofs (needing a lot of correction, for libel was still worrying everyone concerned) reached Blair by mid-November, yet the title and the pseudonym were still not decided. Gollancz favoured 'The Confessions of a Down and Out', but Blair protested that 'I don't answer to the name of down and out, but I will let it go if he thinks seriously that it is a taking title.'[26] He favoured 'The Confessions of a Dishwasher'. Very much as a compromise, Gollancz decided on 'Down and Out in Paris and London', a decision made so late that the first edition was printed with 'Confessions of a Down and Out' as the running title on the pages. He let Blair retain a line from Chaucer as a legend: 'O scathful harm, condition of poverte.' 'As to a pseudonym, a name I always use when tramping etc. is P. S. Burton,'* he wrote to Moore, 'but if you don't think this sounds a probable kind of name, what about Kenneth Miles, George Orwell, H. Lewis Allways. I rather favour George Orwell.'[27] And so did Victor Gollancz.

Thus was born 'George Orwell', luckily not 'H. Lewis Allways'. The Orwell was a river that he knew and liked, the whole name had a manly, English, indeed country-sounding, ring to it with perhaps an undercurrent of industry in the buried ore. Certainly one of his characteristic themes became the price of progress: that the elimination of poverty can threaten nature and tradition. Be that as it may, he continued to review and write articles under his real name for two more years. To his old friends, he remained Eric Blair; but gradually he became 'George Orwell' and George to new friends. He didn't reserve Orwell for a public face: he was happy to be George. Before long he was answering to both and signing himself by either name according to how he was addressed. But Eric Blair remained the name he used in all legal and domestic contexts – signing cheques, leases, contracts, and getting married.

Advance copies of *Down and Out* reached George Orwell three days before Christmas 1932. Somewhat naïvely he asked Moore 'What does "a recommendation of the Book Society" on the cover mean?' and humbly and unnecessarily asked that 'one copy should be sent for review to the *Adelphi*? They know me and I write for them sometimes, so they would give it a sympathetic review, I expect.'[28] He carried copies with him up to Southwold where he had agreed to spend Christmas – rather than, as the year before, trying to get into prison. He met Eleanor Jaques at Liverpool Street Station to travel back together.

The book was published at 8s 6d on 9 January 1933 and got good notices. Orwell wrote to Moore and said he would leave one hundred pages of his novel (*Burmese Days*) in his office when on the way back

---

*Not always, he had been 'Edward Burton' to the Whitechapel magistrates. (Some echo of Burton the explorer who went native to reach Mecca?)

to school from Southwold and added: 'I have seen a number of notices about the other book, and they were very much better than I had expected, particularly those in the *Evening Standard* and the *Daily Mail*. I believe there was a good one in the *Morning Post* ... No libel actions hitherto, I hope? The book was listed in this week's *Sunday Express* among "best sellers of the week". Does that mean anything definite. I suppose it will go some weeks before you can tell whether it is selling or not?'[29]

At first it looked hopeful. After a modest first printing of 1,500, there was a second impression of 500 that January, and then a further 1,000 printed, probably in February. But then it stuck. A similar thing happened with the American edition published by Harper Brothers in June: they printed 1,750 but by February 1934 had remaindered it, selling off the remaining 383 copies cheap. There was to be a French edition by Gallimard in 1935 (5,500 copies – not exhausted by 1953), and a Czech translation that same year.[30] Its great fame came only in 1940 when Penguin printed 55,000 sixpenny copies, classifying it both on the cover and in their trade list as 'Fiction'. (No records survive either at Penguin Books or in Orwell's papers that throw any light on this misclassification – for in subsequent reprints it appeared on the non-fiction list and in the non-fiction colours.)

Not too bad, in fact, for a first book. Gollancz must have hoped for better, but he realized that he had good growth stock on his hands if not an instant success. For though he made no attempt to cultivate Orwell personally as he tended to do his star authors, yet he kept pressing Moore for news of Orwell's next writings.

The money problem was not solved. The most Orwell could have made out of the book, spread over two years, was between £150 and £200: not enough to give up 'foul teaching'. Yet the notices heartened him. W. H. Davies, the poet and sometime tramp, said in the *New Statesman and Nation* for 18 March 1933: 'This is the kind of book I like to read, where I get the truth in chapters of real life ... his book is packed with unique and strange information.' C. Day Lewis, the poet soon to join the Communist Party, told readers of the *Adelphi:* 'Orwell's book is a tour of the underworld, conducted without hysteria or prejudice ... a model of clarity and good sense ... The facts he reveals should shake the complacence of twentieth century civilization, if anything could; they are "sensational", yet presented without sensationalism' (February 1933). The *Manchester Guardian* saw the moral aptness of the style. 'M.H.' commented: 'He has ... so much to say in that quiet, level voice of his that he has written a book which might work a revolution in the minds of those who are totally unable to look on down-and-outs as other than something entirely unlike themselves' (January 1933). *The Times Literary Supplement* thought well of it as 'a vivid picture of an apparently mad world'.[31] The dust-jacket of the first American edition could quote J. B. Priestley saying: 'Uncommonly good reading. An excellent book and a valuable social document'; and Compton Mackenzie wrote: 'A clearly genuine human document which at the same time is written with so much simple force that in spite of the squalor and degradation thus unfolded, the result is curiously beautiful with the beauty of an accomplished etching on copper.'

Only the anonymous reviewer of the *New English Weekly* had doubts and wanted to know more about the author and if it all really happened to him: 'This book ... is forcefully written and is very readable. Yet it fails to carry conviction. We wonder if the author was really down and out. Down certainly, but out? ... A most interesting book, which does not, however, bear comparison with one or two recent publications of the same kind' (16 February 1933).

The older generation at Southwold must have received the book with considerable reserve. A friend and neighbour remembers that Ida Blair was puzzled by it and said that it was not the Eric she knew. Richard and Ida Blair were glad that their son was writing under a pseudonym. They would have been still more grateful had they known about his novel on Burma. Avril remembered that 'they were rather surprised at the outspokenness of the language' but were 'not in any way shocked' (or if so, they did not show it, she probably meant). The Blairs were not a family to discuss such things. One suspects some careful understatement when she says:

In his relations with his family, my brother had always been detached and one almost might say impersonal. There was never any discussion of sex or his love affairs or anything of that nature at all. So when all those matters came out in his book, it almost seemed as if it had been written by a different person. Although there was this element of surprise about *Down and Out* when we read it, it didn't mean that there was ever any estrangement in the family ...[32]

His Southwold friends, Dennis, Eleanor and Brenda, however, were enthusiastic about the book, and Dennis even wanted to write to *The Times* when a hotelier 'of forty years experience' challenged *Down and Out*'s authenticity. Perhaps Eleanor restrained him. By now the triangle may have been vibrating somewhat.

Back in Hayes, Orwell wrote in triumph to Eleanor to say that Moore was 'very pleased with the hundred pages of the novel I sent to him and harries me to get on with it'.[33] Years later he was to recall: 'I wanted to write enormous naturalistic novels with unhappy endings, full of detailed descriptions and arresting similes, and also full of purple passages in which words were used partly for the sake of their sound. And in fact my first completed novel, *Burmese Days*, which I wrote when I was thirty but projected much earlier, is rather that kind of book.'[34] He is too self-deprecating. Some have seen it as among his very best books. If the characters are two-dimensional, yet they are vivid portrayals of characteristic types and they carry the plot precisely and economically; the sense of time and place is profound and brooding, a rare sociological if not a psychological imagination is at work, and the descriptions of nature are magnificent in their own right and stand symbolically in contrast to both the frailty and the beastliness of man — imperial man at least — and to those he corrupts. But the writing did not come easily. He worked hard. By 7 July he wrote to Eleanor that 'My novel will be about finished by the end of this term, but I don't like large sections of it and am going to spend some months revising it ... God send I'll be able to drop this foul teaching after next year.'[35]

Eleanor had left the job in London that had given them some chance of being together, and that spring and summer they seem to have had only one meeting and walk in the country, to Burnham Beeches. He told her that he was taking a new job at a similar school in the autumn, but that they wanted him to do some vacation teaching, so he would not be back for as long as usual in Southwold. By 30 July, 'I have finished my novel, but there are wads of it that I simply hate, and am going to change.'[36]

What happened that summer in Southwold? Eric told his agent that he was only down for two or three weeks in August. If there were any more letters from him to Eleanor after July they have not survived; and none at all from her to him. All that is certain is that in August of the following year, the *Southwold Recorder* noted the engagement of Hubert Dennis Collings and Eleanor Violet Mary Jaques, and in September their marriage took place at Cambridge. The paper noted that Mr Collings would be leaving for an important post in Singapore (he had left his research post in Cambridge and joined the Colonial Office). How close the true relationship was between Eric and Eleanor is unclear. If she ever thought seriously of marrying him, did she reject the idea because he was poor and seldom with her, whereas her other suitor was closer to hand, and promised to be successful? There is now no way of telling. But two years later, when he came to write *Keep the Aspidistra Flying*, he was able to convey with extraordinary success the rage and self-pity of someone who thinks he is not able to pursue a normal courtship or love life because of lack of money. The hero's degrading poverty and hopelessness as a breadwinner holds him back and nearly spoils everything – until the lady herself, Rosemary, intervenes, brushes him up, and drags him back into the world of commercial employment whether he likes it or not. If there was anything of Eleanor in Rosemary, as there was much of Eric or George in Gordon, she does not appear to have attempted any dragging, even if he did some wretched waiting.

Meanwhile another correspondence had increased in volume and intensity, that with Brenda Salkeld. The gym mistress and Eric became good friends in the early 1930s and remained in touch with each other all his life. The letters are deeply revealing about his literary tastes and development: that is the side of him that interested her. Nearly all his letters to her that survive are in *The Collected Essays, Journalism and Letters*. Miss Salkeld has inadvertently created an unnecessary mystery about them since at her request they each appear labelled 'extract' and carry no salutations or farewells. In fact they are, apart from some trivialities, full texts, only the salutations are missing, which are mainly mild endearments of a kind common among good friends. A few are stronger but have no relation to the content of the letters themselves, and thus seem almost mocking in tone. Possibly he was a little importunate with her, but she would have nothing of him but friendship, so that he, occasionally, like many a lonely and sexually underemployed young man, tried to make her feel guilty and then rudely mocked her. Her letters to him do not survive, but their friendship did all their life.

She must have moved among Shavians, for he turned loose a fine polemic against '. . . any more of your friends who worship Bernard Shaw? Tell them that Shaw is Carlyle and water, that he ought to have been a Quaker (cocoa and commercial dishonesty), that he has squandered what talents he may have had back in the '80s . . . that he suffers from an inferiority complex towards Shakespeare . . .' 'Do you ever see the *New English Weekly*?' he asked in another letter. 'It is the leading Social Credit paper. As a monetary scheme Social Credit is probably sound, but its promoters seem to think that they are going to take the main weapon out of the hands of the governing classes without a fight, which is an illusion.' And he went on to say that a few years ago he had thought it 'rather fun' to reflect that our civilization is doomed, but now it 'fills me above all else with boredom to think of the horrors that will be happening within ten years'. It would either be 'some appalling calamity, with revolution and famine', he said, 'or else all-round trustification and Fordification' in the hands of the bankers.[37] (So Orwell can imagine such a stage towards *Nineteen Eighty-Four* long before he had read James Burnham's *Managerial Revolution*.)

He had obviously been reading the *New English Weekly* very closely. It was the platform of those of Orage's disciples who had stayed true to the relative sanity of his Social Credit period (under the influence of Major Douglas) before Orage had surrendered himself to slavery under the teacher and mystic, Gurdjieff.[38] Major Douglas was forever attacking 'the trusts'. Dislike of big business was no monopoly of socialists. Ezra Pound, for instance, shared such views, as did American populists; and so did Tory anarchists, presumably.

'Have you read *Ulysses* yet? It sums up better than any book I know the fearful despair that is almost normal in modern times. You get the same kind of things, though only just touched upon, in Eliot's poems. With E, however, there is also a certain sniffish "I told you so" implication . . . as the spoilt darling of the *Church Times*.'[39] He had managed to borrow a copy of Joyce's *Ulysses* which was only published in Paris, and was being watched out for eagerly by those custodians of public morality, His Majesty's Inspectors of Customs and Excise. And in December Eric wrote Brenda a huge letter, almost two thousand words, answering her 'What do you think Joyce is after?'. It could have been printed almost as it stood, a highly perceptive and interesting piece of critical writing. The book moved him deeply.

[to answer your question] one has got to decide what a novel normally sets out to do. I should say that it sets out first ... to display or create a character, secondly to make a kind of pattern or design which any good story contains, and, thirdly, if the novelist is up to it, to produce *good writing* which can exist almost as it were in vacuo and independent of subject ... I think *Ulysses* follows this scheme fairly closely, but the queer and original thing about it is that instead of taking as his material the conventional and highly simplified version of life presented in most novels, Joyce attempts to present life more or less as it is lived. Of course he is not trying *merely* to represent life. When *Ulysses* first came out one heard it said on every side that it was an attempt to describe a day in somebody's life, leaving nothing out, etc. etc. It is not that. If one thinks, a complete description of a day, or even of an hour, would be simply an enormous omnium gatherum, quite formless and probably not at all interesting, and in any case would not convey the impression of life at all. Art implies selection and there is as much selection in *Ulysses* as in *Pride and Prejudice*. Only Joyce is attempting to select and represent events and thoughts as they occur in life and not as they occur in fiction.[40]

Orwell shared Joyce's scorn for those who write novels through reading other novels. He appreciated the formal structure of *Ulysses* more than most (many could not see it at all) and yet 'quite apart from the different styles used to represent different manners of thought, the observation is in places marvellous.' Some of the passages 'have haunted me ever since reading them. If you read them aloud you will see that most of them are essentially verse.'

This *Ulysses* letter, while mainly it shows an enthusiast trying to define and convey his growing absorption in the mechanics and craft of fiction, yet also shows a potentiality for real critical ability – as came later in the great essays on Swift, Dickens and Henry Miller. But *Ulysses* proved nearly fatal to his own development as a novelist. Self-consciously and mechanically he wrote *A Clergyman's Daughter* with 'different styles used to represent different manners of thought'; and there are still elements of this, though less gross, in *Keep the Aspidistra Flying*. A year later he confided to Brenda:

I managed to get my copy of Ulysses through safely this time. I rather wish I had never read it. It gives me an inferiority complex. When I read a book like that and then come back to my own work, I feel like a eunuch who has taken a course in voice production ... but if you listen closely you can hear the good old squeak just the same as ever.[41]

The novel he was working on at that time which 'instead of going forward goes backward with the most alarming speed' was *A Clergyman's Daughter*. Joyce stimulated Orwell as a critic but could have been disastrous to him as a writer, if his documentary plain style had not already emerged in *Down and Out* and was there to fall back upon, even to extend and still further purify.

That autumn of 1933 he had had a poem of real quality published in the *Adelphi*:

> A dressed man and a naked man
> Stood by the kip-house fire,
> Watching the sooty cooking-pots
> That bubble on the wire;
> And bidding tanners up and down,
> Bargaining for a deal,
> Naked skin for empty skin
> Clothes against a meal ...[42]

The tale was as simple as the diction. The bargain is struck, the one gets the clothes, the other a meal, the positions are reversed; but the unstated implication is that both are still in a hopeless and pitiable condition. It is far better than the literary and contrived pessimism of the earlier, somewhat religious poem. The following April, the *Adelphi* printed another poem, which was to be included in *The Best Poems of 1934*, published by Jonathan Cape and selected by Thomas Moult. This was 'On a Ruined Farm Near the His Master's Voice Gramophone Factory' (which was at Hayes). He contrasts the ruined countryside:

> As I stand at the lichened gate
> With warring worlds on either hand

to

> The factory-towers, white and clear
> Like distant, glittering cities seen
> From a ship's rail ...

and which seem to generate their own

> Faith, and accepted destiny;

But none to me as I stand here
Between two countries, both-ways torn,
And moveless still, like Buridan's donkey
Between the water and the corn.[43]

A close friend in 1945 was to talk affectionately, thinking of Benjamin in *Animal Farm*, of 'donkey George'. He was already torn between what were to be important themes in *The Road to Wigan Pier*, *Coming Up For Air* and *The Lion and the Unicorn*: progress which could abolish the horrors of poverty and progress which could destroy traditional decencies of an England still close to the countryside – the machine versus nature. But we need both.

By early December he had retyped his revision of *Burmese Days*, after having lent most of the manuscript to Brenda Salkeld to read and comment upon. He had moved that September to Frays College, Harefield Road, Uxbridge, near to Hayes, a far larger and more respectable establishment with about one hundred and eighty pupils, thirty of whom were boarders. The Hawthorns had run into financial difficulties and the proprietor had sold the school to a somewhat larger local establishment, whose head master was soon afterwards arrested and served six years for indecent assault.

Fellow teachers at Frays remember him well. He was popular with the pupils and cordial enough but 'somewhat aloof' with his colleagues, though they remember his courage as a new master in persisting in smoking at the staff table, a practice frowned upon. He did not linger in the Common Room in the evenings but went to his room and typed solidly. H. S. K. Stapley, then a young master there, later to be head master, remembers that he brought a second-hand motorbike which he rode on Sundays dressed only in his old sports coat and grey flannel trousers, no protective clothing whatever. On one ride in the middle of December he got caught in an icy rainstorm. He went down with a chill.[44]

He did not have to endure the new school long, for the chill developed into pneumonia and he was rushed into Uxbridge Cottage Hospital. For a few days there was real anxiety. 'My mother was sent for,' wrote Avril, 'and I drove her down':

He was very ill indeed, but the crisis had passed then, and he was recovering. He was very worried about money, so the nurse told us. He'd been delirious, and he'd been talking the whole time about his money. We re-assured him that everything was all right, and he needn't worry about money. It turned out that it wasn't actually his situation in life as regards money that he was worrying about, but it was actual cash: he felt that he wanted cash sort of under his pillow.[45]

In his tramping days he must have slept with his money under his pillow. If you lost your last ten shillings in those circumstances you might be submerged for ever, not able to reach the next Spike or, in his case, get back to friends or home. However, worry over his actual situation, his miserable job and the disappointing sales of his book might have shown through when his guard was down.

He was still in hospital on 28 December when he wrote to thank Moore for several visits, and said that when he got out in about a week's time, 'I am going straight down to Southwold. Of course I can't go back to school at the beginning of the term, so I am going to chuck teaching, at least for the while. It is perhaps rather imprudent, but my people are anxious that I should do so, as they are concerned about my health, and of course I shall be able to write my next novel in 6 months or so if I haven't got to be teaching at the same time.'[46]

Hospital records of this stay have long been destroyed. One can only surmise that he brought the illness on by overwork, sitting upright typing for hour after hour into the night when already tired. Following the attack of pneumonia, did he perhaps suspect that he had tuberculosis, not simply occasional chronic bronchitis?

This return to Southwold may have been an easier one than his return from Burma. Home is, after all, where you try to be when you are ill. He had published a book, he was reviewing regularly, and having lived on his school master's salary, still had some of the *Down and Out* advance and royalties. He wrote to Moore at the end of January 1934, 'I am much stronger, and have begun doing a little work. By the way, I know that Harper's owe me a few royalties – not much, I am afraid, but about £20 or £30. Do you think it would be possible to get anything out of them say next month? It doesn't matter now, but I may be getting rather hard up in a month or two.'[47]

He seemed to get on better with his father, for they were often seen taking short walks together and working diligently but ineptly, by local working-class standards, on an allotment. 'What he grew on it, I don't know, but he and Eric knew nothing about gardening. They were always coming across to borrow a rake or a shovel or ask what to do. They didn't have a clue – and owning an allotment was an odd thing for a man in his walk of life to do, none of the other retired civil servants did.' Such was the opinion of Mr Percy Girling, whose father owned a pub and rented the Blairs the allotment. When asked what he thought their 'walk of life' was, he replied: 'They were people who had missed their way somewhere, they weren't quite right, do you see? For instance, the allotment. And old man Blair looking so scruffy and lost. There was money there, there *had* been money there, you could tell from the furniture. Lovely carpets, good Georgian furniture. Lovely dining room they had. But they didn't have enough money then ...'[48]

Perhaps the allotment was Eric's idea, but it gave Mr Blair an additional interest to attending the cinema and his club, the Blythe Club, the gentlemen's club, a cut above the Constitutional Club where those in trade gathered. Blair did not care for his wife's bridge parties and whist drives which went on as regularly as before, earning her much affection and acquaintanceship, though the Blair parents do not seem to have made close friends in Southwold. Avril had gone into partnership with a local woman, whose mother ran a sweet shop, to run a 'good class', they said, tea-shop, inevitably called 'The Copper Kettle'. Social paradoxes abounded. Orwell already wore his famous shaggy uniform of sports jacket and grey flannel trousers; but Mr Denny the local tailor remembers that 'they were always beautifully cut and made to measure [by Mr Denny's father]. He was a difficult man to fit off-the-peg, being tall and thin.'[49]

Yet there were tensions in Southwold. A neighbour remembers a 'stand-up row' between Humphrey Dakin and Ida Blair about *Down and Out*, Dakin roaring that Eric knew nothing about the working man, he knew far more and could get on better with them in any pub than Eric. Mrs Blair defended her tall son indignantly, but not perhaps very enthusiastically. What could she have cared whether he understood the working man or not? The neighbour thought that neither of the brothers-in-law were obvious candidates for possession of the common touch, although Eric was always courteous and gentle. She also remembers that some of Ida Blair's friends at this time found Eric 'very outré and were very condescending: "how terrible for Mrs Blair to have a son like that, he looks as though he never washes".'[50] They would have been positively shocked had they known what he was working away at so hard: *A Clergyman's Daughter*; and highly alarmed, especially as so many of them had connections in India, had they known what he had just completed and was trying, with little success, to get published: *Burmese Days*. As V. S. Pritchett was to write long afterwards: 'A scathing and vivid novel with the amusingly old-fashioned title of "Burmese Days": many an Anglo-Indian must have thought it a collection out of *Blackwood*'s and must have had a shock when he read it.' His description is hard to better:

His pictures of the white man have a contempt mingled with pity. On the other hand the Burmese are not pictured as saints. Orwell is in fact not the usual minority man who turns against the British Empire and who makes heroes of the oppressed simply because they are oppressed. Orwell is far subtler and far more honest than that. He is really an active moralist, a preacher who sees that oppression creates hypocrisy, and that hypocrisy corrupts. He scents the decay in civilization with an almost fanatical nose. He detests the decay yet he has too much detachment to be a fanatic. There is a note of flat tiredness too, a note of the wearied saint. This Burmese novel is written on the raw; its realm is as distinct as anything in Kipling or E. M. Forster. It used to be said after the fall of Singapore that the novels of Somerset Maugham had indirectly prophesied it; Orwell went further than Maugham; Orwell's prophecy was savage and direct. And yet, all the time he is interested, more and more absorbed by the dejection of the life he describes. And he writes with a bitter humour and wit, punctuated by sudden bouts of sympathy and pity for the people he has attacked.[51]

Yet that glory was for later. At the time it was a case of:

12 February 1934

My dear Moore,

BURMESE DAYS

I have thought this over again, and I feel that I would really sooner not go further with it. I can't face the sleepless nights.

Yours sincerely,
Victor Gollancz[52]

Gollancz must already have said 'no' once, for Orwell's letter to Moore of 29 January expressed disappointment that Heinemann had turned it down also for fear of libel. The publishing houses moved quickly in those days, or perhaps that was what a good agent could do for a new writer: get a quick decision. Fortunately Eugene Saxton was in London then, the chief editor of Harper Brothers of New York. He saw Orwell and was impressed by the man and the manuscript, despite the disappointing sales of *Down and Out* in America. He proceeded cautiously, but after obtaining some alterations from Orwell, making the very real risk of libel less likely (it was, after all, a bitter attack on 'fictional' individuals, both Burmese and British, in a fully contemporary setting), Saxton agreed to publish it. The book appeared on 25 October in New York. 'My novel is due to come out in New York tomorrow ...', he wrote to Brenda Salkeld. 'Please pray for its success, by which I mean not less than 4,000 copies. I understand that the prayers of clergyman's daughters get special attention in heaven.'[53] The prayers of the rationalist, ex-clergyman's daughter were not quite answered. Harper printed 2,000, there was a second printing (probably of fewer copies), and then it was remaindered in February 1935 with 976 copies unsold.[54] Once again, the sales were out of line with a respectable number of respectful critical notices. Publishing novels in the 1930s (as still today) was highly speculative, either they did well quickly or they were dropped at once, it was simply not worth carrying small stocks to sell in pennyweights over the years.

That same October, Orwell wrote to Moore, saying that he had met Jonathan Cape and had asked him to read *Burmese Days* when they got copies from Harper. He was not optimistic, he said, because Cape used the same solicitor as Gollancz. Nearly all of the publishers did, in fact, because Rubinstein's judgement on libel was excellent, and successful actions could destroy publishers and authors alike, quite apart from the cost of litigation.[55] Gollancz, however, kept the book in mind. When he saw that no one from Burma had tried to make his fortune in the Manhattan courts at Harper's expense, he wrote to Orwell again.

1 February 1935

Dear Mr Blair,

It occurs to me that it might be worth while to consider the Burmese novel exhaustively from the point of view of libel. We could take our time over it and it might be that the points could be cleared up. With this end in view, would you send me the typescript?

Yours sincerely,
Victor Gollancz[56]

By then Orwell no longer had a copy, so Moore had to send him the already amended American edition. This text was followed when the English edition appeared in June 1935, apart from still further changes in name. Lackersteen became Latimer, for instance – seemingly more dangerous as a more common name, unless Orwell had owned up to having an aunt called Limouzin; and all the Burmese and Indian names were mangled into nonsense: Gollancz's fear seems to have been that some Babu, more than some Sahib, would pop up in London to take out a writ because *his* name had been used, or so he would claim. The Penguin edition of 1944 still followed the American version and has become the established English text, since the original manuscript is lost.

Amid all these visions of gain and loss, he was still hard up. He made several more attempts to obtain translation work – all unsuccessful; and through Eugene Saxton he tried to interest Chatto and Windus in commissioning a short biography of Mark Twain. The paradox of the humorist who was also a bitter pessimist must have stirred a chord of empathy in Orwell – perhaps he saw Mark Twain as the Yankee Swift or hoped that 'George Orwell' could become the English Mark Twain.

Brenda Salkeld was teaching away from Southwold most of this time, so meetings got fewer. His letters continued in the same fond vein, however: 'How I wish you were here! I am so miserable, struggling in the entrails of that dreadful book and never getting any further, and loathing the sight of what I have done. *Never* start writing novels, if you wish to preserve your happiness.'[57]

Some time in August, Eric told her that as soon as he finished the present book, he was going to live in London. A friend had offered him part of a flat in Bayswater, but it would 'choke me to live in Bayswater': he wanted to live 'somewhere in the slums for choice'. She must have ticked him off smartly for 'eating worms', for in another letter he denied that he meant living in a slum, only in a slummy part; he did not like 'respectable' areas; 'they make me sick.' He was generally depressed:

I have practically no friends here now, because now that Dennis and Eleanor are married and Dennis has gone to Singapore, it has deprived me of two friends at a single stroke. Everything is going badly. My novel about Burma made me spew when I saw it in print, and I would have rewritten large chunks of it, only that costs money and means delay as well. As for the novel I am now completing, it makes me spew even worse, and yet there *are* some decent passages in it. I don't know how it is, I can write decent passages but I can't put them together ... I nearly died of cold the other day when bathing ...

This age makes me so sick that sometimes I am almost impelled to stop at a corner and start calling down curses from Heaven like Jeremiah or Ezra or somebody – 'Woe upon thee, O Israel, for thy adulteries with the Egyptians' etc etc. The hedgehogs keep coming into the house, and last night we found in the bathroom a little tiny hedgehog no bigger than an orange ...[58]

The image of Jeremiah caring for a baby hedgehog is characteristic and beautiful.

He professed to dislike London. Why he planned to go there is not clear. Probably he went mainly to get away from Southwold, but perhaps also because he thought he could get more reviewing work if he were on the spot. He may have wanted to see more of Richard Rees and the young writers whom Rees encouraged to drop in for tea round the gas fire in the *Adelphi*'s humble office, or whom he occasionally asked to his flat in Chelsea.

He sent Moore the completed manuscript of *A Clergyman's Daughter* on 3 October 1934 with the rather gloomy comment: 'It was a good idea, but I am afraid I have made a muck of it – however, it is as good as I can do for the present. There are bits of it that I don't dislike, but I am afraid it is very disconnected as a whole, and rather unreal.'[59] He told Brenda at the same time that he was only staying in Southwold long enough to rough out an idea for his next novel. So although a lot of the locale of *Keep the Aspidistra Flying* is Hampstead, the mood and themes surrounding Gordon (Jeremiah) Comstock ('I don't know – perhaps I'd sooner sink than rise') must predate his next move. When Orwell wrote to Moore next, saying that he 'knew there would be trouble' over *A Clergyman's Daughter*, the letter was dated 14 November 1934; and the address was 3 Warwick Mansions, Pond Street, Hampstead, London N.W.3 – above the bookshop where he had just found, or rather been found, a part-time job.[60]

CHAPTER EIGHT

BOOKSHOP DAYS

(1934–5)

BOOKLOVERS' CORNER was owned by Francis and Myfanwy West-rope. It is now the Prompt Corner, a chess players' café on the corner of South End Green, Hampstead, but it remained a bookshop until the mid-1950s. South End Green marks the beginning of Hampstead 'proper' when approached up the hill from Kentish Town, a working-class and heavily Irish district. It was social borderland (and boarder-land). In Orwell's day a tram route from the City brought crowds up to the famous Hampstead Heath fairs on Bank Holidays, and brought East Enders for Sunday outings. Hampstead was, and is, a place for intellectuals (both real and pretend) to live; and in the 1930s there were still many houses with cheap bedsitters, a favourite area for young writers and artists on the make or on the mend, as well as for the established who could afford small Georgian or ample Victorian houses.

Hampstead and Chelsea were thought to be, indeed to a large extent were, London's artistic inner suburbs, only yielding intellectual precedence to Bloomsbury. Unlike Bloomsbury, however, Hampstead possessed a broad middle class, less extreme in its social divisions than upper-middle-class true Bloomsbury and déclassé sub-Bloomsbury. Booklovers' Corner sold a range of second-hand books that reflected the broader Hampstead range, and matched the description in the opening pages of *Keep the Aspidistra Flying*: 'There were high brow, middle brow and low brow books, new and second-hand all jostling together, as befitted this intellectual and social borderland.' I bought books there as a student just after the War and it was still just such an extraordinary diversity. Gordon's caustic comments on the merits of the types of books, authors and customers may be taken as Orwell's satiric exaggeration of his own general attitude to contemporary writing: 'dead stars above, damp squibs below. Shall we ever again get a writer worth reading?' Lawrence was 'all right', and Joyce 'even better before he went off his coconut'.[1] Above all he railed at the 'snooty, refined books ... by those moneyed young beasts who slide so gracefully from Eton to Cambridge and from Cambridge to the literary reviews'.[2] 'Beasts' and 'beastly' are somewhat overworked words by Orwell at this time.

The bookshop fortified Orwell's interest in popular culture. Even though Gordon Comstock mocks, George had read and understood emphatically a good deal more of the sources of popular taste than most other intellectuals. So many seemed over-concerned to break with the past, whether seen as the English literary heritage or their own youthful readings, whereas Orwell liked the best of both worlds, Dickens and Wells as well as Joyce and Miller. His main motive, however, in coming to London, to which he was not particularly attached, must have been to enjoy the company of other writers, perhaps of intellectuals generally. He had been through a long period of isolation, thinking a great deal but rarely discussing books and ideas; indeed, there had been few literary friends in his life since his school-days, apart from walks, talks and letters with Eleanor Jaques and Brenda Salkeld. Neither as Blair nor even as Orwell did he like to talk about his current writing. He believed that those who talked about their writing rarely wrote, but in this period in his life he showed the need to talk about other related problems, literary, social or political; and Hampstead was a good place to meet young writers and radicals with whom he could argue as an equal.

Orwell did see more of Richard Rees and others of the *Adelphi* circle. Rees became deeply fond of Orwell. Just before he died, Rees told Melvyn Bragg that he respected Orwell as a writer for not being 'trendy' or for trying to be 'with it' (Rees kept up with new idioms to the last). He was always reliable in a good old-fashioned way, both as a friend and as a contributor.[3] Rees had already noted sadly that there were 'Left Intellectuals who criticized the *Adelphi* for its "rotten Liberal reformism" or its "muddleheaded mystical idealism" ...' and that 'apart from George Orwell' he had met very few 'literary equalitarians of whom it is quite certain that their equalitarianism is even, in the ordinary and simple sense of the word, sincere'. Orwell, Rees asserted, 'had an essentially simple mind ... and was only able to see one point at a time.'[4] If that was so, it had been a rare quality indeed in the kaleidoscopic world of Middleton Murry and Rees in the *Adelphi* days. But perhaps Orwell's mind was neither so simple nor so uncritically friendly, if we assume that 'Ravelston' in *Keep the Aspidistra Flying* is even in part modelled on Sir Richard Rees. Ravelston, the rich socialist editor, masochistically enjoys guilt feelings about the unemployed as he tucks into a thick and bloody steak:

Ravelston lived on the first floor and the editorial offices of *Antichrist* were downstairs. *Antichrist* was a middle-to-high-brow monthly, Socialist in a vehement but ill-defined way. In general, it gave the impression of being edited by an ardent Nonconformist who had transferred his allegiance from God to Marx, and in doing so had got mixed up with a gang of vers libre poets. This was not really Ravelston's character; merely he was softerhearted than an editor ought to be, and consequently was at the mercy of his contributors. Practically anything got printed in *Antichrist* if Ravelston suspected that its author was starving.[5]

If Rees recognized himself in this, he may have blushed a little, but he took no offence. Perhaps in his good Christian heart he expected each fallen mouth he fed to bite his hand a little, and he not merely forgave them but revelled in their independence and, occasionally, success. Others were to say that Orwell was equally soft-hearted when he became literary editor of *Tribune*.

Orwell developed circles of his own in Hampstead partly through the bookshop and partly through Mabel Fierz. Though he made it out to be extravagantly boring, even a bit shoddy and dishonest, his job in fact interested him; and into the shop came some genuinely interesting people, not just as Comstock declaims 'poseurs, bores and lunatics'.[6] Over cups of strong tea, poor coffee or mugs of bottled beer, he would sit with his friends in their rented rooms (he never entertained himself at the Westropes'), talking things over, setting the world aright and damning fashionable reputations. Almost all these friends were younger men, for his years in Burma had made him at 31 older than most of those beginning to make their way as writers.

'With the fine scorn of the unpublished, Gordon knocked down reputation after reputation. Shaw, Yeats, Eliot, Joyce, Huxley, Lewis, Hemingway – each with a careless phrase or two was shovelled into the dustbin.'[7] Either Gordon or George was not wholly consistent about

Joyce. Edwin Muir, the Scots poet, who lived in Downshire Hill, described in his autobiography this time as when 'Hampstead was filled with writing people and haunted by young poets despairing over the poor and the world, but despairing together, in a sad but comforting communion'.[8] Orwell was about ready for this limited form of sociability.

For his first six months in Hampstead, Orwell lived in the West-ropes' own flat in Warwick Mansions, above the bookshop. Jon Kimche (later to become editor of *Tribune*, then of the *Jewish Observer and Middle East Review*) also lodged in the same flat, where he had arrived a month or two before Orwell to work in the shop during the mornings in return, like Orwell, for a rent-free room. So Orwell had the mornings and evenings to write, serving in the shop for the afternoon. He occasionally went out to buy books for the proprietor from private houses, so he must have shown some aptitude in the trade beyond a love of books.

Orwell wrote to Brenda Salkeld about his 'employer's wife' being ill (though according to Kimche it was her husband who was ailing)[9] but he comments quite favourably of her that:

My present landlady is the non-interfering sort, which is so rare among Lon-don landladies. When I came she asked me what I particularly wanted, and I said 'The thing I most want is freedom'. So she said, 'Do you want to have women up here all night?' I said, 'No,' of course, whereat she said, 'I only meant that I didn't mind whether you do or not.'[10]

Apart from being a motherly, pleasant and helpful type, his 'employer's wife' may well have been so indulgent since she was, in fact, a good friend of his Aunt Nellie Limouzin who had written to her on 23 September 1934 from Paris:

I had a letter from Eric yesterday ... He intends finishing his third novel [sic] by the end of this month and will then go up to London and 'stay some months'. I shall give him your address and hope you will be able to see him. I shall advise him to write to you first, for no doubt you are both very busy with the shop, the house and I L P work. He may *possibly* be staying in Golders Green for I know he has a friend there and, if so, would be 'contagious' to you.[11]

Kimche knew the Westropes through their activities in the Independent Labour Party (Left-wing, egalitarian, a strange English mixture of secularized evangelism and non-Communist Marxism) and assumed that Orwell had met them by the same route. Even though they lived in the same house and talked to each other a lot, Kimche did not know that Orwell had met the Westropes through a family connection rather than through ILP meetings at the Conway Hall. And Orwell did not tell Brenda Salkeld either. She can only remember him grumbling, when they met either at Southwold one weekend or in London some time that year, about 'his remote and gradgrind employers' – rather as Comstock does in the novel. When in an essay the following year he actually referred to 'my employer's *kindness* to me', he still said 'employer', not 'friend'.

Orwell did like to keep his small worlds apart. Perhaps in his distortion of the kindly, unworldly and basically poor Westropes, he was trying to act out the hero (or the anti-hero) of his coming novel, suppressing the more benign and mundane real world. Gordon Comstock's life in the bookshop is an imaginative projection of what things could have been if Orwell had had no friends or had not, at last, got his first two books published and a third in the press. If the physical descriptions both of people and places in *Keep the Aspidistra Flying* are transparently Hampstead (Willowbed Road for Willoughby Road and Coleridge Grove for Keats Grove, for instance), most of the acute sense of personal failure and pessimism that permeates the novel must refer back to the four or five previous years of Orwell's life.

The first effect of poverty is that it kills thought. He grasped, as though it were a new discovery, that you do not escape from money merely by being moneyless. [p. 63]

Life on two quid a week ceases to be a heroic gesture and becomes a dingy habit. Failure is as great a swindle as success. [p. 72]

For the rest, in two whole years he had produced nothing except a handful of short poems – perhaps a score in all. It was so rarely that he could attain the peace of mind in which poetry, or prose for that matter, has got to be written. The times when he 'could not' work grew commoner and commoner. Of all types of human being, only the artist takes it upon him to say that he 'cannot' work. But it is quite true; there *are* times when one cannot work. [p. 41]

Gordon Comstock's character, vivid though it is and one of the best Angry Young Men in English literature before John Osborne's Jimmy

253

Porter, yet exhibits somewhat contradictory traits: many of his diatribes seem intended to satirize self-pity, but others show the author's own lingering self-pity. A gloomy man mocks a morbid man. By 1935 Orwell had achieved enough success, self-confidence and hope of living decently by his pen to be ironical about Gordon and his old self, but had not distanced himself enough to take out all auto-biography.

The Westropes' precise political orientation is highly significant and was concealed equally from old and later friends by Orwell. For dramatic effect, as has been shown already, he talked in both *The Road to Wigan Pier* and *Homage to Catalonia* as if he entered the socialist camp, and in the particular Left-wing but anti-Communist way he did, as a direct and immediate consequence of the events he describes. In fact, without committing himself, he had been brooding over such a socialism for a long time. Almost certainly the Westropes and their friends influenced him politically, just as it is certain that he found it congenial to work for people whose political convictions he was coming to share. Kimche does not remember him as talking much about politics then, except that he held forth a great deal about the iniquities of the Roman Catholic Church; he thought of him 'as a kind of intel-lectual anarchist'. Orwell's individualism, his 'Tory anarchism', would not allow him to come near the organized Communist Party; the Labour Party would have appeared in those days of the National Government as both discredited and too milk and water; but he knew a lot more about Marxism than readers of the second section of *The Road to Wigan Pier* might suppose – the ILP Marxists whom he met in Spain all agree on that. Perhaps St Paul had for a long time been ambivalent and broodingly tortured about Christianity but had found his final commitment both easier to explain and more convincing to others if he expressed it in terms of sudden illumination on the road to Damascus.

Mary Myfanwy Westrope had been a member of the ILP since 1905 and by 1935 was a veteran of the women's rights movement. It seems her pacifism kept her out of the militant Pankhurst suffragettes. Francis Westrope was imprisoned as a conscientious objector in the First World War, where he met the pianist Frank Merrick and Fenner Brockway. Merrick says that Westrope and he became interested in Esperanto by accident while in prison: a grammar was the only mind-stretching book available, apart from theological works. Perhaps there was some accident about Westrope's interest, but Esperanto had an ideology of brotherhood of man and international fraternity about it that must have appealed: the tower of Babel, not Mammon or Eve's apple, was to him the primal curse. Given one language, there would be perpetual peace. But the Esperantist cause was nothing if not eclectic and ecumenical: it could sail alongside or take up on board many another great cause or small crankery – including vegetarianism in the Westropes' case. Esperanto led them to meet Nellie Limouzin and Eugène Adam. Like Adam, Myfanwy Westrope had visited the Soviet Union (in 1931), and she too had returned profoundly disillusioned, not with socialism but with what she saw there. She plunged into ILP activity even more heartily on her return.[12]

The ILP was a striking mixture of optimism and pessimism, of heavens and of hells. Domestically, the capitalist system was breaking down, a revolution would occur – it need not be forced – but it would be resisted by counter-revolutionary forces, so these forces had to be anticipated. However, the socialist movement must maintain both internal party democracy and extend to all, not destroy, what the Communist Party called 'mere bourgeois liberty'. The ILP was divided on the Hitler question, whether he was a witness to the last days and death-throes of capitalism or a new autonomous force to be actively resisted by arms. But internationally, most of the ILP saw war as both imminent and as a purely nationalist, capitalist occurrence, a phenomenon of the final era of a capitalism tearing itself apart. This would provoke, after terrible devastation, an international general strike of working men. And in all this, the Communist Party of the Soviet Union and its affiliates had become little better than the new Fascist régimes: an historically specific form of state monopoly capitalism. While not strictly pacifist, the ILP's anti-militarism made working alliances with pacifists easy; and while declaring itself revolutionary, the ILP appealed to Left-wing activists in the existing British Labour movement, still picking itself up slowly after its betrayal by Ramsay MacDonald.

The 'friend in Golders Green' referred to in Nellie Limouzin's letter was of course Mabel Fierz, who herself knew the Westropes. So twice in his early career Orwell was exposed to broadly the same range of ideas that he was to meet, but much more vividly, among the Spanish socialists and anarchists; and exposed indeed to the same association of socialism and assorted crankeries that he was to attack in *The Road to Wigan Pier*. To Brenda Salkeld, if not to Mabel Fierz, he was keeping up his pose of 'Tory anarchist' as late as May 1935, when he told her that he had called on Richard Rees to borrow money, having forgotten it was a Bank Holiday: '. . . but he was at some sort of Socialist meeting and they asked me in and I spent three hours with seven or eight socialists harrying me, including a South Wales miner who told me – quite good-naturedly – that if he were dictator, he would have me shot immediately.'[13] All that can be certain is his proximity at that time to Left-wing socialist ideas, but not yet his full commitment. Mosley's Blackshirts were also very active on the periphery of Hampstead and could have been a powerful negative influence in putting him on the road to Catalonia.

If the political Orwell is beginning to emerge, the literary Orwell was enduring typical difficulties. Gollancz was driven to commission three lengthy opinions. *A Clergyman's Daughter* was a curate's egg – everyone who read it agreed that it was 'good in parts'. Gerald Gould, his chief reader (and a regular novel reviewer for the *Observer*), said that it was 'an extraordinary book', was 'very original', and 'on literary merit I think it certainly ought to be published'; but drew attention to 'snags and difficulties'. These included, again, the fear of libel, since 'the author is so particular and exact in his geographical indications'. The terrible school where Dorothy teaches is said, for instance, to be 'at Southbridge, about twelve miles from London' (as is Uxbridge where Blair had taught). This fear of libel is a good measure of how autobiographical readers assumed the book to be. Despite that, however, Gould found the school-teaching scenes completely implausible and 'quite ludicrous as a representation of what could possibly go on today' (which Orwell was firmly to deny – indeed to show a sardonic delight in the fact that Gollancz and his advisers found it implausible). Gould thought the night scene in Trafalgar Square, when Dorothy loses her memory among tramps, 'extremely powerful' and 'a mixture of James Joyce in the ULYSSES period and O'Casey in his latest mood'. But he saw its 'change of mood and manner' as 'a distinct artistic mistake'.

As usual, Gollancz's solicitor, Harold Rubinstein, to whom it was sent straight away, gave more than legal advice. The difficulties of libel raised by Gould could, he thought, be quite easily overcome; but not those of structure. He said that the book fell into five distinct and far too loosely related sections: (a) Dorothy's life as a drudge for the church and housekeeper for her bigoted and incompetent father; (b) her life as a hop-picker when her memory fails and, following the attempted seduction by the literary gentleman, she runs away; (c) her night in Trafalgar Square with the tramps and down-and-outs; (d) her life as a schoolmistress under the ignorant and despotic proprietor; and (e) her return, somehow defeated, somehow resolute, to the routines of the old parish life. Rubinstein briskly called the first section 'good', the second 'much better', the third 'magnificent', the fourth 'puerile' and the fifth 'unconvincing'. He concluded that the 'fine qualities' of the book would be hopelessly prejudiced if it went out without drastic revision.

Gollancz was in a quandary. He had great faith in Orwell, perhaps not in *A Clergyman's Daughter*; but then a publisher has to keep a new author going, setting his sights on future successes so long as actual loss can be avoided in the present. So he asked for a formal opinion from Norman Collins, his young fellow-director. Collins wrote to him on New Year's Day 1935 to say that it was in many ways the oddest manuscript he had ever read. He agreed wholeheartedly with the solicitor's excellent literary criticism, saw that drastic changes to the structure would improve it, possibly it should be three different books rather than one. But how would the author react?

His reply to such suggestions would, I am convinced, be precisely what O'Casey's reply was to the Abbey Theatre when they turned down his play – and that was a perfectly plain and unequivocal 'Go to hell'. I think then that it is up to us to publish the book, making a ballyhoo of the fact that in many respects this is perhaps the most remarkable novel that we have ever published, etc, etc.

I know nothing of Orwell, but it is perfectly clear (to adopt a convenient phraseology) that he has been through hell, and that he is probably still there. He would certainly be a plum for a practising psycho-analyst. There is in his work, either latent or fully revealed, almost every one of the major aberrations ... The whole of this report adds up to this, I should certainly publish it as it stands rather than let it go, but I would certainly put it up to the author that he makes the sort of alterations which I have suggested ... rather than publish in its present form.[14]

However, Gollancz meanwhile made up his mind to publish with only minor revisions, perhaps fearing that Orwell *would* prove as difficult as O'Casey.* But Orwell, in a letter to Moore six weeks before Collins wrote his report, had already said that he would be willing to do 'a little toning down' of the school scene to meet Gollancz's incredulity; and he had assured him that questions of libel and obscenity were but 'a small matter' to be put right 'by a few strokes of the pen'.[15] By 22 January 1935 Orwell thanked Moore for getting such good terms from Gollancz for the book, asked that a reference to *Burmese Days* be included, and cheerfully remarked 'I am afraid he is going to lose money this time, all right.'[16] He at least did not lose. Four thousand copies were printed and, though the type was distributed, none was remaindered: a good, modest piece of estimating on Gollancz's part. The reviews were very mixed, indeed most reviewers did not know how to place the book, rather like the reports made for Gollancz. Orwell himself had had such doubts when he had told Moore with half-gloomy and half-cheerful frankness, 'It was a good idea, but I am afraid I have made a muck of it.'[17] When he presented a copy to Brenda Salkeld he said that it was 'tripe', apart from the Trafalgar Square night-scene.[18] This was endearingly modest and honest but also obsessively perfectionist. He was to say such things again about his other writings, with far less cause.

Years later when Orwell was putting his affairs in order, he renounced it entirely. He left instructions that it was not to be translated or reprinted, and wrote to a friend that it was a book he was ashamed

---

* The mention of Sean O'Casey's name was to give Gollancz an idea. He sent him a proof copy asking him for a puff for the jacket – a tactic V.G. so often pursued. He must have said something about the Trafalgar Square scene being in the manner of Joyce, for O'Casey replied that 'Orwell had as much chance of reaching the stature of Joyce as a tit has of reaching that of an eagle.' And for fair measure he says that he called it 'a bastard ballet of lamentation'; but by the time he wrote that (in *Sunset and Evening Star*, London, 1954, pp. 133–5), he was working off old scores against Orwell from a book review. (Orwell, to complete the tale, had reviewed his *Drums Under the Windows* in 1945: 'W. B. Yeats once said that a dog does not praise its fleas, but this is somewhat contradicted by the special status enjoyed in this country by Irish nationalist writers ... the basic reason is probably England's bad conscience. It is difficult to object to Irish nationalism without seeming to condone centuries of English tyranny and exploitation ... So literary judgement is perverted by political sympathy and Mr O'Casey and others like him are able to remain almost immune from criticism' – almost (*The Collected Essays, Journalism and Letters*, Vol. IV pp. 13–15)).

of and that: 'This was written simply as an exercise and I oughtn't to
have published it, but I was desperate for money, ditto when I wrote
Keep the A. At that time I simply hadn't a book in me, but I was half
starved and had to turn out something to bring in a £100 or so.'[19]
But his contemporary letters to Brenda Salkeld make clear that he was
writing it for publication and that, while certainly an experiment in
seeing whether different styles and perspectives could be combined in
one narrative as Joyce had done, it was not a mere exercise. He had
already had plenty of exercise in producing writing that did not get
published. Also he was not 'half-starved', even if still very hard up, at
the time he was writing either *A Clergyman's Daughter* in Southwold
or *Keep the Aspidistra Flying* in Hampstead. His worst times had been
in the immediately preceding years. He wanted to make money with
these books, if not enough to live on then almost enough, so he drove
himself hard, and far from 'not having a book' in him, he moved from
one to another with great speed and determination. At this stage in his
life he lacked time, tranquillity and security, certainly, which money
would help provide; but he did not lack ideas.

   A Clergyman's Daughter may not be consistently excellent, but it is
better, in parts, than many, including Orwell himself, were to believe.
The central character of Dorothy, slaving for her useless father, is a real
type and the description of her claustrophobic life rings true, the
sociological detail of middle-class poverty and pretension is fascinating,
even if psychologically the character remains shallow; but he was
simply not that kind of novelist, and there is this other kind of novel.
The breakdown following an attempted seduction that moves her into
the company of tramps and the hop-picking fields is absurdly arbitrary
and implausible; but once established in another closed world, the
description is rich, vivid and compelling. The night scene, written as
dialogue between the tramps in Trafalgar Square, is, in its own right,
astoundingly awful and, as a straight crib from Joyce's *Ulysses* (fully
deserving O'Casey's abuse), embarrassing; it is only interesting for
picaresque detail better placed in his essays and documentaries. Then
her life as a schoolmistress, when she surfaces again, is another compelling creation of a closed world, the remorseless detail of which was
drawn, like the tramping scenes, directly from his own experience.
Someone else must have furnished the details of life in a poor vicarage,
for his own home had nothing of such poverty and despair. But the

three good chapters out of five, all studies in closed societies, have no real relationship to each other and could just as well have been separate short stories. The final chapter, when Dorothy's father allows her home again, is as unresolved and ambiguous as the ending of *Keep the Aspidistra Flying* was to be. She simply forsakes any hope of freedom and resumes the old life, just as Gordon Comstock was to go back to the advertising agency and forsake his poetry. Material circumstances defeat them both. We leave her making cheap costumes once again for the school play:

The problem of faith and no faith had utterly vanished from her mind. It was beginning to get dark, but, too busy to stop and light the lamp, she worked on, pasting strip after strip of paper into place, with absorbed, with pious concentration, in the penetrating smell of the gluepot.

But is she defeated (as Gordon could be said to be) by the Money God, or is she (as Gordon could be said to be) reconciled to what is at least the 'best of all possible worlds'? Is the final tone sardonic mockery or sardonic pity? The author seems undecided. Orwell himself seems unresolved. If mockery, he can only be the spectator, however good a writer; but if pity, then something should be done about it, while remaining a true writer.

Yet if there was no sign of political commitment in the book, the very first paragraph contained symbols and concepts strangely prescient of his very last great work.

As the alarm clock on the chest of drawers exploded like a horrid little bomb of bell metal, Dorothy, wrenched from the depths of some complex, troubling dream, woke with a start and lay on her back looking into the darkness in extreme exhaustion.

Whatever Orwell revealed about himself in *A Clergyman's Daughter* (and Norman Collins plainly read too much into it – had he met Orwell he would have been astonished at how ordinary and commonsensical he appeared), he did not reveal his politics.

Orwell had a girlfriend in Hampstead, who was a member of the Labour League of Youth, but she remembers that he talked very little about politics except to curse the Empire and 'the Scots by whom he appeared to imagine it dominated'. He had several friends at this period with whom he was on occasional 'walking out together' terms, but there were two 'steady' or 'regular' girls. 'Sally' (a pseudonym) seems to have been, like Rosemary in *Keep the Aspidistra Flying*, a commercial artist; but unlike Rosemary she kept the real George more or less at arm's length. She gave way, with some overlap, to Kay,[20] who worked in a secretarial agency near Russell Square. Kay was someone of literary tastes, who liked to do typing for writers and therefore meet them and mingle with their lives. Orwell met her in the late autumn of 1934 when she came into the shop. She lived very close and knew the Westropes. She was both more down to earth and political than the lesser lights, who seemed to Geoffrey Gorer – in a rather suspect collective memory – to be 'arty' types: 'candles and sandals', given to wearing dirndl skirts and carrying the *New Statesman and Nation* like a talisman. Eric liked the role of a kindly, wiser, older brother, a young girl's guide to literature. He must have been pleased to have a girl both serious and merry to talk to, to walk with, and occasionally when luck and circumstances permitted (for it was always 'to leave by midnight' in those dark days beyond recall), go to bed with. He told her to read Dickens and Conrad and to repair lack of knowledge of the great tradition before tackling the moderns, like Lawrence and Joyce.[21] But Kay needed little such advice: she was already widely read and used to splitting her votes between the ancient and the moderns. A contemporary described her as 'a jolly, smiling, warm-hearted, open, marvellously calm lady'.

Orwell did not even talk to Kay about his writing. He was, in fact, somewhat secretive. Making love was nice enough, but it stirred no great warmth in him, no confessions or soul-baring. Somehow a story grew that he carefully closed a big notebook before sharing his bed one night and, on another occasion, placed a tea-towel modestly over a pile of manuscript. Kay did learn that he was writing a verse epic of the history of the English from the times of Chaucer and in a Chaucerian manner. His aspiration to be a poet still lingered. No trace of this epic survives. The only echoes of this in Orwell's work are the title-page device from Chaucer to *Down and Out* – 'O scathful harm, condition of poverte' – and a snatch of dialogue in *Keep the Aspidistra Flying*:

'Have you read Chaucer's *Man of Lawe's Tale*?'

'The *Man of Lawe's Tale*? Not that I remember. What's it about?'

'I forget. I was thinking of the first six stanzas. Where he talks about poverty. The way it gives everyone the right to stamp on you ...'[22]

Orwell talked to Kay mainly about literature or else volubly and knowledgeably about birds as they walked Hampstead Heath together. He loved birds and he also loved cats. He grumbled to her about cats killing birds: he could not accept this contradiction in nature. She can only remember discussions about politics in the company of other friends: it was clear he was strongly 'pacifist', she said, or more likely anti-militarist, and strongly anti-colonialist; but she has no memory of any specific socialism.

By early March Orwell was well into his new novel, and due to the illness of Myfanwy Westrope, he said (Jon Kimche remembered it as Frank Westrope), he had to find rooms outside. The ever-active Mabel Fierz found him a room in a first-floor flat at 77 Parliament Hill, the last house in the road right on the edge of Hampstead Heath: Parliament Hill itself, on which young and old still fly kites, was framed in his window. The flat was owned by a psychologist of Jungian persuasion, Mrs Rosalind Obermeyer (later Mrs Henschel), who was taking the postgraduate psychology course at University College, London. She let out two rooms, the other to a medical student, Janet Grimpson; and the three of them shared the sitting-room. Rosalind Obermeyer had met him briefly a few years before when Orwell was staying at the Fierzs. Now Mabel asked her friend to let Orwell have the room specifically because it would give him fresh air from the Heath that he badly needed for his weak chest. Neither Jon Kimche nor Kay realized that he had a weak chest. 'Just a bit of a cough sometimes, a bit chesty, you know' – people remember Orwell saying things like that, part confiding, part forbidding inquiry and sympathy. Two new friends were only aware that Orwell had bronchitis 'each winter'.

He brought Kay to his room at Parliament Hill to meet these two new friends, Rayner Heppenstall and Michael Sayers. Heppenstall, new to London after reading English at Leeds University, was beginning to write for the *Adelphi*. He became a novelist and a poet, and later a famous producer on the BBC's Third Programme in its early days. One evening earlier that spring, Richard Rees had asked Heppenstall to join him for dinner at Bertorelli's restaurant in Charlotte Street to meet a fellow contributor – George Orwell. Heppenstall brought another writer with him, whose poems were beginning to appear in the *Adelphi*, Dylan Thomas. Both he and Thomas, Heppenstall relates, were 'already pretty well stoked up on Henekey's cider', and 'There was a good deal of nonsense that evening

... but nothing which casts much light upon either Dylan or "George Orwell" '.[23] Almost immediately, Heppenstall and Orwell met again at the house of T. Sturge Moore, a white-bearded poet in a skull cap who was the original of A. E. Housman's much-travelled remark, 'a sheep in sheep's clothing'. Through Heppenstall Orwell met Michael Sayers, poet, writer and Communist fellow-traveller who later emigrated to the United States. He asked them both to dinner, cooked a good steak for them on his newly-purchased 'Bachelor Griller', and they drank beer out of wooden 'tree pattern' mugs that he was then collecting (as Heppenstall states, but Kay is very firm that he collected pewter tankards, and only had one such arty 'tree pattern', that she had given him as a joke).

'Curious,' wrote George to Brenda Salkeld on 7th March,

... that you should mention that review of Joad's book, because Heppenstall, the man who wrote it, stayed at my place the night before last – in fact he was having breakfast with me when I was reading your letter. I did not tell him what you said about 'second-rate highbrows'. As a matter of fact, he is very nice – a Yorkshireman, very young, twenty-four or five, I would say, and passionately interested in the ballet ... I cannot tell you how I am looking forward to coming down next weekend. I do hope it won't fall through.[24]

He also introduced Rayner to Mabel Fierz, who delightedly took him under her wing as a young hopeful, as she had taken Eric some years before.

George and Rayner were welcome, Kay remembers, at literary 'At Homes' given by such as Edwin Muir and his wife, Willa. Orwell refused to go, indeed he crossed the street rather than pass the Muirs, so strong was his irrational dislike, they all noted, of the Scots. (In fact the Muirs came from Orkney and Shetland.) He railed against 'the whisky-swilling Scottish drunks' who misgoverned and maltreated the Burmese; and perhaps some hate lingered from the time when Mrs Wilkes favoured the kilted Scottish lordlings in St Cyprian's days. More speculatively, an obsessively long incident, six whole pages, in *Keep the Aspidistra Flying* might furnish a more specific reason. Gordon, invited to a party by 'Paul Doring' and his wife in 'Coleridge Grove' (Keats Grove is next to Downshire Hill) finds, on his arrival, that the house is empty. He may have got the wrong night but they may have done it to him deliberately.

Otherwise, Orwell seemed to be in a mood for company. He sometimes dined at small restaurants in Soho on half-crown set meals; so even if money was very tight, he was no longer precisely poverty-stricken. At one such dinner, Rayner Heppenstall was impressed by George sending back a bottle of red wine to have the chill taken off. He joked that the experience of the Paris *plongeur* was socially one up on his own student days in Leeds or in provincial France. Nevertheless, without ever quite discussing it, Heppenstall and Sayers thought that Orwell was only half-educated compared with their own fine selves.* Any university degree was better than none, and they were certainly in highbrow mood, Heppenstall attending and writing about ballet and chasing ballet girls, and Sayers leading what he held to be a poet's life. Heppenstall was to claim (something that no one else can remember) that all Orwell's women at that time were ugly, as if there were more than one, and imputes some kind of masochism to his amatory forays. Sayers and he saw something a little comic in Eric, 'a nice old thing, and kindly eccentric', going on and on about Dickens, Samuel Butler and Gissing, and something odd in his collection of comic postcards. Also Orwell was found reading the *Magnet* and the *Gem*,[25] children's comics. Plainly culture had to be defended *against* the masses, even in a Marxist mode, whereas Orwell was beginning to show signs of actually appreciating what Herbert Read was to mean by saying, in the title of a once-famous essay, 'To Hell With Culture'; and his interest in popular culture had something anthropological about it (anticipating the great days of *Picture Post*).

This attitude received reinforcement from a long friendship that followed an unexpected letter from Geoffrey Gorer, the social anthropologist. He had read *Burmese Days* and wrote to its author:

Will you allow me to tell you how very much indeed I admire your novel *Burmese Days*: it seems to me an absolutely admirable statement of fact told as vividly and with as little bitterness as possible. It is difficult to praise without being impertinent; it seems to me that you have done a necessary and important piece of work as well as it could be done. I wonder if you intend

* Michael Sayers' attitude emerges in this sting in the tail of his double review of *Burmese Days* and *A Clergyman's Daughter*. 'One feels he has ideas about the novel, and that his future work is going to be unusually interesting. At present Mr Orwell seems to be most concerned with presenting his material in the clearest and honestest way. Being a man of considerable and diverse experience this problem naturally comes to him before any aesthetic consideration ...' (*Adelphi*, August 1935, p. 316).

your stricture on the Burmese sahib-log who are 'living a lie the whole time' to apply to their domestic counterparts; it seems to me to work admirably.

My most sincere congratulations.

Geoffrey Gorer[26]

This soon led to a meeting (when Orwell cooked him liver and bacon, to his distaste). Years later Gorer recalled:

I found he was one of the most interesting people I've ever known. I was never bored in his company. He was interested in nearly everything. And his attitudes were original. He didn't take accepted ideas ... I would have said he was an unhappy man. He was too big for himself. I suppose if he'd been younger you would have said 'coltish'. He was awfully likely to knock things off tables, to trip over things. I mean, he was a gangling, physically badly co-ordinated young man. I think his feelings that even the inanimate world was against him which he did have at some times, I mean any gas stove he had would go wrong, any radio would break down ... He was a lonely man – until he met Eileen, a very lonely man. He was fairly well convinced that nobody would like him, which made him prickly.[27]

Burmese Days was reviewed by Cyril Connolly in the *New Statesman and Nation*. The prep-school friends had drifted apart at Eton, and there had been no contact since.

Burmese Days is an admirable novel. It is a crisp, fierce and almost boisterous attack on the Anglo-Indian. The author loves Burma, he goes to great lengths to describe the vices of the Burmese and the horror of the climate, but he loves it, and nothing can palliate, for him, the presence of a handful of inefficient, complacent public school types who make their living there. The ... vigour and rapidity of this extremely biased book ... His novel might have been better had he toned down the ferocious partiality of the Lawrence–Aldington school, but personally I liked it and recommend it to anyone who enjoys a spate of efficient indignation, graphic description, excellent narrative, excitement, and irony tempered with vitriol.[28]

This led to an invitation to dinner, 'a *"bifteck aux pommes"* cooked by himself' Connolly remembered. Later he was to admit, with rare empathy, that it was quite natural for their renewed acquaintance to have been so delayed: 'when Orwell came back from Burma he did not care for Oxford and Cambridge intellectuals, the easy livers, "the Pansy Left" as he called them.'[29] 'His greeting was typical, a long but not unfriendly stare and his characteristic wheezy laugh, "Well, Connolly, I can see that you've worn a good deal better than I have". I could say nothing, for I was appalled by the ravaged grooves that ran down from cheek to chin. My fat cigar-smoking persona must have been a surprise to him.'[30] From then on,* Connolly bestirred himself to introduce Orwell to people and, particularly during the War, to encourage and publish his essays. Theirs was a friendship of unlike characters. They must have looked at each other like two strange, noble beasts of different species, happening to share the same waterhole, not hostile but generically remote. Connolly admired Orwell for his integrity, authenticity, and eccentricity; but was faintly condescending about his wasting time over the social question rather than concentrating on high literature, while Orwell admired Connolly for his erudition, his knowingness and sociability, but was faintly condescending about his wasting time with *l'art pour l'art* rather than advancing the good old cause. Both seem to have thought that they were patronizing the other by renewing and pursuing (after thirteen years) their ironical but warm friendship. They each had secondary characteristics, however, which were close to the other's dominant one: Connolly then shared the fashionable Left-trending views, as shown by his enthusiastic account of a brief visit to revolutionary Barcelona the following year (which he republished in *The Condemned Playground*); and Orwell had hoped, in *A Clergyman's Daughter*, to write a novel as an exercise in style. None the less, what Connolly would repeat years after his friend's death sums it up well enough: 'I was a stage rebel, Orwell was a true one.'

A lot of things happened at once. Through Connolly, Orwell was to meet the wife of his last days, but through his landlady he now met the wife of his great creative period. With all these new friends, sociability almost went to the solitary man's head. He decided to give a small party. This meant asking his landlady to let him use some of her space, so it was agreed they would give one together.

After about three months in which we rarely met (I engrossed in my studies, he often writing his latest novel), he asked me one day, could we not give a

---

* Denys King-Farlow said to the editors of *The Collected Essays, Journalism and Letters* that Orwell had told him that 'Without Connolly's help I don't think I would have got started as a writer when I came back from Burma.' (Vol. 1, p. 162) But King-Farlow's memory must have been at fault. On Connolly's own testimony, they did not meet until 1935 when Orwell already had two books out, a good publisher, a small reputation and a known character.

joint party as his bedsitter was too small. I know he said one of the people he would invite was Richard Rees and was it Heppenstall? As far as I can remember, he had not invited any women friends, but I remember clearly inviting Eileen O'Shaughnessy, a fellow student at University College, and a lay psychotherapist, Dr Jennings White, who was on the Committee of the Institute for the psychological treatment of delinquency, where I had obtained work as a social worker, and I invited also one or two men students also in the Psychology Department of University College.

When our very pleasant evening ended, I remember Eric accompanied the guests to the nearby buses and trains at the bottom of the hill – on his return he came into my sitting-room, I had noticed that he had paid a good bit of attention to Eileen and Eric said, 'Now *that* is the kind of girl I would like to marry!' I was delighted to hear this, as I, too, felt they had much to give each other. She was a very attractive, very feminine Irish woman, with lively interests and a gay, infectious laugh. So I replied, 'Fine! I'll invite her when I see her again in two days' time, and you tell me which evenings would suit you, and both come and have dinner with me.'

At College I saw she was already reading *Burmese Days* (perhaps he had lent it to her). Our small dinner party two days after was a very gay affair. I left them quite soon (after the meal) in my sitting-room and went out to nearby friends.[31]

Soon after, George took Eileen horse-riding on Blackheath – some old habits die hard – close to where she lived at Greenwich. Two or three weeks later she told another student who had been at the party, Lydia Jackson,* that he had as good as proposed to her. She had not said yes, but she had not said no.[32]

Eileen Maud O'Shaughnessy was of Irish stock, born in 1905 and brought up in Sunderland on Wearside. She had won a scholarship to St Hugh's College, Oxford, from where she graduated in 1927 with a Second Class Honours degree in English. She tried teaching in a girls' boarding-school but could not stand it, held various odd jobs, including reading to the aged Dame Elizabeth Cadbury and some social work, but then took a secretarial course, eventually taking over sometime in 1931 a small firm herself, 'Murrells Typing Agency' in Victoria Street, London, SW1. The office junior, or 'the oil rag', then 15 years old, remembers her well as a 'vivid personality', happy but

---

* Her pen name was Elizaveta Fen. She was born in Russia in 1899, coming to England in 1925 and meeting Eileen at University College, London in 1934. She remained a close friend of them both.

unbusinesslike. Instead of copy-typing the thesis of a White Russian émigré, she rewrote it: the office thought that she should have got the doctorate. Eileen tried to educate young 'oil rag' and prepare her for university, but the girl's mother would have none of it.[33]

Eileen became interested in psychology, sold the agency and entered University College, London in 1934, passing a qualifying examination for the M A in Psychology. In 1935–6 she completed the course work for the degree, though she was never to finish her thesis (something to do with measuring imagination in school children, undertaken on the advice of the Professor, Cyril Burt). She also acted as secretary during this time to her brother, a surgeon and chest specialist. A fellow student and her experimental partner (it was the high court of scientific and experimental method, allegedly), John Cohen (later Professor of Psychology at Manchester), remembers her as 'rather stiff and austere', but also bright, argumentative and provocative. Her great concern for her brother's work was also evident.[34]

Eileen was socialist in her convictions, but did not belong to any organizations or political parties. Indeed, like her future husband, she distrusted parties even if she was prepared to espouse ideologies. The closest she came to activism was teaching two short courses in Psychology for the Workers' Educational Association while at University College. In appearance, Eileen was small, dark and fine-boned. No one called her 'beautiful' but everyone remembers her as either remarkably 'pretty' or 'handsome' – even Rayner Heppenstall admitted this, allowed her to be an exception to his dubious generalization that George only cared for ugly girls. However, Eileen did not care too much how she dressed, usually in shabby and unbrushed but 'good' black suits. Cyril Connolly remembered her as 'very charming ... intelligent ... and she loved him, and she was independent, and although she didn't wear make-up or anything like that, she was very pretty, and totally worthy of him as a wife; he was very proud of her.'[35] Her friends are vehement that she understood people far better than George, and that her range of interests was almost as wide. They were not to be perfect together, but always a good match. She fought his fights and looked after him as well as he would allow – although she was a woman careless of creature comforts herself. She indulged, even enjoyed, his eccentricities. Brenda Salkeld thought well of her, believed her to be the kind of woman George needed. Some of Eileen's friends, however, were not so sure that George was the right man for her, and were puzzled that such an emancipated and forceful woman was so willing to play second fiddle to what appeared to be a rather self-absorbed and gawky minor novelist.

Eileen gave George a new optimism. So unsure of himself with people, he found it marvellous to be loved by a woman like this who did not nag him to look for a steady job, not try to change his bohemian habits. He is likely to have viewed marriage rather conventionally. Having lived alone for so long, he saw the institution of marriage as partly a surrender of liberty in return for security. He did not think that two 'free souls' such as theirs would, in uniting, make a marriage of a unique kind; rather that marriage was a bit of a compromise, forcing the partners to take on many bourgeois conventions.

Perhaps Eileen's arrival in his life could account for the sudden, strange and rather ambivalent 'happy ending' of Gordon Comstock's odyssey – when he decides to take the soul- or poetry-destroying job in the advertising agency and marry Rosemary. Luckily Orwell did not himself do anything so drastic as look for a full-time job again.

Our civilization is founded on greed and fear, but in the lives of common men the greed and fear are mysteriously transmuted into something nobler. The lower-middle-class people in there, behind their lace curtains, with their children and their scraps of furniture and their aspidistras – they lived by the money code, sure enough, and yet they contrived to keep their decency. The money-code as they interpreted it was not merely cynical and hoggish. They had their standards, their inviolable points of honour. They 'kept themselves respectable' – kept the aspidistra flying. Besides, they were *alive*. They were bound up in the bundle of life. They begot children which is what the saints and the soul-savers never by any chance do.[36]

He wanted children very much, more so than Eileen. But he told Heppenstall one thick night three years later, on a rare occasion when his tongue was loosened by trying to keep up with his Alcibiadian companion, that he believed himself to be sterile (which is confirmed, at least his belief is confirmed, by Eileen telling a friend the same thing).[37] Why he believed this to be true is unclear. Perhaps it was simply that, as he told a woman friend ten years later, they had tried to have children and failed. But odd that he should shoulder the blame so self-critically: it takes two to make a child.

Some time in September 1935 Orwell was to write to Heppenstall,

'You are right about Eileen. She is the nicest person I have met for a long time. However, at present alas! I can't afford a ring, except perhaps a Woolworth's one.' And in October he told him that 'Eileen says she won't marry me as yet' until she had finished her course and was earning some money. 'Perhaps I shall be earning more next year,' he said vaguely. 'On the other hand by next year we may all have been blown sky-high. I was down at Greenwich the other day and looking at the river I thought what wonders a few bombs would work among the shipping.'[38]

Keep the Aspidistra Flying was nearing completion when he wrote these cheerful words which make Comstock and Orwell sound so very close to each other. The work as a whole is not political, the diatribe against the 'money god' is not put in socialist terms but seeks to show the damage done to individual (almost individualist) artistic impulse by both commercialism and sheer lack of money (the two perspectives do not always focus together). But there is a definite recurrent theme which, while it is unrelated to the plot, is an extension of the hero's 'apocalyptic relish'; bombing. Even before the Spanish War many novels and poems worked in the theme of the coming of bombing planes, either in straightforward fear or as a desperate hope for the collapse and purgation of a rotten civilization, as well as odd bits of Futurist servility to anything metallic, shiny and inhuman.[39] But Orwell's concern with bombing reflects some of the specific concerns of the immediate company he kept. By 1935 Orwell, through friends like Michael Sayers and the Westropes, was being introduced more and more to advanced Left-wing thinking. Mrs Westrope's younger brother had even introduced him to the abrasive Reg Groves, one of the first British Trotskyists, who had been Orwell's immediate predecessor in the bookshop.[40] Orwell pretended to Brenda Salkeld that he was keeping his distance from these socialists, who would like to see him shot, but he was not convincing, either to her or to Kay, whom he told that 'what England needed was to follow the kind of policies in Chesterton's *G. K.'s Weekly*' (a kind of anti-capitalist, agrarian 'Merrie England' medievalism). Orwell knew that such retreats were impossible precisely because of the likelihood of a new and specific kind of war.

And the reverberations of future wars. Enemy aeroplanes flying over London; the deep threatening hum of the propellers, the shattering thunder of the bombs. [pp. 23–4]

Gordon squinted up at the leaden sky. Those aeroplanes are coming. In imagination he saw them coming now; squadron after squadron, innumerable, darkening the sky like clouds of gnats. With his tongue not quite against his teeth he made a buzzing blue-bottle-on-the-window-pane sound to represent the humming of aeroplanes. It was a sound which, at the moment, he ardently desired to hear. [p. 29]

You can't look at it without thinking of French letters and machine-guns. Do you know that the other day I was actually wishing war would break out? I was longing for it – praying for it, almost. [p. 106]

The electric drills in our streets presage the rattle of machine guns. Only a little while before the aeroplanes come. Zoom – bang! A few tons of TNT to send our civilization back to hell where it belongs. [p. 282]

In part this imagery of bombing is no more than, once again, that 'this age makes me so sick that sometimes I am almost impelled to stop at a corner and start calling down curses from heaven like Jeremiah'.[41] Indeed, his Burma poem had already called down a violent doom, part retributive and part sadistic, not merely on the Empire but on England herself. The specific images in *Keep the Aspidistra Flying* not only make a remarkably good prophecy put forward in 1935 of events in 1939–45 but also offer a clear anticipation of some of the precise imagery and the general intensity of *Nineteen Eighty-Four*. The anti-militarist and pacifist rhetoric in the novel, however, shows the specific kind of discussions going on in the left-wing circles in which Orwell moved. They all believed, as did many military theorists, that the bombing aeroplane would be utterly, drastically and quickly decisive in any future war. And that from the bombed-out ruins of capitalist civilization, an organized working-class movement would spontaneously arise (to the ILP aerial war, not mass poverty, would mark the breakdown of capitalism). If a Guernica did not occur quite on that scale, all 'thinking people' expected it to happen before it did. The imagery of bombing gives some measure of how much Orwell in 1935 was already penetrated by one other great political theme of his time, war as well as unemployment and poverty.

The main literary consciousness of the mid-1930s was gradually, under the pressure of external events, in danger of becoming wholly or overly politicized. Some writers felt the need, as when Yeats in his poem 'Politics' mocked Thomas Mann, to defend the very existence and irrelevance of poetry (much as Mann himself in the 1920s had defended the 'ivory tower' against his brother's advocacy of descent into the political arena). Jack Common reminisced:

After *Down and Out* ... Orwell was well and truly launched as a novelist. That is he was always well-reviewed and could count on a faithful readership likely to grow. The danger was, this being the Thirties, that [his novels] might come to seem irrelevant. It was typical of the way things were going that the *Adelphi*, formerly a monthly ivory tower sheltering or gathering together the devotees of truth-beauty, beauty-truth in writing, was now a political lighthouse in which doughty polemicists argued about which way to direct the beam.[42]

Along with his immersion in cultural and political pessimism (which was as a tendency quite as evident in contemporary literature as 'commitment'), Orwell remained positive and tender towards nature and the traditions of the common people – in all, an almost pietistic exaltation in the texture of everyday life, aspidistras and all. He was also brooding on themes that we would now call 'environmentalist', looking back with horror at the suburban sprawl over the countryside around such places as Uxbridge. Apart from one poem, these themes did not appear in print until 1939 in *Coming Up For Air*. There was a three-year gap until his next novel (indeed last true novel) during which time the subject matter of his writing became dominated (whether against his natural inclination or not) by his moral reaction to political events; but not before.

That August he began to write regularly for the *New English Weekly* which A. R. Orage had founded in 1932. It is doubtful if Orwell ever met Orage, who died in 1934. It was his successor, Philip Mairet, whom Orwell principally wrote for, two years of a gruelling 'Some Recent Novels' column, appearing about once a month. Mairet knew Orwell well. (Orwell only ceased to write for his weekly when, in 1940, it stuck to a pacifist line and Orwell changed to support for the war.) The *New English Weekly* paid almost nothing, but it was a good way to obtain books. Orwell wrote his column conscientiously, obviously reading all the books carefully. If he was harsh to bad (and especially to pretentious) authors, it was clear that he had suffered in reading their work, not just snatched at the jacket and a few random pages. In December 1935 he made a revealing comment in a brief review of Henry Miller's *Tropic of Cancer* – it showed the general effect he was trying to achieve in *Keep the Aspidistra Flying* – 'Man is not a Yahoo, but he is rather like a Yahoo and needs to be reminded of it from time to time.'[43]

He had moved house in August, perhaps to gain more privacy. Grateful though he must have been to Rosalind Obermeyer for introducing him to Eileen, there were difficulties in having his fiancée's fellow-student as landlady. He was still seeing Kay, who had accepted her secondary role, but perhaps he wanted, nevertheless, to put space between himself and her. But the move was precipitated by Mabel Fierz and Rayner Heppenstall. Rayner had lost his digs because of an intolerant landlady, and rucksack on back had fled to Golders Green and Mabel. She had suggested that the three of them, Heppenstall, Sayers and Orwell, find a flat together – to be her 'junior republic', she said, a joke none of them found very funny. They found a flat at 50 Lawford Road, a working-class area just off Kentish Town High Street, so only twenty minutes away from the bookshop where Orwell continued to work each afternoon. The house was small, a yellow-brick early Victorian semi-detached villa, and their flat of three rooms and a kitchen was on the first floor. On the ground floor there was a tram-driver and his wife, and in the basement a plumber. George took a weekly bath in the public baths, Rayner went up to Mabel's at weekends for his; and Michael only used the flat for assignations.[44]

Part of that summer Heppenstall had been away at the first of the *Adelphi* summer schools at Caerleon, when Middleton Murry, then in mystical Marxist or Christian-Socialist phase,* decided that a 'fellowship' should be founded; and then Heppenstall went to stay with Middleton Murry in Norfolk. George had been driven over to Norfolk from Southwold by his sister Avril (the Blairs could run a small motor-car), and had taken Brenda Salkeld for the ride. Almost as soon as Rayner returned to London that August the thought took him to become a Catholic. He actually went to Oxford for instruction under Father D'Arcy. He soon gave it up. Michael Sayers, as the winds blew him, either veered towards or away from the Communist Party. They made a most unlikely pair of flat-mates for a man who was already anti-

* Murry had concluded a few years before that Marx was essentially a religious teacher: '... Communism is the enemy of all "religions", because it is itself the one religion' (*The Necessity of Communism*, [Cape, 1932], p. 111, a book that Orwell almost certainly had read). 'Murry believed in a change of heart,' wrote Rayner Heppenstall long afterwards: 'He believed in the class war, but insisted that it should be waged without hatred.' (*Four Absentees* [Barrie and Rockcliff, 1960] p. 33).

Catholic and anti-Communist. The presence of Rayner and Michael may prove that friendship knows no barriers, or on the other hand it may have been a sign of his slow ferment in trying to place himself politically and morally. The three of them got on, at first, reasonably well. Heppenstall later admitted that they rather exploited 'old Eric'. The rent-book was in Orwell's name and Michael was forgetful about the rent, though he always paid up in the end; but Rayner often had no money by the end of the week. George was first up each morning. He had a certain dignity and formality: unlike Rayner, he would not attempt any serious writing while unshaven and in his dressing-gown. It was George who cooked breakfast, washed up, did most of the cooking; and Rayner stretched himself to fetch the beer for dinner each evening in a jug from the Duke of Cambridge pub on the corner. He and Michael did not seem to take George too seriously; they continued to think of him as 'a nice old thing'. He was ten years older, indeed, than Sayers and eight than Heppenstall. His time-out in Burma had made him older than most of the young writers still leading this kind of 'floating life'; but it also gave him an emotional detachment from them and immunized him from fashion.

Eileen came to see George on Sundays, and George and she would head off by train or Green Line bus for walks in the country. On one such Sunday they set off for Epsom, George carrying a shooting-stick. Rayner himself (he later wrote in self-deprecatory comic vein) went to the Ballet Club at Notting Hill Gate. The business manager was aware of his over-attentiveness to one of the girls and had been told off to ply him with whisky to divert his attention until the girl had had a chance to dress and depart. On his way home to Kentish Town, Rayner passed out twice and made the final ascent up the stairs on his hands and knees. Orwell was waiting up for him.

'. . . Bit thick you know . . . This time of night . . . Wake up the whole street . . . I can put up with a lot . . . A bit of consideration . . . After all . . .' All exemplary sentiments, but somehow at the time they seemed inappropriate.

'Eric,' I said, 'do shut up and go away.'

'. . . Time of night . . . Put up with a lot . . . Bit thick . . . the neighbours . . . I do think . . .'

'Eric,' I said, 'go away. If you don't go away, I shall hit you.'[45]

Eric did not go away. Rayner swung at him feebly and relates that he came to ten minutes later on the floor with a bloodied nose. Unable to clean the blood off his floor, he crawled into the absent Michael's room and bed. Orwell then locked him in. Rayner started to kick the door; and when Orwell opened it, Rayner saw that he was armed with his shooting stick.

I pushed it [the stick] aside and sprang at him. He fetched me a dreadful crack across the legs and then raised the shooting-stick over his head. I looked at his face. Through my private mist I saw in it a curious blend of fear and sadistic exultation. I moved sideways, caught up Michael's chair. I had raised it sufficiently to receive on it the first crash of the descending metal-fitted stick.[46]

'Sadistic exaltation' is, of course, meant to demolish more of Orwell's achievements than his lack of *Adelphi* Quaker-Marxist virtues in dealing with a difficult friend. Heppenstall was not alone in pointing to this dark side of Orwell's character, even if he may have exaggerated it. The account written some twenty years later raises the same kind of problems as Orwell's own autobiographical writings. The incident certainly occurred, as Mabel Fierz confirms, to whom the battered Rayner retreated the next morning – but she puts it down simply to his 'silly behaviour'.[47] It is more reasonable to infer from it that when Heppenstall wrote this account, he had come to think that Orwell's writings were grossly overestimated or that he intended his account to be a symbolic criticism of Orwell's character, rather than to believe that he saw the incident in just such terms at the time.*

* Rereading my first edition, grateful that some critics reacted well to my deliberately avoiding the overly psychological kind of biography, but noting that some think I have overdone it, that there is a 'sado-masochistic' streak in Orwell that is only implicit in my narrative, I look at this passage again. Heppenstall's account is well known, so I could not ignore it although my scepticism is obvious. But perhaps the fairer criticism is that he appears to me to crystallize, like the accomplished novelist he is, a complicated and recurring matter into a single significant anecdote of seemingly instant illumination.

The complicated matter is surely evident throughout this work, but I may not anywhere have been explicit enough. Orwell certainly from very early days liked to push himself into extreme situations: tramping, the tripe shop in Wigan and the trenches of Catalonia to come, possibly the Burma Police, as well as many small incidents, unpopular stands and difficult ways of doing ordinary things; and all despite his ill health. These can all be rationalized as the needed explorations of a genuine and profound political writer. And Orwell's sense of what was ordinary is not to be judged by the home life of Hampstead and Chelsea literary intellectuals. But none the less, however usefully channelled and exploited from his writing, something odd and disturbing remains. I only say that it is inexplicable, except from stock and *a priori* psycho-

The 'junior republic' broke up, but Orwell and Heppenstall met again, perfectly amicably, the following summer when Orwell went to lecture at Middleton Murry's new *Adelphi* centre in Essex. Heppenstall took the chair for him. They retired afterwards to a pub together, 'with perfect contentment', for Rayner to tell George personal news of an old friend of Hampstead days, days already behind them both. Orwell was by then married, settled in the country, and had returned from a crucial journey. They remained friends, albeit not close friends, and Rayner Heppenstall was a constant visitor in the last days. 'His friendships were constant, but seldom close,' as Cyril Connolly remarked.[48]

---

analytical positions, and that it is to be rejected as an overall 'explanation' or 'reduction' of his literary and moral achievements. I do not mean to imply that it does not exist.

Victor Pritchett's remark, which I quote more than once, that 'he might be described as a writer who has "gone native" in his own country' may have a deeper implication. Orwell was an explorer of 'the lower depths', but like some of the great explorers of Africa or of the Arabian deserts, as well as discovery there was a constant self-testing and a self-mortification, some hang-over of how some great individualists had played their version of the Imperial system's 'great game': to see how much a man could take in extreme situations, self-discovery as well as geographical or, in his case, social and political discovery.

CHAPTER NINE

THE CRUCIAL JOURNEY TO WIGAN PIER

AND HOME TO WALLINGTON (1936)

IN January 1936 Orwell finished *Keep the Aspidistra Flying*. He had to make some last-minute changes in the proofs when it was discovered that all his derisive advertising slogans and names of shoddy, beastly products were, despite his own assurances and indignant denials, frighteningly close to actual well-known slogans and products.[1] Closeness to experience could go too far. Each of his books raised such nominalist worries among publishers and friends. It was finally published on 20 April 1936 – a rich and terrible year for political events, yet his book was essentially unpolitical, despite the raging against the money god and the recurrent images of bombing. The theme was the familiar romantic one of an artist's attempt to maintain his integrity as he struggles with poverty and the temptation of a normal, salaried life. Though the social system stands condemned as exploitative and philistine, there is no suggestion that it can or should be changed by political action: perhaps it may all be blown up, but the dilemmas of the book are those of individual failure or success, authenticity or compromise. The book expressed the mood and concerns of Orwell's immediate past, his life since he returned from Paris, but by the time it had appeared Orwell had become far more politically minded. He still was not sure precisely where he stood, but he was sure that the main dilemmas of his time expressed themselves in political terms.

Keep the Aspidistra Flying was the last of his self-consciously 'literary' books, with passages of pastiche Joyce, Gissing, Lawrence, and Wells clearly identifiable. If these influences were still not fully digested, they did not stand as flagrantly apart from each other as in *A Clergyman's Daughter*. Whether by coincidence or influence, his writing improved greatly after meeting Eileen, becoming a settled, simplified and consistent style. The book is also clearly therapeutic, purging his extreme bitterness, jealousy and sense of failure, even if some of the scars – and perhaps a slight masochism – still remained. His pessimism about inevitable progress and his nostalgia for the era immediately before the First World War were both there, but so was an engrained refusal to muzzle his critical powers – even when discussing causes becoming close to his heart: 'Liberty is telling people what they do not want to hear.'[2]

Victor Gollancz was the *deus ex machina* who decisively tilted the still-uncertain and experimenting Orwell in the direction of becoming a political writer, though Gollancz would later wish to disassociate himself from some of the results. That same January 1936, he commissioned Orwell to write a book about the condition of the unemployed in the industrial north of England. Richard Rees recalled:

There was such an extraordinary change both in his writing and, in a way also, in his attitude after he'd been to the North and written that book. I mean, it was almost as if there'd been a kind of fire smouldering in him all his life which suddenly sort of broke into flame, at that time. But I can't understand it or explain exactly what happened. I just don't know.[3]

Orwell accepted readily Gollancz's suggestion of going north, especially as he offered an advance of £500, a very big advance indeed for the time. Orwell told Geoffrey Gorer that but for the money he would never have gone. Advances are, of course, seldom if ever quite all that the word implies. Some money came on signature of the contract, some on delivery of the manuscript, and some not until publication. The total, however, was about twice the amount Orwell counted on for each year's survival; so he could now plan ahead, and indeed marry Eileen. For the first time he could feel reasonably secure, even modestly successful, as a professional writer. The advance was about the same as his father's pension, and though it was spread over two years it allowed him to give up his job in the bookshop and marry the kind of wife, as Eileen was, who did not mind this student-like subsistence.

Gollancz was never close to Orwell. They never got on to first-name terms nor met socially; books were to be rejected and author and publisher were to quarrel. Gollancz was to declare, though with the sour-grapes of hindsight, that he thought Orwell had been 'enormously over-rated'.[4] But at the time he had great faith in Orwell, as shown by the huge advance; and this faith was crucial. He thought that Orwell would develop into a considerable novelist. He also had this brilliant idea, however, so simple and obvious once stated, of interrupting Orwell's annual flow of novels to send him to report on the conditions of real industrial workers. He wanted the same kind of thing as *Down and Out* but now a book about working men in poverty and unemployment, not tramps and outcasts. The idea was Gollancz's, not Orwell's. It was not commissioned, as has often been said, for the (Communist-dominated) Left Book Club, which was launched in May of that year; the possibility of its inclusion arose later. When Orwell sent the finished manuscript to his agent on 15 December 1936, he said that he thought the chances of Gollancz including it in the already highly successful Left Book Club were small 'as it is too fragmentary and, on the surface, not very left-wing'.[5]

Orwell lost no time in setting straight out from the bookshop to the North. The Puritan daemon drove him hard. Much later, near to his death, he wrote in his notebook that all his writing life 'there has literally been not one day in which I did not feel that I was idling, that I was behind with the current job, and that my total output was miserably small. Even at the periods when I was working ten hours a day on a book, or turning out four or five articles a week, I have never been able to get away from this neurotic feeling, that I was wasting time.'[6] Legends about Orwell in the North have grown, but the facts are reasonably clear. He was only in the North for two months, living with working people in Wigan, Barnsley and Sheffield, from 31 January to 30 March; and that included about a week with his sister and her husband in Leeds. And this was no Tolstoyen or Narodnik coming to dwell and to work among the common people, nor yet a relapse to his own down and out days. He came openly as an established writer and a journalist, engaged on research, carrying letters of introduction from Richard Rees, Middleton Murry (for the *Adelphi* in its most political phase was printed in Manchester and had a 'centre' in Liverpool) and from ILP members in London, probably through the Westropes. However, his old experience stood him in good stead. He had the toughness, sense, curiosity and humility to live with ordinary people, not to put up at the Station Hotel or stay in a middle-class boarding-house. Few journalists, then or now, would have done likewise from choice. Orwell took the simple view, 'how else?'

He set off, however, somewhat in the manner of his days on the road. True, he took a train to Coventry, but then for five days he made his way north to Manchester, partly on foot and partly on buses, through Birmingham and Stourbridge to Macclesfield, through the 'Black Country': in other words, passing through some of the grimmest urban spoil of the first industrial revolution just to see what he could see. He stayed in cheap hotels and common lodging houses. Admittedly his last night in a doss-house was because banks were closed by the time he arrived in Manchester.

In Manchester he stayed for four days with a trades union official and his wife, the Meades, who lived in a new council estate at Brynton Road, Longsight. Meade also had charge of the printing and distribution of the *Adelphi*. Orwell visited their printing office and was sad to find that Middleton Murry's northern supporters were very much divided among themselves, personally and politically. He records in '*The Road to Wigan Pier* Diary' that the Meades were slightly scandalized to learn that he had stopped in a common lodging house, and that Mrs Meade was ill at ease when he tried to help with the washing up: 'Lads up here expect to be waited on.'[7] (This 'Diary', it should be said, is clearly not a diary kept day to day, but must have been worked up afterwards – complete with author's footnotes: it is not the primary source of the final book, but either an intermediate stage or, more probably, a first thought as to how to present the material for publication. *Down and Out* was first written in diary form.[8] 'The Diary' is not necessarily a more literal record of 'what actually happened' than the published book.)

The Meades suggested that Orwell go to Wigan, which had high unemployment through closures and short-time in both the cotton mills and the coal mines, and they gave him the address of Joe (or 'Jerry') Kennan, an electrician in the mines and an ILP member. He was also active in Wally Hannington's NUWM, the National Unemployed Workers' Movement.

There was a knock at the door on Saturday afternoon. We were just having tea. And I opened the door and there was this tall fella with a pair of flannel bags on, a fawn jacket and a mac. And he told me that he had two letters, one from Middleton Murry, who was a pacifist author, and the other from Frank

Meade ... In this letter Middleton Murry wanted me to find him a type of lodgings of a lower class, practically of a slum character. So I asked Orwell in, he came in and he had tea with us. Now later after tea we went down to market square where there was always, every Saturday and Sunday, a series of political meetings. There was the I L P, there was the Communist Party, there was the National Unemployed Workers' Movement and there were also various religious bodies ... I introduced him to some of the lads connected with the Unemployed Workers' Movement ... So we found him – they did find him these lodgings.[9]

In the so-called 'Diary' he describes the house he lodged in, sharing a room, as a small house, overcrowded and none too clean. He calls the owners 'H'. Their real names were John and Lily Anderton, and the address was 72 Warrington Lane, a typical poor street of terrace houses, three rooms up and two down, cold tap only and an outside lavatory. After about a week he moved. 'Changing lodgings as Mrs H is ill with some mysterious malady and ordered into hospital,' said the 'Diary' typescript. 'They have found lodgings for me in Darlington Road, over a tripe shop ... Social atmosphere much as at the Hs but house appreciably dirtier and very smelly.'[10] *The Road to Wigan Pier* says nothing of Warrington Lane and begins in the famous tripe shop; and the sudden appearance there of an 'I', waking to 'the clumping of the mill-girls' clogs down the cobbled street', is as unexplained and as abrupt as in *Down and Out*.

Jerry Kennan's children and surviving friends give a different account. They say that Orwell simply gave up without explanation the 'poor, granted, but clean and decent' lodgings that were found for him. These lodgings had been found for him just because, although the Andertons were unemployed, the house *was* clean and decent. More- over, old Labour movement veterans of the period all give much the same testimony as a former National Union of Mineworkers official and Communist, Mr Jim Hammond: 'He could have gone to any of a thousand respectable working-class houses and lodged with them or stayed right where he was. But he doesn't do that. He goes to a doss- house, just like he's down and out in Paris still. You see, when they've left the upper class, they've got to go right down into muck and start muckraking ... Did he have a taste for that sort of thing?'[11] Mr Hammond, however, shrewd old activist, concedes that Orwell may well just have wanted to make propaganda and for that purpose sought out the very worst he could find. He thought that a mistake, that it actually fed middle-class prejudices, that Orwell was wrong and a bit obsessive to associate working-class poverty with dirt – as indeed he did ('I sometimes think that the price of liberty is not so much eternal vigilance as eternal dirt').[12] In fact, particularly among a group as skilled and proud as the miners, people who were unemployed cleaned their homes almost obsessively, the men helping too, for once – 'keepin' yer end up, like'. Mr Hammond's speculation is very plausible, particularly as he took, for a Communist, a relatively measured and balanced view of the book. The second half he regarded as offensive and ignorant, but the first half, apart from the cleanliness issue, he saw as brilliant propaganda and quite 'awesome' in 'giving the truth about' coalmining, and with so much feeling and accurate detail – especially as it was based on only three trips underground.

Wigan is, to this day, collectively touchy on the tripe shop issue. Mr Hammond's analysis is widely shared, indeed taught in Wigan's schools when the book, year by year, is read. While Orwell himself, in the autobiographical section of the book, was ironical about his old perception of tramps as the essential or typical victims of economic misfortune and social injustice, yet he made something of the same sociological mistake again in relation to 'the tripe shop' – even if it is not, after the first few pages, as central to the actual argument as the long-suffering inhabitants of Wigan suppose. Yet symbolically they have a point. There is no doubt that there *was* a tripe shop and that Orwell lodged there for about two weeks; also, that once the exact house was identified as 22 Darlington Street (now 'Norcliffe's Corsets'), old people in the immediate neighbourhood remembered it, without prompting or hesitation, and confirmed the view of the present owner's mother that it had been 'a right filthy hole, a specially filthy hole'.[13] (The long-dead proprietors and their lodgers should not be named, but their names are to be found in the Wigan Burgess (voters) Lists for 1937 and are euphonious with Orwell's pseudonyms.) Jerry Kennan remembered the place too. He described the table as 'indescribable' – a dozen layers of the local evening newspaper, sodden with tea and greasy with tripe, serving as a tablecloth.

Most people who met Orwell were impressed by his gentle seriousness. He went to a wide range of political meetings. He thought Wally Hannington, the national leader of the NUWM, a poor speaker. Jerry Kennan 'wouldn't say by any means Orwell was a convinced socialist, although he was convinced that drastic changes were required'.

Orwell was taken into many houses, simply saying that he wanted to see how people lived. He made systematic notes on housing conditions and wages. He spent several days in the local Public Library, his name is in the register (as Eric Blair), consulting reports on public health and conditions in the mines. He did his homework as a social investigator. He typed up his notes neatly (which survive), six pages on Wigan (about 4,500 words) categorized under Population, Health, Employment (including rates of pay and unemployment benefits, etc.), Housing, Religion and Miners, with 'Additional Notes on Housing' (i.e., detailed descriptions of twenty houses and the streets they are in). There are also press clippings and copies of reports and some additional notes on mining. Similar notes, though on a smaller scale, are there for Sheffield and Barnsley. And he collected some miners' pay slips with piece-rate calculations; and three of these are rubber-stamped, just as he said in the book, 'Death Stoppage'. As he wrote to Rees, 'I have . . . collected reams of notes and statistics, though in what way I shall use them I haven't made up my mind yet.'[14] (The shape of the book was, indeed, not clear beforehand and was to give him trouble.) And he took part in or listened to innumerable political discussions. Orwell did not conceal who he was, what he had been, or what he was doing – although some of it got a little garbled:

He told me he had been a colonel in the Burmese military police, he'd been educated in Eton, he'd never been in an industrial area in his life, and I distinctly recall him saying that, prior to his journey up north here, he had never seen a large factory chimney or a colliery chimney smoking.

He, as far as his politics were concerned, he was a fella of a cynical character, seemed to be looking and delving for a philosophy. He certainly expressed dissatisfaction with British Imperialism as he had seen it. And he wanted to find out the mood and thoughts of workers. Particularly miners or unemployed workers. And to see the effect of the Means Test and the Anomalies Act which was having such a terrific effect on life in places like Wigan.[15]

So somewhere between 'cynical' and 'delving' was how Orwell struck an intelligent, working–class activist who saw him almost daily for about three weeks.

He did not attempt to submerge himself utterly among the unemployed or, in any sense, to go underground. He wrote to friends, Rees and Connolly, for instance, and he received and corrected proofs of *Keep the Aspidistra Flying* – 'otherwise not doing any work, as it is impossible in these surroundings,' he told Connolly.[16] But he did, of course, since Wigan was coal and cotton, see the need literally to go underground to complete his survey. The descriptions of mining are among the finest passages in *The Road to Wigan Pier*.

I made the arrangements [said Jerry Kennan]. I was working with the electricity department, Wigan Corporation. And we had just electrified that pit. Pit called Cribbens, it was. And we took him down; there was the mains engineer, a Mr Darbyshire, the assistant, Mr Glaidon, meself, and Mr Darbyshire's two boys. Well, we rigged him out in helmet and a lamp, and travelling down the main road which of course I could comfortably stand up in, but the way he took the roof had bent a number of girders. And we hadn't gone more than 300 yards when Orwell just didn't duck his head quick enough. It didn't knock the helmet off; knocked him down. He was flat out. Then we revived him, got him round, and we travelled further in and the further in we travelled, the lower the roof and I would think he travelled the best part of three-quarters of a mile, bent absolutely double. I had to be bent. And we – there had been an 'eavy fall in what they call the ravine mine, and we couldn't get through. And this made a longer detour to the working face. And the working face was I think 26 inches. And by the time we landed there, Orwell was unquestionably exhausted. And I remember him lying down on the coal on the floor and I said to him, it's a so-and-so good job they don't want you down here for to write a book about mining . . . Well, we got back but there were three occasions altogether in which he was completely out.[17]

Coming out of the pit, they had to half-carry the exhausted Orwell. But he recovered enough to have drinks with them in a pub nearby, then vanished for four days, leaving Jerry Kennan worried.

Probably feeling a bad attack of bronchitis coming on, he had taken an early morning working-men's train, across to Liverpool where he had a letter of introduction to two middle-class members of the *Adelphi* circle and of the ILP: John and May Deiner. He appeared unexpectedly:

Very early morning . . . a horrible morning in February, all frosty and fog, and he stood at the door, and he was a strange figure. No overcoat, no hat, no bag and a threadbare coat. Standing there and shivering, he was actually shivering from head to foot. Well, he collapsed, well not quite collapsed, but as near as made no matter. So my husband and I we got him to bed as quickly as we could, and he was really very ill. But he wouldn't have a doctor. So we did the best we could in those circumstances. We gave him hot lemon. Anyway, he got better later on. You see, he was really ill.[18]

It sounds like one of his winter attacks of bronchitis brought on by exhaustion. By getting into a warm and comfortable place, Orwell probably saved himself from a third attack of pneumonia. He would only stay in bed three days. In the 'Diary' he only admits to feeling suddenly 'unwell' and 'being ignominiously sick' on a visit to the Deiners and Liverpool; and he makes the visit sound as if it lasted for only two days, rather than four or five – as May Deiner clearly recalls.

He wanted to meet George Garrett, a seaman turned docker, a Communist, who wrote short stories for the *Adelphi* under the ludicrous pseudonym of Matt Low. Garrett took him down to the docks to see a gang waiting in hope of work. The company agent picked out fifty at random from two hundred hungry and ragged men waiting. There had been fighting among them which brought the police in. These were the blessings of casual labour before the horrors of 'over-manning'. The Deiners drove Orwell and Garrett around for most of a day in their car to tour slums and to see slum clearance, which impressed Orwell (though he repeated in the 'Diary' what must have been Garrett's line about the contractors doing well out of it), before driving him back to Wigan in the evening. They remember stopping at several antique-cum-junk shops at Orwell's request, and he bought two brass candlesticks and a ship in a bottle. He told them that he was thinking of trying to set up a small antique shop in a cottage or shop he was about to rent down in Hertfordshire. He also asked Garrett to look into the possibility of taking a passage back to London by sea from Liverpool in an ordinary cargo ship (so there might have been a chapter on life at sea).

Back in Wigan, Orwell felt that he had seen all he wanted to see, and planned to move on, across the Pennines from Lancashire into Yorkshire. He had delved politically as well as kept his distance as regards personal commitment. He had heard the intellectual theories of the books he had read in London actually argued in Wigan, as if passionately close to experience, by self-educated working men, Communist and ILP. He would listen intensely but not make statements, only ask Socratic questions (what Jerry Kennan saw as 'cynicism'). Both the socialism 'beneath the surface' of the eventual book and his sweeping criticisms of socialism must have crystallized directly from all these talks, far more than from his descriptive social investigations. 'Marxists as a rule are not very good at reading the minds of their adversaries,' he was to write – a cogent remark that could well have come simply from listening to Marxists argue, forever categorizing their opponents, rarely grasping their authentic motives. But by the time he wrote, that summer and autumn, there came to be a semi-colon after 'adversaries', and a brilliant extension of the sentence which had little to do with Wigan, but much to do with his sudden awakening as a political thinker: 'if they were, the situation in Europe might be less desperate than it is at present.' Burma, Paris and studying the classics were not wasted: this very English figure could somehow transcend the insularity of so much English socialism.[19]

Quite apart from socialist theory, he drew from Wigan not only haunting images of the horrors of poverty but also of the goodness and decency of ordinary working-class life – so long as a man has a job. He was taken to watch men leaping dangerously on to the steel trucks, to scramble – 'the wild rush of ragged figures' – amidst the débris and waste being dumped on the tips for bits of coal to heat their homes. Orwell felt and conveyed the special ignominy of an unemployed miner being reduced to this open and dehumanizing thieving when, after all, the whole of our civilization, as we know it, depended on the hard, buried work of the miners: 'In order that Hitler may march the goose-step, that the Pope may denounce Bolshevism, that the cricket crowds may assemble at Lord's, that the Nancy poets may scratch one another's backs, coal has got to be forthcoming.'[20] (The last phrase has a biblical ring of censoriousness.) And there was the famous sight that he claims to have seen from the railway train leaving Wigan:

The train bore me away, through the monstrous scenery of slag-heaps, chimneys, piled scrap-iron, foul canals, paths of cindery mud criss-crossed by the prints of clogs. This was March, but the weather had been horribly cold and everywhere there were mounds of blackened snow. As we moved slowly through the outskirts of the town we passed row after row of little grey slum houses running at right angles to the embankment. At the back of one of the houses a young woman was kneeling on the stones, poking a stick up the leaden waste-pipe which ran from the sink inside and which I suppose was blocked. I had time to see everything about her – her sacking apron, her clumsy clogs, her arms reddened by the cold. She looked up as the train passed, and I was almost near enough to catch her eye. She had a round pale face, the usual exhausted face of the slum girl who is twenty-five and looks forty, thanks to miscarriages and drudgery; and it wore, for the second in which I saw it, the most desolate, hopeless expression I have ever seen. It struck me then that we are mistaken when we say that 'It isn't the same for them as it would be for us,' and that people bred in the slums can imagine nothing but the slums. For what I saw in her face was not the ignorant suffering of an animal. She knew well enough what was happening to her – understood as well as I did how dreadful a destiny it was to be kneeling there in the bitter cold, on the slimy stones of a slum backyard, poking a stick up a foul drain-pipe.[21]

This passage shows his growing skill as a writer, his ability to use, not to be dominated by his material, to keep the essentials in mind, not to lose the wood for the trees. For there is a flatter version of the same incident in 'The Diary'[22] in which the girl, less plausibly, actually does catch his eye: but more plausible is that there he simply sees her walking up 'a horrible squalid side-alley', not taking in all that from the moving train. But the train leaving Wigan is itself a symbol of the writer's almost desperate pain at being merely an observer, a member of another class who, having done his contracted task, is carried off remorselessly and mechanically simply to write about 'what can be done?' In *The Road to Wigan Pier* the passage is immediately followed by a short, lyrical description of something he saw then 'for the first time in my life', simply two crows 'in a bare patch beside the line' courting and copulating. Again this is very much like the juxtaposition of the 'Jeremiah passage' in the letter to Brenda Salkeld with the description of a baby hedgehog: and it serves the same purpose. The sterile doom of industrial ugliness can be redeemed by nature, even the ugliest birds can procreate, even in an urban wasteland. In 'The Diary' the crows also occur and copulate; but in a field high on the moors coming into Sheffield and several days away from the young woman. Their symbolic purpose is less obvious in 'The Diary'. Placing them in the book, however, next to the young woman and the drain shows a poetic sensibility; the plain descriptive style of the documentary was, indeed, a very deliberate artistic creation.

Suppose even, which is unlikely, this whole part of the book, drain and crows, were invented. Does this affect in any way the accuracy

GEORGE ORWELL

and honesty of his portrayal of poverty? If we accept the book as consciously 'literature', it does not matter that the author deals with typical rather than actual events; but if we take it as reportage, then any suspicion of retouching and invention of detail can damage our trust in the author's judgements. (The difficulty is that the whole documentary genre of the 1930s dwells in the borderlands between fact and fiction, sometimes clearly one side of the line, like *Down and Out*, sometimes clearly on the other, like *Homage to Catalonia*; but occasionally like *The Road to Wigan Pier*, parts of a book straddle the border ambiguously.)

A more positive image settled into his mind: 'the memory of working-class interiors...reminds me that our age has not been altogether a bad one to live in.'

There is much in middle-class life that looks sickly and debilitating when you see it from a working-class angle.

In a working-class home – I am not thinking at the moment of the unemployed, but of comparatively prosperous homes – you breathe a warm, decent, deeply human atmosphere which it is not so easy to find elsewhere. I should say that a manual worker, if he is in steady work and drawing good wages – an 'if' which gets bigger and bigger – has a better chance of being happy than an 'educated' man. His home life seems to fall more naturally into a sane and comely shape. I have often been struck by the peculiar easy completeness, the perfect symmetry as it were, of a working-class interior at its best. Especially on winter evenings after tea, when the fire glows in the open range and dances mirrored in the steel fender, when Father, in shirt-sleeves, sits in the rocking chair at one side of the fire reading the racing finals, and Mother sits on the other with her sewing, and the children are happy with a pennorth of mint humbugs, and the dog lolls roasting himself on the rag mat it is a good place to be in, provided that you can be not only in it but sufficiently *of* it to be taken for granted.[23]

This passage is sometimes criticized as sentimental and somewhat narrow as a vision of the good life. But read in its context, such a charge is irrelevant. The past for the common man was one of 'mouldy bread', poverty, disease and fear; the future will be of 'rubber, glass and steel', he said; but at least, within the present, if unemployment can be beaten, there are homely contentments and fraternal virtues which contrast vividly with both middle-class acquisitiveness, competitiveness and propriety and with the restless power-hungry arrogance of the intellectuals. And it is compatible with the 'happy ending' rather than 'artist defeated' reading of *Keep the Aspidistra Flying*. To see some good in the past is, for Orwell, to show hope for a better future: even under poverty and oppression, the human spirit, common pleasures and common decency are hard to crush.

Orwell crossed the Pennines to Yorkshire where wool, not cotton, was king; but still coal-mining country. By 2 March he was in Sheffield to meet William Brown, a partially-crippled man whom he knew to be a Marxist and who wrote occasionally for the *Adelphi*. He turned out to be a Communist. Communists and I L P members could still work together on many local issues. Brown found him lodgings with a miner's family who lived in a typical, small 'back-to-back' in Wallace Street. He was to pay them six shillings a week for full board. He asked Brown, who was unemployed, to show him round Sheffield. Brown did so with zeal, hurrying Orwell round houses, factories, meetings, for three crowded and exhausting days.[24] Since only one chapter of *The Road to Wigan Pier* was on housing, Orwell seems to have spent a disproportionate amount of time looking at houses and typing up his notes on the physical conditions that he found. This suggests that he did not have a clear plan for a book, only a general subject-matter; but the visits to houses also led to a great deal of talk with ordinary people. Even that, however, needs a slight qualification: being taken round by political activists, mainly Marxists, whether of Communist Party, Trotskyist or I L P persuasion, it is likely that the homes they knew they could enter easily would be those of supporters. He was meeting, almost all the time, a special section of the most politically conscious of the working class. Yet he is himself aware of that, or at least aware, in many comments in 'The Diary' and some in the book, that leaders or activists tended to be bourgeois or at least lower-middle-class in their life-style and values, Marxist or not. What became the distinctively Orwellian political judgement was that he thought none the worse of them for that: that from his visit to the North and reaching its peak in the novel *Coming Up For Air* and in his 'war aims' book, *The Lion and the Unicorn*, he developed a theory that the future of socialism depended precisely on the leadership of the lower middle classes and on persuading them that they had an identity of interest with the industrial working class. However, it is also worth noting that most of his political contacts were in a very individualistic context: he gained no sense of the power of the unions, nor of the work of the Labour Party. His I L P contacts actually led him to under-estimate the power of indigenous working-class organization.

Either the arguments or the itinerary of the fiery William Brown left Orwell exhausted, so he cut short his stay in Sheffield after three days and went across to his welcoming sister and hostile brother-in-law in Leeds, where he stayed the best part of a week. 'The Diary' admits this visit,[25] but there is no echo of it in the book. There may have been more stern discussions with his brother-in-law as to which of them now understood the working classes better. He went with them to their cottage on Middlesmoor at the weekend; they took him to see Haworth Parsonage, the Brontë family home, and he was much impressed with the smallness of Charlotte Brontë's lace-up boots, being size twelve himself ('that Trotskyite with big feet,' H. G. Wells was to roar when stung by him). 'The Diary' only makes one comment on the Dakin home relevant to his mission, a simple reminder of the 'elbow-room' present in even a small middle-class house: in a working-class house you are alone '*never*, either by night or day'. Otherwise, he only noted that he attended two stilted discussions in a centre for unemployed men, both supposed to follow BBC talks, one on Galsworthy's play, *The Skin Game*, and the other on a talk entitled 'If Plato Lived Today'. Most people came for the warmth.

On 13 March, he moved down to Barnsley to resume the role of social investigator. Barnsley was a mining town of about 70,000 with less unemployment than Wigan but as much hard poverty. Clogs were still worn, though square-toed, he noted, not pointed as in Lancashire. He stayed there two weeks. Brown had passed him on to Tommy Degnan, another Communist (soon to fight in Spain) who took him over and took him round. Again, as in Wigan, he made no pretences and they knew, as well as he did, what he was doing – 'writing a book about it and us'. He noted in 'The Diary' for 19 March, 'In frightful exhaustion after going down the "day hole", as, of course, when the time came I had not the strength of mind to say I did not want to go as far as the coal face.' But this time there were no after-effects. That was the Wentworth Pit which D. H. Lawrence had been down. (This could have been coincidence or Orwell once again following a literary model into an actual experience, as when he had followed Jack London's route into the abyss of the tramps and Lew Levy's kip.)

Two days later he went down Grimethorpe Pit, an easier journey, only about a quarter of a mile to the face and little bending, he noted; and it was altogether a more modern pit with cutting machinery, electric lights – no Davy lamps – and plenty of showers and lockers up top, so that the miners could go home 'clean and decent'. He saw them going into their baths, admired their physique – they looked so ordinary on the street in ill-fitting clothes – but also he noted that most miners had neither showers at work nor bathrooms at home, so would be black from the waist down six days a week; and that that very week his host had had two narrow misses in Grimethorpe from falls as he loaded trucks underground.[26] Orwell was to depict the miners in words as Josef Herman was to depict them in paint: the extraordinary contrasts between the cubist machinery and the tough, muscular bodies, between pitch-black darkness and artificial illumination; and between the depths of industrial oppression and the heights of human will-power. The miners were not sociologically typical, only symbolically. They grew in his imagination as personifying both the fate and the hopes of the whole working class.

He continued busily visiting houses. One unemployed man whom Tommy Degnan found to take Orwell round, called Firth, enjoyed the task and noticed that Orwell did too. But he became unhappy when Orwell produced a tape-measure to measure up rooms. It reminded him of a detective. To Mr Firth this was no small whimsy. He had been 'on every race course of this country involving a lot of things ... Scotland Yard like' (he had been an illegal bookmaker's runner), so he knew what detectives were like. It really disturbed him to see Orwell measuring up the rooms.[27] Or perhaps there was something in Orwell's manner or the way he went about his investigations which could betray to the sensitive nose the demeanour of the ex-policeman.

One small incident may have had deep consequences. He went to hear Mosley speak at Barnsley Town Hall on 16 March 1936. He thought there were about a hundred Blackshirts, that is uniformed members of the British Union of Fascists. (Only later that year, after the Cable Street march, was the Public Order Act passed to ban uniforms in political demonstrations.)

Mosley spoke for an hour and a half and to my dismay seemed to have the meeting mainly with him. He was booed at the start but loudly clapped at the end. Several men who tried at the beginning to interject questions were thrown out, one of them – who as far as I could see was only trying to get a question answered – with quite unnecessary violence, several Blackshirts throwing themselves upon him and raining blows on him while he was still sitting down and had not attempted any violence. M is a very good speaker. His speech was the usual clap-trap – Empire free trade, down with the Jew and the foreigner, higher wages and shorter hours all round, etc. etc. After the preliminary booing the (mainly) working-class audience was easily bamboozled by M speaking from as it were a Socialist angle, condemning the treachery of successive governments towards the workers... Afterwards there were questions as usual, and it struck me how easy it is to bamboozle an uneducated audience if you have prepared beforehand a set of repartees with which to evade awkward questions.[28]

His new friend, Tommy Degnan, was among those who asked a hostile question and got the treatment from the stewards. Orwell caught up with them outside, Degnan remembers:

I want to have a chat with you, he says. In fact can we go anywhere for a drink. So we went in the Three Cranes and over a glass of beer he disagreed with us heckling and disturbing the meeting and all that kind of thing. So we'd a real discussion about it. I pointed out to him that I was in Germany in 1930 along with Arthur Horner and Bill Allen... at a conference there. And at that time there was a strike on in the Ruhr coal fields. And Hitler was holding a meeting in Essen on this particular night as we were in the hotel, and it got late on, the meeting was over and there were some Social Democratic miners. I knew they were militant enough, they were out on strike and for the strike and all that, and some Party [Communist] miners, and they were arguing. We had an interpreter with us and he was telling us what the argument was about. The Social Democrats said, oh Hitler, it doesn't matter, you know. And the Party lads were saying it were dangerous. So I pointed that out to Orwell... He didn't know whether Mosley was sincere or whether he was just bamboozling the people... It was no danger and you ought to be British, fair play and all that sort of thing, see? He didn't understand what Mosley – and he mustn't have understood what Hitler – what Hitler was doing at the time either. Anyway we had this argument, we didn't fall out, but we'd a strong argument about it and we went about our business after that.[29]

How typical of Orwell (as his own account written at the time shows) to side with the audience who were assaulted, but then to put to the miners a case against disruptive heckling – with all the misunderstandings that can follow from not making clear where you yourself stand before questioning your own side's tactics. However, even if the

Communist misunderstood Orwell and gave himself the best lines,* there is no indication before this incident of any great concern in Orwell with the nature and spread of Fascism. It was soon to become his major concern. Somehow right from the beginning he rejected the conventional Marxist view of Fascism as either part of the 'death-throes of the capitalist system' or as 'the vanguard of late bourgeois capitalism' (a view in fact shared by some Conservatives, if not quite in those terms). He saw that it aspired to be a revolutionary mass movement challenging both capitalism and socialism. He appreciated the appeal of its irrationality and recognized it as an international movement with a reasonably coherent ideology, at a time when most people in Britain still saw the Nazi Party as either a tool of German capitalism or as simply serving conventional national interests. Many people still did not take Hitler seriously and speculated on who was the real cool and rational brain behind the Nazi movement.[30] And from his perception of Hitler's and Mosley's *mixture* of sincerity and ability to bamboozle ordinary people, much as in Thomas Mann's parable of Fascism, 'Mario and the Magician', sprang Orwell's own concern for truth, propaganda and the corruption of ordinary language.

On Thursday 26 March he left Barnsley for a long weekend with the Dakins again, then on the Monday he was back in London. The journey north was over, in a physical sense; but in an intellectual sense it had only just begun. What would he finally say about it? The book was to be written. He never went back and when the book appeared he did not think to send copies to any of the men who had helped him or with whom he had stayed. Jerry Kennan said to an interviewer thirty years later: 'Any of you who'd been shown round for some weeks would at least have seen that they got an autographed copy, wouldn't you. I thought, well what a peculiar type. Wasn't the money I was

---

* Degnan's remark about 'sincerity' may also be misunderstanding (for if Mosley was 'sincere', this, for Orwell, would make matters worse, not better, and make Mosley more dangerous, not less). But Degnan's memory is good. For Orwell wrote to Richard Rees on 20 April 1936: 'Do you know John Strachey personally? I was at school about the same time as him but didn't know him. I would like to have a talk about Mosley with him sometime . . . I heard Mosley speak in Barnsley and his speech though delivered with an excellent platform technique was the most unutterable bollox [sic], but I heard Strachey state in a speech once that Mosley was a very able man . . . I would like to know whether M is sincere in what he says or if he is deliberately bamboozling the public' (*The Collected Essays, Journalism and Letters*, Vol. I, p. 218).

thinking about or anything like that. But I'm not surprised at anything he did.' Would most journalists, however, do so? They build up what seem like personal relationships for the sake of and only for the duration of an interview. Was Orwell's presence in Wigan and Barnsley all that different? However, its consequences were.

The tripe shop proprietor's wife could read fortunes in tea leaves. Had she looked into her lodger's cup, she would have predicted a second crucial journey close at hand for the tall dark stranger. But the first journey had already crystallized many of the political attitudes and convictions often attributed to the second, as is clear from Orwell's correspondence and reviews in the months that followed his return from the North. They show the struggles to find a form in which to express both his sense of shock at things as they were and the moral seriousness of his new belief that society could be reshaped for the better. The famous passage in his 'Why I Write' essay of 1946 now needs reconsidering:

I underwent poverty and the sense of failure. This increased my natural hatred of authority and made me for the first time fully aware of the existence of the working classes, and the job in Burma had given me some understanding of the nature of imperialism: but these experiences were not enough to give me an accurate political orientation. Then came Hitler, the Spanish civil war, etc. By the end of 1935 I had still failed to reach a firm decision. I remember a little poem that I wrote at that date, expressing my dilemma:

> A happy vicar I might have been
> Two hundred years ago,
> To preach upon eternal doom
> And watch my walnuts grow;
>
> But born, alas, in an evil time,
> I missed that pleasant haven...

The Spanish war and other events in 1936–7 turned the scale and thereafter I knew where I stood. Every line of serious work that I have written since 1936 has been written, directly or indirectly, against totalitarianism and for democratic Socialism, as I understand it.[31]

Yet it was 'other events' in 1936, not just the actual experience of 'Wigan' but the reckoning it forced on him of where he stood, which committed him to Left-wing socialism and took him to Spain in the first place. He was fully committed to 'democratic Socialism' (as he so carefully typed the small 'd' and the large 'S') before ever he went, but not to being 'against totalitarianism'. It was Spain, not Wigan, that convinced him that the Communist Party was working irredeemably against the revolution and led him to see similarities between Stalinism and Hitlerism.

Between these two winter journeys, however, came a period of peace. Geoffrey Gorer has said that the only year in which he ever saw Orwell really happy was in the first year of his marriage to Eileen and while living at Wallington. But peace and happiness for Orwell did not imply physical comfort and rest. He drove himself as hard as ever. Like Sidney Webb, he could only see a holiday as a chance to begin a different kind of work. Some friends had found for him a small and ancient cottage, one that had been a failed general store in Wallington, a little Hertfordshire village of two hundred inhabitants two miles off the main London road to Cambridge. He was to live there until 1940. Buses went into Baldock only twice a week, but the five miles were easily bicycled. It was thus a quiet and delightfully isolated village but not entirely inaccessible for anyone determined enough to visit him. Cambridge played no part in his life, but Letchworth, only two miles from Baldock, did. Consider the famous peroration in *The Road to Wigan Pier* against the association of socialism with crankery:

One sometimes gets the impression that the mere words 'Socialism' and 'Communism' draw towards them with magnetic force every fruit-juice drinker, nudist, sandal-wearer, sex maniac, Quaker, 'Nature Cure' quack, pacifist and feminist in England. One day this summer I was riding through Letchworth when the bus stopped and two dreadful-looking old men got on to it. They were both about sixty, both very short, pink and chubby, and both hatless. One of them was obscenely bald, the other had long grey hair bobbed in the Lloyd George style. They were dressed in pistachio-coloured shirts and khaki shorts into which their huge bottoms were crammed so tightly that you could study every dimple. Their appearance created a mild stir of horror on top of the bus. The man next to me, a commercial traveller I should say, glanced at me, at them, and back again at me, and murmured, 'Socialists', as who should say, 'Red Indians'. He was probably right – the ILP were holding their summer school at Letchworth. But the point is that to him, as an ordinary man, a crank meant a Socialist and a Socialist meant a crank.[32]

What was Orwell doing on that bus? Presumably he was himself attending the ILP summer school which was held at Letchworth every July. Letchworth, like Welwyn Garden City just to the south of it, or like Hampstead Garden Suburb where Mabel Fierz lived, had been a favourite dwelling-place in the 1910s and 1920s for 'new lifers' and advanced thinkers of all kinds, though by the 1930s their 'isms' and their 'ologies' were on the wane. Health food shops and progressive schools, however, still survived, even flourished. Orwell would have disliked actually living with such people, but the relative closeness of his cottage to this centre of mental power and progress might suggest that someone from the *Adelphi* circle had found him his new home – Jack Common also lived only about eleven miles to the south on a smallholding. The constellation of Common, Orwell and Letchworth seems more than coincidental. Orwell was annoyed at the cranks, morally and politically; and he made a virtue of being very ordinary, not crankish; but in the 1930s he enjoyed such company and was closer to them, both by acquaintance and by his way of life, than he ever admitted.

The cottage was *very* simple. There was no electricity, only Calor gas for heating and oil-lamps for light; it had a corrugated iron roof, abominably noisy when it rained; the privy was at the bottom of the garden. On the ground floor were two rooms: a sitting-room eleven feet by eleven, with a 'squint door' through which the shop could be seen, and the shop was a room of the same size, except that it had an alcove with a Calor-gas stove on which they cooked. Upstairs were two rooms of similar dimensions and no bathroom. There were few places in the cottage where Orwell could stand upright without banging his head on a beam. But for a rent of only 7s 6d a week it was a bargain. The garden was of a good size, overgrown but basically well-stocked with fruit trees; he soon dug it for vegetables, built a hen-house, bought chickens and later geese. Orwell leased a patch of ground across the road on which to keep goats, milking them, the villagers remember, at first light each day, saying that he had been told on good authority (perhaps by his old Uxbridge curate friend with his 'Holy Goat') that the milk would then taste better.[33] And in the front garden he planted a six-penny Woolworth's rambler rose whose scion still flourishes as a large hedge.

On 3 April, he wrote to tell Jack Common that he had moved in the day before, had bought a new bacon slicer, had asked the villagers if they would like a shop there again: 'I am a bit vague about how one gets in touch with the wholesalers for a "general" shop, but I suppose it isn't more complicated than a bookshop.' But all these intricacies and details of a grocer's life he was to solve for himself. And he discussed with Common the feuds between the *Adelphi* followers in the North: they seem 'savagely jealous of people from other areas', each declaring that 'theirs is the only genuine distressed area and the others don't know what poverty means'; and that at their summer schools 'people from the middle classes and genuine working-class people didn't get on together and ... were annoyed by patronising airs put on by some of the others'.[34] The themes of the second half of *The Road to Wigan Pier* were beginning to take shape. He was conscious of his own politically ambiguous and personally stilted or incomplete, never quite-at-ease, relationship with working men. He and Common, for instance, liked each other, but with obvious and mutual hesitancies: Orwell knew that Common suspected him of being an intellectual who had gone slumming simply for material for his novels; and Common knew that Orwell suspected him of trading on his authentic working-class background – so rare, indeed, among the consciously proletarian writers of the 1930s.

Orwell cycled over one day in April to seek Common's advice about hen-keeping and small shop-keeping (since Common had, for a short while, kept a corner shop in Chelsea). Years afterwards Common recalled:

As our cottage might be hard to find I walked out to the brow of the hill north of the church to await the visitor's coming. He had Datchworth's oaken spire, today shooting up to a sky of silk and summer, to aim at. I leaned against a three-armed signpost which read To Knebworth, Woolmer Green; To Datchworth Green; To Bragbury End. From that last direction and very much downhill there presently appeared a solitary cyclist, a tall man on a tall bike. He could have got off and walked at the worst gradient. Not he. This Don Quixote weaved and wandered this side, that side, defeating windmills of gravity till he grew tall on the hillbrow and tall too that Rosinante of a bicycle, an ancient Triumph that could have belonged to his father.

Fellow-countrymen, men of Herts, we made greetings. It was odd, a new vision, seeing him in these country circumstances. He might have been a seedy Empire-builder, the reality of some character read about in boys' adventure stories, a broken-down ex-officer. Whatever it was I saw that morning, I am sure I had a fuller appreciation of my friend Eric. For the moment I was drowned in talk, country-dweller's talk first. He had far more interest than I'd expected in my efforts to make a garden out of bare meadow. He was negotiating, he said, for a bit of rough land opposite his cottage; he could run hens there and sell the eggs in his village store. We continued this pleasant chat down to the pub.

The landlord, a cheerful drunkard ex-navy rating, called him 'sir' tentatively, expecting me to correct him if this was one of the lads despite his gentility. But I did not – no particular reason. Years later I realised that no pub ever knew my friend as 'Eric' let alone 'George'.[35]

Yet even if the landlord, like the villagers, did not feel wholly at ease with Orwell (and it is equally odd of Common to have confused beery matiness with true fraternity), George did feel at home in Wallington. The villagers liked him, though they did not care for all of his friends who visited at weekends. As for the discomforts or the simplicities, he was neither indulging in masochism nor putting on an act. He told visitors that he found it 'very practical' and 'suited to my needs'.

Mark Benney (the convict alias author alias sociologist) remembers Richard Rees taking him to meet Orwell in the autumn of that year:

We knocked on the door of a little cottage, and it was opened by a tall figure, face and clothes covered with coal smuts, who peered at us through a billowing cloud of smoke; Blair had been trying to light his first fire of the season, to find that the chimney was in some way defective. An examination showed that some bricks were missing from the flue, leaving a hole that caused a downdraught. While Blair shovelled the offending coals from the grate, Richard and I went out to the back garden to search for bricks or stone to fill the hole. We found some quickly, nice old blocks of granite of the right size and shape; but when we came back into the house, Blair looked at our finds, then shook his head regretfully. No, he explained, he couldn't use those pieces, they really came from the field behind the garden, which had once been a cemetery; the bits of granite lying around were fragments of old tombstones. I stared at him and began to ask, 'What . . . ?' But no, he went on reluctantly, he couldn't use those to patch his chimney, he wouldn't feel right about it. I was later to become more familiar with Eric Blair's reverence for traditional things; at the time I simply wrote it off as slightly loony. But later, as we drove back to town, Richard was positively ebullient: he seemed to feel that we had witnessed an impressive demonstration in how to be painfully scrupulous while painfully uncomfortable.[36]

When Jean-Jacques Rousseau achieved sudden fame by winning a prize with an essay defending natural man against civilized and artificial institutions, he resigned his job as secretary to a rich family, gave up wearing gold lace and white stockings and tried to make his own life a public witness to his expressed beliefs in simplicity, spontaneity and living naturally. He did so very consciously. Orwell lived to his beliefs long before the day of his fame, indeed ever since his return from Burma; and he did so far more naturally and less self-consciously than Rousseau. None of those who come to admire him for how he led his life has ever accused him of deliberately making his life emblematic of his ideas. It simply was. If he ever postured, it was in small, venial, comic, rather homely things: he had, for example, dogmatic insistence that beer could only be drunk out of a 'straight glass', as working-men did, never realizing that the class lines divide differently in the 'tankard' controversy depending on what part of the country you are in, or even on which district of London. Like Dr Johnson, his inter-locutory opinions were often excessively decisive, even deliberately provocative in a pedantic kind of way.

That May he settled down to work on *The Road to Wigan Pier* which began more from a primary concern with poverty than a basic concern with class. As was often the case in Orwell's life, many things were happening all at once.

Keep the Aspidistra Flying appeared at last on 20 April, shorn of potentially libellous matter. He had some respectful reviews from good people, Compton Mackenzie in the *Daily Mail*, Richard Church in *John O'London's*, and Richard Rees (somewhat incestuously, but such was the custom of the day) puffed it for the *Adelphi*. It did not sell particularly well: 3,000 copies were printed, of which 484 were left to be re-issued in 1942.[37] Yet he was treated as an established 'promis-ing young writer', someone already with a small following, always worth reading and likely, some day, to do something outstanding. Cyril Connolly gave the book a warm but critical welcome in the *New Statesman and Nation*. He said that in Orwell's *Burmese Days* the hatred of Burma (or of what Burma had become under the British) was redeemed by many beautiful descriptions of landscape, but 'the writer of *Keep the Aspidistra Flying* hates London and everything there'. He liked the vigour and the satire of the book even though 'at times making the reader feel he is sitting in a dentist's chair'; and 'the obsession with money, about which the book is written, is one which must prevent it from achieving the proportion of a work of art'.[38] The points are just, and it is clear what he honestly disliked in his old/new friend's writing.

Turn and turn about, that is the way of the literary world, for by July Orwell was reviewing Connolly's first and only novel, *The Rock Pool*. He called it 'mature and skillful', but he thought that Aldous Huxley and Norman Douglas had already done and done better this type of novel about the anguish of expatriate artists in the Mediterranean.

A more serious objection is that even to want to write about so-called artists who spend on sodomy what they have gained by sponging betrays a kind of spiritual inadequacy. For it is clear that Mr Connolly rather admires the disgusting beasts he depicts, and certainly he prefers them to the polite and sheeplike Englishman; he even compares them, in their ceaseless war against decency, to heroic savage tribes struggling against western civilisation. But this, you see, only amounts to a distaste for normal life, and common decency, and one might equally well express it, as so many do, by scuttling beneath the moulting wing of Mother Church ... I criticise Mr Connolly's subject-matter because I think he could write a better novel if he would concern himself with more ordinary people.[39]

Yet this candid exchange did not affect their renewed friendship. When Anthony Powell told Connolly that he had enjoyed reading Orwell's book,* Connolly at once told him that George Orwell was the Eric Blair who had been two years ahead of him in College at Eton. Powell then wrote 'a fan letter' at Connolly's suggestion thinking that Orwell needed 'cheering up'. 'His answer, perfectly polite and friendly, had also about it something that cast a faint chill, making me feel ... that Orwell was not for me.'[40]

Paul Beard reviewed the book in the *New English Weekly*, again a somewhat inside job, since Orwell was their chief reviewer of novels *en masse*; but he was very perceptive:

---

* In his memoirs he wrote: 'I liked the novel for its violent feelings, and presentation of a man at the end of his tether, rather than for form or style, both of which seemed oddly old-fashioned in treatment, as did many of the views expressed in the story' (*Infants of the Spring*, p. 130). The comment is true, but it is odd for Powell to condemn for being 'oddly old-fashioned'. Comstock–Orwell would have harshly retorted that only 'monied beasts' can afford to be fashionable.

With Mr Orwell we reach the complete realist. He is one of those fortunate writers for whom, like Arnold Bennett, any object at all, by its mere existence, thereby acquires a vivid and exciting virtue ... His realism cheerfully undergoes even the repetitiveness of life, the tedium of which it tides over by an unfailing fund of verbal liveliness, and by an awkward *enfant terrible* frankness.[41]

'Any object at all by its mere existence' – he had caught a kind of pietism in Orwell towards natural objects, perhaps even closer to still-life painting than to literature, which Orwell himself was to recognize in his essay 'Why I Write' ('So long as I remain alive and well I shall continue ... to take pleasure in solid objects and scraps of useless information'). He was to give Winston Smith a life-line to the past from 1984 by picking up a useless coral paperweight in a junk shop. He was to tease his fierce readership of *Tribune* by spending space on the beauty of sixpenny rose bushes and of toads mating. Orwell thought that man should be as one with natural objects, like Rousseau he disliked the artificiality of the city. Paul Beard's 'awkward *enfant terrible*' frankness was a good phrase too and its coexistence in Orwell's naturalism and piety towards things was, if arresting and curious, certainly somewhat contradictory and odd, as Powell had seen so clearly.

A letter to Orwell from John Lehmann, doubtless arising from reviews of the book, brought an immediate *enfant terrible* response. The eventual result, however, was an essay which marked a sudden stylistic and moral maturity, only latent or fragmentary in earlier works.

Dear Mr Lehmann
... I am writing a book at present & the only other thing I have in mind is a sketch, (it would be abt 2000–3000 words), describing the shooting of an elephant. It all came back to me very vividly the other day & I would like to write it, but it may be that it is quite out of your line. I mean it might be too low brow for your paper & I doubt whether there is anything anti-Fascist in the shooting of an elephant! Of course you can't say in advance that you would like it, but perhaps you could say tentatively whether it is at all likely to be in your line or not. If not, then I won't write it; if you think it might interest you I will do it & send it along for you to consider. I am sorry to be so vague but without seeing a copy of *New Writing* I can't tell what sort of stuff it uses.

Yours very truly,
George Orwell[42]

Luckily John Lehmann replied civilly. He was used to Gordon Comstock and perhaps he remembered Blair at the Wall Game; and so 'Shooting An Elephant' was written and appeared that autumn in the second number of the already famous *New Writing*. This essay did more than any of his books to demonstrate Orwell's unique character and powers as a writer to editors and other writers. The tone as well as the style, a sad common sense expressed in clear, plain uncluttered colloquial English, became that used in the first part of *The Road to Wigan Pier* (experience fully digested), while the style of the second part, despite its political content, was still close to that of *Keep the Aspidistra Flying*, and showed signs of padding and afterthoughts. It oscillated violently from plain style to literary-decorated, and back, for the ideas were powerful but as yet undigested.

Lehmann's intervention may have secured the style of the first half of the book. But a letter from Geoffrey Gorer told Orwell more what he wanted to hear and sounded a key note for the content of the second half of *Wigan Pier*:

... to tell you how very much indeed I admire your *Aspidistra*. It is an astounding and horrible performance, as far as my inadequate knowledge goes, unique in the last century of English writing. Since Swift I do not think any book has been so certain to make 99% of its readers uncomfortably guilty. You have committed the supreme blasphemy – you have mocked Our Lord the golden calf – and from what I have seen of the reviews (Sunday papers) His servants, however humble, are springing to His defence.[43]

Orwell wanted to be both a good 'new writer' and to be Swift reborn. Gorer's letter was a deliberate, friendly and knowing exaggeration.

Everything happened at once. His literary powers were maturing, his political standpoint becoming more clear, his new friendships and old ones too were burgeoning, and marriage was approaching.

He had written to Connolly from Wigan that he would like to have stayed in the North longer but for being away from 'my girl'. Some time in May he told Gorer:

I am getting married very shortly – it is fixed for June 9th at the parish church here. This is as it were in confidence because we are telling as few people as possible till the deed is done, lest our relatives combine against us in some way & prevent it. It is very rash of course but we have talked it over & decided I should never be economically justified in marrying so might as well be unjustified now as later. I expect we shall rub along all right – as to money I mean – but it will always be hand to mouth as I don't see myself ever writing a best-seller. I have made a fairly good start on my new book.[44]

Another face from school-days re-emerged. The former joint editor with Blair of the *Election Times* had returned from America, heard about Orwell from Connolly, so wrote inviting him to a birthday party. Orwell replied to Denys King-Farlow on 9 June 1936:

Dear King-Farlow,

Of course I remember you ... I'm afraid I can't possibly come along on the 11th, much as I would like to, first of all because it's always difficult for me to get away from here, secondly because like the chap in the N[ew] T[estament] I have married a wife and therefore I cannot come. Curiously enough I am getting married this very morning – in fact I am writing this with one eye on the clock and the other on the Prayer Book, which I have been studying for some days past in hopes of steeling myself against the obscenities of the wedding service.[45]

Presumably they married in church partly for the reason that many non-believers did and do, to please families. Neither his nor Eileen's agnosticism was of the strident religiously anti-religious kind, and he had a liking for the forms and traditions of 'the Church by law established'. Not a thought for a marriage day, but he was to ask in his will to 'be buried (not cremated) according to the rites of the Church of England'.

The occasion was very simple. Eileen and he walked down the road from the cottage together. George vaulted over the churchyard wall so as to be standing inside the gate to pick up Eileen and carry her to the church door, having plainly got his folk-lore muddled. Two of Eileen's friends remembered things she told them much later: 'After their wedding there was a lunch in a pub and George's mother and sister took Eileen upstairs and told her they were very sorry for her, she was taking on something. She knew but she didn't mind.' And somebody had given them a special pot of marmalade. Eileen put the pot on the table. George objected: it should be decanted into a jam dish. Eileen objected that they hadn't got one, he said they must get one forthwith. 'This amused Eileen very much as George had warned her that they were going to live like the working class, but she discovered that there were a lot of gentilities that George set great store by.' George had furnished the cottage gauntly with a table or two, a few chairs and two bed-frames. Eileen brought curtains, cushions and covers, and she cooked for him substantially, with large English breakfasts to begin each day – rather as if she saw or feared a need to try to build him up. She did not, however, take much care of herself and no one yet foresaw any special need. Her standards of comfort were also fairly austere, and she could readily adapt to odd circumstances, with a quite conscious amusement – which was as well, for the chimney smoked, the kitchen was makeshift and few doors or window-frames fitted properly, so that it was bitterly cold, even in June. Some friends found their weekends there a test of physical endurance.

Birds built their nests between the ceiling and the roof, and although their singing was delightful in the morning, at night they would sometimes stamp and struggle overhead like an army of demons. 'People think they are *rats*,' George told me with the characteristic smile he had whenever he indulged in being mildly sadistic, and expected you to be frightened and shocked.[46]

Lydia Jackson saw that her friend was sacrificing her own chance of a career to looking after George (she even ran the poor little shop, a trickle of village children asking for halfpennyworths of sweets) for she had to curtail her work for her surgeon brother; but she also noted that Eileen was no mere doormat. She stood up to George in things big and small, restraining his characteristic flights:

We were having eggs and bacon for breakfast when George remarked that every villager ought to have his own pig and cure his own bacon. 'But,' he added, 'they are not allowed to keep pigs unless they satisfy a set of complex sanitation regulations. Bacon manufacturers had seen to this ...' Eileen gave me a quick glance and a smile. 'Now what made you say this?' she exclaimed. 'Isn't it rather a sweeping statement to make?' The look in George's face showed that he was both amused and a little embarrassed, but he stuck to his guns. 'It is in the interests of bacon manufacturers ...' he began. 'Yes, I know, but have you any evidence to show that they were responsible for the sanitary regulations?' He had not, and she added: 'That's the kind of statement an irresponsible journalist would make.'[47]

So the days were passed in cooking, gardening, shop-keeping and, for him, writing. When King-Farlow paid them a visit, charmed by them both but somewhat rattled by the simplicity of the arrangements, Orwell told him that he had taken up prison visiting. (He makes no other reference to this and his name cannot be found in the Home Office lists of prison visitors in that area.)

In July, he attended part of an I L P summer school in Letchworth and in August went over to the *Adelphi* summer school at Middleton Murry's new home and centre of light and friction at Langham in Essex. He gave a lecture at the *Adelphi* school, Rayner Heppenstall taking the chair for him. This was their first meeting since the Kentish Town brawl. They were reconciled; but he cannot remember what Orwell lectured on. Richard Rees made the claim that Orwell 'astonished everybody, including Marxist theoreticians, by his interventions in discussions. Without any parade of learning, he produced breathtaking Marxist paradoxes and epigrams, in such a way as to make the sacred mysteries seem almost too obvious and simple.' A leading Marxist theoretician, he said, eyed Orwell with 'a mixture of admiration and uneasiness'.[48] This is unlikely. 'Leading Marxist' and 'theoretician' must have been relative terms among Middleton Murry's followers, even though there was a Marxist faction (mainly I L P) in the *Adelphi* and Middleton Murry himself was still preaching his lofty synthesis of Marx and of Christ. To judge by the second half of *The Road to Wigan Pier*, Orwell had not studied the classic texts of Marxism closely; and there is no evidence elsewhere in his writings, letters or among the books he possessed that his knowledge of Marxism was anything but secondary. Probably he had picked up most of what he knew from the 'oral tradition' (like so many students in the 1960s), by meeting Marxists and listening attentively and seriously as they argued, albeit irritated by their abstractions and their rigidity. *The Road to Wigan Pier* none the less shows that he has some claims to understand the Marxist mentality, even if not the sacred texts; and that his positive anger at the Communists did not come until Spain.[49]

His attitude to Marxists while writing *The Road to Wigan Pier* can be seen best in two book reviews. He said of Alec Brown's *The Fate of the Middle Classes* that an account of the English class system expounded by an 'orthodox Communist ... is like watching somebody carve a roast duck with a chopper'; and 'the statement that "every ideology is a reflection of economic circumstances" explains a good deal, but it does not explain the strange and sometimes heroic snobbishness that is found in the English middle classes ... it fails to take account of the stratifications within middle class itself'.[50] This is a measured criticism, not outright rejection, the kind of criticism that some modern Marxists, followers of Gramsci for instance, would readily accept, or even claim to be the true young Marx. But in reviewing Philip Henderson's *The Novel Today*, Orwell hit hard at Communist aesthetic theory, accusing Marxist reviewers of employing 'a double set of values' in dodging from political rejection of a book to aesthetic rejection as it serves their purposes, without having 'the guts to say outright that art and propaganda are the same thing'. He listed Right-wing bourgeois novelists of excellence whom Communists reject utterly – 'this kind of thing is very depressing to anyone who cares for the cause of Socialism'. The only literary critics as bad as the Marxists, he said, are those in Roman Catholic papers. 'The basic trouble with all orthodox Marxists is that, possessing a system which appears to explain everything, they never bother to discover what is going on inside other people's heads. That is why in every western country, during the last dozen years, they have played straight into the hands of their adversaries.'[51] By the time he wrote this in December, he had finished *The Road to Wigan Pier* in which that passage appears that is almost identical in meaning, but fully Orwellian in style: 'Marxists as a rule are not very good at reading the minds of their adversaries.' (A seemingly judicious understatement meant to strike straight and hard.)

Though for a year he worked on this second documentary, the year in which his lasting political stance became clear, he did not think for one moment that he was ceasing to be, above all else, a novelist – even if he was only to write one more true novel (excluding *Nineteen Eighty-Four* as something *sui generis*). For that, events were mostly to blame. It was his far-sighted moral reactions to events that were to create, albeit as the side-product of the novels and his political writing, the essays, and these may be his most lasting literary achievement. He carried on reviewing novels all that year, he wrote an essay in two parts called 'In Defence of the Novel' (not so much about the novel as a genre as about its abuse by bad, hasty and promiscuous reviewing);[52] and he entered into a brief but revealing and mutually respectful correspondence with Henry Miller, whose *Tropic of Cancer* and *Black Spring* he had grown, after initial doubts about the former, to admire greatly.[53] (Neither book could then be legally imported into England, thanks to the literary criticism practised by His Majesty's Inspectors of Customs and Excise.) Orwell admired Miller for his rhythmic English, his frankness and what he saw as his control of fantasy.* It was a practical example of why he detested Marxist criticism and of his own resolute dualism: he could praise Miller's writing while he plainly disliked his cynicism and his apolitical stance. Miller teased Orwell for his earnestness, beginning one letter 'Dear Erik Blair', though it turned into a thoughtful discussion of naturalism, realism and surrealism.[54] He had already 'waded through' *Down and Out* and found it a 'great treat'. He liked its accuracy, though:

I don't think your argument holds water, but I like it enormously. I don't for one minute believe that we will ever get rid of the slave class, or rid of injustice. For example, I would criticise your attitude throughout the book, if I were to be harsh and just, and say that what you endured was largely the result of your own inadequacy, your false 'respectability' or your bloody English education.

None the less, he promised to 'foist it ... on my friends ... even ram it down their throats' and affably remarked that its 'dismissal in a brief paragraph by a shit of a Compton Mackenzie makes my blood boil'.[55]

George Orwell, unlike Henry Miller, both followed and reacted to political events. Early in 1936 a general election in Spain had created a coalition of Left-wing and republican parties as a 'Popular Front' government. The Spanish constitution of 1936, turning its back on monarchy, dictatorship and the Church, became famous among socialists and liberals throughout the world. But the government, not always acting wisely or prudently, found itself plunged into continual crises. On 17 July, the Spanish generals had rebelled. They marched on Madrid, notable among them Franco's column of Moorish regiments, and had expected, the world expected, an easy victory, as in so

---

*In the letter of 26 August, Orwell told Miller that he admired the way in *Tropic of Cancer* he would 'wander off into a kind of reverie where the laws of ordinary reality were slipped, just a little but not too much', whereas in *Black Spring* 'on the whole you have moved too much away from the ordinary world into a sort of Mickey Mouse universe where things and people don't have to obey the rules of space and time'. He made the same point in a review (the *New English Weekly*, 24 September 1936) but added: 'the written word loses its power if it departs too far ... from the ordinary world where two and two make four'. So here is not just the first use in Orwell of the last touchstone of truth in *Nineteen Eighty-Four*, but a discussion of naturalism and fantasy that anticipates the epistemology on which the whole book was to be based.

many military *coups d'état* in Spain or South America, whose politics Spain shared rather than those of the rest of Europe. The government was forced to arm the factory workers and, to everyone's surprise, the rebel generals were checked. What had promised to be a quick *coup d'état* suddenly turned into a prolonged and bloody civil war, indeed in some parts of Spain, notably Catalonia, into a workers' revolution – a kind of counter-counter-revolution, something far more radical than the republican policies that had provoked that military rebellion. Little or nothing is known about Orwell's immediate reactions, only that King-Farlow visiting Eileen and him in September remembers that Orwell was following events in Spain closely and was well-informed. Like many others he cursed the arms embargo by the British and French governments, thought that the German and Italian support for Franco was the first move in a second world war, and noted that an International Brigade had been formed. Desire to save the republic or to forward the revolution swept through the British Left and divided society bitterly. Even Cyril Connolly had visited Spain and brought back a glowing account of the Spanish anarchists in Barcelona.

... the feeling one gets in this city. The pervading sense of freedom, of intelligence, justice, companionship, the enormous upthrust in backward and penniless people of the desire for liberty and education, are things that have to be seen to be understood. It is as if the masses, the mob in fact, credited only with instincts of stupidity and persecution, should blossom into what is really a flowering of humanity.[56]

At some stage that winter Orwell decided to go to Spain, but primarily to fight, not to write. Like a sensible author he decided to finish his current book before he left (W. H. Auden's visit to Spain followed the same timetable). If Eileen wished her husband not to go or if they quarrelled over it, there is no indication. Most probably she supported him. She, like her husband, was of the William Blake 'tribe of the tiger *and* the lamb'. The only known tensions between them were over her determination to visit her brother for a few days from time to time, to help him edit and type his scientific papers. There is no indication of jealousy on George's part, only the obvious surmise that her absence affected his progress on *The Road to Wigan Pier* – having to do for himself at their cottage in Wallington, not to mention having to cope with the remorseless knockings on the shop door, asking for pennyworths of sweets and small groceries, while his mind brooded on socialism and on Spain.

On 11 December he wrote to Moore telling him to deal with Eileen about all his literary affairs while he was away 'and accept her decision as my own'. On 15 December he sent the manuscript with the comment that he was 'fairly pleased' with it, but doubted if Gollancz would select it for the Left Book Club.[57] Four days later he got a telegram from Gollancz asking him to come in at once to discuss his hope to make it a Left Book Club choice.

Since the book fell into two halves, Gollancz first tried to persuade Orwell's agent to allow a small public edition of both halves to appear in hard covers, and the large Left Book Club edition to be simply the descriptive first half on Wigan. For the second half contained matter that would not please the brothers, as John Strachey strongly complained to Gollancz. They would not like to associate with diatribes against 'the astute young social literary climbers who are Communists now, as they will be Fascists five years hence', as Orwell had written, 'because it is all the go, and all that dreary tribe of high-minded women and sandal-wearers and bearded fruit-juice drinkers who come flocking towards the smell of "progress" like bluebottles to a dead cat'. Nor would they welcome a neophyte's claim that British socialists had endorsed the Soviet model of industrial progress at any price, thus replacing the older moral language of socialism ('liberty, equality, fraternity and justice,' he said) with images of society as a machine to be controlled like a machine. Indeed his attack on machine civilization went even wider than its association with Soviet Communism: 'the goal to which we are already moving,' he wrote, 'the logical end of mechanical progress is to reduce the human being to something resembling a brain in a bottle.' He feared the removal of man from nature, virtually the denaturing of man, much as Aldous Huxley had done four years before in *Brave New World*.[58]

Moore and Eileen refused to allow this denaturing of the book; and Orwell himself had had time for a preliminary talk with a worried Gollancz who, once again, must have read it eagerly and almost overnight. Admittedly, there was padding and hasty afterthought in the second section, but none the less it contained serious if unpopular criticism, revealing Orwell's own character and fierce integrity. Gollancz got round the difficulty by himself writing an extraordinary introduction to the book, which appeared, for 'technical reasons', he said, on the public edition as well as on the Club edition.[59] The introduction praised the first half warmly but warned that the second half was very eccentric and disputatious and that 'no reader must forget that Mr Orwell is throughout writing precisely as a member of the "lower-upper-middle class"'. Pot calling kettle black, indeed. Orwell, he said, acted as a 'devil's advocate for the case against Socialism'. He made a dozen interesting criticisms of the book he was publishing and offered another dozen highly prejudicial half-truths, mentioning, for instance, Orwell's 'general dislike of Russia – he even commits the curious indiscretion [sic] of referring to Russian commissars as "half-gramophones, half-gangsters"', thus giving even greater currency to one of Orwell's finest thrusts of satire to date. While he shrewdly drew attention to Orwell's 'intellectual anti-intellectualism', his own pre-occupations as a fellow-travelling tightrope walker prevented him from making the more obvious, indeed consequent, criticisms: that Orwell was obsessed by Marxist intellectuals and said nothing about the broad trades union and Labour movement or about non-Marxist or liberal Marxist democratic Socialist theorists. Many of the points that Orwell was painfully and, as yet, none too clearly discovering for himself had already been well made. For instance, Orwell came to know R. H. Tawney only after writing *The Road to Wigan Pier* [60] and his discussion completely ignores even the writings of Shaw and Wells (which he knew well) and of Laski, the Coles and the Webbs (which he probably did not). The German revisionists and Austro-Marxists were to him a closed book. Democratic Socialist theorists were to be found had Orwell read more widely: accidents of personal acquaintance and experience led him to see 'the struggle' as being between the Communist Party and the ILP and Marxists and non-Marxists in the ILP.

When the book was published in March 1937 and Orwell's copy reached Barcelona, he was in the trenches before Huesca. He wrote to thank Gollancz for his introduction. 'I liked the introduction very much, though of course I could have answered some of the criticisms you made. It was the kind of discussion of what one is really talking about that one always wants and never seems to get from the professional reviewers.'[61] His letter sounds a bit naïve, as if he thinks that Gollancz is being as honest as himself in making fair objections publicly; but Sonia Orwell has said that George told her years later that he was only being polite, that he did see through it and was privately angry. Years later, however, he may have felt that he had been naïve at the time.

The first edition for the Left Book Club was an astonishing 43,690 copies, and it was twice re-issued, though with a public edition of only 1,750.[62] Gollancz then made a unique offer to club members of the first half of the text for one shilling as a supplementary book for May, urging them to buy it to send to friends 'as one of the best weapons in rousing public conscience'. (This was presumably with Orwell's permission, though no correspondence survives.[63]) The Left Book Club bulletin for May 1937 used *Wigan Pier* as an example of how to run a good discussion, and carried a testimonial, 'one of our speakers writes', that could have been written by Gollancz himself as carrying just the right blend of praise and reproof of Orwell, together with an avuncular admonishment of the comrades for occasionally boring their readers:

In regard to *The Road to Wigan Pier*, I think this book has exercised our wits more than any other of the previous books. Perhaps you might tell this to Mr Gollancz and ask him to let us have a book of that kind at least once in six months. Why I say this is, that although some of the books have been excellent, they haven't given us grounds for controversy. When we have finished reading Palme Dutt's brilliant historical analysis, or Strachey's splendid, crystal-clear outline of the theory and practice of Socialism, all we can do is to nod our heads and say, 'yes, comrades, you are right'. But when Orwell shows us in the second part of his book what is going on in his mind, he enrages even the most pacific among us, and then we sit up and sharpen our brains so as to refute his erroneous notions.[64]

All this is to anticipate. The controversy it aroused continued long after Orwell had returned from the Spanish War.

He went out to fight, not to write. In the end he did both. Jack Common remembered him saying: 'After all, there are not such a terrific lot of fascists in the world: if we each shot one of them ...' And he looked at Common to see how this provocatively simplistic remark would be taken. 'He used these naiveties as a testing to see whether the man who argued the good cause was capable of the crudity of action for it or would wince from the violence he thought inevitable.'[65] Philip Mairet, the editor of the *New English Weekly*, Orage's disciple and successor, recalls:

Near the end of 1936 Orwell came clumping into my tiny ... office in Rolls Court. Dressed and shod evidently for some sort of expedition, he deposited a heavy strapped portmanteau on the floor, and as much of his lanky frame into the visitor's chair as it would hold, and said: 'I'm going to Spain'. 'Why?', I asked. I knew already, of course; so many young men were enlisting in the International Brigade; but he had said nothing to prepare me for the loss of his valuable co-operation. 'This fascism' he said, 'somebody's got to stop it'.[66]

He pawned his share of the Blair family silver to equip himself, and Eileen told Ida and Avril when they visited her that the knives and forks had been sent away to be engraved with the Blair family crest.[67]

CHAPTER TEN

SPAIN AND 'NECESSARY MURDER'

(1937)

IN March 1940 Orwell published with Gollancz *Inside the Whale*, a book of essays, in which the title essay looked back over the debate about artists and political commitment in the 1930s. He criticized two famous stanzas from the original 1937 version of W. H. Auden's poem 'Spain', to be much revised and finally disowned.

> Tomorrow for the young poets exploding like bombs,
> The walks by the lake, the winter of perfect communion;
> > Tomorrow the bicycle races
> Through the suburbs on summer evenings: but to-day the struggle.
>
> To-day the deliberate increase in the chances of death;
> The conscious acceptance of guilt in the necessary murder;
> > To-day the expending of powers
> On the flat ephemeral pamphlet and the boring meeting.

Orwell said that he had seen bodies of murdered men. 'I don't mean killed in battle' and 'To me, murder is something to be avoided. So it is to any ordinary person. The Hitlers and the Stalins find murder necessary, but they don't advertise their callousness.' So they didn't call it murder, only 'liquidation' or 'elimination' or 'some other soothing phrase. Mr Auden's brand of amoralism is only possible if you are the kind of person who is always somewhere else when the trigger is pulled. So much of left-wing thought is a kind of playing with fire by people who don't even know that fire is hot.' The general point is just, but Orwell may have belaboured Auden with the wrong end of the stick, for the poet probably did mean (though the whole poem is astonishingly ambiguous and ambivalent compared to its reputation) merely 'killed in battle' when he says 'necessary murder'. Auden revised the deterministic 'necessary murder' that so angered Orwell into the more existential (and evasive) 'fact of murder'; and he did so after Orwell's first criticism had appeared.[1]

Orwell himself was not a squeamish liberal when it came to 'necessary murder', he was more like an old Roman Republican or (at last) a Cromwellian Puritan (for the guilt was there too); but he discovered that the simple duty of defeating Fascism and of atoning for his complicity in class oppression by taking up arms was befouled by the acceptance of murder within the republican camp. Not that he took a simple view of Fascism: he was one of the very few on the Left who saw it not as 'advanced capitalism' but as a grim perversion of Socialism, a genuine mass movement with an élitist philosophy but a popular appeal. He knew about the Moscow trials before going to Spain and shared the views of the I L P Press that these were political murders; but he did not yet think that the whole international Communist movement was involved in or would condone these aberrant Russian terrors and follies; and still less did he suspect that Fascism and Bolshevism could have anything in common.

Being misinformed that people entering Spain to fight needed papers from some Left-wing organization, he had applied to John Strachey (whom he had met through Richard Rees) who took him to see Harry Pollitt, the General Secretary of the British Communist Party. Pollitt would have known of Orwell because the row with Gollancz was already on, unbeknown to Orwell, about how or whether to publish *The Road to Wigan Pier*; and Strachey, as the most active selector for the Left Book Club, cleared all difficulties with Pollitt. 'Pollitt after questioning me,' said Orwell, 'evidently decided that I was politically unreliable and refused to help me, also tried to frighten me out of going by talking a lot about Anarchist terrorism.' When asked if he would join the International Brigade, Orwell replied that he wanted to see for himself what was happening first. Pollitt then refused to help, says Orwell, but 'advised me to get a safe-conduct from the Spanish Embassy in Paris, which I did'.[2] This was not entirely unhelpful of Pollitt; it was naïve of Orwell to have gone to him – even though his mind was more open at this stage about the practical effectiveness of the Communist effort in Spain than has usually been supposed. So Orwell 'rang up the I L P, with which I had some slight connections, mainly personal, and asked them to give me some kind of recommendation'.[3] Fenner Brockway gave him letters to their representative in Barcelona. He made contact with the official I L P contingent who were then gathering in London, meeting in pubs and cafés near the I L P Headquarters in the Farringdon Road, spending their time collecting funds and organizing public meetings. But impatient to be off, he went on ahead of them, alone.

Orwell left London about 22 December and was in Barcelona by the 26th (the Blairs rarely seem to have celebrated Christmas as a family reunion), two weeks ahead of the I L P main contingent. He only stopped a day in Paris, just long enough to collect Spanish travel documents. But he found time in the afternoon, before catching the midnight express to the Spanish border, to pay a call, perhaps a little incongruously in the circumstances, on Henry Miller.

For Miller not merely took no interest in the Spanish War whatever, he genially told Orwell that it was the act of an idiot to go to Spain, that anyone who went from a sense of obligation was plain stupid: all those ideas about defending democracy, etc., were 'baloney'. They discussed 'liberty'. To Miller, it was something entirely personal, to be defended against whimsical beliefs in public obligations and responsibilities, and civilization was, in any case, doomed to take a nasty turn for the far worse whatever brave boy scouts like Orwell did about it. To Orwell, liberty and democracy went together and, among other things, guaranteed the freedom of the artist; the present capitalist civilization was corrupt, but Fascism would be morally calamitous. Political argument drew them apart, but there was sufficient sympathy between them as writers for Orwell to confide to Miller his feeling of guilt at having served in Burma (though he was to say this publicly in *The Road to Wigan Pier*); and for Miller boldly but sympathetically to ask Orwell, feeling for him and admiring his *Down and Out*, whether he had not punished himself enough already. Such psychological probing brought 'the classic reply', recounts Alfred Perlès, Miller's Boswell, 'that ... where the rights and very existence of a whole people are at stake, there could be no thought of avoiding self-sacrifice. He spoke his convictions so earnestly and humbly that Miller desisted from further argument and promptly gave him his blessing.'

Since Orwell was wearing a blue suit, presumably to look respectable at the Consulate, the blessing took the form of the gift of a corduroy jacket which, though not bullet-proof, Miller avowed to be warm and to be his contribution to the republican cause: 'Henry discreetly refrained from adding that Orwell would have been welcome to the jacket even had he chosen to fight for the opposite side.'[4] A man who travels light often gathers strange burdens.

Visiting Miller he was upset by an absurd quarrel with a taxi-driver who got aggressive and abusive on being asked by Orwell, in innocence and ignorance, to drive him a very short distance and then presented with a large bank-note which he could not change. Orwell reminisced that he must have appeared to the taxi-driver as 'a symbol of the idle, patronizing foreign tourists who had done their best to turn France into something midway between a museum and a brothel'. He was to contrast this incident to what happened when he boarded the train for Spain that night, virtually a troop-train full of tired Czech, German and French volunteers, and to the following morning when 'as we crawled across southern France, every peasant working in the fields turned round, stood solemnly upright and gave the anti-Fascist salute'. He concluded that the motives of the 'polyglot army . . . of the peasants with raised fists . . . my own motive in going to Spain, and the motive of the old taxi-driver in insulting me, were at the bottom all the same', all part of 'the wave of revolutionary feeling'. Writing in 1944, he may have predated his own revolutionary feelings as distinct from a fierce commitment to the defence of the republic.[5]

Orwell carried letters of introduction to John McNair (1887–1968), a Tynesider who had worked in France for twenty-five years, but otherwise devoted his life to the socialist cause (he became General Secretary of the Independent Labour Party from 1939–55). He ran the ILP office in Barcelona where he coordinated the money, materials and men raised in England by the ILP for the benefit of the POUM (*Partido Obrero de Unificación Marxista*, the United Marxist Workers' Party), whom they regarded as their sister party. The POUM had its own militia, though they were the smallest of the political militias. So did the Communists who, thanks to Russian aid, were the best equipped. The largest of the militias were those controlled by the official trades union federation, the CNT–UGT, an alliance of two federations, the anarcho-syndicalist *Confederación Nacional de Trabajadores* and the socialist *Unión General de Trabajadores*.

Communists would join the UGT and POUM members would

join the CNT. As the CNT had led the revolution in Catalonia, its alliance there with the cautious UGT worked badly. The CNT anarchists in Catalonia had their own militia, but some preferred to enlist with the POUM militia, which was a slightly more disciplined body and must have been one of the most politically conscious militias ever. The Communists helpfully simplified the situation by calling everyone in the POUM and their militias 'Trotskyites'. Some had been, like their leader Andrés Nin, and a few still were in spirit; but Nin had broken with Trotsky long before, finding him too egocentric and dogmatic, and had not been in correspondence with him since 1934. In 1936 Nin argued, however, that Catalonia should offer Trotsky political asylum; but that was to be an act of compassion, not to seek his leadership: the POUM was an independent Marxist force.[6] They were the ILP's ideal self image.

John McNair wrote towards the end of his life that one late December afternoon the POUM sentry at his door said, 'There's a great big English-man who wants to see you.'

A moment later Orwell followed him in. He drawled in a distinctly bourgeois accent, 'I'm looking for a chap named McNair, I've got a couple of letters for him.' At first his accent repelled my Tyneside prejudices and I curtly replied, 'A'am the lad ye're looking for.' He handed me his two letters, one from Fenner Brockway, the other from HN Brailsford, both personal friends of mine. I realized that my visitor was none other than George Orwell, two of whose books I had read and greatly admired ... I asked him what I could do to help and he replied, 'I have come to Spain to join the militia to fight against Fascism.' I asked him if he had ever been a soldier and he mentioned that he had been a police officer in Burma and could handle a rifle. I told him that I remembered this from *Burmese Days*. For the first time he smiled and the atmosphere became friendly ...

He took careful note of my description of the militia bodies and then added that he would like to write about the situation and endeavour to stir working-class opinion in Britain and France. I suggested the best thing he could do would be to use my office as his headquarters, get the atmosphere by going to Madrid, Valencia, and the Aragon front where the POUM forces were stationed and then get down to the writing of his book. He then said that this was quite secondary and his main reason for coming was to fight against Fascism.[7]

So McNair, taking Orwell at his word, took him straight along to the POUM barracks and he signed up on the spot. Victor Alba, who has written a history of POUM, was then a young journalist of 20 and he was asked, because he spoke French, to show Orwell round Barcelona. He remembers him as a 'silent, taciturn, not a good humoured man', giving no impression of being an interesting person; but he noted that he had enlisted voluntarily, that he was not simply paying a visit, as were so many English and French intellectuals.[8]

When McNair was interviewed, however, at about the same time as his written account, he did not even say 'book'; but simply that Orwell had talked about doing 'some articles' for the *New Statesman and Nation*.[9] That accords with the memories of two others. But what is reasonably clear is that for Orwell at that time writing was, indeed, a quite secondary motive for coming to Spain; and it is quite certain that Fred Warburg was mistaken when he claimed in his autobiography that Orwell came to him to discuss *Homage to Catalonia* before going to Spain.[10] When the book began to take shape in Orwell's mind months later he offered it to Gollancz who, knowing what it would say and probably anxious to placate Strachey and Pollitt, turned it down sight unseen.

Each of Orwell's documentary books and his essay or story 'Such, Such Were the Joys' have posed a problem for the biographer. As with 'Shooting an Elephant' and 'A Hanging', they are a compound of fact and fiction, honest in intent, true to experience, but not necessarily truthful in detail. *Down and Out* was far from a literal record of 'what actually happened', and *The Road to Wigan Pier* was less a straight documentary than often supposed. *Homage to Catalonia* is, however, closer to a literal record than anything he wrote; for in order to controvert the many existing false accounts (he was not breaking new ground, only in the way he wrote) he had to get the facts right and give himself no artistic licence. It poses no general problem of genre, only lesser problems of some particular questionable judgements; and while he warns his readers that Catalonia was not the whole of Republican Spain, he did not always take his own advice. His account of his own motives both contains some hindsight and a reversal of cause and effect once again for dramatic effect: 'I had come to Spain with some notion of writing newspaper articles, but I had joined the militia almost immediately, because . . . in that atmosphere it seemed the only conceivable thing to do.' And he was to admit to having written somewhat uncritically about the POUM because they had been so slandered and vilified in the international Press.[11] But the purpose of the book, to expose Communist folly and wickedness and to cry to the conscience of mankind to save the Republic, demanded that nothing in it could be faulted as fact, even if it was also 'art'. The names he gave of his comrades in the line and back in Barcelona are real names, and survivors have confirmed all of the main incidents he describes, whether of trench warfare or street-fighting.

His humility, fine simplicity and courage in joining the POUM militia irradiate his book. What does not emerge is that from the beginning he both assumed and had thrust on him positions of minor leadership, and that in a militia where commands had to be persuasive rather than arbitrary. He tells of 'what was comically called instruction' but not of his own instructing. This was by virtue both of his own training and of his character. The Burma Police had been, after all, a kind of militia. Part of his job had been the training of native constables in small arms, drill, hygiene and field movements as well as in police routines. When McNair went round to the Lenin Barracks three days after Orwell had enlisted (as 'Eric Blair', of course) to see how he was getting on:

... there was George forcing about fifty young, enthusiastic but undisciplined Catalonians to learn the rudiments of military drill. He made them run and jump, taught them to form threes, showed them how to use the only rifle available, an old Mauser, by taking it to pieces and explaining it. Gone was the drawling ex-Etonian, in his place was an ardent young man of action in complete control of the situation. When the two hours drill was over, he chased the lads off to the bathing pool, jumped in first himself and they all followed him.

Good officer stuff, but working with anarchists and socialists: Orwell was in his element. McNair asked him how he had succeeded in establishing this ascendancy and twenty-eight years later claimed to remember 'practically word for word' his reply:

'When I got here four nights ago they seemed to think I was a bit of a curiosity. They had hardly ever seen a foreigner. After our meal I noticed they were whispering behind my back. I just rolled a cigarette, sipped my wine and waited ... I tumbled to their game, they were going to make the big Englishman drunk. They tried very hard. Bottle after bottle of the rough Spanish wine came up and we all kept on drinking. They did not know that I had worked for a year and a half in Paris in hotels and pubs and know all about cheap red wine which the French call *"Gratte-gorge"* (throat-scraper). One by one they began dropping out and stumbled away to their bunks. We were only three or four left so I said quietly, "Well, boys, we've had a nice friendly drink so I'll just toddle off if you'll show me where I sleep." They understood my French. I managed, but only just, to get to bed quietly . . . A strange commentary on life that I was only able to obtain their respect because I could drink most of them under the table.'

'Next morning they all had a hang-over so I decided to jump in. My Catalonian being inadequate I got the man in charge to translate from my French. "Now, young fellows, we had a jolly good night but we're not here to booze, we're here to smash the fascists. You will now all drill under my orders and follow what I do." To my surprise and joy they all agreed, they soon got over their hangovers, and since then they think I'm somebody and treat me with comradeship and respect.'[12]

'Comradeship and respect' is what Orwell found everyone showing each other in Barcelona. The bourgeoisie seemed to have vanished. It was a working-class town, no one 'well dressed' and everyone addressing each other as 'Comrade', and using the second-person familiar 'thou' in place of the distancing 'you'. He did not realize, in fact, that the revolutionary phase of the red flags or the anarchist red and black flags was nearly over – republican normality was about to be restored by the central government for the sake of a united war effort and to placate foreign opinion, particularly that of the British and French governments.

Orwell went to the trenches in the Aragon front at Alcubierre. He was in the hills about two hundred miles west of Barcelona and on a salient in line about midway between Saragossa and Huesca. He was part of the 'Rovira' or 29th division and the neighbouring divisions were all composed of Anarchist militias. 'I had dropped more or less by chance into the only community of any size in Western Europe where political consciousness and disbelief in capitalism were more normal than their opposites.'[13] His *centuria* or battalion was commanded by an affable Belgian irregular, Georges Kopp, an ex-engineer who had manufactured arms in Brussels for the Spanish government until the embargo. McNair had to order two pairs of size twelve boots from England specifically for Orwell. The *centuria* was 'an untrained mob composed mostly of boys in their teens'; he was made a *cabo* or corporal, in charge of a section of twelve men. It was a quiet part of the line, as he wrote: boredom and cold were the main enemies. He admitted to suffering bitterly from the cold, his winter bronchitis never left him: 'Firewood was the one thing that really mattered', and was in short supply – he risked snipers' bullets to pull in branches of bushes from between the lines. It was as well that the Fascists were not active in that part of the line, for the POUM had little with which to resist them beyond enthusiasm and fifteen rounds of ammunition each. Every cartridge had to be separately tested in the breech to see if it would fit, for three different types of rifle were in use. Orwell's was a Mauser of 1890 vintage – not a good year, he thought. Food, wine, candles, cigarettes and matches were in reasonable supply most of the time but 'we had no tin hats, no bayonets, hardly any revolvers or pistols, and not more than one bomb between five or ten men ... no range-finders, no telescopes, no periscopes, no field-glasses except a few privately owned pairs [like his own], no flares or Very lights, no armourers' tools, hardly even any cleaning materials'.[14] The list is poignant. They were left in the line, in badly constructed trenches, for debilitatingly long periods until their leave was due. No regular alternation of line and reserve was ever organized. In eighty days, he was able to get his clothes off only three times. Sanitary or medical services were poor to non-existent. Many of the recruits simply defecated in the trenches where they stood, neglecting or refusing to dig latrines. 'One of the essential experiences of war is never being able to escape from disgusting smells of human origin.'[15] That January it was too cold as yet for lice, they came later in March. 'The men who fought at Verdun, at Waterloo, at Flodden, at Senlac, at Thermopylae – every one of them,' he reflected, 'had lice crawling over his testicles'; but before the lice returned, rats and mice abounded. 'The dirt never worried me. Dirt is a thing people make too much fuss about. It is astonishing how quickly you get used to doing without a handkerchief and to eating out of the tin pannikin in which you also wash.'[16] But dirt did worry him, whether among tramps, in the tripe shop or in the trenches; he used it as a symbol of oppression throughout his writings, and he deliberately forced himself to endure dirt in order better to understand, he thought, the condition of the poor and the oppressed.

Firing was not continuous, only spasmodic sniping, for both sides were short of ammunition. Orwell often crawled forward on patrol far into no-man's-land to observe the Fascist lines – it relieved the boredom; but fighting patrols were not used. Both sides were simply holding the line in preparation for a possible big push. 'Georges Kopp, on his periodical tours of inspection, was quite frank with us. "This is not a war," he used to say, "it is a comic opera with an occasional death." '[17] The English contingent called the war 'a bloody panto-mime'. A friendship (which was to last) sprang up between Orwell and Kopp. Kopp had sent for him on being intrigued to see on the company roll 'Eric Blair: grocer'. They had a similar sardonic humour and it helped to pass the time away. Orwell could well have written with the same tragic irony as the Communist poet, John Cornford, killed only the month before on the Cordoba front, 'This is a quiet sector of a quiet front.'[18]

The militia he was in, like the others, had been hurriedly raised in the early days of Franco's revolt the previous year by trades unions or political parties, and the soldiers owed their allegiance to these more directly than to the central government. Indeed the POUM's Marxists were as opposed to centralist state control in practice as the Anarchists were in theory. Both saw the Communists as a party corrupted by state power. *La Batalla*, the POUM's newspaper, alone in Catalonia had denounced the Moscow trials of July 1936 and Stalin's executions of the 'Old Bolsheviks' in August; indeed they claim it to have been the first paper anywhere to realize what was happening.[19] The POUM militia was 'in theory at any rate... a democracy and not a hierarchy' as if every *centuria* was a soviet or commune. There were officers and NCOs, orders were given and were expected to be obeyed; but they were given by one comrade to another and had to be given for clear and obvious reasons, not just to test 'blind obedience'. So 'there was no military rank in the ordinary sense; no titles, no badges, no heel-clicking and no saluting', Orwell recalled. Everyone drew the same pay, had the same food, wore the same uniform, lived in the same quarters. 'The essential point of the system was social equality between officers and men. Everyone ... mingled on terms of complete equality ... Of course there was not perfect equality, but there was a nearer approach to it than I had ever seen or than I would have thought conceivable in time of war.' Describing his feelings three months later he said: 'I was breathing the air of equality, and I was simple enough to imagine that it existed all over Spain. I did not realize that more or less by chance I was isolated among the most revolutionary section of the Spanish working class.' And that June from hospital he was to write to Cyril Connolly: 'I have seen wonderful things and at last really believe in Socialism, which I never did before.'[20] Orwell did believe in socialism before, as *The Road to Wigan Pier* and reviews written at that time prove. But he did not '*really* believe': it had been an intellectual matter and a moral compassion for other people's sufferings. In Catalonia he experienced it for himself. He was no longer condescending, he was engulfed in comradeship. Nothing that happened later could ever take away that extraordinary experience. He personified it all in the opening paragraph of *Homage to Catalonia* where he described shaking hands with an unknown Italian militiaman, simple, candid and ferocious, whose language he could not even speak, and they only met for a moment – 'Queer, the affection you can feel for a stranger'; and in the last paragraphs of his essay of 1942, 'Looking Back on the Spanish War', the verses he wrote in his memory express the same feeling:

> But the thing that I saw in your face
> No power can disinherit:
> No bomb that ever burst
> Shatters the crystal spirit.

George Woodcock was to apply these last three words to Orwell himself.

Two Catalan writers include a section on Orwell in a recent life of Josep Rovira, the commander of the 29th Division in which Orwell (and one of themselves) fought. Some of it is simply commentary on *Homage to Catalonia* (the accuracy and authenticity of which they applaud, while distancing themselves from what they assume to be Orwell's more moderate political position); but parts of it are based on talking to fellow Catalans who had either met him or met people who had:

You could immediately see in him a desire to observe like a curious child. His introverted stare was no impediment because immediately he could establish a warm and human relationship. The majority of the militiamen were young and playful, how he himself described them, and none of them suspected that the long-legged foreigner who always had to bend down when the others walked about in the trenches, was an intellectual, a writer who noted details of everything around him, including the psychological traits of the human beings whose life he shared in good and open comradeship ...

Unlike other foreign volunteers associated with the militia ... Orwell had come to take part in the fight, the outcome of which to him was quite uncertain and problematic, not as an adventurer looking for honours and distinctions. All the time he was at the front, he never moved from the trenches except once when he was wounded and another time for a short leave – that is to say, he never looked for contacts in the army hierarchy, nor with politicians or journalists, many of whom were attached to the divisions, more or less near the fighting line. Those who lived with him in the months he was in the firing line never saw him go near the column, brigade or divisional headquarters. If as he declared in his book he had come to Spain with the vague idea of writing newspaper articles, it would appear that once he got to know something of the reality of trench life and the human types with whom he shared it, the natural thing would have been to change his place and exchange the discomfort and dangers of the trenches for the relative comfort of being a journalist at staff headquarters.[21]

Even if the psychological description of the first paragraph is a little idealized – some would doubt that he could establish 'immediately ... a warm and human relationship' even in Catalonia at this time – yet the second paragraph makes an irrefutable and impressive moral point.

Towards the end of January, Orwell and a solitary Welsh working man, Robert Williams, were transferred a few miles further west to Monte Oscuro, overlooking the town of Saragossa. They joined the ILP contingent who had just come out from England and had finished their two weeks' training in Barcelona. There were about thirty of them in all, commanded by Bob Edwards, an ILP Parliamentary candidate in the 1930s (Labour MP since 1955), who had visited Moscow and although without military experience had been made honorary colonel in the Red Army, an empty compliment which led to his being made a company commander in Spain. This dismayed a few old soldiers.

Edwards describes the first appearance of Orwell:

All six foot three of him was striding towards me and his clothing was grotesque to say the least. He wore corduroy riding breeches, khaki puttees and huge boots, I've never seen boots that were so large, clogged in mud. He had a yellow pigskin jerkin, a coffee coloured balaclava hat and he wore the longest scarf I've ever seen, khaki scarf wrapped round and round his neck right up to his ears, on his shoulder he carried an old-fashioned German rifle, I think it must have been fifty years old; and hanging to his belt were two hand grenades. Running beside him, trying to keep pace, were two youths of the Militia, similarly equipped; but what amused me most was that behind Orwell was a shaggy mongrel dog with the word POUM painted on its side.

And he notes Orwell's eccentricity and courage:

He was absolutely fearless. About seven hundred yards from our lines and very close to a Fascist machine-gun post was a huge crop of potatoes. The war had interfered with the harvesting and there were these lovely potatoes. Orwell worked it out that a man, crawling on his stomach, could just not be hit by machine-gunners at that distance. With a sack – about three times a week, yes – he'd say, 'I'm out for potatoes' and I'd say 'For goodness sake, you know, it's not worth the risk.' He said, 'They can't hit me, I've already proved it.' And they shot at him, you know, every time he went out for potatoes, they were shooting all the time. But he'd worked it out that they just couldn't hit a man at this distance, and he was quite right, they couldn't.[22]

As George walked along his section of the trenches, there were continual shouts of 'Get your head down'. Because of his height he protruded above the parapet, drawing the enemy's fire. But he claimed to have worked it out rationally that the range was too great, as with the potatoes, for anything but an accidental hit. He was more concerned with rats than with bullets: 'If there is one thing I hate more than another it is a rat running over me in the darkness. However, I had the satisfaction of catching one of them a good punch that sent him flying.' Bob Edwards made a bit more of this, or of a similar incident.

He had a phobia against rats. We got used to them. They used to gnaw at our boots during the night, but George just couldn't get used to the presence of rats and one day late in the evening he caused us great embarrassment which resulted in the loss of some very valuable material and equipment. A particularly adventurous rat had annoyed George for some time and he got out his gun and shot it. But the explosion in the confines of his dug-out vibrated – it seemed throughout the whole front, and then the whole front and both sides went into action. The artillery started, we threw patrols out, machine-gun nests got going and after it all our valuable cookhouse had been destroyed and two buses that had brought up our reserves.[23]

This sounds a tall tale, but others confirm it. Even if old veterans often gild the same lily, they all see it as very Orwell-like.

Edwards, indeed, portrayed Orwell as a slightly comic figure. He plainly disliked him, suspecting him, he later admitted, of being another 'bloody scribbler' getting colour for a book.[24] Others remember his exact words as 'a bloody middle-class little scribe'. Certainly Orwell wrote a great deal, sitting outside his dug-out when warm enough or inside by candlelight. (People have speculated about what he was writing and sending on to Eileen – 'diaries', it is said, but this is pure speculation and it is very unlikely that he got whatever it was out of Spain.) John ('Paddy') Donovan, a new recruit, remembered how they suffered in his dug-out through Orwell's incessant smoking of cigarettes while he wrote, rolled from the strongest, coarsest black shag pipe tobacco. He kept a rope cigarette lighter hanging from his belt all the time. But he was always inter-ruptable for a chat or an argument with anyone, and he 'mucked in' totally and efficiently. The youngest of them was Stafford Cottman, an 18-year-old who had moved into the Young Communist League from the Labour Party's Guild of Youth, but who had none the less joined the POUM (the lines were not so tightly drawn at first). He now comments 'how funny people are about Orwell, a much simpler person than he's made out to be, so ordinary and decent'.[25] Despite his 'Eton accent' he found him unaffected and straightforward, easy to get on with. Paddy Donovan, who had been in the First World War, a very unpolitical working man (perhaps there for the job and the scrap), remembered him in the same way. Certainly the ILP contingent respected his military competence, for when Bob Edwards left the unit at the end of March to attend the ILP annual conference, they promptly elected Orwell as their group representative or commander in his place (by the time Edwards had finished his business in England, he was advised not to try to return).

Years after, Orwell told the tale that, crawling close to the enemy trenches, he got a Fascist soldier in his sights who was holding up his trousers as he ran. Orwell could not pull the trigger: 'I had come here to shoot at "Fascists"; but a man who is holding up his trousers isn't a "Fascist", he is visibly a fellow creature.'[26] This was not opting out of the business of killing. In an account of the night raid on the enemy trenches, Orwell made clear that grenades that he threw almost certainly proved deadly. He had also tried to bayonet a man running away down a communication trench as he ran along the top, but could not catch up. Then came the counter-attack:

I had no bombs left except the Fascist ones and I was not certain how these worked. I shouted to the others to know if anyone had a bomb to spare. Douglas Moyle felt in his pocket and passed one across. I flung it and threw myself on my face. By one of those strokes of luck that happen about once in a year I had managed to drop the bomb almost exactly where the rifle had flashed. There was the roar of the explosion and then, instantly, a diabolical outcry of screams and groans. We had got one of them, anyway; I don't know whether he was killed, but certainly he was badly hurt. Poor wretch, poor wretch! I felt a vague sorrow as I heard him screaming.[27]

This account of the action is confirmed by a story printed shortly afterwards in the ILP's journal, the *New Leader*, gleaned from letters sent to John McNair by members of the contingent. The main difference in the accounts is that his comrades singled out 'Eric Blair's' personal bravery (the ILP editor made no attempt to exploit the writer's name, probably had no idea who he was):

A Spanish comrade rose and rushed forward. '*Pour ellos –Ariba!*' (For the others – charge!) 'Charge!' shouted Blair... In front of the parapet was Eric Blair's tall figure coolly strolling forward through the storm of fire. He leapt at the parapet, then stumbled. Hell, had they got him? No, he was over, closely followed by Gross of Hammersmith, Frankfort of Hackney and Bob Smillie, with the others right after them.

The trench had been hastily evacuated. The last of the retreating Fascists, clothed only in a blanket, was thirty yards away. Blair gave chase, but the man knew the ground and got away. In a corner of a trench was one dead man; in a dugout was another body.[28]

Frank Frankford [sic] remembers the man in the blanket and Orwell chasing him with his bayonet. In a more properly conducted war there might have been a medal, but such a 'mention in despatches' must have given the new socialist far more pleasure.

In mid-February, Eileen suddenly went to Spain to be near George and to work as secretary to McNair and the ILP office in Barcelona. She also began typing manuscripts or diaries for George, but whatever they were, they were lost in the troubles to come. Perhaps she came primarily to be nearer her man, but it showed a strong commitment to the cause on her side. She found him at Monflorite, attending a field hospital with a poisoned hand. 'The doctor is quite ignorant and incredibly dirty,' she wrote to her mother. It healed, however, in about ten days. Eileen could only spend three days with her husband near the front, and Georges Kopp drove her back to Barcelona. Orwell wrote to her just after she left: 'Dearest, you really are a wonderful wife. When I saw the cigars my heart melted away.' But there was, guardedly, more serious matter in the letter. He was due for leave in Barcelona at the end of the month, and wanted her at 'some opportune moment' before then to say something to McNair about 'my wanting to go to Madrid, etc.'.[29]

Madrid was the most active section of the line. But the Madrid front was the preserve of the International Brigade, mostly Communists, entirely under Communist control.

The 'etc.' in his letter to Eileen must refer to the political and military debate that was raging in the ILP contingent. The POUM and the Anarchist trades unions of the CNT held that the war could only be won by continuing the revolution that had been sparked off by the Fascist rebellion. They held that it must be, as in the days of Danton or of Trotsky, a revolutionary war: 'We must go forward or we shall go back!' was their slogan. The official Republican Government, backed by the far larger UGT unions and, above all, by the Communist Party, grown disproportionately powerful since Stalin was almost the only supplier of arms to the Republic, tried to contain, even to suppress, the revolutionary fervour. They feared that the call of the extreme Left for the expropriation of property would alienate both the middle classes and foreign investors: the war was to be fought simply to save the Republic. Middle-of-the-road parties took the same view, but so, tactically, did the Communists, since Stalin wanted to defeat German and Italian intervention in Spain without antagonizing the British and French governments, whom he still hoped would see the need for a European anti-Fascist defensive alliance, something just as important as lifting the arms embargo against Spain. And the Communists had been strengthened by the affiliation of the Socialist Youth Movement – a militarily important body, since its age limit reached up to 35.[30] This is to put the case at its best; but also the Spanish Communist Party, under Russian orders, were after power and would stop at nothing to prevent the Anarchists and the 'Trotskyites' (that is, in their eyes, the POUM) from retaining their local dominance in Catalonia. Three days before Andrés Nin had been expelled from the Spanish Government, *Pravda* itself on 16 December 1936 somewhat prematurely announced that 'In Catalonia the elimination of Trotskyites and Anarcho-Syndicalists has begun. It will be carried out with the same energy as it was carried out in the Soviet Union.'[31]

Most of the ILP contingent were strongly anti-Communist even before they arrived in Spain. They shared the view of Nin (who was soon to be killed by Russian agents) that Stalin had betrayed the revolution and was even willing to connive in a purely nationalistic and imperialistic war against Germany, at least a war that would have nothing to do with advancing socialism. Orwell, while he did not share the Communists' view that Fascism in Spain was the same as that in Germany and Italy (Franco, he shrewdly saw, wished more to restore feudalism than to impose modern fascism),* did share their tactical view of how the war should be run. He found socialism among the Catalan militia but he saw the practical international case for the Communist slogan, 'The war first, the revolution afterwards', a slogan derided by both POUM and the Anarchists. This seemed to him common sense, and he maintained this minority viewpoint in the long hours of debate with which the ILP contingent pursued continuous political education, or fought off boredom. He was firm enough in his own mind and tough enough in discussion to hear and accept all the POUM and the ILP denunciations of Stalin's tyranny and yet to say that had nothing to do with the tactical situation in Spain. Two of his comrades remember this well, and he soon made no secret of his intention to transfer, during the coming leave, to the International Brigade. Others would have gone with him, because they too wanted to be with the real action and to have the modern weapons with which the Russians favoured their own.[32] Again there is need to remember that, while he had criticized the Marxist mentality in *The Road to*

---

* 'Franco was not strictly comparable with Hitler and Mussolini', his was not a revolution but a 'military mutiny backed up by the aristocracy and the church . . . not so much to impose Fascism as to restore feudalism' (*Homage to Catalonia*, p. 49). Interestingly this was the only passage that the censor (in Franco's lifetime) deleted from the first Catalan translation in 1970 (see J. Coll and J. Pané, *Josep Rovira: una vida al servei de Catalunya i del Socialisme* (Ediciones Ariel, Barcelona, 1978), p. 135 and for Orwell's views on Fascism see Chapter Nine, p. 293, note 30 above).

Wigan Pier, he had had good personal relations with the Communists in the North of England, and had respected their practical activism. In Chapter 5 of *Homage to Catalonia*, when he came down strongly in favour of POUM's revolutionary strategy, none the less he said quite plainly – what so many have ignored –

I do not want to suggest that in February I held all of the opinions that are implied in what I have said above ... It is easy to see why, at this time, I preferred the Communist viewpoint to that of the POUM. The Communists had a definite practical policy, an obviously better policy from the point of view of the common sense which looks only a few months ahead ... On the whole I accepted the Communist viewpoint, which boiled down to saying: 'We can't talk of revolution till we've won the war.'[33]

Orwell's views were far from eccentric. Willy Brandt (the future prime minister and SPD leader) was in Catalonia at this time (they only met very briefly) as a young German exile, and he expressed the dilemma thus:

The POUM in partial agreement with the Anarcho-syndicalists ... supported the view that the revolution was the overriding concern. The Communists, in partial agreement with the 'bourgeois' Democrats, took the opposing view that the demands of the war took precedence. In trying to arrive at a view of my own I fell out with the revolutionaries, who seemed to me to have overshot the target by a wide margin, but I disagreed even more violently with those who sought to exploit the discipline which the military situation demanded by establishing a system of one-party rule.[34]

But it was not the 'debate in the trenches' that was to move Orwell like Brandt against the Communist Party, while retaining his respect for the revolutionaries; his attitudes were to change when he took a spectacularly unrestful leave back in a changed Barcelona after one hundred and fifteen days in the trenches.

There were a few days of peace, however. Eileen wrote to her brother on 1 May: 'George is here on leave. He arrived completely ragged, almost barefoot, a little lousy, dark brown and looking very well. In the previous twelve hours he had been in trains consuming anis, muscatel out of anis bottles, brandies and chocolate.' So he was ill for two days, she related, and thus 'still persuadable to having a quiet day'. In the same letter, she mentioned that he had actually applied for a discharge and planned to re-enlist with the International Brigade in Madrid.

On 3 May, the Government's 'Civil Guards', said Orwell,* attempted to take over the telephone exchange from the Anarchist CNT unions who controlled it. He recalled:

About midday on 3 May a friend crossing the lounge of the hotel said casually: 'There's been some kind of trouble at the Telephone Exchange, I hear'. For some reason I paid no attention to it at the time.

That afternoon, between three and four, I was halfway down the Ramblas when I heard several rifle-shots behind me. I turned round and saw some youths, with rifles in their hands and the red and black handkerchiefs of the Anarchists round their throats, edging up a side-street that ran off the Ramblas northward. They were evidently exchanging shots with someone in a tall octagonal tower – a church, I think – that commanded the side-street. I thought instantly, 'It's started!'[35]

No one would ever be sure why it happened or quite what happened, though trouble was in the air. It may have been the Anarchists behaving in a tactically undisciplined way. They, like the POUM militia, kept their own arms and ammunition dumps, defended their own localities, and were deeply suspicious of central civil or strategic military commands. The Anarchists may well have been tapping the phones. Some were anxious for a showdown in Catalonia with the Communists, and vice versa. In any case, they were not subject to much control by their leaders. The Anarchists believed to a man that the Communists provoked their people to riot in order to force the central government to suppress and disarm them. The Communist leaders spread the tale in Spain that the Anarchists and the POUM had been infiltrated by Fascist *agents provocateurs* who, indeed, long afterwards claimed credit – as such people will. Broué and Témime in their great study of the Communist role in the Civil War sanely comment: 'Such a discussion is a complete waste of time: provocation by one, two or even ten agents is only effective if the situation lends itself to it. As we have seen, it did lend itself to it.'[36]

* Orwell appears to have confused the Civil Guard, the national armed *gendarmerie*, with the *Guardia de Asalto*, the *Asaltos* – an even tougher lot. These assault Guards had been founded in 1931 as a small *corps d'élite* specifically for emergencies and for the 'defence of the republic'. See Alberto Corazon, his Introduction to the first Spanish translation of *Homage to Catalonia, Homanje a Cataluña* (Ediciones Ariel, Barcelona, 1970), pp. 11–12.

The Communists spread the tale abroad that the POUM were secretly allied to the Fascists, even receiving arms from them across the lines at night, and that the Anarchists were 'objectively Fascists'; and this canard was repeated without question by Left-wing and even by some Liberal newspapers in Britain, to Orwell's great disgust and anger when copies reached him in Barcelona. By 9 May the Communist Party secretary, José Diaz, had established the line: 'our principal enemies are the Fascists. However, these not only include the Fascists themselves, but also the agents who work for them . . . Some call themselves Trotskyites . . . If everyone knows this, if the government knows it, why doesn't it treat them like Fascists and exterminate them pitilessly.'[37]

As the fighting spread, Orwell could not get up the Ramblas to the Hotel Continental where Eileen was staying. It was situated on the corner of Plaza de Catalunya where the telephone exchange was, so he headed for the Hotel Falcon down the other end of the Ramblas, which was used by POUM militiamen on leave. Most of the ILP platoon gathered there. Confusion reigned. No one really knew what was happening. The Anarchist parliamentary leaders were publicly calling for a truce, but barricades had already gone up and local groups were heavily involved in street fighting. No one knew or could see if it was an Anarchist rising or a Government attempt to wipe them out. If it was a rising, it was most incompetently planned; but if it was a deliberate purge, that too was ill-prepared, spasmodic and halfhearted.

John McNair appeared that night with supplies of cigarettes and news. The following day Orwell, issued with a rifle and ammunition as well as tobacco, managed to work his way up the Ramblas, despite snipers' bullets, to the Continental to find Eileen. He also found Georges Kopp. Kopp, a soldier of fortune in all things, was perhaps a little over-attentive to his comrade's wife; he saw it as being equally fond of them both; but she kept him at a comradely distance. Kopp busied himself to prevent bloodshed in their block. Close to the Continental were the offices of the POUM. Next door was the Café Moka in which twenty to thirty 'Civil Guards', said Orwell, had barricaded themselves when the fighting started, more in fear than in offence. Some German POUM Shock Troopers were bowling hand-grenades down the pavement at the café. Kopp ordered them to stop. He then with a studied casualness strolled up to the café, to the alarm of his men, and reached a local cease-fire agreement with the

Asaltos, restoring their confidence by swopping a crate of beer for a rifle they had lost. He ordered the POUM building to be defended against any attack, but otherwise there was to be no firing. Orwell was sent across the road into a small, ornamental conservatory or cupola on the roof of the *Poliorama* cinema. From there he guarded the approaches for three almost sleepless days and nights; but they were not attacked. Jon Kimche, visiting Spain as chairman of the ILP League of Youth, found Orwell there, 'lounging in the cupola', but there was little time to talk; or if so, of what they talked is forgotten – just as in the bookshop.

Elsewhere from all over the town sounds of machine-gun and rifle fire and of exploding hand-grenades came in spasmodic gusts, even the occasional crash of artillery. Orwell only fired once, to destroy an unexploded grenade on the pavement. By the time the unhappy Prime Minister had agreed with the Communists to send strong Government reinforcements to Barcelona and the Anarchists on 8 May had finally obeyed a desperate appeal by their leaders to take down the barricades and disperse, at least four hundred people had been killed and a thousand wounded. Orwell was to describe with impressive honesty and objectivity what happened to him and what he saw. At first the tone is dry:

I was in no danger. I suffered from nothing worse than hunger and boredom, yet it was one of the most unbearable periods of my whole life. I think few experiences could be more sickening, more disillusioning or, finally, more nerve-racking than those evil days of street warfare ... Sometimes I was merely bored with the whole affair, paid no attention to the hellish noise, and spent hours reading a succession of Penguin Library books which, luckily, I had bought a few days earlier; sometimes I was very conscious of the armed men watching me fifty yards away. It was a little like being in the trenches again; several times I caught myself, from force of habit, speaking of the Civil Guards [sic] as 'the Fascists'.[38]

His tone became more angry, a cool hard anger, only in the next chapter of the book, where he discussed the reporting of all this in the Communist and international press. Two examples are enough. He quoted the *Daily Worker* of 11 May, an article that began, 'The German and Italian agents, who poured into Barcelona ostensibly "to prepare" the notorious "Congress of the Fourth International", had one big task' which was to provoke so much bloodshed, 'in co-operation with the local Trotskyists', that the Germans and Italians would have an excuse for direct naval and military intervention on the Catalan coast. He also quoted the Liberal *News Chronicle*, whose foreign staff had been heavily penetrated by Communists (as when Arthur Koestler became a correspondent for them in Spain), a story that began '. . . This has not been an Anarchist uprising. It is a frustrated *putsch* of the "Trotskyist" POUM'; and cheerfully ended 'Barcelona, the first city of Spain, was plunged into bloodshed by *agents provocateurs* using this subversive organization'.[39] It is still hard to recall how vile, gross, and fabricated such propaganda was. Orwell saw before his own eyes not merely the distortion of evidence through differing perspectives but the sheer invention of history. One aspect of *Nineteen Eighty-Four* was already occurring.

Again Orwell admits that the lesson of these events took some time to sink in. 'Orwell was affected less by the May fighting,' the historian Raymond Carr has written, 'than by the ruthless use the Communists made of a political post-mortem in order to destroy their enemies.'[40] Not knowing fully what the fighting was about, Orwell instinctively took up arms with his POUM comrades:

The poorer classes in Barcelona looked upon the Civil Guards [sic] as something rather resembling the Black and Tans, and it seemed to be taken for granted that they had started this attack on their own initiative. Once I had heard how things stood, I felt easier in my mind. The issue was clear enough. On one side, the CNT, on the other side the police. I have no particular love for the idealized 'worker' as he appears in the bourgeois Communist's mind, but when I see an actual flesh-and-blood worker in conflict with his natural enemy, the policeman, I do not have to ask myself which side I am on.[41]

The Burma policeman who claimed to have struck servants with his fists had travelled a long way.

The outbreak of fighting could just have been a ghastly series of muddles and misunderstandings. Only after the fighting ended did Orwell become aware of what malignant lies and simplicities were being written in the Communist press. He says that rank-and-file Communists on the spot were unhappy at what they read but stuck to their own side none the less.

Our Communist friend approached me once again and asked me whether I would not transfer into the International Column.

I was rather surprised. 'Your papers are saying I'm a Fascist,' I said, 'Surely I should be politically suspect, coming from the POUM.'

'Oh, that doesn't matter. After all, you were only acting under orders.'

I had to tell him that after this affair I could not join any Communist-controlled unit. Sooner or later it might mean being used against the Spanish working class. One could not tell when this kind of thing would break out again, and if I had to use my rifle at all in such an affair I would use it on the side of the working class and not against them. He was very decent about it. But from now on the whole atmosphere was changed.[42]

Another pair of size twelve boots which he had ordered from a local cobbler the day before the fighting began were ready the day after it ended. On 10 May Orwell returned to the line near Huesca with the POUM, and was made lieutenant of the ILP platoon in Bob Edwards' continued absence.

Only the year before, John Cornford had written for Margot Heinemann in the poem 'Heart of the heartless world' that '... if bad luck should lay my strength/into the shallow grave...' Orwell, in a grim way, had good luck. Ten days after returning to the front, at 5 in the morning on 20 May, 'Eric was standing there talking to us, at dawn "Stand To", telling us of his experiences in the brothels in Paris... then it got light', remembers Frank Frankford, 'and his tall head was right above the parapet and all of a sudden, down he goes, shot through the throat'.[43] A single shot had rung out. A sniper, aiming well or damned lucky, had put a bullet right through his neck, just under the larynx. 'Roughly speaking it was the sensation of being *at the centre* of an explosion ...' Orwell recalled, 'my first thought, conventionally enough, was for my wife. My second was a violent resentment at having to leave this world which, when all is said and done, suits me so well ... The meaninglessness of it! To be bumped off, not even in battle, but in this stale corner of the trenches, thanks to a moment's carelessness.'[44] Luckily he was hit, as recounted by Kopp, by a high velocity modern rifle from fairly close range: the speed and heat of the bullet left a clean and cauterized wound, there was little haemorrhaging and no infection set in.

The doctors told him that if the bullet had been but a millimetre to the left he would have been dead. They also told him, quite wrongly, that the vocal chord was broken and that he would never speak normally again. At the field hospital two of his comrades came, as was customary, to take the wounded man's pistol, watch, torch and knife. Such things were common property, only privately possessed for public use. They found him very calm but they took it for granted that he would die. He was then jolted down to the divisional hospital at Barbastro. This was so horribly overcrowded that the very next morning, without further treatment, he was shipped down by train to Lerida. He drily commented that people with abdominal or internal wounds were usually killed by the jolting on the badly made and shell-scarred roads, so he was lucky to have gone by train.

Eileen and Georges Kopp found him at Lerida from where, after three or four days, he was sent on to Tarragona. He claimed this was a mistake and that it was meant to be Barcelona. After a week there, Eileen staying by him every minute, he was declared out of danger and ended up in a POUM convalescent hospital, Sanatorium Maurin, in a suburb of Barcelona (named after the famous POUM leader). His voice came back after electrotherapy, but low and hoarse: when he was fully recovered, he had a lasting, flat tonelessness of speech. Eileen had sent a telegram to his father at Southwold only four days after the wound: 'ERIC SLIGHTLY WOUNDED PROGRESS EXCELLENT SENDS LOVE NO NEED FOR ANXIETY EILEEN'. The Blairs would have read this as if he had got 'a Blighty wound' and that their strange son would soon be home. At that stage she must have been desperately worried herself, but probably feared that one of the ILP contingent might send a more alarming message. On 31 May, Eileen got Georges Kopp to send a full medical account to her surgeon brother, an eight-page description and narrative, requesting him to write to the Spanish specialist, anticipating that George would be leaving Spain for further treatment in England.[45]

In the hospital, there were old comrades from the unit: Arthur Clinton, Robert Williams and Stafford Cottmann, the youngest of the ILP contingent. George could get into Barcelona in the afternoon on the tram to meet Eileen. But he realized that everything was turning sour. The military truce of the POUM and CNT with the police and civil authorities had been observed, but a vicious post-mortem filled the Communist and Government Press, 'there was a peculiar evil feeling in the air, and veiled hatred'. The Communists had become the dominant power in the local administration. POUM members on leave felt themselves viewed with suspicion, discriminated against in small ways. On returning to the front from leave, Orwell had learned that another member of the ILP contingent, Bob Smillie (the grandson of the great Scottish miners' leader), had been arrested after coming back to Spain from a propaganda tour in England. Smillie was in prison in Valencia (and he was to die there, though whether from acute appendicitis or murdered by the Communists has never been cleared up). It was known that Smillie had been carrying documents, so Cottman and Orwell anxiously destroyed pamphlets and maps, anything that could be regarded by hopeful Communists or ignorant police as incriminating. Somewhat disillusioned, unsure if the full use of his voice would ever return, very tired, Orwell applied for his discharge. It was readily given on medical grounds; but it had to be counter-signed by divisional military commanders back in the field, a measure introduced to guard against malingering and desertion. It took Orwell six days, from 14 June, to get his discharge, as he was shunted from one office and one town to another, hitch-hiking lifts on military vehicles. He was back in Barcelona on 20 June and walked into the Hotel Continental.

Eileen was waiting anxiously in the foyer. She immediately bustled him straight out again into the street, and told him that the police had begun a purge of Anarchist and POUM activists and their foreign supporters. The POUM had been declared illegal and the Anarchists had been disarmed by sudden raids. The news had been kept from the front for several days, so that POUM units returning on leave were either disarmed and disbanded or arrested. Her own room had been searched by the police a few nights before, but with typical Spanish manners neither her person nor the bed on which she was lying – in which she had concealed ILP documents. Eileen told him who had been caught and who not. McNair and Cottman were hiding out, but Georges Kopp, although a battalion commander now, had been arrested.

That night Orwell slept out, hiding in a ruined church. The next morning Eileen arranged that McNair, Cottman and he should all meet at the British Consulate. His two friends brought news that Smillie had died in prison and rumours, which soon proved true, that Andrés Nin had been kidnapped and killed by Russian agents. The memory of the martyred Nin stayed with Orwell: he left a 'testament' too, like Goldstein in *Nineteen Eighty-Four* who is Nin quite as much as Trotsky.[46]

That same afternoon, he and Eileen visited Kopp in prison. In the confusion of the mass arrests, ordinary prison rules, allowing a daily visit before trial, were still being observed: the political prisoners were not yet incommunicado. Kopp told them that he had been carrying an important letter from the Ministry of War to a colonel of Engineering on the eastern front which the police had confiscated. Orwell went straight to the War Department in Barcelona and, with difficulty, found the colonel's office. He explained to the aide-de-camp that Major Kopp had been arrested by mistake while carrying an important letter to his colonel. The ADC was startled, if not scared, to learn what unit they were from, but he took Orwell with him straight to the office of the Chief of Police. After a fierce argument, the officer retrieved the letter. But for Kopp, he could do nothing: only promise that 'proper inquiries' would be made. The little ADC shook hands with Orwell in front of the police before they parted. Orwell thought that very brave of him. The whole episode shows the Orwells as incredibly brave too, almost foolhardy. They could do little or nothing to get their friend out of prison and yet had risked being rounded up themselves.

The men spent another night hiding and a day walking the boulevards as if they were tourists. Hotels had to report all guests to the police. They ran into several old comrades or acquaintances on the streets, also on the run or lying low – among them Willy Brandt. They tried to persuade Brandt to come with them to England but he refused. Cottman remembers Brandt then in a mood of despair at 'working men killing working men', pitying the poor among the Fascists, almost turning pacifist in his sadness at the sweet cause gone sour. In the evening Eileen, having got papers and passports together, and paid back personal money she was holding for various ILP members still at large, met them at the station at the last possible moment before the evening train left for France – which they then found, incredibly for Spain, had left early. So a third night was spent hiding out before the four of them got on the morning train together and sat confidently in the restaurant car, as if they were tourists or delegates returning from some conference. They crossed the frontier tensely but without incident. Orwell's discharge papers had only the number of his regiment on it and the frontier guards had not yet been told that it was a POUM formation. The four of them grieved for Kopp and other friends, but McNair knew that they could all do more good raising the alarm outside – if anyone would listen.[47]

At Perpignan on the French side of the frontier they ran into Fenner Brockway, the General Secretary of the ILP, coming into Spain again to try to get some of the others out. Brockway had met Orwell only once before, but now found him 'far more mature as a socialist'. The five of them talked deep and anxiously into the night. They talked about Spain and discussed where articles and letters could be published to warn the other elements in the Popular Front of the Communists' actions and to bring pressure for the release of their imprisoned comrades. They talked about the issues of international politics and readily agreed, according to Brockway, that the British Government was more interested in combating Communism and Socialism than Fascism, so that if war did come with Germany, it would be a purely imperialist and capitalist struggle for markets, nothing that should gain the support of genuine socialists. Orwell said that he intended to support the I L P strongly and practically. He also asked Brockway's advice about a publisher for a book on Spain, since he already knew that Gollancz was 'distressed' at his POUM connection. Brockway suggested that Fredric Warburg was just the man, not afraid to publish books from the independent Left wing, iike Brockway's own *The Workers' Front*. He was already nicknamed, very misleadingly, 'The Trotskyite publisher'.*

* Fredric Warburg in his autobiography, *An Occupation for Gentlemen* (Hutchinson, London, 1959), says that 'Orwell came to see me in December 1936 to discuss a visit to Spain and a book on the Spanish War ... "I want to go to Spain and have a look at the fighting", he said, "write a book about it. Good chaps, those Spaniards, can't let them down. Can probably give you the book a month or two after I get back."' (p. 231) And he also has an account of John McNair hiding the manuscript 'when the police ransacked his flat during the Barcelona rising' (p. 236) – which conflates the rising with the subsequent purge and credits Orwell with a superhuman speed of writing. Warburg's memory must be at fault on both counts. Orwell had written to Gollancz from Barcelona as early as 9 May 1937, saying 'I hope I shall get a chance to write the truth about what I have seen ... I hope to have a book ready for you about the beginning of next year' (*The Collected Essays, Journalism and Letters*, Vol. I, p. 267). But Gollancz must have rejected this offer, for Orwell told Rayner Heppenstall in a letter of 31 July 1937: 'I am also having to change my publisher, at least for this book. Gollancz is, of course, part of the Communism-racket, and as soon as he heard I had been associated with the POUM and Anarchists and had seen the inside of the May riots in Barcelona, he said he did not think he would be able to publish my book, though not a word of it was written yet.' And an unpublished letter to his agent of 1 September 1937 is conclusive: 'Herewith the signed draft of the agreement, for which many thanks. I trust I shall get the book done by December 31st, as agreed. If Secker and Warburg want to know how it is getting on I could let them have some specimen chapters in a few weeks, providing they understand that this is the rough draft and I always alter a great deal in rewriting.' (Whatever it was that McNair may have told Warburg that he hid from the police, it cannot have been the manuscript of *Homage to Catalonia*. Even if there was an earlier version, or notes towards one, it did not get out of Spain; their lives had depended on crossing the frontier with nothing incriminating on them.)

In the morning Brockway departed for Barcelona, McNair and Cottman for Paris, and George and Eileen had three days' rest at Banyuls.[48] 'Rest', once again, is a relative term. He sent a telegram to the *New Statesman and Nation* offering an article, received an encouraging reply and began to write 'Spilling the Spanish Beans'.

By the first week in July the Blairs were back in the house in Wallington, which Jack Common had been looking after for them. Orwell got down to *Homage to Catalonia* almost at once and Eileen got down to putting the house and garden in order. He must have been pleased to find on his return a copy of the *News Chronicle* for 10 June 1937 with a large photograph and long extract from *The Road to Wigan Pier* – as fourth of a series of five 'giving the work of young writers already famous among critics, less well-known by the public'. The others were Arthur Calder-Marshall, Tom Harrisson, Stephen Spender, and – coupled together – W. H. Auden and Christopher Isherwood. But his article for the *New Statesman and Nation* was rejected. He might growl and be suspicious as to their motives, but it was, after all, submitted on spec, not commissioned. So he published it in two parts in his old stand-by, the *New English Weekly*, on 29 July and 2 September. He told of the 'reign of terror' that the Government, backed by the Communist Party, had unleashed against 'its own revolutionaries'; he said that the real struggle in Spain was between revolution and counter-revolution in the Government camp. He went so far as to accuse the Republican middle class of favouring a negotiated peace with Franco for fear that outright victory would mean the revolution. For good measure he argued that the British Government, by its fear of 'communism' (misplaced in this case) and sympathy with Spanish Fascism, had brought a new world war closer, but it would clearly not be fought as an anti-Fascist war, but simply as a capitalist and nationalist reaction to German military and commercial expansion. The Communist purge of the POUM had brought Orwell right round to the Anarchist, POUM, Trotskyite and ILP line that the Spanish War could only be won through a revolution, indeed that the future, impending and inevitable, European or world war could only be won by the élan and dedication of a people's revolution, neither by phoney national coalition nor by popular front. The articles appear to have had no popular impact.

The *New Statesman and Nation*, however, sent him for review as a kind of softener Franz Borkenau's *Spanish Cockpit*. 'Dr Borkenau,' wrote Orwell, 'is a sociologist and not connected with any political party.' Borkenau, in fact, had been an Austrian Communist who had worked for the Comintern in Moscow, lost his faith when he saw the megalomania of Stalin and the power hunger and cynicism of the bureaucrats; then he studied at Frankfurt under Adorno; was an exile in Panama and then Mexico, before going to Spain a few weeks after the outbreak of rebellion, and writing what is still a classic book on the war. His *Spanish Cockpit* both analyses the reasons for its outbreak and gives an eye-witness account of the revolution in Catalonia that, even before Orwell arrived in Spain, exposes the hostility and conspiracy of the Communists against their Left-wing rivals. He was imprisoned at Communist instigation and was lucky to get out. The experience took him to places and enabled him to see connections hidden to Orwell. But the argument was the same: the needs of Spain perverted and ruined by the dogmatic rigidity and the power hunger of Moscow. Borkenau had a deep influence on Orwell who reviewed equally enthusiastically two of his later books, *The Communist International* (1938) and *The Totalitarian Enemy* (1940).[49] Borkenau, like Ignazio Silone, Arthur Koestler and George Orwell himself, had come to see that, however horrible and paradoxical it might be, Stalinism and Fascism had something in common both in style and methods. The word that Mussolini had used as a boast they used as an insight into the unique aspirations of some modern autocracies: 'totalitarianism'.

Orwell's review of Borkenau appeared, however, not in the *New Statesman and Nation*, but in *Time and Tide* (31 July 1937), for Kingsley Martin, the editor of the *New Statesman and Nation* had rejected it.

29 July 1937

Dear Mr Orwell,

I am sorry that it is not possible for us to use your review of *The Spanish Cockpit*. The reason is simply that it too far controverts the political policy of the paper. It is very uncompromisingly said and implies that our Spanish correspondents are all wrong. I have, in fact, done my best to present a balanced view of the Spanish situation and published an article taking much the same view as yours by Liston Oak, followed by two very judicial articles by Brailsford, who made this controversy one of his particular subjects of investigation while he was in Spain.

I should add that our reviewers are always left a good deal of latitude and there is free controversy in the correspondence columns, but it is no use publishing reviews that too directly contradict conclusions that have been very carefully reached in the first part of the paper.

We shall, of course, send you payment in the usual way.

Yours sincerely

Kingsley Martin[50]

The Literary Editor, Raymond Mortimer, claimed to have rejected the review for the different reason that it simply stated Orwell's own view, not Borkenau's (they were, in fact, very much the same); but he apologized profusely to Orwell the following year when he learned for the first time of Kingsley Martin's letter.[51] Martin never seemed to grasp the enormity of his action, particularly reprehensible as he never denied that Orwell's facts were true, only that he believed that to publish them would damage the Popular Front.[52] His biographer talks about a proper sense of expediency, but Orwell thought that such 'expediency' was toleration of 'necessary murder' and showed 'the mentality of a whore' – a willingness to string along at any price.[53] Long before Orwell's difficulties in getting *Animal Farm* accepted in 1944, there were objective reasons to believe that many prominent Left-wing intellectuals were not as dedicated to truth and liberty as they were to the illusion of being close to the future levers of power if they kept the company of the communists. Bertrand Russell accused them of worshipping the power as well as the sense of purpose of the Soviet Union. There is not the slightest ground for imputing persecution mania or paranoia to Orwell on this score. The socialist camp had gained as a recruit its most earnest and difficult free spirit.

Looking back in his essay 'The Prevention of Literature' of 1946 he said: 'To write in plain, vigorous language, one has to think fearlessly and if one thinks fearlessly one cannot be politically orthodox.' In 'Why I Write' of the same year he had stressed the primacy of 'taking a stand' and having something to say. But whether his heterodoxy led to the plain style or the plain style to the heterodoxy, it was in Spain that they fused in his character and in his craft and in *Homage to Catalonia* that they appeared in their fullest and most perfect expression – with the sole possible exception of *Animal Farm*.

For the next few years, public controversy and Orwell walked hand in hand. He had come back to England to read the reviewers' warfare that had greeted *The Road to Wigan Pier*. It was internecine strife. The second half of the book had divided the Left. It was, indeed, wide open to criticism: he generalized about the psychology of the Left without so much as mentioning the Labour Party and the TUC, and he portrayed the Left's ideas or rather 'mentality', for it was all from talk rather than from books, as if the whole world of socialist theory were composed either of official Marxists (the Communist Party) or provisional Marxists (the ILP). None the less, he made deep and shrewd criticisms. If he exaggerated the influence of intellectuals, yet the middle classes, especially the lower middle classes who needed to be won over, made the same mistake. He realized that ordinary people were more appalled by the apparent crankery of socialists than they were attracted or repelled by socialist doctrines. Orwell made a virtue of ordinariness and common decency; the Lord had not come into the world to save those who were righteous already. Some reviewers saw this, in whole or in part. Ethel Mannin had snorted in the ILP's *New Leader* that it was 'a great pity ... he did not confine himself to facts and figures'.[54] Harold Laski in the Left Book Club's journal gave faint praise to the first half and damned the second half for ignorance of socialist theory.[55] But Arthur Calder-Marshall wrote a very respectful review in *Time and Tide* in which, however, he pointed out two grave faults: that the stress on the squalor of the lodging house underestimates 'the humanity of even the most poverty-stricken working-class homes'; and that of all the reasons both plausible and strange that Orwell gives for the disarray of the socialist movement, he fails to mention the most obvious: the lack of militant leadership by the Labour party and the TUC.[56]

This sort of fair criticism did not suit Pollitt or Strachey. Pollitt himself reviewed the book in the *Daily Worker* – a sign of the importance he attached to it:

Here is George Orwell, a disillusioned little middle-class boy who, seeing through imperialism, decided to discover what Socialism has to offer ... a late imperialist policeman ... If ever snobbery had its hallmark placed upon it, it is by Mr Orwell ... I gather that the chief thing that worries Mr Orwell is the 'smell' of the working-class, for smells seem to occupy the major portion of the book ... One thing I am certain of, and it is this – if Mr Orwell could only hear what the Left Book circles will say about this book, then he would make a resolution never to write again on any subject that he does not understand.[57]

The attack was repeated several times in the summer, an attack of such a kind that Orwell wrote to Gollancz. The letter is a characteristic mixture of honesty, straightforwardness, pugnacity and simplicity (or is the apparent naïveté ironical?)

The Stores, Wallington, Nr Baldock, Herts
20.8.37

Dear Mr Gollancz,

I do not expect you will have seen the enclosed cutting, as it does not refer to anything you published for me.

This (see underlined words) is the – I think – third reference in the 'Daily Worker' to my supposedly saying that the working classes 'smell'. As you know I have never said anything of the kind, in fact have specifically said the opposite. What I said in Chapter VIII of 'Wigan Pier', as you may perhaps remember, is that middle-class people are brought up to *believe* that the working classes 'smell', which is simply a matter of observable fact. Numbers of the letters I received from readers of the book referred to this and con-gratulated me on pointing it out. The statement or implication that I think working people 'smell' is a deliberate lie aimed at people who have not read this or any other of my books, in order to give them the idea that I am a vulgar snob and thus indirectly hit at the political parties with which I have been associated. These attacks in the *Worker* only began after it became known to the Communist Party that I was serving with the POUM militia.

I have no connection with these people (the 'Worker' staff) and nothing I said would carry any weight with them, but you of course are in a different position. I am very sorry to trouble you about what is more or less my own personal affair, but I think perhaps it might be worth your while to intervene and stop attacks of this kind which will not, of course, do any good to the books you have published for me or may publish for me in the future. If therefore at any time you happen to be in touch with anyone in authority on the *Worker* staff, I should be very greatly obliged if you would tell them two things:

1. That if they repeat this lie about my saying the working classes 'smell' I shall publish a reply with the necessary quotations, and in it I shall include what John Strachey said to me on the subject just before I left for Spain (about December 20th). Strachey will no doubt remember it, and I don't think the CP would care to see it in print.

2. This is a more serious matter. A campaign of organized libel is going on against people who were serving with the POUM in Spain. A comrade of mine,* a boy of eighteen whom I knew in the line, was recently not only

---

* This was Stafford Cottman who said that his home was picketed on his return by local Communists denouncing him as a Fascist.

expelled from his branch of the YCL for his association with the POUM, which was perhaps justifiable as the POUM and CP policies are quite incompatible, but was also described in a letter as 'in the pay of Franco'. This latter statement is quite a different matter. I don't know whether it is libellous within the meaning of the act, but I am taking counsel's opinion, as, of course, the same thing (i.e. that I am in Fascist pay) is liable to be said about myself. Perhaps again, if you are speaking to anyone in authoritative position, you could tell them that in the case of anything actionable being said against me, I shall not hesitate to take a libel action immediately. I hate to take up this threatening attitude, and I should hate still more to be involved in litigation, especially against members of another working-class party, but I think one has a right to defend oneself against these malignant personal attacks which, even if it is really the case that the CP is entirely right and the POUM and ILP entirely wrong, cannot in the long run do any good to the working-class cause. You see here (second passage underlined) the implied suggestion that I did not 'pull my weight' in the fight against the Fascists. From this it is only a short step to calling me a coward, a shirker etc., and I do not doubt these people would do so if they thought it was safe.

I am extremely sorry to put this kind of thing upon you, and I shall understand and not be in any way offended if you do not feel you can do anything about it. But I have ventured to approach you because you are my publisher and may, perhaps, feel that your good name is to some extent involved with mine.

> Yours sincerely, Eric Blair[58]

Gollancz replied to Orwell at once with unusual brevity, 'Many thanks for your letter, which I am passing on to the proper quarter'; and to the proper quarter in King Street he wrote: 'My dear Harry, you should see this letter from Orwell. I read it to John over the telephone and he assures me that he is quite certain that he said nothing whatever indiscreet. Yours ever, Victor.'[59] The attacks, for the moment, did cease. What Strachey said, alas, we will never know. He might actually have said something critical of the party line.

Sometimes the Communist movement, however, got its wires crossed badly. In May 1937 Orwell had received a letter from the Moscow periodical *International Literature* asking for a contribution and a copy of *Wigan Pier*. He sent the book, promised a contribution, but explained that he was recovering from a wound he had had while serving with the POUM militia. He received, at length, this remarkable reply:

25.VIII.37

Mr George Orwell
The Stores
Wallington

Sir,
The Editorial Office of the International Literature has received your letter, in which you answer our letter dated May 31st. You are right to be frank with us, you are right to inform us of your service in the militia of the POUM. Our magazine, indeed, has nothing to do with POUM-members; this organization, as the long experience of the Spanish people's struggle against insurgents and fascist interventions has shown, is a part of Franco's 'fifth column' which is acting in the rear [of] the heroic army of Republican Spain.
> International Literature[60]

As in the worlds of *Animal Farm* and *Nineteen Eighty-Four*, the discredited rival is not just labelled 'objectively Fascist', he becomes perceived as Fascist.

That summer and autumn, into the next year in fact, anxious letters went to and fro trying to discover what had happened to missing members of the ILP contingent in Spain. One letter from a man just out of prison, Harry Wilton, said that he had heard that Georges Kopp had been moved to Madrid at the end of July and had been 'knocked off'; and Eileen's brother had been sent by Kopp a copy of an ultimatum he had presented to the Chief of Police in Barcelona at the beginning of that month threatening to go on hunger strike if not given a hearing – a letter which Eileen passed on to John McNair to publicize. Forgotten men are more easily killed. Some months later came a letter to Eileen from Robert Williams, who had spent longer in prison, informing 'My dear Comrade Blair' that Kopp was still alive. Yet in May 1938, she got a letter from Alexander Smillie, thanking her for sending him a copy of *Homage to Catalonia*, talking sadly of his dead son, George's comrade, either killed by the Communists or allowed to die by neglect in prison, and linking 'poor Kopp' to his 'poor Bob' as among the ranks of the martyrs for the 'good old cause'.

Not all men are made of the stuff of martyrs. On 14 September the *Daily Worker* carried a long statement alleged to have been signed by F. A. Frankfort who had been in prison in Barcelona (though for a civil, not a political charge – he says). The statement said that when the ILP contingent was near Alcubierre under Kopp's command: 'Every night at 11 p.m. the sentries heard the rattle of a cart' and they could tell from its light that it came from the Fascist lines, and 'we were ordered never to shoot at this light, and when we grew inquisitive about it we were forbidden to try to find anything out'. He implied that these arms were then used in the May riots. 'In their political work, also, the POUM was similarly working for Fascism ... Had my political education not been so backward, I should not have let myself be led so far. But my ignorance in May still so great,' the statement went on, 'that I committed the crime of taking part in the armed rising of Fascists against the anti-Fascist Government.' (Could this specifically, as well as the Moscow trials generally, have given Orwell the idea for the bizarre and pathetic confessions of the animals in *Animal Farm*?) Two days later the *Daily Worker* said that they had been asked by him to correct certain points: the spelling of his name, Frankford not Frankfort; that he had not been kept in the POUM by force; and that he was not *certain* that the carts actually crossed the line, nor had he *himself* actually seen Kopp returning from the Fascist lines.[61]

First John McNair attacked Frankford in the ILP's *New Leader*, and a week later Orwell wrote a precise and angry refutation of each of the charges which was signed by fourteen other members of the contingent, all those the editors could contact at short notice.* The heading stated that he was 'not a member of the ILP'. Orwell speculated that 'all these wild words ... were put into Frankford's mouth by Barcelona journalists, and that he chose to save his skin by assenting to them'. And Fenner Brockway asserts that a few days after the article 'the boy' came to London, saw McNair and 'broke down crying and begged forgiveness'. He too conjectures that he 'had been imprisoned in Barcelona and presented with the document to sign as a condition of freedom'.[62]

Both these suppositions seem reasonable, but Mr Frankford denies that he ever broke down or asked forgiveness; says that he never signed anything, but simply gave an interview to Sam Lessor of the *Daily Worker* which he embellished, and he sticks to his story that there was fraternization and crossing of the lines on occasion (which seems

---

* Their names were Bob Edwards, Charles Doran, John Donovan, Douglas Moyle, George Gross, Charles Justessen, Mike Milton, John Braithwaite, Stafford Cottman, Harry Thomas, Philip Hunter, Uriah Jones, Tom Coles and John Ritchie. *Floreat semper eadem.*

plausible), but he is 'not sure' whether he ever thought that guns rather than fruit and vegetables ever figured in such movements, though 'there are things still to be explained'. (When I asked him if he was not angry at the *Daily Worker* for putting words into his mouth, Mr Frankford replied: 'Quite legitimate in politics, I am a realist.')[63]

Such an incident not merely strengthened Orwell's affection for the ILP but must also have set his mind working on the necessity of telling the truth in politics and the dangers of ideological approaches that deal only in '*the* truth' or in 'the *objective* truth'.

Orwell did not join the ILP until the following year, but he attended part of their summer school and various other activities. The summer school was in the first two weeks of August at St Christopher School, Letchworth. McNair, Cottman, Paddy Donovan, Douglas Moyle and Jock Braithwaite were there, as well as Fenner Brockway. Officials from the POUM and the CNT spoke. Among other speakers were George Padmore, Reginald Reynolds, and James Maxton. One evening was given over to a report from the contingent members. *New Leader*'s conference report only mentioned 'There was Eric Blair, an intellectual, his voice still weak from a bullet wound in the throat,'[64] and that he spoke briefly. Others remember him making occasional brief and impressive interventions in other discussions, but that his voice was low and he was not always audible. Fenner Brockway walked with him on the lawns one evening and Orwell offered to write regularly for *New Leader* – an offer that was turned down, 'to my everlasting regret', says Lord Brockway. 'I made one of the two great mistakes of my life. I turned him down because *New Leader* was a propaganda sheet for the factory floor, and it did not seem to me that this was his kind of writing.'[65] But he may also still have distrusted Orwell as a 'literary man' or a Johnnie-come-lately to Fenner's stern version of the socialist camp.

The ILP had organized a camp that summer for refugee Basque children. They lived under canvas at Kelvedon in Essex while they were taught English and found families. A then 16-year-old member of the Barking Branch of the ILP Guild of Youth remembers Orwell. He must have gone down to help for at least one week, possibly several weekends as well. He helped them draw up their appeals for money. On her part, it was a case of calf-love at first sight. She did not realize that he was married. He did not volunteer the information, but nor did he take advantage of her, 'he was so gentlemanly'. He was 'so gentle, so wise, so well-informed and so dedicated'. Her Guild of Youth thought of themselves, she said, as a POUM group through his influence.[66] Who was following whom is not clear, but both McNair and Cottman remember 'the girl from Essex' as being in the lorry when volunteers from the London area went to help organize a meeting at Bristol one weekend, and the lorry came off the road into a ditch. They both laughed, remembering George as being 'shy with women', for she seemed to want close comfort in the upset night, and he would only proffer a brotherly shoulder. Perhaps he was a little bit shy, but he was also a gentleman, defending the weak, not taking advantage of them.

Many ordinary people began to write to Orwell at this time about *The Road to Wigan Pier*, how it had brought them to socialism, or at least to the realization that something needed to be done about unemployment, poverty and the constraints and conceits of class. Some in the cause already pointed out in friendly criticisms that conditions in other parts of the country were very different from those in South Lancashire and the West Riding. Only a few of his replies survive, but enough to suggest that he replied patiently and at length to them all, rather humbly admitting the complexity and variety of poverty. (Sometimes one does learn something more about a subject after writing a book about it.)

Old friends were eager to talk about Spain. Connolly had visited Spain briefly before Orwell and Richard Rees had plunged in actively as an ambulance driver. His letters to old friends at this time are among the fullest he ever wrote, but they largely anticipate or repeat the matter of *Homage to Catalonia*. He was also reviewing many books on Spain, now that far more political books came his way than novels. He could not afford to turn anything down, however: money was getting very tight again. One can see him working out ideas for the book, or that became part of the book, in letters and reviews. He always thought aloud, as it were, in minor book reviews about the major themes of his next book.

That autumn, he and Eileen stayed at Southwold for three weeks with his parents; they sowed more spring vegetables at Wallington, aiming to become self-sufficient, and they bought a dog whom they christened 'Marx' – a black poodle, but the manly, hunting-dog sort, not a lap-dog poodle. All in all, it is a wonder he was able to finish the book that year; but by the turn of the New Year, 1938, driving himself hard, it was done.

A letter to Geoffrey Gorer, however, showed more clearly than is explicit in the book how Orwell saw his Spanish experience in the perspective of the I L P, virtually the Trotskyist, theory of international relations. This involved an opposition *both* to Fascism *and* to preparation for war against Germany, a view-point which he held until September 1939.

The Popular Front boloney boils down to this: that when the war comes the Communists, labourites etc., instead of working to stop the war and overthrow the Government, will be on the side of the Government, provided that the Government is on the 'right' side, i.e. against Germany. But everyone with any imagination can foresee that Fascism, not of course called Fascism, will be imposed on us as soon as the war starts. So you will have Fascism with Communists participating in it, and, if we are in alliance with the U S S R, taking a leading part in it. This is what has happened in Spain. After what I have seen in Spain I have come to the conclusion that it is futile to be 'anti-Fascist' while attempting to preserve capitalism. Fascism after all is only a development of capitalism, and the mildest democracy, so-called, is liable to turn into Fascism when the pinch comes. We like to think of England as a democratic country, but our rule in India, for instance, is just as bad as German Fascism, though outwardly it may be less irritating. I do not see how one can oppose Fascism except by working for the overthrow of capitalism, starting, of course, in one's own country. If one collaborates with a capitalist-imperialist government in a struggle 'against Fascism', i.e. against a rival imperialism, one is simply letting Fascism in by the back door. The whole struggle in Spain, on the Government side, has turned upon this. The revolutionary parties, the Anarchists, P O U M, etc. wanted to complete the revolution, the others wanted to fight the Fascists in the name of 'democracy', and of course, when they felt sure enough of their position and had tricked the workers into giving up their arms, re-introduce capitalism. The grotesque feature, which very few people outside Spain have yet grasped, is that the Communists stood furthest of all to the Right, and were more anxious even than the liberals to hunt down the revolutionaries and stamp out all revolutionary ideas.[67]

The language is extreme: far to the Left of the ordinary Labour movement. If he was not yet a member of the I L P, he was certainly its fellow-traveller; and he shared the revolutionary socialism of its international section (perhaps so extreme because most of the I L P were stubbornly parochial and let the Fenner Brockways 'get on with it'). But leaving the rhetoric aside, the basic policies and contradictions were also those of the majority of the Parliamentary Labour Party at that time: opposition both to Hitler and to rearmament. That Orwell was not just trying out newly read ILP ideas on Gorer is suggested by Paddy Donovan's memory that Orwell told him in Spain that a war between Britain and Germany would just be 'one band of robbers against another'.

The Anarchists tried to woo Orwell. He had said in *Homage to Catalonia* that 'As far as my purely personal preferences went I would have liked to join the Anarchists.' And he called them 'the main revolutionary force'. Emma Goldman wrote to Rudolf Rocker, 'For the first time since the struggle began in 1936 someone outside our ranks has come forward to paint the Spanish anarchists as they really are.' But he remained outside, although critically sympathetic. Emma Goldman did persuade him to join a kind of anarchist front organization, the International Anti-Fascist Solidarity Committee, which brought him into contact with such British libertarians as his fellow sponsors Ethel Mannin, Rebecca West, John Cowper Powys and Herbert Read who had been similarly influenced by Spain. And he met for the first time Vernon Richards, the writer and journalist, very active in the formal Anarchist movement.[68]

Orwell's love of literature did not diminish. He was beginning to see the connection between clarity of language and truth which was soon to bring his two great concerns together. He looked forward, however, to being able to begin work on 'my next novel', and he welcomed the chance of broadening his literary acquaintance, even in unlikely directions. 'Yes,' to Geoffrey Gorer, 'I should like to meet Edith Sitwell very much, some time when I am in town'; and 'thanks' to Cyril Connolly, 'I would like to come to lunch on Friday very much. I would also like to meet Stephen Spender if he is free. I've often said rude things about him in print etc.,* but I daresay he won't know or won't mind'.[69] And some time later when he was 'in town' Connolly recalled:

I remember him coming to a cocktail party we gave in the Spanish wartime, and we had quite a lot of Right-wing friends, rather nice, jolly girls with lots

---

* Not actually by name, but by genus: 'Parlour Bolshevik', 'fashionable successful person' and 'Communist sympathizer'. See his letter to Spender (*The Collected Essays, Journalism and Letters*, Vol. I p. 313); or 'The Nancy poets' for whom the miners sweat their guts out (*The Road to Wigan Pier*, p. 35).

of money who were unpolitical, and then there were one or two Left-wing political people, and poets ... And he came along, looking gaunt and shaggy, shabby, aloof, and he had this extraordinary magical effect again on these women. They all wanted to meet him and started talking to him, and their fur coats shook with pleasure. They were totally unprepared for anyone like that and they responded to something ... this sort of John the Baptist figure coming in from the wilderness and suddenly the women feel it doesn't matter what his political views are, he's a wonderful man.[70]

Such excursions into the rarefied atmosphere of the world of Cyril Connolly were fairly rare. He spent most of his time amid the rural smells of Wallington actually writing; and it did matter very much what his politics were.

After the ordeals of Spain and writing the book about it, most of Orwell's formative experiences were over. His finest writing, his best essays and his great fame lay ahead. From 1937 onwards he knew where he stood, what he was capable of doing and he was able to give out great riches from the store of his experience, he no longer needed to seek out new experiences even though, on two occasions at least, he sought to do so, but as if out of habit rather than for the necessities of writing. Before 1937 a confusion or fusion of autobiography, fiction and documentary was typical of his writing and has needed to be disentangled slowly and critically; but from now on there were to be fewer ambiguities of that kind in his major writings (with the notable exception of 'Such, Such Were the Joys') and they speak for themselves clearly, if they are read in the context of his entire production, including the political journalism as well as the literary essays. As he became more of a public figure, he assumed that people knew where he stood and what his presuppositions were; would have read his journalism and his essays as well as his novels. That was not always to be a sensible assumption.

1 (*top left*). Ida Mabel Blair (*née* Limouzin), 1897

2 (*top right*). Eric Blair, six weeks old

3 (*above left*). Ida Blair, Marjorie and Eric, in the garden of 'The Nutshell', Henley-on-Thames, 1906

4 (*above right*). Three years old

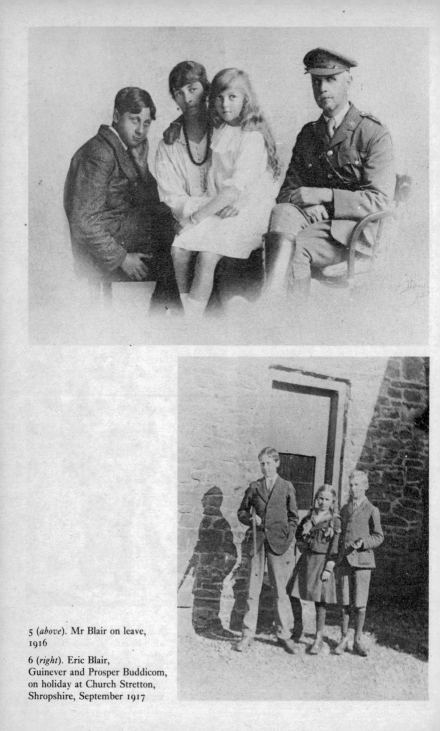

5 (*above*). Mr Blair on leave,
1916

6 (*right*). Eric Blair,
Guinever and Prosper Buddicom,
on holiday at Church Stretton,
Shropshire, September 1917

7 (*above*). At 'Athens'
after swimming, summer 1919
(Steven Runciman second from left,
Eric Blair far right)

8 (*left*). Asking for trouble,
summer 1919

9 (*above*). Before an Eton Wall Game, 1921 (Eric Blair top left)

10 (*below*). Burma Provincial Police Training School, Mandalay, 1923
(Eric Blair standing third from left)

11 (*above*). Montague House, Southwold, where the Blairs lived from 1932 to 1939

12 (*below*). Mrs Blair and dog with friend, Southwold High Street, mid-1930s

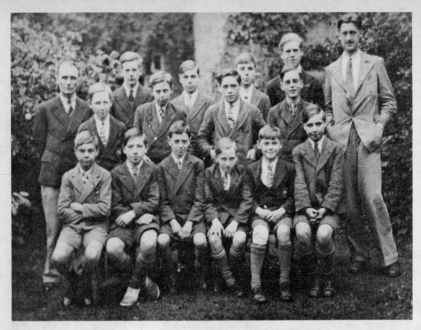

13 (*above*). Teaching at The Hawthorns, 1933

14 (*right*). Southwold beach, 1934

15. The POUM *centuria* leaving Lenin barracks, Barcelona, January 1937 (Orwell in the rear)

16 (*above*). Eileen Blair visits Eric and the I.L.P. contingent at the front near Huesca, March 1937

17 (*below*). Spanish comrades meet again, I.L.P. Summer School at Letchworth, 1937. (Left to right) John MacNair, Douglas Moyle, Stafford Cottman, George Orwell, Jock Braithwaite

SIGNALEMENT

Taille I.82
Front moy.
Nez rect.
Bouche moy;
Menton rond
Visage ovale
Cheveux cht.
Barbe rasée
Corpulence moy.
Yeux cht.
Teint clair

Marques particulières apparentes

_____

_____

Nom et prénoms de la femme :
Ellen Maud O'SHANGHNESSY

Prénoms des enfants âgés de moins de 18 ans :

_____

_____

_____

G 21202

SIGNALEMENT

Taille Im 65
Front bombé
Nez rect.
Bouche moy.
Menton rond
Visage ovale
Cheveux chat.
Barbe
Corpulence moy.
Yeux ch.
Teint clair

Marques particulières apparentes

_____

_____

Nom et prénoms XXXXXXX l'époux
BLAIR Eric Arthur

Prénoms des enfants âgés de moins de 18 ans :

_____

_____

_____

G 21202

18. Identity papers at Marrakesh, September 1938

19 (*above*). Feeding Muriel
at Wallington, summer 1939

20 (*right*). Eileen Blair, *circa* 1941

NATIONAL UNION OF JOURNALISTS

7 John Street, Bedford Row, London, W.C.1

'Phone:
HOLborn 2258

Telegrams:
Natujay Holb, London

This is to certify that

Mr. GEORGE ORWELL

of The Tribune

is a member of the T. + P.
Branch of the National Union of Journalists.

Leslie R. Aldous Branch Sec.

(Address) 66. Priory Gdns. N.6.

Member's Sig.

21 (*left*). Union card,
dated 29 December 1943

22 (*below*). 'VOICE' –
the monthly radio magazine
programme in the Eastern Service
of the B.B.C. (Left to right,
sitting) Venu Chitale,
J. M. Tambimuttu, T.S. Eliot,
Una Marson, Mulk Raj Anand,
C. Pemberton, Narayana Menon;
(standing) George Orwell,
Nancy Barratt, William Empson

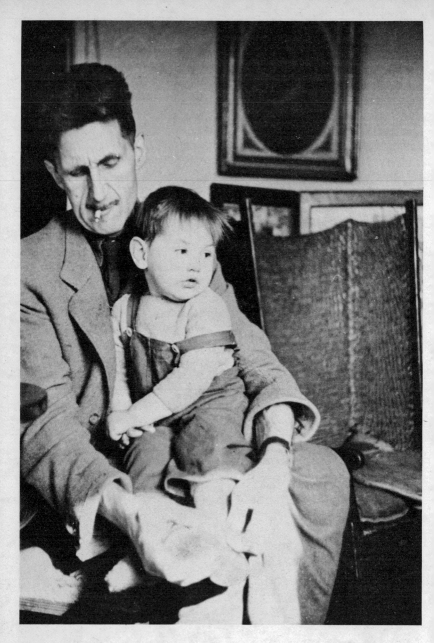

23. Orwell with Richard, Islington, winter 1945

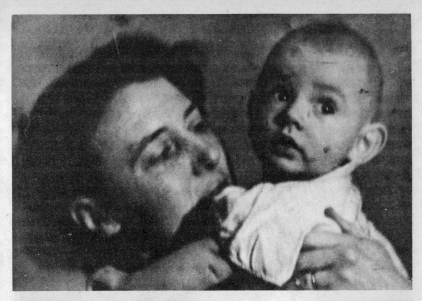

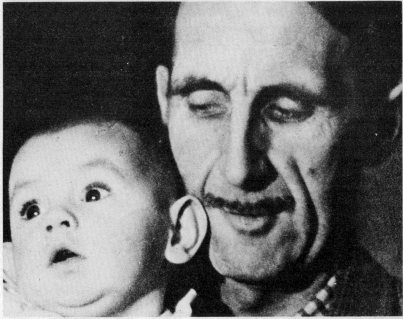

24 (*above*). Eileen and baby Richard, 1944
25 (*below*). Orwell and baby Richard, 1944

26 (*above*). Talking in his flat in Islington, winter 1945

27 (*left*). Sonia Blair (*née* Brownell), on the left; last day in *Horizon* and just married, October 1949

28 (*opposite*). Taking a break from writing, winter 1945

29 (*above*). Typing in his flat in Islington, winter 1945

30 (*below*). Barnhill, 1948

CHAPTER ELEVEN

COMING UP FOR AIR (1938-9):

THE POLITICAL WRITER

DURING 1938 in the thick of two distinct but related polemics, one against the Communist account of the Spanish Civil War and one against the Government's preparation for a Second (imperialist) World War, Orwell nearly fell behind in his self-imposed task of a book a year. Towards the end of the year he wrote: 'What with all this illness I've decided to count 1938 as a blank year and sort of cross it off the calendar. But meanwhile the concentration camp looms ahead and there is so much one wants to do.'[1] As usual, his judgements on literary productivity were highly relative and personal. In fact, he wrote a lot that year and it should be recognized that he had to write a lot from economic as well as psychological necessity. For while he had now achieved a distinctive literary voice* and was coming into demand as an occasional writer, yet he was, if well known, not famous, and so what he was asked to do, whether by way of book reviewing or essays, paid badly: they were distracting necessities. A volume of critical essays, however, began to be a distinct possibility, also a new novel. The novel would somehow warn against war, demonstrate the decency and common sense of ordinary people and show some faint hopes for the future. At the same time it would warn against severing

---

* John Lehmann in his survey *New Writing in Europe* (Penguin, 1940) was to say that Orwell had 'hammered out a direct and colloquial style', and he contrasted the elaborate, literary style of Edward Upward as 'the very opposite of the close-to-conversation style which Isherwood and Orwell were developing at the same time' (pp. 81-3 and 51) – which is presumably why he put them almost side by side in the first three contributions to his *Penguin New Writing I* of that same year.

links with what was good in nature and in English traditions in the name of technological progress.

He showed every sign of wanting to begin writing again; he even, against principles and habit, paid someone to do the heavy winter digging for him – Paddy Donovan, one of his old ILP comrades in Spain who was out of work and hard up. He took up the cudgels in a published letter deploring 'the unnatural agreement' of Left Book Club writers, and drew attention to a 'Left-wing but non-Communist' standpoint favoured by Secker & Warburg, 'who are coming to be known, rather inaccurately, as "the Trotskyist publishers"'.[2] (They were shortly to publish his friend Jack Common's 'straight-talking' or garrulous polemic, *The Freedom of the Streets*, as well as his own *Homage to Catalonia*.) But then a curious and revealing episode occurred – or rather did not occur – which betrayed either wander-lust or a continuing need to expiate the guilt of his Burmese days.

Two days after Christmas 1937, he received out of the blue a letter from a South African Liberal journalist, Desmond Young, who was editor of the *Pioneer*, a weekly journal in Lucknow in India. He wanted Orwell to come out to be his assistant editor and chief leader writer. He offered a 'poor salary', he said, but 'cheap living' and 'some time left for your own writing'. Although it was owned by 'landlord and vested interests', Orwell would have a free hand 'and I don't think it is so dull or reactionary that its policy would turn your stomach'. Orwell could have seen from copies in London that the *Pioneer* favoured a moderate version of the Congress Party's demand for Indian self-government – perhaps by the end of the century. (Mr Young neglected to tell Orwell that the journal secretly received a government subsidy.) Orwell must have replied positively, for on 27 January 1938 Young wrote to A. H. Joyce, Director of Information at the India Office, Whitehall.

I want you to do me a favour. A few weeks ago, on the strength of his very excellent novels, I wrote and made an offer to George Orwell, whose real name is Blair, to come out here as Assistant Editor and leader writer.

I know nothing whatever about him except that he was once in the police in Burma and that he is to my mind the best writer in England since Somerset Maugham.

He has replied to say that he would like to come but he warns me that he has had a good deal to do with left-wing politics and politicians in England and as he has recently been fighting in Spain on the side of the Government he thinks that it is quite possible that there may be a dossier about him and that the Government of India might possibly make difficulties about his admittance. Personally I don't suppose that anything of the sort would happen in these days but it is quite possible that someone, in order to make mischief here, and trouble for me, might write to the Government of India or the local Government and say that he is an undesirable person – which I am quite sure from his books that he is not. I have, therefore, written to him by to-day's Air Mail telling him to call on you and explain the position so that you can judge whether there is any likelihood of difficulties being created.

At the same time I would be grateful if when you have seen him you would send me a short cable to say what you think of him, of course, for my private information only. I am quite prepared to believe that he may be a bit difficult as he has had a very hard life (his first book was 'Down and Out in London and Paris' which you may remember) but I am prepared to make a good many allowances for anyone who can write as good, clear and forcible English as he can.[3]

Orwell wrote to Joyce on 12 February, a short, dignified and wholly unaggressive biographical letter. He was explicit about his politics: 'I am of Socialist sympathies, have been associated to some extent with the ILP, and when in Spain was with the ILP contingent ... My object in going to India is, apart from the work on the *Pioneer*, to try and get a clearer idea of political and social conditions in India ...' He would 'no doubt write some book on the subject afterwards' and try to contribute occasional articles to the English press. His only suppression was that he did not mention his tramping or his ill-health, so that 1929–33 became 'four years' teaching'.[4]

Joyce replied to Young on 18 February – an interesting and intelligent appraisal of Orwell (there evidently had been no dossier on him, but one was now being compiled).

> India Office
> Whitehall, SW1
> 18 February, 1938

Infn.Offr. 108/38.
By Air Mail
Personal

My Dear Young,
Many thanks for your letter of 27th January. I have seen Blair and today despatched to you the following cable:

'Blair keen for twelve months. Leadering ability
undoubted but probably temperamental, unbusinesslike.
Writing.'

In order that I might have something on which to base enquiries, I asked
Blair to let me have a note showing briefly what he had been doing since
he resigned from the Indian Police, and I enclose a copy of the letter received
from him. There is no doubt in my mind as to his ability as a leader writer,
though I think you may have to be prepared, in view of what I assess to
be not merely a determined Left Wing, but probably an extremist, outlook,
plus definite strength of character for difficulties when there is a conflict of
views. It is clear that he is anxious to take on the job, partly in order that
he may gain some practical newspaper experience, but chiefly because he wants
to have an opportunity of studying present conditions in India. The pay you
have offered him will leave little or no margin, and it is his intention to
contribute on Indian affairs to one or two papers in this country if he can
fix up contacts, and to gather material for a new book. He has, as you no
doubt realise, been living almost the life of a 'down and out' during recent
years and, on that account, I am doubtful whether his health would stand
up to anything more than a comparatively short period.

From what I have been able to gather, there is no question of obstacles being
put in the way of his going to India, but in view of his record official circles
there will no doubt be somewhat apprehensive. If you decide to give Blair
a trial, I would be inclined, in all the circumstances, to make the arrangement as tentative as possible until you are able to satisfy yourself that he
fits into the picture. I am sorry that I cannot be more definite in my estimate
of him and I hope that I have not in any sense been unfair to a man whose
intellectual standard is very high, but whose outlook has become soured by
circumstances of hardship, though they may have been of his own seeking.
With all regards and good wishes,

Yours sincerely,[5]
[A. H. Joyce]

Mr Young was dealing with subtle and civilized paymasters who left
their servants their dignity, offering hints to be taken rather than
official prohibitions to be obeyed. The hint was not strong enough
for Mr Young, who did not drop the matter but displayed good liberal
indecision.

The Pioneer
Lucknow
2nd March 1938

A. H. Joyce Esq.
India Office
Whitehall
London S.W.1

My Dear Joyce,
Thank you so much for your letter of February 18. I quite expected that Blair would not be easy and I have no doubt that I should be taking a chance by bringing him out here.
Fortunately it so happens that I am leaving for England by KLM on April 21 so that I shall have an opportunity of meeting him before I finally commit myself. I shall also look forward to seeing you.
With kind regards,

   Yours sincerely,[6]
   [Desmond Young]

Joyce, however, had not based his reply of 18 February solely on Orwell's letter and their interview. Orwell had received a security vetting. These papers are not available, for they contain the names of informants.* There was nothing to make the India Office wish to prohibit his entry, as they, or rather the Government of India, had power to do. But when the reports were appraised in India, it was felt that Orwell's appointment would serve as a source of embarrassment both to the Government and to the *Pioneer*. The appraiser expressed the shrewd concern that if for any reason his appointment were terminated, he might turn to extremist (i.e. nationalist) political work on however small a salary, and it would be difficult to get him out of India. So it was agreed that when Young came to London, Joyce should try harder to discourage him from making the appointment and convey to him discreetly the Government of India's views. By the time Young and Joyce met in early May, Young had got the message, for he told Joyce that he had had to turn Orwell down on medical grounds. But he was probably only trying to get credit for

---

*I am grateful, none the less, to Dr David Owen, then Secretary of State for Foreign and Commonwealth Affairs, for instructing the India Office Librarian to prepare for me a helpful summary of the closed section of the file, on which this paragraph is based.

'acting responsibly', for Orwell had already turned himself down on medical advice.*

On 8 March, a tuberculous lesion on Orwell's left lung suddenly began to bleed badly. Eileen got her brother, Laurence O'Shaughnessy, to see him. O'Shaughnessy was friendly with the director of a sanatorium in Kent, where he was himself a consultant surgeon. After some debate about the risk of moving him, the director, Dr J. B. McDougal, took him into Preston Hall, Aylesford, Kent. Eileen described the incident in a letter to Jack Common, written from her brother's house:

24 Crooms Hill
Greenwich, SE 10 [no date]

Dear Jack,

You'll probably have heard about the drama of yesterday. I only hope you didn't get soaked to the skin in discovering it. The bleeding seemed prepared to go on for ever and on Sunday everyone agreed that Eric must be taken somewhere where really active steps could be taken if necessary – artificial pneumothorax to stop the blood or transfusion to replace it. They got on to a specialist who visits a smallish voluntary hospital near here & who's very good at this kind of thing & he also advised removal, so it happened in an ambulance like a very luxurious bedroom on wheels. The journey had no ill effects, they found his blood pressure still more or less normal – & they've stopped the bleeding, without the artificial pneumothorax. So it was worth while. Everyone was nervous of being responsible for the immediate risk of the journey, but we supported each other. Eric's a bit depressed about being in an institution devised for murder but otherwise remarkably well. He needn't stay long they say, but the specialist has a sort of hope that he may be able to identify the actual site of haemorrhage and control it for the future.

This was really to thank you for being so neighbourly from such a distance, in such weather. One gets hysterical with no one to speak to except the village who are not what you could call soothing. I'll let you know what happens next. I have fearful letters to write to relations. Love to May & Peter,
Eileen[7]

---

*The file on Orwell was then closed, only to be opened once more on 6 December 1943 when the same A. H. Joyce sent a Memo up to his chief: 'You may have noticed that "George Orwell" has joined *The Tribune* as Literary Editor. Some of his recent stuff (such as his review of Wagg's book) has not been too bad. I don't know whether any use can be made of him?' But his chief scribbled in the margin: 'If he applies for material or advice, certainly. As to use, we already know by personal acquaintance and contact, making use of him is difficult.'

The calm factual, slightly ironic but none the less evasive under-statement of this letter shows how very much alike they were. They shared a deep reluctance to accept help even from their families, certainly felt ashamed to admit it, especially to someone like Jack Common in case he regard it as middle class nepotism.

Orwell was in the sanatorium for nearly six months. Preston Hall was run by the British Legion for ex-servicemen, and the patients knew that Orwell was the consultant's brother-in-law – they remarked on the fact that he got 'preferential treatment', a single room as soon as he arrived, whereas most of them had to wait for one for months. So there may have been some embarrassment on his part about his admission there, mirrored in Eileen's letter to Jack Common which made it seem impersonal and accidental that Preston Hall was chosen. Orwell took his breakfast alone, but insisted on 'mixing in with the boys', a fellow patient remembers, for all other meals.[8] 'The boys' came to accept him, he asked them lots of interesting questions about themselves, their experiences in other sanatoria and during the war, about their jobs and homes, but Mr Victor Stacey, who spent quite a lot of time in Blair's company (for he was Blair, not Orwell, in hospital), recalls with some surprise that he contrived to say very little about himself.

Patients could go out, of course. Orwell was soon taking the bus to some nearby ponds, where he resumed his favourite boyhood pastime of fishing. Perhaps he actually caught a fish or two; perhaps he just enjoyed the activity, quietly contemplating the water to see if the fish came up for air.

I remember one summer afternoon using the footpath through a nearby field of hay which was ready for cutting, at some distance I by chance saw Eric Blair's head among the waving hay. He appeared to be in fits of laughter. Catching my eye, he beckoned me over, having been amused by two large caterpillars performing antics on the long stems of grass.[9]

He appears like some Buddhist monk laughing at the aptness of the small things of creation. Orwell was not allowed to undertake any serious work or use his typewriter, so he finally turned down a proposition from Thomas Nelson, the publishers, which had reached contract stage, to write a book on *Poverty in Practice*; and though by midsummer the basic ideas and structure for *Coming Up For Air* were in his mind, he could not begin work on it. He was allowed to do occasional reviews, however, so a small stream of these emerged from the sanatorium, particularly for *Time and Tide*, for which he was now writing more regularly than for the *New English Weekly*. 'I still haven't done a stroke of work,' he told Connolly, 'but keep toying with the idea of starting my novel. One good effect the rest has had on me is that it has made me feel I can write a novel again, whereas when I came here I felt my novel-writing days were over.'[10]

Eileen could visit him only once a fortnight. It was a long difficult and, for them, costly journey from Wallington, north of London, to Aylesford in Kent to the south-east. She would have liked to stay with her brother in Greenwich, an easy halfway point, but someone had to feed the now unwanted goats, chickens and poor Marx, the masterless dog. 'I met Mrs Blair on the occasion of her visits,' writes Mr Stacey, 'a charming lady who was much interested in us. We were all aware of the comings and goings of lots of people visiting E.B. Some looked well-off, others extremely poor. We, of course, never knew who they might be.' Among the poor would have been Jack Common, Rayner Heppenstall and some of the Spanish ILP contingent who hitched their way down to see their strange, brave and unlucky comrade. Among the middle class were Max and Dorothy Plowman, who brought their friend, the novelist L. H. Myers, with them, an admirer of Orwell's writing. This was a visit which was to have a good consequence. Among the well off or seeming well off were Richard Rees and his friend Cyril Connolly; and somewhere betwixt and between, Stephen Spender, who paid Orwell at least one visit. They had already exchanged two interesting letters that year.

> 11 Queen Mansions
> W.6
> [no date]

Dear Eric Blair,

Thank you for your letter. On getting it, I rang up the *London Mercury* and have arranged to review your book [*Homage to Catalonia*] for them – so I shall read it & get a free copy. The two chapters you sent me did not strike me in the way you describe: on the contrary, I was impressed very favourably, and I think that unless you are treated *à la* Gide, what you have said should do good & not be aimed against the Spanish Govt. It depends a good deal,

I suppose, on how the critics handle your book. I hope they will not try to force you & it into a position of opposition.

There are one or two things I would like to discuss with you. I've never read any of your attacks on me, but I am puzzled as to why when knowing nothing of me you should have attacked me; and equally puzzled as to why when still knowing nothing of me, but having met me once or twice, you should have withdrawn these attacks. After all, I am bourgeois & most of the things you imagined, I should think. I am very pleased that you should feel differently now, but I should like to talk this over some time. Meanwhile, I am very sorry to hear that you have TB. If you are bored in hospital, I would like very much to come down & see you, in about a fortnight's time. I was very upset when Cyril told me you were ill & would have written then, had I known your address.

I am sending you a copy of my play, as you may care to read it in bed, if you have little else to do. If you can't bear the thought of it, don't look at it: I won't be offended.

Yours, Stephen Spender[11]

Jellicoe Pavilion
Preston Hall,
Aylesford, Kent.
Friday [15? April 1938]

Dear Spender,

... You ask how it is that I attacked you not having met you, & on the other hand changed my mind after meeting you. I don't know that I had exactly attacked you, but I had certainly in passing made offensive remarks abt 'parlour Bolsheviks such as Auden & Spender' or words to that effect. I was willing to use you as a symbol of the parlour Bolshie because (a) your verse, what I had read of it, did not mean very much to me, (b) I looked upon you as a sort of fashionable successful person, also a Communist or Communist sympathiser, & I have been very hostile to the CP since about 1935, & (c) because not having met you I could regard you as a type & also an abstraction. Even if when I met you I had not happened to like you, I should still have been bound to change my attitude, because when you meet anyone in the flesh you realize immediately that he is a human being & not a sort of caricature embodying certain ideas. It is partly for this reason that I don't mix much in literary circles, because I know from experience that once I have met & spoken to anyone I shall never again be able to show any intellectual brutality towards him, even when I feel that I ought to, like the Labour MPs who get patted on the back by dukes & are lost forever more.

It is very kind of you to review my Spanish book. But don't go & get into trouble with your own party – it's not worth it. However, of course you can disagree with all my conclusions, as I think you would probably do anyway, without actually calling me a liar ...

Yours, Eric Blair[12]

'Intellectual brutality' is a good phrase: Orwell saw himself as a violent unmasker of published pretentiousness, hypocrisy and self-deceit, telling people what they did not want to hear; but in private he was a gentle and tolerant man. His new friendship with Spender, whom he had *not*, in fact, attacked by name, did not prevent him on several occasions from returning to attacks on 'the nancy boys of literature' and 'the pansy Left' which Spender would have thought distasteful and indiscriminate. Orwell wanted literature to be *relevant* but he objected to an artist totally committing his talents and reputation to parties or causes, like the Communist Party, that scorned freedom and elevated certain lies (such as those about the POUM) to be 'ideologically correct'. Orwell objected equally strongly, however, to pure aestheticism or *'l'art pour l'art'*. Hence he was defending, in a truculent way, an essentially 'centrist' or moderate position in the Art and Society debate of the 1930s. The importance of the subject-matter or the sincerity of the writer can never excuse bad writing, but equally good writing is unlikely to come from someone with nothing to say about morality and society or who cultivates a delicate morality. So he was firing at both flanks at once, but the phrase 'pansy Left' could for a moment focus both enemies in his sights. The attack unfairly ignored Right-wing effeminacy in England, even if by 'pansy' and 'nancy' Orwell probably meant to mock 'irresponsible aestheticism' rather than active homosexuality – though the innuendo was in line with the aggressive heterosexuality of the ILP, some of whom were apt to see sodomy in the wearing of sandals. Be all that as it may, firing at such broad and ambiguous targets is not the nicest aspect of Orwell.

Why was Spender attracted to Orwell? Perhaps because he was already beginning to agree with him, beginning to reconsider his own commitment to Communism and his Left Book Club *Forward from Liberalism* published the previous year – now a remarkable document to re-read. He, too, was beginning to think of the relevance, rather than the fusion of artistic and political activities. Spender was deeply impressed, indeed influenced, by *Homage to Catalonia*; and refused to join in the hue and cry against it which the Party required from its famous names and its fellow-travellers.[13]

Homage to Catalonia was published on 25 April. *The Times Literary Supplement* and *Manchester Guardian* gave it respectful but perfunctory reviews. The *Daily Worker* savaged it in a few words, giving a lead followed by the smaller Left-wing journals. Again and again it was pictured as a defence of 'Trotskyites and anarchists' who betrayed the Republican cause. Understanding and appreciative reviews only appeared in the two journals where Orwell himself wrote regularly: Philip Mairet in the *New English Weekly* and Geoffrey Gorer in *Time and Tide*.[14] An anonymous review in the *Listener* praised his 'masterly description of war' but said that he was politically 'muddle-headed and inaccurate', accused him of an apologia for Trotskyist tactics which 'amounted to treachery', and asserted that 'to such proportions did the ultimate maleficence of the Trotskyists grow that it is credible that, indeed, they formed a part of the Fifth Column of whom General Franco has so constantly boasted'. Orwell replied vigorously. The reviewer countered that by 'Fifth Column' he only meant that they were weakening the authority of the central government and 'thus aiding the enemy'. The editor, J. R. Ackerley, unusually added a note: 'We are bound to say, in printing our reviewer's reply, that we consider it hardly meets the points raised by Mr Orwell, to whom we express our regrets.' A little victory for honesty and decency.[15] But the fighting though fierce was limited, and the book did not give rise to a general Press war, as Fred Warburg had hoped: the book, indeed, did not sell. Fifteen hundred copies were printed and there were still copies in stock when it was reprinted in 1951 as part of the Uniform Edition of Orwell. Not until 1952 did it make its first American appearance.[16] Critics are slow to recognize any literary merit in political writing, and as a political tract the standpoint in *Homage to Catalonia* was unusual, only appealing in its entirety to the ILP, to Trotskyists like Reg Groves (who called it 'the best thing that ever happened to us'), and to some non-political people.

Three private letters must have given Orwell great pleasure. Franz Borkenau, now in London, wrote: 'To me your book is a further confirmation of my conviction that it is possible to be perfectly honest with one's facts quite irrespective of one's political convictions.'

Shortly afterwards he visited Orwell. Herbert Read wrote that, although a 'hardened professional reader', the book 'moved me deeply ... by far the best book that I have seen on this Spanish war ... I don't see how anyone can doubt your honesty and objectivity', and 'I couldn't help comparing my own war experiences with yours', which he then did, frankly and sadly. Naomi Mitchison wrote from Argyll that the book delighted her for its truthfulness, while disturbing her politically, and that she was going to give copies of it to her eldest son and his friends who were tending to be 'orthodox Communist', looking for 'the moral security of thinking they are 100% right'.[17] Small sales but such praise from such free spirits must have strengthened Orwell in his new and lasting self-image as moral conscience of the Left.

Perhaps it was the controversy over *Homage to Catalonia* that made Orwell move from being an ILP fellow-traveller into becoming a card-carrying member. His card was issued on 13 June 1938, just in time for 'Why I Join the ILP' to appear in their weekly, *New Leader*, on 24 June. The piece was short, only about 800 words: he put himself on record but it was not, either in style or content, one of his best efforts. Writers, he said, wanted to keep out of politics, but the new age of 'rubber truncheons and concentration-camps' would not allow this luxury. One had to stand up for freedom or be cut down by Fascism. Capitalism meant imperialism and unemployment. Only a Socialist régime would 'in the long run ... dare to permit freedom of speech'.

Why the ILP more than another?

Because the ILP is the only British party – at any rate the only one large enough to be worth considering – which aims at anything I should regard as Socialism.

I do not mean that I have lost all faith in the Labour Party. My most earnest hope is that the Labour Party will win a clear majority in the next General Election. But we know what the history of the Labour Party has been, and we know the terrible temptation of the present moment – the temptation to fling every principle overboard in order to prepare for an imperialist war.

It is vitally necessary that there should be in existence some body of people who can be depended on, even in the face of persecution, not to compromise their Socialist principles. I believe that the ILP is the only party which, as a party, is likely to take the right line either against imperialist war or against Fascism when this appears in its British form.[18]

So far from not having 'lost all faith in the Labour Party', it is the first sign anywhere in his writings or letters that he had ever had any at all. Thinking more widely about politics during and after Spain, he plainly did not want to sound too sectarian or fanatical. The phrase indicates his agreement with those in the ILP who saw themselves as the temporarily suppressed conscience of the Labour Party, rather than a true Marxist vanguard that would one day head a revolutionary mass movement. But if relatively realistic in regard to domestic politics, he was dogmatic in his espousal of the Left ILP and the POUM, virtually the Trotskyist, theory of international relations.

War was coming, but it would be an imperialist struggle for markets between Britain, France, Germany and Italy. If Russia were involved, it would be purely to defend her territory, not to foment a revolutionary situation in Europe: indeed her national self-interest led her more, as she had shown in Spain, to attempt to defuse than to ignite. As the war would be unprecedentedly destructive, but probably short and sharp because of the bomber plane, an insurrectionary opportunity would be given to the working classes in Europe and the oppressed peoples in the Colonies. If it was to drag on, the democratic super-structure of British capitalism would turn Fascist and a grimmer counter-action would be necessary. Pamphlets in Orwell's possession* show this to be common ILP and Trotskyite doctrine. The link between the two appears to have been the dead, the martyred, Andrés Nin. (Much of Goldstein's testimony in Nineteen Eighty-Four seems to derive from pamphlets by or about Nin, rather than – as has been supposed – directly from Trotsky.)[19] This view was often called pacifist, but 'anti-militarist' is more accurate, for though working alliances were entailed with the Peace Pledge Union and other pacifist organizations, the ILP in theory believed in being prepared to fight a revolutionary war (even though in practice it never came to the caching of arms, only to talk of hiding a printing press: the anarchist Freedom Press, for instance, had Herbert Read's basement near Beaconsfield in mind as the final refuge for their last fight). Orwell,

---

*About this time he began to collect political and secularist pamphlets, many on war and peace, also on Spain, and on pacifism and militarism. He thought them important enough to have them listed by a secretary in 1946. They are now in the British Library.

indeed, had paid a membership subscription to the Peace Pledge Union the previous December, but there is no record of his renewing it. He may only have wanted their pamphlets.

There is no doubt that Orwell shared these views, though some of his later friends and editors have played them down as repetitive or as an aberration.[20] In a letter of 26 May 1938 to the *New English Weekly*, he spoke of the hope of 'producing an effective anti-war movement in England. It is a question of mobilizing the dislike of war that undoubtedly exists in ordinary decent people, as opposed to the hack-journalists and the pansy left'. The ILP actually denounced the Popular Front as being pro-war, for urging the British and French Governments to enter into a formal treaty of mutual defence with the USSR. And in a letter to Jack Common in October he said:

Did you see Kingsley Martin's ... article in last week's *NS* about the condition on which the LP should support the Government in war? As though the Government would allow any conditions. The bloody fool seems to think war is a cricket match. I wish someone would print my anti-war pamphlet I wrote earlier this year, but of course no one will.

No trace of this pamphlet survives, the only important writing for publication that has gone missing since the days of Orwell's obscurity. He continued to hold these views until the Hitler–Stalin pact of August 1939, when he changed overnight into support of the coming war and began to lecture Left-wingers on the virtues of a revolutionary patriotism.[21]

That spring and summer in the sanatorium gave him time for reading and thinking. The concept of 'totalitarianism' was becoming clearer to him. It had some links with both his anti-war thoughts and his somewhat speculative, more personal sympathy with the anarchists. Modern centralized states, he came to feel, often had more in common through their commitment to oppressive self-perpetuation, than their different ideologies might suggest. Reviewing Franz Borkenau's *The Communist International* reinforced these thoughts which he shared with Jack Common.[22] In reviewing Bertrand Russell's *Power*, Orwell doubted whether 'the huge system of organized lying upon which dictators depend' would put them at a disadvantage: 'it is quite easy to imagine a state in which the ruling caste deceive their followers without deceiving themselves'. With state control of radio and education '"the truth is great and will prevail" is a prayer rather than an axiom'.[23] Later that year he elaborated this thought in another review of a book on Russian government:

The terrifying thing about the modern dictatorships is that they are something entirely unprecedented. Their end cannot be foreseen. In the past every tyranny was sooner or later overthrown, or at least resisted, because of 'human nature' which as a matter of course desired liberty. But we cannot be at all certain that 'human nature' is constant. It may be just as possible to produce a breed of men who do not wish for liberty as to produce a breed of hornless cows. The Inquisition failed, but then the Inquisition had not the resources of the modern state. The radio, press-censorship, standardized education and the secret police have altered everything. Mass-suggestion is a science of the last twenty years, and we do not yet know how successful it will be.[24]

And that summer he had noticed very favourably Eugene Lyons' book *Assignment in Utopia*, a thoughtful analysis of Stalinism. This passage must have stuck in his memory:

Optimism ran amuck. Every new statistical success was another justification for the coercive policies by which it was achieved. Every setback was another stimulus to the same policies. The slogan 'The Five-Year Plan in Four Years' was advanced, and the magic symbols '5-in-4' and '$2 + 2 = 5$' were posted and shouted throughout the land.

The formula $2 + 2 = 5$ instantly riveted my attention. It seemed to me at once bold and preposterous – the daring and the paradox and the tragic absurdity of the Soviet scene, its mystical simplicity, its defiance of logic, all reduced to nose-thumbing arithmetic ... $2 + 2 = 5$ in electric lights on Moscow housefronts.[25]

Not all reading, thinking, and writing were political, however. The hospital at Aylesford had a small library consisting entirely of safe classic or didactic authors and of histories of the First World War. Orwell took out their *Collected Works of Charles Dickens* and kept it in his room. Henry Miller wrote to him again, a teasing, affectionate letter.

Terribly sorry to learn of your illness. You seem to have tough luck indeed. And yet one feels confident somehow that you will survive everything and anything – even the plague! Perhaps all you need is a rest – stop thinking and worrying about the external pattern. One can only do his bit – you can't shoulder the responsibilities of the whole world. (That's for guys like Hitler and Mussolini – they thrive on it.) Do nothing! You'll find it's very difficult at first – then it becomes marvellous and you get to really know something about yourself – and thru yourself the world. Everyone is micro- and macrocosm both, don't forget that . . .[26]

A tiresome and odd correspondence, but a small mark of his growing reputation, drew a sad admission that an old ambition had been abandoned. C. D. Abbott, of the Lockwood Memorial Library, State University of New York at Buffalo, wrote to him asking for manuscripts of his poems. Orwell replied, tersely but politely, that he was not a poet. Abbott persisted: 'Your name was given to me recently in London as a poet whom it would be most unwise of us to neglect.' Orwell replied: 'It might possibly have been Dylan Thomas or Rayner Heppenstall, both of whom I remember liked a poem of mine, or possibly it was Richard Rees. But anyway, I don't really write verse.'[27]

The Eton College (reunion) Dinner guests on 7 July 1938 sent Orwell a signed menu card. 'Greetings and regrets you were not here'. Collegers of his Election were beginning to realize who 'George Orwell' was. But he must have regretted the truth of his reply to the American library more than his necessary absence from the Eton reunion Dinner.

Orwell made good progress. The lesion seemed to have healed. In the middle of July, the hospital let him have his typewriter back. For a while he cut down his heavy smoking, but the doctors evidently feared that another bout of his usual winter bronchitis could reopen the trouble, so they advised him to spend the winter abroad in a warm climate. Financially this was impossible, so there must have been anxious consultations among his friends. Then L. H. Myers, who had visited him that once in the sanatorium, asked the Plowmans to act as intermediaries as if from an unknown benefactor. He gave them £300 for Orwell. It was not a loan, even though Orwell insisted years later, in his brief time of relative prosperity, on repaying it.[28]

After a weekend at Southwold, and a last week in the sanatorium, George and Eileen sailed for Morocco from Tilbury on 2 September on SS *Stratheden*, a P & O liner bound for the East via Gibraltar. The journey may have both stirred old memories for George and given him new ideas, for ten years later the last story he ever planned to write, after finishing *Nineteen Eighty-Four*, was to have been 'A

Smoking Room Story', set on board ship returning from the East, a microcosm of the class society. Why Morocco? No evidence survives. Probably there was no positive reason, it would have been chosen by a process of elimination. For as war clouds gathered, 'South' could no longer mean Spain or Italy; Morocco was not that far from England, and there were European doctors in case he had another haemorrhage. So they travelled from Gibraltar to Tangier, Casablanca, and finally to Marrakesh. After some time in hotels, the Orwells rented a small villa with a servant who came in each day, acquired a goat for milk, a few hens for eggs, and set about sowing vegetable seeds as if, mercifully on a smaller scale, they were still at Wallington. Orwell kept a diary of the half-year spent in Morocco, but it was a formal and stilted record of domestic events; and though he contrived to work knowledgeable references to North Africa into reviews and minor wartime writings, the experience did not affect him in any other obvious way. All his journeys had either been for experience from which to write a book or had resulted in a book; but this time he came to write a book already premeditated and unconnected with his temporary habitat. He remained intellectually remote, even if characteristically curious about the everyday life of the North African poor. So while they lived much like other 'long-stay' tourists, George began to write *Coming Up For Air*, the most English of all his novels in which alarms of war mingled with idyllic images of a Thames-side Edwardian childhood.

Orwell did write one 'set piece' on Marrakesh for John Lehmann's *New Writing*. It was overwritten, beginning (almost like self-parody): 'As the corpse went past, the flies left the restaurant table in a cloud and rushed after it, but they came back a few minutes later'; and it was somewhat contrived and external, ending with a description of Senegalese troops marching by while 'every white man' was supposed to be speculating 'How long before they turn their guns in the other direction?'[29]

So the enforced sojourn in Morocco led to no new themes. His anti-imperialism could have been strengthened a little, but it was strongly there already. His letters home, to Common, Connolly, Read and Gorer, were full of thoughts of impending war and dry half-jokes about returning to go straight into a concentration camp. A letter of 5 March to Herbert Read went over the now familiar ground that 'war preparation', let alone war, would lead to 'some kind of Austro-Fascism' in England: 'I doubt whether there is much hope of saving England from fascism of one kind or another, but clearly one must put up a fight, and it seems silly to be silenced when one might be making a row merely because one failed to take a few precautions beforehand. If we laid in printing presses etc. in some discreet place ...' He could help, but not financially. He wondered if Roland Penrose or Bertrand Russell might put up the money.[30] To Common, who had taken over the cottage at Wallington, he also wrote in great detail about the health of his Moroccan hens and gave agricultural and sanitary advice: the pullets would need a forcing mash and the mating of Muriel the goat was long overdue – 'a most unedifying spectacle – if you happen to watch it'. He should have warned them that using thick toilet paper would block up the lavatory. Then, as now, the simple life proved highly complex.

He wrote to John Sceats, an I L P member and insurance salesman whom he had met, asking for details of the life of a rep, because he wanted a plausible job for a '£5 a week and a house in the suburbs' man who would have the opportunity of driving around a bit and could be pictured as 'slightly bookish'. This was the birth of George Bowling.[31]

The domestic diary he kept was very bald and practical, mainly a record of planting, cooking, excursions, etc., but occasionally there were entries of more interest. 'Tortoises', he noted on 13 November, 'do not seem to stay under water long without coming up for air.' What is the meaning of this phrase, the title of his coming novel? In the novel, is it the fish reviving themselves and a hope that humanity by returning to nature can emerge from darkness and oppression? Much of the novel is pessimistic. Industrialism and capitalism have killed the best of old England. Echoing the cadences of Hugh Latimer's great sermon before Edward VI on the destruction of the yeomanry by the enclosures, Bowling lamented:

Where are the English coarse fish now? When I was a kid every pond and stream had fish in it. Now all the ponds are drained, and when the streams aren't poisoned with chemicals from factories they're full of rusty tins and motor-bike tyres.

Also there were massive and new external threats. 'George Bowling' put the totalitarian hypothesis of Borkenau, Orwell, Silone and Koestler in homely terms:

> Old Hitler's something different. So's Joe Stalin. They aren't like these chaps in the old days who crucified people and chopped their heads off and so forth, just for the fun of it. They're after something quite new – something that's never been heard of before.

There were further prophecies of doom, as intense as anything in *Keep the Aspidistra Flying*, but now public and plausible, less personal:

> I saw this street as it'll be in five years' time, say, or three years' time (1941 they say it's booked for) after the fighting's started. No not all smashed to pieces. Only a little altered, kind of chipped and dirty-looking, the shop windows almost empty and so dusty that you can't see into them. Down a side street there's an enormous bomb-crater and a block of buildings burnt out so that it looks like a hollow tooth. Thermite. It's all curiously quiet and everyone's very thin ... I see it all. I see the posters and the food queues, and the castor oil and the rubber truncheons and the machine guns squirting out of bedroom windows.

As in *Nineteen Eighty-Four*, which these passages clearly foreshadow, the implication is not that these things will necessarily happen, but that they could happen if we do not stand up and fight in time.

> The world we're going down into, the kind of hate-world, slogan world. The coloured shirts. The barbed wire. The rubber truncheons. The secret cells where the electric light burns night and day and the detective watching you while you sleep. And the processions and the posters with enormous faces, and the crowds of a million people all cheering for the Leader till they deafen themselves into thinking that they really worship him, and all the time, underneath, they hate him so that they want to puke. It's all going to happen. Or isn't it? Some days I know it's impossible, other days I know it's inevitable.[32]

However, also as in *Nineteen Eighty-Four*, something hopeful is stirring beneath the surface. While the novel satirized lower-middle-class suburban life, it was part of an Orwellian argument that people like Bowling should be the natural leaders, if only they could cease to wallow in nostalgia and actively grasp their identity of interest with the workers, as both are equally exploited. 'The prole suffers physically,' ruminates Bowling, 'but he's a free man when he isn't working.' There are forces of common sense and decency in the characters and traditions of the English working class with which, if they realized their power and had the right leadership, drawn from the lower middle classes, they could shake off exploitation, avoid war and build something better. As with the submerged tortoise, there is both power and hope in the common people, however sluggish they appear. To espouse the despised *petit bourgeoisie* as the socialist leaders of the working class could seem a deliberate perversity or a kind of Puritan romanticism, but Orwell was fully serious in thinking that he had made a profound discovery about English class structure and social movements.

A cool but loving voice beside him was not so sure, however, that such faith in the people would be effective. Eileen wrote to her sister-in-law: 'Eric, who retains an extraordinary political sympathy in spite of everything, wants to hear what he calls the voice of the people. He thinks this might stop a war, but I'm sure the voice would only say that it didn't want a war but of course would have to fight it if the government declared war.'[33]

Part of the excellence of *Coming Up For Air*, which some see as his best novel, is that the argument that hope lies in the common people is subtle and implicit, but it is certainly there: the pessimism is explicit, and hence is deliberately overdrawn. It was a novel of warning, not an emanation of total pessimism. Orwell's political pessimism at this time did not fill his whole life, nor did it arise from his basic personality plus ill-health and colour all his views.[34] His pessimism was precisely political: the world was running downhill out of control into war because political wisdom had not been applied; but it could have been. Brutal, anti-human, in a word 'fascist', forces had been encouraged and released by these failures, even in our own midst. But there were other values: a crisis might remind us of what they were and what we could do. There is no evidence, despite Orwell's illness and his political pessimism, that he was anywhere near to clinical depression. Such pessimism was perfectly rational in 1938 to 1939: optimists were becoming fatuous. Indeed what is remarkable at this period is the irrepressible energy and the sardonic humour of the man. He had the ability to enjoy actual, concrete, natural things: caterpillars on a blade of grass moved him to laughter, tortoises under water led him to reflection, just as years before (in the letter to Brenda Salkeld) Jeremiah had paused amid his denunciations to contemplate a baby hedgehog with love.

In December a letter came from a man they had given up for dead. Georges Kopp wrote from Toulon to tell them that he had been released after '17 months and 17 days of Communist Party jail. I had a very hard time and am afraid my health is probably ruined for ever.' He had lost seven stones in weight, suffered scurvy and blood poisoning. He asked if they could influence the ILP to lend him £50: political exiles in free countries have mundane difficulties. He wrote again in January delighted to have read *Homage to Catalonia*; and thanked Eric for his attempt to get him released by going to the Police HQ in Barcelona: 'awfully brave and some sort of heroical'. Kopp was trying to get a passport so he could get to Greenwich. Eileen had obviously persuaded her surgeon brother to look after him for a while. (He reached Greenwich late in January and wrote an account of his Spanish experiences, but he returned to France to enlist before the Orwells themselves returned to England.)[35]

Just after Christmas, a festival Eileen and George again ignored, he finished the first draft of the novel and they took a week's holiday at Taddert in the Atlas Mountains. Shortly after they returned to Marrakesh, Orwell fell ill again for three weeks, having to spend ten days in bed. Neither the diary nor letters reveal what the illness was. The diary shows Eileen having two different weeks of unspecified 'illness' while in Marrakesh. All was not well physically with either of them. They were, however, keen to return to England.

Fear that war was coming was shared not only by political activists. Back in October, Orwell's sister Marjorie had written from Bristol, where she and her family had moved, a letter nominally reporting on Marx 'being perfectly good except for such natural wickedness as will never be eradicated', but also a letter full of preparations for war: collecting the children's gas-masks, reporting that all the parks in London have been dug up for shelters, 'England is swept clean of corrugated iron and sand bags'. She wondered whether to hoard food or not and noted that Devon and Cornwall 'are simply packed with evacuees'.[36] The Orwells wanted to be back despite George's jokey pretence that it was good to be well out of it and his black humour at what he feared could happen – at the least that they would be prevented from getting home.

15.1.39

... I must say I was very thankful to be out of Europe for the war crisis

... I suppose the next bit of trouble will be over the Ukraine, so perhaps we may get home just in time to go straight into the concentration camp if we haven't been sunk by a German submarine on the way. I hope and trust it won't be so ... I trust when next we meet it won't be behind the barbed wire.[37]

In February came the news of the collapse of Spanish Republican resistance on the Catalan front and the newspaper photographs of the refugees streaming across the Pyrenees into France; and in March came the final surrender everywhere. On 26 March the Orwells sailed from Casablanca, arriving in London four days later with the completed manuscript of *Coming Up For Air*: George Orwell and George Bowling would both be home in time for the showdown. The Orwells had left for Morocco just before the Munich crisis and Chamberlain's surrender to Hitler ('peace with honour') of the Czech Sudetenland, and they returned just after the final disintegration of the Czechoslovak federation and the start of the German occupation.

George and Eileen paused in London long enough to deliver the manuscript to Victor Gollancz, who still kept his contract and faith in Orwell as a novelist, but was all too happy to see his non-fiction go elsewhere. They went to Southwold for ten days, Orwell going down with a heavy cold or bronchitis almost at once, spending a week in bed. His father was seriously ill, permanently bedridden, and his mother had bouts of phlebitis. Avril coped, competently and sardonically. She probably let Eric and Marjorie know how lucky they were not to have to look after the parents. All in all, it cannot have been the happiest of homecomings for George, with family sickness, the final Spanish defeat and impending general war.

They must have been relieved to reach Wallington and to plunge into the old tasks of gardening, clearing, digging and planting. The Commons had evidently not coped with the primitive conditions and the complex instructions as well as the Orwells might have hoped. For the first three weeks in May they visited Eileen's brother at 24 Crooms Hill, Greenwich. This was a rest for them both and also an opportunity for George to be thoroughly examined by Laurence O'Shaughnessy and to have tests made at local hospitals. Orwell appears to have been willing to accept his brother-in-law's advice, from up to the time of O'Shaughnessy's death at Dunkirk Orwell seems to have had no other regular GP. For the present it would seem his health was all right (no records have survived), for he underwent no further treatment.

During the last week in May, the Orwells returned to Wallington. The domestic diary shows a distinct shift in the balance of the economy from vegetables to flowers: lobelias and dahlias abounded; but there were still hens, ducks and goats. Some time that May Orwell began work on a volume of essays, of which the one on Henry Miller, political responsibility and English writers in the 1930s (already looking back to an era) gives the title to the whole work: *Inside the Whale*. On 24 June he was called urgently, but not unexpectedly, to Southwold. On 28 June his father, Richard Walmesley Blair, died of cancer. The death certificate further notes: 'E. A. Blair, son, present at the death'.

Orwell's values had become totally different from his father's, but he saw that as no reason to break (like some of his friends of Hampstead days) with either his family or the family as an institution. He did not resent his father having sent him to St Cyprian's and Eton. He disapproved of the decisions but respected the conventional motives. There may have been disappointment on both sides at the other's behaviour, but in the main each probably had a tolerant respect for the other and no expectation that the relationship of father and son needed any rationalizing or intellectualizing.

Three days later he returned to Wallington, thus almost immediately after the funeral. Although he felt deeply for his mother, visiting home more often than many of his contemporaries, he, like the rest of the Blairs, seemed to practise an ethic of practicality, having little liking for or apparent need of emotional gestures. One imagines that he asked his mother after the funeral if there was anything he could do for her, and she replied no, in the customary manner with them: so he left to get back to his book of essays.

On 12 June, just before his father's death, *Coming Up For Air* had been published. It received good notices and did moderately well: 2,000 copies were printed and a reprint of another 1,000 was made that same month.[38] It sold out in a couple of years. Reviewers noted that it had similarities with the early novels of Wells and also called it 'Dickensian', often praising the author's ability to put social philosophy into the commonsense mouth of a lower-middle-class commercial traveller. Certainly George Bowling is a most subtle and well-rounded creation, a considerable feat of imagination, showing that Orwell could emancipate himself from autobiography. There was, however, something slightly condescending in many of the reviews, both about the author and about the non-intellectual anti-hero who could have serious thoughts about war and peace and appreciate the 'golden country' of the pre-industrial landscape. No one speculated that Orwell, like Dickens and early Wells, may have been not merely writing about the lower middle class but actually aiming his book at them, trying to stir them up, wanting them to assert themselves and the real England. Taking it in the same context as his essays on Charles Dickens and Boys' Weeklies that appeared in his next book, *Inside the Whale*, it is overwhelmingly likely that the ILP supporter was trying to get his ideas across to the 'newly literate' market (despoiled by the cinema, radio, and 'romantic trash' available from the twopenny circulating libraries), especially as Orwell's hope for a patriotic English revolution centred on this marginal class. Reviewers also assumed that the nostalgia of George Bowling was exactly the same as George Orwell's, and later critics have pointed to Bowling's nostalgia as a contradiction of Orwell's socialist hopes. No one pointed out that the gross nostalgia of George Bowling may well have been intended to show both what held him back from being an effective man and what prevented his class from fulfilling an active and distinct political role. Orwell had nostalgia himself, certainly, but in balance, not to excess as he deliberately portrayed in Bowling. So the nostalgia of the novel as a whole was deliberately ambivalent. Critics tend to over-identify Orwell with his characters. There are so many good things in the past that we should preserve, the novelist says, but clinging to the past indiscriminately is no solution.[39] As propaganda, *Coming Up For Air* was, with its sales of 3,000 copies, a clear failure; but as a novel it was highly accomplished. (It had one technical eccentricity: he had decided that it could all be done without semi-colons.)

July saw the publication of another violently anti-war article, 'Not Counting Niggers', which brought his old anti-imperialism into loud harmony with his new ILP quasi-Marxist ideas. He mocked the anti-fascist alliance of 'Quakers shouting for a bigger army, Communists waving union jacks, Winston Churchill posing as a democrat'. Schemes for the democracies to stand together against the dictatorships always forgot, he argued, 'six hundred million disenfranchised human beings'. He objected to lumping together the British and French Empires as 'democracies' when they were 'in essence nothing but mechanisms for exploiting cheap labour'. He ended:

Nothing is likely to save us except the emergence within the next two years of a real mass party whose first pledges are to refuse war and to right imperial injustice. But if any such party exists at present, it is only as a possibility, in a few tiny germs lying here and there in unwatered soil.[40]

That he wrote, whether consciously or not, 'germs' instead of 'seeds' hardly argues much real hope.

Time was running out. From 24 August to 3 September 1939 Orwell was the guest of L. H. Myers at his house at Ringwood, Hampshire. Myers did not disclose that he was the anonymous benefactor who had provided the money for Orwell to winter in the south. The dates are interesting, for on the day before he went down to Hampshire, the Nazi–Soviet Pact had been announced, totally without warning. Stalin's agreement to remain neutral if Germany was involved in a war, obviously in effect an agreement to carve up Poland between them (as swiftly happened), was an event that, among other things, changed every relationship and assumption of the English Left Wing. Orwell's basic attitude to the war did not change overnight, but his policy and behaviour did. The war was still tainted, likely to be fought on imperialist, not anti-Fascist, lines; but now that the two totalitarian enemies had combined together, Orwell suddenly saw the need – in the words of C. Day Lewis – 'to defend the bad against the worse'. If the Soviets could so cynically embrace the Nazis and finally renege on international socialism, it was positively honest to defend the lesser evil of Chamberlain's England against Hitler's Germany. At the same time he bore his Spanish experience in mind and tried to ensure that it became a war both for and by democracy. After the Hitler–Stalin pact he renounced his anti-militarism or crypto-pacifism for much the same reasons as many intellectuals renounced the Communist Party.

His patriotism became very much linked to defending 'the country' as symbolized in the countryside. Only a crisis brought his two images of his own personality, latently so contradictory, decisively together:

the countryman and the citizen. Though he kept no diary of a personal or a literary kind, yet there are two domestic diaries, running from 9 March 1938 to 29 April 1940, which contain brief observations on the weather, flowers, birds, animals, egg production, and occasionally cooking or preserving recipes. Not even the outbreak of war was mentioned. He wanted to be both public and private man, but he had wanted to keep the two spheres apart.[41]

CHAPTER TWELVE

THE CHALLENGE
AND FRUSTRATION OF WAR

(1939–41)

IN the autumn of 1940 after the fall of France, when the eight or nine months of the 'phoney war' were over, a short essay of Orwell's, 'My Country Right or Left', appeared in John Lehmann's Penguin *Folios of New Writing*.

For several years the coming war was a nightmare to me, and at times I even made speeches and wrote pamphlets against it. But the night before the Russo-German pact was announced I dreamed that the war had started. It was one of those dreams which, whatever Freudian inner meanings they may have, do sometimes reveal to you the real state of your feelings. It taught me two things, first, that I should be simply relieved when the long-dreaded war started, secondly, that I was patriotic at heart, would not sabotage or act against my own side, would support the war, would fight in it if possible. I came downstairs to find the newspaper announcing Ribbentrop's flight to Moscow. So war was coming, and the Government, even the Chamberlain Government, was assured of my loyalty.

He could give reasons, he said, for supporting the War: that the only alternative to resisting Hitler was surrender. It was better to resist. Anything else would make nonsense of the Republican resistance in Spain or of the Chinese resistance to the Japanese. But he recognized that this was a purely utilitarian argument: 'the emotional basis' of his actions, he dared to argue, was 'patriotic ... what I knew in my dream that night was that the long drilling in patriotism which the middle classes go through had done its work, and that once England was in a serious jam it was impossible for me to sabotage'. But patriotism had nothing necessarily to do with Conservatism: 'it is devotion to something that is changing but is felt to be mystically

379

the same'. Change could even imply revolution, would have to imply revolution, he argued, if the War was to be won (carrying into the England of 1940 the ideas of Catalonia in 1936).

Within two years, maybe only a year, if only we can hang on, we shall see changes that will surprise the idiots who have no foresight. I dare say the London gutters will have to run with blood ... But when the red militias are billeted in the Ritz I shall still feel that the England I was taught to love so long ago and for such different reasons is somehow persisting.[1]

Thus the crypto-pacifist of 'Not Counting Niggers' was reborn as the revolutionary patriot of *The Lion and the Unicorn*, a work which was to expand the themes greatly – the only book that has ever been written about the possibility of revolution in terms of English national character.

The cynicism and opportunism of the Russo-German pact turned Orwell to support of the War just as it led others to leave the Communist Party; but never having been in the Party, Orwell could continue to argue for the revolution while appreciating and advocating the need to defend a minimal democracy; and he had no cause to forgive and forget when Hitler invaded Russia in 1941. The leaders of the ILP continued to call the War a capitalist-imperialist conspiracy; so Orwell, like many of its rank and file, quietly resigned.

The outbreak of war was in some ways congenial both to Orwell's character and to his circumstances. Generally it removed uncertainties, gave each individual a sense of a job to be done and created, at least after nine months when Chamberlain went and Churchill came in, a tense atmosphere of common endeavour. To Orwell, the War became, from school days, the 'supreme sacrifice'; from Burma days, the final round of 'the great game'; and from Spanish days, it was 'the last fight' against Fascism. The power of the Empire in tearing down Fascism would destroy itself and a purged and democratic England arise from the ruins. Orwell could also plausibly believe that he personally, from his para-military training in Burma and from his discovery of a relationship between ideology and military effectiveness in Spain, had more to contribute to the war effort than most, whether in action or by advice: so his frustration was all the greater when no one wanted his services. Spain might have purged many of Orwell's own guilt feelings about imperialism, but his early wartime writings show a great sensitivity towards themes of national punishment, penance, sacrifice, a rational understanding of the appeal of the irrational.

[Hitler] has grasped the falsity of the hedonistic attitude to life. Nearly all western thought since the last war, certainly all 'progressive' thought, has assumed tacitly that human beings desire nothing beyond ease, security and avoidance of pain. In such a view of life there is no room, for instance, for patriotism and the military virtues. The Socialist who finds his children playing with soldiers is usually upset, but he is never able to think of a substitute for the tin soldiers; tin pacifists somehow won't do. Hitler, because in his own joyless mind he feels it with exceptional strength, knows that human beings *don't* only want comfort, safety, short working-hours, hygiene, birth-control and, in general, common sense; they also, at least intermittently, want struggle and self-sacrifice, not to mention drums, flag and loyalty-parades ... Whereas Socialism, and even capitalism in a more grudging way, have said to people 'I offer you a good time', Hitler has said to them 'I offer you struggle, danger and death', and as a result a whole nation flings itself at his feet.[2]

This was written at least two months before Churchill's first speech as Prime Minister: 'I have nothing to offer but blood, toil, tears and sweat'. But neither Churchill nor Orwell was Hitler. Both were, in very different ways, archetypal Englishmen who, in order to defend common sense, common decency, ordinary virtues, saw the need to recognize their limits and to act for the emergency with uncommon brutal resolution.

The extremities of war intensified Orwell's belief in the virtues of the ordinary. 'The intellectuals who are at present pointing out that democracy and fascism are the same thing,' Orwell wrote to Gollancz in January 1940 (forgetting that he himself had done so in 'Not Counting Niggers'), 'depress me horribly. However, perhaps when the pinch comes the common people will turn out to be more intelligent than the clever ones.'[3] Orwell, again like Churchill, was more of a Roman republican than a modern liberal: the hardships and excitements of war had some positive appeal for him, and he saw a national war as a school of virtue and civic courage. He scorned the pacific and the overscrupulous.

Yet if the War stimulated Orwell's public spirit, the private man was bitterly depressed that he could neither serve effectively nor write what he wanted. After Spain, he knew clearly what he was: primarily,

though by no means exclusively, 'a political writer'. He had forged
his famous plain and colloquial style, and he had found his major
themes. He had no need to respond to the invitation to go to India
for the sake of his writing; it was only his new socialist morality that
drove him to think seriously of doing so. He was all ready for major
writing when war created the need or desire to serve actively. However,
the scars and record of his tuberculosis prevented him from enlisting
or from finding relevant war work. Conscription and paper-rationing,
moreover, had brought about the shrinkage or closure of many journals
which had up until then provided Orwell with most of his income,
so he was forced back into whatever casual reviewing and journalism
he could get. He lost both the time and the tranquillity to write more
novels, as he had hoped. With the outbreak of war he 'entered on
a period of waste and frustration'⁴ – at the very time when he had
so much to give drawn from his past experiences. None the less, Blair
being Orwell, he wrote an astonishing amount, turning more and more
to the essay as his main genre. The two masterpieces to come, *Animal
Farm* and *Nineteen Eighty-Four*, were, of course, deeply influenced
by the War and its immediate aftermath; but their roots lay in his
Spanish experience and in the reception of *Homage to Catalonia*.
Orwell was turning over the integral ideas of these books, developing
and sharpening them, in many essays, even in routine book reviews.

Immediately the War began, Eileen took a job in the Censorship
Department in Whitehall and came to Wallington only at weekends.
Orwell told friends that she had to do this to help make ends meet,
since so many of the little magazines on which he depended were now
closing down 'for the duration'; but it is also likely that she wanted
to keep her sister-in-law, Gwen, company at Greenwich, for her
brother Laurence, in the Territorial Army, had been called up into
the Royal Army Medical Corps. George at first only planned to stay
behind in Wallington for a few weeks to finish *Inside the Whale* before
enlisting or finding a relevant war job, just as he had carefully finished
The Road to Wigan Pier before going to fight in Spain. The 'Domestic
Diary' showed him on 14 September resolved to sell off all the fowls,
explaining to himself (or to the puritan god of diary-keepers) that 'we
should only be able to come down here at weekends'. But events
interrupted him. By the end of the month he had changed his mind

and decided to keep the older fowls to breed from – a sign that he intended longer occupancy – and he did not finish the book until December.

So his 'old life', which in truth had always been much interrupted, continued for another half-year. He wrote, did jobs around the house and garden, presumably still milked Muriel at dawn and took his poodle Marx out to chase rabbits (bourgeois rabbits?) while he picked blackberries. Eileen came down at weekends. Her hours were long, the travelling exhausted her, she began to look frail and tired. He wanted her to give up the job, but she also wanted to do something for the war effort and, in any case, to have given up would have been economically unrealistic with his income now badly reduced. They spent two weeks together at Greenwich that Christmas, before he returned to Wallington in January: but by the end of the month he was back in Greenwich again laid up for six weeks with what he would only admit to being 'flu'. Whether he really believed that the Army would take him is hard to tell, but he tried hard and he grumbled to Geoffrey Gorer: 'I have so far completely failed to serve HM government in any capacity, though I want to, because it seems to me that now we are in this bloody war we have got to win it and I would like to lend a hand. They won't have me in the army, at any rate at present, because of my lungs.' The poet Paul Potts remarked later that 'the War Office had more trouble keeping him out of the army than it did in getting hundreds of others to join'.[5] After his illness Orwell told Gorer that 'I am trying very hard to join a Govt training centre and learn machine draughtsmanship, partly because I want a job, partly because I think it would interest me ... and partly because I think it might be well to come out of the war having learned a trade.' But nothing came of it for Orwell. He must have had the Government Training Centre at nearby Letchworth in mind where Mark Benney was then learning how to use hacksaw, file and lathe for munitions work.[6] Here was some sign that 'small-holder' Orwell saw a need for a 'mechanic' Orwell to match and balance his belief that people should welcome the scientific and urban future while also preserving the best of the values of the rural past. He disliked the machine, but he saw its necessity. He disliked London, preferring countryside, but when it was clear during the retreat from France that the bombing planes would soon be coming (as he had prophesied in his last two novels), he moved to London with no more substantial a job than a weekly column, first on theatre, then on film, then theatre again, for *Time and Tide*. Plainly he had little liking for the journal, he would have found it excessively literary, liberal, eclectic – that is spineless and non-committed. '*Time and Tide*', it was said, 'wrote for no man'.* He simply felt he had to be in London at the time of crisis.

Before the overwork, the deprivations, the edginess, the dangers and the fatigue of wartime London took over, there was a last literary interlude. *Inside the Whale* was published on 11 March 1940 and was well received. For the first time his critical powers showed themselves clearly. He was not just an interesting novelist and an interesting reviewer, he was beginning to be recognized as a major essayist and as one of the best writers of English prose of his day. Dr Q. D. Leavis wrote a long review in *Scrutiny*, saying just that, praising his non-fiction highly but asking him to give up trying to write novels. He was already a fine 'critic of literature' and he might even grow to be, with the full *Scrutiny* seal of approval, a 'literary critic'. 'But one thing above all there is to his credit,' she concluded, 'if the revolution here were to happen that he wants and prophesies, the advent of real Socialism, he would be the only man of letters we have whom we can imagine surviving the flood undisturbed.'[7] The Communist pursuit of Orwell continued, only now the more respectful and discriminate hand of Arthur Calder-Marshall put the knife in, accusing him, after much diversionary praise, of sharing Miller's quietism rather than simply and pointedly tolerating it.[8]

The volume showed the full range of his interests. His essay on 'Boys' Weeklies' studied the politics of popular culture, a pioneering essay. 'I find this kind of semi-sociological literary criticism very interesting and I'd like to do a lot of other writers,' he told Geoffrey

---

*Nowhere is *The Collected Essays, Journalism and Letters of George Orwell* more selective. Sonia Orwell and Ian Angus have drawn a decent veil over this eighteen-month stint. Their literary judgement is hard to question. The writing, with few exceptions, is hasty, heavy-handed and banal. Plainly Orwell did the reviews as a job and had little liking for either theatre or film; and rather surprisingly he never made use of the material for any essay on popular culture, even the film reviews, as he had drawn a little gold out of dross from each of his former pot-boiling episodes. Only reviews of a film of Wells' *Kipps*, of Chaplin's *The Great Dictator*, and of the blue comedian Max Miller ('The Cheeky Chappie') at the Holborn Empire deserve a place in the canon.

Gorer, 'but unfortunately there's no money in it. All Gollancz would give me in advance on the book was £20.'[9] Orwell did not attack comics as such, as a highbrow might, but enjoyed them and saw them as a good beginning to literacy. Nor did he condemn the fact that they contained ideology, but rather condemned the particular ideology which preached subservience, snobbery, acquisitiveness, and smothered the masses with irrelevant distractions (the origins of Prolecult). 'It is possible ... to imagine a paper as thrilling and lively as the *Hotspur*, but with subject matter and "ideology" a little more up to date.'[10] He actually had an abortive correspondence with the writer Geoffrey Trease about the possibility of founding an artfully disguised Left-wing comic.[11]

The title essay discussed the failure of political sense and responsibility of intellectuals in the 1930s, gloomily prophesying the rise of totalitarian societies in which free literature would be impossible. None the less, he held up Henry Miller as an extreme case of a writer so good that he has to be defended despite his cynicism and, something worse than simple political irrelevance, his positive mockery of public, republican values. The essay is not wholly consistent. Orwell argued for the preservation of free literature but thought that 'literature, in the form in which we know it, must suffer at least a temporary death'; and ended by speaking of a demonstration of the *impossibility* of any major literature until the world has shaken itself into a new shape.[12] Yet the grim pessimism in this overstated essay, with its famous talk of liberal concepts of freedom and progress being exposed as 'fraud', is at first sight hardly compatible with a traditional radical optimism, even when put with deliberate understatement in his essay in the same volume on 'Charles Dickens':

His radicalism is of the vaguest kind, and yet one always knows that it is there. That is the difference between being a moralist and a politician. He has no constructive suggestions, not even a clear grasp, of the nature of the society he is attacking, only an emotional perception that something is wrong. All he can finally say is, 'Behave decently', which, as I suggested earlier, is not necessarily so shallow as it sounds. Most revolutionaries are potential Tories, because they imagine that everything can be put right by altering the *shape* of society; once that change is effected, as it sometimes is, they see no need for any other. Dickens has not this kind of mental coarseness. The vagueness of his discontent is the mark of its permanence. What he is out against is not this or that institution but, as Chesterton put it, 'an expression on the human face'.[13]

So 'Inside the Whale', as in *Nineteen Eighty-Four*, gave a frighteningly plausible warning of total defeat, but also supported a thin red line of hope. This either/or dichotomy *is* a philosophically tenable position. Logically one may argue that only one or other of two extremes is possible: sociologically certain conditions exclude any middle positions. Machiavelli argued thus: either a Republic or a Prince. But to put the contradiction so rationally would not do justice to an agonized psychological tension in Orwell at this time between the progressive, revolutionary libertarian (looking forward to a free, but socially responsible, literature and society) and the Jeremiah or foreteller of catastrophe (who could only enjoy, like Henry Miller, art for art's sake and memories of the past until the end came). The balance does come down in favour of the libertarian – as in his famous description of what he imagines Dickens ideally to look like, which is so often taken as an unconscious self-portrait (as surely it is):

I see a face which is not quite the face of Dickens' photographs, though it resembles it. It is the face of a man of about forty, with a small beard and a high colour. He is laughing, with a touch of anger in his laughter, but no triumph, no malignity. It is the face of a man who is always fighting against something, but who fights in the open and is not frightened, the face of a man who is *generously angry* – in other words, of a nineteenth-century liberal, a free intelligence, a type hated with equal hatred by all the smelly little orthodoxies which are now contending for our souls.[14]

'We *could* make a real improvement in human life,' Orwell replied to a letter from Humphrey House, the Dickens scholar, 'but we shan't do it without the recognition that common decency is necessary. My chief hope for the future is that the common people have never parted company with their moral code.'[15] Even so, he did not offer any guarantee of success either for the 'generously angry' or for 'common decency': he only stated that this was the proper way to behave, whether to succeed or to go down. (This correspondence may have led to the invitation to speak that May at the annual conference of the Dickens Fellowship, with Compton Mackenzie in the chair.)

And so, as in the past, he prepared to go on to his next book. But for once Orwell made a different kind of virtue of necessity. 'I dare say we *could* get by,' he wrote to Gorer in April 1940, 'if I stuck simply to writing, but at present I am very anxious to slow off and not to hurry on with my next book, as I have now published eight in 8 years which is too much.' Back in January, he had already told Gorer, 'I am sort of incubating an enormous novel, the family saga sort of thing, only I don't want to begin it until I'm all set.'[16] Again in April 1940, he told Rayner Heppenstall, 'I haven't touched my novel but am kept very busy doing reviews which help to keep the wolf a few paces from the backdoor.'[17] And a few days later, he wrote again to Heppenstall to congratulate him on the birth of a child ('What a wonderful thing to have a kid of one's own, I've always wanted one so'); and adds, 'I am buried under books I keep reviewing and not getting on with my own book. God knows whether it will ever get written or whether such things as publishing novels will still be happening two years hence.'[18] It is doubtful if he ever started writing it, almost certainly not in 1940. What is the lost book? There is one clue. An autobiographical note he wrote that same month for an American directory ended: 'I am not at the moment writing a novel, chiefly owing to the upsets caused by the war. But I am projecting a long novel in three parts, to be called either *The Lion and the Unicorn* or *The Quick and the Dead*, and hope to produce the first part by some time in 1941.'[19]

What was this 'enormous novel', a 'family saga' and in 'three parts'? Each of Orwell's previous books had arisen from his immediately previous experiences and was highly autobiographical, so it is odd that all trace of what this trilogy was to have been about has vanished from his letters or, with one exception, from the pages of his notebooks. The answer may be found by considering these pages in relation to what were his main intellectual and moral concerns in 1940. Some twenty pages of an unpublished notebook, almost certainly written in 1943, have the heading 'For "The Quick and the Dead"'.[20] The rest of the small notebook – apart from a few pages of notes on distortions of words and political usages – contains an early but clear outline of *Nineteen Eighty-Four*, under its first projected title, 'The Last Man in Europe'. (See Appendix A.) The notes on 'The Quick and the Dead' are for an account of a hard-up middle-class childhood, once again, somewhat in the manner of Gordon Comstock's and George Bowling's. They tell of the unreality through a child's eyes of the horrors of the

First World War; and give an account of childhood sexual beliefs, which shows the torment and fantasy that can follow into late adolescence from quite astonishing ignorance. There are long lists of commonplaces and proverbial sayings found in middle-class households, very much of the kind that Winston Smith and the old shopkeeper who betrays him try to remember.

Could Orwell have been planning as early as 1940 a trilogy of which something like *Nineteen Eighty-Four* would have been the third volume? Logically this account of the final totalitarian society would follow a volume on how the revolution was betrayed (*Animal Farm*), itself following on from volume one ('The Quick and the Dead') which would show through the childhood of Winston's father how the old order (which Orwell/Winston both loved and hated) had decayed and collapsed. And the abandoned title, 'The Last Man in Europe', would make more sense if Winston Smith was the last of a family, of whom we had already heard, whose decay and demise parallel that of a free if corrupt, imperfect and self-destructively competitive society. In *Nineteen Eighty-Four* many of the flashbacks to the far past are awkward, not merely because objective history and truthful memory are being abolished but because the author seemed to try to squeeze too much into too small a space. Many critics have pointed out that his thesis, that a totalitarian society once allowed to develop cannot be overthrown internally, is made less plausible by there being no account of how it came to develop in the first place. There is only the awkward interpolation of Goldstein's testament, which it is difficult to know how far, if at all, to take seriously as social analysis since it is a mixture of truth and parody. But such objections ignore *Animal Farm*. This work already stands in just such an intellectual relationship to *Nineteen Eighty-Four*, even if the literary form is so pleasantly different: the Inner Party are the pigs in power perpetually. Also the partisan history in Goldstein's testament would gain more point if it had originally been intended as an ironic juxtaposition to a true interpretation of what had happened in the past with which the reader was already familiar. Certainly the main intellectual concern of Orwell in 1940 and 1941 was with the totalitarian hypothesis: that the Nazi and Bolshevik régimes would move towards a common form of 'oligarchical collectivism'[21] and with the possibility of human freedom being preserved by the common people, not the power-hungry intellectuals, holding on to the best of the purged and harrowed past. He used the title 'The Lion and the Unicorn' for a quite different book, an essay on the English national character, on the war and on revolution. But the assertion that the ornamental brass buttons of British soldiers would continue to be worn even after the revolution, has the same symbolic meaning in the essay as the useless coral paperweight that Winston Smith of the novel finds in the year 1984: an irrational but human and beautiful artefact of a past not wholly malign. Memory preserves us from Big Brother's control and manufacture of history itself. All this is speculative. In the mood of his essay on Dickens in *Inside the Whale* rather than in that on Henry Miller, Jonah could simply have been planning a socialist Forsyte Saga.

Whatever it was he finally or temporarily abandoned, Orwell closed up Wallington for the duration of war and some time in the middle of May Eileen and he moved into 18 Dorset Chambers, Chagford Street, NW1 – near Regents Park, people politely said. So it was, but it was the most miserable two-room fourth-floor flat, above shops, backing on to garages in a mews, with no lift, little light, cheap second-hand furniture, gas water-heater and shared bathroom. But it was central and must have been cheap, particularly with the flight of Londoners from the centre. (They soon let Wallington to Eileen's friend, Lydia Jackson, and her flat-mate, Patricia Donahue, when they were bombed out; but the Orwells kept the use of the house for occasional weekends.)

Orwell began his weekly stint of theatre reviewing for *Time and Tide*, continued his book reviewing for them, and began to review regularly for *Tribune*, mainly a page to himself, both novels and political books, but usually as a review *en masse* as he had once done for the *New English Weekly*, now turned pacifist and anti-war. He schooled himself to write reviews straight on to the typewriter without drafts or revisions. Their style thus became even more colloquial, colourful and relaxed.

He began to keep a diary on 28 May, the day news began to come through of the surrender of the Belgian Army and of the British Army's retreat to Dunkirk.* '28 May ... For days past there has been no

*The diary covers the period 28 May 1940 to 28 August 1941, then resumes from 14 March to 15 November 1942 (see *The Collected Essays, Journalism and Letters*, Vol. II, pp. 339-450, which reprints it almost completely, with the editors' headnote on

real news and little happening ... 29 May. One has to gather any
major news nowadays by means of hints and allusions ... 30 May.
The BEF are falling back on Dunkirk ... Borkenau says that England
is now definitely in the first stage of a revolution ... Still no evidence
of any interest in the war ... 31 May. Last night to see Denis Ogden's
play *The Peaceful Inn*. The most fearful tripe ... 1 June. Last night
to Waterloo and Victoria to see whether I could get any news of [Eric]
... 'Eric' was Laurence O'Shaughnessy. Orwell must have plunged
into the confusion of the unscheduled trains coming into the London
stations from Channel ports, trains full of bewildered French and
Belgian refugees and exhausted Allied troops, a few in formation but
mostly ragged and looking for their units; some British troops
snatching a quick couple of days with their families before reporting
back to their depots, everyone expecting the bombers and the invasion
to follow quickly on their heels. Only one unit of Marines, marching
in perfect order, recalled childhood memories to Orwell of 1914 'when
all soldiers seemed giants to me'. But amid what then looked more
like a defeated rabble than an organized army, he could gain no news
of Eileen's brother. The news came a few days later. He had been
killed on the beaches while tending the wounded.

Eileen was deeply attached to her brother. His death struck her hard.
'I believe that Eileen's grip on life', wrote Lydia Jackson, 'loosened

---

p. 339 explaining minor deletions). It was intended for publication jointly with the
novelist and journalist Inez Holden (1904–74) whom he met in 1940 through Fred
Warburg. They could not agree on editing his part of it (though they became close
friends), so she published separately (*It Was Different At The Time*, Bodley Head,
1945) and his 'diary', according to her, was rejected for publication by Warburg. It
is a rather stilted commentary on the wartime news, at times amusingly tendentious,
but often inaccurate and rarely personal, falling rather clumsily between 'what the papers
should have said' and (all too little of) 'what I saw myself'. It is curious how many
false starts Orwell made with either diaries for publication or the diary as a literary
device: the lost first version of *Down and Out*, the diary version of the first part of
The Road to Wigan Pier, probably what he worked on in the trenches in Catalonia
that Eileen typed up in Barcelona but did not survive (see p. 326 above); and now
this 'wartime diary'. Finally there was Winston Smith's attempt to set down the truth
– which Orwell never seriously attempted to do in a diary. The above are all highly
literary while the Wallington and Jura diaries are bare records of planting, purchases
and domestic events. A page or two of his 'hospital notebook' of 1949 (see p. 539 below)
is perhaps a partial exception.

considerably after her brother's death.' Eileen had told her he was the only person on whose immediate help she could absolutely count when in difficulties. 'If we were at opposite ends of the world and I sent him a telegram saying "Come at once" he would have come. George would not do that. For him his work comes before anybody.' 'It was undoubtedly so,' Lydia Jackson added: 'For Orwell his work was more important than any personal relationship, and I believed that he cared for himself only in his capacity as a writer.'[22]

Eileen looked after George with a fierce but undemonstrative protectiveness, however hard-driven herself, knowing of his illness; but he seems only intermittently to have noticed her ill-health, and when he did, put it down entirely to the job and wartime conditions. (Laurence's death, indeed, deprived the Orwells of any regular medical advice – they were not the sort to trust doctors, or to go to them until something was obviously and badly wrong.) Very few of Eileen's letters have survived and the testimony of her friends is inevitably tinged with hindsight; but it is curious that there is no mention of Eileen's brother's death in any of Orwell's letters; nor does the diary, though there is an entry for each of the relevant days, refer to it. Is this mastery of feeling or some lack of feeling? Eileen seemed to share with Eric, indeed with the Blairs generally, an almost terrible public stoicism but privately she grieved bitterly. Perhaps family death coloured his diary entry for 8 June – an unusually interesting one:

Stephen Spender said to me recently, 'Don't you feel that at any time during the last ten years you have been able to foretell events better than, say, the Cabinet?' ... Where I feel that people like us understand the situation better than so-called experts is not in any power to foretell specific events, but in the power to grasp what *kind* of world we are living in. At any rate, I have known since about 1931 (Spender says he has known since 1929) that the future must be catastrophic.

Orwell kept on trying to enlist. He told John Lehmann that 'I was informed at the W[ar] O[ffice] that it is no longer held against a man to have fought in the Spanish civil war';[23] but still no medical board would pass him. The best he could do was to join that June the Local Defence Volunteers, which later became known as the Home Guard. Orwell soon came to attach great significance to it; he saw it as through blood-red spectacles as a potential people's militia. In April 1941 he was still trying to find full-time war work: a letter from the Air Ministry informed him that there was no vacancy in the office of Director of Public Relations. His suspicion that there was discrimination against men who had fought in the Spanish Republican ranks was not unreasonable: Eileen had reported that her colleagues in the Censorship Department tended to see all Reds as equal and as equally dangerous. Some people were, indeed, not quite sure which war they were fighting.

Some literary life continued. Orwell now met Connolly more often and became a regular contributor to *Horizon*, the literary monthly that from January 1940 to New Year 1950 graced English Letters and carried, right from the beginning, so many of Orwell's best essays and reviews. He contributed to nearly every issue in 1940. And from January 1941 until the summer of 1946 he wrote a regular 'London Letter' for *Partisan Review* of New York, a Left-wing but anti-Communist journal. He enjoyed the freedom which the letter form allowed (with occasional interventions from the wartime censors), writing mainly on politics and the war effort; and belabouring the pacifists with almost indecent fervour, considering his own recent change of heart. He commented with humour on the London literary scene. The articles were a somewhat long-winded trial run for the masterpieces of discursive and polemical column journalism that he was soon to write for *Tribune*. His first contribution to *Partisan Review* recalled: 'the day in September when the Germans broke through and set the docks on fire, I think few people can have watched those enormous fires without feeling that this was the end of an epoch. One seemed to feel that the immense changes through which our society has got to pass were going to happen there and then. But to an astonishing extent things have slipped back to normal.'[24]

Connolly was to recall the Orwell of this period with affectionate mockery and typical inaccuracy about dates and facts:

Orwell was a political animal. He reduced everything to politics; he was also unalterably of the Left. His line may have been unpopular or unfashionable, but he followed it unhesitatingly; in fact it was an obsession. He could not blow his nose without moralizing on conditions in the handkerchief industry ... Orwell slipped into the last war as into an old tweed jacket. He settled down in 1939 to the BBC or the Literary Editorial Chair of *Tribune*, or as London correspondent to *Partisan Review* (NY) to watch his dream come true – a People's War. He had seen it nearly happen in Spain, now it seemed inevitable. This time the gamble must come off, *Revolution or Disaster*.

A series of defeats would topple the British ruling class; in the nick of time the People would kick them out and take control, snatching victory at the last moment, as happened in revolutionary France. Churchill must go, even Cripps must go. Red Guards in the Ritz! Long live the People's Army and the socialist home-guard.

This point of view, apart from not being borne out by the facts, limited Orwell... He felt enormously at home in the Blitz, among the bombs, the bravery, the rubble, the shortages, the homeless, the signs of rising revolutionary temper.[25]

But Connolly was also to praise Orwell for having dispelled from *Horizon* a tendency to being itself a 'Left-wing "school magazine"'.[26]

It must have been about this time that the literary editor and novelist, V. S. Pritchett, first met him.

He was an expert in living on the bare necessities and a keen hand at making them barer. There was a sardonic suggestion that he could do this but you could not. He was a handyman. He liked the idea of a bench. I remember once being advised by him to go in for goat-keeping, partly I think because it was a sure road to trouble and semi-starvation; but as he set out the alluring disadvantages, it seemed to dawn on him that he was arguing for some country Arcadia, some Animal Farm, he had once known; goats began to look like escapism and, turning aside as we walked to buy some shag at a struggling Wellsian small trader's shop, he switched the subject sharply to the dangerous Fascist tendencies of the St John's Wood Home Guard who were marching to imaginary battle under the Old School Tie.[27]

'9 August 1940. The money situation is becoming completely unbearable ... Wrote a long letter to the Income Tax people pointing out that the war had practically put an end to my livelihood while at the same time the government refused to give me any kind of job ... 19 August. A feature of the air raids is the extreme credulity of almost everyone about damage to distant places ... 23 August ... Have got my Home Guard uniform, after $2\frac{1}{2}$ months ... 26 August (Greenwich)... We were watching at the front door when the East India docks were hit ... 10 September ... Most of last night in the public shelter, having been driven there by recurrent whistle and crash of bombs not very far away ... Frightful discomfort due to overcrowding ... 12 September...a youth of about twenty in dirty overalls, perhaps a garage hand. Very embittered and defeatist ... He spoke bitterly about the people rendered homeless in South London, and eagerly took up my point when I said the empty houses in the West End should be requisitioned for them ... 24 September. Oxford Street ... the late afternoon sun shining straight down the empty roadway and glittering on innumerable fragments of broken glass. Outside John Lewis's, a pile of plaster dress models, very pink and realistic, looking so like a pile of corpses that one could have mistaken them for that at a little distance. Just the same sight in Barcelona, only there it was plaster saints from desecrated churches ... 19 October. The unspeakable depression of lighting the fire every morning with papers of a year ago, and getting glimpses of optimistic headlines as they go up in smoke ...' And so on through the tense summer of the Battle of Britain and the long winter suffering of the bombing of London.

Yet intellectual life continued. Some time that winter, Arthur Koestler, straight from his escape from Europe and eager to meet the author of *Homage to Catalonia*, the reading of which had strengthened his own rejection of the Communist Party, appeared from one world[28]; and from another world, a country house in Northamptonshire, came a courteous letter from Sacheverell Sitwell thanking Orwell for sending him an account of supernatural occurrences: 'I wish we could meet some time. My sister, who is staying here with me, wants me to tell you that she is a great admirer of yours and has read with admiration nearly everything you have written.'[29] Orwell had an almost equally incongruous brief encounter at about the same time with Anthony Powell, who had been a year behind him as an Oppidan at Eton. Inez Holden had taken the Orwells to supper at the Café Royal. She knew the Powells, who happened to be there, and asked them over to her table to meet the Orwells. Powell quite wanted to meet him, but felt embarrassed at being overdressed for the occasion, in his regiment of the Line 'blues' (patrol uniform or regimentals, brass buttons and a high collar). 'Orwell's first words, spoken with considerable tenseness', Powell recalled 'were "Do your trousers strap under the foot?" ... "Yes." Orwell nodded. "That's really the important thing." "Of course." "You agree?" "Naturally." "I used to wear ones that strapped under the boot myself," he said, not without nostalgia. "In Burma. You knew I was in the police there? These straps under the foot give you a feeling like nothing else in life."' What their wives must have thought of this regression is unrecorded, but not merely had social disaster been avoided, foundations had been laid for what grew, three years later when Powell was back in London, into a genuine friendship. Powell remembered him as 'Tall – as has been more than once remarked, closely resembling Gustave Doré's don Quixote.'[30]

Powell's eagerness to meet Orwell led Inez to reflect in her private diary on his growing reputation:

Sept. 11th '41

It's strange the way a writer's fame begins slowly creeping up to him and then racing so that after a while he seems to be a poor relation of his own fame. People of taste and sensitiveness, writers, political workers and actors (who are now showing signs of being extremely left wing) socialist doctors, factory workers and technical instructors in touch with their labour organizations are all well aware of Orwell.

Yesterday at the PEN world congress lunch I sat at a table with Koestler, Cyril Connolly, Stevie Smith, Guy Chapman, Koestler's girl friend Miss Hardy ... René Avord, of *La France Libre*, who has some other name, and a German refugee writer. Koestler was betting that Orwell would be the greatest best seller in five years time and our bet was five bottles of burgundy.[31]

There may be some exaggeration in this of her new friend's fame and of Koestler's prescience, but the entry is undoubtedly genuine and contemporary, it is not hindsight.

More in his usual ambience than the Café Royal, though also odd for the company he had to keep, Orwell appeared twice in the repentant Victor Gollancz's anthology *The Betrayal of the Left: An Examination and Refutation of Communist Policy*, published in March 1941. Laski contributed a Preface, Gollancz wrote the lion's share, the equally repentant John Strachey wrote three chapters, on espousing 'The Social-Democratic Way' against Leninism and another on 'Totalitarianism': Johnnie-come-lately but Johnnie did well to point to a parallel between 'Fascist uniformity' and 'Soviet uniformity', although this was ground already well covered by Silone, Borkenau, Koestler, Malraux and Orwell. Gollancz and Strachey attacked their old ally, Harry Pollitt, with the zeal – to them – of yet another new cause. Orwell, tactfully avoiding the tone of 'told you so' of his fellow-contributors, wrote on 'Fascism and Democracy', to rub in the still unwelcome truth that Fascism has a popular base and following. He also wrote an essay on 'Patriots and Revolutionaries', urging that the Left should not scorn patriotism and had as much claim to the name of patriotism as the Right.* The book has been claimed as a watershed in British Left-wing thought, but in fact it marked the beginning of the end of the Left Book Club. The Club lingered on with a low pulse rate until just after the war, but only 500 copies of *The Betrayal of the Left* were printed for the club edition and 1,300 for public sale. There was, however, a second impression of 500 and 200 copies respectively.[32] Many of the fellow-travellers at whom it was aimed forgave and forgot the sins of the Communist Party when Stalin, thanks to Hitler, entered the war.

Orwell took the Home Guard very seriously. He joined on 12 June 1940 what became C Company of the 5th County of London Battalion (the St John's Wood company). He was made a sergeant immediately and had to train a section of ten men. Based on St John's Wood (a fashionable area that bordered on poor areas), the section was a remarkable social mix. It originally consisted of two wholesale dealers from Covent Garden, a garage proprietor and his son, a Jewish piano manufacturer and his 17-year-old nephew, a van-driver, a factory worker, a plumber and an unemployed old soldier. Later Orwell sent the Company Sergeant-Major, who was commissionaire of a nearby block of flats in which Fred and Pamela Warburg lived, to recruit the famous tenant. By night, three nights a week and Sunday mornings, Warburg said 'Sir!' smartly to the Sergeant-Major, by day vice versa.[33]

As well as lack of uniform and arms, there was at first lack of any clear definition as to what the Home Guard were meant to do. It was agreed that an invasion was imminent, but were they to be an auxiliary force like the Territorials deployed in the field with the regular army, were they simply to be armed civilians for guard duty and to provide pockets of last-ditch defence in their own localities, or were they, beyond the latter task, to be a guerrilla force, trained to survive and operate behind enemy lines? Unless there was clarity about their tactical role, there could be no clear training programme. Naturally enough, as Orwell grumbled both in the section post and in print, they were officered in the main by retired veterans of the First World

* Neither of these essays is reprinted in *The Collected Essays, Journalism and Letters*. Admittedly the same ground is covered in *The Lion and the Unicorn*, but not including them permits a misleading and depoliticized picture of the balance and nature of his writing in 1940 and 1941.

War who stuck to ideas of trench warfare and were slow to assimilate
the lessons of the German *Blitzkrieg*, if they thought of tactics at all.
So the Home Guard spent most of its time on weapon-training and
drill. Orwell intimated that the first was all right, if there were weapons;
but the latter, being used as toy soldiers by 'Colonel Blimps', was a
total waste of time.

The role he characteristically saw for the Home Guard was clear
right from the beginning in a letter he wrote in June to *Time and Tide*
urging the slogan 'ARM THE PEOPLE', an unusual line for their drama
critic to take. He claimed that the Spanish War had shown 'that the
advantages of arming the population outweigh the danger of putting
weapons in the wrong hands'. Specifically he urged the issue of
hand-grenades 'within the next three days' as the key to street-
fighting and as capable of rapid manufacture (he quickly found an
empty garage and put his section to work making their own petrol
bombs out of milk bottles, by methods no longer safe to describe);
the issue of all shotguns, etc., from gunsmiths' shops; the blocking of
fields against aircraft landings; the painting out of place-names everywhere; and the giving of radio receivers to all LDV: 'as with weapons,
the Government should not hesitate to requisition what it needs'.[34]
The last three items on his list were to become commonplace and
Government policy; but Orwell was quick off the mark in identifying
them as necessary. Perhaps he hoped to attract official attention and
to become some sort of adviser on guerrilla, militia and street warfare?

Some people of similar mind were more successful, and Orwell made
contact with them. When in December he wrote a piece in *Tribune*
urging Left-wing socialists to join the Home Guard, not to think of it
as a 'Fascist organization' (or if so, by joining to make it less so), he
could refer to two schools of thought in the 'Home Guard. One was
simply the regular (auxiliary) army mentality; but 'one school (for a
long while centred round the Osterley Park training school, run by
Tom Wintringham and other veterans of the Spanish Civil War) wants
to turn it into a democratic guerrilla force, like a more orderly version
of the early Spanish Government militias'. He urged his readers to join
and to 'give a shove in the right direction ... from below'. And there
followed these naïvely disguised inflammatory words:

Let no one mistake me. I am not suggesting that it is the duty of Socialists
to enter the Home Guard with the idea of making trouble or spreading sub-

versive opinions. That would be both treacherous and ineffective. Any Socialist who obtains influence in the Home Guard will do it by being as good a soldier as possible, by being conspicuously obedient, efficient and self-sacrificing. But the influence of even a few thousand men who were known to be good comrades *and* to hold Left-wing views could be enormous. At this moment there is not even in the narrowest and most old-fashioned sense of the word, anything unpatriotic in preaching Socialism.

We are in a strange period of history in which a revolutionary has to be a patriot and a patriot has to be a revolutionary...

The Communists, ILP, and all their kind can parrot 'Arms for the Workers', but they cannot put a rifle into the workers' hands: the Home Guard can and does. The moral for any Socialist who is reasonably fit and can spare a certain amount of time (six hours a week, perhaps) is obvious.[35]

At some stage, Orwell attended the Army's famous and controversial Osterley Park School for small-scale infantry tactics (set up hurriedly after Dunkirk when all sorts of desperate ideas were given a try). He met Tom Wintringham there and also Hugh Slater,* whose *Home Guard for Victory!* (Gollancz, 1941) he reviewed twice, once in the *New Statesman and Nation* and then in more than three pages in *Horizon*.[36] Orwell praised the technical portions of the book on street-fighting, etc., and Slater's balanced view on the discipline question, showing how they were linked to the author's view (which was true but had been kept beneath the surface – Orwell let the cat out of the bag) that the Home Guard should develop into 'a quasi-revolutionary People's Army'. Orwell already held this view, he did not derive it from Slater. It can be read between the lines of the article printed the previous year in *Time and Tide*, whose readers were anything but revolutionary socialists. And Orwell wrote a centre-page article for the

---

*Humphrey (Hugh) Slater (1906–58) was a product of Sedbergh and Tonbridge schools who studied at the Slade, spent some months in the USSR in 1930, went to Berlin in 1932, became an active Communist journalist in the 1930s, fought in Spain, became Chief of Operations in the International Brigade (though his disillusionment with the Party began then). In 1940 he initiated with Tom Wintringham, who had also fought in Spain, the training of the Home Guard at Osterley Park, after which he entered the regular army, being invalided out in 1944 with the rank of major. He became an intimate friend of Inez Holden, another link with Orwell, and founded *Polemic* in 1945, to which Orwell contributed 'Notes on Nationalism', 'Second Thoughts on James Burnham', 'Politics and Literature: An Examination of *Gulliver's Travels*' and 'Lear, Tolstoy and the Fool' – four of his best essays. Slater was often brilliant and charming, if devious and not always trusted.

Evening Standard (which, though Lord Beaverbrook was in the Government, was constantly gunning for the 'old guard' at the War Office), headed 'Don't Let Colonel Blimp Ruin the Home Guard'. This began as a reasonable statement, with only a few socialist overtones, of the Osterley Park new 'battle-drill' case under Wintringham as against the parade-ground school. It was a statement of the social needs for a citizen militia spirit in place of the old Territorial Army mentality. But at the end, he went right over the top (which the sub-editor actually emphasized by either allowing or imposing capitals):

Even as it stands, the Home Guard could only exist in a country where men feel themselves free.

The totalitarian states can do great things, but there is one thing they cannot do: they cannot give the factory-worker a rifle and tell him to take it home and keep it in his bedroom. THAT RIFLE HANGING ON THE WALL OF THE WORKING-CLASS FLAT OR LABOURER'S COTTAGE IS THE SYMBOL OF DEMOCRACY.

IT IS OUR JOB TO SEE THAT IT STAYS THERE.[37]

This sounds ridiculous only in hindsight. If the Germans had invaded, the Wintringhams, the Slaters and the Orwells were surely right. And the Home Guard did need a political dimension: any volunteer army does, and it may then excel the professionals. But in a national war for survival, simple patriotism (as Churchill knew) was almost enough. Orwell helped the Left to respect patriotism, but he could not guide the patriots towards socialism. To impute permanent political aims to the Home Guard was not so much ludicrous as, in the event, unneeded – especially on the purely military argument that Orwell, Wintringham and Slater tried to use.

Among Orwell's unpublished papers are about fourteen pages of tightly written, detailed notes for lectures that he gave either to the Home Guard units or to other audiences on the theme of the Home Guard. Three of them are on techniques of 'Street-Fighting', both attack and defence, and on 'Field Fortifications'. They seem to synthesize Slater's views, army manuals' instructions, and his own ideas. They are devoid of political content, but show how deeply he studied the tactical problems, what care he took. Two sets of notes, however, deal with the 'Rôle of the Home Guard', though there is no clue to whom they were delivered: they state the case for a mobile militia force, are against the kind of officers they are getting, and argue for the compulsory 'political instruction' on the origins of the war and on war aims, indeed examination in these subjects before promotion. He did not specify, in the notes at least, what kind of political instruction; but again his underlying view was clear, that there was an indissoluble link not merely between high strategy and politics but also between tactics and politics. Such an analysis was far from eccentric.

The Home Guard section in St John's Wood was not aware of the full sweep of his revolutionary views: even if they read their *Evening Standard* from front to back, they did not read *Tribune* – not even the young intellectual who was heir to the piano factory. There was a great amount of time spent sitting around with cups of tea and talk. Orwell was, as usual, reticent about his own background and experiences. The young man, questioned closely and rather sceptically by Orwell about Zionism and the beliefs of British Jews, only gradually pieced together that here was an Old Etonian who had fought in Spain and was against the system.[38] With the others Orwell was scarcely an active propagandist, usually limiting himself to dark implications that respect for private property, which stopped them setting up fire-posts or pill-boxes with the best lines of fire across St John's Wood, also prevented the immediate rehousing of the bombed-out poor in the deserted homes of the rich.

Fred Warburg has written an entertaining and essentially accurate report of what it was like to serve as corporal under Sergeant Orwell.[39] Orwell's earnestness had its funny side. But the prominence that Warburg gives to Orwell's responsibility for one typical army muck-up in training can give a false impression. The wrong training-charge was put into a trench mortar, unsecured on a garage floor, so that the recoil smashed out a poor fellow's teeth. Warburg's stress on this episode has led some to embroider a picture of a dear, sincere but mechanically inept Sergeant Orwell who would have made a good extra character in the BBC's 'Dad's Army'. But the testimony of others in his section points to his efficiency with weapons and to the knowledgeable and realistic training he gave his unit in street-warfare and fieldcraft, though his deliberate neglect of and sardonic attitude towards drill and spit-and-polish has also been remembered.[40] Certainly he had the respect of all surviving members of the Home

Guard section: he knew what he was talking about and taught them relevant things. His enthusiasm, like theirs, faded away as the likelihood of invasion diminished. Eileen remarked to a friend about the Home Guard period that 'I didn't mind bombs on the mantelpiece, but didn't like the machine-gun under the bed'.[41]

He obtained his discharge in November 1943 for 'medical reasons'. Even so late, after his three years in the Home Guard, he wrote two pieces for the *Observer* urging that a more democratically organized Home Guard should continue, even after the War, and should replace the Territorial Army.[42]

Readers of *Partisan Review* had to share Orwell's twin obsessions, expressed with less inhibition than to readers of the London *Evening Standard*: he believed that a revolution was beginning to take place in Great Britain and that the 'Home Guard' would form its militia.[43] Orwell saw it as the commonsense of the matter that political war aims were needed: patriotism was necessary but in its traditional form it was not enough. He became a revolutionary patriot.

These thoughts were strengthened by a remarkable conjunction in London at that time of people who shared these ideas, which led to Orwell's fullest statement of his own political and social beliefs.

Tosco Fyvel was one of the new friends Orwell made at the beginning of the War. T. R. Fyvel, born in 1907, had spent part of the 1930s in Palestine, where his Zionist parents had emigrated from Vienna. He had been sent to school in England, returning to work as an assistant to Golda Meir in the Histadrut at the time of the Arab Rebellion of 1936. He met Orde Wingate then, a man who combined military genius with a profound belief in Zionism. Wingate urged Fyvel to return to Britain for the War, to spread like a young prophet his doctrine of the over-riding importance of war aims, the primacy of the political over the military. While waiting to be called up (Fyvel served in Psychological Warfare in the Middle East with Richard Crossman), he took this message to a sympathetic Fred Warburg, who had published his *No Ease in Zion*. Warburg introduced him to Sebastian Haffner (an anti-Nazi refugee, later German correspondent of the *Observer*) and to George Orwell. The four men formed a little 'War-Aims Group' and sat in Warburg's garden in London or Fyvel's garden in Twyford during the summer of 1940, watching the smoke trails of the Battle of Britain and discussing who should say what in, of course, 'an important new series'.[44]

Fyvel and Orwell became joint editors of a series of pamphlets called 'Searchlight Books' published at 2s each. Orwell worked hard with Fyvel on the series, finding and persuading authors and reading their manuscripts. It was a good list.* They called on H. G. Wells to try to interest him, but that day found a tired old man who just rambled on about the country going to the dogs. The 'Publisher's announcement' of the series said:

Nazism has plotted and organized for twenty years ... We cannot defeat Germany unless we have first freed ourselves from our own weaknesses. It is the aim of SEARCHLIGHT BOOKS to do all in their power to criticize and kill what is rotten in Western civilization and supply constructive ideas for the difficult period ahead of us. The series ... will stress Britain's international and imperial responsibilities and the aim of a planned Britain at the head of a greater and freer British Commonwealth, linked with the United States of America and other countries, as a framework of world order. The books will be written in simple language without the rubber-stamp political jargon of the past. They will seek to appeal to the new generation which is fighting this war whether on the battlefields or in the factories and to all those who can recognize the spirit of the new world prospects which are opening before us.[45]

Orwell's mind and hand are obvious – except in the Germanic noun-clause of the last sentence.

Fyvel persuaded a somewhat reluctant Orwell himself to write for the series. He still wanted to fight, not write. None the less, in the

---

* The other books published were Sebastian Haffner, *Offensive Against Germany*, 1941; Ritchie Calder, *The Lesson of London*, 1941; Cassandra, *The English at War*, 1941; T. C. Worsley, *The End of 'The Old School Tie'*, 1941; Arturo Barea, *The Struggle for the Spanish Soul*, 1941; Joyce Cary, *The Case for African Freedom*, 1941; B. Causton, *The Moral Blitz: War Propaganda and Christianity*, 1941; Olaf Stapledon, *Beyond the 'Isms'*, 1942; and Stephen Spender, *Life and the Poet*, 1942. Books were commissioned from Michael Foot, Cyril Connolly, Tosco Fyvel, George Catlin, Arthur Koestler, and François Lafitte, but never published or finished before Secker & Warburg's printers at Portsmouth were destroyed in 1942 with most of their stock and all of their paper, bringing the series to an end. Orwell's book and Cassandra's (William Connor of the *Daily Mirror*) did best, Orwell selling over 10,000 copies. In wartime conditions, new and topical books being in short supply were passed from hand to hand. Fred Warburg estimates reasonably that at least 50,000 people must have read it.

autumn Orwell wrote *The Lion and the Unicorn* at great speed, the first in the series: a neglected book whose significance is often ignored.* When he wrote *Animal Farm* and then *Nineteen Eighty-Four*, he must have assumed that people knew already where he stood politically, would recognize the assumptions behind his satires. He could not have foreseen that the great success of these books would bring him a far wider readership who knew little or nothing of the small but intense literary and political world of wartime London. He would have been astounded to learn that anyone could read *Animal Farm* as simply anti-socialist and *Nineteen Eighty-Four* as a certified prophecy rather than as a qualified warning.

Even critics who knew and respected Orwell's pre-war novels and cultural essays often disregarded the body of what they considered to be his minor political writings and journalism – well-written, voluminous and repetitive though it was.[46] This has led to such great misunderstandings, both of his political position and of what he intended his two last great works to mean, that it is necessary to repeat the argument of *The Lion and the Unicorn* at some length, despite it being still in print.†

He began the first part, 'England Your England': 'As I write, highly civilized human beings are flying overhead, trying to kill me.' They are 'kind-hearted law-abiding men' who would never dream of 'committing murder' were it not for the force of patriotism. Yet Orwell immediately hinted, a shock to the Left, that patriotism was not to be scorned. It was a human necessity and whether it is good or bad depends on its particular content. So he examined, from his own observation and in simple terms, the English national character. 'The

---

* For instance, Jeffrey Meyers only bothers to quote one review of it in his book, *George Orwell* (Routledge & Kegan Paul, 1975) in the 'Critical Heritage' series; and in his *A Reader's Guide to George Orwell* (Thames and Hudson, 1975), he deals only with the first part of the book, the essay on national character. But Koestler stressed its importance in an obituary notice: 'Among all the pamphlets, tracts and exhortations which the war produced, hardly anything bears re-reading today, except, perhaps, E. M. Forster's *What I Believe*, a few passages from Churchill's speeches, and, above all, Orwell's *The Lion and the Unicorn*' (*Observer*, 29 January 1950).

† *The Lion and the Unicorn* has been kept in print by Secker & Warburg but, alone of his major works, Penguin did not reprint it separately until 1982, since it was included in, perhaps somewhat submerged in, *The Collected Essays, Journalism and Letters*, Vol. II.

English are not intellectual. They have a horror of abstract thought . . . They have a certain power of acting without taking thought. Their world-famed hypocrisy – their double standard towards the Empire, for instance – is bound up with this . . .' But there is a popular culture, of gambling, beer and bawdy jokes that resists the official respectability and hypocrisy. Also 'the gentleness of English civilization is perhaps its most marked characteristic . . . It is a land where the bus conductors are good-tempered and the policemen carry no revolvers.' He contrasted the anti-militarism of the British public with the goose-step: 'one of the most horrible sights in the world . . . it is simply an affirmation of naked power; contained in it, quite consciously and intentionally, is the vision of a boot crashing down on a face'.[47]

For all its gentleness and individualism, England was, however, 'the most class-ridden country under the sun . . . ruled largely by the old and silly'. Yet it has not driven 'hundreds and thousands of its nationals into exile or the concentration camp'. *Peace News* could be sold in the middle of a war for survival.

Patriotism takes different forms in different classes, but it runs like a connecting thread through nearly all of them. Only the Europeanized intelligentsia are really immune to it . . . England is perhaps the only great country whose intellectuals are ashamed of their own nationality . . . All through the critical years many left-wingers were chipping away at English morale, trying to spread an outlook that was sometimes squashily pacifist, sometimes violently pro-Russian, but *always anti-British*.

The intellectuals had been as much to blame as the Chamberlain appeasers for making the Fascists believe that democracy, even of such a kind, was decadent. 'The Bloomsbury high-brow, with his mechanical snigger' at the expense of anything typically English was 'as out of date as the cavalry colonel. A modern nation cannot afford either of them. Patriotism and intelligence will again have to come together.'[48]

Notice that Orwell did not denounce intelligence or possibly intellectualism, only the behaviour of a specific kind of intellectual. He was no anti-intellectual as such, only against most of the self-styled intellectuals of the 1930s vintage. He loathed mere fashion and those who pretended to break completely with all aspects of tradition – except those that guaranteed their own security. Also he showed considerable historical sense in seeing that 'patriotism' in England had

radical roots: 'our country' that *we* work with *our* hands, as the eigh-
teenth- and nineteenth-century radicals had thought, tainting the
aristocracy with cosmopolitanism. When Dr Johnson had roared that
'Patriotism, Sir, is the last refuge of a scoundrel', he was not dottily
reneging on his own Toryism, he was sounding off again at 'that
devil Wilkes' whose followers called themselves 'the patriots', imitating
the dissident American radicals who, in turn, took it from the tradition
of the Roman Republic.[49]

The second section, 'Shopkeepers at War', began with the stirring:
'The war has demonstrated that private capitalism ... *does not work*.
It cannot deliver the goods.' Then followed the already familiar
argument, from his *Tribune* and *Betrayal of the Left* contributions, that
only through a social revolution could the war be won; and 'it is only by
revolution that the English people can be set free'. 'England', he
said, was 'a family', but one 'in which the young are generally
thwarted and most of the power is in the hands of irresponsible
uncles and bed-ridden aunts'. He grasped that something was
happening that fell short of revolution, something that became a
commonplace in the Labour election campaign of 1945 and had
impressed itself on the consciousness of the rank and file of the Army
and of the Civil Defence workers long before it reached the Treasury
or Lord Beveridge: the war effort was proving that planning was
possible, could work for the common good, and need not threaten basic
liberties. People who did not believe in the possibility of planning
before the war, let alone its desirability, were now actually planning on
a huge and reasonably effective scale. 'War', wrote Orwell in the final
section, 'is the greatest of all agents of change. It speeds up all
processes, wipes out minor distinctions, brings reality to the surface.
Above all it brings home to the individual that he is *not* altogether an
individual.' Orwell thus first stated what has become another sober
commonplace of the Welfare State: social change owed more to the two
World Wars than to the initiatives of Asquith and Attlee – a proposition that up until then would have appeared, and did appear to his
old *Adelphi* associates, reactionary, Nietzschean nonsense. So even
'the shopkeepers' could be convinced both of the viability and the
desirability of socialism and planning. But Orwell served up a warning:
'common ownership of the means of production' is not in itself a
sufficient definition of Socialism:

Centralized ownership has very little meaning unless the mass of the people are living roughly upon an equal level, and have some kind of control over the government. 'The State' may come to mean no more than a self-elected political party, and oligarchy and privilege can return, based on power rather than on money.[50]

This characterization of what he had already called 'oligarchical collectivism' preceded his reading of James Burnham, and was not derived from it.

The third and final section of *The Lion and the Unicorn*, called 'The English Revolution', bravely began: 'The English Revolution started several years ago, and it began to gather momentum when the troops came back from Dunkirk.' And the opportunity lay in social change. Orwell did not simply rely on his argument that patriotism could prove stronger than class hatred (like every Left-winger then, in proportion to his hope for popular revolution he feared a counter-revolution). He pointed to specific factors of social stratification, and to a new class on which he pinned so much hope.

After 1918 there began to appear something that had never existed in England before: people of indeterminate social class. In 1910 every human being in these islands could be 'placed' in an instant by his clothes, manners and accent. That is no longer the case. Above all, it is not the case in the new townships that have developed as a result of cheap motor cars and the southward shift of industry. The place to look for the terms of the future England is in light-industry areas and along the arterial roads. In Slough, Dagenham, Barnet, Letchworth, Hayes – everywhere, indeed, on the outskirts of great towns. The old pattern is gradually changing into something new ... To that civilization belong the people who are most at home in and most definitely *of* the modern world, the technicians and the higher paid skilled workers, the airmen and the mechanics, the radio experts, film producers, popular journalists and industrial chemists. They are the indeterminate stratum at which the older class distinctions are beginning to break down ...

In England there is only one Socialist party that has ever seriously mattered, the Labour Party. It has never been able to achieve any major change, because except in purely domestic matters it has never possessed a genuinely independent policy. It was and is primarily a party of trade unions, devoted to raising wages and improving working conditions ...

If it can be made clear that defeating Hitler means wiping out class privilege, the great mass of middling people, the £6 a week to £2,000 a year class, will probably be on our side. These people are quite indispensable, because they include most of the technical experts. Obviously the snobbishness and political ignorance of people like [that] ... will be a very great difficulty ... The only approach to them is through their patriotism. An intelligent Socialist movement will *use* their patriotism, instead of merely insulting it, as hitherto.

But do I mean that there will be no opposition? Of course not. It would be childish to expect anything of the kind.

There will be a bitter political struggle, and there will be unconscious and half-conscious sabotage everywhere. At some point or other it may be necessary to use violence ... But just because the English sense of national unity has never disintegrated, because patriotism is finally stronger than class hatred, the chances are that the will of the majority will prevail.

He then suggested that a six-point programme was needed. First, the nationalization of land, mines, banks, railways and major industries; second, the limitation of incomes 'so that the highest tax-free income in Britain does not exceed the lowest by more than ten to one', three, reform of education 'along democratic lines'; four and five, the giving to India of immediate Dominion status, with the power to secede when the War was over, and the formation of 'an Imperial General Council in which the coloured peoples are to be represented'; and six, the declaration of a formal alliance with China, Abyssinia 'and all other victims of the Fascist powers'.[51] (Alas, if most of this is a pretty good synthesis of Labour Left-wing policy, yet the idea of a ten to one differential of *tax-free* income shows that his amateur economics did not match his amateur sociology – this would have been a far more stratified society than the one he lived in.)

What, he finally asked, would a real Socialist government in Britain look like in power? It would 'transform the nation from top to bottom' and yet it would 'still bear all over it the unmistakable marks of our own civilization'.

It will not be doctrinaire, not even logical. It will abolish the House of Lords, but quite probably will not abolish the Monarchy. It will leave anachronisms and loose ends everywhere, the judge in his ridiculous horsehair wig and the lion and the unicorn on the soldier's cap-buttons. It will not set up any explicit class dictatorship. It will group itself round the old Labour Party and its mass following will be in the Trade Unions, but it will draw into it most of the middle class and many of the younger sons of the bourgeoisie. Most of its directing brains will come from the new indeterminate class of skilled workers, technical experts, airmen, scientists, architects and journalists, the people who feel at home in the radio and ferro-concrete age. But it will never lose touch with the tradition of compromise and the belief in a law that is above the State. It will shoot traitors, but it will give them a solemn trial beforehand and occasionally it will acquit them. It will crush any open revolt promptly and cruelly, but it will interfere very little with the spoken and written word. Political parties with different names will still exist, revolutionary sects will still be publishing their newspapers and making as little impression as ever ... It will show a power of assimilating the past which will shock foreign observers and sometimes make them doubt whether any revolution has happened.

But all the same it will have done the essential thing. It will have nationalized industry, scaled down incomes, set up a classless educational system. Its real nature will be apparent from the hatred which the surviving rich men of the world will feel for it. It will aim not at disintegrating the Empire but at turning it into a federation of Socialist states, freed not so much from the British flag as from the moneylender, the dividend-drawer and the wooden-headed British official. Its war-strategy will be totally different from that of any property-ruled state, because it will not be afraid of the revolutionary after-effects when any existing regime is brought down.[52]

Orwell summed up this book in a sentence at the beginning of the third section: 'We cannot establish anything that a Western nation would regard as Socialism without defeating Hitler; on the other hand we cannot defeat Hitler while we remain economically and socially in the nineteenth century.'[53]

It is endlessly debatable whether Orwell's theories were half-right, that he understood the conditions that would give rise to unexpected Labour victory in 1945 and to the limited social revolution of the post-war period, or whether they were half-wrong, that no revolution of any kind occurred, though the opportunity had been there. The very openness of this question at least reflects his own view that even radical change in England would take traditional forms. But his own values, whether capable of realization or not, were plainly stated and can only wilfully be misunderstood (as when he is claimed for the camp of the Cold War, *Encounter* magazine and the CIA). He was a revolutionary and an egalitarian, a revolutionary in love with the past, but a revolutionary none the less, who urged discrimination when embracing 'all of the past' or 'all of the future'. The difficulty is that he only gave vivid examples of likes and dislikes, not criteria for consistent value-judgements. He was also a libertarian, but of a specifically democratic Socialist kind – both tolerance and emancipation must go together. He was of a republican rather than liberal frame of mind: he was neither joking nor ridiculous when he said the State would have to shoot traitors, after a trial, and that it would crush open revolt promptly and cruelly, while interfering very little with free speech. He was both an egalitarian and a libertarian.

Orwell was a moralist, but a social moralist. His position has its difficulties, but also its attractions. This is not the place to debate them. The biographical question, however, is, did Orwell ever change this position? And did he ever change the parallel views expressed in 'Inside the Whale': that while the artist must be defended even when he is socially irrelevant or positively irresponsible, he must at the same time strive to be, indeed has a duty to be, socially relevant?

What sort of person, the 'man of letters' who now acted as a socialist propagandist, did Tosco Fyvel think had written that remarkable book, *The Lion and the Unicorn*?

I saw an extremely tall, thin man, looking more than his years, with gentle eyes and deep lines that hinted at suffering on his face. The word 'saint' was used by one of his friends and critics after his death, and – well – perhaps he had a touch of this quality. Certainly there was nothing of the fierce pamphleteer in his personal manner. He was awkward, almost excessively mild. Both about him and his wife (who was also not in very good health) . . . there was something strangely unphysical.[54]

Did anyone, except Richard Rees when he turned Christian, really think of Orwell as 'saintly'? If so, perhaps only in a Cromwellian sense, when there were whole regiments of stern and upright 'saints' ('warts and all'). Almost everyone agreed that there was this marked contrast between Orwell's public fierceness and his private gentleness.

A few years later, Fyvel wrote:

This may be guessing, or reading too much into hints he let drop, but I often felt that 'George Orwell' was like the mask of a writer which he took on as he had taken on a Sahib's mask in Burma. There was always the marked contrast between the uncompromising ruthlessness of his political views and his mild manner at home and his readiness to be reasonable and make individual allowances in his personal and working life. The two characters were never quite harmonized. Even outwardly he looked a curiously composite figure. Partly he dressed like a seedy Sahib, partly like an imitation of a French workman of his Paris days, with his dark-blue shirts, small moustache and the cigarettes he rolled from dark, acrid tobacco. Perhaps the creation of

George Orwell, this not quite real personality, which differed from Eric Blair, gave him special strength as a writer.[55]

This 'guessing' proved seminal, for much has been built on Fyvel's alleged dichotomy between 'Blair' and 'Orwell'. Was there really a split or an incompleteness in the man whom people met called George Orwell compared with the one they knew as Eric Blair? Suppose, on the contrary, that Blair grew into Orwell. Dr Q. D. Leavis had congratulated him on 'growing up' compared to the fixations with their adolescence, she said, of the Connolly circle.[56] There were unusual combinations in Orwell's character, but if someone makes his friends feel morally uncomfortable, it is too easy to imply that it is he who wears a mask or is incomplete according to the conventional mould. The mould itself can be cracked or badly fitting. Even if, however, 'Orwell' was partly a mask, Blair (like Lord George Hell in Max Beerbohm's fable) became remarkably like him.

Julian Symons, another good friend though of the last years of the war, did not believe in this duality of character or in the significance of his pseudonym, except that 'George Orwell felt a freedom of comment that would never have come easily to Eric Blair' – implying that family restraints had to be taken into account. With increasing years and the attention paid to his writings, Orwell simply developed or 'grew up': '... certainly the relaxed and friendly George Orwell known to many people during the last decade of his life bore little relation', Symons suggests, 'to the eccentric, prickly and lonely figure who was regarded at least by some people who met him after he came back from Burma, as "a wrong-headed young man who was vain enough to think he could be an author"'.[57] Symons was more aware than most of Orwell's later friends how exceptionally long it had taken him to mature, both as a writer and as a man.

Orwell at this time felt reasonably at one with himself, despite his real frustrations both about novel-writing and war service, as can be seen by part of the biographical entry he made for a reference book in April 1940:

... I served four months on the Aragon front with the POUM militia and was rather badly wounded, but luckily with no serious after-effects. Since that, except for spending a winter in Morocco, I cannot honestly say that I have done anything except write books and raise hens and vegetables.

What I saw in Spain, and what I have seen since of the inner workings of left-wing political parties, have given me a horror of politics. I was for a while a member of the Independent Labour Party, but left them at the beginning of the present war because I considered that they were talking nonsense and proposing a line of policy that could only make things easier for Hitler. In sentiment I am definitely 'left', but I believe that a writer can only remain honest if he keeps free of party labels.

The writers I care most about and never grow tired of are Shakespeare, Swift, Fielding, Dickens, Charles Reade, Samuel Butler, Zola, Flaubert, and, among modern writers, James Joyce, T. S. Eliot and D. H. Lawrence. But I believe the modern writer who has influenced me most is Somerset Maugham, whom I admire immensely for his power of telling a story straightforwardly and without frills. Outside my work the thing I care most about is gardening, especially vegetable gardening. I like English cookery and English beer, French red wines, Spanish white wines, Indian tea, strong tobacco, coal fires, candle light and comfortable chairs. I dislike big towns, noise, motor cars, the radio, tinned food, central heating and 'modern' furniture. My wife's tastes fit in almost perfectly with my own. My health is wretched, but it has never prevented me from doing anything that I wanted to, except, so far, fight in the present war. I ought perhaps to mention that though this account that I have given of myself is true, George Orwell is not my real name ...[58]

Not a very deep self-portrait, but coherent and convincing as a picture of a man mature and secure enough to articulate clearly what he liked, even if less clear as to why he liked them.

Orwell was beginning to be seen publicly as a 'character'. He was aware of this and, as the above litany of likes and dislikes shows, played up to it a little. He *was* a naïve and humble man, but, rather in the way that Abraham Lincoln had nourished 'honest Abe', Orwell the essayist and publicist used rather than concealed this simplicity. He must have been delighted, therefore, when he read the respectful teasing of V. S. Pritchett's lead review of *The Lion and the Unicorn* (in his old enemy, the *New Statesman and Nation*):

Mr George Orwell has many of the traits of the best English pamphleteers: courage, an individual mind, vehement opinions, an instinct for stirring up trouble, the arts of appealing to that imaginary creature the sensible man and of combining original observations with sweeping generalization, of seeing enemies everywhere and despising all of them. And like the two outstanding figures of our tradition of pamphleteering, Cobbett and Defoe, both of whom had his subversive, non-conforming brand of patriotism, he writes a lucid conversational style which wakes one up suddenly like cold water dashed in the face. The sting of it is sometimes refreshing; sometimes it makes one very angry. For Mr Orwell likes his friends no better than his enemies and in the name of common sense is capable of exaggerating with the simplicity and innocence of a savage. His virtue is that he says things which need to be said; his vice that some of those things needed saying with a great deal more consideration. But, damn thoughtfulness! Pamphleteers have to hit the bull's-eye every time, or, failing that, somebody else's eye. Mr Orwell's standards of accuracy and judiciousness are in the tradition and may be compared with those of Shaw, the greatest pamphleteer of our time. I will give one key example from *The Lion and the Unicorn* and be done with it:

'It is a strange fact, but it is unquestionably true, that almost any English intellectual would feel more ashamed of standing to attention during "God Save the King", than of stealing from a poor box.'

'"Unquestionably"', Pritchett concluded, 'is the word I like in that sentence . . .'[59]

The first part of *The Lion and the Unicorn* is an easy mixture of humour and moral earnestness that from now on was to be the mark of Orwell's best writing. Here was an English eccentric who deserved to be taken very seriously both in what he said and in how he said it.

CHAPTER THIRTEEN

BROADCASTING DAYS

(1941-3)

ORWELL in 1941 seemed once again poised to use adversity as the source of a flood of new writing, even if essays and pamphlets rather than novels, when the devil granted him his wish. After a final attempt to join the Army, which earned him a definitive Grade 4 National Service Card from the Willesden Medical Board, he found what was classified as 'essential war work' at the BBC. He had broadcast only once before, a scripted interview on the Home Service with Desmond Hawkins called 'The Proletarian Writer'.[1] But a letter dated 18 August 1941 offered 'E. A. Blair' a standard contract as a temporary Talks Producer in the Empire Department. Then for two precious years his talents were mainly wasted, his colleagues later agreed, in producing cultural programmes for intellectuals in India and South-East Asia, heard by few and unlikely to have influenced even them.

That autumn he went to the BBC's crash course for new producers, mainly intellectuals who knew little or nothing about radio, even as listeners, and held at Bedford College in Regents Park. Among his fellow students he got to know William Empson and Henry Swanzy, who was to remain with the BBC after the war. Swanzy recollected that he must have been about the only person out of the twenty-odd people on the course who did not know that Eric Blair was George Orwell.

As a consequence, I treated him as a normal person, not with the somewhat hushed wariness, not to say obsequiousness, that some at least of our companions showed. He then enjoyed a rather curious status: well known as a journalist and a writer, but rather looked down upon by the pundits, and particularly by the poets, whom he resented. This direct, human treatment

413

seemed to please him ... I remember our going on top of a bus to Marble Arch ... and talking about the fringe problems of class – being 'the poorest boy in the school', which he knew at Eton and I at my own school, about the mass media, and various kinds of snobbery. At tea with his wife in his flat, he talked about Dickens, whom I scarcely knew. I can remember the distortion of his voice, caused by the wound in Spain, and the drawling 'You see' at the end of every generalization, as he rolled his cigarettes in a little machine.[2]

It was essential war work, of a kind, close to propaganda, and it is possible that someone showed some guile in recruiting him. Yet who was using whom is unclear. After he had been there a year, the following internal memoranda circulated.

FROM ESD [Eastern Service Director] Subject: 'George Orwell' to broadcast 15/10[42]
TO AC(OS) [Assistant Controller (Overseas Services)]

Mr Brander has suggested that as Blair does in effect write the News Commentary for India (weekly) he should deliver it himself and thus enable us to 'cash in' on the popularity of 'George Orwell' in India. I mentioned this to Mr Blair, and the result is this characteristically honest and straightforward note.

On the points that Mr Blair raises, I see no difficulty in practice. He and I can, by discussion, always arrange a *modus vivendi*. In fact I feel strongly inclined to try the experiment.

Is there any difficulty about a Corporation employee broadcasting under a pen-name? (If the matter has to be referred to the Establishment side, may I suggest that Blair's note should *not* be forwarded? It was written for my own eye (and I know he would like you to see it also): but to people who do not know him as you and I do, it might be misleading!)

LFRW [L. F. Rushbrook Williams]

From: Eric Blair, Indian Section
Subject: Weekly News Commentary
To: Eastern Service Director

15 October 1942

With reference to the suggestion that I should write and broadcast the weekly news review [to India] in English over my own name, i.e. George Orwell. The four speakers who are at present doing this in rotation have contracts up to 7 November, after which I will gladly take this on. But there are one or two points which it would be better to define clearly beforehand.

If I broadcast as George Orwell, I am as it were selling my literary reputation, which so far as India is concerned probably arises chiefly from books of anti-imperialist tendency, some of which have been banned in India. If I gave broadcasts which appeared to endorse unreservedly the policy of the British Government I should quite soon be written off as 'one more renegade', and should probably miss my potential public, at any rate among the student population. I am not thinking about my personal reputation, but clearly we should defeat our own object in these broadcasts if I could not preserve my position as an independent and more or less 'agin the government' commentator. I would therefore like to be sure in advance that I can have reasonable freedom of speech. I think this weekly commentary is only likely to be of value if I can make it from an anti-Fascist rather than imperialist standpoint and avoid mention of subjects on which I could not conscientiously agree with current Government policy.

I do not think this is likely to cause trouble, as the chief difficulty is over Indian internal politics, which we rarely mention in our weekly news commentaries. These commentaries have always followed what is by implication a 'left' line, and in fact have contained very little that I would not sign with my own name. But I can imagine situations arising in which I should have to say that I could not in honesty do the commentary for that week, and I should like the position to be defined in advance.

From: Asst. Controller (Overseas Services)
Subject: Commentaries by George Orwell
To: ESD

23/10/42

I have discussed this matter with C(OS). There is no difficulty about a member of the Corporation staff broadcasting under a pen-name, but he should not be announced or billed as a member of the Corporation staff, and the normal conditions about staff contributions to programmes should apply. C(OS) suggests, however, that in this instance it would be advisable to make sure – presumably through the India Office – that the Government of India are not going to raise objections to broadcasts by a man whose books they have banned. The propaganda advantages of Orwell's name are obvious and I should hope they would be appreciated.

R. A. Rendell

RAR/ML
1. AC(OS)   2. c(OS)   29/10/42

I have consulted Mr Joyce* and his colleagues, and they feel that it would be useful to take advantage of 'Orwell's' name. In view of the fact that several people whose books have fallen under the displeasure of the G[overnment] of I[ndia] do in effect speak for us, and that their contributions are appreciated, Mr Joyce feels that it would be mistaken to refer the matter specifically to the G. of I. If *asked*, the G. of I. might feel called upon to adopt a critical attitude. If the question is not raised, Mr Joyce thinks they are very unlikely to object!

L. F. Rushbrook Williams[3]

Until then, Orwell's only delivery of news had been a weekly summary he broadcast to Singapore, but Laurence Brander admitted afterwards that 'it is probable that no one except Japanese monitors heard these talks'. Brander went to India early in 1942 to discover who was listening, and found that few of the students at whom they aimed their early Third Programme style *mélange* possessed radio sets; and that anyway the programme went out with a very weak signal at a time of day when few people were listening.† He carried this depressing news back to London where Orwell was already organizing 'impressive processions of literary men and professors ... hurrying through the BBC, broadcasting to India'.[4] It was arranged that some of these talks, doomed to be unheard, should be published in India.

None the less, Brander found Orwell 'invaluable' as a colleague. Everyone respected and liked him in the India section; he 'laughed very readily at the nonsense that went on, and made it tolerable'; he prepared his scripts well and carefully, his lucid English being admirable for the purpose (as so many students have continued to find); but a great handicap was his own voice: 'Thin and flat, it did not go over well on short wave broadcasting.'[5] I. J. Bahadur Singh, a regular broadcaster at that time (later India's Ambassador to Egypt), had a rather different impression.

---

*This is the same Mr Joyce who had vetted Orwell in 1938 (see pp. 354–7).

†Some people were listening. The same Mr Frankford, who had taken such a dim view of Orwell in Spain, heard a broadcast by Orwell himself when a soldier in India waiting to go to Burma: 'He was introduced as an intellectual of the Left, which shook me rigid.'

My memories of Eric Blair were of a rather withdrawn and preoccupied person giving an impression of being generally bored with what he was doing. It appeared that he was doing a job of work without having his heart in it and with not much enthusiasm.

Blair was supervising broadcasts to India which were aimed at stimulating Indian interest in the War effort, particularly at a time when the Japanese army was at India's doorstep. In his conversation with me and other Indian friends, one got the impression that he expected the UK Government to do more to reassure the Indian National Congress that independence would be achieved after the war. He was disappointed that this was not being done. Of course, in the broadcasts for which he was responsible he had willy-nilly to stick to the overall directives of the BBC. Perhaps, this accounted for his lack of enthusiasm and interest. Because of his personal involvement in that country, he was also very distressed by the fate of Burma.[6]

Such 'overall directives', however, were fairly general and favoured the soft touch, the indirect approach, the keeping of educated Indians entertained by British culture. So Orwell or Blair was left pleasantly free, in one way, to gather the best men of English letters to read their poems or discuss their novels – out into the ether. Eventually he became depressed with the whole activity, so few listeners and so many implicit constraints, and came to regard it as meaningless. (He made free use of the BBC's physiognomy in constructing *Nineteen Eighty-Four*'s Ministry of Truth, but he never seriously suggested that the one was a step to the other – for good or ill, he came to see broadcasting only in negative terms.) At first, however, he enjoyed his licence to broadcast whoever he thought good and true in English literature, and to ask T. S. Eliot to read his poems, or E. M. Forster to give talks – both of whom accepted, doing their bit. Milton had, after all, Orwell told William Empson, who was heading the Chinese section in the partitioned room next door, been a propagandist for the Commonwealth.[7] He took on Dylan Thomas as a poetry reader, and doubtless drank with him after the programme (Orwell had a good head for drink), either at The George, a pub much used by BBC men, or another later known, when the American officers moved on to France, as The Whores' Lament.

Bernard Shaw, when asked permission to broadcast a passage from *The Doctor's Dilemma*, only favoured him with a terse 'I veto it ruthlessly';[8] but most famous men cooperated, as did the producer's own friends, such as Inez Holden; and Stephen Spender, Herbert Read and Cyril Connolly, who fitted both categories, also contributed. Most of Orwell's own scripts were characteristically and recognizably his, quirky, lucid and competent, but they rarely matched the best of his occasional pieces for journals.

With some difficulty Orwell persuaded the Canadian writer and anarchist, George Woodcock, to broadcast. Years afterwards, Woodcock wrote, 'In a discussion I had with him at the time he defended his activities by contending that the right kind of man could at least make propaganda a little cleaner than it would otherwise have been, and I know he managed to introduce one or two astonishing items into his broadcasts, but he soon found there was in fact little he could do, and he left the BBC in disgust.' At the time he wrote a firm letter to Orwell telling him that even if the broadcasts were intended by him to keep the Fascists out of India, they were also intended by the system to keep India in the clutches of the British nabobs; that he himself had only broadcast, fearing a trap, out of curiosity to see what went on – and that he had returned his fee.[9] These two proud and prickly men soon got to know each other, and Woodcock was to write a fine account of Orwell's politics.[10]

Orwell must have thought that Woodcock was being a bit sanctimonious, but it was true that some brother officer or Big Brother was always watching and listening:

Memorandum from the BBC War Office Liaison Officer
Subject: MEET MY FRIEND No. 5

22 June 1942

As I explained to you on the telephone, the India Office does not like the underlying tone of this script and believes that the suggestion that Anglo-Indians look upon this country as an alien land in any real sense of the term is untrue ... In the circumstances, would you be good enough, if it is not bothering you too much, to let me know what you decide to do with this script?

Mackarness, G. S., Major[11]

This could have been some of the 'nonsense' that Brander reports Orwell as laughing at, but at other times such surveillance and stupidity made him depressed or angry.

A colleague who found Orwell far less sympathetic was John Morris, who headed the Japanese section. Morris wrote an essay on Orwell at the BBC called 'Some are More Equal Than Others', published soon after his death. He saw Orwell as a difficult colleague. The closeness of their rooms, which were really cubicles with apertures, made it difficult to telephone in privacy. Orwell would, he claims, often shout through the aperture, 'For God's sake shut up!', but never apologize; rather he would then 'offer ... one of the horrible cigarettes which he himself made from a particularly pungent and acrid shag'. He dragged Morris into a pub, though Morris disliked pubs, and mocked him for not knowing how to order beer like a working man, ignoring his obvious riposte that he was *not* a working man. Morris was a former Indian Army officer who had resigned when he developed a taste for literature, 'but, unlike Orwell, had ... in no way turned ... against my own class, and certainly I had no feelings of shame about it'. He remembers that in the staff canteen Orwell poured his tea into the saucer and drank it 'with a loud, sucking noise. He said nothing but looked at me with a slightly defiant expression when I continued to drink my own tea in the normal fashion. The two door-keepers who were also occupying our table looked somewhat scandalized, and after a few minutes got up and left.'[12] Pamela Warburg used to tell similar stories of occasional provocation and embarrassing proletarian affectations. Even Empson, whom Morris also disliked, spoke of Orwell's 'formalized cockney'.* Yet the same facts could be construed differently: either that Orwell was pulling Morris's leg, or being deliberately rude.

Morris also recalls asking Orwell to dinner with L. H. Myers who so admired Orwell's writing and who had paid for his winter in Morocco. Orwell refused to arrive in time for a meal together, but joined them both afterwards, shabbily dressed, made a sarcastic remark that they had probably dined at Boulestin's (a very expensive restaurant) and then lapsed into utter silence, leaving soon after on some thin pretext, to Myers' distress. John Morris is a man of the utmost rectitude: something went wrong with the evening, but it can hardly have been quite as he said. He said that Orwell knew that Myers had been his benefactor, and obviously resented it – which would make

---

*'The FACK that you're black ... and that I'm white, *has nudding whatever to do wiv it*,' Empson heard him say during disputes with Indian script-writers. ('Orwell at the BBC', in *The World of George Orwell* edited by Miriam Gross, p. 96.)

Orwell's behaviour doubly awful. But when Orwell wrote in 1946 (two years after Myers' death) to Max Plowman's widow, Dorothy, returning a first instalment of the money, he was clearly unaware who it was who had been his benefactor.[13] He referred warmly to Myers in a review in *The Times Literary Supplement* in 1948. John Morris seemed to assume that they had not met before, except briefly, whereas Orwell had spent a week at Myers' house as a guest immediately before the outbreak of war. The episode is a curious one, obviously showing some antagonism on Orwell's part to either Myers or Morris, more probably Morris.

Morris's last complaint at Orwell's uncouth behaviour and ill manners may give a clue to what really happened. After Orwell left the BBC, Morris was surprised that he sent him some books to review for *Tribune*. They met by chance in the street and Morris reminded him that he had never paid him. ' "Oh" he said, smiling rather sardonically, "we don't pay for reviews you know; it's all for the Cause." '[14] A political confidence trick? Perhaps, or another incident showing that Orwell simply thought Morris pompous and was teasing him – 'ragging him' is almost the word, just as young Eric had reacted to authority at Eton. He probably saw the whole of the BBC in rather similar light as part of the establishment, tolerant but none the less authoritarian.

Orwell did see the funny side of his war service. Malcolm Muggeridge wrote in his memoirs:

Under the auspices of the BBC, Orwell was similarly engaged, his special territory being India and South-East Asia. We often used to talk about this when I got to know him. From a studio deep under Oxford Street, he beamed at listeners in Cawnpore, Kuala Lumpur and Rangoon – assuming, of course, that there were any – *Areopagitica*, *The Waste Land* read by the author in person, and other gems of Western culture, with a view to enthusing them for the Allied cause. When I delicately suggested that this may well have failed to hit its target, the absurdity of the enterprise struck him anew, and he began to chuckle, deep in his throat, very characteristic of him and very endearing.[15]

Orwell enjoyed many aspects of BBC life, however, in spite of the long and irregular hours. He met interesting people, joined in the literary and political gossip in the pubs. The social life was not entirely uncongenial to him: BBC gossip from those days insists that he had a brief affair with a secretary – rather as if out of a sense of duty or as if he thought it a normal part of office life. Some images of BBC days entered into *Nineteen Eighty-Four*: the look of the main building in Portland Place was certainly a model for 'Mini Truth', though the (once) modernistic Senate House of the University of London in Malet Street could share the same distinction. There was a perpetual smell of cabbage in the BBC Oxford Street staff canteen, too.

The only time when one hears people singing in the BBC is in the early morning, between 6 and 8. That is the time when the charwomen are at work. A huge army of them arrives all at the same time. They sit in the reception hall waiting for their brooms to be issued to them and making as much noise as a parrot house, and then they have wonderful choruses, all singing together as they sweep the passages. The place has a quite different atmosphere at this time from what it has later in the day.[16]

This experience was transformed into the singing of the prole woman, the last hope for humanity.

On 24 September 1943 he wrote to the Eastern Services Director a letter of resignation, making clear that he was not resigning because of any disagreement over 'BBC policy' or 'any kind of grievance', but 'because for some time past I have been conscious that I have been wasting my own time and the public money on doing work that produces no result'. He wanted to go back to his 'normal work of writing and journalism' where he 'could be more useful'. But he ran the risk of another period of unemployment and frustration, for when he resigned he had no other job arranged: he did not leave the BBC 'for *Tribune*' as has often been said.[17] *Tribune* simply happened to be his next job. In fact he wanted to be a war correspondent, he had confided this to William Empson and hinted as much to Dwight MacDonald in a letter to *Partisan Review*.[18] A possibility arose, mentioned in correspondence with the BBC about the precise date of his leaving, that the *Observer* might send him to Algeria and Sicily. But since war correspondents at that time were attached to the Army, they needed to pass a medical examination. Among his papers there is a War Office medical card dated 22 October 1943 tersely declaring him 'unfit for service overseas due to condition of chest'. So he had to stay at home and could not go adventuring again. He did not finally leave the BBC until 24 November; and by that time he had been offered the Literary Editorship of *Tribune*, a job that might have seemed hand-made for his character and talents. But meanwhile private life continued, and as he had never before worked in offices, the public and the private had never been so divided, with only a few points of contact.

One of his friendships made at the BBC was with Stevie Smith, the poet, who lived with an aunt in Palmers Green and worked as a secretary in central London.

14.10.42

Dear George,

Herewith my proof poems which may be more easy for you to handle than the typescript ones, also it gives me great pleasure to say there are considerably *more* of them, in fact never before have I managed to get so many to the page and vol. One hears you have the idea of doing a funny number some time, some of these are funny. You know by now I suppose that I did not hear one word about that last broadcast until 20 minutes before it went on the air. Jolly good show, BBC! And if you want to know what I feel about you at this moment, take a look at the drawings on p. 54.*

Love and fond messages,

Stevie

My address, which may be of interest to your secretary, is attached.

17 October 1942

Dear Stevie,

I don't know what you are grizzling about! I told you a long time back that we hoped you would take part in that programme and gave you the date verbally. We then picked the poems you were to read and you typed out a copy and sent it to me. A few days before the broadcast, my secretary sent a PC reminding you of the date and time, to the only address of yours which she had. I suppose the fact was that the address which you had previously given us was actually Inez's. My secretary did not know that you worked at Newnes' until I told her so on the actual morning of the broadcast. I assumed that you knew all about it and merely sent the PC as a formality.

---

*Two of her stylized, Edward Lear-like drawings: one of a lean-faced, angry-looking man ('Consumed by so much hate,' says the poem) with a shock of untidy hair (but no moustache, so Orwell-like, not Orwell exactly); the other of a hungry wolf. (And 'The Wild Dog' on p. 42 is similar.) See Stevie Smith, *Mother, What is Man?* (Cape, London, 1942), p. 54.

I am sorry about this, but the programme went off all right and Read read your poem quite nicely.

> Yours
> (Eric Blair, Talks Assistant)

20th October 1942

Dear George,

Lies are the most irritating thing in the world and would make an angel grisel and you are the most persistent liar and these fibs are always coming back to me from other people. You never gave me a date for the bloody broadcast or breathed one word about my reading my own poem. I sent the poems to you from this address and also the three short stories you've had since last March. I never gave you Inez's address, why the hell should I, specially as she was on the point of leaving? I'm sorry about it, but not very, as I'm sure [Herbert] Read read better than I should as I've never broadcast before or had a rehearsal. I'm bored to death by the lies.

> Stevie[19]

Anthony Powell includes a curious anecdote about Orwell in his autobiography. '"Have you ever had a woman in a park?" he asked me once. "No – never." "I have." "How did you find it?" "I was forced to." "Why?" "Nowhere else to go."'[20] Malcolm Muggeridge also relates that Orwell told such a tale over a masculine lunch *à trois*.[21] The name of Stevie Smith has, in male literary gossip, been persistently linked with this tale. But a mutual woman friend of Stevie Smith and Orwell is very sceptical:

George was definitely one of Stevie's chums. The position of being a Stevie chum was peculiar. She liked boyish men and in a girlish way enjoyed chummy relationships, but would have got nervous if it got too sexual, although she was sometimes so damned close, holding hands and friendly intimate, that it was also at times pretty provocative behaviour on her part.[22]

She poured scorn on the 'in the park' gossip as being out of character with them both. Orwell must, she thinks, have simply been boasting or teasing his two worldly and fastidious friends.* George did,

---

* If so, he was quoting from his fictional self: 'They had nowhere to go, except the open air. There are so many pairs of lovers in London with "nowhere to go"; only the streets and the parks, where there is no privacy and it is always cold. It is not easy to make love in a cold climate when you have no money.' (*Keep the Aspidistra Flying*, p. 151)

423

however, like taking his lady friends to the cinema and, rather shyly, holding hands. But another friend is sure that she remembers Eileen telling her that she had both Inez Holden and Stevie Smith sobbing on her not entirely sympathetic shoulder about their unrequited loves for George[23] – though this seems improbable, oddly out of character with both ladies: names are so easily transplantable and memories stretch as well as contract.

Certainly Stevie Smith's portrait of Basil-cum-Eric or George, in her novel *The Holiday*, shows she must have known him well, and included 'two characters who divide between them', she wrote in a letter, 'many of George's opinions and characteristics as I saw them. I seem to remember I had the idea at the time that splitting George into two might lessen the danger of libel, not much of a danger really.' One of the Orwells is clearly identifiable in 'Basil', a man monologuing with an eccentric, polemical exaggeration, trying an idea out, like a first run at one of Orwell's *Tribune* columns. Several friends have described this way he had of going on and on if he spoke at all, but no one else has ever given an example.

Basil ... said that very soon the population would be only forty million. He said that the cruelty of the Germans was nothing to what the cruelty of the English would be if the English were really up against it in the matter of losing their property, that is their goods and their money and a chance for the kids ... Basil said that eventually England would have to choose between money and kids, because under capitalism people would not have kids, it was too much to ask, and he began to inveigh against our ex-Ally which put me for once in a good humour with them. He said that America would be the ruin of the moral order, he said that the more gadgets women had and the more they thought about their faces and their figures, the less they wanted to have children, he said that he happened to see an article in an American woman's magazine about scanty panties, he said women who thought about scanty panties never had a comfortable fire burning in the fire-place, or a baby in the house, or a dog or cat or a parrot ...
Or a canary, I said.
Or a canary, went on Basil, and he said that this was the end of the moral order.[24]

Small signs of fame and its attendant penalties began to appear in Orwell's life. The Hampstead Garden Suburb Ward of the Hendon Labour Party had asked him in October 1941 if they could put his name forward as their prospective parliamentary candidate. There is no record of his reply, but he must have declined. Nothing could have been less congenial to him than the life of a parliamentary candidate, unless it was the life of a Member of Parliament; and, in any case, it was a hopeless seat.[25]

Two letters from C. K. Ogden attempted to convert Orwell to the cause of Basic English.[26] Tom Wintringham consulted him on the drafting of a pamphlet urging immediate Home Rule for India if the Congress Party was not to be disaffected and Calcutta to fall, as had Singapore and Rangoon.[27] A letter from B. H. Liddell Hart took issue with a review of Orwell's that had misunderstood his views, and added placatingly 'I was recently told that you were the author of "Bless 'Em All".'[28] Such would have been real fame – and evidently 'Orwell' was beginning to have such tales attached to him; but it was not true.

Orwell was invited to give one of five Fabian Autumn Lectures for 1941, and he chose the title of 'Culture and Democracy'. The lecture moved rather abruptly from a diatribe against the British upper classes and the capitalist system for being dependent on cheap colonial labour into a noble defence of literature against totalitarianism. Orwell protested that it had been 'transcribed from shorthand notes ... and grossly altered without my knowledge'; but it sounds reasonably authentic, and is the only record of his lecturing manner.[29] Some passages are closer to Stevie Smith's Basil than to Orwell at his most reflective.

Orwell must have had some scheme for winning the war, or perhaps, as William Empson remembered, for organized guerrilla warfare if there were a German invasion. He received a short acknowledgement on 26 March 1942 from Tom Jones, CH, Lloyd George's famous Cabinet Secretary: 'your memorandum will be read by the Secretary of State himself. It seems plain sense – too plain I suppose.' No trace of the memorandum or clue to its subject matter survives in either Orwell's or Jones' papers, and as Jones held no official position then and wrote from his private address it is not clear even which Secretary of State it was for, though presumably that for War.[30]

In March 1942 Orwell made his first contribution to the *Observer* for which he was to write regularly until his death. Young David Astor was trying to liven the paper up from under the dead and defeatist hand of its editor, J. L. Garvin, soon to be dismissed. Astor nagged his father, the owner, to let him have a column called 'Forum' on the front page to express strong views by different people from all (nearly all) political directions. Who should write the first? On the advice of Cyril Connolly, who was filling in for the Literary Editor, he met Orwell. Astor had already read and admired ('without necessarily sharing all its opinions') *The Lion and the Unicorn*. He took to Orwell at once for his 'absolute straightforwardness, his honesty and his decency', so Orwell was commissioned to write two of these anonymous short columns. Astor says that Orwell pulled no punches; perhaps not in conversation, but somehow in print both pieces seemed over-judicious, a bit boring even, rather than provocative.

Astor then pushed strongly for Orwell to appear on the literary pages, at first somewhat against the grain of the old hands responsible for the pages; but he soon became accepted by the staff as a versatile and reliable regular contributor. When Astor came back from the Army to the *Observer* in 1945 he commissioned more articles and on occasion used him as a 'special correspondent'; but he admitted that Orwell never found his best form in the *Observer*. Perhaps he found it *too* liberal. It is, indeed, hard to rub such tolerant fur the wrong way; or perhaps David Astor's friendship inhibited him, he would be letting his friend down if he cut loose. He may have toned down the articles in advance, as others have done, to avoid the constant and irritating attrition from sub-editors on the telephone. Moderation has its perils.[31]

The friendship that grew up between Orwell and Astor is interesting. Astor would drop in on him to talk about politics and world events, and to ask his advice on general issues of policy. Several times he shared the friendly uncertainties of wartime cooking at the Orwells and made use of their camp-bed when the air-raids and the black-out made return to his own home impractical. He became a true and helpful friend, ever sensitive that Orwell might resent even the suspicion of patronage. Some people would have exploited the opportunities of friendship with the future proprietor and editor of a great and good newspaper, and would have tried to become an *éminence grise*. Not Orwell. He behaved to Astor much as he did to any other of his friends – speaking with frankness, making no demands, treating ideas on their merits, not for their suitability to the image or mission of the *Observer*. If he played up to Astor at all, it was in his old natural role of

Jeremiah: prophesying the definite collapse of the old order and a possible coming of a new. And Astor, in turn, seems to have treated Orwell as a surrogate conscience. So the quality of Orwell's own writing for the *Observer* might have been affected by a feeling that he was there partly under false pretences, due to a misunderstanding: that Astor had taken his patriotism and his libertarianism seriously, but not his socialism. So Orwell was happiest reviewing books or reporting for the *Observer*, not writing articles which might prove divisive.

His connection with the *Observer* nearly foundered at the beginning. Ivor Brown, the Deputy Editor, intervened to reject the third book review that Orwell wrote for them in October 1942; it was of O. D. Gallagher's *Retreat in the East*. Orwell quoted passages which Brown said would 'play into the hands of a few ill-disposed Americans', that is, those who did not see the war as concerned to save the British Empire.[32] People did censor themselves pompously and foolishly – as Orwell was to discover with *Animal Farm*. Orwell indignantly returned another book he had been given to review for them, and would do no more for the literary pages until the following September, though he wrote three articles for the political pages in the meantime.

Recognition could take strange forms. Orwell's wartime Diary for 27 March 1942 has the cryptic entry: 'Abusive letter from H. G. Wells, who addresses me as "you shit", among other things.' In the August number of *Horizon* the previous year, Orwell had let fly at some newspaper articles by Wells written at the beginning of 1941, reprinted in his book *Guide to the New World*, in which Wells argued that Hitler's power was spent. Why, asked Orwell, did Wells always so underestimate Hitler? Not all of his answer had much to do with Wells.

The people who say that Hitler is Antichrist, or alternatively, the Holy Ghost, are nearer an understanding of the truth than the intellectuals who for ten dreadful years have kept it up that he is merely a figure out of comic opera, not worth taking seriously. All that this idea really reflects is the sheltered conditions of English life. The Left Book Club was at bottom a product of Scotland Yard, just as the Peace Pledge Union is a product of the navy. One development of the last ten years has been the appearance of the 'political book', a sort of enlarged pamphlet combining history with political criticism, as an important literary form. But the best writers in this line – Trotsky, Rauschning, Rosenberg, Silone, Borkenau, Koestler and others

427

– have none of them been Englishmen, and nearly all of them have been renegades from one or other extremist party, who have seen totalitarianism at close quarters and known the meaning of exile ... The people who have shown the best understanding of Fascism are either those who have suffered under it or those who have a Fascist streak in themselves. A crude book like *The Iron Heel*, written nearly thirty years ago, is a truer prophecy of the future than either *Brave New World* or *The Shape of Things to Come*.[33]

It could seem that Orwell dared to find imaginatively such a streak, for the purpose of his writing and of political understanding, even in himself.

Wells, said Orwell, could not face the fact that his advocacy of a rational science and State control of industry had been taken over for the military and despotic purposes of barbarism; that his advocacy of a 'World State' had sapped the patriotism of liberals and was now being attempted by savages; and above all that man could not live by hedonism alone, as Hitler knew and we must all quickly learn.

Orwell wrote that it was 'a sort of patricide for a person of my age (thirty-eight) to find fault with H. G. Wells'; no one's mind would be the same but for Wells, and no writer of English had influenced the young so much between 1900 and 1920. The careful back-dating of the tribute must have angered Wells.

When Wells was young, the antithesis between science and reaction was not false. Society was ruled by narrow-minded profoundly incurious people, predatory businessmen, dull squires, bishops, politicians who could quote Horace but had never heard of algebra ... Back in the nineteen-hundreds it was a wonderful experience for a boy to discover H. G. Wells. There you were, in a world of pedants, clergymen and golfers, with your future employers exhorting you to 'get on or get out', your parents systematically warping your sexual life, and your dull-witted schoolmasters sniggering over the Latin tags; and here was this wonderful man who could tell you about the inhabitants of the planets and the bottom of the sea, and who *knew* that the future was not going to be what respectable people imagined. A decade or so before aeroplanes were technically feasible Wells knew that within a little while men would be able to fly. He knew because he himself *wanted* to be able to fly, and therefore felt sure that research in that direction would continue.[34]

Wells, Orwell concluded, 'is too sane to understand the modern world'. The essay was a classic criticism of rationalism in politics. Bertrand Russell, of all people, was to praise it highly.[35]

Inez Holden, having been bombed out, had been offered by Wells a flat attached to his house off Regents Park. The Orwells had visited her there and George had had supper one evening with Wells and Inez. Knowing of Orwell's admiration for Wells and how much Wells liked admirers, but forgetting about the essay, Inez persuaded H. G. to accept an invitation to dine with the Orwells. Only a day or two before this dinner, Wells heard about the essay and asked her for a copy. Thunder-clouds gathered. Typically, Orwell did not think the article was any reason to cancel the dinner. Her wartime diary for 30 August 1941 tells the story.

In the evening I went down to the Orwells. It was nine o'clock. H. G. had had his dinner with [them]. He was sitting quietly in his high chair there, looking half good half pettish. Orwell had the look of an embarrassed prefect. It was easy to see that the row had not started up yet. The poet Empson was sitting in a chair. He was slightly drunk ... H. G. in an ominous way said to me 'Thank you for that document.' Soon he trotted off and got out a copy of *Horizon* from his coat pocket and Orwell got out another one and slapped it down on the table opposite Wells.

Wells began to read. First Orwell's quotation of him and then what Orwell himself said, putting in stamping parenthesis 'So says Orwell' and 'this is Orwell'. When he spoke of Orwell's defeatism I raised one over-bred eyebrow and H. G. said 'No I want to have this out with Orwell.' On with the argument. 'The Germans aren't all over the Balkans,' said H. G.; 'Of course they are,' answered Orwell, 'look at the map.' Another thing H. G. said 'What sort of world Orwell wants we are going to hear soon. Soon we shall [be] told all about the Orwell world and the Orwell Utopia.' Orwell started to tell him and H. G. interrupted and Orwell said, 'Every time I try to tell you how, you ask me what; and every time I try to tell you what, you ask me how.' Finally it seemed agreed that they both wanted much the same world, H. G. was concerned with what, Orwell with how to get it. The poet Empson said that H. G. should take back the word defeatist considering Orwell had seen a considerable amount of fighting under the worst conditions.

H. G. was clearly outraged and hurt by the wording of Orwell's article calling him old-fashioned and his world state scheme and Sankey declaration 'the usual rigmarole'. Orwell had put some whiskey and snuff between them, he tried to keep it on as friendly as possible a footing. He never got rude or impertinent, although it was agreed that his manners were not so good on paper. H. G. enjoyed the evening. He stayed quite late and we set off home taking with him the poet Empson who was now ... pretty well drunk.

Empson had considered he should say that Orwell's effort should be appreciated and so he said 'Great man Orwell. I think we should appreciate his effort, there he is an Etonian and his honesty and fight against his upbringing compels him to say anything he wants in a rude manner. He is an Etonian. I am a Wykehamist, I can't write about anything that matters.' ... I remember H. G. saying it was not because Orwell was rude that he had been angry with him but because his values were wrong.

Empson said, 'No it was because Orwell was rude that H. G. had been angry.' So ended the evening. H. G. on saying Good Night to me said 'I was sorry to take you home early but I have to work tomorrow.' He said it was an amusing evening.[36]

What occasioned the abusive letter from Wells six months later was the appearance in the *Listener* of the best of Orwell's BBC talks, 'The Rediscovery of Europe' where, in passing, Wells was lumped together with Shaw, Housman and Hardy, indeed 'nearly all English writers of that time', as having 'complete unawareness of anything outside the contemporary English scene'. And he added, for good measure (redoubling, in Wells' eyes, the sin of his original patricide), that when Wells wrote a history of the world, he 'looks at the past with the same sort of surprised disgust as a civilized man contemplating a tribe of cannibals'. Orwell contrasts Wells' generation with that of Eliot and Joyce.

Their revulsion from a shallow conception of progress drove them politically in the wrong direction, and it isn't an accident that Ezra Pound, for instance, is now shouting antisemitism on the Rome radio. But one must concede that their writings are more grown-up, and have a wider scope, than what went immediately before them. They broke the cultural circle in which England had existed for something like a century. They re-established contact with Europe, and they brought back the sense of history and the possibility of tragedy. On that basis all subsequent English literature that matters twopence has rested, and the development that Eliot and the others started, back in the closing years of the last war, has not yet run its course.[37]

Wells had evidently felt that he had dealt with an unruly but talented disciple at that dinner, and viewed continued criticism as, he told Inez Holden, 'treachery'. Orwell, on the other hand, as his earlier brush with Stephen Spender shows, somewhat naïvely or primly never saw why public criticism, when it was not total rejection, should prevent social intercourse. Wells railed against the literary manners of this

'Trotskyist with big feet' – a remark that delighted Eileen when it came to her patient ears. Hetta Empson heard about it too and protested that her feet were even bigger – measuring them up against George's at one of the once famous Saturday night 'Come all ye's' that she and her husband gave in Hampstead.

The Orwells had moved to a more pleasant flat at 111 Langford Court, Abbey Road, St John's Wood, a few months before the dinner with Wells. It was on the fifth floor of an eight-storey modern block, with a lift, although still with only one bedroom, so visitors and bombed-out friends slept on camp-beds in the living-room. They had been more or less bombed out themselves from their flat near Baker Street. Langford Court was full of 1930s refugees. Eileen told a friend that she met an Englishwoman in the lift and they embraced in mutual surprise. In the winter Orwell was laid up from time to time with heavy colds, influenza or bronchitis. Eileen left him lunch or quite often dashed home from Whitehall to cook him something quickly. Obviously he could, as he had for so long, look after himself, but she knew that when he was writing he neglected himself, so she always made sure he had a hot meal at midday. Perhaps her brother had given such advice to her before his death. At that time Eileen was neglecting her own health, although Eric either did not notice how run down she had become or did not know what to do. They both drove themselves hard and were mutually loving but she was the more perceptive. Orwell had nothing against proper or even good food; if someone else entertained him he did not feel uncomfortable or guilty. Smart restaurants he took in his stride; but he rarely sought them out, nor seemed particularly aware of what he was eating. They entertained reasonably well, but their mutual domestic economy must have been fairly miserable. Wartime canteen food he pronounced as 'really very good', Victory Pies and all. He once absentmindedly ate a dish of boiled eels that Eileen had left for the cat, so the cat ate the shepherd's pie she had left for him, presumably with the same indifference. But even on boiled eels, serious opinions can differ.

Mark Benney entertained them just after their move from Baker Street. The Benneys laid on 'quite a spread to console them for their ill luck' in being bombed out, a plump chicken and a rare bottle of claret.

We had just taken our places at the dining table under the big 'picture' window when a bomb fell some fifty yards away and we were lifted out of our seats by the blast. When we picked ourselves up the room was covered with the fine splinters from the shattered window, and the only light came from the incendiary bombs burning in the street outside, but none of us was hurt. Eileen said, incredulously, 'No, no – not *again*!' I said, looking with relief at the bottle still in my hand, 'At least the wine's safe!' Eric said glumly, 'If we'd been in one of those working-class hovels round the corner we'd be dead as mutton now!' . . . The perverse distortions of guilt were . . . the very meat of his mind; he wanted to believe that he and his upper-middle-class kind were inescapably corrupt and evil; he scrutinized his world with the eye of a Savonarola for evidence of such corruption, and when he could not find it, he sometimes invented it. In one of his 'Letters from London' for *Partisan Review* for example, he reported the tearing down of railings in the drive for scrap metal, and alleged that, while working-class parks and squares were being enthusiastically derailed by the authorities, upper-class squares were being left with their iron privacies untouched. This was patently untrue, but he waved aside my objections with the defence that 'Anyway, it was *essentially* true.'[38]

The railings rumour was, however, widely believed. The more apt comment would have been that Orwell the polemical journalist did not always trouble to check his facts, a not uncommon fault of journalists, not that he invented them.

They moved again in the summer of 1942 to a larger flat, a ground floor and basement, 10a Mortimer Crescent, Maida Vale, about a mile north, in a pleasant, seedy, small area of mid-Victorian villas just off the junction of Maida Vale and Kilburn High Road. It was the kind of lower-middle-class ambience that Orwell thought was London at its best. The warm bustle in the big shops in Kilburn High Road on a late Saturday afternoon in winter still had the air, indeed still does, of an urban village, certainly of the London where ordinary people live. It was the same area where Henry James placed Princess Casamassima when she embraced the anarchists' cause. The flat was large, so it was easier to put people up; but it was desperately cold and draughty. 'If George and I didn't smoke so much,' Eileen told a friend, 'we'd be able to afford a better flat.'[39] When David Astor came to supper and because of air-raids had to spend the night there, he discovered that any warmth in the morning depended on George being woken up in the small hours by a reliable air-raid so that 'I may as well restoke the boiler while I'm up.' Anthony Powell had the same experience 'the night we dined at Kilburn'.

'If I have a dog, I always think my dog is the best dog in the world,' he used to say, 'or if I make anything at carpentry, I always think it's the best shelf or bookcase. Don't you ever feel the need to do anything with your hands? I'm surprised you don't. I even like rolling my own cigarettes. I've installed a lathe in the basement. I don't think I could exist without my lathe.'[40]

Anthony Powell slept on a camp-bed beside the lathe.*

At the end of June 1942, Orwell was persuaded to do a unique and uncharacteristic thing. He took a holiday. He went fishing for a week at Callow End, Worcestershire. Some time that summer, his mother and sister moved down to London from Southwold so that Avril could find war work. They moved into a flat close to George and Eileen, who just seem to have accepted the new situation and taken it in their stride. Avril found work in a sheet-metal factory behind Kings Cross Station – an abrupt transition from a tea-shop in a small Suffolk town. Perhaps even more remarkable was that Ida Blair, wanting to help the war effort again, though now sixty-seven and in poor health, took a job as a shop assistant in Selfridge's. All the Blairs had a certain civic toughness or stubbornness about them.

Avril met some of Orwell's friends. He did not try to keep them apart, although Avril was not an intellectual and, indeed, at that time still rather aggressively regarded her brother as a failure who had let the Blairs down. She met David Astor, Humphrey Slater, Inez Holden and others, enough for them to remember her quite well. Mrs Blair let Arthur Koestler have her set of *Encyclopaedia Britannica* which he fetched from their flat in Alexandra Road himself. She caught up with her reading of her son's books (which Avril did not do until after his death). She had the Penguin 1940 edition of *Down and Out* by her bedside. Perhaps she was reassured that they had classified

---

*It argues a great restraint on Powell's part that there is only the merest whiff of Orwell, small but distinct, in the twelve volumes of his *A Dance to the Music of Time* – in the physical description of Alf, Viscount Erridge, Earl of Warminster, the eccentric and erratic, high-minded revolutionary, living in squalor and an old corduroy jacket and surrounded by spongers and Left-wing hangers-on. (See Hilary Spurling, *Handbook to Anthony Powell's Music of Time* (Heinemann, 1977) p. 55, for a concise description of Alf Warminster, though she does not note the parallel.)

it as 'fiction'. But her health was deteriorating in London, and she died in New End Hospital, Hampstead, following a heart attack on 19 March 1943. The death certificate notes that Eric Blair was present. Before she died she would have learned that her son had developed great talent and, despite the odd way he lived, was beginning to be recognized. She liked and trusted Eileen, so may well have died reasonably happy about the life her tall son led and the fruits of his strange career, so different from that of most of the Limouzins and Blairs.

Just before they moved to Mortimer Crescent, Eileen changed jobs. She now worked in the Ministry of Food preparing recipes and scripts for 'The Kitchen Front', which the BBC broadcast each morning. These short programmes were prepared in the Ministry because it was a matter of Government policy to urge or restrain the people from eating unrationed foods according to their official estimates, often wrong, of availability. It was the time of the famous 'Potatoes Are Good For You' campaign, with its attendant Potato Pie recipes, which was so successful that another campaign had to follow immediately: 'Potatoes are Fattening'. Many features of the Ministry of Truth in *Nineteen Eighty-Four* owe as much to Eileen's experiences in the Ministry of Food, particularly the snappy slogans, as to George's in the BBC Far Eastern Service. The Orwells never suffered from a shortage of potatoes, for they occasionally went down to Wallington at weekends to their vegetable patch which they kept going without regard to the dialectics of the official line.

Eileen's work was more interesting than in her previous job, the hours more regular, and at the Ministry of Food she had some interesting companions. She worked with the writer Lettice Cooper, who wrote a novel in 1947, *Black Bethlehem*, which describes life in a wartime Ministry. The character of 'Ann', despite being made a novelist and given red hair, is clearly based on Eileen.

When you speak to her she generally looks at you for a minute before answering, and then answers very slowly, as though anything you said to her needed careful consideration and was of the greatest importance. At first we thought her affected, and were impatient of waiting for her comments. Later we realized that everything was important to her because her sense of life was so intense that she got the full impact of anything that turned up and saw it not isolated but with all its connections. I find it very difficult to put down what I mean about this, but I think that most people skim over most things. They only really get the impact of certain things that are specially interesting to them. Perhaps they have to be like that to get through the day in this crowded world. Certainly Ann finds it hard to get through the day. She does her work very well, but she almost always stays late to finish it. She goes home at night without meat or vegetables which she meant to buy in her lunch hour, but had not bought because she had not finished what she was saying at lunch. In the flat when she cooks and cleans for her brilliant, erratic husband and their friends, she is generally washing up at midnight ... Ann ... attracts crises. Her own friends are constantly ringing up to say that they wish to be divorced, are going to have babies or nervous breakdowns, or have quarrelled with their husbands or lovers ... His friends, too, have crises. They are bankrupt, turned out of their flats, unable to stop drinking or unable to get drink, called up or looking for jobs; bitterly wounded by each other or betrayed by their wives. They all come to tell Ann about it ...

'I hope it isn't a long meeting,' Ann said, 'I haven't had breakfast.' 'Oh, Ann!' 'Well, there wasn't any. Charles Campion came in about midnight and said his flat had been hit earlier in the evening and he had nowhere to live. So we made him a bed on the floor, and of course he hadn't had anything to eat, so he had to have the bacon and bread and marmalade. It was all there was. Then we sat talking till two because he was a bit shaken and didn't feel like going to bed ...' You feel about Ann that she is not only used to actual war, but is fundamentally used to the idea of war ...

'Where would Dawson sleep?' 'Oh, that would be all right. He and Charles could have camp-beds in the sitting-room. We've got two. They're really very comfortable and I do generally cook a hot meal at night, even though it isn't always ready till about nine.'

Ann and Christopher have the standards of comfort of soldiers on the march. Something to eat and somewhere to lie, and a share of anything they've got for any fellow-campaigner. I often think they are the real citizens of the new world. I like my comfort, but oh how much more I like privacy! And I know that my belief in the brotherhood of man — the only religion most of us have got left nowadays — isn't strong enough to make me willing to take anybody into my home just because they are uncomfortable where they are.[41]

Eileen's friends of the Ministry days are all very firm that she was a remarkable person in her own right, who supported George completely, but did not allow her personality to be submerged by his, and kept her affection towards him while standing up to him, bringing him down to earth on small matters of fact. Her friends felt that Orwell neglected what was to them (or how much of this is hindsight?) the visible decline in Eileen's health, or that he simply didn't notice it, putting her tiredness down vaguely and comprehensively to 'the War'. If he went shopping for some necessity in short supply, whether matches, razor blades, soap or off-the-ration food, he never thought of going to another shop if the first was sold out, but accepted the melancholy fact of wartime shortages and went home empty-handed – the effort had been made, mission incomplete. But the Blairs were alike in that, and in some ways both throve on the War.

One source of both mutual sorrow and of tension between them was not at this time apparent to their friends. Orwell wanted them to have a child, which they were both convinced they could not have. He had the strange conviction that he was biologically sterile, but it is likely that there were more substantial reasons on her side connected with her health. He began to press her to adopt a child, but she resisted, though whether she spoke, as many women did then, of wanting to wait until after the War, whether she was worried about money if she gave up work – particularly as she wanted George to avoid routine jobs and get back to real writing again – or whether she spoke frankly about her condition cannot be known.

Despite his long hours at the BBC, the Home Guard, friends, family, *Partisan Review* and the *Observer*, Orwell astonishingly found time to write considerable essays. There was the elegaic 'The Art of Donald McGill' in Cyril Connolly's *Horizon*, superficially about 'rude' seaside postcards, more profoundly about the uncrushable life-force of the common people. He meant to put just that kind of vulgarity and contempt for authority into the character of the Proles. 'If you look into your own mind, which are you, Don Quixote or Sancho Panza? Almost certainly you are both. There is one part of you that wishes to be a hero or a saint, but another part of you is a little fat man who sees very clearly the advantages of staying alive with a whole skin. He is your unofficial self, the voice of the belly protesting against the soul.'[42]

He also wrote a long review in *Horizon* of T. S. Eliot's *A Choice of Kipling's Verse*. Did Orwell coin the phrase 'a good bad poet' in this review, or was it already current? It must have helped Queenie Leavis solve her lofty problem as to whether Orwell was merely 'a good critic of literature' or could ever be termed a 'literary critic'. It was literary criticism: structure, language, content and context were all given their due. And 'The Rediscovery of Europe' was a mature recognition of a broader 'great tradition' than F. R. Leavis'. The theme of the 1941 Fabian Autumn Lecture, 'Culture and Democracy', was expressed with greater clarity in a small essay in *Tribune* (before he joined their staff):

Left Wing literary criticism has not been wrong in insisting on the importance of subject-matter. It may not even have been wrong, considering the age we live in, in demanding that literature shall be first and foremost propaganda. Where it has been wrong is in making what are ostensibly literary judgements for political ends. To take a crude example, what Communist would dare to admit in public that Trotsky is a better writer than Stalin – as he is, of course? To say 'X is a gifted writer, but he is a political enemy and I shall do my best to silence him' is harmless enough. Even if you end by silencing him with a tommy-gun you are not really sinning against the intellect. The deadly sin is to say 'X is a political enemy: therefore he is a bad writer.' If anyone says that this kind of thing doesn't happen, I answer merely: look up the literary pages of the Left Wing press, from the *News Chronicle* to the *Labour Monthly*, and see what you find.[43]

T. S. Eliot, Orwell sensibly if unfashionably insisted, was a reactionary *and* a good writer.

The importance and difficulty of telling the truth was beginning to be a *leitmotif* in Orwell's writings. 'Looking Back on the Spanish War' (a long essay which he wrote gratis for *New Road*, a small socialist yearly anthology) marked another intellectual stage along the road to his full theory of totalitarianism expressed in *Nineteen Eighty-Four*.

I saw, in fact, history being written not in terms of what happened but of what ought to have happened according to various 'party lines' ...

This kind of thing is frightening to me, because it often gives me the feeling that the very concept of objective truth is fading out of the world. After all, the chances are that those lies, or at any rate similar lies, will pass into history. How will the history of the Spanish War be written? ...

If the leader says of such and such an event, 'It never happened' – well, it never happened. If he says that two and two are five – well, two and two are five.[44]

437

However, polemical zeal could occasionally lead him into writing what he could only have rationalized as 'essentially true' rather than literally true. In his 'London Letter' of January 1942, for instance, he told readers of *Partisan Review* that 'pacifism is objectively pro-Fascist' and, with a wild fling of guilt by association, quoted the appearance of the Duke of Bedford, Alex Comfort, Julian Symons and Hugh Ross Williamson together in an anti-war pamphlet as showing 'the overlap between Fascism and pacifism'.[45] Some pacifists may have been silly in their logic as well as noble in their aims, but to be called 'Fascist' was unjust, and for Orwell to use the Marxist formulation of 'objectively' was not to follow, for once, the high standards he had set himself. A more profound criticism of pacifism occurred in his essay 'Lear, Tolstoy and the Fool' of 1947: 'Creeds like pacifism and anarchism, which seem on the surface to imply a complete renunciation of power, rather encourage this habit of mind. For if you have embraced a creed which appears to be free from the ordinary dirtiness of politics – a creed from which you yourself cannot expect to draw any material advantage – surely that proves that you are in the right?'[46]

Orwell stirred up in the pages of *Partisan Review* a hornet's nest of controversy about pacifism. The fight spread across the waters to have Orwell trading quasi-Byronic stanzas with 'Obadiah Hornbooke', alias Alex Comfort, over fifteen verses each in the pages of *Tribune*, both men piling Pelion on Ossa with the gloves off.

> But you don't hoot at Stalin – that's 'not done' –
> Only at Churchill; I've no wish to praise him,
> I'd gladly shoot him when the war is won,
> Or now if there were someone to replace him.
> But unlike some, I'll pay him what I owe him;
> There was a time when empires crashed like houses,
> And many a pink who'd titter at your poem
> Was glad enough to cling to Churchill's trousers.
> Christ! how they huddled up to one another
> Like day-old chicks about their foster-mother!
>
> I'm not a fan for 'fighting on the beaches',
> And still less for the 'breezy uplands' stuff,
> I seldom listen in to Churchill's speeches,

> But I'd far sooner hear that kind of guff
> Than your remark, a year or so ago,
> That if the Nazis came you'd knuckle under
> And peaceably 'accept the *status quo*'.
> Maybe you would! But I've a right to wonder
> Which will sound better in the days to come,
> 'Blood, toil and sweat' or 'Kiss the Nazi's bum' …[47]

But typically Orwell made peace privately with Comfort; they met each other and corresponded amicably, mainly over *Tribune* contributions. Orwell was meeting other anarchists, particularly through using their Freedom Bookshop, and Comfort introduced him to a few more. He actually apologized to Julian Symons for the 'London Letter', sent him books to review, and soon the two men became close friends.

Just as he was leaving the BBC, he allowed himself one serious reflection on the institution, nominally a reflection on the advantages as well as the disadvantages of trying to popularize poetry over the air; but it turned into yet another defence of the intellectuals, more like his defence of Henry Miller than his near-rejection of them all in *The Lion and the Unicorn*. Again it looked forward, though more optimistically, to greater themes to be treated in *Nineteen Eighty-Four*:

The British government started the last war with the more or less openly declared intention of keeping the literary intelligentsia out of it; yet after three years of war almost every writer, however undesirable his political history or opinions, has been sucked into the various Ministries or the BBC and even those who enter the armed forces tend to find themselves after a while in Public Relations or some other essentially literary job. The Government has absorbed these people, unwillingly enough, because it found itself unable to get on without them … No one acquainted with the Government pamphlets, ABCA lectures, documentary films and broadcasts to occupied countries which have been issued during the past two years imagines that our rulers would sponsor this kind of thing if they could help it. Only, the bigger the machine of government becomes, the more loose ends and forgotten corners there are in it. This is perhaps a small consolation, but it is not a despicable one. It means that in countries where there is already a strong liberal tradition, bureaucratic tyranny can perhaps never be complete. The striped-trousered ones will rule, but so long as they are forced to maintain an intelligentsia, the intelligentsia will have a certain amount of autonomy.[48]

Not a very lofty defence of the intellectual, but a shrewd perception that the defence of liberty sometimes has as much to do with 'loose ends and forgotten corners' as it does with barricades and manifestos. Since he could not go adventuring as a war correspondent, he was well fitted, as preacher and critic, for his new job.

CHAPTER FOURTEEN

TRIBUNE AND THE MAKING

OF ANIMAL FARM

(1943–5)

By the end of November 1943 Orwell had begun work as Literary Editor of *Tribune*. He had first begun reviewing for *Tribune* at the end of March 1940, continuing for the rest of that year, but then producing nothing until September 1942 when, despite his BBC contract, both polemical essays and reviews appeared regularly. *Tribune*'s Managing Editor was Jon Kimche, who had been Box to Orwell's Cox when they both worked as half-time assistants in the Hampstead bookshop in 1934–5.

He had gone on to manage the ILP bookshop in Ludgate Circus and to write for the *Evening Standard*. The very active editorial directors were two Left-wing Labour MPs, George Strauss (who put up most of the money) and Aneurin Bevan (who embodied what it stood for). Strauss and Bevan were both anti-Government and also anti-leadership in their own party, but they stood for a more aggressive conduct of the War, greater participation by Labour in the Home Front, and while they eulogized 'the heroic Russian people' they were boldly and – at the time – uniquely critical of Soviet policy. They knew Orwell only from his writings, recognized him as a kindred spirit and became good colleagues, though never personal friends. The weekly editorial meetings must have been extraordinary: Bevan and Strauss went on about the great questions of the day, but left to others the humble decisions about what actually to put in the paper. Then there was less a *Tribune* line than a *Tribune* style of argument, which suited Orwell perfectly.[1] Orwell joined the NUJ and preserved his membership card proudly – though it was left unsigned.

As a job it paid less than the BBC, probably only £500 a year; but as Orwell only needed to go in to the office in the Strand on three days a week, it left him more free to write. He began work on *Animal Farm* almost at once. But far from giving all his spare time to it, he began that December to write a weekly column about books for the *Manchester Evening News*, then a fine and literate middle-brow paper, which he kept up until November 1946.

In the same month his occasional contributions to the *Observer* were put on a regular footing, appearing fortnightly until May 1946, and then occasionally until his death. He became, from the days of his grim poverty, almost compulsive about taking on work when offered, though all the while worrying himself by knowing quite well that he should be concentrating his energies. But he may also have felt a special need for more money at this time to let Eileen stop work and adopt a child.

The number of book reviews he wrote in this period is astonishing. Some of them, not surprisingly, are pedestrian. Yet despite this great burden of work, whether self-imposed or not, every review has something characterful, quirky or thoughtful to say. He seemed simply to enjoy reading as he had as a schoolboy; it would have been all that he wanted to do had the authorities at St Cyprian's not constrained and harried him with their oppressive lessons, all designed simply to pass exams. Orwell's book reviewing both continued his own education and became almost a public extramural course in Politics and Literature. He thought aloud about all the main current concerns he had: all of the dominant themes of both *Animal Farm* and *Nineteen Eighty-Four* occur in the reviews of these years. To read them makes it impossible to believe that either book was a sudden inspiration, except perhaps for the invention of the precise allegory that became *Animal Farm*.[2] His passionate concern with preserving the clarity of the English language is a recurrent motif and a dominant cultural theme emerged, which is only implicit in the books: literature *should* be relevant to social questions but, even when not, *must* be defended from mere partisan judgements.

If a few of the reviews are thin and hasty, not all benefiting from 'his straight on to the typewriter' informality, virtue did not always flow from necessity, yet the *Tribune* 'As I Please' columns gave him a marvellous opportunity to pull all his interests together. Julian Symons' description of the weekly column cannot be bettered:

... he discussed a hundred subjects, ranging from the comparative amounts he spent on books and cigarettes or lamenting the decline of the English murder from the days of Crippen to a casual wartime killing to the spawning of toads in spring. Some of these pieces were seriously conceived, others were week-to-week journalism, but all of them showed an idiosyncratic freedom in putting down things that interested him, often combined with a previously unsuspected humour.

One of the most attractive features of his personality was a childlike simplicity which had been revealed only rarely in the iron grey puritanism of the work he produced before the war, and now this had full play. The love of fishing and country walks that he had tried rather awkwardly to incorporate in novels came through clear and charming now that he spoke in the first person. The puritanism remained an important element in his writing, but in the *Tribune* pieces particularly he was able without any shamefacedness to record his pleasure in seeing a kestrel flying over Deptford gasworks and hearing a blackbird in the Euston Road, and to deprecate the idea that this was sentimentality. To those who attacked his distrust of mechanization as that of a Lollard crying out for the past he replied that 'By retaining one's childhood love of such things as trees, fishes, butterflies ... one makes a peaceful and decent future a little more probable, and by preaching the doctrine that nothing is to be admired except steel and concrete, one merely makes it a little surer that human beings will have no outlet for their surplus energy except in hatred and leader-worship.'[3]

The joy he felt at being Literary Editor of *Tribune* lay largely in his own writing. He was an excellent editor of his own copy and was always on time. When dealing with unsolicited contributions, however, he had too soft a heart, so he accepted more than could be used and manuscripts piled up on the table or were thrust into his desk drawer. Often books were sent out for review, or taken out by callers, more according to the poverty of the reviewer than his talent. Yet he also tried for the big names he admired irrespective of politics. On taking up the editorial chair, he wrote grandly, or naïvely, to T. S. Eliot, saying they would be honoured if he would send them something: 'we are able to print poems up to the length of a page'.[4] He sent similar letters, with more effect, to Henry Treece and – burying the hatchet – to Alex Comfort, but adding a sententious postscript: 'The subject-matter of a poem isn't as a rule all-important, but we can't undertake to print direct pacifist propaganda.'[5] He could always lay down the law for others but not always follow it himself. Tosco Fyvel, who was already contributing to

Tribune and followed Orwell as Literary Editor, remembers the problem he had clearing up the back-log of unacknowledged manuscripts and over-commissioned articles stuffed into desk drawers. Paul Potts, a poor poet whom Orwell befriended, despite other friends regarding him with impatience, remembers him slipping a ten-shilling note or a pound from his own pocket into the envelope containing some rejected poems. Orwell himself recognized his own limitations: 'It is questionable whether anyone who has had long experience as a free-lance journalist ought to become an editor. It is too like taking a convict out of his cell and making him governor of the prison.'[6] His own writing was always the most important to him, and the column ranged widely. In all he wrote, as well as book reviews and special essays, 71 'As I Please' columns covering, to be precise, 232 separate topics. He wrote for the faithful of the Labour movement, yet he refused to preach; rather he became adept at stinging them into thought, at being the Socratic gad-fly to prevent 'complacency and sloganizing'. The column gained him fame and notoriety throughout the Labour movement – for in the circumstances of the wartime party truce, it was *Tribune* that best expressed the views of the non-Communist (and then usually non-Marxist) Left-wing opposition. For some old Labour Party grass-roots activists Orwell is solely the *Tribune* Orwell, and his last two books are only a disturbing rumour. He became a Dr Johnson of the *Tribune* Left.

I had better not continue too long on this subject, because the last time I mentioned flowers in this column an indignant lady wrote to say that flowers are bourgeois . . .

How many a time have I stood watching the toads mating, or a pair of hares having a boxing match in the young corn, and thought of all the important people who would stop me enjoying this if they could. But luckily they can't. So long as you are not actually ill, hungry, frightened or immured in a prison or a holiday camp, spring is still spring . . . the earth is still going round the sun, and neither the dictators nor the bureaucrats, deeply as they disapprove of the process, are able to prevent it.

But one has the right to expect ordinary decency even of a poet. I never listened to Pound's broadcasts, but I often read them in the BBC Monitoring reports, and they were intellectually and morally disgusting.

I have often advocated that a Labour government, i.e. one that meant business, would abolish titles while retaining the Royal Family.

Examples of futile slogans, obviously incapable of stirring strong feelings or being circulated by word of mouth, are 'Deserve Victory', 'Freedom is in Peril, Defend it with all your Might', 'Socialism the only Solution', 'Expropriate the Expropriators', 'Austerity', 'Evolution not Revolution', 'Peace is indivisible' ...

But it reminded me of how tiny is the number of slaves of whom anything whatever is known. I myself know the names of just three slaves – Spartacus himself, the fabulous Aesop, who is supposed to have been a slave, and the philosopher Epictetus, who was one of those learned slaves whom the Roman plutocrats liked to have among their retinue. All the others are not even names.

I would not deny that the 'managerial' class *might* get control of our society, and that if they did they would lead us into some hellish places before they destroyed themselves. Where Burnham and his fellow-thinkers are wrong is in trying to spread the idea that totalitarianism is *unavoidable*, and that we must therefore do nothing to oppose it.

In the last analysis our only claim to victory is that if we win the war we shall tell less lies about it than our adversaries. The really frightening thing about totalitarianism is not that it commits 'atrocities' but that it attacks the concept of objective truth: it claims to control the past as well as the future.

Don't imagine that for years on end you can make yourself the boot-licking propagandist of the Soviet regime or any other regime, and then suddenly return to mental decency. Once a whore, always a whore.[7]

   This last unspecified jibe brought Kingsley Martin, as editor of the *New Statesman and Nation*, shouting down the phone threatening *Tribune* with a libel action. The Foreign Editor, Evelyn Anderson (an anti-Nazi refugee who had studied at Frankfurt in its great Weimar days), remembered Kimche patiently explaining to Kingsley Martin that an action would make him look ridiculous and that Orwell was not the man to retract, but would probably compound the libel and then claim justification in open court. Nothing more was heard from their sister journal.[8] Protests from readers were frequent, both at the frivolous use he made of his column and at his frequent attacks on the Soviet Communist Party. Bevan defended Orwell, partly because he shared his views on the Soviet betrayal of socialism and partly because, though he thought him tactless and obsessive, he knew him as a brilliant writer and absolutely honest. Jennie Lee (Baroness Lee) remembers her husband saying to other directors: 'George has alighted on our desk, as he'll be when he leaves, free as a bird. We'll be glad when he's with us. We'll accept the fact that there will be times when he will fly off.'⁹

Without Bevan's support Orwell (despite his growing fame) might not have lasted – even though the circulation manager coolly reported that those who wrote in regularly threatening to cancel their subscriptions were rarely subscribers. The rest of the small staff quickly learned that any attempt to persuade Orwell not to expose Communist tyranny so persistently would only lead to more of the same, only stronger. 'Liberty is the right to tell people what they do not want to hear', he was to write in defence of *Animal Farm* – which is just what he practised in his *Tribune* column. The staff all got on well with him, all commenting on the strange mixture of his personal gentleness and ferocious writing. None of the friendships went beyond the office, except for Fyvel's, already established. He volunteered Eileen's help to Evelyn Anderson in correcting her English for a book; and the same help was also extended to Franz Borkenau, a mutual friend and a former fellow-student of Evelyn's.

Small wonder that neither George Strauss nor Michael Foot, who followed Bevan as Editor in 1945, can remember whether 'As I Please' was supposed to be part of the literary pages or of the political pages (although Kimche, who had to put the paper together, is firm that he sub-edited 'As I Please' as Political Editor, and not Orwell himself as Literary Editor). Orwell, however, *did* do much as he pleased, and his failure to pay attention to the conventional distinction between politics and literature has perpetually irritated some and pleased others. The columns were, indeed, a perfect expression of Orwell's interests and personality, of his moral seriousness and quirky humour, and deserve reprinting in full. George Woodcock recalled:

I used to be surprised to watch Orwell writing an almost perfect 'As I Please' piece straight on the typewriter, with no second version, but I think the reason for this facility as well for his productivity under the circumstances of his life lay in the extent to which his writing was tied into his existence. By this I do not mean that he wrote about his major experiences, though that was true and important, for he was always a memoirist rather than a novelist. I mean rather that he liked to talk out his ideas in long monologues over cups of strong tea and hand-rolled cigarettes of black shag, and not long afterward one would see the evening's talk appearing as an article, and not long after that the third stage would be reached when it was incorporated into a book, as many of his conversations during 1946 and 1947 found their final form in *Nineteen Eighty-Four*.[10]

Orwell did not talk like this with everyone. Being now a well-known writer, he met an increasing number of people, or rather from now on many interesting people can remember occasional encounters with him on semi-public occasions, over *Tribune* business, at protest meetings, and at pubs and parties. There is the most remarkable conflict of testimony as to whether he was talkative or silent on such occasions. Some give portentous accounts of what he said to them and how well he said it, while others give self-deprecatory and comic accounts of him lurking in the background, saying little or nothing, a dumb or sulky lion even when bearded. From Woodcock's observation we might deduce that both may be right. He was often silent when not among his intimate friends, but if he spoke at all he tended to monologue, sometimes as if rehearsing an actual *Tribune* column. May not even Dr Johnson have refused, on occasion, to rise to bait and remained silent in his depths? All we can ever have are occasional memories and records of what people did say. The column journalist must agonize each day that he will dry up or not have anything sparkling to write about, so he is forever alternating between bouts of listening and of talking to try his ideas out. Kingsley Martin was like that. His sincere conversational spontaneities of Monday, Tuesday and Wednesday appeared in the Friday *New Statesman*'s 'Diary', and friends were made even crosser when their confidences to him also appeared.[11] But Orwell never broke a confidence, and used neither gossip nor crumbs from great men's tables. His stance was that of Everyman, not Insider, airing plain common sense either on matters of public record in the newspapers or from his own experience.

Stereotyped letters of abuse from party hacks he ignored, but he appears to have spent a lot of time answering genuine worries from genuine people. Enough examples survive to show that he would answer an unknown correspondent as carefully as a famous writer. *The Collected Essays, Journalism and Letters* prints one letter that he wrote to a Mr H. J. Willmett. Nearly all the essential thesis of *Nineteen Eighty-Four* was stated in explaining why he thought that further growth of totalitarianism and leader-worship were likely even after the war. He told Mr Willmett that he believed 'very deeply, as I explained

447

in my book *The Lion and the Unicorn*, in the English *people* and in their capacity to centralize their economy without destroying freedom in doing so'. But Britain and the USA had not really been tested, either by defeat or prolonged severe suffering. He feared that 'the intellectuals are more totalitarian in outlook than the common people'. They had opposed Hitler 'but only at the price of accepting Stalin. Most of them are perfectly ready for dictatorial methods, secret police, systematic falsification of history etc. so long as they feel that it is on "our" side.' To say that there was no fascist movement in Britain 'largely means that the young, at this moment, look for their *führer* elsewhere'. He hoped, even trusted, that the common people in ten years' time would not think as the intellectuals did then; but one could not be sure; there were struggles ahead; and 'if one simply proclaims that all is for the best and doesn't point to the sinister symptoms, one is merely helping to bring totalitarianism nearer'.[12]

The postbag also brought in an angry letter from the great mentor of his youthful editors, Middleton Murry, angry to be called pro-Soviet just because he was pacifist. Again, as with Symons, Orwell re-read, reconsidered and apologized 'very deeply ... for misjudging your attitude'.[13] A dozen or more violently anti-Semitic letters followed an *Observer* review of 30 January 1944 of a book called *The Chosen People*; and his *Tribune* piece of 11 February about these letters touched off another barrage. His comments show him fully purged of the mild and conventional, but none the less clear, anti-Semitism which appeared early in *Down and Out in Paris and London* and lingered in his 'War-Time Diaries'. More pleasantly and fruitfully, a piece on Soviet falsification of history drew an appreciative letter from Gleb Struve, an American scholar of Soviet literature.[14] Struve told Orwell about Zamyatin's anti-Utopian novel, *We*, which so interested Orwell, because by then he was planning his own anti-Utopia, that Struve took trouble to find him a French translation. It was more grist to the mill, but neither the grain nor the stone.[15]

The *Tribune* days were, in the main, good days. Orwell had congenial, comradely colleagues who accepted him as he was – a strange mixture of the eccentric and the ordinary; and he had a pulpit from which to preach anti-sermons, one that could have been made to measure. '*Tribune*' he wrote in 1947 for its tenth anniversary, was not perfect, but was 'the only existing weekly paper that makes a genuine effort to be both progressive and humane – that is, to combine a radical Socialist policy with a respect for freedom of speech and a civilized attitude towards literature and the arts'.[16]

While at *Tribune* he also had more time for his literary friends. He still wrote for *Horizon* and met Connolly and Spender and their friends quite frequently – including Connolly's extraordinarily beautiful assistant, Sonia Brownell. She was always vague and evasive when asked when they first met or got to know each other well. Sometimes she talked of a continuous friendship since 1940 when she had first copy-edited his contributions to *Horizon*, at other times it was 'the end of the war'; but always it was 'when everyone was talking about *Burmese Days*' (which would be the Penguin reprint of 1944, although a friend claims to have given her an old Gollancz copy in 1940).

As Anthony Powell and Malcolm Muggeridge came back from overseas to finish the war in London, they took to lunching regularly with Orwell, usually at the Bodega just off the Strand, sometimes joined by Julian Symons who seemed at that time almost to be Orwell's true disciple, and occasionally by David Astor. He met Vernon Richards and other British anarchists at the Freedom Bookshop or in pubs near the Conway Hall, where anarchists haunted and harangued secular meetings of all kinds – a kind of pacifist blood-sport that Orwell enjoyed listening to, up to a point. He did not accept anarchism in principle, but had, as a socialist who distrusted any kind of state power, a speculative and personal sympathy with anarchists. And he spent beery and argumentative evenings in the pubs of 'Fitzrovia' and Soho where the sub-Bloomsbury of young, poor or hard-up writers congregated.[17] As always, he kept these circles in the main well apart from each other. Even true and good friends are still surprised to discover whom else he knew. The happiness of the *Tribune* days can be seen in the serenity of tone, conveying a bitterness of content, of *Animal Farm*. *Tribune* days were happy days partly because he knew they would soon come to a natural end. He told several friends long before the success of *Animal Farm* that he would like to live in the country after the War, even mentioning vaguely 'the Hebrides' – that is as far as possible from London, telegrams and anger. If Dr Johnson could visit them, why could he not actually live in them? He was sure that he could live off his pen reasonably decently, by his standards, even without *Tribune*.

*

In the same month as he joined *Tribune*, November 1943, Orwell began writing *Animal Farm* and he had finished by the end of February 1944. He knew that it would be a short book, for he wrote to Philip Rahv in December 1943, 'I have got another book under way which I hope to finish in a few months.'[18] He was perfectly clear both what it was about (which could not always be said of his pre-war novels) and that it would cause trouble: 'I am writing a little squib', he told Gleb Struve on 17 February 1944, 'which might amuse you when it comes out, but it is not so OK politically that I don't feel certain in advance that anyone will publish. Perhaps that gives you a hint of its subject.' And in the very same letter he reverted to his interest in Zamyatin's *We*: 'I am interested in that kind of book, and even keep making notes for one myself that may get written sooner or later.'[19] This is the first concrete evidence that he was planning *Nineteen Eighty-Four* even before he began to write *Animal Farm*. Some of these notes have survived. (See Appendix A on p. 582 below.)

The relationship between the two books is much closer than many critics have supposed. The form that each took was very different, but there was an intellectual continuity between the story of the revolution betrayed and the story of the betrayers, power-hungry in each case, perpetuating themselves in power for ever. And it was no boast on his part to say: '*Animal Farm* was the first book in which I tried, with full consciousness of what I was doing, to fuse political purpose and artistic purpose into one whole.'[20] It was to become, its political message quite apart, sometimes indeed forgotten, the very model of good English prose almost everywhere English is learned; and even in the Soviet bloc it circulates in several widely read *samizdat* versions.

He explained the purpose and origins in a preface he wrote in 1947 for a Ukrainian edition:

... for the past ten years I have been convinced that the destruction of the Soviet myth was essential if we wanted a revival of the socialist movement.

On my return from Spain I thought of exposing the Soviet myth in a story that could be easily understood by almost anyone and which could be easily translated into other languages. However the actual details of the story did not come to me for some time until one day (I was then living in a small village) I saw a little boy, perhaps ten years old, driving a huge cart-horse along a narrow path whipping it whenever it tried to turn. It struck me that if only such animals became aware of their strength we should have no power over them, and that men exploit animals in much the same way as the rich exploit the proletariat.

I proceeded to analyse Marx's theory from the animals' point of view . . .[21]

Thus he reminded his readers, just as he was beginning to write *Nineteen Eighty-Four*, that *Animal Farm* had been 'in my mind for a period of six years before it was actually written'. He took pains to assert the political continuity and coherence of his writing after 1936 when he became both fervently Socialist and fervently anti-Communist. But he also warned his readers that though *Animal Farm* took various episodes from the Russian Revolution, the demands of the story came before literal history. The final scene of Pilkinton and his men dining with the Pigs, for instance, was not meant to show reconciliation but discord. 'I wrote it immediately after the Tehran Conference which everybody thought had established the best possible relations between the USSR and the West. I personally did not believe that such good relations would last long.' The division of the world at Teheran and Yalta between superpowers who then fell out also underlies the plot of *Nineteen Eighty-Four*.

There was a peculiarity about the actual composition of *Animal Farm* compared to that of Orwell's earlier books. He discussed it in considerable detail with Eileen. She had been, she told her friends, always a bit disappointed that he did not want her to read through and criticize his manuscripts before typing them out; only rarely, even back in Wallington days, did he even ask her to type for him. After Eileen's death, he told Dorothy Plowman that 'she was particularly fond of and even helped in the planning of *Animal Farm*'.[22] He read his day's work to her in bed, the warmest place in their desperately cold flat, discussed the next stage and actually welcomed criticisms and suggestions, both of which she gave. Never before had he discussed work in progress with anyone. Then the next morning Lettice Cooper and Eileen's other women friends at the Ministry of Food waited eagerly for a paraphrase of the latest episode.[23] Eileen seemed excited by it. And they shared not just her pleasure in the story, but also a mischievous delight in speculating about the trouble that lay ahead for the reckless author. Intelligent people did not miss the black comedy of Government propaganda, particularly when it was Churchill's government, pumping out plaudits to those 'heroic Russian people' who so shortly before had been 'the dupes of the Bolsheviks in alliance with Hitler'. Had not Churchill himself said, the day after Hitler's invasion of Russia, that if Hitler were to invade Hell he would pay a graceful tribute on the floor of the House of Commons to the Devil? But for most people propaganda seemed to have obliterated all bad memories of the Russian purges and the carving up of Poland and the Baltic States with Hitler. That it was all *pour raison d'état* or 'for the emergency' seemed forgotten, even among some British Conservatives, let alone among the Left. Many English Conservatives of the old breed never really took ideology seriously: politics was all a matter of national self-interest, so Russia could be dealt with as Russia. To think of Stalin as 'Uncle Joe' might be going too far, but to keep on reminding people that he was a totalitarian was as irrelevant as reminders of his crimes were imprudent. But Orwell was not so much attacking sins of the past, still less the conduct of a wartime ally; rather he was trying to clear men's minds of cant and power worship so as to guard against what he feared would be a future even more threatened by totalitarianism.

When the book was completed Orwell had no doubts of its merits. For the first time he was fully pleased with what he had done. He also had no doubt that he did not want Gollancz to publish it – though quite unfairly he would include Gollancz in his future execrations against those who had seen its worth but had not had the guts to publish it, or who had set themselves up as censors.

10a Mortimer Crescent,
London N.W.6
19.3.44

Dear Mr Gollancz,

I have just finished a book and the typing will be completed in a few days. You have the first refusal of my fiction books, and I think this comes under the heading of fiction. It is a little fairy story, about 30,000 words, with a political meaning. But I must tell you that it is – I think – completely unacceptable politically from your point of view (it is anti-Stalin). I don't know whether in that case you will want to see it. If you do, of course I will send it along, but the point is that I am not anxious, naturally, for the MS to be hanging about too long. If you think that you would like to have a look at it, in spite of its not being politically O.K., could you let either me or my agent (Christy & Moore) know? Moore will have the MS. Otherwise, could you let me know that you *don't* want to see it, so that I can take it elsewhere without wasting time?

> Yours sincerely,
> Eric Blair

Gollancz replied to this provocative letter with understandable huffiness.

March 23rd 1944

Dear Mr Blair,
Certainly I should like to see the manuscript.

Frankly, I don't begin to understand you when you say 'I must tell you that it is – I think – completely unacceptable politically from your point of view it is anti-Stalin'. I haven't the faintest idea what 'anti-Stalin' means. The Communists, as I should have thought you were aware, regard me as violently anti-Stalinist, because I was wholly and openly opposed to Soviet foreign policy from the Nazi–Soviet pact until Russia came into the war, because I have been highly critical of illiberal trends in Soviet internal policy, and because the last two issues of the 'Left News' have been very largely devoted to uncompromising criticism of the Soviet proposals about East Prussia, Pomerania and Silesia. Personally, I think it both incorrect and unwise to label that anti-Stalinism; I call it the kind of criticism, whether of the Soviet Union or of any other State, that no socialist can renounce. There is, on the other hand, the anti-Stalinism of Hitler, Lord Haw-Haw, and the more reactionary Tories. With the latter, of course, I can have nothing whatever to do – and I should be surprised to learn that you can.

I suppose I ought rather to pat myself on the back that you apparently regard me as a Stalinist stooge, whereas I have been banned from the Soviet Embassy for three years as an 'anti-Stalinist'.

> Yours sincerely,
> Victor Gollancz

Orwell then sent it to him with a covering note asking for a speedy decision, reiterating that he did not think 'that it is the kind of thing you would print' and saying that, naturally, he was 'not criticizing the Soviet regime from the Right, but in my experience the other kind of criticism gets one into even worse trouble'.[24]

Gollancz did give a commendably speedy decision.

Eric Blair Esq.,
10a Mortimer Crescent
London N.W.6

April 4th 1944

My Dear Blair,
You were right and I was wrong. I am so sorry. I have returned the manuscript to Moore.

Yours sincerely,

Dictated by Mr Gollancz, but signed in his absence.

He said a little bit more to Orwell's agent.

April 4th 1944

My Dear Moore,
Here is the manuscript of ANIMAL FARM, together with my note to Blair. I am highly critical of many aspects of internal and external Soviet policy: but I could not possibly publish (as Blair anticipated) a general attack of this nature.

Yours sincerely
[Victor Gollancz]

Years later Gollancz maintained that Orwell was a 'much over-rated writer'. This may have been sour-grapes, but it is plain that Gollancz turned down the book as a matter of policy and principle. Even if he had had prophetic powers of the book's incredible sales he would probably have made, though with agony, the same decision. It was his own firm and he simply did not like the book's standpoint.

Then at the suggestion of George Mikes, who had met Orwell attending meetings of Hungarian refugees, he gave it to André Deutsch, then working for Nicholson and Watson, run by J. A. C. Roberts. Deutsch was enthusiastic, but Roberts told Orwell to his face that he did not know what he was talking about as regards Russia. Orwell then offered it to Deutsch himself to publish, but though he was tempted, he was not then ready to go it alone. He suggested that Orwell try Cape.[25]

Only then did Orwell's rage and alarm, despite his anticipation of trouble, begin to mount. Cape's chief reader and literary adviser, Daniel George (who also reviewed novels regularly for *Tribune*), shrewd and experienced, favoured it, despite some uncertainty about 'its real purpose':

This is a kind of fable, entertaining in itself, and satirically enjoyable as a satire on the Soviets. The characters of Marx, Lenin, Trotsky and Stalin can clearly be recognized, and incidents in recent Russian politics are cleverly parodied. There is no doubt that it would find many appreciative readers, though these might not be of the class of which the author publicly approves, and its real purpose is not made clear. Publication of it is a matter of policy. I cannot myself see any serious objection to it.[26]

Veronica Wedgwood, although about to leave Cape, also read it and was strongly in favour of publication.

Jonathan Cape must have been eager to publish it for he wrote anxiously to Gollancz about the copyright position. Gollancz had Orwell under contract for his next three novels, and wished to hold him to that; so he told Moore and Cape that *Animal Farm* was both not a 'novel' and was below the normal length for a novel (he had no interest in or rights over Orwell's non-fiction). Cape then began to discuss the terms of a contract with Moore, but also seeing it as 'a matter of policy' thought it best to talk it over with a friend of his, 'a senior official' in the Ministry of Information. The name of this official cannot, alas, be discovered. But to think it incredible that Cape sent the manuscript at all would be hindsight. The chronicler of his firm wrote: 'It is not easy to recall now the force of moral rather than governmental pressure which deterred publishers from risking damage to the common war effort...'[27] The friend, in fact, followed up their conversation with a personal letter strongly imploring Cape not to publish a book that would so damage good relations with Russia. Cape was deeply upset and agonized over the decision, but fairly quickly, to the dismay and annoyance of Daniel George and Veronica Wedgwood, wrote to Moore as follows.

19 June 1944

My Dear Moore,
Since our conversation the other morning about George Orwell, I have considered the matter carefully and I have come to the conclusion that, unless the arrangement that exists whereby our author has to offer two works of fiction to another publisher can be waived, it would be unwise for us to enter into a contract for his future work. However, it does not seem to me unlikely that some compromise could be reached with Gollancz so far as this matter is concerned.

I mentioned the reaction that I had had from an important official in the Ministry of Information with regard to ANIMAL FARM. I must confess that this expression of opinion has given me seriously to think. My reading of the manuscript gave me considerable personal enjoyment and satisfaction, but I can see now that it might be regarded as something which it was highly ill-advised to publish at the present time. If the fable were addressed generally to dictators and dictatorships at large then publication would be all right, but the fable does follow, as I see now, so completely the progess and development of the Russian Soviets and their two dictators, that it can apply only to Russia, to the exclusion of other dictatorships. Another thing: it would be less offensive if the predominant caste in the fable were not pigs. I think the choice of pigs as the ruling caste will no doubt give offence to many people, and particularly to anyone who is a bit touchy, as undoubtedly the Russians are ... I think it is best to send back to you the typescript of ANIMAL FARM and let the matter lie on the table as far as we are concerned ...

> Yours sincerely,
> Jonathan Cape[28]

Orwell was torn between rage and laughter at Cape's procedure. In the margin of a copy of the letter, where it suggested some other animal than pigs, Orwell wrote laconically 'balls'. (It is debatable whether the word 'pig', offensive enough anywhere, is peculiarly offensive to Russians, but that is not the point. Cape had turned it down, not asked for innocent revisions.)

Something nearly came of it. Veronica Wedgwood was leaving to become Literary Editor of *Time and Tide* (a Liberal journal – in a very Right-wing sense). She asked the editor and proprietor, Lady Rhondda, a formidable lady, whether it would be possible to serialize the book. She was taken with the idea, even though it would have meant sacrificing almost all the literary pages for many weeks. But when Veronica Wedgwood took this proposal to Orwell, he expressed gratitude but said that the politics of *Time and Tide* were far too far to the Right for him, he felt it to be the wrong background for the book.

So Orwell then sent the manuscript to T. S. Eliot as a director of Faber and Faber.

10a Mortimer Crescent,
NW6
(Or 'Tribune' CEN 2572)
28 June 1944

Dear Eliot,

This MS has been blitzed which accounts for my delay in delivering it and its slightly crumpled condition, but it is not damaged in any way.

I wonder if you could be kind enough to let me have Messrs Fabers' decision fairly soon. If they are interested in seeing more of my work, I could let you have the facts abt my existing contract with Gollancz, which is not an onerous one nor likely to last long.

If you read this MS yourself you will see its meaning which is not an acceptable one at this moment, but I could not agree to make any alterations except a small one at the end which I intended making anyway. Cape or the MOI, I am not certain which from the wording of his letter, made the imbecile suggestion that some other animal than pigs might be made to represent the Bolsheviks. I could not of course make any change of that description.

> Yours sincerely
> Geo. Orwell

P.S. Could you have lunch with me one of the days when you are in town?[29]

Even before Eliot replied, Orwell had made a hidden flick at Cape in a *Tribune* 'As I Please' column of 7 July:

Nowadays this kind of veiled censorship even extends to books. The MOI does not, of course, dictate a party line or issue an *index expurgatorius*. It merely 'advises'. Publishers take manuscripts to the MOI and the MOI 'suggests' that this or that is undesirable or premature, or 'would serve no good purpose'. And though there is no definite prohibition, no clear statement that this or that must not be printed, official policy is never flouted. Circus dogs jump when the trainer cracks his whip, but the really well-trained dog is the one that turns his somersault when there is no whip. And that is the state we have reached in this country, thanks to three hundred years of living together without a civil war.[30]

Orwell's language was intemperate, but his description was all too accurate.*

T. S. Eliot replied on 13 July.

I know that you wanted a quick decision about 'Animal Farm' but the minimum is two directors' opinions, and that can't be done under a week. But for the importance of speed, I should have asked the Chairman to look at it as well. But the other director is in agreement with me on the main points. We

---

*Sir Stanley Unwin relates in his memoirs how his services as the Publishers Association representative on the Press and Censorship Bureau (of the Ministry of Information): '. . . were never required. In doubtful cases publishers voluntarily and gladly submitted typescripts or proofs, and the censors dealt with them expeditiously. The expression of opinions remained free.' (Sir Stanley Unwin, *The Truth About a Publisher* [Allen & Unwin, 1960].) Here is double-think indeed.

agree that it is a distinguished piece of writing; that the fable is very skilfully handled, and that the narrative keeps one's interest on its own plane – and that is something very few authors have achieved since Gulliver.

On the other hand, we have no conviction (and I am sure none of the other directors would have) that this is the right point of view from which to criticize the political situation at the present time. It is certainly the duty of any publishing firm which pretends to other interests and motives than mere commercial prosperity, to publish books which go against the current of the moment; but in each instance that demands that at least one member of the firm should have the conviction that this is the thing that needs saying at the moment. I can't see any reason of prudence or caution to prevent anybody from publishing this book – if he believed in what it stands for.

Now I think my own dissatisfaction with this apologue is that the effect is simply one of negation. It ought to excite some sympathy with what the author wants, as well as sympathy with his objections to something; and the positive point of view, which I take to be generally Trotskyite, is not convincing. I think you split your vote, without getting any compensating strong adhesion from either party – i.e. those who criticize Russian tendencies from the point of view of a purer communism, and those who, from a very different point of view, are alarmed about the future of small nations. And after all, your pigs are far more intelligent than the other animals, and therefore the best qualified to run the farm – in fact, there couldn't have been an Animal Farm at all without them: so that what was needed (someone might argue) was not more communism but more public-spirited pigs.

I am very sorry because whoever publishes this will naturally have the opportunity of publishing your future work: and I have a regard for your work, because it is good writing of fundamental integrity . . .[31]

Orwell bore Eliot no personal ill will for this. They corresponded on routine editorial matters without rancour later in the year. Yet the letter was in some ways a very strange one. Eliot offered such a variety of arguments, not all consistent with each other, to the same conclusion, but at least he took the book very seriously, which must have disarmed Orwell's personal anger. Plainly he says, in his complicated Eliot-like way, that 'it is not our kind of book' and that further, whatever its literary merits, a polemical political book needs some positive conviction behind it from the firm. It would have been as odd for Faber and Faber to publish a revolutionary tract as for Victor Gollancz, at that time even, to publish an anti-Russian conservative one. The Trotskyite attribution is neither unfair nor entirely unexpected from Geoffrey Faber and T. S. Eliot's standpoint, and it is a more accurate reading than that it was to receive from some future Cold War warriors across the Atlantic (including his future main American publishers). The insistence on the inevitability of élites, however, that pigs are with us always, so preferably 'public-spirited' pigs, is extraordinarily narrowing for any satirist, especially one capable of 'good writing of fundamental integrity'; and the point about the integrity of small nations, precisely one of Orwell's own concerns, is either a sad misreading or a bad red-herring. The favourable comparison with Swift's skill and with *Gulliver* itself (how right Eliot was, how specific is the influence of the Yahoos and the Houyhnhnms on Orwell's fable) should surely have settled the matter, if literary merit was the touchstone. Swift too could have been viewed as untimely, imprudent and essentially negative. Eliot was lucky that Orwell never wrote a parody Eliot letter of rejection to Swift.

The touchstone, however, was not purely literary: Orwell had encountered a 'political writer' almost as complicated as himself. If, that is, the letter of rejection is necessarily to be taken as Eliot's views in all respects: it could be a composite of several people's views. He was, after all, a partner of Faber and Faber, but Geoffrey Faber was the owner and took the financial risks. Eliot was punctilious and precise in never recommending publication, only commenting on a book's merits. Geoffrey Faber made the hard decisions, but he did not like writing difficult letters of rejection, such disagreeable tasks he often left to the loyal Eliot. What exactly happened in this case is obscure, but it is a simplification to say that 'T. S. Eliot' turned down *Animal Farm*. It was rejected by the firm, a different and not wholly consistent animal.[32]

Four days after Eliot's letter arrived, Orwell told Moore that 'Warburg again says he wants to see it and would publish it if he can see his way to getting the paper, but that is a big "if" '. If that falls through, he said, he was not 'going to tout it round further publishers ... but shall publish it myself as a pamphlet at 2s. I have already half arranged to do so and have got the necessary financial backing.'[33] Why did he not take it to Warburg in the first place, a publisher who had already handled two of his books? The answer must lie in Orwell's confidence in the merit of the book and his desire to see it published by one of the two best publishing houses in England. Years before, with far less justifiable confidence, he had sent Faber and then Cape the first and the rejected versions of *Down and Out in Paris and London*. He wanted that kind of recognition, at least for this book. Secker and Warburg, before their faith in Thomas Mann, Franz Kafka and Orwell had paid off, looked a very different house – small, lively but precarious and still nicknamed, however unfairly, because of their courage and persistence in bringing out difficult Left-wing books, 'the Trotskyite publisher'. Political though the fable was, Orwell thought its literary merits should carry it to a wider readership.

It is odd that he lost heart too soon. Perhaps he was shocked that his new reputation did not prevent such a sudden return to the problems of how to get published at all that he had suffered in his youth. To be turned down by two great publishing houses,* and to be as yet unwilling even to show the manuscript to Fred Warburg, seemed an inadequate reason for desperate measures like publishing it himself. Perhaps he felt that if the two most distinguished houses had not recognized its merit he would show the lot of them, he would eat worms and do it himself in thoroughly radical fashion. And he may have been affected by American rejections too. At some stage that year it was sent to the Dial Press who returned it, according to Orwell, with the comment that 'it was impossible to sell animal stories in the USA.'[34] It is possible, of course, that he believed that the hand of the MOI, once alerted, would reach everywhere; and also that he believed the rumours, as his excitable *Tribune* friends did, that Victor Gollancz was on the phone warning London publishers that this time that man had gone too far and was damaging the national interest.

Orwell may not have intended literally to publish it himself, although he approached David Astor, with much diffidence, for a loan of £200. Astor was willing but thought the project hare-brained: he counselled him to have patience with real publishers.[35] But Orwell may have wanted the money more as a subsidy, for he next offered it to anarchist friends. George Woodcock was a member of the board of the Freedom Press, managed by Vernon Richards and Marie Louise Berneri; and he remembers sounding them out. She objected to it strongly, so it is doubtful it was ever formally submitted. Vernon Richards and others are sure that it was never submitted, but the

---

*Michael Meyer says in his essay in *The World of George Orwell*, ed. Miriam Gross, p.131, that he also offered it to Collins, although the firm has no record of this and neither is it mentioned in any of Orwell's letters to his agent.

Anarchists were being prosecuted at that time and their affairs were in confusion.[36] Probably one or other of them advised Orwell that it would not stand a chance if formally submitted, for the board contained many belligerent pacifists who knew his early wartime writings and attacks on them as pacifists only too well. Whatever their common hatred of Stalinism, of all 'oligarchic collectivism' and their common ground with Orwell that there had been a revolution but it had been betrayed, they had not liked being called 'objectively Fascist' in relation to the war effort. They may have neither forgiven nor forgotten. Their feelings are understandable. However, associated with them was Paul Potts who published and sold poems in pubs on broadsheets, mainly his own. (This enterprise grew, for a while, into a pleasant little imprint, the Whitman Press.) In a perceptive, if idiosyncratic, chapter on Orwell called 'Don Quixote on a Bicycle' in his *Dante Called You Beatrice* (1960), Potts claims:

At one point I became the publisher of *Animal Farm* – which only means that we were going to bring it out ourselves. Orwell was going to pay the printer, using the paper quota to which the Whitman Press was entitled ... We had actually started to do so. I had been down to Bedford with the manuscript to see the printer twice. The birthplace of John Bunyan seemed a happy omen. Orwell had never spoken about the contents. I had not liked to ask as any questions might appear to have an editorial accent. He had, however, talked about adding a preface to it on the freedom of the Press ... That essay on the freedom of the Press was not needed as Secker and Warburg, at the last minute, accepted the book.[37]

The sentimental prose of *Dante Called You Beatrice* raises some of the same problems as Jacintha Buddicom's writing about Orwell's early years: the style has been taken as grounds for doubting the memories and judgements. Mr Potts' book has its moments when fact and fiction blend rather uneasily and the chronology is a bit wobbly; but he knew Orwell well and he is a valuable and important source. The essential truth of Potts' account is shown by his being the only person who had ever heard of or who could remember 'the Freedom of the Press' – a fiery preface to *Animal Farm* which Orwell did in fact write as a blast against self-censorship, but fortunately did not use. It was lost until 1971.[38] People either did not believe Potts or did not notice his claim that there was a lost major essay (reviewers often have to work at such speed).

In the end the much-handled, dog-eared manuscript was sent to
Fred Warburg late in July. The dramatic account Warburg gives in *All
Authors Are Equal* of it coming to him out of the blue, of Orwell turning
up during his lunch one day and dumping the manuscript on him with
an urgent explanation of its contents, is contradicted by Orwell's letter
to Moore in the previous month (already quoted), in which he says that
Warburg knew about it, had not seen it but wanted to publish it.
Probably Orwell came to him, rather shamefacedly, as a last resort. But
Orwell's letter raises a problem. However enthusiastic Warburg may
have been about Orwell, it is unlikely that he would have taken
anything sight unseen. He had already, not surprisingly, turned down
Orwell's 'War-time Diary'. Perhaps Orwell was merely making excuses
to Moore for not wanting to send it directly to Warburg, as would have
seemed to Moore to be less trouble, more sensible and even proper,
from the start. Warburg is, however, amusingly frank about his hesi-
tations once he had read it. Its merits were obvious, but so were the
dangers of being its publisher in wartime. Warburg in his autobiography does not crow over Cape or Faber. He saw the dilemma very
much in their terms but, despite some strong opposition to accepting
the book within his firm, decided to run the risk. Under the rationing
system, however, he was desperately short of paper, as he had already
warned the suspicious Orwell.[39]

The book was over a year in production and it was not published
until August 1945, which was a very long time in those days, especially
for such a short book. Orwell wrote to a provincial Labour journalist,
Frank Barber, on 3 September 1945, 'I have been surprised by the
friendly reception *Animal Farm* has had, after lying in type for about
a year because the publisher dared not bring it out till the war was
over.'[40] And on 19 August he had written in a letter to Herbert Read
that he had stopped writing for *Tribune* while away in France 'and
didn't start again because Bevan was terrified there might be a row over
Animal Farm which might have been embarrassing if the book had
come out before the election, as it was at first intended to'.[41] These
two statements must be taken with a large pinch of salt in the absence
of other evidence. It had not been 'lying in type for about a year', for
Orwell wrote in a letter to T. S. Eliot on 5 September 1944: 'Warburg
is going to do that book you saw but he probably can't get it out until
early next year because of paper.'[42] Letters between Orwell and his

literary agent show that complications about signing the actual contract also dragged on into March 1945. Orwell may well have been laying it on a bit thick about the delay after the difficult experience he had had in getting his masterpiece accepted at all.

For a moment George Orwell seemed to relapse into being Gordon Comstock again and lashed out in all directions. His feeling of being persecuted for plain speaking was heightened by the rejection in March of a review he wrote for the *Manchester Evening News* of Harold Laski's *Faith, Reason and Civilization*. He had agreed with Laski that the Soviet Union, for all its faults, was the 'real dynamo of the Socialist movement', but he had criticized him for closing his eyes to 'purges, liquidations, the dictatorship of a minority, suppression of criticism and so forth'. The editor felt that this was against the national interest. Dwight Macdonald got to hear about it in New York and wrote an editorial in his *Politics* warning 'how seriously the feats of the Red army have misled English public opinion about Russia'.[43]

So Orwell's harsh and bitter comment in the last paragraph of the unused preface is understandable, given the provocation and the circumstances.

I know that the English intelligentsia have plenty of reason for their timidity and dishonesty, indeed I know by heart the arguments by which they justify themselves. But at least let us have no more nonsense about defending liberty against fascism. If liberty means anything at all it means the right to tell people what they do not want to hear. The common people still vaguely subscribe to that doctrine and act on it. In our country ... it is the liberals who fear liberty and the intellectuals who want to do dirt on the intellect; it is to draw attention to that fact that I have written this preface.[44]

As soon as Orwell had finished writing *Animal Farm* in February he began work on a somewhat pot-boiling commission for which he had signed a contract with Collins the previous August, to write a small booklet of 48 pages, *The British People*, in their 'Britain in Pictures' series.[45] By May he had completed it, a fine and characteristic essay, although it was a fairly obvious reworking of the first section on national character of *The Lion and the Unicorn*. (It was not published until August 1947.)

In early June something far more important happened. Eileen had given up her job on 'The Kitchen Front' at the Ministry of Food, and agreed at last, despite feeling run down and perpetually tired, to adopt a baby. Her sister-in-law Gwen, a doctor like her late husband, had found a baby boy for them from the Newcastle area where she had a house. She had sent her own children up there in the care of the old O'Shaughnessy family nurse during the flying bomb raids on London. The baby had been born on 14 May and they named him Richard Horatio Blair when they adopted him in June. Rayner Heppenstall soon obliged by casting his horoscope.[46]

George was delighted with Richard and talked about him endlessly to his friends like any proud parent. He took his turn at getting up at night and changing nappies. His carpentry might not be much good (rickety bookshelves abounded), his cooking was somewhat plain, but he mastered the domestic arts of fatherhood with skill and pleasure. Eileen was plainly willing and able, but less enthusiastic. She did it for George, she told her friends, rather than for herself; and at first conveyed much the same attitude of sardonic and critical affection to Richard that she showed to her husband. But before long the child had won her over, and she accepted him as if her own, warmly, completely and protectively. Her friends soon found that unquestioning baby-worship was required rather than critical sympathy.

Yet if *Tribune* days were, on the whole, happy days and if he was full of joy at being a parent, there was, none the less, some inner tension or sexual frustration in him. He would sometimes go on his own to William and Hetta Empson's Saturday night parties or At Homes at Hampstead. They would ask respectable, distinguished, sometimes unsuspecting literary friends or acquaintances in for a drink or a coffee; but other more bohemian friends meanwhile were drinking in pubs on Haverstock Hill, Rosslyn Hill and Pond Street before surging into the Empsons after closing time, bringing in tow whoever wanted to carry on drinking – pick-ups, drop-outs, strangers and all. The Empsons' warm and hospitable parties were a fine and famous mix of all the diverse social types whose company Orwell enjoyed separately and in small doses but normally kept well apart. One June or July evening, the merest acquaintance from BBC days, who had only come across Orwell before as a rather quiet and melancholy figure in the background at BBC pubs, met him again at the Empsons, sitting on his own in a corner, drinking fairly heavily. When neither was able to get a taxi, Orwell insisted, very much against her inclination, as she was young and was nervous of him, on walking her home and then trying, while crossing the Heath, to make love to her far too persistently, somewhat violently even. To keep him off, she promised to meet him again when next she was in London, but on not keeping the unlikely rendezvous, she received a violent letter of formal reproach, actually trying to make her feel guilty, she said, about the social solecism of breaking an appointment. Certainly his marriage, so firm in most ways, perhaps in what really mattered, had its ups and downs, frustrations and infidelities.

Nothing went easily for the Orwells, even as a household. On 28 June their flat was bombed. One of the 'doodle-bugs' or flying bombs landed nearby and brought down ceilings, windows and roof. It cracked the main walls, rendering the house uninhabitable. Avril had moved in with them not a week before when her own flat was damaged. None of them was injured and they were able to salvage all their possessions, including George's papers and his pamphlet collection. Inez Holden, who was ill at the time and living in the country, lent them her flat at 106 George Street, near Portman Square, a good flat in a pleasant, even fashionable area. They stayed there until they found a place of their own to rent in Islington, at 27b Canonbury Square, but Avril moved back, almost at once, to her damaged flat. What is now a very smart and expensive area of restored late Georgian and early Victorian terraces was then a run-down and seedy part of London even without the effects of the War, a lower-middle-class enclave into working-class territory, a kind of borderland to the East End.

Already some intellectuals and professional people were beginning to move in, attracted by the style of the houses and the easy access to both the City and West End. It was the kind of marginal area Orwell loved. The flat was quite a good flat, with a breakfast room, a small workroom, two bedrooms and a good-sized living-room. But it was on the third floor, making for difficulties with a baby, pram and shopping. Friends liked visiting them there, but thought it a foolishly impractical place to bring up a child. Both the Orwells, however, maintained that as soon as the War was over they would leave London for the country, hopefully before Richard began to walk.

Orwell began to make inquiries. David Astor, whose family owned land on the island of Jura, put him in touch with Margaret Fletcher, one of the other lairds, who had a remote farmhouse to rent called Barnhill – to rent very cheaply, for the main object was to prevent dilapidation rather than to make money. Margaret Fletcher, now Mrs Nelson, thinks that Orwell came up to see them with David Astor late in 1944 and Astor thinks that Orwell went up alone, although there is no other record of any visit then, but certainly Mrs Fletcher was in correspondence with Eileen early in 1945, who did not seem as enthusiastic as her husband to move north. Margaret Fletcher remembered that Eileen impressed her by the sensible questions she asked about what conditions were like and what they would need to bring. So Orwell had planned to move to Jura in Eileen's lifetime and even before he could be sure of the financial success of *Animal Farm*. His 'War-time Diary' entry for 20 June 1940 shows that the general area was long premeditated: 'Thinking always of my island in the Hebrides, which I suppose I shall never possess or see.'[47]

That winter in Canonbury Square many people visited them. Orwell liked playing host. They both looked tired and ill, friends said, but also happy with the baby, with Orwell's writing (despite the difficulties over *Animal Farm*) and his *Tribune* column. Paul Potts describes the ambience:

Nothing could be more pleasant than the sight of his living room in Canonbury Square early on a winter's evening at high tea-time. A huge fire, the table crowded with marvellous things, Gentleman's Relish and various jams, kippers, crumpets and toast. And always the Gentleman's Relish, with its peculiar unique flat jar and the Latin inscription on the label. Next to it usually stood the Cooper's Oxford marmalade pot. He thought in terms of vintage tea and had the same attitude to bubble and squeak as a Frenchman has to Camembert. I'll swear he valued tea and roast beef above the OM and the Nobel Prize.

Then there was the conversation and the company, his wife, some members of his family or hers, a refugee radical or an English writer. There was something very innocent and terribly simple about him. He wasn't a very good judge of character. He was of roast beef, however. He loved being a host, as only civilized men can, who have been very poor. There was nothing bohemian about him at all. However poor he had been it did not make him precarious. But he tolerated in others faults he did not possess himself.[48]

More famous friends were invited to dinner occasionally, but Orwell's real pleasure was high tea. Besides, people tended to stop too long after dinner and he liked to go to bed reasonably early, about eleven o'clock, for he was up and at work by half past six in the morning, pausing for a cooked breakfast later, then writing until midday, on the days when he did not have to go into *Tribune*. On *Tribune* days he worked in the evening, so sometimes people who dropped in would sit talking to Eileen, who would firmly leave her husband unmolested in his study. They would hear the constant pounding of his typewriter as they talked.

He was immensely productive, and just how much so can be quantified for he kept a 'Payment Notebook' of his writings from July 1943 to December 1945. He gave a length to each article listed and they add up to 99,850 words for an income of £597 19s. (which he miscast as £586 4s.), of which a mere £45 represented an advance on *Animal Farm*. During 1944 he wrote one hundred and ten reviews or short articles for the *Manchester Evening News*, *Tribune*, and the *Observer*, not counting many smaller journals.

When in October it was clear that Warburg would publish *Animal Farm*, Orwell began to plan another book of essays, which became his *Critical Essays*, which he completed by January 1945. He reprinted the essays on Dickens and on Boys' Weeklies from *Inside the Whale* (now out of print), together with the best of his *Horizon* essays (on comic postcards, Kipling, Koestler, Wells, Yeats, 'Raffles and Miss Blandish'), and a new essay on Dali and obscenity. From his essay on 'Wells, Hitler and the World State', he was developing in his new essays the theme of the inadequacy of 'mere hedonism', both as an account of good and of bad actions. This theme linked his character with his political ideas. Love of 'power' seemed often a sufficient reason for bad actions – although Orwell wavered, influenced by and yet critical of James Burnham, as to whether régimes based on 'power' for its own sake divorced from ideology were ever possible. Perhaps he never resolved this. Are we meant to think that O'Brien in *Nineteen Eighty-Four* has revealed a secret that the Inner Party stand for nothing except possession of power? Or are we meant to think that such a belief is absurd and part of the 'satire', he was to call it, of the book? But certainly Orwell rejected even the perversion of happiness, which Aldous Huxley in *Brave New World* and Zamyatin in *We* both made the motivating forces, as an adequate account of the new despotisms.

Orwell's critique of hedonism and how it relates to political alternatives appears at its clearest in two paragraphs from his essay on 'Arthur Koestler':

GEORGE ORWELL

To take a rational political decision one must have a picture of the future. At present Koestler seems to have none, or rather to have two which cancel out. As an ultimate objective he believes in the Earthly Paradise, the Sun State which the gladiators set out to establish, and which has haunted the imagination of Socialists, Anarchists and religious heretics for hundreds of years. But his intelligence tells him that the Earthly Paradise is receding into the far distance and that what is actually ahead of us is bloodshed, tyranny and privation. Recently he described himself as a 'short-term pessimist' ... Since about 1930 the world has given no reason for optimism whatever. Nothing is in sight except a welter of lies, hatred, cruelty and ignorance, and beyond our present troubles loom vaster ones which are only now entering into the European consciousness. It is quite possible that man's major problems will *never* be solved. But it is also unthinkable! Who is there who dares to look at the world of today and say to himself, 'it will always be like this: even in a million years it cannot get appreciably better'? So you get the quasi-mystical belief that for the present there is no remedy, all political action is useless but that somewhere in space and time human life will cease to be the miserable brutish thing it now is.

The only easy way out is that of the religious believer, who regards this life merely as a preparation for the next. But few thinking people now believe in life after death ... The real problem is how to restore the religious attitude while accepting death as final. Men can only be happy when they do not assume that the object of life is happiness.[49]

In a letter to a *Tribune* reader Orwell had already set out the character of new regimes that would go beyond mere hedonism.

I think you overestimate the danger of a 'Brave New World' – i.e. a completely materialistic vulgar civilization based on hedonism. I would say that the danger of that kind of thing is past and that we are in danger of quite a different kind of world, the centralized slave state, ruled over by a small clique who are in effect a new ruling class, though they might be adoptive rather than hereditary. Such a state would not be hedonistic, on the contrary its dynamic would come from some kind of rabid nationalism and leader-worship kept going by literally continuous war ... I see no safeguard against this except (a) war-weariness and distaste for authoritarianism which may follow the present war, and (b) the survival of democratic values among the intelligentsia.[50]

Also he linked power and hedonism in a profound essay on pornography and violence, 'Raffles and Miss Blandish' which first appeared in *Horizon* in October 1944. He asked why there is such 'an immense difference in moral atmosphere' between the two books.

468

Raffles, the gentleman crook, has no religious beliefs, but he still observes the rules of a traditional code of decency and behaviour. But in the (then) semi-pornographic crime novel *No Orchids for Miss Blandish* not merely have these taboos vanished, but the author openly seeks to attract the readers by violence, cruelty and sexual sadism. Orwell argued a direct connection between pornography and power worship:

The interconnection between sadism, masochism, success worship, power worship, nationalism and totalitarianism is a huge subject whose edges have barely been scratched, and even to mention it is considered somewhat indelicate ... Fascism is often loosely equated with sadism, but nearly always by people who see nothing wrong in the most slavish worship of Stalin. The truth is, of course, that the countless English intellectuals who kiss the arse of Stalin are not different from the minority who give their allegiance to Hitler or Mussolini, nor from the efficiency experts who preached 'punch', 'drive', 'personality' and 'learn to be a Tiger man' in the nineteen-twenties, nor from the older generation of intellectuals, Carlyle, Creasy and the rest of them, who bowed down before German militarism. All of them are worshipping power and successful cruelty. It is important to notice that the cult of power tends to be mixed up with a love of cruelty and wickedness *for their own sakes*.[51]

He further added that 'the common people, on the whole, are still living in the world of absolute good and evil from which the intellectuals have long since escaped.' (Two more of the themes of *Nineteen Eighty-Four* are clearly set out.)

As so often the critique is clearer than the remedy. Did he really imagine that 'the traditional code' of the world of Raffles embodied ideas of 'absolute good and evil' that could be specified and universalized? Gentlemen have ever been relativists in their morals. But he opened up a speculation which was, indeed, then and now, 'considered somewhat indelicate'. He made much the same point about the art of Salvador Dali.

If you say that Dali, though a brilliant draughtsman, is a dirty little scoundrel, you are looked upon as a savage. If you say that you don't like rotting corpses, and that people who do like rotting corpses are diseased, it is assumed that you lack aesthetic sense ...

One ought to be able to hold in one's head simultaneously the two facts that Dali is a good draughtsman and a disgusting human being. The one does not invalidate or, in a sense, affect the other. The first thing we demand of a wall is that it shall stand up. If it stands up, it is a good wall, and the question of what purpose it serves is separable from that. And yet even the best wall in the world deserves to be pulled down if it surrounds a concentration camp.[52]

Another essay of this time not merely shows his belief that political liberty and simplicity of language are closely linked, but that common sense can actually be discovered as well as asserted. In 'Propaganda and Demotic Speech' he wrote:

The whole idea of trying to find out what the average man thinks, instead of assuming that he thinks what he ought to think, is novel and unwelcome. Social surveys are viciously attacked from Left and Right alike. Yet some mechanism for testing public opinion is an obvious necessity of modern government and more so in a democratic country than in a totalitarian one. Its complement is the ability to speak to the ordinary man in words that he will understand and respond to.[53]

Even when Orwell was talking of giving up his literary editorship anyway to give more time to his own writing and even with the end of the War in sight, he felt his old desire growing to be somehow in the thick of the action. David Astor asked him to act as a war correspondent for the *Observer* to cover the liberation of France and the early occupation of Germany. Despite his writing, the new novel he was now actively planning, despite Eileen and the child, despite his health and her health, he leaped at the chance of getting out of England and seeing the last phase of the war. The moral problems of vengeance in liberated France and of how to treat the Germans would obviously fascinate him; and Astor was shrewd enough to hope that he would get no ordinary, descriptive reportage from Orwell. If the Allies behaved in a meaningless, brutal way that would preclude re-education and reconciliation, who better than Orwell to sound the alarm? So Orwell gave up the *Tribune* job, but not *Tribune*: he wrote almost as regularly and as much in the next two years as he had in the period when he was Literary Editor. He must have loved the journal very much for it always paid badly and sometimes not at all.

On 15 March 1945 Orwell, however, at last set off to catch up with the War. He was dressed in the officer's uniform of a war correspondent, carried his typewriter and a single large suitcase. This time the requirement of an Army medical seems to have been overlooked or waived. He used the Hotel Scribe in Paris as his base, until in the fourth week of March he went off to Cologne. The Hotel Scribe was packed full of war correspondents, most of whom he found very boring. All but one – as Paul Potts remembers Orwell telling him:

To his delight he found Hemingway's name. He had never met him. He went up to his room and knocked. When told to come in, he opened the door, stood on the threshold and said 'I'm Eric Blair'. Hemingway, who was standing on the other side of the bed, on which there were two suitcases, was packing, and what he saw was another War Correspondent and a British one at that, so he bellowed, 'Well what the ying hell do you want?' Orwell shyly replied 'I'm George Orwell'. Hemingway pushed the suitcases to the end of the bed, bent down and brought a bottle of Scotch from underneath it and still bellowing said 'Why the zing hell didn't you say so. Have a drink. Have a double. Straight or with water, there's no soda'.[54]

Equally oddly, he met the philosopher A. J. Ayer in the same hotel. Ayer did not really know who Orwell was, nor Orwell Ayer, but they took to each other, finding they shared an admiration of Dickens, Kipling and Hopkins – a somewhat odd trio.

'His moral integrity made him hard upon himself and sometimes harsh in his judgement of other people', wrote Ayer, 'but he was no enemy to pleasure. He appreciated good food and drink, enjoyed gossip, and when not oppressed by ill health was very good company. He was another of those whose liking for me made me think better of myself.'[55] Ayer noted that Orwell had no interest whatever in philosophy and Orwell seemed to indicate that it would be better for Ayer to interest himself in the future of humanity. They discovered that they had both been to Eton and had had Gow as tutor. In 1946 they met quite often in the company of their mutual friends, Humphrey Slater and Celia Kirwan. Here were two vastly different men of near genius who each recognized the quality in the other without being quite sure what it was. Another conjunction of different worlds was a lunch with P. G. Wodehouse, on his uppers and fearing prosecution for a wickedly silly wartime broadcast from occupied France that the Germans had flattered him into making. Orwell reassured him that he was an idiot and defended him vigorously in print.[56]

From Paris Orwell conducted last-minute correspondence about the proofs of *Animal Farm*: he instructed Roger Senhouse, Warburg's partner, to change, when the windmill that the animals have so laboriously built blows up, 'all the animals including Napoleon flung themselves on their faces' to 'all the animals except Napoleon'. Orwell's sense of fairness extended even to Stalin who had, he told Senhouse, stayed in Moscow during the German advance.

His dispatches to the *Observer* must however, have disappointed David Astor. Before going on to Cologne, he had sent three stories from Paris (3, 10, and 17 March), all rather cramped and uneasy mixtures of reporting and moral speculation. In Cologne on 24 March he wrote a thoughtful and worried dispatch on 'Creating Order Out of Cologne Chaos', about the problems of physical reconstruction while dealing with the political uncertainty of how to treat the Germans. Then Orwell was taken ill. It is not clear what happened, whether it was bronchitis, pneumonia again, or another haemorrhage of the lung. He was ill enough to draw up 'Notes for My Literary Executor', making clear what he wanted republished and what he did not. He rejected *A Clergyman's Daughter* and *Keep the Aspidistra Flying*, which he called 'silly pot-boilers' and said that he had already refused Penguin permission to reprint the latter. He dated the memorandum 31 March 1945 and sent it back to Eileen for her to have witnessed and to retain.[57] The name of the O'Shaughnessy family nurse, Joyce Pritchard, appears as a witness. She was with Eileen at Gwen O'Shaughnessy's house in Newcastle, where Eileen had taken baby Richard shortly after George left for France. His letter and the memo would have crossed two letters from Eileen – had hers ever been posted.

CHAPTER FIFTEEN

FAMOUS AND SOLITARY MAN

(1945–6)

INSTEAD of the letters from Eileen, he received a wire from the *Observer* saying that she was dead. She had died on 29 March in Newcastle, under anaesthetic during what he told his friends was a routine operation. He doped himself heavily with M & B tablets (generally used against heavy infection before penicillin became widespread), discharged himself from the hospital in Cologne and returned to London. Shivering and haggard, wrapped in an army greatcoat, he was on Inez Holden's doorstep in George Street while she was still trying to find out how to send him the news. He must have got a lift in a military aircraft, he was in England so quickly. He went straight on up to Stockton-on-Tees, and he found an unfinished letter from Eileen.

Fernwood House
Clayton Road
Newcastle-on-Tyne
29.3.45 ·

Dearest I'm just going to have the operation, already enema'd, injected (with morphia in the *right* arm, which is a nuisance), cleaned and packed up like precious image in cotton wool and bandages. When it's over I'll add a note to this and it can get off quickly. Judging by my fellow patients it will be a *short* note. They've all had their operations – annoying, I shall never have a chance to feel superior. I haven't seen Harvey Evers [the surgeon] since his arrival, apparently Gwen didn't communicate with him and no one knows what operation I am having! They don't believe that Harvey Evers really left it to me to decide as he always 'does what he thinks best'. He will of course. But I must say that I feel irritated to be thought of as a *model* patient. They think I'm wonderful, so placid and happy they say. As indeed I am once I can hand myself over to someone to deal with.

473

This is a nice room – quite low so one can see the garden. Not much in it except daffodils and some crocus but a nice little lawn. My bed isn't next the window but it faces the right way. I also see the fire the clock

Time had run out, they had come to fetch her.[1]

He was back in London four days later, after the funeral. Some people he met that week were disconcerted at his stoic calm. 'You know my wife has died,' he said; even, it is claimed, 'Such a shame, she was a good old stick,' almost as if he were talking about someone else. All he said to Julian Symons was 'My wife died last week. She was going to have a minor operation. She died while having it.' But Geoffrey Gorer and Paul Potts assert that with each of them he mourned openly and bitterly; and Lydia Jackson and Inez Holden each say that for a brief private moment his tears could not be checked. Gorer claims that he told him that her death was especially tragic because she was sure that she was going to have a baby of her own. If indeed he said so, he must have shared the common belief that barren women who adopt a child often soon conceive; and his own sad suspicion that he was sterile must have been shaken. That week Potts heard him call two women by Eileen's name. Theirs was 'a real marriage', wrote Potts, 'not perfect. But nothing except her death, that came so suddenly and too early, would have broken it up.'[2]

Those who thought Orwell unmoved were indeed friends, but by being office or literary friends, camaraderie and first names at midday and at six o'clock in pubs, they were not likely to pierce the reserve of such a man. Yet domestic friends may sometimes claim too much: it is hard to tell in such grievous matters.

Orwell gave the news to Anthony Powell in a letter thus:

I tried to get in touch with you when I was in London last week, but failed. I don't know whether you will have heard from some other source what has happened. Eileen is dead. She died very suddenly and unexpectedly on March 29th during an operation which was not supposed to be very serious. I was over here and had no expectation of anything going wrong, which indeed nobody seems to have had. I didn't see the final findings of the inquest and indeed don't want to, because it doesn't bring her back, but I think the anaesthetic was responsible. It was a most horrible thing to happen because she had had five really miserable years of bad health and overwork, and things were just beginning to get better. The only good thing is that I don't think she can have suffered or had any apprehensions. She was actually looking forward to the operation to cure her trouble, and I found among her papers a letter she must have written only about an hour before she died and which she expected to finish when she came round . . .[3]

He appears to have given everyone he met much the same account, for instance in a letter three months later: 'very suddenly and unexpectedly . . . [an] operation which should not have been very serious in itself . . . No one had anticipated anything going wrong';[4] and to his old Spanish comrade, Stafford Cottman, a year later: 'The only good thing was that I don't think she expected anything to go wrong with the operation. She died as a result of the anaesthetic . . . I was in France at the time, as neither of us had expected the operation to be very serious.'[5] Only to Lydia Jackson did he say a little more – in a letter on 1 April from Stockton-on-Tees, thus the very day he reached the North:

I do not know if you will have heard from anyone else the very bad news. Eileen is dead. As you know she had been ill for some time past and it was finally diagnosed that she had a growth which must be removed. The operation was not supposed to be a very serious one, but she seems to have died as soon as she was given the anaesthetic and, apparently, as a result of the anaesthetic . . . It was a dreadful shock and a very cruel thing to happen, because she had become so devoted to Richard and was looking forward to living a normal life in the country again as soon as the war was over. The only consolation is that I don't think she suffered, because she went to the operation, apparently, not expecting anything to go wrong, and never recovered consciousness.[6]

He was using Eileen's typewriter.

Orwell told no one else about 'the growth which must be removed', and Eileen had not told him. Perhaps it was just a decent privacy about the ugly facts of death. But it is more likely that he did not want to admit, even to himself, that there had been a disagreement between them about whether or not she was to have a hysterectomy, also about the cost of it all, which might have delayed her seeking specialist advice. When she finally wrote to tell him that she was having the hysterectomy she had said, 'yesterday I had a phase of thinking that it was really outrageous to spend your money on an operation of which I know you do not approve'.[7] Perhaps also, looking back on it, he felt guilty, or ashamed at his obtuseness in ignoring or misinterpreting certain obvious symptoms. Even before he went away he must have known that the operation was likely to be more serious than he gave Powell to believe. Perhaps he really did not read, as he told Powell, 'the final findings of the inquest': 'Cardiac failure whilst under anaesthetic of ether and chloroform skilfully and properly administered for operation for removal of uterus.' Joyce Pritchard, the O'Shaughnessy family nurse, never doubted that the operation was for cancer.[8] Eileen, however, had also given differing accounts of the need for the operation to her friends. Lydia Jackson had understood only that a small operation was needed to restore the balance of red to white corpuscles because of her anaemia.[9] At first Eileen told Lettice Cooper that she had gone North, on Gwen's advice, to rest and prepare herself for a hysterectomy, but then she wrote to her more fully:

... I went to see a Newcastle surgeon because as Richard's adoption was through I thought I might now deal with the growth (no one could object to a growth) I knew I had. He found it or rather them without any difficulty and I'm going into his nursing home next week for the removal. I think the question about the hysterectomy is answered because there is hardly any chance that the tumours can come out without more or less everything else removable. So that on the whole is a very good thing. It was worth coming to the north country because there is to be none of the fattening up in hospital before the operation that I was to have in London. London surgeons love preparing their patients against unknown consequences. I think they're all terrified of their knives really ... In London they said I couldn't have any kind of operation without a preparatory month of blood transfusions etc., here I'm going in next Wednesday to be done on Thursday. Apart from its other advantages, this will save money, a lot of money. And that is as well ...[10]

Both women knew, and he must have done, that she had long suffered from persistent bleedings, fatigue and internal pains. Yet it would have been in character with them both and in accordance with the conventions of the time if they had never fully discussed together the fuller implications of her symptoms; and even as to the simple hysterectomy, she may only have known that he disapproved, still hoping for a child of their own; he may not actually have said so.

Eileen had, however, also written a long, long letter to him earlier in the last week of her life (though it is not certain that he ever read it). She also wrote letters to friends and made her will which was witnessed by the nurse and the housekeeper. In that long letter, even sadder in its way than the short, unfinished one, she admitted to him for the first time quite explicitly, though obviously she still had some hope of surviving, what it was that she had known or suspected for a long time.

The first page of the letter, typed, she said, on a warm spring day in the garden at Greystones while Richard sat up in his pram, was amusing, light and wholly unworrying, all about Richard and his progress, telling a tale of how the husband of the housekeeper's predecessor had, with incredible incompetence, shot himself at a pigeon shoot. 'This convinced me not that Richard must never have a gun but that he must have one very young so that he couldn't forget how to handle it' – almost as Jacintha's Aunt Lilian had once reassured Mrs Blair about the young Eric; and as if shooting was still to be part of the education of a member of the 'lower-upper-middle class' which, as Orwell had once patiently explained, meant 'the upper-middle class without money'. But the second and third pages of her letter, though embedded in friendly chat, had more matter in them:

Gwen rang up Harvey Evers and they want me to go in for this operation at once. This is all a bit difficult. It is going to cost a terrible lot of money. A bed in a kind of ward costs seven guineas a week and Harvey Evers' operation fee is forty guineas. In London I would have to pay about five guineas a week in a hospital but Gwen says the surgeon's fee would be higher. The absurd thing is that we are too well off for really cheap rates – you'd have to make less than £500 a year. It comes as a shock to me in a way because while you were being ill I got used to paying doctors nothing. But of course it was only because Eric [her brother] was making the arrangements. I suppose your bronchoscopy would have cost about forty guineas too – and I must say it would have been cheap at the price, but what worries me is that I really don't think I'm worth the money. On the other hand of course this thing will take a longish time to kill me if left alone and it will be costing some money the whole time ... Anyway, I don't know what I can do except go ahead and get the thing done quickly. The idea is that I should go in next week and I gather he means to operate quickly – he thinks the indications are urgent enough to offset the disadvantages of operating on a bloodless patient; indeed he is quite clear that no treatment at all can prevent me from becoming considerably more bloodless every month. So I suppose they'll just do a blood transfusion and operate more or less at once.

So far two things are clear: that they both knew that she was in for a serious operation (if simply for removal of fibroids, 'routine'; but with her anaemia, 'serious'); and that Orwell did not know that it might be critical. Her letter continued with an account of a rash and quick visit she had paid to London the previous week – nominally to see Gwen and also George Mason, a consultant who had been a close friend of her brother's; and to deliver a corrected manuscript of Evelyn Anderson's to *Tribune*; but also, quite obviously, to see her close friends once more, just in case the worst should happen. On this rash visit she collapsed with pain. She related all this in the letter, except for her collapse, but then went on:

One very good thing is that by the time you get home I'll be convalescent at last and you won't have the hospital nightmare you would so much dislike. You'd more or less have to visit me and visiting someone in a ward really is a nightmare even to me with my fancy for hospitals – particularly if they're badly ill as I shall be at first of course. I only wish I could have had your approval as it were, but I think it's just hysterical. Obviously I can't just go on having a tumour or rather several rapidly growing tumours. I *have* got an uneasy feeling that after all the job might have been more cheaply done somewhere else but if you remember Miss Kenny's fee for a cautery, which is a small job, was fifteen guineas so she'd certainly charge at least fifty for this. Gwen's man might have done cheaper work for old sake's sake, but he's so very bad at the work and apparently he would have wanted me in hospital for weeks beforehand – and I'm morally sure I'd be there for weeks afterwards. Harvey Evers has a very high reputation, and George Mason thinks very well of him and says Eric did the same, and I am sure that he will finish me off as quickly as anyone in England as well as doing the job properly – so he may well come cheaper in the end. I rather wish I'd talked it over with you before you went. I knew I had a 'growth'. But I wanted you to go away peacefully anyway, and I did *not* want to see Harvey Evers before the adoption was through in case it was cancer. I thought it just possible that the judge might make some enquiry about our health as we're old for parenthood and anyway it would have been an uneasy sort of thing to be producing oneself as an ideal parent a fortnight after being told that one couldn't live more than six months or something.[11]

So she had feared cancer for a long time, even before Richard's adoption, but had not told George – 'I wanted you to go away peacefully'. She had hoped to recover but had rationally prepared for death. She clearly hoped to recover because most of the letter was a practical account of negotiations, left in her hands, either to take Mrs Fletcher's property at Barnhill on Jura, depending on the rent and the cost of repairs, or to find somewhere else in the country; and if that fell through, perhaps to ask Lydia Jackson to give Wallington up and to go back there temporarily, however small it was for the three of them.

She thought it 'essential that you should write some book again' and stop 'editing', 'do much less reviewing and nothing but specialized reviewing if any'; and to 'get into the country'. She asked him to take seriously how much she hated life in London – 'I don't think you understand what a nightmare the London life is to me'; she was 'now so confident of being strong in a few months that I'm not actually frightened as I should have been of living a primitive life again'; and he needed peace and quiet for real writing and she 'can't breathe the air' and 'can't read poetry in London'.

Eileen thus tried very hard and selflessly not to make her husband feel guilty at having gone adventuring and having left her at such a time – whatever was to happen. He did not know that her condition was critical but it was imperceptive not to have seen, long before he went away, that Eileen's health was in a serious condition. This would remain true even if, as is just possible, he never received this letter – that it was compassionately concealed from him in his lifetime and only added to his papers after his own death. No one remembers. Gwen cleared up Eileen's personal possessions, not George. If this is so, he did not deceive his friends, but he had deceived himself to an extraordinary degree.

Eileen's letter shows how strongly he must have pressed her to adopt a child. Did he simply close his eyes to the possible dangers to her health? Certainly with a great writer the writing comes first. One thinks of Thomas Hardy, subtle in his characters but obtuse to the actual suffering of his first wife. Hardy sat in his study and wrote, but for Orwell *Tribune* had only been a part-time job. Playing at war correspondent was hard on Eileen, dangerous to his own health and no ascertainable help to his writing. Having had a clear plan of 'The Last Man in Europe' or 'Nineteen Eighty-Four' in a notebook since late in 1943 and since all the essential ideas in it were already crystallized, to visit France and Germany (unlike Burma, Spain and the North of England in relation to his other books) added or created nothing. If he had hoped that it would, no sign remains either in his correspondence or in the text of *Nineteen Eighty-Four*.

She did not wish him to feel guilty. But could he have been so blind to what she could not conceal, even when trying to: how much his continued worries about money were needlessly worrying her too? Yet to be fair it is difficult now to recall, quite simply, how acute and obsessive were worries about the cost of bad illness among the middle classes in Britain before the National Health Service.

So guilt must have mingled with grief. George and Eileen were, of course, much alike both in not finding it easy to talk about personal things and in neglecting themselves; but while Eileen could see George's needs, he was less perceptive about hers. Her friends did not blame him strongly. They recognized that both of them were as they were, and that Eileen had gone into the marriage with her eyes open from the very beginning. Long afterwards they were sad that both of the Orwells could have lived longer had they not neglected themselves. Perhaps too, though the ground is delicate and speculative, Eileen's known symptoms, growths in the uterus, bleeding and fatigue, may account in part for his infidelities in the last few years of the war. Some of her friends knew of these and suspected that she did too, and one of them was, indeed, herself involved – disturbed but not always able to resist his repeated importunities. A year after Eileen's death he wrote to a woman to whom he had proposed:

I don't much care who sleeps with whom, it seems to me what matters is being faithful in an emotional and intellectual sense. I was sometimes unfaithful to Eileen, and I also treated her very badly, and I think she treated me badly too at times, but it was a real marriage in the sense that we had been through awful struggles together and she understood all about my work, etc.

After making temporary arrangements for Richard, Orwell went back to Europe. 'I felt so upset at home,' he said in a letter to Powell, 'I thought I would rather be on the move for a bit.' So a week in Paris, two weeks in south Germany, based on Nuremberg, then Stuttgart, another week in Paris, then to Austria before returning home at the end of May. He sent weekly dispatches to the *Observer* and some to the *Manchester Evening News*. It was all good descriptive writing, evoking what it all looked like in Germany and Austria, the pathos and chaos of ruined cities and a countryside still full of a surrendered army. But, again, not distinctively Orwell. Reporting and essay writing are different things. It is odd that the papers used him on the news pages rather than for less frequent but longer feature articles. He did the job well enough, indeed did not intrude his own personality – as was the whole game of 'As I Please' – but the net result was a column which, while professionally written, could have been done equally well by many others. He earned his salt but he did not shine.

There is a curious lack of letters to any of his friends while in France and Germany and none of them can remember him talking about the time. One could suspect either that he was in a deep depression or somehow felt for once a fish out of water, in an artificial position, somehow unable adequately to relate to the great events and the ghastly devastation. It is puzzling.

He returned to England in time to cover the General Election campaign in London constituencies, contributing the leading political story on 24 June and 1 July – 'a fortnight of electioneering, in which most of my waking hours were spent in the streets or in pubs, buses, and tea-shops, with my ears pricked all the time'. He made no attempt to interview leading politicians and candidates nor to accept or relay their generalities about 'what the public is really thinking' – as is customary on these occasions. But alas, this solitary and deliberate attempt at 'Mass Observation', for he had followed closely such attempts to discover 'public opinion', failed: 'I only twice overheard a spontaneous comment on the election'.[12] The humour of this bathos was clearly unintentional.

More lively was the *Observer* Profile of Aneurin Bevan which he wrote anonymously. The characteristic which he admired came across clearly:

He is more of an extremist and more of an internationalist than the average Labour M.P., and it is the combination of this with his working-class origin that makes him an interesting and unusual figure ... Bevan thinks and feels as a working man. He knows how the scales are weighted against anyone with less than £5 a week ... But he is remarkably free – some of his adversaries would say dangerously free – from any feeling of personal grievance against society. He shows no sign of ordinary class consciousness. He seems equally at home in all kinds of company. It is difficult to imagine anyone less impressed by social status or less inclined to put on airs with subordinates ... He has the temperament that used to be called 'mercurial' – a temperament capable of sudden low spirits but not of settled pessimism. His boisterous manner sometimes gives casual observers the impression that he is not serious and his warmest admirers do not claim that punctuality is his strong point. But in fact he has a huge capacity for work ... He does not have the suspicion of 'cleverness' and anaesthesia to the arts which are generally regarded as the mark of a practical man. Those who have worked with him in a journalistic capacity have remarked with pleasure and astonishment that here at last is a politician who knows that literature exists and will even hold up work for five minutes to discuss a point of style.[13]

Bevan was the one politician whom Orwell thoroughly respected, partially identified with and whose ear he would like to have had.

That was the last of his 'special assignments'. Perhaps Eileen's death and Richard's needs shocked him into a sense of priorities. He settled down to a fortnightly long review for the *Observer*, a weekly review in the *Manchester Evening News* (among his most thoughtful), and also wrote weekly in *Tribune*, sometimes a book page, sometimes an essay (such as 'The Sporting Spirit' or 'Decline of the English Murder', again among some of his finest writing); and in November 1946 he took over his old 'As I Please' column from Jennie Lee until the following April. He kept himself very busy. His writing flowed as easily and as well as before, with what E. M. Forster was to call 'his peculiar mixture of gaiety and grimness'; but some of his old friends saw something terrible in the pace at which he drove himself. Again, economic as well as psychological reasons are obvious: he needed to employ a house-keeper-cum-nurse for Richard. His friends expected him to give Richard up, but he clung to him tenaciously and lovingly, doing all that needed to be done when temporary arrangements broke down. There could be, however, a more radical solution to the problem of looking after Richard.

Partly for economic and 'rational' reasons, partly from loneliness and inward grief, he began to propose to women he knew or met. Within little more than a year of Eileen's death he had proposed to at least four women, possibly more, and had been gently rejected. They were all considerably younger than he was. That winter he began to see more of Sonia Brownell. She was a friend of artists and literary men, had been painted by William Coldstream, had worked for John Lehmann on *New Writing* before joining Cyril Connolly on *Horizon*: very beautiful and sought after, very self-contained and 'enigmatic', it was said, yet full of energy and, wrote Lehmann, 'her daring, gay, cynical intelligence and insatiable appetite for knowing everything that went on in the literary world: her revolt against a convent upbringing seemed to provide her life in those days with a kind of inexhaustible rocket fuel'.[14] Sonia Brownell had learned from Connolly and shared many of his attitudes to literature, a world remote from that of Orwell's *Tribune* friends (few moved, as he did, so easily between both worlds). They were both strong characters with strong commitments of a very different, but complementary, kind. Someone remembers them in the

Canonbury flat both talking rapidly and excitedly about different things, almost comically across each other, but plainly stimulating each other. What did she see in him – beyond the books and the *Horizon* essays which she had edited? He had honesty, straightforwardness, sincerity and – in her circle – a rare practicality. She said that he was the only intellectual she knew who could mend a fuse or an iron. What did he see in her? Probably youth, beauty, the life force, intelligence. They had a brief affair; but when he proposed to her, she turned him down, gently, saying that though she was very fond of him, she did not love him.

He had accepted an invitation to spend Christmas 1945 and the New Year of 1946 with Arthur and Mamaine Koestler, who had taken a farm house near Blaenau Ffestiniog in Merionethshire not far from Bertrand Russell. They had also invited Mamaine's twin sister Celia Kirwan, then separated from her husband and seeking a divorce. Celia and Mamaine (*née* Paget) were identical twins, then 29 years old, very beautiful, intelligent ladies. Orwell had not met Celia before, even though she was a first cousin of Inez Holden and was then working as editorial assistant on *Polemic*, a magazine dealing with contemporary thought, and edited by Humphrey Slater, to which he had already contributed. They met on the platform, he carrying Richard on one arm while grasping an old and bulging suitcase with the other. They travelled down together, sitting opposite each other. They must have looked a strange sight together: he so shaggy, she so elegant. Celia recounts that she was immediately very strongly drawn to him and sensed that there was something wonderful about him. Later she recalled his own words in the first pages of *Homage to Catalonia*: 'Queer the affection you can feel for a stranger!'

There were long walks and talks that Christmas. Orwell would carry Richard along on his hip and Celia noticed how competently he coped with the little boy, bathing and changing him as if to the manner born, relaxed and unanxious about him – practical abilities very unusual in fathers of his generation. Thinking of wise old Benjamin in *Animal Farm*, she and Mamaine used to refer to him as Donkey George. Koestler observed his growing friendship with Celia with precipitate pleasure. How marvellous it would be to have as brother-in-law the very Englishman he most liked and respected, the first writer he had sought to meet when he reached England. Celia, however, had a mind of her own and did not see her brother-in-law's passion for coincidences as a sufficient ground for marriage. She thought Orwell attractive, however, for his character and personal qualities, though he was not what is usually considered 'an attractive man', as he himself was aware: when Arthur, Mamaine and he were discussing the attributes they would most like to have, he said, 'I should like to be irresistible to women'.

They saw quite a lot of each other when they returned to London and Celia's affection and sympathy for him increased. 'I had a very deep and special feeling for George', she wrote later. 'If I call it love (as I do) it might give the impression that I was in love with him, but it was just because I wasn't that I didn't agree to marry him or to have an affair with him.' She was glad that he wanted none the less to go on seeing her often, and they remained friends until his death (she telephoned him on the day he died to arrange a visit). When asking her to marry him, he stressed his disadvantages: that he was in poor health with what he called his bronchiectasis; that he was fifteen years older than her; that she might be a widow in ten years' time, at the difficult age of 39; and that he believed himself to be sterile. He did not mention the possible advantages of being the widow of a now distinguished and successful author. Celia found no trace of self-pity in his remarkable proposals, only decency, honesty and a touching altruism, all of a piece with his natural qualities.[15]

A somewhat different state of mind comes out in an almost similar proposal he made to someone on first meeting her, some time in March 1946. Anne Popham shared a flat in the same building as Orwell with a friend who had met him through Connolly, and they asked him to dinner, together with V. S. Pritchett – a successful reunion for the men, although the women felt rather left out of things. Anne Popham was somewhat in awe of him as already an almost legendary character, so she spoke little. She was returning to Germany with the Control Commission, but on the last morning of her leave, the morning after the dinner-party, ran into George on the stairs. He asked what she was doing and she told him. An hour or so later, she found a typewritten note, asking if she could look in perhaps at teatime as there was something he wanted to say to her. She went up apprehensively, they had tea together with Richard and Susan Watson, the housekeeper, who were then dismissed. He immediately asked her to sit beside him on the bed, said that he was very attracted to her, kissed her and asked if she would consider marrying him. Touched and flattered, though embarrassed and a little shocked by his dispassionate precipitancy, she disengaged herself, and after a little polite if tense conversation about Richard and about her life in Germany, he asked if he might write to her, and she left. Ten days later, he wrote her a good letter, long and chatty, telling of his own activities and Richard's ebullience; and then:

I wonder if you were angry or surprised when I sort of made advances to you that night before you went away. You don't have to respond – what I mean is, I wouldn't be angry if you didn't respond. I didn't know till you told me about your young man [who was killed in the RAF]. I thought you looked lonely and unhappy, and I thought it just conceivable you might come to take an interest in me, partly because I imagined you were a little older than you are ... There isn't really anything left in my life except my work and seeing that Richard gets a good start. It is only that I feel so desperately alone sometimes ... Of course it's absurd a person like me wanting to make love to someone of your age. I do want to, but, if you understand, I wouldn't be offended or even hurt if you simply say no. Anyway, write and tell me what you feel.

She replied negatively, if confusedly, not wishing to hurt him; and after a while received another letter, similar but perhaps even more sad and revealing:

I wonder if I committed a sort of crime in approaching you. In a way it's scandalous that a person like me should make advances to a person like you, and yet I thought from your appearance that you were not only lonely and unhappy, but also a person who lived chiefly through the intellect and might become interested in a man who was much older and not much good physically. You asked me what attracted me to you in the first place. You are very beautiful, as no doubt you well know, but that wasn't quite all. I do so want someone who will share what is left of my life, and my work. It isn't so much a question of someone to sleep with, though of course I want that too, sometimes. You say you wouldn't be likely to love me. I don't see how you could be expected to. You are young and fresh and you have had someone you really loved and who would set up a standard I couldn't compete with. If you still feel you can start again and you want a handsome young man who can give you a lot of children, then I am no good to you. What I am really asking you is whether you would like to be the widow of a literary man. If things remain more or less as they are there is a certain amount of fun in this, as you would probably get royalties coming in and you might find it interesting to edit unpublished stuff etc. Of course there is no knowing how long I shall live, but I am supposed to be a 'bad life'. I have a disease called bronchiectasis which is always liable to develop into pneumonia, and also an old 'non-progressive' tuberculous lesion in one lung, and several times in the past I have been supposed to be about to die, but I always lived on just to spite them, and I have actually been better in health since M and B. I am also sterile I think – at any rate I have never had a child, though I have never undergone the examination because it is so disgusting. On the other hand if you wanted children of your own by someone else it wouldn't bother me, because I have very little physical jealousy.

You are young and healthy, and you deserve somebody better than me: on the other hand if you don't find such a person, and if you think of yourself as essentially a widow, then you might do worse – i.e. supposing I am not actually disgusting to you. If I can live another ten years I think I have another three worthwhile books in me, besides a lot of odds and ends, but I want peace and quiet and somebody to be fond of me. There is also Richard. I don't know what your feelings are about him. You might think all this over. I have spoken plainly to you because I feel you are an exceptional person.[16]

Here he seems to have crossed the divide between self-knowledge and self-pity. (Indeed, the mixture of self-pity and of trying to make the reader feel guilty is reminiscent of and is a lapse back to some much earlier letters to Eleanor Jaques and Brenda Salkeld.) What he wanted was, of course, all very sensible, a mother for Richard and for himself a mistress, housekeeper, nurse, and a literary executor, with the compensation for his wife, if he did live longer than might be the case, that she would inherit a good income, since *Animal Farm* was published and already showing clear signs of becoming a best seller. This was all very rational of him, and in those days some plain, literary lass might have seen it as a proper mission in life to take on George and his Richard; but it was hardly the way to woo beautiful and emancipated women. His persistence shows, though his fine and even his comic writings flowed on, how deeply distraught, inwardly unwrought, he was by Eileen's death; but perhaps the lack of passion in half-businesslike half-kindly wooings also speaks of some guilt towards her. It could also point to some lack of perceptiveness on his part towards women.

Animal Farm was finally published on 17 August 1945. The first impression of only 4,500 copies soon sold out (Warburg must have been very short of paper, unless he was less certain about it than he later believed). Not until November could a second impression, now of 10,000 copies, appear – from which time it has never stopped reprinting.[17]

Neither Moore, Orwell's agent, nor Warburg had succeeded in finding an American publisher before publication. Even by the end of the year after publication, according to Warburg, 'twelve or more American publishers ... had rejected it, including such top firms as Harper, Knopf, Viking and Scribner' – some on the grounds that it was too small to publish on its own, but others, presumably, on political grounds.* It happened, however, that Frank Morley, who had been with Faber before the War and had joined Harcourt Brace in New York, had come to Britain as soon as he could at the end of the War to see what readers were currently interested in. He asked to serve for a week or so in Bowes and Bowes, the Cambridge bookshop. On his first day there customers kept asking for a book that had sold out – the second impression of *Animal Farm*. He left the counter, read the single copy left in the postal orders' department, left for London and bought the American rights. 'Which American publisher is it?' bellowed the deaf Moore down the phone to Warburg in Morley's hearing: 'All the best ones have turned it down.' On his return to New York he was met by a far from enthusiastic reception from the head of his firm who was worried that most people would not get the point, and also worried that some people would. But he changed his mind when it was selected by

* Could there really have been time for 'twelve or more' rejections? But certainly there were a lot. Arthur Schlesinger, Jr, remembers bringing a copy enthusiastically from London to Angus Cameron, the senior Little, Brown editor who turned it down flat on political grounds. Dwight Macdonald in *Politics* and Philip Rahv in *Partisan Review* blamed 'Stalinism' – as did Orwell.

Certainly there was some Fellow-Travelling amongst American publishers, more than liberals liked to admit in the McCarthy era. But also many would have still been under the spell of wartime solidarity; and also suspicious that any British author attacking the USSR was really defending the Empire. Also had '*we*' not dropped the atom bomb? America was more polarized than Great Britain: the fierce anti-Communism of 'middle America' drove many intellectuals to the other extreme – though 'Stalinist' and anti-Stalinist socialists hated each other almost as much. More subtly, those liberals (in the American sense) who were beginning to get worried about Russian policy in Eastern Europe would not want to publish anything that could be used as a weapon by nativist, isolationist anti-Communists, already beginning to stir again powerfully in Congress. And some conservative-minded publishers presumably took the Cape and Faber 'national interest' line though this was less common in America.

the Book-of-the-Month Club, since when in the States, too, it has continued to be more than a season's sensation.[18] '*Animal Farm*', said Fred Warburg replying to the toast at his eightieth birthday dinner, 'made me as a publisher.'

Overnight Orwell's name became famous. Orwell-like became a synonym for moral seriousness expressed with humour, simplicity and subtlety intertwined. Four years later 'Orwellian' became a synonym, somewhat mistakenly, for 'ghastly political future'. His fame did not spread, however, in a simple way, but as the product of a reviewers' war that was soon to echo across the Atlantic and then, in a flood of translations, around the world.

Animal Farm was widely reviewed and most English reviewers noticed it warmly and nearly all praised the style. Comparisons with Swift were common, Cyril Connolly alone making clear why: 'the feeling, the penetration, and the verbal economy of Orwell's master Swift'. (He knew from prep school days how much his friend had lived with Swift.) On the content there was, for such a simple-seeming book, surprising disagreement. Some saw it simply as anti-Soviet or anti-Stalin polemic, and praised it on those grounds, just as others, fellow-travellers and Communists, on the same grounds damned it. The comrades still pursued him – memories were long – venomously and persistently. A letter of 3 January 1947 in the *Daily Worker* was to say: 'In response to a magnificent gesture by the Soviet Union, Lord Montgomery is going there as a guest of the Red Army ... Is this why the Third Programme is busily preparing to broadcast that anti-Soviet farrago: George Orwell's *Animal Farm*?' But the best reviewers saw that, while the allegory followed the Russian Revolution fairly closely, its condemnation of tyranny was universal; and that there was a second, more positive theme, that of 'revolution betrayed'. Most English reviewers knew something of Orwell's previous books, even if not all knew his *Tribune* essays, so they realized and stated – except in some provincial papers – that he was a socialist. But many American reviewers missed this (as some of the New York publishers who rejected it may have feared) and used the book as a polemic against socialism in general. Some even said that it was significant that the book had appeared after the British General Election. How could the book be read that way, considering the terms of Old Major's prophecy of the end of oppression and the coming of a realm of fraternity and justice, the constant recurrence of this vision and at the end of the book the clear theme of 'revolution betrayed' rather than of 'revolution' impossible or undesirable? Ideological preconceptions in the United States, however, were not merely very strong but subtly different to those in Britain; so an American Right-winger who did not know Orwell's political position could embrace the book wholeheartedly as being anti-revolutionary, presumably thinking Old Major's speech was intended either as specious nonsense or as pie in the sky. One can imagine Republicans saying 'That fellow knows socialism is good in theory but impossible in practice.' And if later they learned that the fellow was a socialist, then they assumed that he must have unwittingly forsaken his socialism rather than that they had misread the text.

English reviewers, however, in recognizing the secondary theme of the book as 'revolution betrayed', did not necessarily endorse it. Cyril Connolly reviewed the book warmly but critically in *Horizon* as restoring 'the allegorical pamphlet to its rightful place as a literary force', and as showing 'that Mr Orwell has not entirely been seduced away by the opinion-airing attractions of weekly journalism from his true vocation, which is to write books'. But he added that the thesis of 'the betrayed revolution' in Orwell, as in Koestler, missed the fact that 'every revolution is "betrayed" because the violence necessary to achieve it is bound to generate an admiration for violence which leads to the abuse of power'.[19] Connolly seems to have thought that Orwell argued for a Leninist rather than for a populist or Communard revolution (Anarchist reviewers read Orwell's intended meaning more accurately); but his criticism is a fair one on the issues raised by the book (the Anarchists would have replied that the State itself abuses power in repressing genuine democratic movements – Orwell's opposition to centralization or 'oligarchical collectivism' came close at this time to some aspects of anarchist thought).

Several English Conservative reviewers, unlike American Republicans, saw clearly what he was saying, so could praise him for his 'down with tyranny!' but accused him of inconsistency for his 'revolution betrayed'. Robert Aickmann, for example, wrote that Orwell had not learned that 'private property is an essential condition of personal freedom; that personal freedom is an essential condition of any other more up-to-date kind of freedom; that the attempt to live by bread alone is the quickest way to go breadless; that the expropriators are expropriated; that the counter-revolution begins inside the revolution . . .'[20] Perhaps a more subtle point that nobody made would be that while the book cannot fairly be read as a satire against revolution, it does not follow that it must be read as a case for revolution. There is such a thing as political reflection as well as political advocacy: 'All revolutions are failures, but they are not all the same failure,' Orwell had written in his essay on Arthur Koestler in September the previous year.

Because the American publication was a year later than the British, Orwell was not at first aware that his book could be seen as or used as anti-socialist propaganda. He was more concerned that some English reviewers had given him the old Trotskyite label, seeing Napoleon as Stalin and Snowball as Trotsky, but not noticing the compliance of Snowball/Trotsky with the original and crucial violation of animal equality, special rations for the pigs – the revolution's first betrayal: 'all the pigs were in agreement on this point, even Snowball and Napoleon'.

'Comrades!' he cried. 'You do not imagine, I hope, that we pigs are doing this in a spirit of selfishness and privilege? Many of us actually dislike milk and apples. I dislike them myself. Our sole object in taking these things is to preserve our health. Milk and apples (this has been proved by Science, comrades) contain substances absolutely necessary to the well-being of a pig. We pigs are brain-workers. The whole management and organization of this farm depend on us. Day and night we are watching over your welfare. It is for *your* sake that we drink that milk and eat those apples. Do you know what would happen if we pigs failed in our duty? Jones would come back! Yes, Jones would come back! Surely, comrades', cried Squealer almost pleadingly, skipping from side to side and whisking his tail, 'surely there is no one among you who wants to see Jones come back?'[21]

Orwell marked this passage in a copy he gave to Geoffrey Gorer, telling him that it was the key passage. Tom Hopkinson gave the same passage pride of place in a famous reassessment of *Animal Farm*, just after Orwell's death, in which he said: 'I know only two present-day works of fiction before which the critic abdicates: one is Arthur Koestler's *Darkness at Noon*, the other Orwell's *Animal Farm*.'[22] No one committed himself quite that strongly at the time*; critical opinion tends to gather confidence from success. The terms of a private letter from Herbert Read may have pleased Orwell more than all the published notices and increasing sales:

Thank you very much indeed for *Animal Farm*. I read it through at a sitting with enormous enjoyment. My boy of seven and a half then spotted it, and I tried chapter 1 on him. He has insisted on my reading it, chapter by chapter, every evening since, and he enjoys it innocently as much as I enjoy it maliciously. It thus stands the test that only classics of satire like *Gulliver* survive.

What seems to me to be its rare quality is its completeness. The cap fits all round the head: everything is there and yet there is no forcing of the story – it is all completely natural and inevitable. I do most heartily congratulate you.[23]

William Empson, about to depart to China, had reservations, not unlike Connolly's, but from a political stance closer to Orwell's own:

160a Haverstock Hill
NW3

24 Aug/45

My Dear George,
Thanks very much for giving me 'Animal Farm' – It is a most impressive object, with the range of feeling and the economy of method, and the beautiful limpid prose style. I read it with great excitement. And then, thinking it over, and especially on showing it to other people, one realizes that the danger of this kind of perfection is that it means very different things to different readers. Our Mr Julian [his son] the child Tory was delighted with it; he said it was very strong Tory propaganda.

Your point of view of course is that the animals ought to have gone on sharing Animal Farm. But the effect of the farmyard, with its unescapable racial differences, is to suggest that the Russian scene had unescapable social differences too – so the metaphor suggests that the Russian revolution was always a pathetically impossible attempt. To be sure, this is denied by the story because the pigs can turn into men, but the story is far from making one feel that any of the other animals could have turned into men ...

I certainly don't mean that that is a fault in the allegory; it is a form that

---

*Except perhaps Simon Watson-Taylor: 'It is related of Jonathan Swift that, at the end of his life, on being handed a copy of the *Tale of a Tub*, he remarked "Good God! What a genius I had when I wrote that book". Likewise I am prepared to claim, on behalf of Mr Orwell, that *Animal Farm* is of far greater significance than its unassuming title would suggest' (*Freedom*, 25 August 1945).

has to be set down and allowed to grow like a separate creature, and I think you let it do that with honesty and restraint. But I thought it worth warning you (while thanking you very heartily) that you must expect to be 'misunderstood' on a large scale about this book; it is a form that inherently means more than the author means, when it is handled sufficiently well.

Bill Empson[24]

Orwell should have pondered Empson's point about allegory and ambiguity before he embarked on his next book. *Nineteen Eighty-Four* raised in more acute form the very same problems and the same diversity of political interpretations. Orwell had been reasonably sure of the preconceptions of his familiar British readers when writing *Animal Farm* when his sales were small. Also its main target was quite clear. In his essay on Koestler of 1944 he spoke of 'the sin of nearly all left-wingers from 1933 onwards' of being that 'they have wanted to be anti-Fascist without being anti-totalitarian'. His British readers knew him for what he was – a *Tribune* socialist – and would read the book in that light; but it was not sensible of him to expect the same understanding of his book from a world readership. Certainly an emanation of the tradition of 'English socialism', for such it was (egalitarian, nonmarxist, moralist, craft- rather than class-conscious, obsessed with the balance of 'town' and 'country'), which could also be plausibly read as Trotskyist, Anarchist, Tory or as Cold War anti-Communism, had its peculiarities and its own types of ambiguity.

Orwell told Dwight Macdonald that when Queen Elizabeth, the Queen Mother, whose literary adviser was Sir Osbert Sitwell, sent the Royal Messenger to Secker & Warburg for a copy in November, they were completely sold out, so he had to go in top hat and carriage to the anarchist Freedom Bookshop in Red Lion Street. But alas, according to George Woodcock and others, it was only a man in a bowler hat and a taxi.[25]

After the success of *Animal Farm* and by appearing regularly in *Tribune* and the *Observer*, Orwell was now, in a small but distinct way, a public figure – already 'almost a legend to the younger generation' (as the woman to whom he sent the proposal was to say). Fame brought an inevitable invitation to dine with Lord Beaverbrook, a risk increased by his having written nine pleasant pot-boilers for the *Evening Standard* in the winter of 1945: on the politically contentious subjects of Christmas, open fires, English cooking, evening dress, junk-shops, how to make tea, popular songs, rudeness, the English weather and the ideal pub. He pleaded the lack of a dinner jacket and was asked to lunch instead.[26] Nothing is recorded of what was said, although Orwell told Koestler beforehand that he wanted to talk to Beaverbrook about Stalin, whom Beaverbrook had met.

Fame also brought a letter from John Betjeman artfully praising his 'The Common Toad' essay in *Tribune*: 'I have always thought you were one of the best living writers of prose.'[27] Orwell tried to help other writers whom he thought were in difficulties, which led among other things to a complicated correspondence with Rebecca West, who did not seem to share his view that Henry Miller was in any special difficulties and needed help. He also had correspondence with P. G. Wodehouse, whom he had met in Paris and defended in print against sententious charges of being a collaborator.[28] Many poorer and lesser writers found they could approach him for money – his second wife destroyed a sizeable list of such gifts and loans after his death.

His old friend Rayner Heppenstall had surfaced as a leading producer of the early days of the BBC Third Programme. He roped Orwell in to write a fine adaptation of Charles Darwin's *The Voyage of the Beagle* in March 1946, and a very stilted version of *Animal Farm* which was transmitted the following year.[29] He was asked to address many socialist and literary societies, most of which invitations he turned down – he knew he was a poor speaker. Since his wounds in Spain, he had a weak and monotonous voice: but when he did speak, he was usually clear and sincere. He is remembered, for instance, lecturing on international relations early in 1946 to the Red Flag Fellowship. They were all Left-wingers, more ex-Communists among them than Communists, including many Marxist and Social Democratic exiles. Orwell speculated about the possibility of a world war between the USSR and the USA. The coming of the atom bomb might tempt either side into it. He argued clearly that it would be better to fight than go down; and that if there was such a war, he would choose to be on the side of America rather than Russia because, with all the faults of an uncontrolled capitalism, at least they had liberty. Where there was some liberty, it could be extended; but he took the view that the Soviet Union was so despotic that there was little hope of liberty ever emerging there. He argued what struck the audience as a very pessimistic thesis, that despotism almost always led to war. Rather surprisingly the fellowship took this quietly. Few of them *agreed* but few seemed shocked that he said it. His speech was 'rather disorganized, no variation in tone, but sincere and important stuff, so generally regarded as a "good talk",' said one of the audience. Reg Groves remembers it as 'a matter-of-fact speech, not a poor one – contrasted well with some flamboyant oratory before.'[30]

Orwell accepted a commission to write for a short-lived magazine for schools, *Junior: Articles, Stories and Pictures*. It did a survey of 'World Affairs, 1945'. Although not included in *The Collected Essays, Journalism and Letters*, this article is important as the most clear and simple statement of his real views on international relations. Written as 'the leaders of the Big Three are conferring at Potsdam', he expected the world to be divided into three armed and hostile camps, no longer a multiplicity of nation states. Only a world organization could prevent it, which would depend on the voices and votes of common people everywhere. That was put forward as a real but not very likely alternative. The tone was a tempered pessimism. So he already had the scenario for *Nineteen Eighty-Four* in his actual reading of world events in 1945. He added a preface to the text after Hiroshima, anticipating that soon each of his three power blocs would have the bomb and the world could be on the edge of utter disaster.[31] Then in *Tribune* in 'You and the Atom Bomb' he made two shrewd forecasts – on a level of abstraction somewhere between what has actually happened and the plot of *Nineteen Eighty-Four*:

But suppose – and really this is the likeliest development – that the surviving great nations make a tacit agreement never to use the atomic bomb against one another? Suppose they only use it, or the threat of it, against people who are unable to retaliate? In that case we are back where we were before, the only difference being that power is concentrated in still fewer hands and that the outlook for subject peoples and oppressed classes is still more hopeless ...

If as seems to be the case, it is a rare and costly object as difficult to produce as a battleship, it is likelier to put an end to large-scale wars at the cost of prolonging indefinitely a 'peace that is no peace'.

In the same article he remarked, in passing, that the essential thesis of James Burnham's *Managerial Revolution* was turning out to be correct, after all: a tripartite division of the world, each unit ruled by a 'self-elected oligarchy'.

James Burnham's theory has been much discussed, but few people have yet considered its ideological implications – that is, the kind of world-view, the kind of beliefs, and the social structure that would probably prevail in a state which was at once *unconquerable* and in a permanent state of 'cold war' with its neighbours.[32]

He was already considering these implications himself.

David Astor paid him the great compliment of circulating in April 1946 his essay 'Politics and the English Language' to all those who wrote for the *Observer* and its Foreign News Service – with a new title, 'What Do You Mean?' and a headnote: 'We reproduce it for private circulation – without insinuation or apology . . .'[33] (His argument that liberty and good plain style go together influenced a whole generation of journalists but not, alas, students of the social sciences.) As ever, Orwell asked no favours of Astor, except for one thing that always worried him before he travelled anywhere: how to get some size twelve boots. He asked Astor to get some from America, he would pay for them, of course. Letters went out to the office of the Astor Estate in New York. Why Orwell thought that America was good for size twelve boots, as Pinter's tramp thought of the Monks at Luton, is not clear, but while Astor was searching, Orwell had Malcolm Muggeridge (visiting Washington) and Dwight Macdonald (in New York) undertaking the same mission, and soon the firm of Harcourt Brace turned its collective mind to the problem.

The Duchess of Atholl asked him to speak for the League for European Freedom, but he firmly replied in November 1945:

I cannot associate myself with an essentially Conservative body which claims to defend democracy in Europe but has nothing to say about British imperialism. It seems to me that one can only denounce the crimes now being committed in Poland, Yugoslavia, etc. if one is equally insistent on ending Britain's unwanted rule in India. I belong to the Left and must work inside it, much as I hate Russian totalitarianism and its poisonous influence in this country.[34]

(Such would have been his reply to many subsequent bodies who use his name too freely.)

He took an active part in protesting against the harrying and prosecution of British Anarchists. He had a curious relationship with Anarchists and Anarchism. On returning from Spain he had joined the ILP but had felt some closeness to the Anarchists: it was the Spanish

Anarchists who had shown him, he said, that socialism was possible. During the war he opposed them bitterly, as he opposed the I L P for pacifism and opposition to the war effort. Yet towards the end of the war he had many friends and acquaintances among Anarchists, such as Herbert Read, George Woodcock, Marie Louise Berneri, Vernon Richards (whose photographs of Orwell in Canonbury became so famous) and their friend Julian Symons. After the War, he resumed a general, if critical, sympathy with them. He wrote a book review for *Freedom* and first published (gratis) his 'How the Poor Die' in George Woodcock's journal *Now* in November 1946.[35] He was never for a moment a card-carrying member of the Anarchists, but his thought was tinged with an active ambivalence towards anarchism. Even in 1946, in a review of such literature he wrote in the *Manchester Evening News*, Orwell criticized anarchism and pacifism strongly. He saw it as 'a kind of primitivism' incompatible with an industrial society and 'high living standards', implying that the kind of State needed for industrial society is inevitably oppressive and coercive. Further, pacifism actually weakens those countries who tolerate it most. 'But in a negative sense', he continued, their criticism had been useful: 'They have rightly insisted that present-day society, even when the guns do not happen to be firing, is not peaceful and they have kept alive the idea – somewhat neglected since the Russian Revolution – that the aim of progress is to abolish the authority of the State and not to strengthen it.'[36] He himself was more than a little ambivalent on whether the State should be strengthened for welfare or diminished for liberty; and on whether power as such was evil or only the abuse of power.

When the Anarchists themselves were attacked, however, he had sprung to their defence unambiguously. Towards the end of 1944, the Special Branch of Scotland Yard had raided the offices of *War Commentary*, the predecessor of *Freedom*, and taken away membership and subscription lists. The raid evoked many protests. Orwell wrote about it in *Tribune* and signed a letter circulated by Herbert Read with T. S. Eliot, E. M. Forster and Stephen Spender, among others, as signatories. Then in 1945 just before the end of the War in Europe, the Director of Public Prosecutions, perhaps with time on his hands, charged the editors of *War Commentary* under the Defence Regulation for attempting to 'undermine the affections of members of His

Majesty's Forces'. Three of the accused were sentenced on 27 April to nine months in prison each. Orwell was outraged. He regarded the Government's decision to prosecute as a political decision which promised badly for freedom of speech in peacetime. (It was probably connected with the decision to continue conscription.) He signed a letter of protest which appeared in *Tribune* on 4 May.[37] Later that year he wrote a noble piece also for *Tribune*, 'Freedom of the Park', when anarchist and pacifist newspaper-sellers were arrested for obstruction at Speakers' Corner, Hyde Park – which he praised as 'a sort of Alsatia where outlawed opinions are permitted to walk'.[38]

These incidents were not very important in themselves. He, however, was one of several people who noticed how useless the National Council for Civil Liberties was, indeed how positively hostile the Council was to the Anarchists and the free Left. The NCCL was one of many 'good causes' at that time which had become virtually a Communist Front organization, certainly reluctant to defend the critics of the comrades. So it led him into the only voluntary body in which he was ever active: he became Vice Chairman of the Freedom Defence Committee of which Herbert Read was Chairman. Among the sponsors on the letterhead appeared E. M. Forster, Bertrand Russell, Cyril Connolly, Benjamin Britten, Michael Tippett, Henry Moore, Osbert Sitwell and Augustus John. It did some good, surviving until 1949, by which time counter-purges had been successful in the NCCL.[39] 'Orwell may have become a name to conjure with by then, but typically, having joined, he took his duties seriously, contributing several "sizeable donations" ', said George Woodcock who seems, as Secretary, to have masterminded it all.

Orwell found that the Freedom Defence Committee was too narrowly concerned with defending British Left-wingers prosecuted for political reasons, so while he remained Vice Chairman, the following year found him involved, at Arthur Koestler's urging, in a complicated four-cornered negotiation between himself, Koestler, Bertrand Russell and Victor Gollancz in an attempt to set up a broader 'League for the Dignity and Rights of Man'. Orwell drafted a fine two-page manifesto of aims and objectives. The League should have the two-fold task of (a) theoretical clarification and (b) practical action. The first task of clarification would be to redefine the word 'democracy'. It had to go beyond nineteenth-century liberalism.

The starting point of the discussion should be to regard as the main functions of the State:
(1) To guarantee the newborn citizen his equality of chance.
(2) To protect him against economic exploitation by individuals or groups.
(3) To protect him against the fettering or misappropriation of his creative faculties and achievements.
(4) To fulfil these tasks with maximum efficiency and a minimum of interference.[40]

Its practical actions would include, of course, a quarterly magazine, eventually a monthly, and lobbying on behalf of political prisoners and against repressive laws everywhere. Contact should be made with groups in other countries, or help be given to found them. Unfortunately, it all depended on the social conscience of an Australian-born man of wealth, Rodney Phillips, who had appeared in Humphrey Slater's circle in London and seemed anxious to patronize Left-wing and libertarian causes, including the financing of *Polemic*. But while the four allies argued about what to do with his money, Phillips suddenly shifted his interests to the kind of revues that had showgirls in them. If these ideas collapsed at the time, it is reasonably certain that they bore some strange fruits. Through Koestler and some American contacts, the Congress of Cultural Freedom emerged; and more happily some of the ideas reappear in the early documents of Amnesty International.[41]

Koestler and Desmond MacCarthy tried to tempt Orwell into joining P E N, the international writers' organization. Koestler said that Storm Jameson wanted to put him up for President of the British branch, but Orwell in a letter of 13 April 1946 firmly squashed the suggestion. The sick infant Freedom Defence Committee and the abortive League for the Rights of Man had been enough: 'I *cannot* do that sort of work.' He had taken Eileen's last advice to heart: 'It is just throwing one's time and abilities down the drain. In any case as you know I am going away for the whole summer and cutting loose from all this. Everyone keeps coming at me wanting me to lecture, to write commissioned booklets, to join this and that, etc. – you don't know how much I pine to get free of it all and have time to think again.'[42]

He had been driving himself as hard as ever. The 'Payment Notebook' for July 1943 to December 1945 shows that he wrote 109,850 words in 1945, ten thousand up on 1944, and that his annual income had increased at a greater rate – from £597.19s. to £961.8s.6d.

(As only £79 of this income arose from the royalties on *Animal Farm*, this shows that much of his journalism and essays were now commanding better prices in more prestigious journals – though he continued to write for nothing or for very little, as for *Tribune*, if he liked the people or the cause.)

Inwardly a solitary man, Orwell had always liked company at times of his own choosing. Reserved or inhibited about his real feelings as he was, even with intimate friends, yet he liked to spend part of the day hearing good talk about books and politics – without, of course, seriously disrupting his work timetable. Lunches were the solution.

His occasional lunches with Powell and Muggeridge grew into a weekly institution at this time, each asking along one guest if he chose. Sometimes they ate at the Bodega off the Strand and sometimes at the Bourgogne in Soho. There is a confusion of rival claims and memories about who else were regulars. Orwell also lunched regularly with Julian Symons, a man who bridged Orwell's two main worlds of politics and literature, a very perceptive friend and admirer. Memories of what was said on these occasions are very general. If Orwell had something of Dr Johnson's didacticism, yet he neither dominated the table nor produced memorable epigrams; or perhaps he lacked a Boswell (Julian Symons was too much a person in his own right); and certainly he lacked volume in his utterances. If too many sat down round the table, his weak voice often could not be heard at all amid the clamour of gossip and rival opinions. If few sat down, he would occasionally dominate the conversation, not always on politics or literature, often – a friend remarked with affectionate irritation – on 'homely talk' that was a cross between Ripley's 'Believe it or Not' (a newspaper column) and a home improvement manual. He had an endless delight in 'small scraps of useless information', just as in his home he collected objects for their curiosity value – like his Victorian commemorative mugs – rather than for their convenience or beauty.

Michael Meyer once took him out to dinner to meet a future Labour Minister. The man talked loudly, incessantly and without showing the slightest interest in the opinions of the rest of the company. Orwell made no attempt to stop the flow, suffering in silence, behaving with perfect politeness, thanking his host gravely 'for a quite interesting evening'.

For a *tête à tête*, Orwell liked the small restaurants of the Charlotte

Street area of north Soho, now called Fitzrovia. His favourite was the Akropolis, which was opposite Sonia Brownell's flat and Hetta Empson's studio. He took George Woodcock to a celebratory lunch on the day he heard that the Book-of-the-Month Club had taken *Animal Farm*, but after carefully catching the head waiter's eye, he stalked across the road to the rival Little Akropolis – for the other establishment had requested the previous week that he wear his jacket despite the heat. Orwell then sat in the Little Akropolis in his braces, happy at his twin triumphs. Once while lunching there with Malcolm Muggeridge he asked him to change places: Kingsley Martin had come in and Orwell said that he could not bear to have to look at 'that corrupt face' all through a good meal.

Michael Meyer, then recently down from Oxford, had met Orwell through Tambimuttu, the Ceylonese poet and editor who judged poems and poets nightly at the Wheatsheaf pub in Rathbone Place. Meyer dared to bring a famous older friend, Graham Greene, together with Orwell for lunch at the Csarda in Dean Street. The meeting was agreeable if not epochal: even though they talked politics, Orwell tactfully kept off religion. Being now able to keep his own end up, Orwell asked Meyer and Greene back to lunch, to the Elysée in Percy Street, slightly better than the Little Akropolis. But Greene outtrumped them both with a final lunch at Rules. Orwell wore a suit on that occasion. Greene was then editing a series for Eyre & Spottiswoode. Could Orwell think of any neglected writers of merit? 'Yes, Leonard Merrick', he replied. It was agreed on the spot that he should write an introduction to a re-issue of *The Position of Peggy Harper*, which he did; but the series was wound up and it never appeared. Alas, poor Merrick.[43]

If Orwell liked a beer before or after lunch in one of the literary pubs of that area, like the Wheatsheaf, the Fitzroy in Charlotte Street, the Bricklayer's Arms (or 'Burglar's Rest') in Gresse Street, he did not suffer from what 'Tambi' vainly warned Julian Maclaren-Ross was 'Sohoitis' – the contagious disease of staying there day and night, talking books but never getting any work done.[44] (Others called it 'Potts' Disease'.) He had established a new iron régime of work for himself, only enjoying or wasting, as luck would have it, the middle part of the day. Far more rarely would he go out to dine in the evening.

From the time of his return to England after Eileen's death, his private life was dominated by his utter determination to hang on to young Richard. He brought the baby back from the North and left him with Gwen O'Shaughnessy's half-sister Doreen who had married no other than Georges Kopp (Gwen and Laurence had put him up in Greenwich in 1939). The Kopps had introduced the Orwells to Canonbury Square, where they lived themselves. Orwell seems, however, despite Kopps' adventurous spirit, to have grown less fond of him – and anyway, it was only a temporary arrangement. So he looked around for a nurse-cum-housekeeper, until he was able to remarry, as he plainly intended to do.

Susan Watson was aged 25 and with a daughter of 7, recently separated from her husband a Cambridge don, then a Scientific Civil Servant. She had a debility which made her lame. Looking for a job, her daughter being at boarding-school, she was recommended to Orwell by mutual friends, Rayner Heppenstall and Hetta Empson. Susan Watson looked after George and Richard for about a year, thus saw more of them in a domestic situation than anyone else had ever done except Eileen and Avril. She grew to admire Orwell greatly, but found him a difficult person, not easy to live with at all. She had no thought then that he was or would be a great writer, so here was a very intelligent housekeeper and observer whose memories seem unclouded by hindsight or by literary positions of her own. She found him 'a conflicting mixture of emotional inhibition and intellectual expansiveness': his first instruction to her was 'You must let him play with his thingummy.' His second was 'Can you make scones?' which she could not; but as she saw that it was important to him to have things done in the way that he was used to, she got a recipe and made scones.[45]

He was generous with the housekeeping money, £10 a week and £7 for herself – which was good pay in those days. He was strict about keeping to his own rations and would never look or encourage her to look for off-ration extras. But he liked what he liked, roast beef cooked very rare and Yorkshire pudding dripping with gravy on Sundays, and 'good Yarmouth kippers' frequently for high tea. When he entertained for dinner, which was rarely, or when he asked people in for high tea, which was about once a week, he gave careful instructions about the quality of food to be offered, graded according to how welcome they were. He gave good friends everything he liked himself, which sometimes led to odd results – such as Cyril Connolly loyally munching

Scottish oat cakes and even attacking black pudding with mashed potatoes when his friend said, 'By Jove, this looks good.' He liked his tea as well as his tobacco strong, sometimes putting twelve spoonfuls into a huge brown pot that needed both hands to lift and steady it.

After high tea and playing for half an hour or so with Richard, he began work. Cocoa was made at ten o'clock sharp every evening, in a special Victorian Jubilee mug and made in a special way to his instructions. Cadbury's cocoa was strongly preferred, he would only accept Fry's as, to him, a very poor second choice if Cadbury's had utterly vanished from the shops. Milk then had to be *almost* on the boil and frothing before the chocolate was added to the milk and stirred with a *wooden* spoon. He would then work until three o'clock in the morning. Susan Watson grew so used to the typewriter that she would wake in alarm if it was not being pounded. He was to be woken at a quarter to eight. She usually sent in Richard, crawling, to tickle his feet. He had to be woken gently for he suffered from nightmares, sometimes screaming in his sleep. The outward stoic calm and tranquillity of his last years covered some inner tensions. They had breakfast together at half past eight, and each day he made the same little joke. While he held up the tray himself with a white teacloth over his arm as if he were a waiter, she would load the cups and plates. Then he would work until it was time to go out to lunch; or if no lunch was arranged he would pop into the pub on the corner for beer and sandwiches. He usually pottered around in the early afternoon, he liked browsing in second-hand bookshops, indeed second-hand shops of all kinds, in which that area of London was rich. Or he would do some carpentry. Susan Watson defends his carpentry as 'seeming pretty good to me'; but others remember a chair whose four legs could never touch the ground all at once; and when Michael Meyer, whose father was in the timber business, got him some fine lengths of cherry-wood to make book-shelves, Meyer was appalled to meet them again not merely painted white but also sagging for lack of centre supports. (Meyer's account rings true, but some other sceptics of his practicality were unlikely to have been as experienced in carpentry as they were in literature.)

An aunt from Streatham used to visit him, a funny old lady wrapped in black satin and jet beads. Susan thought that she remembered the name 'Nellie Limouzin'. When she came he used to get his great collection of McGill post-cards out of the drawer to make her laugh.

Susan was instructed never to bring in the tea until his aunt had finished looking at and laughing at the cards. He did not want Susan to see her enjoying these 'improper' objects. He had some strangely old-fashioned figures of speech mixed with modern ideas. When Tambimuttu came to tea one day he called him somewhat dismissively 'a regular coughdrop'.

Apart from mealtimes, briefly after tea, and on Tuesdays when Susan had her day off, Orwell did not see a great deal of Richard, being so engrossed in work, but she realized that there were periods between Eileen's death and her coming to Canonbury when he had had Richard wholly to himself and made a good job of looking after him. Friends trembled when they saw him – six foot three inches – striding down the street towards them with Richard on his shoulders, fearing infant decapitation from every tree branch or street sign. (This was the time when Vernon Richards took a series of photographs, fine and now quite famous character studies, of Orwell with Richard, and Orwell at his desk, cigarette and typewriter, and at his workbench, chisel and wood, equally absorbed.) Orwell discovered, like many a one-parent family, the pleasures of dropping in on married couples at teatime where there were young children, whether Anthony and Violet Powell or Rayner and Margaret Heppenstall (both kindly friends if sceptics about some of his ideas and writing). Orwell worried a good deal about Richard's backwardness, as he did not talk clearly nor walk securely until he was nearly two, but then he caught up with a rush. Orwell intervened spasmodically in his toilet training, tending to be a bit strict, obviously thinking that Susan, as a modern mum herself, was *laisser faire, laisser passer*.

Towards her he behaved very properly, if a little stiffly, never quite sure whether to treat her as a trusty old housekeeper-nurse or as young daughter. But he plainly did not like her boyfriends visiting, and only suffered them calling for her. It obviously upset whatever image he had built up for her. When a friend called for her one evening and began to play with Richard on the floor, Orwell picked his son up and abruptly left the room. 'Something very innocent was suddenly made to seem rather indecent.' But she got her own back, by chance, when she brought in more tea accidentally at the very moment he was proposing to Anne Popham whom he had met at dinner the night before.

He was strict and formal about some strange things. They had a char,

GEORGE ORWELL

a Mrs Harrison, a real Islington Cockney lady with a little boy called Kenny, always covered in bread and jam, who would play with Richard. Kenny said 'Mum', so Richard began to call Susan 'Mum'. 'Can't have Richard calling you "Mum",' he said. 'Oh, he'll soon stop,' said Susan. 'I'd like him to call you Nana.' But since neither Richard nor Susan seemed to respond to this Edwardian whimsy word, it was settled that Richard would call Susan 'Susan'. That winter of 1945–6 was so cold and fuel was so short that Orwell chopped up some of Richard's toys for firewood. This annoyed Susan, she thought it a melodramatic and slightly sadistic act, as if he wanted to be able to write that 'things got so bad in the winter of 1945–6 that . . .' She felt sure that wood could have been found, had he tried as hard as some others. Avril, who visited from time to time, remembered the incident, but saw nothing strange about it.

He was punctilious about her free time. Only once did he ask her to change her fixed day off, when he had been asked to lunch with 'the old Earl', as he called Bertrand Russell. But he wanted punctuality from others. For a while he had a part-time secretary – Siriol Hugh Jones. His demands for punctuality at quarter past nine in the morning were quite beyond her. She fled in the middle of an article to work on a Communist magazine, so Orwell phoned her mother in Wales and Mrs Hugh Jones came all the way to London by train to deliver the pages to the *Observer* offices, which he had meanwhile redone and taken in himself. But at least she made a good list of his pamphlet collection which is now in the British Library.

His clothes were famously casual. His wardrobe consisted of 'an awful pair of thick brown corduroy trousers', a pair of thick grey flannel trousers, a 'rather nice' black corduroy jacket, a shaggy and battered old greeny-grey Harris tweed jacket, and a 'best suit' of dark grey to black herringbone tweed of old-fashioned cut. During the War, she learned, Eileen had once lost her handbag with their year's supply of clothing coupons in it. They never bothered to claim new ones. He told Tosco Fyvel early in 1946 that he was fed up with wearing old clothes and, now he had a little money, would buy some new ones. But he never seems to have got around to doing so. He asked Susan to dye his khaki Home Guard shirts and beret black and the overcoat brown – despite her protests that it would make him look like a Fascist. It did. He had no colour sense at all. The woollen beret shrank so much that, when he put it on, he was overcome with laughter; and he took a Burmese sword down from the wall and did a comic dance around the table. He was capable of sudden outbursts of droll humour, but not very often. He once took Susan to Collins Music Hall on Islington Green. But when he took her out to dinner at a good restaurant in Baker Street, he instructed her to order a drink and then deserted her for several minutes while he conducted an experiment to see whether waiters would serve women on their own as willingly as men. The experiment must have been inconclusive for nothing on this great social question appeared in *Tribune* or even in the *Evening Standard*.

Susan Watson remembers Sonia Brownell, Celia Kirwan and Inez Holden visiting the flat from time to time, each more than once pressed into minding Richard for a little while on a Tuesday afternoon, as well as being entertained in company at more social hours. Some men of letters remember vividly dinner-parties there at this time, but don't remember her, nor she them. Either he entertained a good deal on Tuesday evenings, cooking for himself, or they gild in memory those high teas with the very best kippers and Gentleman's Relish on toast. Certainly Susan kept very much in the background, knowing that he liked it that way.

It was that Christmas that he and Richard visited the Koestlers in North Wales and he met Celia Kirwan. They had all enjoyed reading in the Christmas number of *Tribune* an example of Orwell's comic self-mockery, 'Old George's Almanac', which prophesied unrelieved and epochal disasters for 1946, yet ended by saying that at least the coming year could not possibly be as bad as the last six. And since Celia worked for Humphrey Slater on *Polemic*, to which both Koestler and Orwell contributed, they almost certainly discussed an attack on *Polemic* made in the December number of *Modern Quarterly*: 'for persistent attempts to confuse moral issues, to break down the distinction between right and wrong'. Orwell thought that these were odd words coming from a 'Communist-controlled' journal, so he seized the opportunity to turn the tables by replying in an anonymous *Polemic* editorial to an essay in the same number of *Modern Quarterly* by Professor J. D. Bernal, the famous physicist, crystallographer and Marxist. Bernal had written that 'A radical change in morality is ... required by those new social relations which men are already entering into in an organized and planned society', and said that 'those based on excessive concern with

individual rectitude need reorientating in the direction of social responsibility'. Further, Orwell quoted Bernal, 'Because collective action in
the industrial and political fields is the only effective action, it is the
only virtuous action.'[46] This provoked one of Orwell's finest polemics.
He accused Bernal of misusing his scientific reputation to assert that
'almost any moral standard can and should be scrapped when political
expediency demands it'. He reminded Bernal of a time in 1939 when
Moscow Radio had denounced the British blockade of Germany as an
inhuman measure that struck at women and children, 'while in 1945,
those who objected to some ten million German peasants being driven
out of their homes were denounced by the same radio as pro-Nazi'.
Thus, he countered:

... it is evident from Professor Bernal's point of view that any virtue can
become a vice, and any vice a virtue, according to the political needs of the
moment ... [He held] the doctrine that an action – at any rate in political and
industrial affairs – is only right when it is successful ... Right action does not lie
in obeying your conscience, or a traditional moral code: right action lies in
pushing history in the direction in which it is actually going ... To put it even
more shortly: anything is right which furthers the aims of Russian foreign
policy.

Orwell concluded by repeating one of the great themes of his last period
by pointing to how 'pompous and slovenly' was Bernal's English: 'It is
not pedantic to draw attention to this, because the connection between
totalitarian habits of thought and the corruption of language is an
important subject which has not been sufficiently studied.'[47]

Apparently innocent of reading either J. S. Mill or Karl Popper,
Orwell had reached the same conclusions for himself, rejecting 'the
fallacy of infallibility' and seeing that there was a connection between a
deterministic view of scientific method and the rejection of 'an open
society'. But there was no explicit philosophical grounding for his
characteristic views on politics and ethics, only the invocation of
'conscience' and 'traditional moral code'. He left off where philosophers should begin, but unlike many of them he did get to the right
starting point. And in rejecting Bernal's scientific socialism, he did not
reject socialism, though he began to ground it more in tradition and a
common-sense morality than in theory.

That January of 1946 he wrote a full-page review for the *Manchester*

Evening News of a group of books on socialism. He asked whether the old ideas of 'human brotherhood', involving hopes to abolish 'war, crime, disease, poverty and overwork' were being abandoned for a 'new kind of caste society in which we surrender our individual rights in return for economic security?' – which he saw as the Soviet way. Socialists, he said, 'are not obliged to believe that human society can actually be made perfect', only 'that it could be made a great deal better than it is' and that 'most of the evil that men do results from the warping effects of injustice and inequality'. The basis of socialism was humanism, it could co-exist with Christianity, but not with the belief that man is inherently a fallen creature. He pictured among those who believe in 'the possibility of human progress a three-cornered struggle between Machiavellianism, bureaucracy and Utopianism'. He came down on the side of the utopians.

If one studied the genealogy of the ideas for which writers like Koestler and Silone stand, one would find it leading back through Utopian dreamers like William Morris and the mystical democrats like Walt Whitman, through Rousseau, through the English diggers and levellers, through the peasant revolts of the Middle Ages, and back to the early Christians and the slave revolts of antiquity.

The pamphlets of Gerrard Winstanley, the digger from Wigan, whose experiment in primitive Communism was crushed by Cromwell, are in some ways strangely close to modern Left Wing literature.

The 'earthly paradise' has never been realized, but as an idea it never seems to perish, despite the ease with which it can be debunked by practical politicians of all colours.

Underneath it lies the belief that human nature is fairly decent to start with, and is capable of indefinite development. This belief has been the main driving force of the Socialist movement, including the underground sects who prepared the way for the Russian revolution, and it could be claimed that the Utopians, at present a scattered minority, are the true upholders of Socialist tradition.[48]

Certainly there is a shift here from the quasi-Marxist viewpoint of *The Lion and the Unicorn* of 1941 when he argued that revolution was needed and was near at hand, even if many of the results would have continuities with good things in the past. But it is a shift in expectations, not in values. His values are optimistic, even utopian, but his expectations are now pessimistic; but pessimistic about the time-scale and about human perfectability, not pessimistic in the sense of despairing or of abandoning a belief in radical betterment. He was a moderate only as to means, not as to ends.

This flow of reviews was temporarily interrupted. Some time just before 13 February, his regular feature failed to appear in the *Manchester Evening News* 'due to Mr Orwell's illness': he had had a haemorrhage. Susan Watson heard him go down the corridor in the middle of the night. He simply said, 'Ice and cold water in a cloth please, and put it on my head.' He was in bed, she remembers, for about a fortnight; but possibly longer, for his Manchester column also did not appear on 14 March. His regular fortnightly piece appeared a week late in the *Observer*, but somehow he kept going his weekly contributions to *Tribune*. He would not allow Susan to bring in a doctor. But he was ill enough to stay in bed, not to shave and not to eat, except semolina pudding flavoured with lemon and vanilla, of which he was very fond. Only when Richard got a cold, towards the end of Orwell's illness, was a doctor summoned. He examined the child, then had a quick look at the sick man and pronounced, Orwell contemptuously told Koestler later, that he had 'gastritis'. But he cannot even have told the doctor that he had tuberculosis and that he had had a recent haemorrhage.[49]

He was soon out and about, however, making light of it, brushing off inquiries about his health and actively planning the move to Jura. Not quite a complete move as yet, for he planned to return to London in the winters, and indeed did for the first winter.

Critical Essays was published in London that February and as *Dickens, Dali and Others* in New York at the end of April. From mid-April Orwell gave up all journalism for six months and attempted to take a complete rest until the end of July (though Susan remembers him working steadily). So his not calling a doctor can hardly be seen as pretence that he was not ill; rather he had persuaded himself that it was something episodic, which could be recovered from each time it occurred with what seemed to him a reasonable amount of rest.

On 3 May his older sister Marjorie died at the early age of 48 of a kidney disease. A few days after attending her funeral he set off alone for Barnhill on Jura, taking his old Burmese metal-lined chest filled with flour, arriving there on 23 May. His younger sister Avril unexpectedly followed a week later to help him. On his way north he visited Eileen's grave and he stayed for one week with Georges and Doreen

Kopp on a farm they had taken at Biggar, near Edinburgh. Kopp sold Orwell an old lorry, the condition of which, when it was finally collected and driven to Jura, proved a source of some tension between them. At the beginning of July he dashed down to London to collect Susan and Richard.

CHAPTER SIXTEEN

JURA DAYS

BARNHILL was an abandoned farmhouse with outbuildings near to the northern end of the island of Jura. It lay at the end of a five-mile, heavily rutted track from Ardlussa, where the laird or landowner, Margaret Fletcher, lived and where the paved road, the only road on the island, came to an end. Her husband, Robin Fletcher, was a former Eton master who had survived Japanese prisoner of war camps and the Burma Road. The Etonian connection was a coincidence: they did not realize for some weeks that their tenant, recommended to them by David Astor, had been in College at Eton. More relevant, Robin Fletcher until his death in 1960 was an 'improving landlord' or, as the islanders simply said, 'a good laird'. That meant a great deal in the small island of some 250 inhabitants suffering steadily from depopulation. For 'improvement' meant that he cared more for the crofters than, in contrast to the three bigger lairds of Jura, the deer. He put farming before shooting, trying to improve the land and fence out the deer, pushing back the margin of cultivation.

To repair and tenant Barnhill, which had too little arable land itself to be worth farming, was part of a plan to make two cottages at Kinuachdrach, where the land was good, more attractive to labourers and their wives – Kinuachdrach was two miles beyond even Barnhill, and neighbours made all the difference, particularly neighbours who might have a car or lorry of their own. Transport was the problem, for Craighouse, which had a general store and a hotel, and where the steamers from the mainland then came in, was twenty-five miles away. The local doctor lived there, a Dr Sandiman, an old man whose qualifications were ancient. Ardlussa at that time had no telephone, the nearest one being a further fifteen miles down the road. Post came up to Ardlussa from Craighouse three times a week and an estate worker took it on to Barnhill and Kinuachdrach twice a week. Guests for Barnhill would often get stuck and be put up overnight in Ardlussa, so the Fletchers came to see most of – what were to the ordinary islanders – Barnhill's interesting comings and goings. Orwell's guests were different from the sort of people the islanders had seen before, and the islanders, slow, gentle, stubborn, kindly and reserved, did not mingle, but observed and remembered.

The climate was mild. Elaborate critical theories of Orwell's character and of his last writings have been built on isothermic fantasy. The West coast of Scotland at that latitude is not like the East coast: the Inner Hebrides are not Aberdeen. The islands lie in the Gulf Stream and have a prevailing south-westerly wind. Frost and snow are rare. Twenty miles down the Sound, for instance, lies the island of Gigha and Achamore House Gardens with one of the finest rhododendron, camellia and azalea collections and arboreta in the British Isles. 'Mad and suicidal sojourn', wrote one critic, 'death wish' wrote others, of Orwell's long premeditated and quite sensible decision to get as far away from London as he could.[1] Certainly he neglected himself. He was aggressively antihypochondriac. He tried all the time to carry on as if he was in normal health, but not to make matters worse. He disliked the cold intensely and would not have gone to Jura without making careful inquiries. He was methodical, commonsensical and prosaic enough, unlike some quasi-Freudian scholars, to have also consulted rainfall charts and isotherms in any good atlas. Eileen had asked all the right questions in correspondence with Mrs Fletcher. David Astor must have described the climate to him carefully, and Astor knew Orwell's general condition well enough. If there was folly in going to Barnhill, it was the simple folly of being so far from a hospital, a good doctor, and being so far from a telephone. In any case, Orwell returned to London that first winter and originally planned to do so for the second winter too.

The house looked more spacious than it was. On the ground floor there was a large kitchen-breakfast-room with a separate pantry and laundry-room, and a large dining- or sitting-room. Upstairs were four small bedrooms all much the same size, one of which Orwell used as a study-bedroom in winter, though he tended to work downstairs in summer if there were no visitors. The kitchen was usually the living-room and the living-room, a difficult room to heat in winter, was used as an extra bedroom in summer when guests arrived. There were some outbuildings, and a single field separated the house from the sea, an easy scramble down to where a small boat could be moored. There was land for a vegetable garden and also two fields which were farmed from Kinuachdrach.

Planning on taking a holiday before he got down to work on *Nineteen Eighty-Four*, Orwell found instead that he had over-extended himself that first summer in the matter of hospitality. At various times that summer Richard Rees, Inez Holden and Sally McEwen, a former secretary at *Tribune*, visited Barnhill. Perhaps he did not expect his casual invitations to be taken up. As Avril was following him up a week after he arrived, Paul Potts was also on his way. Avril plainly found him an impossible person who talked incessantly, frankly and freely on nothing but difficult or improper subjects. Years afterwards she re-counted, with a humour she plainly did not show at the time, how when sent for wood he promptly cut down the only tree near Barnhill that bore nuts. In *Dante Called You Beatrice*, Potts recounts this incident as a fine example of his friend's forgiving nature. He may have noticed that his friend's sister viewed him differently, but armoured in the spirit of his poetic vocation, he endured what he doubtless took to be the normal reaction of a philistine daughter of the English bourgeoisie. His admiration for Orwell was, however, unbounded: 'he carried independence to such lengths that it became sheer poetry'. Some furniture had to be taken from Ardlussa to Barnhill. 'Some very rich people, friends of Orwell's, who had a hunting lodge on the other side of the island, had a whole garage full of brakes and station wagons and jeeps – five I believe – yet he refused to borrow the use of one for a few hours. We had to pack those chairs and that table on our backs across seven [five] miles of some of the most beautiful scenery in Europe.'[2]

What Avril called 'a very dilapidated Ford van', the one that Kopp had sold to Orwell, had not yet reached Jura (perhaps there was some life left in it after all for Kopp to expend), so Orwell made do with a motorbike, as he had over twenty years before in Burma. The five miles of rutted track between Barnhill and Ardlussa must have made this extraordinarily uncomfortable and exhausting. At the beginning of July he made a quick visit by train to London to bring up Susan Watson and Richard. Shortly afterwards Sally McEwen and her child arrived. Not merely did she bring no supplies with her, but she was a militant vegetarian which posed problems in a kitchen where venison, rabbit and lobster were the staple foods. Sally McEwen and Avril found only one thing in common: dislike of Paul Potts. Potts tolerated them all, with bemused puzzlement as to why there should be tension in this earthly paradise presided over by his benign friend. Orwell, as tensions mounted, retreated into his room in the evenings and defended himself with his typewriter, taking it up again earlier than he had intended. His days were full with digging a vegetable garden, putting up shelves, helping with the hay-making, fishing, shooting rabbits, tending his lobster pots, learning the way of the boat with its outboard motor, exploring the north of the island, cutting up venison, plucking geese, making jam, searching for lost hens, fetching milk from Kinuachdrach, all the pottering, do-it-yourself and country pursuits that he loved so much.

Susan had not expected to find Avril entrenched at Barnhill. Avril, sadly on her own after her mother's and then her sister's deaths, had decided to dedicate herself to looking after her difficult brother and his child. She disapproved of Susan from the start. The public version was that Barnhill was too difficult a place for a young woman with a physical handicap. The private version was that 'she was no good with children' – a suspect judgement for a childless spinster to make about a young mother. Plainly the hearth, the kitchen, the farm and the island were too small for the two women. 'Call yourself a nurse,' said Avril, 'and you can't even darn socks.' Susan did not call herself a nurse. It was a different world for Susan from Canonbury Square. Even the time-honoured way of waking George (by sending Richard in to tickle his feet) was declared unsuitable; and whereas she thought that George should sleep longer taking a rare holiday, Avril remorselessly had him up at half past seven because 'that's what he has always done'. George was not 'George' even: he was Eric, Avril firmly and naturally insisted. For her 'George Orwell' was only a pen name. (It is somewhat odd that he had let Susan use the pen-name at Canonbury.) Orwell had, naturally, corresponded with the Fletchers as Eric Blair, and he was known as Mr Blair to all the islanders; and while he had talked about changing his name legally, he had never done so. Donald Darroch, for instance, a farm-worker who was their neighbour at Kinuachdrach, knew he wrote books under another name, 'but that seems a sensible thing to do when the man has a family'.[3] George was apologetic to Susan about what she regarded as Avril's unexpected appearance. He told Susan that he would like her to stay, but he could not send Avril away. She says that he admitted that Avril was behaving oddly, ceasing to put salt into any of the cooking even, but she had had a hard life having to work in a tea-shop (though joint-owner was closer to the truth, and it had been moderately profitable). He felt he owed it to her to let her stay if that was what she wanted and to honour her belief that he couldn't get on without her. He obviously felt guilty about her. However, as often in family tensions, innocent onlookers got struck by forked lightning. Paul Potts was the first to go.

One account is that Avril simply told him to go and said 'something unforgivable'. Another is that Sally McEwen wrote something hurtful about him in a letter and left it open where he would see it. But all accounts agree Potts left suddenly in the night. An estate worker at Ardlussa still remembers being woken in the small hours by footsteps on the road and seeing 'the nice Canadian poet' (poets are held in respect in the Gaelic cultures) with a rucksack on his back and a suitcase in his hand walking towards Craighouse. 'I don't know why or even how he went,' said Avril, 'I so resented those people who wasted Eric's time.'[4]

Susan only lasted another month. During that time first Brenda Salkeld visited, at Avril's invitation. They had all been friends in Southwold days and had never quite lost touch. Brenda was probably Orwell's oldest friend apart from Connolly. Then came Inez Holden, bringing with her, Avril acidly commented, 'not scarce necessities but all sorts of useless luxuries' – among which was a cat, a 'lady cat'. This led to howling fights with Barnhill's tom and his regular paramour. Orwell got quite upset that all this noise would scare away the birds, about which he discoursed monotonously over meals. Inez Holden invented, said Avril, 'the absurd game of shouting "cannibals" whenever strangers appeared'. Strangers were, in fact, not uncommon in the summer. Remote though the house was, both sleek yachtsmen and tough hikers, possibly challenged by its very remoteness, would call from time to time as if, Avril said with conscious exaggeration, 'it was a Public House' or as if they were doing them a favour. Her brother did not welcome such casual callers. The cottagers at Kinuachdrach said they often wished for winter to come to avoid 'the constant knocking on the door' for milk, eggs or tea from people who said, 'Aren't you lonely?' All things are relative, however; such intrusions probably occurred no more than two or three times a month. Orwell welcomed the real islanders, however, when the men from the cottages north of Barnhill came down. In the manner of the islands, the kettle was always boiling on the hearth and strong tea and scones were dispensed. When someone brought supplies up from Craighouse or the post from Ardlussa, they were offered 'a wee dram' (a stiff double, in fact). Most of the islanders liked him, one of his neighbours recalled: 'He seemed a kindly man and he kept himself to himself and interfered with no one' – which the crofters see as a great virtue among their own kind, and even more as how the gentry should treat them. (Orwell saw himself as potentially one of them; but they firmly saw him as 'a peculiar and kindly gentleman'.)[5]

Writing to ask Celia Kirwan to visit, he told her:

... the journeys one makes are quite astonishing. Susan's child came up here yesterday, and I was supposed to go to Glasgow to meet her. I set out the day before yesterday morning, but punctured my motor bike on the way and thus missed the boat. I then got a lift first in a lorry, then in a car, and crossed the ferry to the next island in hopes there would be a plane to Glasgow, however the plane was full up, so I took a bus on to Port Ellen, where there would be a boat on Friday morning. Port Ellen was full to the brim owing to a cattle show, all the hotels were full up, so I slept in a cell in the police station along with a lot of other people including a married couple with a perambulator. In the morning I got the boat, picked the child up and brought her back, then we hired a car for the first 20 miles and walked the last five home. This morning I got a lift in a motor boat to where my bike was, mended the puncture and rode home – all this in 3 days ... With all this you can imagine that I don't do much work – however I have actually begun my new book and hope to have done four or five chapters by the time I come back in October.[6]

She would have visited, but her job as editorial assistant on Humphrey Slater's *Polemic* (for which Orwell wrote four of his finest essays*) kept

---

* 'Notes on Nationalism' (Oct. 1945), 'The Prevention of Literature' (Jan. 1946), 'Second Thoughts on James Burnham' (May 1946), and 'Politics vs Literature: An Examination of *Gulliver's Travels*' (Sept. 1946), all reprinted in *The Collected Essays, Journalism and Letters*, though the Burnham essay is retitled 'James Burnham and the Managerial Revolution'.

her in London. An elegant lady, then as now, she denies being put off by the details:

Don't bring more luggage than, say, a rucksack and a haversack, but on the other hand do bring a little flour if you can. We are nearly always short of bread and flour here since the rationing. You don't want many clothes so long as you have a raincoat and stout boots or shoes. Remember the boats sail on Mondays, Wednesdays and Fridays, and you have to leave Glasgow about 8 a.m.[7]

Susan made an awful mistake. She asked a friend, on leave from the Army, to stay, albeit with Orwell's permission. She warned him not to get into arguments with Orwell, for the young David Holbrook was still a Communist. But somehow he did, whether he picked on Orwell, as she said, or whether Orwell picked on him, as he said. And their somewhat uninhibited behaviour plainly upset Avril. Certainly Holbrook got two very cold shoulders. He saw Orwell as an intrinsically cold and morose man, indeed saw brother and sister as much the same. In a chapter of an unpublished early novel he has 'Burwell', a gloomy masochist resenting young visitors from an outside world he had left 'to perish for its fecklessness'. Burwell exulted in domestic disaster and inconvenience and, a symbolic *pièce de résistance*, blew the head off a goose with a shotgun. When his sister had 'reduced it to a deep brown carbonized relic ... Mumbling with taut lips and wheezing, Burwell, with every line in his face turned down in contented displeasure, carved off meat baked as hard as bootlaces.' Other visitors found Avril's cooking pleasant, even good, but Orwell could have that effect on some people's perceptions.[8]

Susan and her friend departed as suddenly as had Potts, after a violent row with Avril. They too carried their luggage to Ardlussa by hand where she arrived exhausted, to be helped on her way by a concerned Mrs Fletcher. Neither Susan not Orwell bore each other any ill will. She collected her belongings from Canonbury Square and faithfully sent on to him a parcel of the Nosegay Black Shag from which he rolled his strong and incessant cigarettes. Katie Darroch, who kept house for her brother at Kinuachdrach, remembers how upset Richard was at Susan's departure: 'the poor wee laddie, he cried and he cried.'[9]

Orwell could not have driven them down to the ferry himself, anyway, for when the van purchased from Georges Kopp had arrived the previous week, it could not be driven off the ferry: it had to be lifted off by hand – as is well remembered in the oral history of Jura. The engine had boiled dry and seized up. It was abandoned by the quay, where parts of it could be seen until at least 1976.

Orwell, in spite of all these interruptions, had begun to work again. For a long time he had had a clear plan for his new book, but just as the 'complete holiday' plan had broken down, so concentration on one big task seemed not to be possible. He was now receiving many invitations to write for well-known American journals, some of which were too highly paid to resist. This was hardly a sign of that conscious race with death to produce a political testament which has so often been pictured. He behaved as if he thought he had fully recovered from his winter's illness and had many years ahead of him. For the first time his sister showed signs of being impressed by her brother, saw from his public standing that he had not been wasting his time entirely all those years. In any case, she mellowed greatly after Susan had gone and when it was clear that a Blair family, of a sort, were once again together. She had no idea what he was writing, however, and nor did she ask. She had in fact read very little of her brother's writings. After his death she read his books and essays widely and then with considerable understanding and insight. Sometimes we only get to understand people when it is too late.

They returned to Canonbury Square in the autumn. He must have been missing his London friends for he wrote ahead to Humphrey Slater asking him to lunch on Sunday, 13 October, the very morning that he arrived back on the night-sleeper from Glasgow: 'if possible bring one of our mutual friends with you?' – presumably either Celia Kirwan or Inez Holden. And he grumbled typically but revealingly:

I haven't really done any work this summer – actually I have at last started my novel about the future, but I've only done about fifty pages and God knows when it will be finished. However it's something that it is started which it wouldn't have been if I hadn't got away from regular journalism for a while. Soon I suppose I shall be back at it, but I am dropping some of it and am going to try to do mostly highly-paid stuff which I needn't do so much of ...[10]

Avril and Richard returned a day or two ahead of them, carrying a goose for the lunch, since he broke his journey to visit Eileen's grave. But if inwardly he was desolated, he kept it to himself. He re-established his routines much as they had been the previous year, although he did more entertaining that winter and now Avril, not Susan (Richard searched the flat for Susan), looked after him and, unlike Susan, presided at his high teas and dinners. He took for granted that Avril would be there, behaving affably enough to her about the meals – complimenting her formally almost as if she were the hostess and he a guest; but he did not let her somewhat austere presence inhibit the flavour of his talk. She was quite pleased to meet people she had heard of, vaguely: Anthony Powell and Malcolm Muggeridge, not unknown to the general public even then; and someone bright and merry, who worked for Cyril Connolly (a name she remembered from childhood), called Sonia Brownell. Some, of course, she had met before in Mortimer Crescent. They found good qualities in 'old Av'', some qualities like Eric's: a great integrity and a refusal to take the fashion-able viewpoint, sticking to her view sometimes even, like her brother, when the initial premise was palpably absurd or mistaken – then similarly retracting at the next meeting, after considerable reflection, some point that others had by then forgotten. She also had a certain literal-mindedness and pedantry about her, again similar to Eric's. Guests learned that if they said, 'The sauce was marvellous! how *do* you do it?' they would probably get a letter from Avril two days later setting out clearly how white sauce or brown sauce is made.

Sonia Brownell was a fairly frequent visitor, and Orwell visited her in Percy Street; but it was far from an exclusive attachment on either side.

At Tosco Fyvel's suggestion, who was now Literary Editor, Orwell took up his 'As I Please' column in *Tribune* again, replacing Jennie Lee; and he made it lively and various as before, as serious and comic, provocative and common-sensical. Only one column echoed his Scot-tish experience:

Up to date the Scottish Nationalist movement seems to have gone almost unnoticed in England ... In some areas, at any rate, Scotland is almost an occupied country. You have an English or anglicized upper class, and a Scottish working class which speaks with a markedly different accent, or even, part of the time, in a different language. This is a more dangerous kind of class division than any now existing in England. Given favourable circumstances it might develop in an ugly way, and the fact that there was a progressive Labour Government in London might not make much difference ... I think we should pay more attention to the small but violent separatist movements which exist within our own island. They may look very unimportant now, but, after all, the Communist Manifesto was once a very obscure document, and the Nazi Party only had six members when Hitler joined it.[11]

On 31 January he had written for their tenth birthday, 'As I Pleased', a comprehensive account of his relationships with *Tribune*, including a comic admission of his inadequacy as a Literary Editor. It had a valedictory air about it, although his last column was not until 4 April when he dealt with the Royal Commission on the Press, patent medicine advertising, the legality of growing and curing one's own tobacco, and pidgin English. Correspondence arising from the column dragged on for another three weeks, however, including belated replies to a previous query of his as to what was the 'Woodwele that sang' of the Robin Hood ballads – at last he had got his readership to enjoy that kind of thing, not to denounce it as unsocialist or irrelevant to the class struggle. And the previous November he had given up his weekly book column in the *Manchester Evening News* – some sign of trying to concentrate his powers.

Fyvel relates that Orwell offered to write for *Tribune*, however, a long article that was to be bitterly critical of the Labour Party for not having immediately abolished (i) the public schools, (ii) the House of Lords and (iii) titles. Fyvel persuaded him that this was not the most tactful or relevant thing to do in the difficult post-war circumstances, so it was never written. But in talking about it Orwell expressed himself as very critical of Aneurin Bevan for having lost himself in 'all this administration about housing and hospitals'. Orwell plainly attached a great priority to symbolic actions and felt let down that Bevan, whom he believed to share this view, was willing to play along, he thought, with Attlee's cautious Fabianism.

Orwell's correspondence with his agent increased greatly that winter. Secker & Warburg were planning a uniform edition of his works in which *Coming Up For Air* would be the first and *Burmese Days* the second, and he was fascinated by questions of printing and production. There was complicated correspondence with Victor Gollancz, who finally agreed to relinquish his contractual right to Orwell's next three novels.

27b Canonbury Square
Islington N1

9 April 1947

Dear Gollancz,
I should have written several days earlier, but I have been ill in bed. Very many thanks for your generous action.

> Yours sincerely
> Geo. Orwell[12]

So there was some illness that winter, famous for its bitter cold, the shortage of coal and widespread electricity breakdowns which began the decline in popularity of the Labour Government. Avril only recalled that it was 'Eric's usual bout of bronchitis, no worse'. Later he was to blame the cold of that winter for the final collapse of his health, but there is no sign that anything occurred as bad as the haemorrhage of the previous winter.

He continued to write essays. This is the time he wrote 'Lear, Tolstoy and the Fool', a profound comparison of the didacticism of Tolstoy with the tolerant humanism of Shakespeare; and his second essay on James Burnham, written for the *New Leader* of New York.[13] There was no indication that he was still working on *Nineteen Eighty-Four*, it was as if he had set the major task aside until he returned to what he hoped would be the tranquillity of Jura. There was a good deal of correspondence with George Woodcock and others about the affairs of the Freedom Defence Committee of which he was still Vice Chairman. He knew well that such time-consuming work caught his conscience and could not be, should not be avoided while he remained in London. But if he set the unfinished manuscript aside that winter, he was still working out the themes, or echoing what he already concluded in various earlier essays. In 'The Prevention of Literature' in the January number of *Polemic* an idea occurred which only needed a little extension or satiric exaggeration to become the machines of the Ministry of Truth churning out porn to distract and debase the Proles:

Of course, print will continue to be used, and it is interesting to speculate what kinds of reading matter would survive in a rigidly totalitarian society. Newspapers will presumably continue until television technique reaches a higher level, but apart from newspapers it is doubtful even now whether the great mass of people in the industrialized countries feel the need for any kind of literature ... perhaps some kind of low-grade sensational fiction will survive, produced by a sort of conveyor-belt process that reduces human initiative to the minimum.

It would probably not be beyond human ingenuity to write books by machinery. But a sort of mechanizing process can already be seen at work in the film and radio, in publicity and propaganda and in the lower reaches of journalism.

The theme of truth and the possibility of falsification which was to become the last interrogation of Winston Smith, 'the last man in Europe', also occurred in the same essay:

A totalitarian society which succeeded in perpetuating itself would probably set up a schizophrenic system of thought, in which the laws of common sense held good in everyday life and in certain exact sciences, but could be disregarded by the politician, the historian, and the sociologist. Already there are countless people who would think it scandalous to falsify a scientific textbook, but would see nothing wrong in falsifying an historical fact. It is at the point where literature and politics cross that totalitarianism exerts its greatest pressure on the intellectual.[14]

Could he possibly have picked up something from Freddy Ayer in Paris or London about 'the verification principle', which had been his sole criterion of meaning in his *Language, Truth and Logic* of 1936?

In a piece he wrote that winter, called 'Toward European Unity', he had as a possible effect of the coming of the atom bomb:

That the fear inspired by the atomic bomb and other weapons yet to come will be so great that everyone will refrain from using them. This seems to me the worst possibility of all. It would mean the division of the world among two or three vast super-states, unable to conquer one another and unable to be overthrown by any internal rebellion. In all probability their structure would be hierarchic, with a semi-divine caste at the top and outright slavery at the bottom, and the crushing out of liberty would exceed anything that the world has yet seen. Within each state the necessary psychological atmosphere would be kept up by complete severance from the outer world, and by a continuous phony war against rival states. Civilizations of this type might remain static for thousands of years.

This is *Nineteen Eighty-Four*, but if the vision is pessimistic (remembering that he had already begun writing the book), it was only a possibility, 'the worst possibility' indeed: there was an alternative, some hope at least – the only hope:

... to present somewhere or other, on a large scale, the spectacle of a community where people are relatively free and happy and where the main motive in life is not the pursuit of money or power. In other words, democratic Socialism must be made to work throughout some large area. But the only area in which it could conceivably be made to work, in any near future, is western Europe. Apart from Australia and New Zealand, the tradition of democratic Socialism can only be said to exist – and even there it only exists precariously – in Scandinavia, Germany, Austria, Czechoslovakia, Switzerland, the Low Countries, France, Britain, Spain and Italy. Only in those countries are there still large numbers of people to whom the word 'Socialism' has some appeal and for whom it is bound up with liberty, equality and internationalism.[15]

He saw this tradition of 'liberty, equality and internationalism' as only existing, however precariously, in Western Europe; in the USSR 'there prevails a sort of oligarchical collectivism'; in North America 'the masses are contented with capitalism, and one cannot tell what turn they will take *when* capitalism begins to collapse'; 'the Asiatic nationalist movements are either Fascist in character, or look towards Moscow, or manage to combine both attitudes'; and at present, he said, 'all movements among the coloured peoples are tinged by racial mysticism.'

Here is a curious mixture of idealism and pessimism. *Nineteen Eighty-Four* may have severed itself, to some degree at least, from its author's intentions, as Empson thought *Animal Farm* had done; but of his intentions, or rather his political stance while writing it, there can be little doubt. This tempered pessimism is also apparent in 'Lear, Tolstoy and the Fool':

A normal human being does not want the kingdom of Heaven: he wants life on earth to continue. This is not solely because he is 'weak', 'sinful' and anxious for a 'good time'. Most people get a fair amount of fun out of their lives, but on balance life is suffering, and only the very young or the very foolish imagine otherwise.[16]

This is still the same position that he had taken in *Tribune* in 1943, the year he first planned *Nineteen Eighty-Four*:

The danger of ignoring the neo-pessimists lies in the fact that up to a point they are right. So long as one thinks in short periods it is wise not to be hopeful about the future ... The answer, which ought to be uttered more loudly than it usually is, is that Socialism is not perfectionist, perhaps not even hedonistic.

Socialists don't claim to be able to make the world perfect: they claim to be able to make it better. And any thinking Socialist will concede to the Catholic that when economic injustice has been righted, the fundamental problem of man's place in the universe will still remain. But what the Socialist does claim is that that problem cannot be dealt with while the average human being's preoccupations are necessarily economic. It is all summed up in Marx's saying that after Socialism has arrived, human history can begin.[17]

On 29 December Orwell planned a quick dash up to Jura 'to plant fruit trees', as he told his sister and his 'Domestic Diary';* but he had the misfortune the following day to miss the steamer, and there was not another that could get him to Jura until 2 January. Thus while he did, in fact, plant some fruit trees, he had missed whatever ceilidh he had obviously hoped to join on New Year's Eve. However, by 11 April, Orwell was back on Jura with Avril and Richard.

All Richard Blair can remember of Canonbury Square is the bitter cold when he was in his pushchair, a little pain from an electric shock as he stuck his fingers into the old dry-cell batteries that worked the bell, and playing with his father's tools until his aunt, alarmed and protective, stopped him.[18]

The day after they arrived at Barnhill, Orwell wrote to Sonia Brownell, pressing her to come. Nothing could sound more intimidating than the instructions he sent for the forty-eight-hour journey and the need for stout boots, gum boots, oilskins and to be sure to bring her rations and a little flour and tea.

I am afraid I am making this all sound very intimidating, but really it's easy enough & the house is quite comfortable. The room you wld have is rather small, but it looks out on the sea. I do so want to have you here. By that time I hope we'll have got hold of an engine for the boat & if we get decent weather we can go round to the completely uninhabited bays on the west side of the island, where there is beautiful white sand & clear water with seals swimming abt in it. At one of them there is a cave where one can take shelter when it rains & at another there is a shepherd's hut which is disused but quite livable where one could even picnic for a day or two. Anyway do come & come whenever you like

*He had begun to keep a Domestic Diary again, but as in Wallington in 1939–40 the contents are almost entirely records of weather, planting, birds and animals etc. (They cover the periods 7 May 1946 to 5 January 1947, then 12 April to 24 December 1947 – the last volume of the three being continued to May 1948 in Avril's hand.)

for as long as you like, only try to let me know beforehand. And meanwhile take care of yourself & be happy.[19]

Lovers' letters should make light of difficulties, not underline them; and camping was not Sonia's style. But anyway, she was not able to go.

While they had been away, there had been changes made at the end of the island. It was difficult to keep cottagers from leaving Kinuachdrach. One tenant, Donald Darroch, was a hard and capable worker, but in the neighbouring cottage was an Irish road worker called 'Francey' Boyle who had somehow got stranded in Jura and had sent for his wife. They were not the stuff that pioneers are made of, so they moved down the island. (Besides he had lost an eye striking a match at night to find where the petrol was leaking from a lorry.) Tony Rozga, a Polish ex-serviceman, and his wife from Midlothian, desperate for a cottage anywhere, replaced them. The Fletchers also answered an advertisement in the *Oban Times*, and as a result an extra man was taken on who lodged with the Darrochs. His name was William Dunn, a young ex-Army officer back from the war with a wooden leg, scion of a good Scottish family, well educated but penniless. He put in for the labourer's job on the whimsical grounds that he needed somewhere desolate to practise the pipes. In fact he wanted to go in for farming himself and needed to learn virtually from the bottom up. He had found the right place.

Bill Dunn saw a good deal of the Blairs. He was sceptical about Orwell's skills as farmer, gardener or handyman, although there was little love lost between himself and the islanders on these matters either. Orwell was still suffering from the effects of his winter bronchitis, and was not out of the house much for the first month after their return, so Avril was grateful for Bill Dunn's help in and out of the house. Dunn welcomed the company of a gentleman, even a rather stiff – he thought – and reserved Left-wing writer; but he was pleased to notice that the sister, though perfectly loyal, did not share all her brother's values, obsessions and political views.

Richard Rees was to come for a long stay that summer, but had not yet arrived. By the end of May, Orwell began to get out and about again, though he did not feel in good health until midsummer. Bill Dunn reminisced: 'I thought he was a very nice chap, very vague, terribly vague, he certainly didn't look well, but he was always jolly game. I remember going out to Scarba with him.' Scarba was only a mile north of Jura, but was across the famous Corryvreckan, a tidal race and whirlpool.

We landed in a sort of shingly bay and the first thing we saw was a dirty great adder, an enormous thing and Eric quickly planted his boot right on top of its neck and anchored it to the ground and I fully expected that with the other foot he would grind its head into the ground too – he was obviously intent on destroying it – but he got out his penknife and quite deliberately opened and proceeded more or less to fillet this wretched creature, he just ripped it right open with the thing – quite deliberately. I must say, it surprised me terribly because he always really struck me as being very gentle to animals, in fact I think he was a very gentle, kindly sort of man.[20]

Bill Dunn was no intellectual, but he knew quite well what he meant to imply by telling that tale to Rayner Heppenstall in a radio broadcast: so similar to, and with the same ambiguities about Orwell's and the narrator's motives, as Heppenstall's own tale of being beaten up by Orwell in Hampstead days. There was this sadistic streak in Orwell's character – which usually he mastered. (Are men to be judged by single aspects of their nature taken separately or by how, on most occasions, they master them together?) Curiously Dunn's somewhat inconsequential remark at the end, 'he was ... a kindly man', is what all the islanders who met Orwell say; and that is about all they will say. If a man is not 'nice' or a 'kindly' man, however, they will say nothing or, more harshly and only very rarely: 'Well opinions did differ, and for myself I could not say.'

By the end of May he was writing to tell Warburg that he was about a third of the way through a rough draft of the book, had been 'in wretched health ... (my chest as usual) and can't quite shake it off'. He hoped to get a draft finished by October and complete it early in 1948, 'barring illnesses'.

I don't like talking about books before they are written, but I will tell you now that this is a novel about the future – that is, in a sense a fantasy, but in the form of a naturalistic novel. That is what makes it a difficult job – of course as a book of anticipations it would be comparatively easy to write.

And he added that he was sending him separately 'a long autobiographical sketch which I originally undertook as a sort of pendant to Cyril Connolly's *Enemies of Promise*, he having asked me to write a reminiscence of the preparatory school we were at together ... I think it should be printed sooner or later when the people most concerned are dead ...'[21] This was, of course, 'Such, Such Were the Joys', his bitter account of how prep school had warped a young life and left the writer perpetually with a sense of failure. As has been argued,* it was not a literally true, autobiographical account and was closer to *Down and Out in Paris and London*, arising from but surpassing solidly based fact and genuine experience, than it was to *Homage to Catalonia* which sought to tell the verifiable truth, the whole truth and nothing but the truth. Some parts are closer to a short story, while others to a dramatized confession.

When was it written? Even that is not clear. The point is important for those who, like Anthony West, would see *Nineteen Eighty-Four* as a sado-masochistic fantasy arising from childhood trauma at St Cyprian's, not as a rational work of political reflection. To claim that it was his last major essay written immediately before, or actually in the middle of, the composition of *Nineteen Eighty-Four* is, however, only conjecture. It could have been written, in a first version at least, far earlier. The balance of probability points to late 1938 or to the early years of the war. (See Appendix B.)

Even if 'Such, Such Were the Joys' was written, or heavily revised, in 1946 or 1947, the text is a shaky foundation on which to build theories of the origin and the 'real meaning' of *Nineteen Eighty-Four*. Now that it is known that he had an outline of *Nineteen Eighty-Four* as early as 1943, the relationship between the two writings, if any, must at least be seen as less direct than has been suggested. And even if there is a significant relationship, then it is by no means clear which is cause and which is effect. Did the essay lead to the book or did he need, in order to imagine the claustrophobic world of Winston Smith, to write, revise or even simply to re-read this essay? The difficulty with purely psychological arguments is that they are so often reversible. The child is father to the man, but the man remembers the child. Finally, to my mind a decisive point: the world of Winston Smith is a totalitarian world with no possibility of escape, but both the actual world of St Cyprian's and the recreated world of the essay were authoritarian worlds, cruel and

*In chapter 1, 'And I Was a Chubby Boy', p. 41 (especially note 3); and in chapter 2, 'The Joys of Prep School and the Echoing Green', pp. 64 ff.

oppressive but not total, and Orwell knew that the inhabitants could always, as one or two did, go over the wall if they could not hold out until the holidays. In so far as the imaginary world of the 'I' in the essay does seem on occasion to convey a total world with the utter hopelessness of escape or rebellion, that would not be a true memory of childhood but a product of a mature man's recognition and theory of totalitarianism.

None of the summer visitors to Jura remember his talking either about what book he was writing or about school-days. They just heard the typewriter pounding away in his room. Gwen O'Shaughnessy came for a week with her children. That summer Humphrey Dakin, now a widower, sent his daughters, teenage Lucy and her elder sister Jane, just leaving the Women's Land Army, to stay with their aunt and uncle for a longer holiday. Their elder brother Henry also turned up, then a second lieutenant in the Army on leave. They liked their uncle Eric, though for days on end they hardly saw him, just like at Leeds when they were small children, except at mealtimes since he worked almost without interruption.[22]   Richard Rees had arrived at about the same time, and promptly decided that Barnhill was the place for him and that if he put a bit of money into it, the land could be properly farmed and become 'self-sufficient'. He was somewhere between a pioneer of the 'good earth' folk of the 1960s and a survivor of the 'simple-lifers' of the 1920s. Certainly Barnhill was, even without adding to its land, getting a bit much for Orwell to manage on his own; and he was probably sufficiently attracted by Rees' vision of pantisocracy at least not to discourage him from talking about it to Bill Dunn. Rees was to put up the capital, Dunn to supply the skill and the labour – though Rees and his friends might wield a hay fork on a summer's day. Rees in fact spent most of the summer painting landscapes.

To make up for neglecting his nephew and nieces, Orwell proposed an expedition, the same one he had promised Sonia. Here is Henry Dakin's narrative of an event that even got into the *Daily Express* – albeit in garbled form: the near-death of the author of *Animal Farm* was worth a paragraph.

He decided to camp on the other side of the island and four of us went round in a boat, Eric, Lucy, Ricky [Richard was now 3 years old] and me, with the camping gear and tent. We had a couple of days there, Eric liked fishing, we stayed in fact in a kind of hut there. On the way back, there was much looking up of dates and tides, but he must have misread them. Jane and Avril had walked back, but when we turned round the point there was already a fair swell, the boat was rising and falling a lot, but we were not worried because Eric seemed to know what he was doing and he did spend a lot of time mending and caulking the boat, and we had an outboard motor. But as we came round the point obviously the whirlpool had not receded. The Corryvreckan is not just the famous one big whirlpool, but a lot of smaller whirlpools around the edges. Before we had a chance to turn, we went straight into the minor whirlpools and lost control. Eric was at the tiller, the boat went all over the place, pitching and tossing, very frightening being thrown from one small whirlpool to another, pitching and tossing so much that the outboard motor jerked right off from its fixing. Eric said, 'the motor's gone, better get the oars out, Hen. Can't help much, I'm afraid'. So I unshipped the oars and partly with the current and partly with the oars, but mostly with the current, tried to steady her and we made our way to a little island. Even though that bit of it was very frightening, nobody panicked. Eric didn't panic, but nobody else did either. Indeed, when he said he couldn't help you very much, he said it very calmly and flatly. He was sitting at the back of the boat, he wasn't particularly strong, I was younger and stronger and sitting near the oars.

We got close to a little rock island and as the boat rose we saw that it was rising and falling about twelve feet. I had taken my boots off in case I had to swim for it, but as the boat rose level with the island, I jumped round with the painter in my hand all right, though sharp rocks painful on the feet, turned but saw the boat had fallen down. I still had my hand on the painter but the boat had turned upside down. First Lucy appeared, Eric appeared next and cried out, 'I've got Ricky all right'. Eric had grabbed him as the boat turned and pulled him out from under the boat. He had to swim from the end of the boat to the side of the island, still hanging on to Ricky. He seemed to keep his normal 'Uncle Eric' face the whole time, no panic from him or from anyone. And they were all able to clamber up on to the island ... So we were left on this island about a hundred yards long and I could not see all of it because the rocks rose in folds – we were left with the boat, one oar, a fishing rod and our clothes. Eric got his cigarette lighter out, never went anywhere without it, and put it out on a rock to dry. We had not been there three minutes when he said he would go off and find some food. A slightly ridiculous thing, it struck me afterwards, because we had had breakfast only two hours before and the last thing that any of us was thinking of was eating or of hunger. When he came back, the first thing he said was, 'Puffins are curious birds, they live in burrows. I saw some baby seagulls, but I haven't the heart to kill them.'

'I thought we were goners', he concluded. He almost seemed to enjoy it. We waved a shirt on the fishing rod about, and after about one and a half hours a lobster boat spotted us and picked us up. Picked us up with some difficulty, because he could not come up close to the island because of the swell and had to throw a rope across and we clambered along the rope one by one, Eric taking Ricky on his back.

The lobsterman landed us at the north of the island and we just walked about a quarter of an hour or twenty minutes and came across Avril and Jane working hard hoeing in a field. They said to us, 'What took you so long?'[23]

Bill Dunn read this account and his only correction was that Avril and Jane were hay-making, not hoeing, when the survivors returned. Avril, like her brother, seemed to take little notice of the incident.

The incident was far from trivial, however. Orwell's bravery, stoicism and eccentricity come across, but also his lack of common prudence, indeed excessive self-confidence or recklessness in practical matters. He cannot have secured the outboard motor properly and to go on such an expedition at all, to take children in an open boat across such a famous tidal race – legendary in the Western Isles – without being sure of the tides, could appear almost crazily irresponsible. Mr Donald Darroch did not agree with such a direct criticism of a former neighbour: 'It could have happened to anyone. But perhaps he might better first have taken advice from one who knew, who would have warned him or taken him over himself.' And Mr Ian McKechnie, who was then the boatman at Ardlussa and had been out with Orwell several times lobster-fishing, said that Orwell knew well enough what he was doing, even through the Corryvreckan, yet did not need advice but had simply misread the tide tables: 'easy enough to do'.[24] Orwell's own Domestic Diary records the event flatly and clinically with no hint of alarm for himself or others, 'only serious loss, the engine and twelve blankets' – all in a day's work.[25]

It was a cool reaction for a man who could also be melodramatically over-protective. Susan Watson remembered that when a lorry came to Barnhill to fetch a bull (*Gille Cruinn*, 'Round Laddie', was his name, the islanders recall), Orwell locked Richard and Susan in a bedroom while he stood at the door of the house with a loaded service revolver in his hand. The bull trotted eagerly up the plank into the lorry without trouble or struggle.

Richard had had a bad fall during their first summer in Jura and gashed his head. They got him to Ardlussa in the huge, second-hand Austin saloon car they had bought ('big as a tank, it could hold the track' said Tony Rozga); it took six hours in all before Dr Sandiman arrived to stitch him up. This accident should have warned Orwell of the trouble that could lie ahead. The islanders who knew him all agree that the climate was no harm to him, even claim that it was good for tubercular people, a view fiercely contested by Bill Dunn, incidentally, who says that the dampness was obviously harmful; but the remoteness from a doctor 'was not wise – but of course we all felt that, particularly those with old people or children in the house', two of them said.[26]

Orwell clearly intended to settle in Jura, even if he also intended to return to Islington for a short while each winter. His business affairs needed managing, he now needed an accountant as well as an agent, for the tax man was beginning to notice his belated success and the usual prolonged arguments began about the year to which his earnings were attributable. In July, however, he gave up the lease of Wallington at last, giving his sub-tenant, Lydia Jackson, apologetic notice to quit. Lydia had also used Barnhill while he was away in the winter.[27]

He told several friends in letters, for instance George Woodcock, that 'I can work here with fewer interruptions, and I think we shall be less cold here. The climate, although wet, is not quite as cold as England, and it is much easier to get fuel.'[28] And to Anthony Powell: 'I know that if I return to London and get caught up in weekly articles I shall never get on with anything longer.'[29] That September he was near to finishing the first draft of *Nineteen Eighty-Four*, so 'anything longer' must be the next book. Typically he was already looking ahead. But he also told Powell that: 'One seems to have a limited capacity for work nowadays and one has to husband it.' He was getting more realistic for that autumn he felt ill health returning.

Towards the end of October he wrote to Celia Kirwan that he did not have time to write anything for *Polemic*, that he was still 'struggling with this novel' which he had not got on with as fast as he wanted because 'I have been in lousy health most of this year, my chest as usual'.[30] And on the last day of the month he admitted to Moore that 'I am writing this in bed (inflammation of the lungs), so I shan't be coming up to London in early November as planned.'[31]

Orwell finished the first draft of *Nineteen Eighty-Four* by the end of October, and at once took to his bed exhausted.

It was a cold blowy day in April, and a million radios were striking thirteen. Winston Smith pushed open the glass door of Victory Mansions, turned to the right down the passage-way and pressed the button for the lift. Nothing happened. He had just pressed a second time when a door at the end of the passage opened letting out a smell of boiled greens and old rag mats, and the aged prole who acted as porter and caretaker thrust out a grey, seamed face sucking his teeth and watching Winston malignantly.

'Lift ain't working,' he announced at last.[32]

There was, as Orwell had always said, a lot of work still to be done between a first draft and the final version. But he had broken the back of it.

Before Richard Rees left at the end of September, he had entered into a formal agreement with the Fletchers for Bill Dunn to farm at Barnhill in partnership with him. So Bill Dunn had moved down and was living in Barnhill. He grumbled sadly that of the £1,000 that Rees put up for equipment, livestock and seed, Rees had promptly wasted £350 in buying a uselessly large army lorry. Intellectuals did not know the needs of practical farmers, and should leave them to make their own decisions. Avril sympathized. Orwell agreed that it would be sensible for Bill Dunn to live in for he was preoccupied with his work and with the decline in his health again (after a good summer, the summer guests all agreed, whatever he had said in letters). Avril needed a man about the house.

Hearing only that Orwell was mildly ill and would be staying in Jura that winter, David Astor had sent up to Barnhill on loan a pony called Bob and a trap, knowing that the road could become impassable in winter even to a heavy car. Bob, however, never took kindly to the trap, refusing the shafts, though he was useful for Bill Dunn to ride when rounding up sheep and cows.

By the end of November, 'still on my back', Orwell told Powell, still running a temperature, he was unable or did not risk going to the mainland to consult 'my usual chest specialist'. It is doubtful, however, whether he had had a regular specialist since Eileen's brother had died at Dunkirk, despite many examinations by Army medical boards and local G Ps. So 'I've now arranged for a man to come from Glasgow and give me the once-over ... I think I'll have to go into hospital for a bit, because apart from the treatment there's the X-raying etc., and after that I might have a stab at going abroad for a couple of months if I can get a newspaper assignment to somewhere warm.'[33] Incredibly, he was thinking seriously of a suggestion of the *Observer*'s (David Astor could not have known how ill his friend was) of doing a tour of Africa for them to study the South African elections and report on prospects and progress of decolonization elsewhere.[34]

By the end of the first week in December, all such hopes or fantasies had gone. He wrote to Celia:

I've been in bed 6 weeks, & was feeling unwell some time before that. I kept trying to get just well enough to make the journey to London – finally I brought a chest specialist here. He says I have got to go into a sanatorium, probably for about 4 months. It's an awful bore, however perhaps it's all for the best if they can cure me. I don't think living in Jura has had a bad effect on my health – in any case the sanatorium I'm going to is near Glasgow, which is the same climate. Actually we've had marvellous weather this year & very dry. Even now I'm looking out on what might be a spring day if the bracken was green.[35]

He was basically right about Jura, but he sounded very defensive about it. Some of his friends must have been worried. Avril wrote to Humphrey Dakin on 14 December with typical Blair understatement or a partly imperceptive stoicism; 'Eric is far from well.' Years later when asked whether he was not writing against time, she replied: 'I don't think so, because I don't think he was the sort of person who ever thought he was going to die. Not immediately. He knew he was ill. I don't think he ever entertained what is commonly known as the death wish.'[36]

He made a last entry in his Domestic Diary in the early morning of December.

Sharp frosts the last two nights. The days sunny and still, sea calm. A[vril] has very bad cold. The goose for Xmas disappeared, then was found swimming in the sea round at the anchorage, about a mile from our own beach. B[ill] thinks it must have swum round the head and had to follow it with a dinghy and shoot it. Weight before drawing and plucking, $10\frac{1}{2}$lbs. Snowdrops up all over the place. A few tulips showing. Some wallflowers still trying to flower.[37]

That same day they set off, and on Christmas Eve 1947 he entered Ward 3 of Hairmyres Hospital, East Kilbride, near Glasgow. He was, however, to return to Jura, but not for long. The longed-for Jura days were almost over.

'Orwell is the odd man out in English writing', Orwell must have been cheered to hear that V. S. Pritchett had broadcast about him earlier that year: 'He is the most original of his contemporaries. He might be described as a writer who has "gone native" in his own country.'[38] Alas, there were to be no more explorations or forays.

CHAPTER SEVENTEEN

THE LAST DAYS AND

NINETEEN EIGHTY-FOUR

ORWELL was to be in Hairmyres Hospital for seven months. From the beginning he knew that it would be a long stay. His worries about getting size twelve boots were now replaced by the difficulties of getting one of the new Biro ballpoint pens. The day after Christmas he wrote to Julian Symons enclosing £3 for the purchase of one (the early models were expensive). The doctors had firmly taken his typewriter away from him.

No less than four letters to Symons had as their pretext Biro pens and refills.[1] But they all contained other matters. In the first he told him: 'For two to three months I've really been very sick indeed and have lost one and a half stones in weight, and I have of course not done a stroke of work' – this, as ever, was a statement relative to Orwell's extraordinary work habits and demands on himself.

He was more frank when writing to Tosco Fyvel on New Year's Eve: 'Like a fool I decided not to go to a doctor as I knew I'd be stuck in bed and I wanted to get on with the book I was writing. All that happened is that I've half-written the book, which in my case is much the same as not starting it.'[2] The same day he wrote to David Astor, who had asked about visiting hours, and told him much the same, but added: '[the treatment] is one that must take a long time.' He apologized for writing in pencil because his Biro had run dry. There was no mention of *Observer* business in the letter, but in his letter to Fyvel the reason for the urgency about the Biro becomes clear: 'I'm shortly going to start a little book reviewing for the *Observer*' – he had only missed writing three of his fortnightly pieces – 'I might as well make a bit of money while I'm on my back.' This was not just the protestant work ethic still eating him up, he must have been worried about money for Richard and Avril's sake. The royalties from *Animal Farm* were growing, but they might not remain enough to live on without a little journalism – not a lot, as he could now command top rates. The economy of Barnhill, despite Bill Dunn's hard work and Richard Rees' capital, hardly broke even, so that though it was no drain on Orwell's resources, it could not have supported Richard and Avril as well if he were incapacitated.

He describes his treatment at Hairmyres clinically in a letter to his sister-in-law:

I thought you'd like to hear how I was getting on. I believe Mr Dick [the consultant] sent you a line abt my case. As soon as he listened to me he said I had a fairly extensive cavity in the left lung – & also a small patch at the top of the other lung – this I think, the old one I had before. The X-ray confirms this, he said. I have now been here nearly a fortnight and the treatment they are giving me is to put the left lung out of action, apparently for abt 6 months, which is supposed to give it a better chance to heal. They first crushed the phrenic nerve, which I gather is what makes the lung expand and contract, and then pumped air into the diaphragm, which I understand is to push the lung into a different position and get it away from some kind of movement which occurs automatically. I have to have 'refills' of air in the diaphragm every few days, but I think later it gets down to once a week or less. For the rest, I am still really very ill and weak, and on getting here I found I had lost one and a half stone but I have felt better since being here, don't sweat at night like I used and have more appetite. They make me eat a tremendous lot. At present I am not allowed out of bed because apparently one has to get adjusted to having the extra air inside. It is a nice hospital and everyone is extremely kind to me. I have also got a room to myself, but I don't know whether that will be permanent. I have of course done no work for 2–3 months, but I think I may be equal to some light work soon & I am arranging to do a little book reviewing.[3]

The only inaccuracy is that the 'pneumoperitonium' machine injected below, not through, the diaphragm. The discomfort must have been intense. He never complained.

That and other letters show concern that Richard might be tubercular. He and Avril had been trying to get a TT tested cow, so far without any success: they had been boiling all the milk and he was going to have the boy examined in London soon. Also they had kept Richard out of his room for fear of infection when he had been in bed for so many weeks at Barnhill. The poor little boy was now finally allowed to visit his father, but the journey was long and difficult so only one visit took place. Avril sent photographs of him to her brother during that half-year.

Serious work was out of the question. Orwell told Warburg in February:

Before taking to my bed I had finished the rough draft of my novel all save the last few hundred words, and if I had been well I might have finished it by about May. If I'm well and out of here by June, I might finish it by the end of the year – I don't know. It is just a ghastly mess as it stands, but the idea is so good that I could not possibly abandon it. If anything should happen to me I've instructed Richard Rees, my literary executor, to destroy the MS, without showing it to anybody, but it's unlikely that anything like that would happen.[4]

However ill he was he coped with a great deal of routine correspondence as well as letters to his friends. Requests to translate *Animal Farm*, to reprint his essays and to commission for new ones, made it impossible for Moore not to have to write frequently. Orwell was particularly concerned with *Animal Farm*, what kind of house would publish it and how to ensure that the translations were not tendentious or cut. Moore and Orwell themselves pursued a highly political strategy in licensing translations: '*I did not want any fee for 'Animal Farm' from the Poles or any other Slavs,*' Orwell firmly underlines, 'but I don't see why they should not pay a small fee ... if they decided to [translate] one of the other books.'[5] American editors, particularly, once having discovered his address, pursued him with attractive offers; and some were sadly persistent, considering that he courteously and personally replied that he was far too ill. Mr S. M. Levitas, the editor of *New Leader*, was particularly pressing: 'the only publication of the "left" in this great, big country of ours which has combatted totalitarianism for the last 25 years'.[6] Orwell seemed to enjoy, however, hearing from and writing to Dwight Macdonald, who convinced him that Henry Wallace's Presidential candidature should be the hope of the world – though he had to fight off Macdonald too as regards any more writing for his journal, *Politics*.[7] Even Fred Warburg asked him to write a blurb for John Prebble's *The Edge of Darkness* and to read manuscripts, which he also politely declined, in another unnecessary letter.[8] But though he quibbled about the binding and the jackets, Orwell was plainly very happy at Secker & Warburg's beginning a uniform edition of his best books. And he was genuinely sorry not to continue writing for *Partisan Review* as he had done all through the War. Orwell grumbled a bit to Philip Rahv about Koestler, who had taken over the London Letter in *Partisan Review* from him: 'squealing at petty discomforts like petrol rationing that don't touch the mass of the people'; and he told him that he was about to try 'the new American drug streptomycin'.[9]

This drug, which was soon to end tuberculosis as a fatal disease, was discovered in the United States in 1944 and was only being tested in Britain by the Medical Research Council, not available to doctors. Currency restrictions were harsh on imports. Mr Bruce Dick had read favourable reports of it and probably did not have much hope for the treatment he was prescribing. He realized that one of Orwell's first visitors was David Astor. Orwell asked a rare favour.

1.2.48

Dear David,

Thanks so much for your letter. Before anything else I must tell you something Dr Dick has said to me. He says that I am getting on quite well, but slowly, and it would speed recovery if one had some streptomycin (STREP-TOMYCIN).

This is obtainable in the USA, and because of dollars the B[oard] O[f] T[rade] (or whatever it is) won't normally grant a licence. He suggested that you with your American connections might arrange to buy it and I could pay you. He wants 70 grammes and it costs abt £1 a gramme ... I suppose it will mean paying out about 300 dollars. If you want to be repaid in dollars I think I have enough, as I had started building up a reserve of dollars in the US, otherwise I can pay you in sterling, I must in either case pay you for it is a considerable sum and of course the hospital can't pay it ...[10]

Astor, who had been having food parcels from America and butter and eggs from his estate on Jura sent to the hospital, leaped at the chance to help his friend more seriously. A cable was sent from the *Observer* to the office of the Astor Estate in New York – also requesting a pair of hand-made size twelve boots, which Orwell had not asked for, but Astor knew the problem of old.[11] Boots would make an acceptable small present to herald the sudden hope for Orwell's recovery.

Either Dick or Orwell felt it was urgent enough, however, on not hearing from Astor for a few days, to send a telegram with the same request. This crossed a letter saying that he had already cabled to New York. Astor wrote directly to Mr Dick offering any help he could, urging him to ignore any scruples of his patient about money and to come to him directly. He also spoke to Nye Bevan, who was Minister of Health, to ensure that there were no obstacles to importing the drug.[12]

At first the drug seemed to work well. Towards the end of March, Orwell wrote to Julian Symons asking for a refill for his Biro again, enclosing a postal order for 3s 6d. 'I have been having the streptomycin for about a month and it is evidently doing its stuff. I haven't gained much weight, but I'm much better in every way.' He evidently needed the refill because, he told his friend, he had been well enough to write a short article for *Politics and Letters*, in a series on 'Writers and Leviathans'. A notebook he used in hospital which survives includes notes for this article, the theme of which was, as his notes indicated:

Corruption of aesthetic standards by political motives ... Conclusion: must engage in politics. Must keep issues separate. Must not engage in party politics *as a writer*. Recognition of our own prejudices only way of keeping them in check.

If his political beliefs were still the same, certainly a more sombre realism came into their formulation in the published version:

... most of us still have a lingering belief that every choice, even political choice, is between good and evil, and that if a thing is necessary it is also right. We should, I think, get rid of this belief, which belongs to the nursery. In politics one can never do more than decide which of two evils is the lesser, and there are some situations from which one can only escape by acting like a devil or a lunatic. War, for example, may be necessary, but it is certainly not right or sane. Even a General Election is not exactly a pleasant or edifying spectacle. If you have to take part in such things – and I think you do have to, unless you are armoured by old age or stupidity or hypocrisy – then you also have to keep part of yourself inviolate.*[13]

* Contrast this to the end of his review of Hayek's *Road to Serfdom* when he says there is no way out of the equally unpalatable consequences of capitalism or of collectivism 'unless a planned economy can be somehow combined with freedom of the intellect, which can only happen if the concept of right and wrong is restored to politics.' (*The Collected Essays, Journalism and Letters*, Vol. III, p. 119.)

Is this final maturity as a political thinker? Or is it depression feeding on disease? Perhaps only a man in pain, however, or with a great imagination for pain, can grasp the harshness of political dilemmas of war and peace.

'I've had a bad time with the secondary effects of streptomycin,' he told Moore in the middle of April, 'but the TB seems definitely better.'[14] To Julian Symons he wrote that he had 'a bad fortnight' with it: 'I suppose with all these drugs it's rather a case of sinking the ship to get rid of the rats.'[15] Indeed a month later he told Celia Kirwan that it seemed to have killed all the germs, he was getting up for two hours a day and they were hoping he might be able to leave by August.[16] The side-effects, however, had been drastic and Dick had had to discontinue the drug, since nobody then knew how to control such hypersensitive reactions. Orwell seemed to have thought the treatment had come to a natural end. With much precious streptomycin still in hand, Mr Dick gave it, with Orwell's ready agreement, to two doctors' wives in the same hospital, whom it cured completely.[17] The side-effects had been horrible. Orwell recalled them dispassionately in the last notebook he ever kept:

24.3.49. Before I forget them it is worth writing down the secondary symptoms produced by streptomycin when I was treated with it last year. Streptomycin was then almost a new drug & had never been used at that hospital before. The symptoms in my case were quite different from those described in the American medical journal in which we read the subject up beforehand.

At first, though the streptomycin seemed to produce an almost immediate improvement in my health, there were no secondary symptoms, except that a sort of discoloration appeared at the base of my fingers & toe nails. Then my face became noticeably redder & the skin had a tendency to flake off, & a sort of rash appeared all over my body, especially down my back. There was no itching associated with this. After about 3 weeks I got a severe sore throat, which did not go away & was not affected by sucking penicillin lozenges. It was very painful to swallow & I had to have a special diet for some weeks. There was now ulceration with blisters in my throat & in the insides of my cheeks, & the blood kept coming up into little blisters on my lips. At night these burst & bled considerably, so that in the morning my lips were always stuck together with blood & I had to bathe them before I could open my mouth. Meanwhile my nails had disintegrated at the roots & the disintegration grew, as it were, up the nail, new nails forming beneath meanwhile. My hair began to come out, & one or two patches of quite white hair appeared at the back (previously it was only speckled with grey).

After 50 days the streptomycin, which had been injected at the rate of 1 gramme a day, was discontinued. The lips etc. healed almost immediately & the rash went away, though not quite so promptly. My hair stopped coming out & went back to its normal colour, though I think with more grey in it than before. The old nails ended by dropping out altogether, & some months after leaving hospital I had only ragged tips, which kept splitting, to the new nails. Some of the toenails did not drop out. Even now my nails are not normal. They are much more corrugated than before, & a great deal thinner, with a constant tendency to split if I do not keep them very short. At that time the Board of Trade would not give import permits for streptomycin, except to a few hospitals for experimental purposes. One had to get hold of it by some kind of wire-pulling. It cost £1 a gramme, plus 60% Purchase Tax.

This could have been Darwin in the *Beagle* noting minute variations in the birds and animals of the Galapagos, or J. B. S. Haldane noting his own reactions as he experimented upon himself with dangerous drugs – not a desperately sick man.

All the while he struggled painfully to continue writing, fearful that he might no longer be able to, as this extract from the same notebook shows:

30.3.48

When you are acutely ill, or recovering from acute illness, your brain frankly strikes at work and you are only equal to picture papers, easy crossword puzzles etc. But when it is a case of a long illness, where you are weak and without appetite but not actually feverish or in pain, you have the impression that your brain is quite normal, your thoughts just as active as ever, you are interested in the same things, and you seem able to talk normally, and you can read anything that you would read at any other time. It is only when you attempt to write, even to write the simplest and stupidest newspaper article, that you realize what a deterioration has happened inside your skull.

At the start it is impossible to get anything on to paper at all. Your mind runs away to any conceivable subject rather than the one you are trying to deal with, and even the physical act of writing is unbearably irksome. Then, perhaps, you begin to be able to write a little, but whatever you write, once it is set down on paper, turns out to be stupid and obvious. You have also no command of language, or rather you can think of nothing except flat, obvious expressions; a good, lively phrase never occurs to you and even when you begin to re-acquire the habit of writing, you seem to be incapable of preserving continuity. From time to time you may strike out a fairly good sentence, but it is extraordinarily difficult to make consecutive sentences sound as though they had anything to do with one another. The reason for this is that you cannot concentrate for more than a few seconds and therefore cannot even remember what you said a moment ago. In all this the striking thing is the contrast between the apparent normality of your mind, and its helplessness when you attempt to get anything on to paper. Your thoughts, when you think them, seem to be just like your thoughts, at any other time, but as soon as they are reduced to some kind of order they always turn out to be badly expressed platitudes.

In his letters to his friends, as in the two 'hospital notebooks', there is no complaint or self-pity, only precise observation and commentary on his health (though he admitted to no one that the side-effects had been so drastic) and normal discussion of all his usual interests. Richard Rees, who was now living in Edinburgh, visited him regularly and must have seen something of the suffering, but if so kept it to himself. Fred Warburg had come up from London to see Orwell at the end of February, but obviously before the worst of the drug's side-effects were apparent. He saw no immediate cause for worry. Orwell, who greeted him with a smile 'both welcoming and wintry', only complained mildly of the pain of the injections of antibiotics in his arm.[18] In early February, he had actually had his right arm put in plaster for a while, though whether from the effect of the injections or to reduce pressure on the one good lung is not clear. It could even have been done to stop him from writing; but he quickly learned to use the Biro with his left hand.[19] Such a man is hard to stop.

He may or may not have had the manuscript of the first draft of the new book by him, but in the hospital notebook he wrote several pages of analytical notes on 'Nineteen Eighty-Four' or 'The Last Man in Europe' which look like a writing plan but by that stage are more likely to have been reminders to himself of the main themes and symbols, checking that they were all there in the manuscript in the right order. There were notes to 'interpolate' this and that, or themes 'to be brought in' in the redraft, particularly in relation to sections 6 and 7, called chapters in the notebook, that seemed to be causing him difficulty. These were the sections when Winston Smith is writing in his forbidden diary on paper and trying at the same time to recall the lost past in his own mind.

The notebook also contains a huge list of 'Foreign words and phrases unnecessarily used in English'; also that unfinished poem about child-hood and the plumber's daughter of long ago, which included:

> We played the games that all have played
> Though most remember not,
> And the plumber's daughter who might be seven,
> She showed me all she'd got

and which ended, 'When good King Edward ruled the land/And I was a chubby boy.' And odd notes on this and that. Here is one page:

21.5.48
9.45 am. The following noises now happening simultaneously. A radio. A gramophone. Vacuum cleaner running intermittently. Orderly singing inter-mittently. Noise of hammering from outside. Usual clatter of boots and trolleys, whistling, cries of rooks & gulls, cackling of hens in the distance, taps running, doors opening & shutting, intermittent coughing.

Things not foreseen in youth as part of middle age.
Perpetual tired weak feeling in legs, aching knees. Stiffness amounting to pain in small of back & down loins. Discomfort in gums. Chest more or less always constricted. Feeling in the morning of being almost unable to stand up. Sensation of cold whenever the sun is not shining. Wind on the stomach (Making it difficult to think). Eyes always watering.
As painful as a grapestone under a dental plate.
As noisy as a mouse in a packet of macaroni.
As haughty as a fishmonger.

The symptoms he describes are physiologically more typical of old age than of middle age.

By May, however, he really seemed to be on the mend. The hospital let him have his typewriter back. He resumed correspondence with George Woodcock about the Freedom Defence Committee, anxious that they would defend minority rights of all kinds, even Fascist and Communist against each other.[20] He made careful notes for an article on 'The Labour Government after Three Years' for *Commentary*. He lamented that the Labour Government had not been able to bring about any fundamental changes in British society but, on the whole, inclined to defend them as doing about as well as could be expected, in face of the fact that the Labour Party was a trades union rather than a socialist party and, above all, in light of Britain's grave economic crises. The pressing issues, he said, were not so much between Conservative and Socialist as those concerned with immediate economic survival. And, once again, he pointed to a fundamental contradiction between decolonization, which should be and had to be done, and the maintenance of a high standard of living for the Western industrial worker. As in that article on Burma published so long ago in *Le Progrès civique* (1929), he saw Western prosperity as dependent on an exploitative imperialism: he rather naïvely assumed that economic domination would end with formal independence. *Commentary*'s editor gave it the title 'Britain's Struggle for Survival'.[21] Not one of his best pieces – a pot-boiler in fact, but it does show clearly where he stood politically in the very middle of writing *Nineteen Eighty-Four*: less stalwart and aggressive than in 1942, but basically he still held the same values. The attainment of socialism would be a longer haul than once he had hoped. The Labour Government had missed so many opportunities of fortifying and extending that egalitarian ethic which had arisen throughout society, however briefly, during the War. So much would now have to be begun all over again as if for the first time. His values had not changed, but he held them in a mood of realistic sadness. His beliefs were not dead, far from it, but he found that they no longer led him directly into action.

The third article he wrote from his hospital bed, almost the last real essay he was to write, was on an old love of his, George Gissing the novelist. Despite its (what would soon be called) 'Orwellian' beginning, this is tempered pessimism:

In the shadow of the atomic bomb it is not easy to talk confidently about progress. However, if it can be assumed that we are *not* going to be blown to pieces in about ten years' time, there are many reasons, and George Gissing's novels are among them, for thinking that the present age is a good deal better than the last one.[22]

The comic spirit, even mockery, of his own pessimism – as in *Tribune* at Christmas 1946 – is still evident. He replied to a letter from Celia, now working in Paris, 'I must say anything connected with UNESCO sounds pretty discouraging. Anyway, I should knock all the money you can out of them, as I don't suppose they'll last much longer.'[23]

He was allowed out for three hours a day, then more, playing croquet, wandering round the hospital, looking forward to finishing 'this blasted novel', and finding 'no one much to talk to here'. He had found that the editor of *Hotspur*, the children's comic, was a fellow patient, 'but he's rather dull'.[24] Soon, although he was warned to take things very, very easy, he could be discharged. There seemed no need for him to have further out-patient treatment. He could return to Barnhill if he treated himself as an invalid. He wrote to George Woodcock:

23.7.48

Dear George,

I'm leaving hospital at last, so my address will be, as before, i.e. Barnhill, Isle of Jura, Argyllshire. Of course I've got to go on living an invalid life for six months or so, perhaps more, but at any rate I'm much better. I've got your book to review for the *Observer*, but I haven't done it yet. Please remember me to Inge. Yours,

George[25]

On 28 July he was back on Jura. Avril had brought an excited Richard down to Glasgow to meet him. Bill Dunn was waiting with the giant second-hand Austin at Craighouse.

For six hot and glorious summer weeks he was at least a long shadow of his old self. He played with Richard more than before. The boy was now $4\frac{1}{2}$, a big lad for his age. 'Though I only get up half the day,' Orwell told both Celia Kirwan and Michael Meyer, so could take no boat trips or long walks or help around the farm. He did not feel up to riding the frisky Bob, yet walked to Kinuachdrach several times to fetch milk and butter and pottered in the vegetable garden. And he revised his book. If he had to spend half the day in bed, yet 'I have got quite used to working in bed', he told Meyer. He asked Celia to come and visit in September (although again it proved impossible); but put Michael Meyer off by saying that the house was so crowded that people were even overflowing into tents.[26] Avril said that this was a 'white lie'. She and her brother were determined not to be disturbed, even by good friends, until his book was finished. The Rozgas remember (and a photograph confirms) that there was a tent that summer, but he slept in it himself on a camp-bed, wanting all the fresh air he could get.

Things seemed very relaxed and easy. Avril had fought off visitors, except Richard Rees, who was no trouble and who respected Orwell's working habits – indeed, George liked having him vaguely around.

Avril seemed to be more relaxed, even a little skittish. Orwell had not liked having Bill Dunn in the house too much, though he agreed that the arrangement was sensible and practical; and he rather disapproved of Bill's familiarity with his sister. As with Susan Watson, he was not quite sure whether to treat him as one of the family or not.

He was somewhat shocked when he discovered the obvious reason for Avril's happiness and Bill's familiarity. He thought that as the elder brother he should have been consulted, or should have guarded his 'younger sister' (of 41) more zealously. He tried to say something to Avril about the ten-year difference in their ages not being quite decent, but perhaps on seeing a glint of battle in her eyes or on feeling a rare stab of hypocrisy in his own troubled heart, he desisted. Typically, Orwell soon mastered his lower-upper-middle class prejudices and saw the bright side of it, growing to accept the situation. But he refused to discuss the matter with amused or delighted callers. 'It was a family matter' he firmly concluded.

He got down to work, although the usual load of correspondence continued. After he returned the post bag to Barnhill got heavier, the islanders remembered. But there were few real distractions and, apart from his book reviews for the *Observer*, he wrote only one major article that autumn, 'Reflections on Gandhi' for *Partisan Review*. He gently demolished the views that Gandhi was a progressive and that his aggressive *Satyagraha*, 'a sort of non-violent warfare', could be equated with either passive resistance or pacifism, and concluded:

And if, as may happen, India and Britain finally settle down into a decent and friendly relationship, will this be partly because Gandhi, by keeping up his struggle, obstinately and without hatred, disinfected the political air? That one even thinks of asking such questions indicates his stature. One may feel, as I do, a sort of aesthetic distaste for Gandhi, one may reject the claims of sainthood made on his behalf (he never made any such claim himself, by the way), one may also reject sainthood as an ideal and therefore feel that Gandhi's basic aims were anti-human and reactionary: but regarded simply as a politician, and compared with the other leading political figures of our time, how clean a smell he has managed to leave behind![27]

As in his *Observer* profile of Nye Bevan, there could be an autobiographical touch in this: 'keeping up his struggle, obstinately and without hatred' and disinfecting 'the political air'.

Yet all was not well. His own words can tell the story.

9.10.48

Dear David,

... You were right about my being not very well. I am a bit better now but felt very poorly for about a fortnight. It started funnily enough with my going back to Hairmyres to be examined, which they had told me to do in September. Mr Dick seemed to be quite pleased with the results of his examination, but the journey upset me. Any kind of journey seems to do this. He told me to go on as at present, i.e. spending half the day in bed, which I quite gladly do as I simply can't manage any kind of exertion ... so long as I live a senile sort of life I feel all right, and I seem to be able to work much as usual. I have got so used to writing in bed that I think I prefer it, though of course it's awkward to type there, I am just struggling with the last stages of this bloody book ... There is an eagle flying over the field in front. They always come here in windy weather.[28]

22.10.48

Dear Fred,

... I shall finish the book, D V, early in November, and I am rather flinching from the job of typing it, because it is a very awkward thing to do in bed, where I still have to spend half the time ... I can't send it away because it is an unbelievably bad MS and no one could make head or tail of it without explanation. On the other hand a skilled typist under my eye could do it easily enough. If you can think of anybody who would be willing to come, I will send money for the journey and full instructions ...

I am not pleased with the book but I am not absolutely dissatisfied. I first thought of it in 1943. I think it is a good idea but the execution would have been better if I had not written it under the influence of TB. I haven't definitely fixed on the title but I am hesitating between NINETEEN EIGHTY-FOUR and THE LAST MAN IN EUROPE.

I have just had Sartre's book on antisemitism, which you published, to review. I think Sartre is a bag of wind and I am going to give him a good boot ...[29]

29.10.48

Dear Julian,

... I shall finish my book, D V in a week or ten days, but I am rather flinching from typing it, which is a tiring job and in any case can't be done in bed where I have to be half the day. So I am trying to get a good stenog. to come here for a fortnight ... it's not easy to get typists for short periods nowadays, at least good ones, and some might funk the journey ...

In another year or so I shall have to be thinking about Richard's schooling, but I am not making any plans because one can't see far ahead now. I am not going to let him go to a boarding school before he is ten, and I would like him to start off at the elementary school. If one could find a good one. It's a difficult question. Obviously it is democratic for everyone to go to the same schools, or at least start off there but when you see what the elementary schools are like, and the results, you feel that any child that has the chance should be rescued from them ... However I am taking no decisions about Richard one way or the other. Of course we may all have been blown to hell before it becomes urgent, but personally I don't expect a major shooting war for 5 or 10 years. After the Russians have fully recovered and have atomic bombs, I suppose it isn't avoidable. And even if it is avoided, there are a lot of other unpleasantnesses blowing up ...[30]

29.10.48

Dear Moore,
I wired a week ago to ask Warburg if he could find me a good stenog to come here and type my book ... I haven't heard from Warburg yet, but if he can't find anyone possibly you might be able to help me? Of course it's awkward nowadays to find people to take on a job for a fortnight, with two gos of seasickness thrown in ...[31]

Some time the following week he finished revising the manuscript. He came downstairs, opened the last bottle of wine in the house with Bill and Avril, then took to his bed again in a state of collapse. He had typed the first draft, neatly and accurately, as he always did, with double-spacing and good broad margins. So when he had sat up in bed that autumn revising it, he worked with a pen or with Biro, sometimes even pencil, on the same sheets, but made so many corrections and amendments and wrote so tightly into the margins that it must have been difficult even for him to re-read the final manuscript coherently. Obviously a lot of further detailed revision would be needed as the final typing went along. Hence his very real doubts that the job could be farmed out without his presence.

The general problems of the first draft seem to have been of two kinds. Firstly, there was a general slackness and prolixity in the texture of the writing, at least by his formidable standards, signs of speed and tiredness – most of which he firmly corrected in the final version. Secondly there was a tendency to miss out or gloss over in the speed of the actual writing, in the telling of the actual story of Winston and Julia, concepts and ideas about totalitarianism that he had carefully noted down beforehand to be included. These notes demonstrate a much more systematic and theoretical conception than has often been appreciated. The jottings in the 1948 hospital notebook seem to be reminders to himself of what he had left out or stressed too lightly. He had rewritten completely and thus retyped cleanly relatively few pages in the work of revision between August and October; it all needed retyping.

Any exertion was now giving him high temperatures and he felt inflammation of his lungs or lung again. He realized that he would have to go back into a sanatorium. He was already in touch with Bruce Dick about that when it became clear that there was going to be no typist.

19.11.48

Dear Moore,

... I don't think I'll trouble you about the typist. It is all rather a muddle. I asked Warburg to get someone for me, and Roger Senhouse set his niece who lives in Edinburgh on to the job. I still haven't heard from her, but she might at some moment produce a typist and it would then be rather awkward if I had meanwhile engaged somebody from London. Meanwhile I am getting on with the job myself and should finish it before the end of the month, or not much later than that. I am in better health, but I am trying to arrange to go into a private sanatorium for the worst of the winter, i.e. January and February ...

15.11.48

Dear Tony,

... I can work, but that is about all I can do. To walk even a few hundred yards promptly upsets me ... I am just on the grisly job of typing out my novel. I can't type much because it tires me too much to sit up at table ... It's awful to think I've been mucking about with this book since June of 1947, and it's a ghastly mess now, a good idea ruined, but of course I was seriously ill for 7 or 8 months of the time ...[32]

In that same week he replied to a letter from David Astor in much the same terms as he wrote to Anthony Powell, also adding that it proved impossible to get 'a stenog.'. How sad that he had not turned to Astor in the first place. He could have found someone. Fred Warburg and his partner had tried hard, but at that time there was a shortage of labour and the winter season was against them: 'I had to cable my failure to Orwell, who finished the revision early in November, and typed the Ms. himself. On December 4 he posted it to me. This failure on my part still haunts me. It was perhaps the last straw.'[33]

Orwell must then have decided, as Warburg suggests, to take a gamble with his health and to type the final draft himself – to get the damned thing out of the way, the book that had begun to devour him. But he probably thought that the worst he had to fear was another relapse. (Some time that November, for instance, he took the trouble to renew his driving licence.) He could have gone down to London to supervise the revision, but after the Glasgow journey he felt that such a journey would tire him too much. So partly in bed, partly on a kitchen chair in his room, he typed out a top copy plus two carbons in two or three weeks; and to make matters worse, said Bill Dunn, he heated his room with a Valor paraffin-stove in bad repair, smelly and giving off heavy fumes. And while he was working hard, he went back to heavy smoking. The physical effort must have been appalling. If a secretary could have been found for him or if he had had a dictating machine, he might have lived longer. On the last day of November he wrote a long apologetic letter to Moore, who had indeed sent him two names of possible typists, that he had been waiting to hear from Senhouse's niece in Edinburgh; he thought that she had first claim, and so got on with it himself when he did not hear from her. 'I do hope the two women whose names you suggested have not been inconvenienced or put off other engagements or anything like that. It really wasn't worth all this fuss. It's merely that as it tires me to sit upright for any length of time I can't type very neatly and can't do many pages a day.'[34]

This was, however, Orwell's natural courtesy and his consideration for an old man. He must have remembered how Moore had come to see him fifteen years ago, when he scarcely knew him and had only just taken him on as a young author, at Uxbridge Hospital at Christmas 1933. In fact the physical effort of the typing, not the mental effort of the revising or the sombreness of the theme, brought him near to physical collapse. For the whole of December he was bed-ridden. He corresponded with Bruce Dick and then Gwen to try to find a suitable sanatorium – it must be a private sanatorium for he had to have a 'room to myself, otherwise I can't work'. And like Eileen, he worried a bit about the money: 'I can't of course pay things like 30 guineas a week, but can pay anything reasonable. Do you know of anywhere?'[35]

Four days before Christmas, he confessed in identical words to Fred

Warburg and David Astor 'I am really very unwell indeed.' From 7 January his address would be 'the Cotswold Sanatorium, Cranham, Gloucestershire'. 'I'm glad you liked the book,' he told Warburg (a considerable understatement of Warburg's astounded reaction, as will be seen). 'I am trying to finish off my scraps of book reviewing etc. and must then strike work for a month or so. I can't get on as at present. I have a stunning idea for a very short novel which has been in my head for years, but I can't start anything until I'm free from high temperature etc. Love to all. George.'[36]

He polished off an outstanding review for the *Observer*, a pleasant piece on Nicolas Bentley and Leonard Russell's *English Comic Album*. He liked the book: 'the most jaded reader can hardly glance through it without laughing several times,' he concluded, as if daring the publisher to quote that in advertisements. He complained that Max Beerbohm and Thackeray were not well represented, but observed that 'even if there is no Rowlandson or Cruikshank alive today, a period in which Low, Giles, Nicolas Bentley, Ronald Searle and Osbert Lancaster are all at work simultaneously is not doing so badly'.[37]

Orwell wrote to Roger Senhouse, criticizing the proposed dust-jacket copy or 'blurb' for *Nineteen Eighty-Four*. Warburg was moving with great speed, obviously worried that Orwell might die, needing him to read the proofs, wanting him to see the final result and to enjoy the success that Warburg confidently expected.

26.12.48

Dear Roger,

Thanks so much for your letter. As to the blurb. I really don't think the approach in the draft you sent me is the right one. It makes the book sound as though it were a thriller mixed up with a love story & I didn't intend it to be primarily that. What it is really meant to do is to discuss the implications of dividing the world up into 'Zones of influence' (I thought of it in 1944 as a result of the Teheran Conference), & in addition to indicate by parodying them the intellectual implications of totalitarianism. It has always seemed to me that people have not faced up to these & that, eg., the persecution of scientists in Russia is simply part of a logical process which should have been foreseeable 10–20 years ago.[38]

Whatever blurb Senhouse had sent, he was hardly now going to rewrite it as something about the effect of the Teheran Conference on international relations. Orwell might have remembered Empson's warning about allegory in relation to *Animal Farm*: the author's intentions may be different from his effect. But 'parodying ... the intellectual implications of totalitarianism' was closer to the mark. Several times in the coming year, Orwell called the book 'a satire'. Certainly he intended it to be what it was, a parody or a satire and not a prophecy. Or if a prophecy, only what his friend Freddy Ayer and the philosophers would call an 'If/Then proposition': *if* A is not done, then B will follow.

Warburg would have noted Orwell's gloomy remark in October that 'it is a good idea' but 'the execution would have been better' but for the TB (although he had heard that from Orwell, as Gollancz had before him, on the occasion of every book's delivery). Orwell had told Powell in November that it was 'a good idea ruined'; and in February he was to write to Julian Symons that 'My new book is a Utopia in the form of a novel. I ballsed it up rather, partly owing to being so ill while I was writing it, but I think some of the ideas in it might interest you.'[39]

Certainly the execution could have been better. Perhaps he did 'balls it up' in *some* aspects of the writing: the characterization is weak, Goldstein's testimony and the full account of Newspeak are clumsily interpolated or tacked on, and the sociology of the Proles, considering their importance as the sole vehicle of hope, is sketchy and, as it stands, implausible. But the basic ideas had been so long pondered and pre-meditated, even sketched out in that early notebook of 1943, that any effect of the tuberculosis, even bearing in mind that the disease was widely believed to create morbid states of mind, was far more likely to be on the execution of it than in the great overall conception. Biographically, this is reasonably clear.* Yet the overall execution of the concept was masterly: a seemingly naturalistic fantasy that creates lasting terror, however many times one reads it, that humanity *could* come to that.

False biographical problems have been set by the tendency of some

---

* Cf. 'I hope to write another [novel] fairly soon. It is bound to be a failure, every book is a failure, but I know with some clarity what kind of book I want to write.' ('Why I Write', 1946, in *The Collected Essays, Journalism and Letters*, Vol. I, p.7.) And he had said in his essay on Koestler that 'all revolutions are failures, but they are not all the same failure' (*The Collected Essays*, Vol. III, p.244). So his reflection is a very general one. None of his books, except *Animal Farm*, measured up to his great expectations.

critics to play down the artistic achievements of the book, its intrinsic coherence as a self-contained imaginary world, simply because its extrinsic message (irrelevant to its artistic achievement) is so un-comfortable. People reject things by explaining them away. Suppose, however, it was all a morbid fantasy of a fatal illness and not some-thing long and rationally premeditated: the real questions still remain. Is it, in some sense, true? Is it authentic? Whatever the defects, it does ring true as a theoretically coherent model of what a régime would look like that blended the techniques of Communism with those of Nazism for no other purpose than to perpetuate a power-hungry élite of intellectuals in power. And it is authentic as a plausible nightmare that has haunted us ever since, more than any other of the anti-Utopias of this century whether by Wells, London, Huxley or Zamyatin, from all of whom Orwell borrowed, but greatly improved and transcended.

Certainly his letter to Warburg just before Christmas showed that it was no conscious last testament: he was planning a new novel already, as if to try to put the clock back on all the events that had turned him into primarily a 'political writer'. He also told Astor that 'I must try and stay alive for a while because apart from other considerations I have a good idea for a novel'.[40] *Nineteen Eighty-Four* was no last testament: it was simply the last major book he wrote before he happened to die.

By now everyone, including himself, faced the fact that he would die if he did not surrender himself, for a while at least, to a sanatorium. He had at last found one. Even the journey had complications and could have proved fatal. Bill and Avril were to drive him down to spend the night at the hotel in Craighouse before catching the morning boat. Starting rather late in the day the car slipped in the dusk into an enormous pot-hole. On a wet and bitterly cold night, leaving Orwell in the car to comfort Richard, Bill and Avril walked back four miles to Ardlussa to get help. With difficulty and exertion they were pulled out by a tractor, and set on the road again. Ever since that haemorrhage of January 1946, it had been folly for Orwell to live so far from town, however much he loved the country.

They met Richard Rees on the mainland, and he accompanied Orwell (whose essays he had first printed twenty years before) down to Gloucestershire on the train.

*

'I hope the poor fellow will do well. It is now obvious he will need to live a most sheltered life in a sanatorium environment. I fear the dream of Jura must fade out.' Thus Dr Bruce Dick wrote to David Astor commenting on Orwell's relapse and assuring him that he was in good hands at Cranham.[41]

Cranham was a private sanatorium 900 feet up, almost the highest the South of England can manage, in the Cotswold hills between Stroud and Gloucester with views right across the Bristol Channel to the mountains of Wales. The patients were in individual chalets with central heating; for rest, altitude and fresh air, cold air indeed, were then generally believed to be relevant treatments for tuberculosis. Orwell grumbled to Richard Rees at the end of January that while the doctors came round each day, they would not tell him anything: 'I want an expert opinion on how long I am likely to live, because I must make my plans accordingly.' When Brenda Salkeld came to visit him he said the same thing. But he really knew the score: 'The one chance of surviving, I imagine, is to keep quiet. Don't think I am making up my mind to peg out,' he told Warburg in mid May. 'On the contrary, I have the strongest reasons for wanting to stay alive. But I want to get a clear idea of *how long* I am likely to last, and not just be jollied along the way doctors usually do.'[42] What more could they tell him but that he had 'to keep quiet and rest', not to work? Only the occasional review now for the *Observer* – less for the money than to express his gratitude to Astor who kept sending him little comforts, anxious inquiries, and helpful suggestions. 'Have you ever considered the idea of using the wire-recorder machine?' he asked when they took Orwell's typewriter away in March and April, since he seemed to be overworking. No more articles, but his correspondence with his agent got ever longer and more complex.

Moore and Orwell exchanged several long letters a week about translation rights for *Animal Farm* (now appearing in nearly every major language), about reprinting, magazine reprint rights, a new book of collected essays, and complex dealings with Harcourt Brace, the American publishers of *Nineteen Eighty-Four* (as it was to be, not 'The Last Man in Europe' as they had favoured: not even '1984'). Having an agent seemed to save Orwell little work. Perhaps he could not shake off the habit, even pleasure, of wanting to follow every detail as in earlier times when he was desperately anxious to find out how well last year's book was doing and what were the prospects for the next one. Perhaps Moore had simply given up trying to shelter Orwell, knowing his interest in the whole process of publishing; and certainly many political questions arose which he would never have decided without his client. Were cuts to be allowed in a version for Argentine to get through the censorship? Would Orwell actually subsidize a Russian translation by an émigré group if they could guarantee to get copies into the Soviet Union? The Book-of-the-Month Club in the USA wanted to take on *Nineteen Eighty-Four*, but with cuts: the appendix on 'The Principles of Newspeak' and the thirty pages of Goldstein's 'The Theory and Practice of Oligarchical Collectivism'. Orwell utterly refused. Perhaps he had not solved the structural problem of integrating these two things into the narrative or perhaps their unintegrated documentary appearance was fully deliberate; but they are very much part of the meaning of the book, and if readers could not see their significance, they could not understand the book. 'Orwell must have known that this selection must have been worth at this time a minimum of £40,000,' wrote Warburg afterwards. Faced with Orwell's refusal, the Book Club changed its mind. 'So that shows that virtue is its own reward,' Orwell told Rees, 'or honesty is the best policy, I forget which.'[43] 'Would every author have taken the risk, especially at a time of critical illness, when he feared he might be an invalid for the rest of his life?' commented a visibly impressed and relieved Warburg.[44] Certainly Orwell must have feared what would happen to his earning power if he was permanently in sanatoria under such restrictions. He told both Rees, now named as his literary executor, and Gwen, as a trustee of his will, that he had already salted away enough money in insurance policies to cover a good education for Richard.

Unavoidable correspondence also multiplied because Harcourt Brace, as anxious as Secker & Warburg to get *Nineteen Eighty-Four* out quickly, were setting the American edition themselves, so he had two different sets of proofs to deal with; and he was most anxious to correct them himself – although he had Richard Rees in reserve in case he broke down. He was suspicious that silly things would be done, as when the New York copy-editors, either missing the point or thinking that Attlee's England was already under the iron heel, turned all the harsh metric measurements of the year 1984 back into familiar feet and inches. An increasing stream of letters came from editors of periodicals. To all he replied personally and to most negatively – although in April the Medical Superintendent did have some duplicate letters typed: 'Mr George Orwell is seriously ill and is unable to write the article which he had promised you . . .' He made a few notes for instance on an article he planned to write about Evelyn Waugh for *Partisan Review*; but it was never written. And he wrote many letters to his friends. Partly he wrote because he had nothing else to do: his letters are fuller, more reflective and discursive than before, not less – as if the energy and imagination once used in journalism and essay writing now found another outlet. But he also wrote such letters simply because people wrote to him, friendly, anxious, gossipy letters to entertain and distract him; and he, being the man he was, felt obliged to reply equally and in kind to reassure them.

The doctors held out no hopes of new cures, could do little but describe his condition, so had little to tell him. But he seems to have accepted, not just known, the score: 'It looks as if I may have to spend the rest of my life, if not actually in bed,' he told Tony Powell, 'at any rate at the bath-chair level.' He discussed with Richard Rees how to keep on Barnhill, if Avril wanted to: 'Of course I may never be strong enough for that kind of thing again even in summer.'[45] He did not 'rage against the dying of the light' but waited 'with humour and stoicism'. Up until Cranham he had thought of his tuberculosis as a winter disease, that they could 'patch him up' each time after he over-exerted himself; and that he would be good for a fair amount of work in the summers. But now he had just to rest until they were sure that the one more-or-less good lung was recovering and see what kind of restricted régime he could then sustain; any more trial and error on his own judgement could kill him. He could sustain the thought of pain and suffering, but not of a régime that would allow him no work at all.

The doctors did try streptomycin again at the beginning of April when he seemed to be suffering a relapse. 'They had been afraid of it because of the secondary effects, but they now say they can offset these to some extent with nicotine, or something, and in any case they can always stop if the results are too bad.' However, 'this time only one dose of it had ghastly results'.[46] They stopped it at once. He had simply to rest and hope. While he worried that he would never work again, he realized that the only chance of some active life was to try to wait patiently and quietly and not to pound away on the typewriter or to write letters for half the day. But somehow he did not seem to think that handwritten letters counted. Jane Dakin visiting him with her father formed a poor impression of Cranham, thinking it seedy, ramshackle and ill-supervised. They were horrified when he cheerfully produced a bottle of rum from his locker to greet them.

Many people came to visit him, some fearing that he was dying, others simply to entertain him in his isolation. Powell and Muggeridge, who did their share of visiting, persuaded Evelyn Waugh, who neither knew Orwell nor particularly cared for his writing, to visit him; simply because he lived nearby. As one worthy in the world of English letters to another, he did this kindness several times. 'I should have loved to see them together,' wrote Muggeridge, 'his country gentleman's outfit and Orwell's proletarian one both straight out of back numbers of *Punch*.'[47] A fellow-pillar of English socialism, R. H. Tawney, who had a cottage not far away, also came to see him. Tosco Fyvel saw him – the last link with *Tribune* days. Celia and Inez got down from time to time. Orwell refused to meet the *Time-Life* correspondents when *Nineteen Eighty-Four* was published, but the occasional English journalist visited him. He complained that Charles Curran of the *Evening Standard* had argued with him and left him exhausted – which he had done to many fitter men. Some of his old Spanish War and ILP friends came, after reading in the newspapers where he was. Paul Potts hitched down to see him and found his friend much as usual. 'Almost the first thing he said to me ... was, "I see we have lost Haifa." I had an awful job not to bend down and begin looking for it under his bed.' Orwell wrote to editors on Potts' behalf. When Orwell heard that the Freedom Defence Committee had folded up, now that the National Council for Civil Liberties (shaken by E. M. Forster's resignation) had ceased to be Communist-dominated, he wrote to Vernon Richards that the Freedom Press could keep Eileen's typewriter.[48] He worried about Communist infiltration elsewhere, however, and kept a notebook of suspects.[49] And he wrote to the *News Chronicle* on 3 March protesting that Enrique Marco Nadal, a Spanish republican who had re-entered Spain, was under sentence of death.

Orwell made arrangements with Avril to bring Richard down for a month, leaving him in the care of Lilian Wolfe, a 73-year old veteran of the British anarchist movement who lived at the nearby anarchist and craft colony, Whiteway. When at the beginning of March the sanatorium told Orwell that he must stay in bed and totally rest for at least another two months, he wrote to Rees:

I don't know that it matters except for being expensive and not seeing little R. I am so afraid of his growing away from me, or getting to think of me as just a person who is always lying down and can't play. Of course children can't understand illness. He used to come to me and say 'Where have you hurt yourself?' – I suppose the only reason he could see for always being in bed.[50]

'Always in bed' was, indeed, what he thought would be the worst that could happen, unless they could give him some idea of how long he had, so that he would know what he could finish in the time. They let him use his typewriter again for a few hours each day.

She did not come to see him, but Orwell was astonished and delighted to get a letter from Jacintha Buddicom who had only recently become aware, from something Aunt Lilian had read in a literary weekly, that 'George Orwell' was Eric Blair. He replied at once, a simple, lengthy but rather dry account of his life after Shiplake and Henley days, typically ending, 'I am afraid this is a rather poor letter but I can't write long letters at present because it tires me to sit up for a long time.' But it must have set his mind turning back to the 'golden country' of childhood memories, for the next day he added another quite different letter to the envelope, saluting her in childhood fashion:

Tuesday [15.2.49]

Hail and Fare Well, my dear Jacintha

You see I haven't forgotten. I wrote to you yesterday but the letter isn't posted yet, so I'll go on to cheer this dismal day. It's been a day when everything's gone wrong. First there was a stupid accident to the book I was reading, which is now unreadable. After that the typewriter stuck & I'm too poorly to fix it. I've managed to borrow a substitute but it's not much better. Ever since I got your letter I've been remembering. I can't stop thinking about the young days with you & Guin & Prosper & things put out of mind for 20 or 30 years. I am so wanting to see you. We must meet when I get out of this place, but the doctor says I'll have to stay another 3 or 4 months.

I would like you to see Richard. He can't read yet & is rather backward in talking, but he's as keen on fishing as I was & loves working on the farm, where he's really quite helpful. He has an enormous interest in machinery, which may be useful to him later on. When I was not much more than his age I always knew I wanted to write, but for the first ten years it was very hard to make a living. I had to take a lot of beastly jobs to earn enough to keep going & could only write in any spare time that was left, when I was too tired & had to destroy a dozen pages for one that was worth keeping. I tore up a whole novel once & wish now I hadn't been so ruthless. Parts of it might have been worth rewriting, though it's impossible to come back to something written in such a different world. But I am rather sorry now. (''An' w'en I sor wot 'e'd bin an' gorn an' done, I sed coo lor, wot 'ave you bin an' gorn an' done?') I think it's rather a good thing Richard is such an entirely practical child.

Are you fond of children? I think you must be. You were such a tender-hearted girl, always full of pity for the creatures we others shot and killed. But you were not so tender-hearted to me when you abandoned me to Burma with all hope denied. We are older now, and with this wretched illness the years will have taken more toll of me than of you. But I am well cared for here & feel much better than I did when I got here last month. As soon as I can get back to London I do so want us to meet again.

As we always ended, so that there should be no ending

> Farewell and Hail
> Eric[51]

But he never saw her in London, nor did she visit him. It was all such a long time ago. Perhaps the warmth of his letter made her nervous: 'Are you fond of children?' How casual a question was that?

One diary-like entry from his last notebook tells of the routine at Cranham:

21 March 1949

The routine here (Cranham Sanatorium) is quite different from that of Hairmyres Hospital. Although everyone at Hairmyres was most kind & considerate to me – quite astonishingly so, indeed – one cannot help feeling at every moment the difference in the *texture* of life when one is paying one's own keep.

The most noticeable difference here is that it is much quieter than the hospital & that everything is done in a more leisurely way. I live in a so-called chalet, one of a row of continuous wooden huts, with glass doors, each chalet measuring abt 15′ by 12′. There are hot water pipes, a washing basin, a chest of drawers & wardrobe, besides the usual bed-tables etc. Outside is a glass-roofed verandah. Everything is brought by hand – none of those abominable rattling trolleys which one is never out of the sound of in a hospital. Not much noise of radios either – all the patients have headphones. (Here these are permanently tuned in to the Home Service. At Hairmyres, usually to the Light.) The most persistent sound is the song of birds.[52]

And another entry shows that the old radical George had not faded away.

17 April 1949
Curious effect, here in the sanatorium, on Easter Sunday, when the people in this (the most expensive) block of 'chalets' mostly have visitors, of hearing large numbers of upper-class English voices. I have been almost out of the sound of them for two years, hearing them at most one or two at a time, my ears growing more & more used to working-class or lower-middle-class Scottish voices. In the hospital at Hairmyres, for instance, I literally never heard a 'cultivated' accent except when I had a visitor. It is as though I were hearing these voices for the first time. And what voices! A sort of over-fedness, a fatuous self-confidence, a constant bah-bahing of laughter abt nothing, above all a sort of heaviness & richness combined with a fundamental ill-will – people who, one instinctively feels, without even being able to see them, are the enemies of anything intelligent or sensitive or beautiful. No wonder everyone hates us so.[53]

Thus he balanced the advantages and disadvantages of the class system.

Sonia visited him quite often. Perhaps she was one of those 'strongest reasons for wanting to stay alive' of which he had written to Fred Warburg. She was very fond of him and was upset to see the tall and upright man struck so low and helpless. Temperamentally she would want to try to do something to help. She must have known the medical prognosis, some hope of something if he rested, but also known that to want to live he must have hope of some work and some support, some normal life. She would have seen how much, despite the self-sufficient exterior, he wanted to be loved. Once he had to write putting a visit off:

24.5.49

Dear Sonia,
I was so very sorry to put you off but at the time I was in a ghastly state. Now I seem to be somewhat better I do hope you'll come and see me soon. Any day would suit me except the day you think Cyril might be coming,

on the 29th., when I think someone else is coming. But any way when and if you can come let me know in advance because of sending a car.

I've just had what is called a 'second opinion', incidentally the doctor who attended D. H. Lawrence in his last illness. He says I'm not so bad and have a good chance of surviving, but it means keeping quiet and doing no work for a long time, possibly a year or more. I don't mind so much if I could then get well enough to do say another 5 years work. Richard is coming down soon to stay near here. He will start going to kindergarten school in the mornings, and can sometimes come over and see me in the afternoons.

Please give everyone my love. By the way I cut the enclosed out of the NY Times. If you see Stephen, tell him to get another photo taken for the honour of English letters. Looking forward to seeing you.

> With love
> George[54]

The 'second opinion' had been solicited by Fred Warburg from a personal friend, Andrew Morland. Pamela, Warburg's wife, had begun to form a poor opinion of Cranham. Morland was a Harley Street chest specialist and a consultant at UCH (University College Hospital, London), one of the best hospitals in the country. Morland wrote to Warburg about Orwell, and must have told the patient much the same:

Dear Fred,   25 May, 1949

Mr Eric Blair (George Orwell)

I have just returned from seeing this man at the Cotswold Sanatorium. I found that he has rather severe disease of the left lung and a relatively slight amount on the right. He has made some progress in the right direction since January but his improvement has been slow and undulating.

I discussed his outlook with him as fully and frankly as possible but in a case like this prognosis is hazardous.

Provided he rests properly he should continue to improve but it may well be that after a number of months he will stagnate or even relapse. One point I am quite clear about is that if he ceases to try to get well and settles down to write another book he is almost certain to relapse quickly.

With further rest I do not anticipate a cure but he might well reach a stage at which he could do several hours writing a day combined with physical rest. He would then reach the stage which we call the 'good chronic' i.e. able to potter about and do a few hours sedentary work.

His resistance must be fairly good as he stabilized well last year and should not have broken down had he not foolishly over-exercised.

> Yours sincerely,
> Andrew Morland[55]

The warning was clear, a relapse could occur, and this must have been known to those close to him. But there was now more hope than any of them had read in the generalities and silences of the Cranham doctors. The prospect of even 'several hours writing a day' would not merely fortify Orwell's will to live but, quite as important, reconcile him to being a good patient meanwhile and prevent him from prematurely trying to get down to work on the next, what would then certainly be the last novel. The prospect did reconcile him, and he began to plan for the future. The phrase 'good chronic' must have appealed to his sense of humour, though he did not add it to the long lists of neologisms in his notebook.

He wrote no more reviews. His last in the *Observer* had appeared on 6 February, a review of F. R. Leavis' *The Great Tradition*, and his last review ever was a long one for *New Leader* (New York) on 14 May 1949 of *Their Finest Hour*, the second volume of Winston Churchill's War memoirs. But he did cheat the doctors a little by making a few notes in his notebook, even drafting a few paragraphs of 'A Smoking Room Story' (set on board ship returning from the East – could this have been an attempt to recreate the youthful novel that he told Jacintha Buddicom he had torn up?). It is possible that this could have been written later in UCH where, eventually, after he had had a momentary relapse, he was transferred on 3 September. For Warburg had been able to persuade Morland to take him in under his own personal supervision.

A week after *Nineteen Eighty-Four* was published, a triumphant if worried Warburg visited Orwell and then dictated a memorandum for the eyes of his closest colleagues:

CONFIDENTIAL

Visit to George Orwell on 15 June 1949
Health
He is undoubtedly better than at his low point of some weeks ago when he saw Dr Andrew Morland. The high temperature of that date, the general feeling of exhaustion and disintegration, appear to have been due to pleurisy rather than a worsening of the tubercular infection. George's present condition is of course shocking, but he is hopeful, and prepared at the moment to do whatever the doctor tells him for a period of up to twelve months. If he does not or cannot improve within this period there cannot in my opinion

be much hope. He is thinking of moving to a sanatorium nearer London when he is feeling better, in two or three months time, provided he feels that his stay in a sanatorium must be continued over a longish period.

Sales & Prospects

I told him of the position and suggested to him that from British and American sources digest rights etc., he would make very large sums of money, probably between £10,000 and £15,000. He spoke reassuringly of the auditors who handle his financial affairs, and told me they were turning him into a Limited Company. Until this is done he is not anxious to receive further royalties, and I shall therefore instruct Miss Murtough to withhold the payment of £800 odd due to Christy & Moore on publication. Obviously this payment is merely withheld for a month or two.

Statement

I took down from him a note on the American cables and have already given over the phone to 'Life' a summary. The statement is typed on the attached sheet, and a copy is being sent to George for his approval. Subject to this it can be used I imagine in any way that appears useful.

Literary Work

He has quite come round to the idea of a new volume of essays, but these will be more miscellaneous than the earlier volume, CRITICAL ESSAYS. He could give us material for a volume right away, approximately 40,000 words, but is anxious to include one or two new essays not hitherto printed. One of these would be a piece he did for 'Politics & Letters' on Gissing, which has been lost during the liquidation of this little company. I suggest JGP gets from George the name of the solicitors who are liquidating it and does a little detective work if he can to find the typescript. Another unprinted contribution would be an essay on Conrad which he has been working on for some months and which he could write quite quickly when he is allowed to do so. The book would probably be called ESSAYS AND SKETCHES and would presumably include the piece about his private school which we have seen here. RS *must* find this during the next few days and hand it to Sonia Brownell or send it to George. This is important.

This material we might wait for until the end of the year, as it is possible that he may do the Conrad essay in the next 8 or 9 months. The idea would then be to publish in the autumn of 1950. I asked him about a new novel, and this is formulated in his mind – a nouvelle [sic] of 30,000 to 40,000 words – a novel of character rather than of ideas, with Burma as background. George was naturally as reticent as usual, but he did disclose this much.

Ability to Write

The effort of turning ideas in his head into a rough draft on paper is, according to George and Dr Morland, work which he cannot afford to attempt for a number of months. At best I doubt whether anything can or should be done by George until the autumn of this year. This about covers the main points that arose, and I am greatly encouraged by my visit. At worst he has a 50/50 chance of recovering and living for a number of years. Probably everything depends on himself and he does at last realize what is involved and what he has got to do.

FJW[56]

Orwell did at last realize what was involved.

Warburg had expected that *Nineteen Eighty-Four* would be warmly received and in all possible senses it was. As Orwell knew, he had printed a first edition of 25,500 copies. It was published on 8 June in London and five days later in New York. A year after publication 49,917 copies had been sold in Great Britain and 170,000 copies in the USA by Harcourt Brace and 190,000 in the Book-of-the-Month Club edition.[57] And, like *Animal Farm*, it never stopped selling: both became modern classics, not seasonal wonders. How Orwell would have relished such details of the trade, quite apart from the power it gave him of complete financial security, freedom now to write what he liked and when he liked, if he was able.

Most English reviewers grasped well enough what the book was all about. Veronica Wedgwood in *Time and Tide* and Julian Symons in *The Times Literary Supplement* (where Anthony Powell had steered it into comprehending hands) saw that Orwell had not written utopian or anti-utopian fantasy in the tradition of Huxley and Wells, but had simply extended certain discernible tendencies of 1948 forward into 1984 (Symons later called it a 'near future' and pointed to how all the grim inventions of that oligarchy were just extensions of 'ordinary' war and post-war things).[58] 'It is no doubt with the intention of preventing his prediction from coming true,' wrote Miss Wedgwood, 'that Mr Orwell has set it down in the most valuable, the most absorbing, the most powerful book he has yet written.'[59] In Germany, Golo Mann, the historian and son of Thomas Mann, writing in the *Frankfurter Rundschau* later in the year, saw clearly both that it was not a prophecy but a warning; and that if it drew mainly from Communist institutions, it also drew significantly from Nazi and Fascist ones. He deplored that some Americans had already turned *Animal Farm* into crude anti-Communist propaganda, distorting its general significance.[60]

V. S. Pritchett saw it as a 'satirical pamphlet' and praised it highly, declaring it to be as fine as anything that Swift had ever written, a savage satire on the 'moral corruption of absolute power'.[61] Symons saw it as a satire too, and he took care to tell the reader about Orwell's earlier work and to describe correctly his political stance. Both he and Pritchett, however, found the torture scenes 'melodramatic', Symons even said 'school-boyish'. 'But the last words about this book,' he concluded, 'must be one of thanks, rather than of criticism: thanks for a writer who deals with the problems of the world rather than the ingrowing pains of individuals, and who is able to speak seriously and with originality of the nature of reality and the terrors of power.' He warned, in a slightly defensive tone, that the English were not used to novels of ideas, preferring the psychological novel of character.[62] The warning was needed because several reviewers rejected it or criticized it strongly for not being their idea of a novel at all, for not being concerned with the interplay of richly differentiated psychologies and familiar circumstances. Most reviewers saw that it was a kind of imaginative treatise on totalitarianism and that its concept of totalitarianism was drawn from tendencies present throughout the modern world, drawing from and cutting across all ideologies. Not so the last Communist pursuit. Kate Carr in the *Daily Worker* and Arthur Calder-Marshall in *Reynold's News* saw it as simple Cold War propaganda, Kate Carr telling her readers with naughty exaggeration that even as a novel it had been received with 'distaste and incredulity' in the liberal bourgeois press. No such subtleties, then, for Arthur Calder-Marshall who said the object of the book was to abuse and stir up hatred against the Soviet Union; and he placed Orwell on 'the lunatic fringe' of the Labour Party.[63] But as a few copies trickled into Eastern Europe, some real *apparatniki* were much impressed by its home truths and prescience.[64]

Across the Atlantic, where it was published simultaneously, there were several reviews as fine and perceptive as anything written by Wedgwood, Pritchett or Symons. Lionel Trilling saw that the book was not an attack on Communism or Socialism in general but on all those factors in modern society that could lead to a life of 'deprivation, dullness and fear of pain'; and he praised the 'intensity and passion' of this 'momentous book'.[65] In the United States, too, some Communists attacked him who could only see themselves in Orwell's somewhat broader mirror for intellectuals. 'Now that Ezra Pound has been given a government award and George Orwell has become a best-seller, we would seem to have reached bottom ... There is a hideous ingenuity in the perversions of a dying capitalism, and it will keep probing for new depths of rottenness,' said Sam Sillen in *Masses and Mainstream*, 'which the maggots will find "brilliant and morally invigorating".'[66]

How Orwell must have enjoyed reading that sort of review – some of his blows had struck home – almost as much as he must have loved some warm and thoughtful private letters of praise that came from old friends and distinguished new admirers: Aldous Huxley, Margaret Storm Jameson, Roy Campbell, Lawrence Durrell, Bertrand Russell and John Dos Passos all wrote to him.

Something far more worrying than Communist abuse, however, had happened with the first wave of reviews. Not only were the Communists seeing it as merely anti-Communist, as did the *Economist* in London and the *Wall Street Journal* in New York; but many other American papers, following *Time* and *Life* magazines, were presenting it as a comprehensive anti-socialist polemic. 'Ingsoc' was identified with the Labour Party and Oceania was being enthusiastically presented as the prophecy of either a Left-winger who had recanted or of a distinguished English author who was writing about what *would* happen if liberty as free enterprise were not firmly defended.

Orwell was greatly distressed. Clippings and cables from New York must have reached him even before Fred Warburg visited Cranham on 15 June, bringing more clippings, his triumph somewhat dimmed by Orwell's unhappiness at these misunderstandings or deliberate distortions. Orwell dictated a statement to Warburg, Warburg making short notes which he then 'dolled up' into a Press Release:

It has been suggested by some of the reviewers of NINETEEN EIGHTY-FOUR that it is the author's view that this, or something like this, is what will happen inside the next forty years in the Western world. This is not correct. I think that, allowing for the book being after all a parody, something like NINETEEN EIGHTY-FOUR *could* happen. This is the direction in which the world is going at the present time, and the trend lies deep in the political, social and economic foundations of the contemporary world situation.

Specifically the danger lies in the structure imposed on Socialist and on

Liberal capitalist communities by the necessity to prepare for total war with the USSR and the new weapons, of which of course the atomic bomb is the most powerful and the most publicized. But danger lies also in the acceptance of a totalitarian outlook by intellectuals of all colours.

The moral to be drawn from this dangerous nightmare situation is a simple one: *Don't let it happen. It depends on you.*

George Orwell assumes that if such societies as he describes in NINETEEN EIGHTY-FOUR come into being there will be several super states. This is fully dealt with in the relevant chapters of NINETEEN EIGHTY-FOUR. It is also discussed from a different angle by James Burnham in THE MANAGERIAL REVOLUTION. These super states will naturally be in opposition to each other or (a novel point) will pretend to be much more in opposition than in fact they are. Two of the principal super states will obviously be the Anglo-American world and Eurasia. If these two great blocks line up as mortal enemies it is obvious that the Anglo-Americans will not take the name of their opponents and will not dramatize themselves on the scene of history as Communists. Thus they will have to find a new name for themselves. The name suggested in NINETEEN EIGHTY-FOUR is of course Ingsoc, but in practice a wide range of choices is open. In the USA the phrase 'Americanism' or 'hundred per cent Americanism' is suitable and the qualifying adjective is as totalitarian as anyone could wish.

If there is a failure of nerve and the Labour Party breaks down in its attempt to deal with the hard problems with which it will be faced, tougher types than the present Labour leaders will inevitably take over, drawn probably from the ranks of the Left, but not sharing the Liberal aspirations of those now in power. Members of the present British government, from Mr Attlee and Sir Stafford Cripps down to Aneurin Bevan, will *never* willingly sell the pass to the enemy, and in general the older men, nurtured in a Liberal tradition, are safe, but the younger generation is suspect and the seeds of totalitarian thought are probably widespread among them. It is invidious to mention names, but everyone could without difficulty think for himself of prominent English and American personalities whom the cap would fit.[67]

Even the outline for this was a good effort from a sick man on a day when there was much other business to discuss, and Warburg had reproduced his leading author's views faithfully: an unambiguous statement of what Orwell meant the book to say.

In fairness, however, to 'some of the US Republican papers' which had tried to use *Nineteen Eighty-Four* as 'propaganda against the Labour Party' (as he told his anarchist friend, Vernon Richards[68]) it must be wondered what Orwell would have said had he known of Warburg's own first reaction to his book back in December. When Warburg first read it he immediately wrote a comprehensive summary of the book so that everyone involved in its production and promotion would know right from the beginning what it was about and how important it was. Four pages summarized the plot, accurately and racily, but he then said:

This is amongst the most terrifying books I have ever read. The savagery of Swift has passed to a successor who looks upon life and finds it becoming ever more intolerable ... Orwell has no hope, or at least he allows his reader no tiny flickering candlelight of hope. Here is a study in pessimism unrelieved, except perhaps by the thought that, if a man can conceive 1984, he can also will to avoid it ...

The political system which prevails is Ingsoc = English Socialism. This I take to be a deliberate and sadistic attack on socialism and socialist parties generally. It seems to indicate a final breach between Orwell and Socialism, not the socialism of equality and human brotherhood which clearly Orwell no longer expects from socialist parties, but the socialism of marxism and the managerial revolution. *1984* is among other things an attack on Burnham's managerialism; and it is worth a cool million votes to the Conservative Party; it is imaginable that it might have a preface by Winston Churchill after whom its hero is named. *1984 should be published as soon as possible, in June 1949* ...

Orwell goes down to the depths in a way which reminds me of Dostoievsky. O'Brien is his Grand Inquisitor, and he leaves Winston, and the reader, without hope. I cannot but think that this book could have been written only by a man who himself, however temporarily, had lost hope, and for physical reasons which are sufficiently apparent.

These comments, lengthy as they are, give little idea of the giant movement of thought which Orwell has set in motion in *1984*. It is a great book, but I pray I may be spared from reading another like it for years to come.

Nothing succeeds like success and bad publicity for a book is better than no publicity, but did Warburg feel no embarrassment at writing down Orwell's memorandum while he could still remember his own (if it was entirely his own, for as with Eliot's rejection of *Animal Farm*, we have to remember that firms are collectivities[69])? He reconsidered the matter nearly twenty-five years later in his memoirs:

There is little in this report which I would today alter, except perhaps my belief that, in describing the 1984 régime as Ingsoc, Orwell was making 'a deliberate and sadistic attack on socialism and socialist parties generally', including even the mild socialism of the UK. This was definitely not Orwell's intention, as he was to make clear soon enough.[70]

History will have to be rewritten more thoroughly than that in 1984.

Yet again Empson's warning on the ambiguities of satire should be recalled. Warburg may have been mistaken, both about the ideological stance of the book and to have begun the myth that the pessimism sprang from sickness (whether from the tubercular bacilli or from childhood traumas), but others also jumped to these conclusions, even if few others did who knew Orwell quite so well. Philip Rahv, Orwell's great American admirer, had praised the book extravagantly in *Partisan Review* as 'the best antidote to the totalitarian disease' so far produced; but then he recommended it specifically to those liberals who still believed, he said, 'that while absolute power is bad when exercised by the Right, it is in its very nature good and a boon to humanity once the Left, that is to say, "our own people" takes hold of it'.[71] He too was distorting, albeit more subtly than Warburg, Orwell's carefully balanced point. Rahv saw the satire as applicable only to the Soviets, and their sympathizers, and not also to the Western way of life whose mass media were already churning out prole-cult for the millions.

Nineteen Eighty-Four is a long premeditated, rational warning against totalitarian tendencies in societies like our own rather than a sick and sudden prophecy about a Soviet or neo-Nazi takeover, still less a scream of despair and recantation of his democratic Socialism.* Its harsh style created as authentic a picture of a state turned by men themselves into hell as the lyrical passages of *Animal Farm* give a picture of a natural, pastoral and egalitarian Utopia. Both are creations of a great writer. *Nineteen Eighty-Four* may show sociological rather than psychological imagination, but imagination of a high order none the less. It is curious that some critics strive hard to identify the *whole* viewpoint of these books with the entire character of the man – as if here was a rare thing indeed, a great writer without imagination, wholly literal-minded and only able to relate, never to transmute, experience. But the persona of the documentary writer and the forthright *Tribune* writer, the George Orwell that went beyond Eric Blair,

* To set it out for the last time with the pedantry that he loved of the lower-case 'd' and the upper-case 'S'.

digs just this trap for himself: he encourages his readers to be literal minded. Empson would never have suggested that all interpretations are equal and that there are not limits to the range of possible meanings to a complex text, nor that Warburg's memorandum stepped outside these limits. But that Orwell's own publisher could at first so misread it showed that Orwell was at best incautious, at worst foolish. After his experience of *Animal Farm*'s reception in the United States, he should have guarded against such misunderstandings and unwanted friends by practising what he always preached so well: unequivocal clarity of meaning in the text. Clarity of meaning was always more important to him as a political writer than beauty of usage or evocativeness. His advocacy of plain English could have its price. It might have been better to have sacrificed some of the formal virtues of the novel and reached a greater clarity of intention, rather than being reduced to producing memoranda for American newspapers and press agencies after the event. If he had 'ballsed it up', as he had written to Julian Symons, it was mainly in that respect.

Memoranda of correction and explanation, even, had their sad hazards. On 16 June, he had responded to a cable from an official of the United Automobile Workers, Francis A. Henson, who wished to recommend the book to his members but wanted some clarification because of the good press it was getting in Right-wing journals.

My recent novel is NOT intended as an attack on Socialism or on the British Labour Party (of which I am a supporter) but as a show-up of the perversions to which a centralized economy is liable and which have already been partly realized in Communism and Fascism. I do not believe that the kind of society I describe necessarily *will* arrive, but I believe (allowing of course for the fact that the book is a satire) that something resembling it *could* arrive. I believe also that totalitarian ideas have taken root in the minds of intellectuals everywhere, and I have tried to draw these ideas out to their logical consequences. The scene of the book is laid in Britain in order to emphasize that the English-speaking races are not innately better than anyone else and that totalitarianism, *if not fought against*, could triumph anywhere.[72]

This, however, is not only a conflated but also a corrected version. What was actually first reproduced comes out in a letter he wrote to Moore in July:

With reference to the *Socialist Call*, I believe all this trouble started with the *New York Daily News*, which I am told wrote up '1984' as an attack on the Labour Government. I issued a sort of dementi through Warburg and something of the same kind in a cable to *Life*. Meanwhile the United Automobile Workers had written saying they were encouraging their members to read the book and asking for a statement. I gave them a few lines of which they then issued a cyclostyled copy. But I see that it contains a stupid slip, either of theirs or mine (possibly caused by my handwriting). I had written 'I do not believe that the kind of society which I described necessarily will arrive, I believe ... that something resembling it could arrive.' The latter phrase appears in their version as 'that something resembling it will arrive'. Yesterday *Life* rang up again and asked whether my statement to the UAW could be quoted. I told them it could and pointed out the error which I trust they will rectify.

Could you tell the *Socialist Call* people as politely as possible that I would gladly write them an article if I were well, but that I am really too ill to write anything and that my statement to the UAW covers my position, provided that it is understood that I wrote 'could arrive' and not 'will arrive'.[73]

Small wonder he was eager to supervise every detail of the publication arrangements and publicity.

Yet he had written a masterpiece of political speculation. *Nineteen Eighty-Four* is to the twentieth century what Thomas Hobbes' *Leviathan* was to the seventeenth. He had characterized and shown the plausibility of, but had also parodied, totalitarian power, just as Hobbes had characterized and tried to justify autocratic power. At St Cyprian's and in Burma Orwell had experienced autocratic systems of government and he constantly scorned and mocked autocratic behaviour in individuals, but his long journey into European politics of the 1930s and 1940s had led him to understand and to fear totalitarian government as the greater menace to humanity. One limits our humanity, but the other could destroy it. This was one of his great themes. If totalitarianism becomes our common way of life, then all other humane values, liberty, fraternity, social justice, love of literature, love of plain speaking and clear writing, belief in a natural moral decency among ordinary people, love of nature, enjoyment of human oddity, and patriotism would perish. He argued for the primacy of the political only to protect non-political values. So while he was primarily a political writer and *Nineteen Eighty-Four* may assume his own and known political values, yet it does not make them explicit. It is a flawed masterpiece both of literature and of political thought.

We need to know why hope lies in the Proles; and we need to know whether he really believes that total power needed no ideology other than power for its own sake (a bleak pessimism indeed) or whether that view is satire on the power-hungry. The book was fully compatible with what he had written before and much of its inspiration arose from what he had done before. It does not summarize his life's work, however; it is not his *summa*, and it is not even a political last testament, or a last testament of any kind. It was, once again, the last great book he happened to write before he happened to die. He would have had much more to write about, just as he had written about other things, great and small.

On 3 September he moved into his last bed at University College Hospital in Gower Street, London. He had a private room for which he paid just over £17 a week. Visitors were supposed to be limited to half an hour a day, but this was not enforced too strictly. Flowers and fruit from David Astor greeted him. Once he would have been embarrassed or amused, now he was touched: he was growing used to the life of an invalid.

Even before he had left Cranham friends knew that something important was afoot, as he had told Warburg in a letter of 22 August.

As I warned you I might do, I intend getting married again (to Sonia) when I am once again in the land of the living, if I ever am. I suppose everyone will be horrified, but apart from other considerations I really think I should stay alive longer if I were married.[74]

He said a little more to David Astor about himself and Sonia.

UCH
5.9.49

Dear David,
Thanks ever so for sending those beautiful chrysanths and the box of peaches that actually met me on my arrival here. I feel ghastly and can't write much, but we had a wonderful journey down yesterday in the most ritzy ambulance you can imagine. This beastly fever never goes away but is better some days than others, and I really quite enjoyed the drive down ...
    I hope you are feeling better and that you will be able to meet Sonia. Morland says I mustn't see people much, but here in London it's easier for people to just look in for half an hour, which they hardly can at Cranham. Sonia lives only a few minutes away from here. She thinks we might as well

get married while I am still an invalid, because it would give her a better status to look after me especially if, eg. I went somewhere abroad after leaving here. It's an idea, but I think I should have to feel a little less ghastly than at present before I could even face a registrar for 10 minutes. I am much encouraged if none of my friends or relatives seems to disapprove of my remarrying, in spite of this disease. I had had a nasty feeling that 'they' would converge from all directions and stop me, but it hasn't happened. Morland, the doctor, is very much in favour of it.

I remember visiting you when you had the sinus but I didn't know it was this hospital. It seems very comfortable and easy-going here. Can't write more.

> Yours,
> George[75]

His second proposal to Sonia had been successful. Mutual friends did not, as George feared, or said he feared, oppose the idea, they rather welcomed it: it would give George something more to live for and leave him in capable and caring hands. Even before UCH the idea had been forming between Morland and Orwell that, when he was strong enough for the journey, he should move to a high-altitude clinic in France or Switzerland: it was then widely believed that with less pressure on the lung, risk of a haemorrhage might be diminished. A letter had reached him in August from a Catherine Karot in Versailles, for instance, recommending a sanatorium in Haute Savoie.[76]

Sonia was much in evidence from then on at the hospital, and began to take routine burdens off Orwell's shoulders. He still sent a few handwritten letters to some old friends, but his typewriter – which was almost an extension of his body-mind – had been taken from him for the last time. Three or four important letters to Moore were apparently dictated. Most of the writing in his last notebook was done at Cranham, such as the outline and some paragraphs for 'A Smoking Room Story' and a few passages for some other novel or short story, of mildly sadistic sexual fantasy. They reflect upon a type of woman who is sexually over-demanding. Apart from these, the extracts printed in *The Collected Essays, Journalism and Letters*, are representative. While 'At 50, everyone has the face he deserves' is a fine and haunting epigram, it cannot truly be presented as the last entry he made. It was not the last entry in the notebook as *The Collected Essays* appear to suggest. Since he moved from page to page, filling in back spaces, leaving long blanks for further additions on some themes, it is simply not possible to be sure what was the last entry. His habit of precise observation, however, continued. At one point he notes down.

Daily Routine of University College Hospital (*Private Wing*)

7–7.30 a.m. Temperature taken. Routine questions 'How did you sleep?'

7.30–8 Blanket bath. Bed made. Shaving water. 'Back' rubbed.

8.45 (about) Breakfast. Newspaper arrives.

9.30 (about) Wing Sister arrives with mail.

10 Temperature taken.

10.30 (at present) my bed is 'tipped'. Ward maid comes to sweep room.

11 (about) Orderly arrives to dust.

12.30 Bed taken down.

12.45 p.m. Lunch.

2 Temperature taken.

2.30 Bed 'tipped'.

3.30 Bed taken down.

3.45 Tea.

5 Temperature taken.

5.30 (about) am washed as far as waist. 'Back' rubbed.

6.45 Dinner.

10 Temperature taken; a drink of some sort.

10.30 (about) Bed 'tipped' & light put out shortly after.

No fixed hour for visits of doctor. No routine daily visit.

Room has: washbasin, cupboard, bedside locker, bed table, chest of drawers, wardrobe, 2 mirrors, wireless (knobs beside bed) electric pipe radiator, armchair & 1 other chair, bedside lamp & 2 other lamps, telephone. Fees 16 guineas a week, plus extra fee for doctor, but apparently including special medicines. Does not include telephone or wireless (Charge for wireless 3/6 a week)

He could now afford to pay in hospital fees each week more than twice what he and Eileen had lived on until the success of *Animal Farm*. How sad the contrast with the mutual worries about the cost of Eileen's operation in 1945.

The same notebook contains his own dispassionate and now famous description of his compulsive work ethic and also records his perpetual 'neurotic feeling that I was wasting time' and that his creative impulse 'is exhausted for good and all'. 'If I look back and count up the actual amount that I have written, then I see that my output has been respectable; but this does not reassure me, because it simply gives me the feeling that I once had an industriousness and a fertility which I have now lost.'[77] Perhaps self-recognition was now his own true therapy: he was becoming almost tranquil.

There is however, though it could have been written at Cranham, an entry headed 'Death Dreams':

Death Dreams very frequent throughout the past two years. Sometimes of the sea or the sea shore or more often of enormous, splendid buildings or streets or ships, in which I often lose my way, but always with a peculiar feeling of happiness & of walking in sunlight. Unquestionably all these buildings etc. mean death – I am almost aware of this even in the dream, & these dreams always become more *frequent* when my health gets worse & I begin to despair of ever recovering. What I can never understand is *why* since I am not afraid of death (afraid of pain & of the moment of dying, but not of extinction), this thought has to appear in my dreams under these various disguises. Cf. also my ever-recurrent fishing dream. Obviously this has a sexual meaning. The water, I suppose, means woman, & the fish are phallic symbols. But why do sex impulses which I am not frightened of thinking about when I am awake have to be dressed up as something different when I am asleep? And then again, what is the point of the disguise if, in practice, it is always penetrable?

Opinions among his visitors varied as to whether he was dying. Some took it for granted. Anthony Powell wrote: 'It was fairly clear that he was not going to recover; only the length of time that remained to him in doubt.'[78] Orwell told both Powell and Muggeridge that he did not think a writer could die if he had one more book in him. And they knew of his plans for marrying and going to Switzerland. 'All a dream,' wrote Muggeridge, 'writers still with things to write *can* die.'[79] Yet this is hindsight. Other visitors were impressed that he was not so much struggling, but resting quietly to live: at last he had seen sense, perhaps just in time. Rayner Heppenstall, who saw him several times in UCH, though he thought that Orwell's last works and time in Jura exhibited a death wish, did not think he was necessarily dying, only gravely ill, touch and go.[80] 'How ill was he? It was difficult to discuss this,' Tosco Fyvel wrote. 'Even while he talked freely and vigorously, his condition looked worrying.'[81]

In fact, however, Morland's junior consultant now says that 'when I first saw him, I had no serious doubt that he was dying'. Morland's diagnoses and letters to patients tended to optimism, indeed this 'give the patient some hope' was the general custom of the day; and there was a specific justification with tuberculosis cases. For while before streptomycin the disease was generally fatal, there was always a chance. Unlike cancer, it was an inflammatory disease and sometimes its progress, quite unaccountably, stopped. On this long chance, it was judged that the morale of the patient had to be kept up – even of such a man who wanted to know the truth and could face it. But this real view of the doctors was not communicated either to Sonia or to George, nor to anyone else.[82]

Orwell must have believed Morland's diagnosis that if he took care he could become a 'good chronic' able to do a few hours' writing each day; and he himself was hoping for no more than that – unless he had a relapse. Orwell knew quite well that if he had another haemorrhage, he would die at once. Otherwise, he thought his chances, if he accepted permanent invalidism – and he had accepted permanent invalidism – were quite good. A man who had courted the pain and humiliation of poverty, had lived with the fear of failure, had for a time experienced failure, who had been close to death several times already from a bullet wound and pneumonia, he could face with calmness the chance of death; but he was determined to act on the equally good chance of life. He prudently prepared for the possibility of death, drawing up precise instructions about which of his books and essays were to be reprinted and which not, lists of small mistakes in *Homage to Catalonia*, and notes on translations and on his collection of pamphlets. Again he repeated, as in 1945, that *A Clergyman's Daughter* and *Keep the Aspidistra Flying* were not to be reprinted, but he now added *The Lion and the Unicorn* and *The English People*; and he picked out the *Tribune* essays he thought worth reprinting, but proscribed his long review of T. S. Eliot's 'Four Quartets' in *Poetry London* (October 1942), 'My Country Right or Left', 'Culture and Democracy', his introduction to *British Pamphleteers* and his essays in Victor Gollancz's anthology, *The Betrayal of the Left*. And though he wanted *Homage to Catalonia* 'not to disappear', he did not want Warburg kept to his contract to republish it since it was 'commercially no good'. He even relented on his old stand against Gollancz's wish to publish only the first half of *The Road to Wigan Pier*: 'The first half of the book many times reprinted as L[eft] B[ook] C[lub] supplement. NB that though the book as a whole would hardly be worth reprinting, the first half is detachable and in particular the first chapter might be put into a book of sketches.' He judged himself so sternly and by such high standards. He was entitled to do so, but he simply did not understand the interest that was already growing in all of his writings because of his best work. It is useless to speculate, however, which of his prohibitions were primarily commercial, political or artistic.[83] But as well as concerning himself with his past writings, he made plans for the future, both personal and literary; and he talked to visitors much as usual about what was going to happen to the Labour Government, Britain, Europe and the world.

Such talk can, of course, be interpreted two ways. 'To accept death as final was for him a test of intellectual honesty,' his Christian friend, Richard Rees, was to write; 'to care passionately about the fate of mankind after your death was an ethical imperative.'[84] And Cyril Connolly was to write:

The tragedy of Orwell's life is that when at last he achieved fame and success he was a dying man and knew it. He had fame and was too ill to leave his room, money and nothing to spend it on, love in which he could not participate; he tasted the bitterness of dying. But in his years of hardship he was sustained by a genial stoicism, by his excitement about what was going to happen next and by his affection for other people.[85]

Orwell may have tasted the bitterness of fearing to die (although he showed no sign of fear or bitterness, only patience and serenity), but that he knew he was a dying man is simply untrue. In fact, in UCH that September he felt that he was getting better.

His marriage took place on 13 October. Marrying in a hospital involved obtaining a 'special licence'. But David Astor handled all the necessary correspondence with the Archbishop of Canterbury. Orwell asked Powell and Muggeridge to find him a smoking-jacket, for even if he was getting married from a hospital bed he could not do it in a dressing-gown. He looked unexpectedly grand and military in a smoking-jacket, as if, son of a poor gentleman, he had pursued his natural career in Burma to a successful end and had never become a political writer. Powell remembers the jacket as crimson corduroy, but Muggeridge as mauve velvet. Memory is so fallible; Sonia said that in the end she bought it for them to give to him. David Astor and Janette Kee (a friend of Sonia's and the wife of Robert Kee) were the witnesses. The occasion was kept short, so as not to tire him. David Astor entertained Sonia and a small party of mutual friends to a wedding luncheon at the Ritz. The signed menu was brought to Orwell. He was 46 years old, the certificate noted, and she was 31.

After the wedding, Orwell at first rallied appreciably, then had some bad days, then good, then bad again; his temperature undulated and he lost weight badly. He wrote only two or three letters in November, and in December none. Celia Kirwan noted that he was reading the Bodley Head's bi-lingual edition of Dante's *The Divine Comedy*. Otherwise he saved his energy for visitors and to be fit for the journey to a sanatorium in Switzerland. A plane was chartered for the last week in January, and a friend of Sonia's stood ready to accompany them.[86] Letters were gradually withdrawn from him, Sonia taking over the correspondence with agent, publishers and editors, as she was well used to do for Cyril Connolly at *Horizon*. Orwell admired her skill and judgement in these matters.

Threads from youth sometimes pull together strangely towards the end of a middle-aged man's life. Jacintha Buddicom had written to him, and now one afternoon old Andrew Gow, Fellow of Trinity, came to see him, using the excuse for his visit that he was in UCH to see a Trinity man and happened to hear that Blair was there too. Years afterwards he could not remember the name of that Trinity man and was probably making an excuse in case his old difficult Etonian pupil thought that he had turned soft. Blair was embarrassed because young Richard, brought by Avril for a last visit before his father left for Switzerland, was recounting a farmyard incident at Barnhill in farmyard language: he did not think this fit for the distinguished classical scholar's ears.[87] The intellectual tramp and truth-teller observed bourgeois proprieties to the last.

Shielding him from all routine business and importuning letters, Sonia brought one letter to him, knowing the pleasure it would give. Desmond McCarthy, the doyen of English critics, had had lunch with her and sent Orwell a note hoping for his recovery, and congratulated him on his writings: 'you have already made an indelible mark on English literature.'[88] He had slowly climbed to such a height.

Friends came to see him in UCH for the last time before he left for Switzerland. He chided Spender that he was wrong to attempt to reply to Communist critics: '"There are certain people like vegetarians and Communists whom one cannot answer. You just have to go on saying your say regardless of them, and then the extraordinary thing is that they may start listening."' On a previous visit he had grumbled to Spender about there being far too many visible signs of wealth in London, despite a Labour Government: to see so many Rolls-Royces annoyed him. Spender said that he had been told by Hugh Gaitskell that most of them belonged to foreigners and the embassies, and that to get rid of them would not help any one much. '"That may be so," he said, "but there shouldn't be visible signs of one class being much better off than another. It is bad for morale."'[89] Julian Symons found him 'worrying, with fine Johnsonian insularity, about the problem of tea. "I don't know if I shall get proper tea in Switzerland," he said. "They have that filthy Chinese stuff, you know. I like Ceylon tea, very strong."' He thought that in Switzerland they might lift the ban on his writing, and he talked to Symons about the short novel he was planning. 'He also elaborated a thesis that the Communist Party's object in putting up a hundred candidates for the coming election was to help defeat the Labour Party. He regretted that he wouldn't be in England for the election.'[90] The last opinion that Rayner Heppenstall heard him utter was that he had changed his mind about the Welsh and Gaelic languages being dying anachronisms: he now thought that they ought to be encouraged and preserved. Perhaps his English patriotism was at last trying to come to terms with a broader concept of the United Kingdom and its nations.[91] Stafford Cottman, the most faithful of the old Spanish war comrades, phoned him up to arrange a visit, after some difficulty, for the hospital did not know 'Eric Blair'; but Orwell said he was tired and would rather see him after his return.[92]

Orwell made out a new will on 18 January 1950 as a precaution before flying to Switzerland, making Sonia and Richard Rees jointly his literary executors, leaving a sizeable insurance policy towards Richard's education, and making Sonia his sole beneficiary. He requested that she should then leave the residue of his estate to Richard in her will. There was no provision for Avril, who was named joint guardian of Richard together with Sonia and Gwen O'Shaughnessy. Avril and Bill Dunn, in fact, were to bring up Richard, Sonia helping financially. 'And lastly I direct that my body shall be buried (not cremated) according to the rites of the Church of England in the nearest convenient cemetery, and that there shall be placed over my grave a plain brown stone bearing the inscription, "Here lies Eric Arthur Blair born June 25th, 1903, died ..."; in case any suggestion should arise I request that no memorial service be held for me after my death and that no biography shall be written.'

Muggeridge noticed that he now had a fishing-rod across the end of his bed, as if ready for mountain streams in Switzerland.

One of the very last people to see him alive was the poorest of his friends, Paul Potts:

... on the eve of going to Switzerland I, like a lot of his friends, called to say good-bye. Cut into the door of his hospital room was a small window. One could look through it, and see him before knocking. That afternoon I saw he had fallen off to sleep. He needed sleep badly, found it hard to come by. I left without waking him, leaving a packet of tea outside the door. After all, he'd be back in a couple of months and up again. Ever since I had known him he'd been given up as hopeless. During that time he'd lived a fuller life than a whole company of A1 recruits. Under his influence all his friends stopped taking the doctors seriously.[93]

Tosco Fyvel must have seen him earlier that same afternoon, 'he seemed particularly cheerful'. They chatted about school days, their different experiences: 'he talked to me about himself at Eton, relating harmless and amusing incidents'. Before Fyvel left, Orwell urged him to visit him in his Swiss sanatorium.[94]

But it was all a dream. He had already climbed as high on his *Zauberberg* or Magic Mountain as he ever would. What Morland had warned could happen at any time did happen. Orwell's lung haemorrhaged on the night of 21 January 1950 and he died at once and alone before Sonia could be found. The world heard the news on the BBC that morning. As the first sentence of the first manuscript version of his last book had said, the radios had all struck thirteen.

The death occurred in London today of Mr George Orwell, the author, at the age of 46. He had been ill for a long time. George Orwell was educated at Eton and later served in the Burma police. He fought on the Republican side in the Spanish Civil War and was wounded. After that he spent most of his time writing. He will, perhaps, be best remembered for *Animal Farm*, a satire on life in the Soviet Union, and for the recently published *Nineteen Eighty-Four*, a grim imaginary picture of a totalitarian Great Britain some 30 years from now, which was highly praised by critics on both sides of the Atlantic.[95]

Even after death, droll difficulties attended the decent, gentle, indignant, awkward spirit, now looking for a last resting place – this man who had 'the independence of Swift mixed up with the humility of Oliver Goldsmith', and was 'the wintery conscience of a generation'.[96] The unexpected request to be buried in a churchyard, when he had no connection with any church, priest or vicar, created problems. Muggeridge had a word, however, with a vicar in Albany Street who had never heard of Orwell (or perhaps of Blair?) but was reassured by the name of the Warren Street undertaker.[97] The separate groups of his friends gathered together for the first and last time: famous literary men and publishers, *Tribune*, *Observer* and BBC journalists, exiles from Europe, veterans from the Spanish War, old ILP comrades, anarchists, members of the Home Guard, unknown and obscure writers, friends of Sonia, relatives of Eileen and odd people he had met in Canonbury or Bloomsbury pubs. Anthony Powell chose the lesson from the last chapter of *Ecclesiastes*: '... man goeth to his long home, and the mourners go about the streets'. The mourners noted that it was a long coffin.[98]

The body was taken to a plot that David Astor had found in the country churchyard of All Saints, Sutton Courtenay, near his family estate. As once the atheist Thomas Hobbes had needed the power of a territorial magnate, of a Duke of Devonshire, to get him buried in sacred ground, so now the Left-wing sceptic needed the power of a friendly newspaper proprietor, one of the magnates of our time. Perhaps Orwell's request was not so surprising. He loved the land and he loved England and he loved the language of the liturgies of the English Church. 'Orwell-like' conveys all these things; 'Orwellian' other things. He should be remembered for both.

Let a paragraph from the same essay that Sonia Orwell and Ian Angus printed at the very beginning of *The Collected Essays, Journalism and Letters* serve as his own epitaph at the end of his first full and unwanted biography:

What I have most wanted to do throughout the past ten years is to make political writing into an art. My starting point is always a feeling of partisanship, a sense of injustice. When I sit down to write a book, I do not say to myself, 'I am going to produce a work of art.' I write it because there is some lie that I want to expose, some fact to which I want to draw attention, and my initial concern is to get a hearing. But I could not do the work of writing a book, or even a long magazine article, if it were not also an aesthetic experience. Anyone who cares to examine my work will see that even when it is downright propaganda it contains much that a full-time politician would consider irrelevant. I am not able, and I do not want, completely to abandon the world-view that I acquired in childhood. So long as I remain alive and well I shall continue to feel strongly about prose style, to love the surface of the earth, and to take pleasure in solid objects and scraps of useless information. It is no use trying to suppress that side of myself. The job is to reconcile my ingrained likes and dislikes with the essentially public, non-individual activities that this age forces on all of us.

'... Our prerogatives as men' wrote Louis MacNeice, 'Will be cancelled who knows when ...?', if we cannot radically alter our relationships with public power; but neither a transformed nor a reformed public realm will be worth having if individual creative values do not flourish, indeed fructify in abundance for the majority of people, not just for the chosen or even the self-chosen few. In striving to keep a deliberate balance between public and private values, between creative work and necessary labour, between politics and culture, Orwell's life and his writings should both guide and cheer us. He hated the power-hungry, exercised intelligence and independence, and taught us again to use our language with beauty and clarity, sought for and practised fraternity and had faith in the decency, tolerance and humanity of the common man. And what is even more heartening, he was all that and yet as odd in himself and as varied in his friends as man can be.

APPENDIX A

THE NINETEEN FORTY-THREE OUTLINE

OF *NINETEEN EIGHTY-FOUR*

This outline is clearly what became *Nineteen Eighty-Four*. It is found under the heading 'The Last Man in Europe' in a notebook (in the Orwell Archive at University College, London) which also contains some notes towards and a few paragraphs of 'The Quick and the Dead' – a possible title he mentions in 1940 for 'a long novel in three parts' (see p. 387). 'The Quick and the Dead' *could* have been a conception that would have linked the themes of 'revolution betrayed' of *Animal Farm* and of the awful consequences in *Nineteen Eighty-Four* to a family saga of the prior decay of the old order (see pp. 387–8). The importance, however, of this outline is that the notebook is certainly no later than January 1944 when he mentioned in *Tribune* a list of 'childhood fallacies' which he had in a notebook – as they are (see p. 42). There is also a reference in the notes towards 'The Quick and the Dead' to a horse called 'Boxer' being whipped to his feet by an army officer and driven to death – which strengthens the hypothesis that the two books were planned at the same time, originally part of the same conception. This outline is surely conclusive that *Nineteen Eighty-Four*, however morbid critics may find it, was not a sudden conception following the collapse of his health. He told Fred Warburg in a letter of 22 October 1948 (see p. 546) that 'I first thought of it in 1943'.

[p.1]   For '*The Last Man In Europe*'

[p.2]   To be brought in:

          Newspeak (one leading article for the 'Times').

Comparison of weights, measures, etc.

Statistics.

Window boxes.

Rectification.

Position of R Cs.

Pacifists.

Interrelation between the party & the Trusts.

Position of the proles.

Sexual code.

Names of B M etc.

Films.

The party [illegible].

Dual standard of thought.

Bakerism & ingsoc.

The party slogans (War is peace. Ignorance is strength. Freedom is slavery).

World geography.

The Two Minutes Hate.

[p.3]   The general lay-out as follows:

PART I   Build up of

    a. The system of organized lying on which society is founded.

    b. The ways in which this is done (falsification of records, etc.).

    c. The nightmare feeling caused by the disappearance of objective truth.

    d. Leader-worship, etc.

    e. The swindle of Bakerism & Ingsoc.

    f. Loneliness of the writer. His feeling of being *the last man*.

    g. Equivocal position of the proles, the Christians and others.

    h. Antisemitism (& terrible cruelty of war etc.).

    i. The writer's approaches to X & Y.

    j. The brief interlude of the love affair with Y.

583

PART II

        a. Declaration of war against East Asia.
        b. The arrests & torture.

[p.4]   *c.* Continuation of the diary, this time not written down.

        d. The final consciousness of failure.

All in long chapters, & therefore the layout more accurately might be this
PART I divided into abt 6 parts, comprising:

      i. Lies, hatred, cruelty, loneliness.
      ii. Pictures of London [?] the swindle of Bakerism.
twice *iii.* Fantasmagoric effect, rectification, shifting of dates, etc., doubts of own sanity.
      iv. Position of the proles, etc.

30,000 words *v.* Successful approach to X & Y.

      vi. Love affair with Y. Conversation with X.

PART II to be divided into 3 main parts comprising:

15,000 words *i.* The torture & confession

15,000 words *ii.* Continuation of diary, mentally.

5,000 words? *iii.* Recognition of own insanity.

The fantasmagoric effect produced by:

Were we at war with East Asia in 1974?
[p.5] at war with Eurasia in 1978? Were A, B & C present at the secret conference in 1976?

APPENDIX A

Impossibility of detecting similar memories
in anyone else. Non-memory [?] of the proles.
Equivocal answers. Effect of lies & hatred
produced by: Films. Extracts of anti-Jew
propaganda. B'casts.

The Two Minutes Hate. Enemy propaganda & writer's
response to it.

APPENDIX B

THE DATING OF 'SUCH, SUCH WERE THE JOYS'

Critics who see *Nineteen Eighty-Four* as the product of a death wish and as a sado-masochistic fantasy with its roots in childhood traumas then leap to the conclusion that the essay was written immediately before the book (see p. 41 and note 3 to Chapter 1). Well may they, for although the editors recognize some uncertainty, they sensibly printed the text in *The Collected Essays, Journalism and Letters* immediately following Orwell's letter of 31 May 1947 to Fred Warburg transmitting the essay. All that Ian Angus properly and cautiously says is that it was 'written by May 1947' (*CE* IV, p. 519). Here, however, is the relevant paragraph of the covering letter which is printed in *The Collected Essays* immediately before the essay (*CE* IV, p. 330).

I am sending you separately a long autobiographical sketch which I originally undertook as a sort of pendant to Cyril Connolly's *Enemies of Promise*, he having asked me to write a reminiscence of the preparatory school we were at together. I haven't actually sent it to Connolly or *Horizon* because apart from being too long for a periodical I think it is really too libellous to print, and I am not disposed to change it except perhaps the names. But I think it should be printed sooner or later when the people most concerned are dead, and maybe sooner or later I might do a book of collected sketches. I must apologize for the typescript. It is not only the carbon copy, but is very bad commercial typing which I have had to correct considerably – however, I think I have got most of the actual errors out.

Consider the language carefully: '... which I originally undertook as a sort of pendant' to Connolly's *Enemies of Promise* (1938), 'he having asked me to write ...' This clearly suggests that at least a first version was written much earlier. Against this are two facts: (i) Orwell says in the last section of the essay, 'All this was thirty years ago and more', which places the composition in 1947 exactly. But the text could have been updated in just such an obvious respect and the heading would also be compatible with a revision in the Jura period, indeed he must then have revised it thoroughly enough to necessitate retyping; and (ii) that the typescript and carbon that survive have on the top right-hand of the first page, 'George Orwell, Barnhill, Isle of Jura, Argyllshire'.

The typescripts give no other clue as to date and the type-face is certainly not that of Orwell's typewriter. The letter implies that he was only sending a carbon, whereas what in fact survives in the Orwell Archive (from which the printed text was set) is a top copy and a carbon, and they are not 'very bad commercial typing which I have had to correct considerably'. The typescripts are, in fact, remarkably clean with only very occasional and small corrections of literals and these not in Orwell's hand. The presumption must be, then, that these typescripts are a retyping in Secker & Warburg's offices (though no one can now remember what happened) of whatever Orwell himself corrected. So they do not help to date the essay. There is, moreover, no record or memory of him farming out any work while at Jura; only in Canonbury did he even briefly use a secretary, and only after Eileen began war work in the autumn of 1939 would he not have had help, which he normally did not need, except when he was himself working full-time at the BBC from 1941–3.

All that can be said confidently about the style is that it was written after his stylistic break-through as regards his book-length work, the vivid, conversational, descriptive realism of *Homage to Catalonia*. But its angry tone, at times its rather ranting 'I'll make yer flesh creep' style, and its uncertain pose between the autobiographical and the polemical, is far more consistent with his bitter and jagged writing of the 1938–43 period, with his mood of failure and frustration, indeed, than with the calm, composed and measured post-war essays.

A number of contemporary references strengthen this hypothesis. Orwell wrote to Connolly on 8 July 1938 (*CE* I, p. 343), 'I wonder how you can write about St Cyprian's. It's all like an awful nightmare to me,' but also on 14 December 1938 (*CE* I, p. 363), 'I'm always meaning one of these days to write a book about St Cyprian's . . . people are wrecked by those filthy private schools.' In 'Inside the Whale' (1940) he mocked Connolly for making virtually the same assertion. Orwell saw him as having accepted 'permanent adolescence' unlike continental intellectuals who have gone out into a real world of 'hunger, hardship, solitude, exile, war, prison, persecution, manual labour' (*CE* I, p. 517). Prejudice against the cult of Scotland, very similar to that in the essay, appeared in a book review in the *New Statesman and Nation* (21 September 1940, p. 290); his only other reference to bed-wetting, as the kind of 'dark secret' that psychological novelists pretend to rip out of one, also occurs in a *New Statesman* book review (7 December 1940, p. 574); and when he reviewed, also in 1940, Stephen Spender's novel, *The Backward Son* (in *Tribune*, 24 May, p. 14) he said 'it is about a "prep school", one of those (on the whole) nasty little schools at which small boys are prepared for public school entrance examination. Incidentally, these schools, with their money-grubbing proprietors and their staff of underpaid hacks are responsible for a lot of the harm that it is usual to blame on the public schools. A majority of middle class boys have had their minds permanently lamed by them before they are thirteen' – which is very close to the precise sentiments and language of the essay. And early in 1942 he began a broadcast on European literature with a reminiscence about how badly he was taught history when at school ('The Rediscovery of Europe', originally broadcast on 10 March 1942, *CE* II, p. 198).

Against these indications of a probable composition around 1940 is a section of *Tribune* 'As I Please' column of 14 March 1947 in which he told an anecdote of the lunacies of learning history by rote, which began: 'The other day I had occasion to write something about the teaching of history in private schools, and the following scene, which was only rather loosely connected with what I was writing, floated into my memory. It was less than fifteen years ago when I witnessed it.' The anecdote would have come from his own teaching days, but the writing to which he refers could only be 'Such, Such Were the Joys'. But again this is compatible with a revision.

An intellectual and a practical consideration also point towards the earlier date. The intellectual point is to ask whether it is sensible for all of Orwell's considerable knowledge about extreme forces in European politics in the 1930s and 1940s to be reduced to the traumas of an English childhood? We have argued in the text that, in any case, the political systems of the true St Cyprian's and of Orwell's

Nineteen Eighty-Four are quite different, one authoritarian and the other totalitarian, a distinction which was clear and important to him. If, moreover, it is argued that the totalitarian aspects of his literary St Cyprian's were, after all, historical (the sense of not being able to escape and having no control whatever over one's life), and thus can be seen as the direct cause of *Nineteen Eighty-Four*, it is at least as plausible to reverse this argument and to argue that because of the needs of plot and characterization in *Nineteen Eighty-Four* he reimagined and recreated 'St Cyprian's' – if it was written or even revised in 1947. The practical point is simply that the essay is very long, all but 20,000 words. Desperately wanting to finish *Nineteen Eighty-Four*, is it likely that Orwell could have paused to dash this off first? If he felt compulsive and obsessional about it, he would have dashed it off; but there is simply no evidence for that, and he mentions the essay in none of his fairly full letters of this period to his friends or to his agent.

Probably he was giving Warburg for safe-keeping a fairly quick revision in 1947 of a manuscript originally written in 1940. His letter shows that he realized that it could not be published until the people concerned were dead. He may have given it to Warburg fearing that, if anything happened, Avril might destroy it, or at least not want it published, as did neither his literary executor (see p. 36) nor Andrew Gow (see p. 79). He may have let the side down with his fine polemic, but I do not believe that he exposed autobiographically the roots of *Nineteen Eighty-Four*; they lay in his whole life, most of all his mature experience, not just in his childhood.

NOTES

Citations from Orwell's own published books are all to the Secker & Warburg Uniform Edition (1948–65), not to the original editions. References to material in *The Collected Essays, Journalism and Letters of George Orwell* edited by Sonia Orwell and Ian Angus, four volumes (Secker & Warburg, London, 1968)) are all rendered '*C E*'. (These should not be confused with the one-volume *Collected Essays*, first published in 1961.)

Material in the Orwell Collection in the Manuscripts and Rare Books Department of University College, London is referred to as 'Orwell Archive'. Reference numbers are not given, since at this moment some questions of access are unresolved which might mean rearrangement of the papers. But the existing finding lists are adequate.

Since many readers will possess the Penguin edition of the *C E* rather than the Secker & Warburg edition (they are identical, apart from pagination, except for a few minor corrections in the Penguin edition), a rough conversion table follows from the Secker & Warburg to the Penguin. (The Harcourt Brace Jovanovich edition is identical to Secker & Warburg's.)

GEORGE ORWELL

Conversion table for page references from Secker & Warburg into Penguin edition of The Collected Essays, Journalism and Letters

VOLUME I

S & W	P		S & W	P		S & W	P		S & W	P
1	23		140	164		280	312		420	460
10	32		150	173		290	323		430	471
20	42		160	183		300	334		440	482
30	52		170	194		310	344		450	493
40	62		180	205		320	354		460	504
50	72		190	216		330	365		470	514
60	84		200	227		340	376		480	525
70	95		210	238		350	388		490	537
80	103		220	249		360	397		500	548
90	113		230	259		370	408		510	559
100	124		240	270		380	418		520	570
110	134		250	281		390	429		530	581
120	143		260	292		400	440		540	591
130	154		270	302		410	449			

VOLUME II

S & W	P		S & W	P		S & W	P		S & W	P
10	24		130	156		250	286		370	419
20	35		140	167		260	298		380	430
30	45		150	177		270	310		390	441
40	56		160	189		280	320		400	453
50	67		170	200		290	332		410	464
60	78		180	210		300	343		420	474
70	87		190	221		310	353		430	486
80	101		200	232		320	364		440	497
90	112		210	243		330	375		450	508
100	123		220	254		340	386			
110	134		230	265		350	397			
120	145		240	276		360	408			

VOLUME III

S & W	P		S & W	P		S & W	P		S & W	P
10	24		120	145		230	266		340	386
20	35		130	156		240	277		350	397
30	46		140	167		250	288		360	408
40	57		150	178		260	298		370	419
50	68		160	189		270	310		380	430
60	78		170	200		280	320		390	441
70	90		180	211		290	331		400	452
80	101		190	222		300	342		406	459
90	112		200	233		310	354			
100	123		210	244		320	364			
110	134		220	255		330	375			

VOLUME IV

S & W	P		S & W	P		S & W	P		S & W	P
10	26		140	170		270	312		400	454
20	37		150	181		280	323		410	465
30	49		160	191		290	334		420	476
40	60		170	202		300	345		430	486
50	70		180	213		310	356		440	497
60	82		190	224		320	367		450	509
70	94		200	235		330	378		460	519
80	104		210	246		340	389		470	530
90	114		220	257		350	400		480	541
100	126		230	268		360	411		490	551
110	137		240	279		370	423		500	562
120	148		250	290		380	434		510	573
130	159		260	301		390	444			

NOTES

1. 'AND I WAS A CHUBBY BOY'

1. *CE* IV, pp. 445–6.

2. *CE* IV, p. 415.

3. The *locus classicus* of this argument is in a review by Anthony West of the first American edition of Orwell's *Keep the Aspidistra Flying* in 1954, reprinted in his essays *Principles and Persuasions* (Eyre & Spottiswoode, London, 1958), pp. 157–9: 'In *Nineteen Eighty-Four* ... the whole pattern of society shapes up along the lines of fear laid down in 'Such, Such Were the Joys' until the final point of the dread summons to the headmaster's study for the inevitable beating. In *Nineteen Eighty-Four*, the study becomes Room 101 ... As these parallels fall into place ... it is possible to see how Orwell's unconscious mind was working. Whether he knew it or not, what he did in *Nineteen Eighty-Four* was to send everybody in England to an enormous Crossgates [St Cyprian's] to be as miserable as he had been ... Only the existence of a hidden wound can account for such a remorseless pessimism.' The reader must judge for himself whether the pessimism was 'remorseless' and the result of a 'hidden wound'; and whether claims to know how another's unconscious mind is working are the 'only' possible explanation of such pessimism, compared, say, to the actual misery and devastation in the external world caused by Stalinism and Nazism and the Hiroshima bomb. West also assumes that the essay was written immediately prior to the book, but see Appendix B, 'The Dating of "Such, Such Were the Joys"'.

Jeffrey Meyers, *A Reader's Guide to George Orwell* (Thames and Hudson, London, 1975), follows West, see pp. 30, 46 and 144–54, in both his psychological reduction of Orwell's argument and his acceptance of the assumed date. T. R. Fyvel, who knew Orwell quite well, had more tentatively suggested links between some aspects of *Nineteen Eighty-Four* and both

Orwell's illness and his childhood experiences, in his influential 'A Writer's Life', *World Review*, June 1950, pp. 7–20.

4. Jacintha Buddicom talking to the author at Bognor Regis, June 1972. See also her 'The Young Eric', in Miriam Gross (ed.), *The World of George Orwell* (Weidenfeld & Nicolson, London, 1971) and her far fuller account *Eric and Us* (Leslie Frewin, London, 1974).

5. 'As I Please', 28 Jan. 1944, *CE* III, p. 85.

6. Anthony West, op. cit., p. 159.

7. The family history is taken from family papers in the Orwell Archive, interviews with Avril Dunn, Orwell's sister, 21 Aug. 1972, 15 April 1974, 6–7 Sept. 1976, and from Ian Angus' notes on conversations with her and her husband, 16–19 April 1964.

8. The original diary is in the possession of Mrs Jane Morgan (*née* Dakin) of Jamaica, a niece of Orwell's. Copy in Orwell Archive.

9. *CE* I, p. 1.

10. 'Songs We Used to Sing', *Evening Standard*, 19 Jan. 1946, p. 6.

11. In a review of the film of H. G. Wells' *Kipps* in *Time and Tide*, 17 May 1941, p. 402.

12. *CE* IV, p. 352.

13. *Horizon*, Sept. 1941, p. 216.

14. *The Road to Wigan Pier*, pp. 129 and 125.

15. ibid., p. 127.

16. 'My Country Right or Left', *CE* I, p. 538.

17. *Coming Up For Air*, p. 40.

18. Letters of 25 Sept. 1976 and 15 Jan. 1977 from Mrs Jane Morgan to the author.

19. loc. cit.

2. THE JOYS OF PREP SCHOOL AND THE ECHOING GREEN

1. For Richard Blair's pension see the Civil Pension Books, 1912–31, Accountant General's Records, India Office Library (the pension remains the same for the whole period covered by these records); and for the comparisons of income see Guy Routh, *Occupational Pay in Great Britain* (Cambridge University Press, 1965), p. 104.

2. Henry Longhurst, *My Life and Soft Times* (Cassell, London, 1972), p. 32.

3. Cyril Connolly, 'George Orwell', in his *The Evening Colonnade* (David Bruce & Watson, London, 1973), p. 373.

4. Longhurst, op. cit., p. 37.

5. 'Such, Such Were the Joys', *CE* IV, p. 359.

6. ibid., p. 349.

7. Anthony West, 'George Orwell', in his *Principles and Persuasions* (Eyre & Spottiswoode, London, 1958), pp. 150–59.

8. *CE* I, p. 1.

9. BBC Eastern Service, 2 Nov. 1942 (BBC Archives). Copy in Orwell Archive.

10. First published with some changes of names in *Partisan Review*, Sept.–Oct. 1952, then not in Great Britain until the *CE* of 1968. Anthony West (op. cit.) and others jumped to the conclusion that it was written close to the composition of *Nineteen Eighty-Four*; but this is highly speculative, it was probably written earlier. See Appendix B.

11. *CE* IV, pp. 360–61.

12. *CE* I, p. 363.

13. Review of Stephen Spender, *The Backward Son*, *Tribune*, 24 May 1941.

14. Cyril Connolly, *Previous Convictions* (Hamish Hamilton, London, 1963), p. 318.

15. *Keep the Aspidistra Flying*, p. 53.

16. *CE* IV, p. 332.

17. 'Mrs Form' would presumably run a 'finishing school' and offer correction on 'the form' in the 'school room' – all terms of the trade in Victorian flagellant establishments and some less specialized brothels, see Ian Gibson, *The English Vice: Beating, Sex and Shame in Victorian England and After* (Duckworth, London, 1978) *passim*. But Ian Gibson tells me that in his extensive reading, he has never come across a Mrs Form and doubts her existence: names of fictional and pseudonyms of real Madames were much more explicit. Perusal of material mentioned in Ronald Pearsall, *The Worm in the Bud: the World of Victorian Sexuality* (Weidenfeld, London, 1969) and in Cyril Pearl, *The Girl With the Swansdown Seat* (Frederick Muller, London, 1955) also reaches a reassuringly negative conclusion. Orwell's account of his beating, however, is so close to the theme of Freud's classic psychoanalytical essay, 'A Child is Being Beaten', that it is possible either that he knew this essay or that elements of an unconscious punishment fantasy of 'the terrible mother, the phallic mother of childhood', intruded on his genuine conscious memories. (See Steven Marcus, *The Other Victorians* (Weidenfeld, London, 1966), chapter 6, for a sane discussion of beating fantasies.)

18. Colin Kirkpatrick, of Salisbury, Rhodesia, who was an exact contemporary of Eric Blair's at St Cyprian's, annotated for this author the margins of Peter Stansky and William Abraham's account of Blair at prep school in their *The Unknown Orwell* (Constable, London, 1972). His criticisms all arise from their following Orwell literally in his 'Such, Such Were the Joys'. The claim that it was another boy who was beaten for bed-wetting is repeated in a letter from Mr Kirkpatrick to the author of 9 Jan. 1973.

19. *CE* IV, p. 333.

20. ibid., p. 334.
21. ibid., p. 331.
22. Cyril Connolly, *Enemies of Promise* (Routledge & Kegan Paul, London, 1938), p. 210.
23. Connolly, *Previous Convictions*, p. 318.
24. Connolly, *Enemies of Promise*, p. 212.
25. Gavin Maxwell, *The House of Elrig* (Longman, London, 1965).
26. Longhurst, op. cit., p. 30.
27. Maxwell, op. cit., p. 71.
28. ibid., p. 87.
29. ibid., p. 85.
30. *CE* IV p. 335.
31. ibid., pp. 347–8.
32. Connolly, *Enemies of Promise*, p. 208.
33. Longhurst, op. cit., p. 26.
34. Letter of Nov. 1972 from Sir John Grotrian to author.
35. 'Notes for Professor Bernard Crick' written by Colin Kirkpatrick, Jan. 1973.
36. 'Such, Such Were the Joys', *CE* IV, pp. 36–7.
37. 'Rediscovery of Europe', first published in the *Listener*, 19 March 1942, then in *CE* II, p. 197.
38. 'As I Please', *Tribune*, 14 March 1947, then in *CE* IV, p. 306, though the incident refers to the time when he himself was teaching in 1932.
39. Maxwell, op. cit., p. 77.
40. Letter of 1 May 1967 from Andrew Gow to Sonia Orwell, Orwell Archive.
41. Letter from David Farrer to Cyrus Brooks of A. M. Heath (the literary agents of the Orwell Estate) of 12 March 1953, Orwell Archive, Papers of Sonia Orwell.
42. Jacintha Buddicom, *Eric and Us* (Leslie Frewin, London, 1974).
43. Letter of 29 May 1974 in Jacintha Buddicom's possession.

3. LEARNING AND HOLIDAYS

1. 'Such, Such Were the Joys', *CE* IV, p. 344.
2. Avril Dunn speaking in 'George Orwell: A Programme of Recorded Reminiscences', arranged and narrated by Rayner Heppenstall, recorded on 20 Aug. 1960 and first broadcast on 2 Nov. 1960 (BBC Archives, Ref. No. TLO 24177). Copy in Orwell Archive.
3. Cyril Connolly, *Enemies of Promise* (Routledge & Kegan Paul, London, 1938), p. 213.
4. ibid., pp. 212–13.
5. ibid., p. 213.
6. 10 May 1948, in *CE* IV, p. 422.

7. Avril Dunn in 'George Orwell', BBC (see note 2 above).

8. *CE* I, p. 536.

9. Jacintha Buddicom, 'The Young Eric', in Miriam Gross (ed.), *The World of George Orwell* (Weidenfeld & Nicolson, London, 1971), p. 2.

10. Jacintha Buddicom, *Eric and Us* (Leslie Frewin, London, 1974), p. 16.

11. ibid., p. 19.

12. ibid., pp. 35–6.

13. Few of his poems, even from the published sources, are included in *The Collected Essays, Journalism and Letters*.

14. Buddicom, 'The Young Eric', in Gross, op. cit., p. 2.

15. *Coming Up for Air*, p. 76.

16. *Evening Standard*, 1 Dec. 1945, p. 6.

17. The first paragraph is from Buddicom, 'The Young Eric', in Gross, op. cit., p. 6, and the second is from Buddicom, *Eric and Us*, p. 53.

18. Buddicom, *Eric and Us*, p. 38.

19. ibid., pp. 38–40.

20. ibid., p. 41.

21. *CE* I, p. 2.

22. Peter Stansky and William Abrahams, *The Unknown Orwell* (Constable, London, 1972), reviewed by Cyril Connolly, *The Evening Colonnade* (David Bruce & Watson, London, 1973), p. 372.

23. ibid., pp. 381–2.

24. Cyril Connolly, *Previous Convictions* (Hamish Hamilton, London, 1963), p. 318.

25. Connolly, *The Evening Colonnade*, p. 374.

4. ETON: RESTING ON THE OARS (1917–21)

1. *CE* II, p. 23.

2. Peter Stansky and William Abrahams, in *The Unknown Orwell* (Constable, London, 1972), devote about a third of the book to a fascinating and fascinated account of Eton. The implication is that it must have had a formative effect on Orwell's character, but the point is never demonstrated and he remains tangential to the narrative.

3. Review of B. J. W. Hill's *Eton Medley* in the *Observer*, 1 Aug. 1948.

4. For instance in a letter to Cyril Connolly, *CE* I, p. 363 (see p. 587); and in a letter to Julian Symons of Oct. 1948, 'I am not going to let him go to a boarding school before he is ten, and I would like him to start off at the elementary school' (*CE* IV, p. 451).

5. Denys King-Farlow, 'College Days with George Orwell', MS. *circa* 1967 (five typed pages in Orwell Archive, Reminiscences).

6. Christopher Hollis, *A Study of George Orwell* (Hollis & Carter, London,

1956), p. 20. See also his *Eton: A History* (Hollis & Carter, London, 1960), p. 299 ff.

7. Denys King-Farlow speaking in 'George Orwell: A Programme of Recorded Reminiscences', arranged and narrated by Rayner Heppenstall, recorded on 20 Aug. 1960 and first broadcast on 2 Nov. 1960 (BBC Archives, Ref. No. TLO 24177). Copy in Orwell Archive.

8. Interview by the author with George Wansbrough at Winchester, 18 Nov. 1976.

9. Hollis, *A Study of George Orwell*, p. 15.

10. Interview by the author with Sir Roger Mynors at St Weonard's, 17 Aug. 1976.

11. George Wansbrough (see note 8 above).

12. Hollis, *A Study of George Orwell*, pp. 13–14.

13. Jacintha Buddicom, *Eric and Us* (Leslie Frewin, London, 1974), p. 58.

14. ibid., p. 74.

15. ibid., pp. 59–60.

16. ibid., p. 58.

17. *The Road to Wigan Pier*, pp. 132–3.

18. *CE* I, pp. 536–7.

19. loc. cit.

20. Letter of Christopher Eastwood to Sonia Orwell, 17 April 1964, in Orwell Archive; and interview with the author, 17 Nov. 1976.

21. Stansky and Abrahams, op. cit., p. 107.

22. King-Farlow, 'College Days with George Orwell'.

23. Cyril Connolly, *Enemies of Promise* (Routledge & Kegan Paul, London, 1938), p. 244.

24. Buddicom, op. cit., p. 76.

25. Interview with Denys King-Farlow by Ian Angus, 20 April 1967.

26. Buddicom, op. cit., p. 74.

27. ibid., p. 71.

28. Cited by Cyril Connolly, op. cit., p. 267.

29. Hollis, *A Study of George Orwell*, p. 15.

30. Buddicom, op. cit., p. 79; and see Orwell's letter to Eleanor Jaques, 19 Sept. 1932, *CE* I, p. 102.

31. King-Farlow, 'College Days with George Orwell'.

32. Interview by the author with Andrew Gow at Cambridge, 18 Dec. 1976.

33. Hollis, *A Study of George Orwell*, p. 17.

34. Interview by the author with Sir Steven Runciman in London, 19 Oct. 1976, and Runciman quoted in Sybille Bedford, *Aldous Huxley: A Biography* (Chatto & Windus, London, 1973), Vol. I, p. 92.

35. Buddicom, op. cit., pp. 77–8 and 90.

36. ibid., p. 87.

37. 'Bernard Shaw' by George Orwell, broadcast in the Eastern Service of the BBC, 22 Jan. 1943, 'Calling all Students' No. 5 (BBC Archives). Copy in Orwell Archive.

38. Orwell Archive.

39. *The Road to Wigan Pier*, pp. 140–41.

40. Buddicom, op cit., p. 91.

41. King-Farlow, 'College Days with George Orwell'.

42. When I interviewed Gow in December 1976 I left Stansky and Abrahams' *The Unknown Orwell* with him, which he had not read, though they had interviewed him. When I called on him on 1 Feb. 1977, he asked me to read the passages that mentioned him. I wrote down his comments in the margin and read them back to him to check.

43. Letter of 1 May 1967 from Andrew Gow to Sonia Orwell (Orwell Archive, Papers of Sonia Orwell).

44. *CE* I, p. 2.

45. This parallel of 'more equal' with *Animal Farm* was pointed out by Mr P. M. Nixon of St Peter's School, York, in a letter to *The Times*, 24 Nov. 1973.

46. Buddicom, op. cit., pp. 96–102.

47. *CE* IV, pp. 274–5.

48. King-Farlow, 'College Days with George Orwell'.

49. Buddicom, op. cit., pp. 102–4.

50. *CE* I, pp. 11–12; and see *The Road to Wigan Pier*, p. 142, which claims that he had read Jack London's account of tramping, *The People of the Abyss*, while still at school.

51. Buddicom, op. cit., pp. 105–8.

52. *The Road to Wigan Pier*, pp. 141–3.

53. *Keep the Aspidistra Flying*, p. 55.

54. *The Road to Wigan Pier*, p. 141.

55. Jack London, *The Iron Heel* (Sagamore Press, New York, reprinted 1957), pp. 82–3. William Steinhoff draws attention both to this and the passage from H. G. Wells, 'The Island of Dr Moreau', amid many other sources of the imagery in *Nineteen Eighty-Four* in Orwell's early reading. See his *The Road to 1984* (Weidenfeld & Nicolson, London, 1975).

56. Buddicom, op. cit., p. 109.

57. Letter to author from Mrs Noreen Bagnall of Hockham Lodge, Shropham, Norfolk, 20 Oct. 1972.

58. Buddicom, op. cit., pp. 110–11.

59. Connolly, op. cit., p. 263; and King-Farlow criticized this account when interviewed by Ian Angus, 20 April 1967.

60. Connolly, op. cit., p. 264.

61. Quoted in Eric Parker, *College at Eton* (Macmillan, London, 1933), pp.

209–11. For him to have quoted the manuscript 'College Annals' in print caused such a stir among Old Etonians, one prominent stirrer being Quintin Hogg (Lord Hailsham), that ever since then strangers have not been allowed to examine the records. The sporting records I quote were extracted from the registers and written down for me by a Captain of School, whom I thank.

62. Stansky and Abrahams, op. cit., p. 112.

63. Buddicom, op. cit., pp. 112–14 and 117.

64. ibid., p. 117.

65. Gow's remarks to me are virtually the same as he wrote to Jeffrey Meyers on 1 Jan. 1969 which Meyers quotes in his *A Reader's Guide to George Orwell* (Thames & Hudson, London, 1975), p. 33.

66. ibid.

67. *Keep the Aspidistra Flying*, p. 96.

68. ibid., p. 53.

69. Interview by the author with Sir Anthony Wagner, Garter King of Arms, 29 June 1977.

70. John Lehmann, *The Whispering Gallery* (Longman, London, 1955), p. 95. The Vice-Provost of Eton, Mr F. J. R. Coleridge, and the Captain of School searched the records for me in March 1978 and while the account of that St Andrew's Day match survives, there was, as usual, no score.

5. AN ENGLISHMAN IN BURMA (1922–7)

1. Interview by the author with Ruth Pitter (tape-recorded) at Long Crendon, Bucks, 10 Nov. 1974.

2. Two letters to the author from Mr R. G. Sharp of Poole, Dorset, 29 Oct. and 7 Nov. 1972.

3. India Office Records, Judicial and Public File 6079, 1922.

4. *CE* IV, pp. 265–6.

5. 'Notes on the Way', *Time and Tide*, 30 March 1940.

6. Roger Beadon interviewed by Pamela Howe, BBC transcript, 5 Dec. 1969 at Bristol (BBC Archives, YBS.47.WJ.455.W).

7. R. G. B. Lawson in Peter Stansky and William Abrahams, *The Unknown Orwell* (Constable, London, 1972), p. 135. Their description of service life in Burma is excellent and they were able to interview or correspond with several of Orwell's contemporaries who were dead by the time I began work. There are discrepancies throughout, however, in the datings of his various postings. I have taken mine from *History of the services of gazetted and other officers serving under the government of Burma, corrected up to 1 July 1928*. Vol. 1 part 1, *Services of gazetted officers* (Government of India Publications, 1928). (A copy is in the India Office Library.) They give no source for their dates.

8. See Sir Herbert White, *A Civil Servant in Burma* (Edward Arnold, London, 1913), p. 153; and Eric Stokes, *The English Utilitarians and India* (Oxford University Press, 1959).

9. *Burmese Days*, p. 69.

10. 'My Country Right or Left', *Folios of New Writing*, Autumn 1940, and *CE* I, pp. 537–78.

11. *The Burma Police Manual*, 4th edn (Government Printing Office, Rangoon, 1926), para. 25. A copy is in the State Paper Room of the British Library.

12. Beadon, BBC interview (see note 6 above).

13. *The Road to Wigan Pier*, p. 129.

14. ibid., pp. 143–5.

15. 'Democracy in the British Army', *Left Forum* No. 36, Sept. 1939, p. 236, reprinted in *CE* I, p. 403.

16. *The Road to Wigan Pier*, pp. 147–8.

17. *CE* I, p. 45.

18. *Report on the Prison Administration of Burma for the Year ...* (Government Printing Office, Rangoon, an annual). The volume for 1926 is missing from both the British Library and the India Office Library.

19. *CE* III, p. 267.

20. Jacintha Buddicom, *Eric and Us* (Leslie Frewin, London, 1974), pp. 143–4.

21. See letters quoted in Stansky and Abrahams, op. cit., p. 151.

22. *CE* III, p. 86.

23. *The Road to Wigan Pier*, p. 110.

24. Stansky and Abrahams, op. cit., pp. 152–3; and letter from R. C. Chorley, who was at a neighbouring post, to this author, 6 Dec. 1972.

25. 'Portrait of an Addict', a review by Orwell of H. R. Robinson, *A Modern De Quincey* (Harrap, London, 1942), in the *Observer*, 13 Sept. 1942.

26. Robinson, *A Modern De Quincey*, p. 24.

27. Maung Htin Aung, 'George Orwell and Burma', in Miriam Gross (ed.), *The World of George Orwell* (Weidenfeld & Nicolson, London, 1971), p. 24.

28. *The Road to Wigan Pier*, p. 149.

29. ibid., p. 143.

30. Letters of L. W. Marrison of Battle, Sussex to author, 24 Oct. 1972 and 13 Nov. 1978.

31. Interview by the author with Mr James Brodie of Greenock, 11 Feb. 1974.

32. In the *New English Weekly*, 23 Jan. 1936, on the occasion of Kipling's death, reprinted in *CE* I, pp. 159–60.

33. Robinson, *A Modern De Quincey*, p. 142. He quoted from Kipling's 'The Young British Soldier' accurately.

34. See William Steinhoff, *The Road to 1984* (Weidenfeld & Nicolson, London, 1975), *passim* for these references.

35. Christopher Hollis, *A Study of George Orwell* (Hollis & Carter, London, 1956) is unfortunately a poor book, hasty, inaccurate, pretentious and claiming special knowledge of Orwell, though Hollis was two years ahead of him in Eton and scarcely knew him. As a prominent Catholic intellectual as well as a Conservative Member of Parliament, he argued that Orwell's thought could be turned towards God and away from socialism. But they did meet in Burma.

36. ibid., pp. 27–8.

37. loc. cit.

38. Stansky and Abrahams, op. cit., p. 158. They give the late E. R. Seeley the pseudonym of 'Lawrence'.

39. Harold Acton, *More Memoirs of an Aesthete* (Methuen, London, 1970), pp. 152–3.

40. Beadon, BBC interview (see note 6 above).

41. *Burmese Days*, p. 39.

42. Beadon, BBC interview (see note 6 above).

43. Interview by the author with Roger Beadon at Bristol, 22 Nov. 1972.

44. *Time and Tide*, 30 March 1940.

45. *Burmese Days*, pp. 24–5.

46. *Listener*, 9 March 1938.

47. Maung Htin Aung, 'George Orwell and Burma', in Gross, op. cit., pp. 26–7.

48. 'Shooting an Elephant', first published in *New Writing*, No. 2, Autumn 1936; also in *CE* I, pp. 235–42.

49. Maung Htin Aung, 'George Orwell and Burma', in Gross, op. cit., p. 29.

50. Stansky and Abrahams, op. cit., p. 166.

51. Letter to author from Mrs Noreen Bagnall of Hockham Lodge, Shropham, Norfolk, 20 Oct., 1972.

52. *CE* IV, p. 114.

53. *The Road to Wigan Pier*, pp. 146–7.

54. *Burmese Days*, p. 33.

55. *CE* I, p. 2.

56. Orwell Archive.

57. *CE* II, p. 23.

58. *CE* I, p. 329.

59. *The Road to Wigan Pier*, pp. 149–50.

60. India Office Records, Services and General Department File 5368/27. Blair's letter is of 26 Nov. 1927 requesting permission to resign from 1 Jan. 1928. For the security vetting in 1938, see pp. 345–7 above.

61. E. A. Blair, 'L'Empire britannique en Birmanie', *Le Progrès civique*, 4 May 1929, pp. 22–4. Copy in Orwell Archive. The original English no longer exists. This is re-translated from the French by Audrey Coppard.

62. Rayner Heppenstall, *Four Absentees* (Barrie and Rockcliff, London, 1960), p. 32.

63. The anti-imperialist Tories, like the 'Little Englanders', are now a largely forgotten breed whom Left-wing thought finds it hard to comprehend, but once they were of some importance. In the early days in India they were commonly more tolerant of native customs than liberal administrators with their rational predilections towards uniformity and efficiency. See Stokes, *The English Utilitarians and India*.

64. In a review of E. R. Curtius, *The Civilization of France* in *The Adelphi*, May 1932, p. 554.

6. GOING NATIVE IN LONDON AND PARIS (1928–31)

1. His autobiographical note written for Stanley J. Kunitz and H. Haycraft (eds.), *Twentieth Century Authors* (W. H. Wilson, New York, 1942), reprinted in *CE* II, pp. 23–4.

2. 'Author's Preface to the Ukrainian Edition of *Animal Farm*', written in 1947, reprinted and translated (the original English version no longer exists) in *CE* III, p. 402.

3. Interview by the author with Ruth Pitter (tape-recorded) at Long Crendon, Bucks, 10 Nov. 1974.

4. Interview by the author with Andrew Gow at Cambridge, 18 Dec. 1976.

5. Jacintha Buddicom, *Eric and Us* (Leslie Frewin, London, 1974), p. 145.

6. Letter of 15 Feb. 1949, in Buddicom, op. cit., p. 152.

7. Ruth Pitter in BBC Overseas Service broadcast on 3 Jan. 1956 (script no. DOX 36610, BBC Archives). Copy in Orwell Archive.

8. Interview by the author with Ruth Pitter (see note 3 above). Stansky and Abrahams had earlier interviewed her, so by the time I saw her she had read their account in *The Unknown Orwell* (Constable, London, 1972), pp. 183–90. She said that they wrote to her 'that they had dolled it up a bit'. She objected to the impression they give that Orwell and she saw more of each other, were generally closer to each other, than in fact they were. 'One doesn't object to a man touching up his own story,' she told me, 'but one does object to historians or biographers, because it was so constantly done in the past. It is one of the few things we do better now. Only the truth is interesting, and a cosmetic biography is a very great pity.'

9. Orwell Archive, Manuscripts and Typescripts.

10. *The Road to Wigan Pier*, pp. 149–50.

11. ibid., pp. 150–51.

12. ibid., p. 151.

13. ibid., p. 153.

14. First published in the *Adelphi*, April 1931 and reprinted in *CE* I, pp. 36–43.

15. Stansky and Abrahams, op. cit., p. 191.

16. Philip Foner (ed.), *Jack London, American Rebel: A Collection of His Social Writings* ... (Citadel Press, New York, 1947), p. 372 (an extract from *The People of the Abyss*). And they both may have drawn from Robert Louis Stevenson's chapter 'Personal Experience and Review' in his *The Amateur Immigrant*.

17. *Down and Out in Paris and London*, p. 129.

18. Ruth Pitter, BBC script (see note 7 above).

19. Letter of 25 Nov. 1971 to Sonia Orwell from Groupe Hôpitalier Cochin, Paris. Orwell Archive.

20. *CE* I, pp. 113–14.

21. *The Road to Wigan Pier*, p. 153 (my emphasis).

22. *CE* II, p. 39; and Orwell also had 'Gordon Comstock' in *Keep the Aspidistra Flying* come across the book and 'read about the starving carpenter who pawns everything but sticks to his aspidistra' (p. 56).

23. *CE* I, p. 114.

24. *CE* III, p. 94.

25. See Richard Mayne, 'A Note on Orwell's Paris', in Miriam Gross (ed.), *The World of George Orwell* (Weidenfeld & Nicolson, London, 1971), p. 41.

26. *Down and Out in Paris and London*, p. 9.

27. Interview with officers of the Esperanto Association, 140 Holland Park Avenue, London W11, June 1978.

28. During the latter years of the war, see *CE* III, pp. 25, 85–6, and 210.

29. 'La Censure en Angleterre', *Le Monde*, 6 Oct. 1928, p. 5. The original English no longer exists. This is rendered back from the French translation.

30. *CE* I, pp. 14–15.

31. Orwell Archive.

32. *CE* I, pp. 36–43, and the letter to Plowman is in *CE* I, p. 15.

33. Orwell Archive.

34. Orwell Archive, Manuscripts and Typescripts.

35. *Keep the Aspidistra Flying*, p. 44.

36. *CE* IV, p. 274.

37. ibid., p. 402.

38. Letter from Ruth E. Graves of New York City to Eric Blair, 23 July 1949. Orwell Archive.

39. Mabel Fierz speaking in a BBC television 'Omnibus' programme of 1970

on Orwell, 'The Road to the Left', produced by Melvyn Bragg (Post Production script No. 06349/1139, pp. 12–13, BBC Archives). Copy in Orwell Archive.

40. *Down and Out in Paris and London*, pp. 15–16.

41. *CE* I, p. 115.

42. Loelia, Duchess of Westminster, *Grace and Favour* (Weidenfeld & Nicolson, London, 1961), p. 225.

43. Interview by the author with Captain Maurice Peters, Dec. 1973.

44. The Register of Faber and Faber notes 'A Scullion's Diary' by E. Blair as received on 14 Dec. 1931 and rejected on 25 Feb. 1932. I am grateful to their archivist, Miss Constance Cruickshank, for this information.

45. *CE* I, p. 19.

46. From an unpublished TS. in the Jack Common Collection in the University of Newcastle Library. I am grateful to Mrs Common for permission to reproduce this and to Dr Eileen Aird of the English Department.

47. loc. cit.

48. loc. cit.; and both Richard Rees, *George Orwell: Fugitive from the Camp of Victory* (Secker & Warburg, London, 1961), and Rayner Heppenstall, *Four Absentees* (Barrie and Rockcliff, London, 1960) use the same phrase of Orwell.

49. Letter of Edouard Roditi to Sonia Orwell, 11 Nov. 1970. Orwell Archive, Papers of Sonia Orwell.

50. Brenda Salkeld speaking in 'George Orwell: A Programme of Recorded Reminiscences', arranged and narrated by Rayner Heppenstall, recorded on 20 Aug. 1960 and first broadcast on 2 Nov. 1960 (BBC Archives, Ref. No. TLO 24177). Copy in Orwell Archive.

51. *The Road to Wigan Pier*, p. 133.

52. Interview with Humphrey Dakin by Ian Angus, 23–25 April 1965.

53. Interview with Mrs Lucy Bestley, 13 Sept. 1976, and letters of Mrs Jane Morgan to author, 25 Sept. 1976 and 15 Jan. 1979.

54. *CE* I, p. 92. Orwell says that 'tapping' means begging, so it does; but he is naïve not to see the crude double-meaning in the song he quotes.

55. From a letter of Jane Morgan to the author of 25 Sept. 1976.

56. Humphrey Dakin interviewed and transcribed (though not broadcast) for Melvyn Bragg's BBC 'Omnibus' programme of 1970 (roll 14/6; see note 39 above).

57. 'Through the Eyes of a Boy: An Impression of George Orwell' by Professor R. S. Peters, a six-page script prepared for a BBC broadcast given on 9 Sept. 1955 (BBC Archives). The memories of Professor Peters and of Captain Peters appear to be identical; they certainly confirm each other's accounts.

58. See Mabel Fierz in Melvyn Bragg's BBC 'Omnibus' programme (see

note 39 above) and interviews by Ian Angus 3 Dec. 1963 and 7 Oct. 1967; and by this author 19 Jan. 1973.

59. *C E* I, p. 33.

60. Letter of Edouard Roditi to Sonia Orwell (see note 49 above).

61. Letter to Leonard Moore of 26 April 1932, *C E* I, p. 77.

62. Orwell Archive.

63. Letter in the possession of Brenda Salkeld.

64. *C E* I, pp. 51–71.

65. See Medway Fitzmoran (ed.), *George Orwell in Kent: Hop-picking* (Bridge Books, Wateringbury, Kent, 1970).

66. *C E* I, pp. 72–3.

67. See his essay 'The Clink', written in August 1932 but first published in *C E* I, pp. 86–94.

68. *Keep the Aspidistra Flying*, p. 224, and *Nineteen Eighty-Four*, p. 240.

69. From an unpublished letter to Miss Brenda Salkeld, in her possession.

70. Letter to Dennis Collings of 12 (?) Oct. 1931, *C E* I, p. 51.

71. T. R. Fyvel, 'A Case for George Orwell?', *Twentieth Century*, Sept. 1956, pp. 257–8.

7. HARD TIMES OR STRUGGLING UP (1932–4)

1. Letter of Mr F. M. Gardner CBE, of Luton, to author of 26 Oct. 1972.

2. *C E* I, pp. 77–8.

3. Peter Stansky and William Abrahams, *The Unknown Orwell* (Constable, London, 1972), pp. 248–9. They even have him obtaining the job through Truman and Knightley Associates, the rivals to Gabbitas-Thring as employment agents for private schools. But it seems very unlikely that such an agency would deal with such a school. Bernard Bergonzi repeats this in good faith in his excellent *Reading the Thirties* (Macmillan, London, 1978), pp. 30–31, which shows how legends grow.

In their second volume, *Orwell: The Transformation* (Constable, London, 1979), Stansky and Abrahams compound the error further. They have now identified the school as 'Evelyn's School' (pp. 19–33 *passim*) and have Blair 'coughing and hacking in the damp gloom of the Hawthorns' (p. 22) which they call 'that genteel rooming-house' (p. 19). There was, indeed, an Evelyn's School (a prep school complete with chapel, etc.) but it had closed by Sept. 1931, the year before Blair came to the area, to move and to amalgamate with Farnborough School in Hampshire. Stansky and Abrahams have even conjured up a 'poor Mr Evelyn' (p. 32) and a 'hapless Mr Evelyn' (p. 33) telling his staff that the school was collapsing. But the school never had a head master of that name – its founder in 1872 was a G. T. Worsley, whose son was christened Evelyn and became head master, but was killed in France

NOTES

in 1916. (See *Middlesex Advertizer and Gazette*, 11 Sept. 1931, for a long retrospective article, 'The Passing of Evelyns'.)

I am indebted to Mr B. T. White, the chairman of the Hayes and Harlington Local History Society, and to Mary Pearce, the Local Studies Librarian at Uxbridge Library, for leading me to this information.

4. Robert Holman's *Outside the Whale* as performed at the Traverse Theatre, Edinburgh, in 1976 and at the Bush Theatre, London, in 1978.

5. Interview by the author with Mr Geoffrey W. Stevens of Hayes, Middlesex on 18 Dec. 1972.

6. In the possession of Victor Gollancz Ltd, quoted by kind permission of Livia Gollancz.

7. loc. cit.

8. *CE* I, p. 84.

9. ibid., pp. 84–5.

10. Keith Alldritt, *The Making of George Orwell* (Edward Arnold, London, 1969), p. 55. See also, for the same thesis or concern, Stansky and Abrahams, *The Unknown Orwell*; John Atkins, *George Orwell* (Calder & Boyars, London, 1954); and T. R. Fyvel, 'George Orwell and Eric Blair: Glimpses of a Dual Life', *Encounter*, July 1959, and more speculatively in his contribution to the special number on Orwell in *World Review*, June 1950.

11. *CE* I, p. 81.

12. ibid., p. 103.

13. Interview by the author and correspondence with Mrs Madge Parker of North Petherton, Somerset, in July 1975.

14. *CE* I, p. 82.

15. ibid., pp. 79–81, 101–2.

16. ibid., p. 118.

17. Orwell Archive.

18. Avril Dunn, 'My Brother, George Orwell', *Twentieth Century*, March 1961, pp. 257–8.

19. Orwell Archive. The two passages I quote are not in the shortened version of this letter in *CE* I, pp. 102–4.

20. Orwell Archive. Most of this letter is reprinted in *CE* I, pp. 107–8, but not the last four sentences.

21. *Keep the Aspidistra Flying*, p. 146.

22. Unpublished letter of 6 June 1933. Orwell Archive.

23. *CE* I, pp. 102, 103 and 105.

24. Copy in Orwell Archive, Manuscripts and Typescripts. A copy of the play was preserved by Mr Geoffrey Stevens who was a pupil of Orwell's and who acted in the play.

25. *CE* I, p. 100.

26. ibid., p. 105.

27. ibid., p. 106.

28. ibid., p. 109.

29. Unpublished letter of 17 Jan. 1933. Berg Collection, New York Public Library.

30. I. R. Willison, 'George Orwell: Some Materials for a Bibliography', submitted to the School of Librarianship and Archives, University of London, for the Diploma in Librarianship (Part III), May 1953, pp. 1–5. Copy in Orwell Archive.

31. These reviews are all from files in Orwell Archive.

32. Avril Dunn, 'My Brother, George Orwell', *Twentieth Century*, March 1961, p. 258.

33. Unpublished letter of 18 Feb. 1933. Orwell Archive.

34. 'Why I Write', *CE* I, p. 3.

35. *CE* I, p. 122. I have reversed the order of these two separate sentences.

36. ibid., p. 123.

37. ibid., pp. 119 and 120–21.

38. See John Carswell, *Lives and Letters* (Faber and Faber, London, 1978) for a masterly study of Orage and his circle.

39. *CE* I, p. 121.

40. ibid., p. 126.

41. ibid., p. 139.

42. ibid., pp. 123–4.

43. ibid., pp. 134–5.

44. Author's correspondence with Mr H. S. K. Stapley in Jan. 1973; and see Stansky and Abrahams, *Orwell: The Transformation*, pp. 34–8. After reading their fuller account, from which I draw in the above paragraph, I regret not having interviewed Mr Stapley back then, as they did. The school is now closed and he cannot be traced to comment on the accuracy of our accounts. But this time they have got the right school and produced some interesting evidence.

45. Avril Dunn, 'My Brother, George Orwell', *Twentieth Century*, March 1961, p. 257.

46. *CE* I, p. 129.

47. ibid., p. 133.

48. Interview by Audrey Coppard with Mr Percy Girling, Southwold, 27 Dec. 1974.

49. Interview by Audrey Coppard with Mr Denny, Southwold, 28 Dec. 1974.

50. Interview by Ian Angus with Mrs Vera Buckler, Southwold, 28 June 1965.

51. V. S. Pritchett on 'George Orwell', in Gilbert Phelps (ed.), *Living Writers: Being Critical Studies Broadcast in the BBC Third Programme* (Sylvan Press, London, 1949), p. 109.

52. In the possession of Victor Gollancz Ltd, quoted by kind permission of Livia Gollancz.

53. From an unpublished letter to Brenda Salkeld, undated, headed 'Tuesday night', probably 20 Oct. 1934. Orwell Archive (under seal).

54. I. R. Willison, op. cit., p. 7.

55. Letter of 25 Sept. 1934 in Berg Collection, New York Public Library.

56. In the possession of Victor Gollancz Ltd.

57. *CE* I, p. 136.

58. ibid., pp. 137–40, a conflation of two letters.

59. ibid., p. 141.

60. ibid., p. 142.

8. BOOKSHOP DAYS (1934–5)

1. *Keep the Aspidistra Flying*, pp. 18–19.

2. ibid., p. 14.

3. Richard Rees interviewed and transcribed (though this part not broadcast) for a BBC television 'Omnibus' programme of 1970 on Orwell, 'The Road to the Left', produced by Melvyn Bragg (Post Production Script no. 06349/1139, BBC Archives). Copy in Orwell Archive.

4. Richard Rees, *A Theory of My Time* (Secker & Warburg, London, 1963), pp. 72, 201 and 180.

5. *Keep the Aspidistra Flying*, p. 100.

6. Compare *Keep the Aspidistra Flying*, chapter 1, with his essay 'Bookshop Memories', *CE* I, pp. 242–6.

7. *Keep the Aspidistra Flying*, pp. 197–8.

8. Quoted in Mavis and Ian Norrie (eds), *The Book of Hampstead* (High Hill Books, London, 1960), p. 103.

9. Interview and correspondence with Jon Kimche, Nov. 1979.

10. Letter of 16 Feb. 1935. Orwell Archive. This passage is not included in the *CE* text of the letter, *CE* I, pp. 147–8.

11. This extract from a letter from Elaine Limouzin was included in a letter to this author from Myfanwy Westrope of 21 Oct. 1972. Unhappily Mrs Westrope died before I was able to meet her.

12. I am indebted to Professor John Saville of the University of Hull, for information about the Westropes and their ILP connections.

13. Unpublished letter to Brenda Salkeld. Orwell Archive (under seal).

14. In the possession of Victor Gollancz Ltd.

15. *CE* I, pp. 142–3.

16. ibid., p. 147.

17. ibid., p. 141.

18. ibid., p. 150.

19. *CE* IV, p. 205.

20. Peter Stansky and William Abrahams were evidently able to interview 'Sally', of whom they give a full and interesting account, see their *Orwell: The Transformation* (Constable, London, 1979), pp. 63–5.

21. Interview with and letters from Mrs Kay Ekevall in Dec. 1973 and May to July 1979.

22. *Keep the Aspidistra Flying*, p. 114.

23. Rayner Heppenstall, *Four Absentees* (Barrie and Rockcliff, London, 1960), p. 46.

24. Letter of 7 March of Miss Salkeld. Orwell Archive (under seal). The passage quoted is not in the extract from the same letter in *CE* I, pp. 150–51.

25. Heppenstall, op. cit., pp. 59–60.

26. Letter from Geoffrey Gorer of 16 July 1935. Orwell Archive.

27. Gorer recorded for Melvyn Bragg's BBC 'Omnibus' production (see note 3 above).

28. Cyril Connolly in the *New Statesman and Nation*, 6 July 1935.

29. Cyril Connolly, *The Evening Colonnade* (David Bruce and Watson, London, 1973), p. 375.

30. Recalled by Connolly in a headnote to some letters of Orwell to him published in *Encounter*, Jan. 1962. In that headnote, however, Connolly speaks of the meeting taking place 'at his rooms in Islington'. Orwell was not in Islington until 1944. Connolly always gave vivid detail in his reminiscences, but much of it is, alas, unreliable, especially regarding time and place.

31. Letter of 12 Nov. 1974 to the author from Mrs Rosalind Henschel (formerly Obermeyer) of Eastbourne.

32. Elisaveta Fen, 'George Orwell's First Wife', *Twentieth Century*, Aug. 1960, pp. 115–16.

33. Letter of Edna D. Bussey to Ian Angus, 19 Sept. 1968.

34. Letter of Professor John Cohen to the author, 5 Dec. 1979; and see also Stansky and Abrahams, op. cit., p. 96.

35. Melvyn Bragg's BBC 'Omnibus' production (see note 3 above), para. 3423.

36. *Keep the Aspidistra Flying*, p. 293.

37. Rayner Heppenstall, 'Orwell Intermittent', *Twentieth Century*, May 1955, p. 473; interview with Lettice Cooper in June 1976; and Orwell also told Anne Popham in a letter in 1945 that he thought he was sterile, see p. 336 above. However to state categorically on this evidence 'that Eric was sterile' (as do Stansky and Abrahams, op. cit., p. 166) seems unwarranted.

38. *CE* I, pp. 153 and 154.

39. 'Apocalyptic relish' is Bernard Bergonzi's phrase in his treatment of the bombing theme in literature in his *Reading the Thirties* (Macmillan, London, 1978), pp. 102–10.

40. Reg Groves, agitator and author, had been active in the 'Balham succession' from the Communist Party which was the beginning of Trotskyism in Britain. (See his *The Balham Group*, Pluto Press, London, 1975.) He only knew Orwell 'vaguely' in the bookshop days, but remembers that the Westropes had a wide circle of 'genuine revolutionary socialists' and 'all sorts of odd cranks'. (Interview by author with Mr Reg Groves, Wandsworth, 15 April 1981.)

41. *CE* I, p. 140.

42. From an unpublished MS. of Jack Common's, 'Orwell at Wallington', in the Jack Common Collection, University of Newcastle. I am grateful to Mrs Common for permission to reproduce this, and to Dr Eileen Aird.

43. *CE* I, p. 155.

44. Heppenstall, op. cit., p. 57.

45. Heppenstall, 'The Shooting Stick', *Twentieth Century*, April 1955, p. 370. There is a similar account in his *Four Absentees*.

46. Heppenstall, *Four Absentees*, pp. 85–6.

47. Interview by author with Mabel Fierz at Surbiton, 19 Jan. 1973.

48. Cyril Connolly, *The Evening Colonnade* (David Bruce & Watson, London, 1973), p. 374.

9. THE CRUCIAL JOURNEY (1936)

1. Orwell grumbles in a letter to Richard Rees (*CE* I, p. 165) that they were making a fuss about nothing, but correspondence in the papers of Victor Gollancz Ltd for Jan. to March 1936 between the firm, their solicitors and an advertising agency makes it clear that Orwell's inventions were all recognizably close parodies and legally extremely dangerous.

2. From 'Freedom of the Press', the unused, draft introduction to *Animal Farm* first published in *TLS*, 15 Sept. 1972.

3. Richard Rees interviewed in BBC television 'Omnibus' programme of 1970 on Orwell, 'The Road to the Left', produced by Melvyn Bragg (Post Production Script No. 06349/1139, BBC Archives). Copy in Orwell Archive.

4. From a letter of Gollancz's in 1956 quoted by Sheila Hodges, *Gollancz: The Story of a Publishing House, 1928–78* (Gollancz, London, 1978), p. 111.

5. Letter of Orwell to Moore, 15 Dec. 1936. Berg Collection, New York Public Library. The papers of Victor Gollancz show that *The Road to Wigan Pier* was commissioned by the firm itself in January 1936 and not by the Left Book Club, contrary to Jeffrey Meyers' account in his *A Reader's Guide to George Orwell* (Thames and Hudson, London, 1975), p. 37. Orwell had sent the completed manuscript to Moore on 15 December and only four days later Gollancz wired Orwell to come to see him at once for he hoped to make

'*Wigan Pier*' a Left Book Club choice. Moore then wrote to Gollancz on 29 December to say that he gathered from Orwell after his visit that it was 'practically certain' to be a Left Book Club choice for March 1937.

6. *CE* IV, pp. 510–11.

7. *CE* I, p. 173–4.

8. The 'Diary' was written up later. There are many incidents in the book which are not in the 'Diary'. There are no day-to-day notes or notebooks among Orwell's papers, except extensive notes on housing conditions. Several critics have pointed to the famous passage of the young woman poking out the drain (see pp. 286–8) as found in both diary and book, to show how the writer turns the raw observations into literature. But these observations were not raw. Orwell's first thoughts must have been that a 'diary' form would appear authentic. Fortunately that must have proved far too restrictive a form, even for Part I. Stansky and Abrahams are not alone in their *Orwell: The Transformation* (Constable, London, 1979) in accepting uncritically that it is an 'unretouched diary' (p. 126), a 'hastily noted first state' (p. 130) and 'no more than "raw material" to be reworked' (p. 149).

9. In Melvyn Bragg, BBC 'Omnibus' programme (see note 3 above).

10. *CE* I, p. 178.

11. Interview by author with Mr Jim Hammond, Wigan, 17 Sept. 1976.

12. *The Road to Wigan Pier*, p. 73.

13. Information given by ladies waiting in the pensions queue at the Post Office a few shops down from 22 Darlington Lane, by the shop-owner's daughter and her grandmother, Sept. 1976. See my full account of the finding of the true tripe shop, 'Return to Wigan', *New Society*, 27 Jan. 1977, p. 195.

14. *CE* I, p. 164.

15. Jerry Kennan, speaking in Melvyn Bragg's BBC 'Omnibus' programme (see note 3 above).

16. *CE* I, p. 163.

17. In Melvyn Bragg, BBC 'Omnibus' programme (see note 3 above).

18. May Deiner, interviewed and transcribed for Melvyn Bragg's BBC 'Omnibus' programme (roll 10/11; see note 3 above).

19. *The Road to Wigan Pier*, p. 185.

20. ibid., p. 35.

21. ibid., pp. 19–20.

22. *CE* I, pp. 177–8.

23. *The Road to Wigan Pier*, pp. 117–18.

24. *CE* I, pp. 190–92.

25. ibid., pp. 196–7.

26. ibid., pp. 206–11.

27. Mr Firth interviewed and transcribed (though not broadcast) for Melvyn Bragg's BBC 'Omnibus' programme (roll 14; see note 3 above).

28. *CE* I, pp. 202–3.

29. In Melvyn Bragg, BBC 'Omnibus' programme (see note 3 above).

30. See Brigitte Granzow, *A Mirror of Nazism: British Opinion and the Rise of Hitler, 1929–33* (Gollancz, London, 1964). Orwell's views on Fascism are first found in the second part of *The Road to Wigan Pier* and more fully developed in 'Prophecies of Fascism', *CE* II, pp. 30–33; in a review of *Mein Kampf*, *CE* II, pp. 12–14, in 'Wells, Hitler and the World State', *CE* II, pp. 139–45; and his protest at the misuse of the term in his *Tribune* column, 'As I Please', 24 March 1944, *CE* III, pp. 111–14.

31. *CE* I, pp. 4–5.

32. *The Road to Wigan Pier*, pp. 173–4.

33. Interview by the author with Miss E. Brook, the present owner of the cottage, 11 June 1976.

34. *CE* I, pp. 214–15.

35. From an undated and unpublished reminiscence by Jack Common in his papers in the University of Newcastle library, obviously written after Orwell's death. I thank Dr Eileen Aird for drawing this to my attention.

36. Mark Benney, *Almost a Gentleman* (Peter Davies, London, 1966), p. 107.

37. I. R. Willison, 'George Orwell: Some Materials for a Bibliography', submitted to the School of Librarianship and Archives, University of London, for the Diploma in Librarianship (Part III), May 1953, pp. 15–16.

38. *New Statesman and Nation*, 25 April 1936.

39. *CE* I, p. 226.

40. Anthony Powell, *Infants of the Spring* (Heinemann, London, 1976), p. 130.

41. Paul Beard in the *New English Weekly*, 25 June 1936.

42. *CE* I, p. 221.

43. Letter from Geoffrey Gorer of 21 April 1936. Orwell Archive.

44. *CE* I, p. 222.

45. ibid., p. 224.

46. Elisaveta Fen, 'George Orwell's First Wife', MS. in Orwell Archive, p. 6, a fuller version than in *Twentieth Century*, Aug. 1960.

47. ibid., pp. 11–12.

48. Richard Rees, *George Orwell: Fugitive from the Camp of Victory* (Secker & Warburg, London, 1961).

49. Alex Zwerdling, in his otherwise excellent *Orwell and the Left* (Yale University Press, New Haven and London, 1974) says that Orwell's work at this period 'indicates that he had read Marx with care and understanding' (p. 20). He gives three references, none of which is convincing: glancing references by Orwell and easily found in many secondary sources. Zwerdling invokes Rees (see note 48 above), but he was no authority on Marx.

50. *Adelphi*, May 1936, pp. 127–8.

51. *CE* I, pp. 256–9.

52. ibid., pp. 249–55.

53. ibid., pp. 227–9. Henry Miller's letters to Orwell are in the Orwell Archive.

54. Letter of Henry Miller to Orwell, 5 Oct. 1936. Orwell Archive.

55. Letters of Henry Miller to Orwell, n.d. (?Aug.) and (?Sept.) 1936. Orwell Archive.

56. Cyril Connolly, 'Barcelona' in his *The Condemned Playground: Essays: 1927–44* (Routledge & Kegan Paul, London, 1945), p. 186.

57. The first letter to Moore is in the Berg Collection, New York Public Library, and the second in *CE* I, p. 256; and see note 5 above for Gollancz's reactions.

58. *The Road to Wigan Pier*, pp. 182 and 200.

59. There are papers and correspondence relating to all this in Victor Gollancz Ltd's office. 'Technical reasons' were presumably for economy in binding. Gollancz's introduction is interesting historically so it is a pity that neither the Secker & Warburg Uniform Edition nor the Penguin edition refer to its existence, let alone reprint it. (Sixteen pages of photographs have also never been reproduced; these make clear how much the book was presented as documentary propaganda.) Jeffrey Meyers, however, reprints the introduction in his *George Orwell: The Critical Heritage* (Routledge & Kegan Paul, London, 1975), pp. 91–8.

60. Ross Terrill, *R. H. Tawney and His Times: Socialism as Fellowship* (André Deutsch, London, 1973), *passim*. This book is good on 'English socialism' generally.

61. *CE* I, p. 267.

62. I. R. Willison, op. cit., pp. 17–20.

63. In some 'Further Notes for Literary Executor' which he wrote in a notebook sometime after January 1949, Orwell said of *The Road to Wigan Pier*: 'The first half of the book many times reprinted as LBC supplement. NB that though the book as a whole would hardly be worth reprinting, the first half is detachable and in particular the first chapter might be put in a book of sketches.'

64. *Left News*, May 1937, p. 352.

65. 'Orwell at Wallington', an undated MS. in Jack Common's papers in the University of Newcastle Library.

66. From a letter of Philip Mairet to Ian Angus, 9 Jan. 1964. When I interviewed Mairet on 10 Nov. 1974 he repeated this tale almost word for word.

67. So Eileen told Anthony Powell (see his *Infants of the Spring*, p. 136).

10. SPAIN AND 'NECESSARY MURDER' (1937)

1. *CE* I, p. 516. The tangled history of Auden's revisions to 'Spain' is at last made clear in Edward Mendelson's *The English Auden* (Faber and Faber, London, 1977), pp. 424–5. Auden by 1940 had changed *inter alia* 'in the necessary murder' to 'in the fact of murder', and 'deliberate increase ...' became 'inevitable increase in the chances of death'. Mendelson points out that Auden's revision was published a month before 'Inside the Whale' appeared, so that he could *not* have been reacting to Orwell's criticism of the two stanzas as some critics have believed. But Orwell, as so often, had written an earlier and cruder version of the same thing. In 'Political Reflections on the Crisis', *Adelphi*, December 1938, p. 110, he had attacked 'this utterly irresponsible intelligentsia', the alliance of 'the gangster and the pansy', had referred to Auden by name, had neither mentioned 'Spain' explicitly nor quoted the two offending stanzas, but had misquoted 'from Auden', he said, '"the acceptance of guilt for the necessary murder"'. So the question remains open.

2. *CE* I, pp. 317–18.

3. loc. cit.

4. Alfred Perlès, *My Friend Henry Miller* (Neville Spearman, London, 1955), pp. 156–9; and Orwell, 'Inside the Whale', *CE* I, pp. 519–20.

5. 'As I Please', *Tribune*, 15 Sept. 1944, p. 11.

6. Victor Alba, *El Marxisme a Catalunya*, Vol. II, 'Historia de POUM' (Editorial Portic, Barcelona, 1974). I am grateful to Mr Miguel Berga for drawing my attention to this book and for translating passages for me from Catalan.

7. John McNair, 'George Orwell: The Man I Knew', p. 10. This is a TS. dated March 1965, based on his MA Thesis, copies in University of Newcastle Library and Orwell Archive. The pages on Spain are from his memory and are authentic if not always fully accurate, but most of the thesis is purely secondary and discursive. His *Spanish Diary*, edited with a commentary by Don Bateman (Independent Labour Publications, Leeds, n.d.) is useful, but it is not a contemporary diary and the editing is uncritical.

8. Victor Alba, *El Marxisme a Catalunya*, pp. 150 ff.

9. Notes on interview with John McNair by Ian Angus and Macdonald Emslie, April 1964.

10. Fredric Warburg, *An Occupation for Gentlemen* (Hutchinson, London, 1959), pp. 231–2. His account is circumstantial, he even remembers Orwell saying 'I want to go to Spain and have a look at the fighting ... write a book about it. Good chaps, those Spaniards, can't let them down.' And he remembers the advance paid. But Orwell only came to him *after* Spain, so memory has transposed one incident, invented the other and imagined the dialogue. See footnote on p. 339 above.

11. *Homage to Catalonia*, p. 2, and a long letter to Frank Jellinek of 20 Dec. 1938, *CE* I, pp. 363–7.

12. McNair, op. cit., pp. 10 and 11–12.

13. *Homage to Catalonia*, p. 111. Orwell's accounts of military matters can be checked in Vicenç Guarner, *El Front d'Aragó*, Documents 15 (La Gaia Ciéncia, Barcelona, 1977). Again I thank Miguel Berga for the reference and translation.

14. ibid., pp. 34–5.

15. 'Looking back on the Spanish War' (written in 1942), *CE* II, p. 249.

16. *Homage to Catalonia*, pp. 79 and 31.

17. ibid., p. 32.

18. From Cornford's poem 'A Letter from Aragon', in Jonathan Galassi (ed.), *Understand the Weapon, Understand the Wound: Selected Writings of John Cornford* (Carcanet Press, Manchester, 1976), p. 41.

19. Victor Alba, *El Marxisme a Catalunya*, pp. 150 ff.

20. *Homage to Catalonia*, pp. 26–7 and 69–70; and letter to Cyril Connolly of 8 June 1937, *CE* I, p. 269.

21. J. Coll and J. Pané, *Josep Rovira: una vida al servei de Catalunya i del socialisme* (Ariel, Barcelona, 1978), pp. 129–30 and pp. 128–41 generally on *Homage to Catalonia*.

22. Bob Edwards speaking in 'George Orwell: A Programme of Recorded Reminiscences', arranged and narrated by Rayner Heppenstall, recorded on 20 August 1960 and first broadcast on 2 November 1960 (BBC Archives, Ref. No. TLO 24177). Copy in Orwell Archive.

23. loc. cit.

24. Bob Edwards, MP, 'Introduction', p. 8, to *Homage to Catalonia* (Folio Society, London, 1970). When I interviewed Mr Edwards (20 Jan. 1975) he insisted that Orwell had come out primarily not just to write a book rather than to fight, but also to report the war for *Tribune*. He sent me to prove this a photocopy of a reproduction in a book of Orwell's NUJ card mentioning *Tribune*. But that card was only issued when Orwell joined *Tribune* in 1943; and he wrote nothing for it earlier than 1940 when it became its modern, independent Left-wing self.

25. Interview by the author with Stafford Cottman, West Ruislip, 21 Aug. 1979.

26. 'Looking Back on the Spanish War', *CE* II, p. 254.

27. For Orwell's account see *Homage to Catalonia*, pp. 91–107; the passage quoted is on p. 103.

28. The ILP account is in 'Night Attack on the Aragon Front', *The New Leader*, 30 April 1937, p. 3.

29. *CE* I, pp. 264–6.

30. See Burnett Bolloten, *The Grand Camouflage: The Spanish Civil War*

and the Revolution (Pall Mall, London, 1968), p. 115 and generally, for a scholarly study of Communist tactics in Spain which supports Orwell's experience and conclusions.

31. Alba, op. cit., p. 162, fn.

32. Stafford Cottman and John ('Paddy') Donovan when interviewed by Ian Angus (28 July 1965 and 27 April 1967 respectively). Bob Edwards (op. cit.) confirms this, but he alone maintains that Orwell's motive to leave for a more active sector was a matter of writing rather than fighting.

33. *Homage to Catalonia*, pp. 59–60, 65 and 70.

34. Willy Brandt, *In Exile: Essays, Reflections and Letters 1933–47* (Oscar Wolff, London, 1977), p. 141.

35. *Homage to Catalonia*, p. 129. Eileen's letter is in the Orwell Archive.

36. P. Broué and E. Témime, *The Revolution and the Civil War* (Faber and Faber, London, 1972), p. 286. Their account of the May riots and of 'The Break Up of the Antifascist Coalition' commands great respect and, incidentally, makes Hugh Thomas' remark that Orwell's account of the riots, 'marvellously written though it is, is a better book about war itself than about the Spanish war' seem ungenerous. (Hugh Thomas, *The Spanish Civil War*, 3rd edn revised and enlarged [Hamish Hamilton, London, 1977], p. 653.) Nothing in Orwell's account is contradicted by Broué and Témime nor by Jose Peirats, *Los anarquistas en la crisis política española* (Buenos Aires, 1964) nor by Manuel Cruells, *Mayo sangriento: Barcelona 1937* (Ariel, Barcelona, 1970), on both of whom Thomas relies heavily in his revised edition. Gabriel Jackson, *The Spanish Republic and the Civil War* (Princeton University Press, Princeton, NJ, 1965) is more just when he says that Orwell 'gives a vivid, sympathetic picture of the situation as seen by the POUM militia, but the reader should bear in mind Orwell's own honest statement that he knew very little about the political complexities of the struggle' (p. 370).

37. Quoted in Burnett Bolloten, 'The Parties of the Left and the Civil War' in Raymond Carr (ed.), *The Republic and the Civil War in Spain* (Macmillan, London, 1971), p. 144.

38. *Homage to Catalonia*, pp. 139 and 141.

39. ibid., pp. 171 and 179–80.

40. Raymond Carr in Miriam Gross (ed.), *The World of George Orwell* (Weidenfeld & Nicolson, London, 1971), p. 70.

41. *Homage to Catalonia*, pp. 131–2.

42. ibid., pp. 155–6.

43. Interview by the author with Mr F. Frankford, Wells, 22 Dec. 1979.

44. *Homage to Catalonia*, pp. 198 and 200.

45. Both the telegram and the medical narrative are in the Orwell Archive.

46. Among Orwell's pamphlet collection, now in the British Library (BM 1899 SS 3 [30]), is a pamphlet by Bertram D. Wolfe, *Civil War in Spain*

(Workers' Age Publications, New York, 1937), which has as an appendix 'The Thesis of Andres Nin', a draft he prepared for discussion at the POUM's planned Second Congress in Barcelona in 1937, which was suppressed. It was published on 5 April in Spain. Wolfe's eulogy of Nin (pp. 92–3) has several obvious parallels to *Nineteen Eighty-Four:*

> Few political papers, since the days when Lenin was at the head of the Communist International, have the revolutionary boldness, the insight, the luminous thought and vivid language that characterize this last important writing from the hands of Nin.
>
> Let the reader compare it with the stale, sausage-machine theses of the ultra-left period and the fuzzy, unscrupulous and treacherous language of Comintern documents today, and he will understand why these preachers of confusion and outworn bourgeois catchwords could not tolerate the existence of a clear revolutionary voice which reminded them of their own past and of the true meaning of the ideals and doctrines in the name of which they profess to speak. That is the reason why Nin lies dead, why his body, like those of Liebknecht and Luxemburg under similar circumstances, was secretly buried in the dead of night in some ditch or sewer on the outskirts of Madrid, why his great voice is stilled and his clear brain had ceased to function in the cause of the working class.

Wolfe says that Nin also took the line that the slogan of 'First win the war, then the revolution' was a deliberate Russian betrayal of the actual working-class revolution in Spain. Another pamphlet or small book in Orwell's collection for the same period takes this line and puts it into the broader context of the history of the Soviet Communist Party and of the blind Russophilia of Left-wing intellectuals: Max Eastman, *The End of Socialism in Russia*, was published by Secker & Warburg in May 1937, so Orwell could well have read it before writing *Homage to Catalonia*, and it would have refortified all he meant to say.

This is not to imply that the ideas of *Homage to Catalonia* are derived from either book directly, only to show that the ideas were common stock among the free Left. Orwell's genius lay in relating these ideas to his direct experience, showing how they indeed arose from his experience: positively, the direct and simple style; and negatively, the avoidance of that theoretical introversion which is typical of the Eastmans and the Wolfes. (There were only brief extracts from Nin's speeches in ILP Publications. A recent work in Catalan contains literary and political essays and a brief biography: Oriol Pi De Cabanyes, *Que Va Dir Andreu Nin* (Editorial Nova Terra, Barcelona, 1978). In English there is only a short pamphlet: Wilebaldo Solano, *The Life of Andres Nin* (Independent Labour Publications, Leeds, n.d.).

47. The narrative in the preceding four paragraphs follows Orwell's account

in *Homage to Catalonia*, pp. 219–48, with some additional detail and complete corroboration from Ian Angus' interviews with McNair (see note 9 above), McNair's thesis (see note 7 above) and my interview with Cottman (see note 25 above).

48. Interview by the author with Lord Brockway, 15 March 1977, and his book *Outside the Right* (Allen & Unwin, London, 1963), p. 25.

49. *CE* I, pp. 348–51 and *CE* II, pp. 24–6.

50. Copy in Orwell Archive.

51. See Orwell's letter to Raymond Mortimer of 9 Feb. 1938, *CE* I, pp. 299–302, and the editors' footnote on p. 299 about the incident. Mortimer's two letters are in the Orwell Archive.

52. Kingsley Martin, *Editor* (Hutchinson, London, 1968), pp. 215–19.

53. C. H. Rolph, *Kingsley* (Gollancz, London, 1973), pp. 225–59; and Orwell's remarks are quoted in Edward Hyams' *The New Statesman 1913–63* (Longman, London, 1963), p. 140. Hyams holds that Martin's action 'was really imposed on him by the logic of the situation'. The last phrase is a fine piece of bourgeois Marxist apologetic.

54. *New Leader*, 12 March 1937.

55. *Left News*, March 1937, pp. 275–6.

56. *Time and Tide*, 20 March 1937.

57. *Daily Worker*, 17 March 1937. Copy in Orwell Archive.

58. In the papers of Victor Gollancz Ltd.

59. loc. cit.

60. Orwell Archive.

61. *Daily Worker*, 14 and 16 Sept. 1937.

62. John McNair, 'The *Daily Worker* and F. A. Frankfort', *New Leader*, 19 Sept. 1937; George Orwell, 'That Mysterious Cart', *New Leader*, 24 Sept. 1937; and Fenner Brockway, *Inside the Left* (Allen & Unwin, London, 1942), p. 317.

63. I did not interview Mr Frankford until 22 Dec. 1979 when this manuscript was virtually ready for the printer. Earlier I had failed to trace him, but then he simply wrote a letter to the *Daily Telegraph* (21 Nov. 1979) to correct a statement by Anthony Powell that Orwell was shot by 'one of the other Leftist groups'. Mr Frankford told me that he had never read Orwell's *Homage to Catalonia* (despite having just taken an Open University degree in History). He has since re-read the *Daily Worker* piece in his name and McNair's and Orwell's attacks. He denies having written the statement or even having signed it, but does not repudiate it because there is 'some hanky-panky' yet to be explained. (Sam Lessor still works for the old firm but does not answer letters or calls from bourgeois professors.)

His attitude to Orwell contrasts vividly with that of Stafford Cottman and Paddy Donovan. He told me that in argument with Orwell:

Basically his attitude was Fascist, he didn't like the workers ... I don't care what he says and what he's written, when you spoke to him he didn't like them, he despised them. That was why I could never understand what he was doing there. In fact we said to him that he was a man of the right and not of the left and that he had never thrown off his Burma police attitude. I'm sure he despised us all, which was why we disliked him ... As far as he was concerned, we were a load of nits. We probably were a load of nits, but no need to have adopted that attitude.

If Mr Frankford did feel like this at the time, I suspect that *one* reason could be that Orwell's Socratic manner, which had ruffled the miners at Barnsley after the Mosley meeting, unused to hearing their own assumptions speculatively criticized, could easily make him appear hostile, rather than both committed and probing.

64. *New Leader*, 13 Aug. 1937.

65. Interview by the author with Lord Brockway, 15 March 1977.

66. Interview by the author with Miss M. Pritchard, South Croydon, Feb. 1977.

67. *CE* I, pp. 284–5.

68. I thank Nicolas Walter for these references, all in his excellent 'Orwell and the Anarchists', *Freedom*, Jan. 1981, pp. 9–12, written in response to my First Edition.

69. *CE* I, pp. 285 and 290.

70. Connolly speaking in a BBC television 'Omnibus' programme of 1970 on Orwell, 'The Road to the Left', produced by Melvyn Bragg (Post Production script No. 06349/1139, p. 33, BBC Archives). Copy in Orwell Archive.

11. COMING UP FOR AIR (1938–9)

1. *CE* I, p. 360.

2. Letter to the editor of *Time and Tide*, 5 Feb. 1938, reprinted in *CE* I, pp. 297–8.

3. India Office Records, Information Department File L/I/1/346.

4. loc. cit., and reprinted in *CE* I, pp. 302–3.

5. India Office Records, loc. cit.

6. loc. cit.

7. Letter of Eileen Blair to Jack Common, n.d. (?10 March) 1938. Orwell Archive.

8. Letter of Mr Victor M. Stacey of Reading, Berks, to the author, 16 Nov. 1972.

9. loc. cit.

10. *CE* I, p. 344.

11. Orwell Archive.

12. *CE* I, pp. 312–13.

13. See Spender's interesting 'reassessment' of *Homage to Catalonia* in the special number on Orwell of *World Review*, June 1950, pp. 51–4. But Spender's autobiography has nothing to say about Orwell at this period.

14. Philip Mairet in the *New English Weekly*, 26 May 1938, and Geoffrey Gorer in *Time and Tide*, 30 April 1938.

15. Reviewed in the *Listener* anonymously on 25 May 1938, and Orwell's letter with the editor's note appeared on 16 June.

16. I. R. Willison, 'George Orwell: Some Materials for a Bibliography', submitted to the School of Librarianship and Archives, University of London for the Diploma in Librarianship (Part I I I), May 1953, pp. 21–7.

17. Each of these letters is in the Orwell Archive.

18. *CE* I, pp. 337–8.

19. British Library pamphlets, 1899 ss 1–21, 23–48, and see note 46 to Chapter 10 above.

20. Robert Klitzke in his 'Orwell and His Critics: an enquiry into the reception of and critical debate about George Orwell's political works' (Ph.D. thesis, London 1977; copy in Orwell Archive) claims that the editors have, especially at this period, a 'literary' bias in their selection which works against Orwell's political writings. He quotes Sonia Orwell, on the very first page of her introduction to the *CE*: 'If political events had made less impact on him, he would have lived in the country, written a book – preferably a novel – a year, pursued his interest in the essay form, and, when money was badly lacking, done straightforward book reviews which, he said, he enjoyed writing.' But political events, said Klitzke, 'did have an impact on him and it is mere speculation to attempt to define what would have happened if times had been different'. Klitzke reasonably claims that the evidence points against saying that Orwell would have preferred not to commit himself, but rather towards: 'Orwell's commitment to the English tradition of Socialism ... the overall impression of Orwell's achievements is quite different from Sonia Orwell's idea. He managed to combine with differing degrees of success a political purpose and an artistic one ... Particularly the omission of the articles on the Home Guard and his contributions to *Betrayal of the Left* and *Victory and Vested Interest* ... gives Orwell's revolutionary period – as it emerged from *The Lion and the Unicorn* – the character of a momentary mood. The exclusion from the collection of such essays as "World Affairs, 1945" and "Britain's Struggle for Survival" suppresses Orwell's political commitment to the English Socialist tradition, and does not allow for the definitive contextual reading of *Nineteen Eighty-Four* to begin' (pp. 255–8). See also on this point Sonia Orwell's controversy with Mary McCarthy over her review of the *CE* (*Nova*, June 1969, pp. 28–46 and July 1969, pp. 18–31).

21. *CE* I, p. 357, for the letter to Common. Back in May 1938 Richard Rees had written to Orwell that 'Eileen tells me you've written a peace pamphlet' (Orwell Archive). When Orwell changed his mind he wrote: 'For several years the coming war was a nightmare to me, and at times I even made speeches and wrote pamphlets against it' ('My Country Right or Left', in John Lehmann (ed.), *Folios of New Writing*, No. 2, Hogarth Press, London, Autumn 1940, reprinted in *CE* I, pp. 535–40).

22. *CE* I, pp. 348–51. And Jack Common in his *The Freedom of the Streets* (Secker & Warburg, London, 1938) saw a merging of Nazism and Bolshevism 'into pyramidal states of negative socialism' (p. 148). He also mocks those middle-class intellectuals who think it easy to say 'let's join the prolies' (p. 160). He and Orwell must have talked together a lot.

23. ibid., p. 376.

24. ibid., pp. 380–81, quoted by William Steinhoff, *The Road to 1984* (Weidenfeld & Nicolson, London, 1975), pp. 183–4.

25. Orwell's review is in *CE* I, pp. 332–4; the passage from Lyons is quoted by Steinhoff, op. cit., p. 172.

26. Letter of 20 April 1938 in Orwell Archive.

27. Letters of C. D. Abbott to Orwell, 20 May and 28 June 1938, and from Orwell to Abbott, 4 and 27 June 1938, in Lockwood Memorial Library, State University of New York at Buffalo.

28. Letter of Dorothy Plowman to Ian Angus, 13 Nov. 1963.

29. *CE* I, pp. 387–93.

30. ibid., pp. 385–7.

31. ibid., pp. 357–9.

32. *Coming Up For Air*, pp. 29–30, 76, 152 and 160.

33. Letter of Eileen to Marjorie Dakin, 27 Sept. 1938. Orwell Archive.

34. John Wain sees Orwell in 1937–40 in 'a state very close to total despair, after the snuffing out of the hope that had flared briefly in revolutionary Catalonia'. (See his 'In the Thirties', in Miriam Gross (ed.), *The World of George Orwell*, Weidenfeld & Nicolson, London, 1971, p. 88.) But the socialist flame of Catalonia continued to burn, at least throughout the Second World War – as will be seen. Orwell's mixture of pessimism and optimism is peculiar, as is the pessimism of the plot of *Coming Up For Air* and the ebullient, Dickensian humour and life-force of the main character, George Bowling. It is far too sweeping, in an otherwise perceptive essay, to say that Orwell himself was near to 'total despair'. (Klitzke – see note 20 above – suggests that Wain's view could have been different if he had not been misled by the omission of some of Orwell's political essays.)

35. Letters of Georges Kopp to Orwell of 14 Dec. 1938 and 10 Jan. 1939 in Orwell Archive. (They are not listed in the general 'Letters to Orwell' sequence but are in a special box on Spain.)

36. Letter of Marjorie Dakin, 3 Oct. 1938. Copy in Orwell Archive.

37. Unpublished letter of Orwell to Frank Simmond, 15 Jan. 1939. Orwell Archive.

38. I. R. Willison, op. cit., pp. 28–32.

39. I am grateful to Dr Sebastian Black of the English Department, University of Auckland, for lending me an unpublished essay of his on *Coming Up For Air* which makes this point. He also makes an even more valuable general point: that just because there is so obviously a strong autobiographical element in Orwell's earlier novels, critics have tended to underestimate his inventiveness and to lose all normal caution about attributing the opinions of a character to its creator.

40. 'Not Counting Niggers' appeared in the *Adelphi*, July 1939 and is reprinted in *CE* I, pp. 394–8.

41. Orwell Archive, Domestic Diaries.

12. THE CHALLENGE AND FRUSTRATION
OF WAR (1939–41)

1. Orwell, 'My Country Right or Left', in John Lehmann (ed.), *Folios of New Writing*, No. 2 (Hogarth Press, London, Autumn 1940), pp. 36–41, reprinted in *CE* I, pp. 535–40.

2. A review by Orwell of Adolf Hitler's *Mein Kampf* in *New English Weekly* for 21 March 1940, reprinted in *CE* II, pp. 12–14.

3. *CE* I, pp. 409–10.

4. Ian Angus in his Chronology to *CE* I, p. 550.

5. Letter to Gorer, *CE* I, p. 410; and Paul Potts, *Dante Called You Beatrice* (Eyre & Spottiswoode, London, 1960), p. 80.

6. Letter to Gorer, *CE* I, pp. 527–9. Among Orwell's papers is a four-page typed memorandum 'The Letchworth Training Centre', unsigned. It is unlikely to be by Orwell, though the style is very similar, because it was not written on his typewriter and begins its denunciations: 'The following observations are based on a two-month attendance at ...' It is probably by Mark Benney who refers briefly in his autobiography, *Almost a Gentleman* (Peter Davies, London, 1966), to being there then.

7. *Scrutiny*, Sept. 1940, pp. 173–6.

8. *Time and Tide*, 9 March 1940.

9. *CE* I, p. 528.

10. Orwell on 'Boys' Weeklies', *CE* I, p. 483.

11. Letters of Geoffrey Trease to Orwell, 5 May 1940, and to Ian Angus, 6 Aug. 1966. Orwell Archive.

12. 'Inside the Whale', *CE* I, pp. 493–527.

13. 'Charles Dickens', ibid., pp. 457–8.

14. ibid., p. 460.

15. ibid., p. 532.

16. ibid., pp. 528 and 410.

17. *CE* II, p. 19.

18. ibid., p. 22.

19. ibid., p. 24.

20. Orwell Archive, Literary Notebooks.

21. Orwell first uses the concept 'oligarchical collectivism' in an important review of Franz Borkenau's *The Totalitarian Enemy* in *Time and Tide*, 4 May 1940, reprinted in *CE* II, p. 25.

22. 'George Orwell's First Wife', p. 19, a typescript in Orwell Archive. This is a fuller version than that published by Elisaveta Fen in *Twentieth Century*, Aug. 1960, pp. 115–26.

23. *CE* II, p. 29.

24. ibid., pp. 54–5.

25. Cyril Connolly, *The Evening Colonnade* (David Bruce & Watson, London, 1973), pp. 382–3.

26. Cyril Connolly, Introduction, p. ix, to *The Golden Horizon* (Weidenfeld & Nicolson, London, 1953).

27. V. S. Pritchett, 'George Orwell' (an obituary notice, *New Statesman and Nation*, 28 Jan. 1950).

28. Interview by the author with Arthur Koestler, 19 Oct. 1972.

29. Letter from Sacheverell Sitwell, 22 July 1940. Orwell Archive.

30. Anthony Powell, *Infants of the Spring* (Heinemann, London, 1976), pp. 131–2.

31. An extract from Inez Holden's diary for 11 Sept. 1941 transcribed for me by her cousin, Mrs Celia Goodman (*née* Paget) who, as Celia Kirwan, was herself to become a close friend of Orwell's, meeting him through her twin sister, Mamaine Koestler.

32. See I. R. Willison, 'George Orwell: Some Materials for a Bibliography', submitted to the School of Librarianship and Archives, University of London, for the Diploma in Librarianship (Part I I I), May 1953, p. 40.

33. Fredric Warburg, *All Authors Are Equal* (Hutchinson, London, 1973), pp. 35–6.

34. *CE* II, pp. 27–8.

35. *Tribune*, 20 Dec. 1940.

36. *New Statesman and Nation*, 15 Feb. 1941, and *Horizon*, March 1941.

37. *Evening Standard*, 8 Jan. 1941.

38. Interview by the author with Mr M. D. Jacobs of St John's Wood, 28 June 1976.

39. Fredric Warburg, op. cit., pp. 37–9.

40. Mr M. D. Jacobs, see above, and letters from or interviews with other survivors of the section.

41. Interview by the author with Miss Patricia Donoghue, 13 Dec. 1977, who shared a flat with Lydia Jackson (Elisaveta Fen) during the war. They were occasional sub-tenants of the Orwells' cottage at Wallington.

42. *Observer*, 9 May 1943 and 15 Oct. 1944, not in *CE*.

43. See his London Letters in *Partisan Review* for July–Aug. 1941, pp. 318–19, and for Nov.–Dec., pp. 494–8.

44. See Fredric Warburg, *An Occupation for Gentlemen* (Hutchinson, London, 1959), pp. 259–60, and *All Authors Are Equal*, pp. 14–15. His account was confirmed and some details added in interviewing T. R. Fyvel in Nov. 1972 and again in Nov. 1979.

45. Quoted by Willison, op. cit., p. 36.

46. See Robert Klitzke, 'Orwell and His Critics: an enquiry into the reception of and critical debate about George Orwell's political works' (Ph.D. thesis, London, 1977), *passim*.

47. *The Lion and the Unicorn: Socialism and the English Genius* (Secker & Warburg, London, 1962), pp. 1–25 *passim*; or *CE* II, pp. 56–66 *passim*.

48. *The Lion and the Unicorn*, pp. 23–40 *passim*; or *CE* II, pp. 65–75 *passim*.

49. For the radical roots of civic patriotism see J. G. A. Pocock, *The Machiavellian Moment: Florentine Political Thought and the Atlantic Republican Tradition* (Princeton U.P., Princeton, NJ, 1975).

50. *The Lion and the Unicorn* p. 49; or *CE* II, p. 80.

51. *The Lion and the Unicorn*, pp. 42–5, 68, 74–5 and 76; or *CE* II, pp. 77–8, 90–91, 95 and 96.

52. *The Lion and the Unicorn*, p. 85; or *CE* II, pp. 102–3.

53. *The Lion and the Unicorn*, p. 67; or *CE* II, p. 90.

54. T. R. Fyvel, 'A Writer's Life', *World Review*, June 1950, p. 18.

55. T. R. Fyvel, 'A Case for George Orwell?', *Twentieth Century*, Sept. 1956, p. 259.

56. In her review of *Inside the Whale*, see note 7 above.

57. Julian Symons in an 'Appreciation', which was a postscript to a book club edition of *Nineteen Eighty-Four* (Heron Books, London, 1970, pp. 321–2).

58. *CE* II, p. 24. It was written for Stanley J. Kunitz and H. Haycraft (eds.), *Twentieth Century Authors* (W. H. Wilson, New York, 1942).

59. V. S. Pritchett, *New Statesman and Nation*, 1 March 1941, p. 216.

13. BROADCASTING DAYS (1941–3)

1. *CE* II, pp. 38–44, printed in the *Listener*, 19 Dec. 1940.

2. William Empson, 'Orwell at the BBC' in Miriam Gross (ed.), *The World of George Orwell* (Weidenfeld & Nicolson, London, 1971), pp. 93–9; and Henry Swanzy in a letter to the author, 31 Oct. 1972.

3. BBC Archives. Copy in Orwell Archive.

4. Laurence Brander, *George Orwell* (Longman, London, 1954), pp. 8–9.

5. loc. cit.

6. A letter of the Rt Hon. I. J. Bahadur Singh of New Delhi, to the author, 19 Nov. 1976.

7. Empson, op. cit.

8. Postcard of 26 Oct. 1943 in Orwell Archive.

9. George Woodcock, *The Writer and Politics* (Porcupine Press, London, 1948; reissued by the Freedom Press in 1967), pp. 116–17; and a letter to Orwell of 18 Nov. 1942 (Orwell Archive).

10. George Woodcock, *The Crystal Spirit: A Study of George Orwell* (Jonathan Cape, London, 1967).

11. BBC Archives. Copy in Orwell Archive.

12. John Morris, 'Some Are More Equal Than Others', *Penguin New Writing*, No. 40, 1950, pp. 90–97.

13. Letter to Dorothy Plowman, *CE* IV, p. 104; and review of B. Rajan's *The Novelist as Thinker* in *The Times Literary Supplement*, 7 Aug. 1948: 'Myers was a lovable man and a delicate and scrupulous writer, but he lacked vitality ...'

14. Morris, op. cit.

15. Malcolm Muggeridge, *Chronicles of Wasted Time*, Vol. I I (Collins, London, 1973), p. 78.

16. *CE* II, p. 430.

17. His letter of resignation is in *CE* II, pp. 315–16; and the letter from Ivor Brown of the *Observer* raising the possibility of his going to North Africa and Sicily for them actually begins: 'I understand that you may be leaving the BBC shortly in order to do more writing ...' (Letter of 28 Aug. 1943. Orwell Archive.)

18. His letter to Dwight Macdonald was as early as 3 Jan. 1943, warning, *à propos* of sending articles to the *Partisan Review*, 'that I may get a job that would take me out of England for a while'. (Orwell Archive.)

19. Another letter from Stevie Smith, 17 Nov. 1942, suggests a 'mid-brow Christmas number' and Orwell replies cautiously, 26 Nov., and then negatively, 30 Dec. BBC Archives, copies in Orwell Archive.

20. Anthony Powell, *Infants of the Spring* (Heinemann, London, 1976), p. 134.

21. Muggeridge in Gross, op. cit., pp. 169–70.

22. Interview by the author with the novelist Kay Dick, Brighton, 23 Jan. 1978.

23. Interview by the author with the novelist Lettice Cooper, West Hampstead, 14 Dec. 1977.

24. Stevie Smith, *The Holiday* (Chapman & Hall, London, 1949), pp. 67–9.

Her own attribution of two characters to Orwell is in a letter of hers to Ian Angus of 6 April 1967 in the administrative papers of the Orwell Archive.

25. Letter of 5 Oct. 1941. Orwell Archive.

26. Letters of 17 Dec. 1942 and n.d. Orwell Archive.

27. Letter of 15 Aug. 1942. Liddell Hart Centre for Military Archives, King's College, London, copy in Orwell Archive.

28. Letter of 8 Aug. 1942. Orwell in his review of Liddell Hart's *The British Way in Warfare* (*CE* II, pp. 246–9) had favoured De Gaulle's claim, as against Liddell Hart's and General Fuller's, to have originated the theory of the Panzer or tank 'lightning war'. Unpublished sentences in Orwell's Wartime Diary for 21 Sept. 1942 show that not merely had Orwell completely misunderstood Liddell Hart, but ungenerously attributed to him defeatist, even 'objectively' pro-German views. (Orwell Archive.)

29. 'Culture and Democracy', in G. D. H. Cole, Harold Laski, George Orwell, Mary Sutherland and Francis Williams, *Victory or Vested Interest?* (Routledge & Kegan Paul, London, 1942), and see his letter to the publishers of 23 July 1942 (Orwell Archive).

30. Letter from Tom Jones, CH, to Orwell of 26 March 1942, in Orwell Archive. Baroness White kindly searched her father's papers in the National Library of Wales, but could not find Orwell's original letter, nor any supporting papers.

31. Orwell's first two contributions to the *Observer* were on 8 March and 19 April 1942, each headed 'Mood of the Moment'. Information from David Astor in interview with the author, 14 Feb. 1973 and from his contribution to Rayner Heppenstall's 'George Orwell: A Programme of Recorded Reminiscences', recorded on 20 Aug. 1960 and first broadcast on 20 Nov. 1960 (BBC Archives, Ref No T L O 24177). Copy in Orwell Archive.

32. Letter of Orwell to Ivor Brown with the review attached, 23 Oct. 1942; and to Cyril Connolly, n.d. (probably Sept.), who was acting Literary Editor of the *Observer*, explaining his 'refusal to write for papers which do not allow at least a minimum of honesty'. (Orwell Archive.) Connolly must have cooled him down.

33. 'Wells, Hitler and the World State', *CE* II, pp. 141–4. The title does indeed seem a deliberately provocative piece of giant-killing.

34. ibid., pp. 143–4.

35. Bertrand Russell in the *World Review*'s memorial number on Orwell, June 1950, pp. 5–6.

36. From Inez Holden's account in her diary (in the possession of her cousin, Celia Goodman, *née* Paget). Michael Meyer, the translator of Ibsen, gave a slightly different account of the quarrel in his interesting 'Memories of George Orwell' in Gross (ed.), *The World of George Orwell*, pp. 128–9. Inez Holden wrote a long letter to the *Listener*, 24 Feb. 1972, correcting his account;

he replied, 2 March 1972, claiming that his account came from the Orwells themselves. It surely did, but, quite apart from the unreliability of memory, Orwell may have polished the tale; and a contemporary diary must always be preferred to memory and hearsay.

37. *CE* II, pp. 206–7.

38. Mark Benney, *Almost a Gentleman* (Peter Davies, London, 1966), pp. 167–8.

39. Interviews by the author with Inez Holden, David Astor, Lydia Jackson and Lettice Cooper.

40. Anthony Powell, *Infants of the Spring*, p. 136.

41. Lettice Cooper, *Black Bethlehem* (Gollancz, London, 1947), pp. 153–4, 177 and 181–2.

42. *CE* II, p. 163.

43. *Tribune*, 4 June 1943, and *CE* II, p. 293.

44. *CE* II, pp. 257–9.

45. *CE* IV, pp. 301–2.

46. See *Partisan Review* correspondence columns for May–June and for Sept.–Oct. 1942 and the symposium on 'Pacifism and the War' of that same Sept.–Oct. number in which D. S. Savage, Alex Comfort, George Woodcock and George Orwell hacked and hewed at each other. The symposium is reprinted in *CE* II, pp. 220–30.

47. *CE* II, pp. 294–303, reprinted in *The Oxford Book of Twentieth Century English Verse*, chosen by Philip Larkin (Oxford University Press, 1973). Dr Frederick Grubb has suggested to me that Orwell, in taking up this epistolary form of a renewed Augustan couplet, was possibly influenced by Julian Bell's 'Epistle on Wittgenstein' (1930), if not by his pacifist satire 'Arms and the Man' (1932), and by Edgell Rickword's satire 'The Encounter' (1931), sometimes known as 'Twittingpan'.

48. 'Poetry and the Microphone', *CE* II, pp. 335–6.

14. *TRIBUNE* AND THE MAKING OF ANIMAL FARM
(1943–5)

1. Orwell's account of his relationship with *Tribune* was in 'As I Pleased', written for an anniversary number on 31 Jan. 1947, see *CE* IV, pp. 276–80.

2. See William Steinhoff, *The Road to 1984* (Weidenfeld & Nicolson, London, 1975), and Mark Reader, 'The Political Criticism of George Orwell', Ph.D. dissertation, University of Michigan, 1966 (copy in Orwell Archive).

3. Julian Symons, 'An Appreciation', which was a postscript to a book club edition of *Nineteen Eighty-Four* (Heron Books, London, 1970, p. 329).

4. Letter of 29 Nov. 1943. Orwell Archive.

5. Letter of 29 Nov. 1943.

6. *CE* IV, pp. 278–9.

7. These passages are to be found, in respective order, in *CE* III, p. 131; *CE* IV, pp. 144–5; *CE* III, p. 85; ibid., p. 81; ibid., p. 136., ibid., p. 198; *Tribune*, 14 Jan. 1944; *CE* III, p. 88; and ibid., p. 227.

8. Interview by the author with Evelyn Anderson, London, 6 Dec. 1976.

9. Telephone interview by the author with Lady Lee, London, 26 Nov. 1976.

10. George Woodcock, 'Prose Laureate', *Commentary*, New York, Jan. 1969, p. 75.

11. See Edward Hyams, *The New Statesman, 1913–63* (Longman, London, 1963).

12. Letter to H. J. Willmett, 18 May 1944, in *CE* III, pp. 148–50.

13. *CE* III, pp. 206–7.

14. Correspondence of the author with Professor Gleb Struve, Oct. and Nov. 1972; a letter of his to Ian Angus, 28 Oct. 1963; and a letter of Struve to Orwell, 19 Nov. 1944 (copy in Orwell Archive).

15. Both William Steinhoff's book and Mark Reader's thesis (see note 2 above) conclusively demolish Isaac Deutscher's polemical claim that 'Orwell borrowed the main elements of *Nineteen Eighty-Four* from Zamyatin'. See Isaac Deutscher, '1984 – The Mysticism of Cruelty', in his *Heretics and Renegades* (Hamish Hamilton, London, 1955).

16. *CE* IV, p. 280.

17. See Robert Hewison, *Under Siege: Literary Life in London 1939–1945* (Weidenfeld & Nicolson, London, 1977); and Julian Maclaren-Ross, *Memoirs of the Forties* (Alan Ross, London, 1965).

18. *CE* III, p. 53.

19. ibid., pp. 95–6.

20. 'Why I Write', *CE* I, p. 7.

21. *CE* III, pp. 405–6.

22. *CE* IV, p. 104.

23. Interview by the author with Lettice Cooper, 14 Dec. 1977.

24. Extract from a letter of 25 March 1944 in possession of Victor Gollancz Ltd.

25. Letter of André Deutsch to *Observer*, 23 Nov. 1980; interview by author 16 Jan. 1981; and letter to author from George Mikes, 31 March 1981.

26. Quoted by Michael S. Howard in *Jonathan Cape, Publisher* (Jonathan Cape, London, 1971), p. 179.

27. ibid., p. 180.

28. Letter of Jonathan Cape to Leonard Moore, 19 June 1944, copy in Orwell Archive; and a letter to the author from Dame Veronica Wedgwood of 19 Sept. 1979.

29. *CE* III, p. 176.

30. ibid., pp. 180–81.

31. A letter in the possession of Mrs Valerie Eliot and communicated by her to *The Times*, 6 Jan. 1969 (copy in Orwell Archive).

32. The suggestion is contained in a letter of Frank Morley (who worked for Faber and Faber in the late 1930s) to the author, 21 Sept. 1972.

33. *CE* III, pp. 186–7.

34. *CE* IV, p. 110.

35. Interview by the author with David Astor at the *Observer*, 14 Feb. 1973.

36. See George Woodcock, 'Recollections of George Orwell', *Northern Review*, Montreal, Aug.–Sept. 1953, p. 18, and a fuller account in a letter to the author, 29 Jan. 1974. And letter from Vernon Richards to this author, 12 May 1972, and subsequent interview.

37. Paul Potts, *Dante Called You Beatrice* (Eyre & Spottiswoode, London, 1960), pp. 76–7.

38. When it was printed as 'The Freedom of the Press', *The Times Literary Supplement*, 15 Sept. 1972, pp. 1037–9, with a commentary by this author, 'How the Essay Came to be Written', pp. 1039–40.

39. Fredric Warburg, *All Authors Are Equal* (Hutchinson, London, 1973), pp. 39–58.

40. *CE* III, p. 402.

41. ibid., p. 401.

42. Letter to T. S. Eliot of 5 Sept. 1944, in the possession of Mrs Valerie Eliot.

43. Dwight Macdonald, *Politics*, Nov. 1944.

44. 'The Freedom of the Press' (see note 38 above), p. 1039.

45. See letter to Orwell from W. J. Turner of Collins, 30 Aug. 1943. Orwell Archive.

46. Rayner Heppenstall, 'Orwell Intermittent', *Twentieth Century*, May 1955, p. 476.

47. Interview by the author with Mrs Margaret Nelson (formerly Fletcher), Jura, 2 Sept. 1976, and *CE* II, p. 352.

48. Potts, op. cit., pp. 72–3.

49. *CE* III, pp. 243–4.

50. Letter to Mr S. Moos of 16 Dec. 1943, now in Orwell Archive, by kindness of the recipient.

51. *CE* III, p. 222.

52. ibid., pp. 160–61.

53. ibid., p. 140.

54. Potts, op. cit., p. 82.

55. A. J. Ayer, *Part of My Life* (Collins, London, 1977), p. 287.

56. See P. G. Wodehouse, *Performing Flea* (Penguin, London, 1961), pp. 126–7 and 159; and Orwell, 'In Defence of P. G. Wodehouse', *CE* III, pp. 341–55.

57. Orwell Archive, General Notebooks.

15. FAMOUS AND SOLITARY MAN (1945–6)

1. Letter of Eileen Blair to Orwell, 29 March 1945. Orwell Archive.

2. Julian Symons, 'Orwell, a Reminiscence', *London Magazine*, Sept. 1963, p. 39, and Paul Potts, *Dante Called You Beatrice* (Eyre & Spottiswoode, London, 1960), p. 75.

3. *CE* III, p. 359.

4. A letter from Orwell to a Mr Byrne refusing a speaking invitation, 22 June 1945. Orwell Archive.

5. *CE* IV, p. 149.

6. Letter of Orwell to Lydia Jackson, 1 April 1945, in her possession.

7. Letter of Eileen Blair to Orwell, 21 March 1945. Orwell Archive.

8. Letter of Joyce Pritchard to Ian Angus, 27 Sept. 1967. Orwell Archive.

9. Elisaveta Fen (Lydia Jackson), 'George Orwell's First Wife', MS. in Orwell Archive, or a shortened version in *Twentieth Century*, Aug. 1960.

10. Interview by the author with Lettice Cooper, London, 15 July 1976; and letter of Eileen Blair to Lettice Cooper, 23 March 1945 (Orwell Archive).

11. Letter of Eileen Blair to Orwell, 23 March 1945 and continued the following day. Orwell Archive.

12. 'The British General Election', *Commentary*, New York, Nov. 1945, p. 65.

13. *Observer*, 14 Oct. 1945.

14. John Lehmann, *I Am My Brother* (Longman, London, 1960), p. 144.

15. Interview by the author with Celia Goodman (*née* Paget) at Cambridge, 3 May 1975, and on 6 April 1979, when she discussed the draft of these chapters with me.

16. I thank Anne Olivier Bell for showing me these letters.

17. I. R. Willison, 'George Orwell: Some Materials for a Bibliography', submitted to the School of Librarianship, London University, for the Diploma in Librarianship (Part III), May 1953, pp. 43–73.

18. Fredric Warburg, *All Authors Are Equal* (Hutchinson, London, 1973), pp. 39–58; and interview by the author with Frank Morley, London, Oct. 1972. There is also some correspondence, relating to *Animal Farm* and a possible reprint of *Burmese Days*, between Orwell and Cass Canfield of Harpers in the Humanities Research Center, Austin, Texas (Harper Files, file 'O').

19. Cyril Connolly in *Horizon*, Sept. 1945, pp. 215–16.

20. Robert Aickmann in *Nineteenth Century*, DXXXVI, 1945, pp. 255–61, quoted by Robert Klitzke, 'Orwell and His Critics', Ph.D. thesis, London University, 1977.

21. *Animal Farm*, p. 29.

22. Tom Hopkinson, in a remarkable reassessment of *Animal Farm* in the *World Review*'s special number on Orwell, June 1950.

23. Letter of Herbert Read to George Orwell, 13 Aug. 1945. Orwell Archive.

24. Letter of William Empson to George Orwell, 24 Aug. 1945. Orwell Archive.

25. Letter of George Orwell to Dwight Macdonald, 3 Jan. 1946 (Yale University Library); and from George Woodcock to author, 14 Jan. 1981.

26. Potts, op. cit., p. 82. And Arthur Koestler remembers the same incident.

27. Letter of John Betjeman to George Orwell, 18 April 1946. Orwell Archive.

28. George Orwell, 'In Defence of P. G. Wodehouse', *CE* III, pp. 341–55.

29. *The Voyage of the Beagle* was broadcast on 29 March 1946 and *Animal Farm* on 14 Jan. 1947. Two further versions of *Animal Farm* were made, one by Peter Duval Smith, broadcast on 3 March 1952, which was subsequently revised by Rayner Heppenstall on 23 June 1957 – a much repeated version. Unfortunately Orwell's voice was never recorded or, if so, not preserved.

30. Interview by the author with Mr Rodney Dobson of Woolwich Polytechnic, 22 March 1976.

31. 'World Affairs, 1945', in *Junior: Articles, Stories and Pictures* (Children's Digest Publications, London). This does not seem to have survived for long, but a copy of Orwell's article is in the Orwell Archive.

32. *CE* IV, pp. 8–10.

33. Originally in *Horizon*, April 1946. *CE* IV, pp. 127–40.

34. *CE* IV, p. 30.

35. A review of W. McCartney, *The French Cooks' Syndicate* in *Freedom*, 8 Sept. 1945. 'How the Poor Die' is in *CE* IV, pp. 223–33.

36. 'Pacificism and Progress', *Manchester Evening News*, 14 Feb. 1946.

37. George Woodcock, *The Crystal Spirit* (Jonathan Cape, London, 1967), pp. 20–21.

38. *CE* IV, pp. 37–40.

39. Woodcock, op. cit., pp. 42–3.

40. Memorandum lent to the author by Arthur Koestler.

41. Arthur Koestler interviewed by Ian Angus, 30 April 1964, and by the author, 19 Oct. 1972. Some of the papers of the abortive league are in the Orwell Archive, others in the possession of Arthur Koestler.

42. *CE* IV, pp. 145–6.

43. Interviews by the author with Julian Symons, Anthony Powell, Malcolm Muggeridge and Michael Meyer, and letters from George Woodcock.

44. Julian Maclaren-Ross, *Memoirs of the Forties* (Alan Ross, London, 1965); and Robert Hewison, *Under Siege: Literary Life in London 1939–45* (Weidenfeld & Nicolson, London, 1977).

45. Interviews by the author with Susan Watson, 6 Aug. and 20 Oct. 1975, and subsequent correspondence. She has kindly checked my account carefully.

46. J. D. Bernal, 'Belief and Action', *Modern Quarterly*, Dec. 1945, quoted by Orwell, *CE* IV, pp. 154–6.

47. *CE* IV, pp. 153–60. There is a good account of the background to this fierce Bernal–Orwell controversy in G. Werskey, *The Visible College* (Allen Lane, London, 1978), pp. 286–9. Werskey points out that the tolerant Orwell had produced for the BBC Indian service in 1942 a series on 'Science, Capitalism and Fascism' which included talks by Bernal, Needham, Crowther and Benjamin Farrington (p. 277).

48. 'What is Socialism?', *Manchester Evening News*, 31 Jan. 1946. In view of some subsequent doubts as to where Orwell 'really stood' at this period, or speculation that he was abandoning socialism (only plausible in the slightest if his minor writings are not known or ignored), this omission from *The Collected Essays, Journalism and Letters* is unfortunate. Some old friends like to feel that he was going the way they have gone.

49. Interviews with Susan Watson (see note 45 above).

16. JURA DAYS

1. The quotation is from Jeffrey Meyers, 'The Autobiographical Strain', in his *A Reader's Guide to George Orwell* (Thames and Hudson, London, 1975), p. 47 and also p. 42. The 'death wish' theme, linked to 'infantile regression', is argued by Anthony West, 'George Orwell', in his *Principles and Persuasions* (Eyre & Spottiswoode, London, 1958). He carries his psychological speculations to extraordinary lengths in trying to reduce Orwell's genius to paranoia: 'As these parallels fall into place, one after another, like the tumblers in a combination lock, it is possible to see how Orwell's unconscious mind was working' (p. 158). How sad the gentle doctor would have been that such crude rationalism can be called 'Freudian'. T. R. Fyvel launched this speculation in his seminal essay of 1950, far more delicately and tentatively, though I still think mistakenly: Fyvel says that by 1947 'forty years of conflict had burnt him out … And as for his uncomfortable life in the rough Atlantic climate – totally unsuitable for a consumptive – and the accidents through which his health finally broke down, it seemed to me at times as though some force in him were driving him to complete the drama' ('A Writer's Life', *World Review*, June 1950, p. 20). Fyvel reviewed West's essay in 'George Orwell and Eric Blair: Glimpses of a Dual Life', *Encounter*, July 1959, pp. 60–65.

2. Paul Potts, *Dante Called You Beatrice* (Eyre & Spottiswoode, London, 1960), p. 73.

3. Interview by the author with Mr Donald Darroch, Jura, 5 Sept. 1976.

4. Interview by the author with Avril Dunn, 7 Sept. 1976.

5. Interview by the author with Francis Boyle, Jura, 4 Sept. 1976; and with Tony and Betty Rozga, on Islay, 4 Sept. 1976.

6. *CE* IV, p. 199.

7. ibid., p. 200; and interview by the author with Celia Goodman (*née* Paget), Cambridge, 3 May 1975.

8. Interview by the author with Mr David Holbrook, Cambridge, 11 June 1976, to whom I am grateful for subsequently and bravely lending me the MS. of his early unpublished novel.

9. Interview by the author with Mrs Katie Darroch, Jura, 3 Sept. 1976.

10. Letter to Humphrey Slater of Sept. 1946. Orwell Archive.

11. *CE* IV, pp. 284–5.

12. *CE* IV, p. 326, and see also Orwell's letter to Gollancz of 25 March, *CE* IV, pp. 308–9.

13. ibid., pp. 313–26.

14. ibid., pp. 69 and 64.

15. ibid., p. 371 which first appeared in the July–Aug. 1947 number of *Partisan Review*.

16. ibid., p. 299.

17. *CE* III, p. 64.

18. Interview by the author with Richard Blair, 7 Dec. 1976.

19. *CE* IV, pp. 328–9.

20. Bill Dunn speaking in 'George Orwell: A Programme of Recorded Reminiscences', arranged and narrated by Rayner Heppenstall, recorded on 20 Aug. 1960 and first broadcast on 2 Nov. 1960 (BBC Archives, Ref. No. TLO 24177). Copy in Orwell Archive.

21. *CE* IV, p. 330.

22. Interview by the author with Lucy Bestall, near Keswick, 13 Sept. 1976.

23. Written up from notes after an interview with Henry Dakin, near Bristol, 7 April 1976, and subsequently checked by him.

24. Interviews by the author with Mr Donald Darroch (see note 3 above) and with Mr Ian McKechnie at Campbeltown, 6 Sept. 1976.

25. The entry is worth quoting in full. The facts are the same as in his nephew's narrative, but the tone somewhat different.

19.8.47. Since 17.8.47 at Glengarrisdale ... On return journey today ran into the whirlpool and were all nearly drowned. Engine sucked off by the sea and went to the bottom. Just managed to keep the boat steady with the oars, and after going through the whirlpool twice, ran into smooth water and found ourselves up abt. 100 yards from Eilean Mor, so ran in quickly and managed to clamber ashore. H.D. jumped ashore first with the rope, then the boat overturned spilling L.D.R. and myself into the sea. R. trapped under the boat for a moment, but we managed to get him out. Most of the stuff in the boat lost including the oars. Eilean Mor is larger than it looks – I should say 2 acres at least. The whole surface completely undermined by puffins' nests. Countless wild birds, including many young cormorants learning to fly. Curiously enough it has a considerable pool of what appears to be fresh water, so there must be a spring. No wood whatever on the island, as there is no place where drift could fetch up. However we managed to get my cigarette lighter dry and made a fire of dead grass and lumps of dry peat, prised off the surface, at which we dried our clothes. We were taken off about three hours later by the Ling fishermen who happened to be bringing picnicers round. We left Glengarrisdale at abt. 10.30, which was abt. 2 hours after high tide, & must have struck Corryvreckan at abt. 11.30, ie. when the tide had been ebbing about three hours. It appears this was the very worst time, and we should time it so as to pass Corryvreckan in slack water. The boat is all right. Only serious loss, the engine and 12 blankets.

26. Mrs Rozga and Mrs Darroch (see notes 5 and 9 above) both made this same comment independently in almost identical words.
27. Unpublished letter from Orwell to Lydia Jackson of 28 July 1947. Orwell Archive.
28. Letter to George Woodcock of 9 Aug. 1947, *CE* IV, p. 376; and also a similar letter of 9 Oct. 1947 to Julian Symons, *CE* IV, p. 381, of which the unedited version in Orwell Archive says 'we are going to spend the winter up here because I can be quieter and also it's a bit easier to get food and fuel up here, and actually the climate is a bit warmer'.
29. Letter of 8 Sept. 1947, *CE* IV, p. 378.
30. Unpublished letter to Celia Kirwan of 27 Oct. 1947. Orwell Archive.
31. Unpublished letter to Leonard Moore of 31 Oct. 1947. Berg Collection, New York Public Library.
32. The manuscript of *Nineteen Eighty-Four* is owned by an American collector who wishes to remain anonymous. A photocopy was sent to me. It is not complete. The scene of the seduction of Winston Smith by Julia of the Anti-Sex League is missing. It is a typescript, heavily corrected by Orwell in pen and Biro; and from this stage he made heavy corrections and changes to many passages as he typed it up himself to send to the publishers.
33. *CE* IV, p. 384.
34. Letter of 18 Nov. 1947 from the *Observer*, unsigned carbon in Orwell's

file in the *Observer*. They proposed a three-month assignment. David Astor, the letter makes clear, was away at the time.

35. *CE* IV, p. 385.
36. Malcolm Muggeridge interviewing Avril Dunn on a BBC television broadcast of 20 Nov. 1965.
37. Orwell Archive.
38. V. S. Pritchett, 'George Orwell', in Gilbert Phelps (ed.), *Living Writers* (Sylvan Press, London 1947), which reprinted a Third Programme Series of 'critical broadcasts', p. 107.

17. THE LAST DAYS AND *NINETEEN EIGHTY-FOUR*

1. Unpublished letter of 26 Dec. 1947, Berg Collection, New York Public Library, and letters of 2 Jan., 21 March and 20 April 1948 in *CE* IV, pp. 393–4, 406–7 and 415–17.
2. *CE* IV, p. 386.
3. ibid., pp. 391–2.
4. ibid., p. 404.
5. Unpublished letter to Leonard Moore of 8 June 1948 (Berg Collection, New York Public Library). When Angus and Willison's long awaited bibliography of Orwell appears, the distribution and timing of translations of *Animal Farm* should tell a most interesting political story if the evidence can ever be found.
6. Letter of S. M. Levitas to George Orwell, 25 May 1948; and six more similar letters while Orwell was in sanatoria or hospital. Copies in Orwell Archive.
7. Letters between Orwell and Dwight Macdonald in Yale University Library.
8. Letter of Warburg to Orwell, 25 Feb. 1948. Orwell Archive.
9. Unpublished letter to Philip Rahv, 4 Feb. 1948. Copy in Orwell Archive.
10. Unpublished letter to David Astor, 1 Feb. 1948. Orwell Archive.
11. Interview by the author with David Astor at the *Observer*, 14 Feb. 1973, and telegram of Astor to New York, 11 Feb. 1948, in the *Observer*'s files.
12. Interview (see note 11 above), and letter of Astor to Bruce Dick of 19 Feb. 1948, in the *Observer*'s files.
13. *CE* IV, p. 413.
14. Letter to Leonard Moore of 17 April 1948. Berg Collection, New York Public Library.
15. Letter of 20 April, *CE* IV, pp. 415–16.
16. ibid., pp. 425–6.
17. Letter of Mrs I. L. Hunter of Edinburgh to the author, 30 Oct. 1972.

18. Fredric Warburg, *All Authors Are Equal* (Hutchinson, London, 1973), p. 99.

19. Unpublished letter of Orwell to David Astor, 1 Feb. 1948. Orwell Archive.

20. *CE* IV, pp. 423–4.

21. *Commentary*, New York, October 1948, pp. 343–9, not included in *CE*.

22. *CE* IV, pp. 428–49.

23. ibid., pp. 425–6.

24. ibid., p. 438.

25. Unpublished letter in Orwell Archive.

26. Unpublished letters to Celia Kirwan of 16 Aug. and to Michael Meyer of 3 Aug. 1948. Orwell Archive.

27. *CE* IV, p. 470.

28. Unpublished letter to David Astor, 9 Oct. 1948. Orwell Archive.

29. *CE* IV, p. 448.

30. ibid., p. 449.

31. Berg Collection, New York Public Library.

32. Letter to Moore (Berg Collection), and to Powell, *CE* IV, p. 454.

33. Warburg, op. cit., p. 102.

34. Letter to Moore. Berg Collection, New York Public Library.

35. Letter to Gwen O'Shaughnessy, 28 Nov. 1948. Orwell Archive.

36. *CE* IV, p. 459.

37. *Observer*, 2 Jan. 1949.

38. *CE* IV, p. 460.

39. ibid., p. 475.

40. Unpublished letter to Astor, 21 Dec. 1948. Orwell Archive.

41. Letter of Bruce Dick to David Astor, 5 Jan. 1949, in file on Orwell in possession of David Astor.

42. Letters to Rees, *CE* IV, p. 473, and to Warburg, p. 500.

43. Letter to Rees, 8 April 1949, *CE* IV, p. 488.

44. Warburg, op. cit., p. 110.

45. Letter to Powell of 11 May 1949, *CE* IV, p. 499, and to Rees of 4 Feb. 1949, p. 476.

46. Letter to Rees of 8 April 1949, *CE* IV, p. 488, and to T. R. Fyvel of 15 April 1949, p. 497.

47. Malcolm Muggeridge, 'A Knight of the Woeful Countenance', in Miriam Gross (ed.), *The World of George Orwell* (Weidenfeld & Nicolson, London, 1971), p. 173.

48. Paul Potts, *Dante Called You Beatrice* (Eyre & Spottiswoode, London, 1960), p. 79. Letter to Vernon Richards of 10 March 1949 (Orwell Archive).

49. A notebook of 1949 (Orwell Archive) contains 86 names of Communists or Communist sympathizers in columns under 'Names', 'Jobs' and 'Remarks'. Most of the entries are by another unidentified hand but with frequent

annotations by Orwell, and some of the original entries are by him. Many of the entries are plausible as possible underground or front members, but a few seem far-fetched and unlikely, listed simply for 'Communist-like' opinions.

50. *CE* IV, p. 479.

51. Quoted in Jacintha Buddicom, *Eric and Us* (Leslie Frewin, London, 1974), pp. 151–2. The original is in her possession.

52. *CE* IV, p. 513.

53. ibid., p. 515.

54. Unpublished letter of 24 May 1949. Orwell Archive.

55. Copy of the original is in the papers of Martin Secker & Warburg Ltd, and it is quoted in Warburg, op. cit., p. 112.

56. Copies in papers of Martin Secker & Warburg Ltd, and in Orwell Archive.

57. Warburg, op. cit., pp. 114–15.

58. Julian Symons in 'An Appreciation', which was postscript to a book club edition of *Nineteen Eighty-Four* (Heron Books, London, 1970).

59. *Time and Tide*, 11 June 1949, pp. 494–5.

60. Quoted and translated by Jeffrey Meyers in *George Orwell: The Critical Heritage* (Routledge & Kegan Paul, London, 1975), pp. 277–81.

61. *New Statesman and Nation*, 18 June 1949, pp. 646–8, quoted by Robert Klitzke in 'Orwell and His Critics: an enquiry into the critical reception of and debate about George Orwell's political works', Ph.D. thesis, London University, 1977, p. 47.

62. *The Times Literary Supplement*, 10 June 1949, p. 380.

63. *Reynold's News*, 12 June 1949, p. 4, quoted by Klitzke, op. cit., p. 49.

64. Czeslaw Milosz, a famous defector from the Polish Communist Party, wrote in his *The Captive Mind* (Knopf, New York, 1953) about Orwell's *Nineteen Eighty-Four*:

> ... because it is both difficult to obtain and dangerous to possess, it is known only to certain members of the Inner Party. Orwell fascinates them through his insight into details they know well, and through his use of Swiftian satire. Such a form of writing is forbidden by the New Faith because allegory, by nature manifold in meaning, would trespass beyond the prescriptions of socialist realism and the demands of the censor. For those who know Orwell only by hearsay are amazed that a writer who never lived in Russia should have so keen a perception into its life. The fact that there are writers in the West who understand the functioning of the unusually constructed machine of which they are themselves a part, astounds them and argues against the 'stupidity' of the West.

65. *New Yorker*, 18 June 1949, pp. 78–81.

66. *Masses and Mainstream*, Aug. 1949, pp. 79–81, quoted in Meyers, op. cit., p. 276.

67. A copy of this statement is in the Orwell Archive; see also Warburg, op. cit., pp. 118–19, for his original notes and an account of the circumstances surrounding the statement.

68. *CE* IV, p. 504.

69. David Farrer may have written part of this memorandum, certainly the political viewpoint was closer to his than to Warburg's and he claims to have read the typescript first. (Interview by the author with David Farrer of Secker & Warburg, Feb. 1974.)

70. Warburg, op. cit., pp. 103–6.

71. Quoted in Meyers, op. cit., p. 273.

72. *CE* IV, p. 502.

73. Unpublished letter to Moore, 13 July 1949. Berg Collection, New York Public Library.

74. *CE* IV, pp. 505–6.

75. Copy in Orwell Archive.

76. Letter from Catherine Karot of 25 Aug. 1949. Orwell Archive.

77. *CE* IV, p. 511.

78. Anthony Powell, *Infants of the Spring* (Heinemann, London, 1976), p. 141.

79. Interview by the author with Anthony Powell, near Frome, 11 Aug. 1976, and with Malcolm Muggeridge, Robertsbridge, 23 July 1976; and Muggeridge in Gross, op. cit., p. 174.

80. Interview by the author with Rayner Heppenstall, Bayswater, 4 Nov. 1972, though in *Four Absentees* (Barrie and Rockcliff, London, 1960), p. 176, he had assumed – if with hindsight – that Orwell was dying.

81. T. R. Fyvel, 'A Writer's Life', *World Review*, June 1950, pp. 7–8.

82. Letter to author from Dr Howard Nicholson of 14 April 1981, and phone conversation of 16 April.

83. 'Further Notes For My Literary Executor'. Orwell Archive.

84. Richard Rees, 'George Orwell', *Scots Chronicle*, 1951, p. 11.

85. Cyril Connolly, *The Evening Colonnade* (David Bruce and Watson, London, 1973), p. 377.

86. Muggeridge in Gross, op. cit., p. 174.

87. Interview with Avril Dunn at Ardfern, Easter 1974.

88. Letter of 29 Dec. 1949 (Orwell Archive), perhaps the last letter to reach him.

89. Stephen Spender, *The Thirties and After* (Fontana, London, 1978), pp. 99 and 173.

90. Julian Symons, 'Orwell, a Reminiscence', *London Magazine*, Sept. 1963, p. 47.

91. Heppenstall, 'Orwell Intermittent', *Twentieth Century*, May 1955, p. 481.

92. Interview by the author with Stafford Cottman, West Ruislip, 21 Aug. 1979.

93. Potts, op. cit., pp. 82–3.

94. Fyvel, op. cit., pp. 8–9.

95. The text of the 'Short Notice' given by the BBC on 21 Jan. 1950. Copy in Orwell Archive, Obituaries file.

96. Fyvel, op. cit., pp. 7–8, and V. S. Pritchett in an obituary notice in the *New Statesman and Nation*, 28 Jan. 1950.

97. Muggeridge in Gross, op. cit., pp. 174–5. The *Daily Telegraph* obituary notice, 23 Jan. 1950, also refers to the fishing rods. The *Daily Herald* noted on the same day the irony of a man 'who had known the acutest poverty' dying on the edge of 'one of the biggest dollar fortunes earned in the United States by a British book'. (Orwell Archive, Obituaries.)

98. *Like It Was: A Selection from the Diaries of Malcolm Muggeridge*, selected and edited by John Bright-Holmes (Collins, London, 1981), p. 376. These include several new passages on Orwell, adding to what Muggeridge has written already. Some are factual, strengthening the view that he clearly *appeared* to be dying when in UCH (he refers to the 'stench of death', has Orwell referring to 'death-bed marriages' and, unlike every other witness, has him 'angry' at the thought of death, not calm and serene). Some of the new passages are speculative and opinionated, that 'he was at heart strongly anti-Semitic' and 'self-pity ... was of course his dominant emotion'. But I have not changed my judgement and have preferred to rely, in part, on Muggeridge's earlier published writings: partly because I think the newly revealed judgements are false, unreliably mischievous and eye- or review-catching; and partly because I suspect that the diary is full of hindsight, difficult to take fully seriously as a contemporary and true record, however well it reads.

INDEX